PERSPECTIVES IN SOCIAL RESEARCH METHODS AND ANALYSIS

We dedicate this book to Maureen, Quinn, Elizabeth, Enrique J., Eric, Edrian, Meg, Tobias, and Jonah for their love and kindness, and to our students, who inspired us to write it.

PERSPECTIVES IN SOCIAL RESEARCH METHODS AND ANALYSIS

A Reader for Sociology

EDITORS

HOWARD LUNE | ENRIQUE S. PUMAR | ROSS KOPPEL

Hunter College   *The Catholic University of America*   *University of Pennsylvania*

⑤SAGE

Los Angeles | London | New Delhi
Singapore | Washington DC

For information:

SAGE Publications, Inc.
2455 Teller Road
Thousand Oaks, California 91320
E-mail: order@sagepub.com

SAGE Publications Ltd.
1 Oliver's Yard
55 City Road
London EC1Y 1SP
United Kingdom

SAGE Publications India Pvt. Ltd.
B 1/I 1 Mohan Cooperative Industrial Area
Mathura Road, New Delhi 110 044
India

SAGE Publications Asia-Pacific Pte. Ltd.
33 Pekin Street #02-01
Far East Square
Singapore 048763

Printed in the United States of America.

Library of Congress Cataloging-in-Publication Data

Perspectives in social research methods and analysis : a reader for sociology/editors, Howard Lune, Enrique S. Pumar, Ross Koppel.

    p. cm.

Includes bibliographical references and index.

ISBN 978-1-4129-6739-6 (pbk.)

   1. Sociology—Research. 2. Social sciences—Research—Methodology. 3. Social sciences—Methodology. I. Lune, Howard, 1962- II. Pumar, Enrique S., 1956- III. Koppel, Ross.

HM571.P47 2010
301.072—dc22   2009019946

This book is printed on acid-free paper.

09   10   11   12   13   10 9 8 7 6 5 4 3 2 1

Acquisitions Editor:	Vicki Knight
Associate Editor:	Sean Connelly
Editorial Assistant:	Lauren Habib
Production Editor:	Karen Wiley
Copy Editor:	Kristin Bergstad
Typesetter:	C&M Digitals (P) Ltd.
Proofreader:	Joyce Li
Indexer:	Holly Day
Cover Designer:	Janet Foulger
Marketing Manager:	Stephanie Adams

CONTENTS

PREFACE

Is the unemployment rate a reliable indicator of economic prosperity? How should we measure unemployment? Is unemployment rising or falling over the course of time? You can find analysts who say both. Then, whom do you believe? And why should the answer depend on who you ask? Why can't we just know? Why are pundits still debating some of these questions that seem easy to answer?

To answer questions like these, we usually have to do some sort of research. Social research helps us find the right questions, judge which sources of data are most valid for what we need to know, ask critical questions about public policy issues and reports, and derive our own conclusions with some degree of certainty. Even when we seek answers in other researchers' findings, we still need to conduct research of our own to assess which of the published reports to trust.

This book shows students the steps involved in the research process, the various strategies for conducting a valid social inquiry, and, perhaps most important, the persuasiveness and elegance of reliable social research. We accomplish these ambitious tasks through the power of benchmark cases from various fields in sociology. Benchmarks are exemplary demonstrations of ways to do things. In social research, benchmark studies are taken as best-case scenarios from which we learn the advantages and disadvantages of particular methodologies and techniques. In this book we have therefore

collected a set of readings that can help us think about how to conduct research. In addition, our introductory sections for each chapter put the readings in the context of each of the steps in the research process. Through the combination of best-case illustrations and a clear framework, we hope students can best understand the research process.

Measuring the social world is a complex process. Social research is concerned with things that keep changing even as we measure them, and that change even more because we measure them. In fact, much of the time we study how things are to provide useful information that will help us change the things we are studying. For example, we use employment rates to refine market policies and to judge the performance of governmental policymaking. We use health data to improve health and health care services. So what was true yesterday might not be as valid today, in part because we are constantly measuring and improving the world (or trying to). That's a quandary of research. The more research we do, the more we need to continue our research to decipher the information we confront every day.

Social research skills are important to us at the individual and community level as well. We (as a society) use such information for many other reasons beyond evaluating social policies, and some of these reasons can create problems in our lives. Elected officials use social data to show that they should remain in power. Corporations use social data to sell products. Individuals use the same information to win arguments. People use information very selectively to support their interests. Some people question whether people ever landed on the moon, or whether slavery was really all that bad for the slaves. ("Since you weren't there," the argument goes, "you don't really know.") So, not only are our data always changing, but we are surrounded by others who want to convince us the information says something very different from what we think it says. How can we, the consumers of information, ever know what's going on?

We can. Sociologist Pierre Bourdieu observed that "sociology is a martial art, a means of self-defense." Social research methods teach us how to see through the noise of information, misinformation, and casual oversimplification to get to the underlying patterns of meaningful data. It is a tool for your personal and social well-being. It's all about managing the data yourself so that you can draw your own conclusions. It's how you know what's going on.

The research articles and excerpts presented in this book will step you through the different stages of research, from asking questions to measuring data to drawing valid conclusions and rejecting alternatives that don't stand up to close examination. Each section will provide you with one carefully crafted tool for your toolbox. In keeping with the book's central purpose and our desire to instruct future researchers with viable illustrations, we organize the readings along the following logic: The first section discusses how to start your research. Here, we review the importance of conceptualizing a research question and the uses of theory to stimulate viable research inquiries and jump-start the research process. The second part tackles the ever-important consideration of how to measure and design a particular study and how to select the population and location for your research. Then, we proceed to weigh the role of ethics and political considerations during the research experience. In the section analyzing data collection, such qualitative and quantitative techniques as *surveys, interviews, focus groups, experiments,* and *fieldwork* (*observations* and *ethnographies*) are illustrated. The data analysis technique readings include both *statistical analysis* (including *secondary analysis of available data*) and *content analysis* (including *historical* and *cultural data*). We conclude with an examination of *evaluation research, case studies,* and *comparative–historical* research as examples of the benefits of mixed methods.

The late Senator Daniel Patrick Moynihan once observed that everyone is entitled to their own opinions, but not their own facts. But how can you tell whose facts are valid? The answer is often found by understanding how those facts were ascertained, that is, the methods used in designing and conducting the research that "determined" those facts. This book, with its examples of sociology's best and most engaging research methods, will help you figure out if the data presented from any study should be believed, rejected, or taken with a boatload of qualifications. This knowledge will also help you design your own research and draw meaningful conclusions from it. We hope it will also show you how creative and exciting good research methods can be. At the very least, no matter what you think of this or that research method, you will improve the ability of one source that you must trust: yourself.

ACKNOWLEDGMENTS

We are grateful for the help and advice of our colleagues, several anonymous reviewers, and our hardworking editor, Vicki Knight. We thank our families for all their endurance while we were working on this manuscript, and our various local coffee shops for their libation, inspiration, and WiFi.

Section I

WHERE TO BEGIN

"Begin at the beginning," the King said, very gravely, *"and go on till you come to the end: then stop."*

Alice in Wonderland—Lewis Carroll

Lewis Carroll's advice is obviously good for telling a story. But it is also good for planning a journey or a research project. We, the authors and editors of this book and the authors whose work is presented, have made this particular journey more than once. Our purpose here is to provide some guidance and advice so that you may plan your own research journey and better understand the research of others. Our advice is practical. We have no vocabulary quizzes for you. We hope that you will begin with your own questions, and end with your own answers.

To help you on your way, we have provided a kind of road map through the research process, shown in Figure 1.1. Throughout the book, we will be checking the map and marking our progress. Some chapters will also have a more detailed close-up of the map for the immediate tasks at hand. But do not be fooled by the straight lines. As with most journeys, you may find that you must frequently double back to the last stage, regroup, and set out again a little bit differently. Some of this backtracking is revealed in the more detailed maps that belie the simplicity of the big map.

MOTIVATION

This section, and this book, begins with the big questions: Why do we do what we do? What's our motivation? Our inspiration? And where do we start? In more practical terms, we ask what makes a good research question and where do we get one? These are also the first things that you need to ask yourself as you begin a new research project. To answer such questions we will begin with the words of some of our profession's current luminaries.

Each year at the annual meeting of the American Sociological Association (ASA), the Association's president has the privilege and responsibility of saying something important to the rest of us about our chosen field of work. Our first two readings are the texts of two recent presidential speeches: Troy Duster's from 2005 and Cynthia Fuchs Epstein's from 2006. These addresses provide a good starting point for how two preeminent scholars conceptualize social science research in their respective fields. Moreover, their insights are important for us because they speak to the relationship between

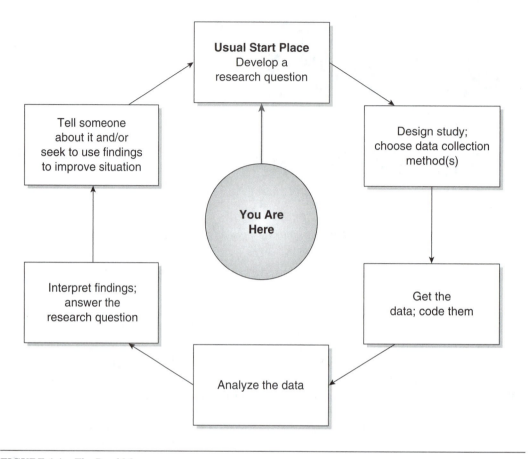

FIGURE 1.1   The Road Map

sociology as a profession and the social world in which we live and work. Their concerns about gaps and weaknesses in the social sciences can guide you to strengthen your work.

Research in the social sciences is different from research in the natural sciences. Most of the natural world behaves according to consistent patterns for reasons that may be studied in controlled laboratory settings. Some of these patterns and reasons are immutable, and therefore considered physical "laws." People aren't like that. The social world is a moving target. As our knowledge of the natural world has increased, human society has gotten only more complex, more interdependent, and more

unpredictable. In addition, humans are sociable creatures, so the actions of individuals cannot be separated from the actions and reactions of others around them. Throw in the larger and more complex forms of association—organizations, corporations, neighborhoods, communities, families, clans, ethnicities, states, nations, and more—and the puzzle becomes a swirl of possibilities.

For some, it may seem "natural" to compare the social sciences to the physical sciences. Thus they propose a scientific inquiry that focuses on observable and recurrent social behavior. But this comparison is troubling on several important, misleading, and even dangerous points. One significant danger is what Troy Duster calls the "reductionist challenge to sociology." *Reductionism* refers to efforts to measure all kinds of complex social phenomena in ways that reduce them to a single dimension. You might, for example, "reduce" the concept of love to the number of times you see people kiss. Clearly it's easier to think about and measure, but it misses the complex reality.

The comparison between the social and natural sciences becomes reductionist in two ways. First, by reducing the concept of "science" to the classic model of laboratory research in the natural sciences, we ignore virtually all of what is unique to sociology. In engineering, you have to measure something only once to know its value. In sociology, the more you measure the more variations you uncover. As we've discussed, this is primarily due to the differences in what the two fields observe. But if we reduce all sciences to only measured facts and calculations, then sociology appears to be a weaker, less reliable science rather than a science of less consistent subject matter.

The second problem follows from the first. If we assume that the measures of the hard sciences are the only correct measures, then we must reduce all kinds of complex social phenomena to things that can be measured in a lab. Broad concepts like one's "state of mind" are reduced to brain scan patterns. Stress is just a physiological response, learning is a series of scores on standardized tests, and antisocial behaviors, or prosocial behaviors, are just genetically coded responses to external stimuli. "Ideas" are pushed aside in favor of "facts," without concern for whether the facts that we have provide the information that we need. Yet, ideas and attitudes clearly are shaped by such things as social norms and historical legacies that are shared within a society even as they are interpreted individually.

Part of Duster's motivation, then, is to ensure that social scientists are able to weigh in on social questions. He also reminds us that we pretty much have an obligation to do so. Duster begins with the observation that it is not possible for us to agree on the "facts" of the social world because we all experience the world differently: "The obvious reason for different interpretations of what people see is that individuals bring very different personal and social histories, perspectives, sexual orientations, religious or secular views, and so forth." Whether the glass is half full or half empty may depend on whether or not you were the one who got to drink the first half.

Duster has also examined the workings of several large, multidisciplinary study panels to explore the question of where our facts come from and how we decide what we need to know. He demonstrates that while it might seem that scientists are looking at the world and "discovering" its workings, in reality social processes determine what we will look for and how we will look for it. These decisions go a very long way toward determining what we will find. Science is a social act. However **objective** our measures may be, our values and interests are reflected in the questions we ask.

Thus, once you have identified the subject matter for your work, the first and most important stage in the research process is to formulate an executable and relevant **research question,** or questions. We can think of this task as having three major parts, as shown in Figure 1.2.

CONCEPTUALIZATION

The research question is the central point of a research project. Above all else, it must be answerable, and that means that the question must be clear, precise, and unambiguous.

Given the uncertainties described above, one of the most important tasks in the social sciences is to figure out what we need to measure in order to answer our research question. Most research starts with **conceptualization** or the formal definition of what our major terms and concepts will mean in the context of our study. Unlike dictionary definitions, which attempt to list all conventional uses of a term, conceptual definitions provide specific working definitions of key ideas as they are to be used for the given study.

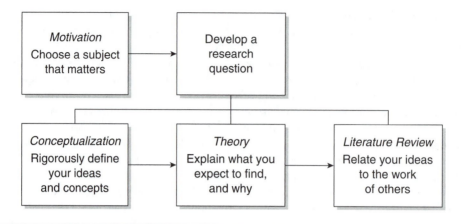

FIGURE 1.2 The Research Question Detail Map

Consider the most familiar of social concepts—gender. In her address to the ASA, Cynthia Fuchs Epstein identifies gender and gender-based inequalities as **social constructs**—concepts that are given meaning in a particular way through choice and experience. Gender differences are commonly represented as "natural" differences based in the biology of sex differences. Gendered inequalities are therefore perceived as inevitable and unchanging. Yet Epstein notes that the conventional descriptions of gender differences are unrelated to biological phenomena, and cannot actually explain differences in social roles, values, or outcomes.

Epstein further demonstrates that the socially defined construct of gender differences consistently devalues the roles of women in society and fosters male privilege. She notes that the **reification** of these concepts means that we do not have to endorse or even agree with these outcomes in order to participate in them.[1] As long as gender inequality is perceived and treated as somehow "natural," we can hardly even perceive it as a set of choices, let alone question

these choices. And of course she demonstrates that the cost of this inequality can be measured not simply through the insults and annoyances that occur within the workplace or on the street, but in lives lost, violence, and poverty.

Among other results, this demonstrates the power of **conceptualization**. This is the stage in the research process where we identify our key concepts and clearly explain both what we mean by those terms and what we don't mean. The conceptualization stage helps us to distinguish the formal assumptions that we're making about our concepts from other ideas that might be out there. In doing so, conceptualization helps us define the scope of our research. Under the once dominant **paradigm** of "functionalism," for example, inequalities were presumed to be natural and useful functions of the social order. The best and smartest researchers, working from this perspective, could then ask what functions inequalities served—how was society improved by such divisions—without really stopping to ask *if* society really is served by them. Drawing more on a "critical" paradigm, gender studies

---

[1]"Reification" is the process of making something real by believing in it. Social differences are real in their consequences, even if they have to be continuously defined and described in order to exist.

and feminist sociology have redefined the concept of inequality as a social **dysfunction**. This minor change in our working definitions opens up a vast new world of research. Inequality is still the same thing, but our conceptual definition of what it means and how it relates to gender has been dramatically altered. Noting this shift, Epstein encourages us to open up newer and broader areas of research that might have been overlooked until recently.

THEORY IN RESEARCH

Research is an empirical quest for knowledge. We collect and analyze data about the social world to understand it better. **Theory** guides our both our questions and our interpretations of any data we find. Our theories about the world suggest ideas that need to be investigated, and our findings raise questions and suggest modifications in our theoretical models. Theory and research are thus partners in the development of knowledge, in constant dialogue with one another.

Theories come in many sizes. In Thomas Kuhn's famous formulation, a paradigm is a grand theoretical framework, or a way of seeing the world overall, within which specific puzzles can be raised and various solutions tested. We also have more manageable propositions within those paradigms, which Robert Merton called macro-, meso-, and micro-theories. Macro-theories tend to address great historical narratives, like the causes of war or revolutions. Meso-theories look at middle-ground ideas, such as how patterns of traffic, or crime, or popular culture change within some social circumstances. Micro-theories tend to favor small events like interpersonal exchanges and the use of gestures and expressions. On a day-to-day basis, each new bit of research has the potential to alter the details of any given theory about any subject, at any of the micro, meso, or macro levels. But the big paradigms, the sets of assumptions about the world, remain fairly stable. When an existing paradigm becomes weighed

down by too many observations and ideas that don't seem to fit, a **paradigm shift** may occur in which the whole perspective is cast down and replaced. Kuhn called such events **scientific revolutions**. One example was the revolution in thinking that occurred when the geocentric model of the solar system (that the Earth is at the center of everything) gave way to the present heliocentric model, with the Sun at the center. Many early astronomers had grappled with the puzzles raised by the assumption that the Earth was stationary, but it took generations of work before such a major shift away from that assumption could take hold.

In our third reading, Herbert Gans raises significant questions about the sociological paradigm of **functionalism**. Functionalism, or structural-functionalism, has roots that go back to Durkheim and was the dominant paradigm in American sociology for much of the mid-20th century. (Gans's article was first published in 1972; earlier versions had been in the works since 1964.) Functionalist analysis begins with the assumption that, over time, society adjusts and regulates itself organically, the way a body heals. At any given moment, we don't have to assume that everything should be perfect, but we would tend to assume that anything that served no useful function at all would eventually be eliminated or discarded. These assumptions frequently seem to work, and they have provided a great deal of guidance to researchers. Robert Merton, for example, noted that many enduring social phenomena appear to be dysfunctional on the surface, but actually provide some other, underlying purpose. He called the surface function "the **manifest function**" of a thing, and it was that part that most closely related to our motives or desires. The **latent function**, on the other hand, often revealed why something lasts even when our motivation appears to be to get rid of it. In a particularly influential application of this idea, Kingsley Davis and Wilbert Moore published a paper in 1945 on "some principles of stratification" in which they attempted to explain why persistent inequalities of socioeconomic status and life chances might be functional to society, even if we all can agree that they cause great harms.

The Davis–Moore piece became one of the most widely cited, and often criticized, theories of its time. For many, their work showed that efforts to help the poor would always fail, that poverty was "natural," and that those who had great wealth probably did little to create the conditions under which others lived in abject poverty. To critics, this thesis simply absolved us, as individuals and as a society, from any responsibility for inequality and more or less blamed the poor, including those born into poverty, for their own troubles.

Taking a lead from Jonathan Swift's *A Modest Proposal* (1729), Gans extends the Davis–Moore thesis to the point where its limitations become visible. Gans suggests 15 ways in which persistent poverty is functional for those members of society who are not poor. None of these functions is likely to be identified by anyone as representing their actual motives, but all are possible. Modestly, Gans offers several possible conclusions from this case. First, instead of asking *whether* or how something is functional for society, we might do better asking *for whom* is it functional. Does some identifiable social group benefit from the persistence of poverty? Do they

have any impact or not on what we do? For that matter, who benefits from a widespread belief in the Davis–Moore thesis? Second, Gans suggests that the latent effects of poverty, those that benefit the rest of us, are so great that we might not want to eliminate poverty if we could. And third, almost as a cautious attempt to be thorough, Gans raises the possibility that functionalism does not actually explain poverty, inequality, or stratification. Hence, it might be about time for a paradigm shift. And indeed, one was taking place during those years while Gans was developing his argument.

Generally, we identify one or more promising theoretical frameworks to explain what we're studying *before* we collect any data, and we use the theories to help decide what data to collect. Choosing a promising theory—including a description of the relations among our concepts—and from that, generating testable predictions (hypotheses) about how those relations will work in our study is called **deductive reasoning**. Whereas choosing to group a number of cases together to find the patterns among them and thereby proposing a new theory to explain those patterns is referred to as **inductive reasoning**. Both involve applying theories to empirical observations in order to explain social events.

Box 1.1 Karl Marx (1818–1883)

Considered one of the intellectual fathers of Communism, Karl Marx also made several noteworthy contributions to social research methods. In his book *The Eighteenth Brumaire of Louis Bonaparte* (1852), Marx developed an important case-study design to interpret the forces that led to Louis Bonaparte's consolidation of power after his coup of 1851. In the *Grundrisse* (1858) he elaborated an innovative approach to the study of political economy. *Das Kapital* could be regarded as the first book employing a world system perspective. Of course, Marx is best known for his contributions to social theory. His claim that political, social, and economic processes followed consistent and measurable rules of conflict and resolution generated new ways of perceiving society that helped merge philosophy with the scientific foundations of the social sciences. Finally, his views on alienation as related to work, control over work, and work processes are still highly influential in research on organizations, the economy, and labor relations.

REVIEWING THE LITERATURE

Where do we get our theories from? In social research, we mostly draw upon previous research to formulate our explanations of the puzzles we observe. Even when we disagree with the reasoning and conclusions of those we read, the exercise of reviewing the existing literature related to our research topic is useful because it forces us to examine and carefully define our assumptions. If, for example, we wished to investigate how jurors evaluate DNA evidence in a trial, we might begin with Troy Duster's research for a theoretical explanation of how nonscientists perceive data from the biological sciences, from which we could make predictions about what a jury would find credible or not. We might incorporate some of the works cited by Gans to understand how subjective judgments bias trials. This would allow us to improve our predictions by considering the role of uncertainty and moral judgment in the decision process. Further, we could include some of Epstein's interpretations of how preconceived notions of gender-appropriate behavior might lead jurors to view certain narratives as more or less believable. Bringing those ideas together, we could propose a theoretical framework that incorporated status, power, and technology in relation to the credibility of evidence.

An illustrative demonstration of the usefulness of doing literature reviews to generate theories can be found in our fourth reading, in which Mark Musick reviews an exhaustive research literature on *theodicy*—"religious beliefs related to the meaning of suffering"—in order to improve our theorizing on the relationships between religion and well-being. His analysis proceeds carefully, from the classic works on the positive functions of religiosity, through more focused research on the individual impacts of specific kinds of beliefs. Focusing these issues further, Musick begins to construct a coherent picture of how different Christian theodicies might impact the lives and well-being of contemporary Americans. This portion of his conceptual review includes matters of comfort, hope, and meaning construction, all of which are viewed in the context of ideas about how we make healthier choices, how we face uncertainty, and how we cope with trauma.

Once the philosophical and practical features of theodicy have been explicated, Musick turns to the question of individual well-being. Having independently established the expected patterns of how specific Christian theodicies operate, he develops a set of interpretive frameworks to explain how well-being might depend on them. Notice that the review presents more than one pattern for the **independent variable** and more than one way that it can affect the variables that depend on it. This is because the literature review portion of a study is not a claim for a single truth. It is a logical argument that while many outcomes are possible, some are more likely than others. The presentation of findings and ideas that have come before this provides the motivation for the actual research that is about to be presented. Researchers use this review, including works with which they disagree, to place their own work in relation to what is known, what is suspected, what is argued over, and what remains to be found. In this way, researchers build on the findings of those who have studied these issues before.

In this case, having established a plausible relationship between types of belief systems and personal health, the author has drawn the reader into a conversation that has long been under way. Here, Musick introduces his third major concept: race. In the United States it is well known that "the Black Church" is different in practice from other churches. (As Epstein might point out, White Christians are able to call their institutions "the church," while African Americans must qualify theirs as the "black" version.) Using existing literature, then, the author has established that race matters, that theodicy matters, and that theodicy tends to differ by race. To this he adds references to show that health outcomes and other measures of well-being also differ by race in the United

States. The seemingly simple review of what is known or observed about several significant concepts, examined together, practically beg the study's research questions: Do church practices and beliefs explain a part of the difference in health? And if so, how might this relationship work?

CONCLUSION

Research begins with a puzzle or a problem to be solved, or something that needs to be investigated. The researcher develops questions based on these topics or issues. A topic can be anything from "how can we build a more just society" to "what's up with all of these reality TV shows?" But the research question has to be something that can be answered through the careful collection and analysis of empirical data.

All this is preparation. We begin with our questions, which suggest relationships among things in the world. We conceptualize our terms and relations, and theorize on the processes that link them. We review what others have found or theorized about our concepts. We decide where our study fits in with this body of past research. Now we are ready to begin our work.

DISCUSSION QUESTIONS

1. If the natural sciences are not the best model for social science research, then what is?

2. What is the role of discovery, and what is the role of creativity in the research process?

3. Let's say your review of the previous research and of the theoretical literature leads you to want to ask very different questions than what you have found so far. What might you do?

4. In these four selections, there is an underlying theme of conflict. Why is "conflict" such a pervasive issue in understanding society? What groups of people in society might be expected to emphasize the role of conflict? (Hint: Think about those with power vs. those without power.)

WEB RESOURCES

The following links can provide you with more detailed information on the topics discussed in this section. You may also go to www.sagepub.com/lunestudy where you will find additional resources and hot-links to these sources.

American Sociological Association Theory Section: http://www.asatheory.org/
International Social Theory Consortium: http://www.cas.usf.edu/socialtheory
York University Critical Social Theory: http://www.fsc.yorku.ca/york/istheory/wiki/index.php/Critical_social_theory
Bibliography and Data Related Literature: http://www.icpsr.umich.edu/ICPSR/citations/index.html

Comparative Perspectives and Competing Explanations

Taking on the Newly Configured Reductionist Challenge to Sociology (2006)

Troy Duster

The centennial of the American Sociological Association (ASA) is an appropriate time to step back and take a full sociohistorical view of how the discipline emerged and developed. Sociologists know well that the ways in which a field of inquiry is organized, professionalized, and institutionalized is a large part of its story—but it is only part of the story. Thus, the history of the association is not coterminous with the history of the discipline (for full history of the association, see Rhoades 1981 and Rosich 2005). There is often some contestation. This may be voiced by members of a group within a larger boundary who try to stretch the field in new and unchartered ways, because they experience their group's perspective as either thwarted or ignored. Those limits are sometimes pushed to the point of secession and reformation.

A clear illustration comes from the origins of the ASA itself as a "breakaway" organization, a recurring theme in the continuous unfolding and remaking of the discipline over the full century. In 1904, sociologists were part of the American Economic Society. The sociologists found the limiting focus upon markets and the economy too restrictive of their intellectual aspirations and research projects, and bolted from the economists to form the American Sociological Society[1] in 1905—holding their first annual meeting in 1906.[2]

Similar to the sociologists' initial breakaway from the economists, the newly founded sociological association would in time reflect the iron law of oligarchic tendencies (Michels 1966). Achieving sufficient professional coherence to patrol the boundaries and shape what was legitimate, the association in turn spawned its

SOURCE: From "Comparative Perspectives and Competing Explanations: Taking on the Newly Configured Reductionist Challenge to Sociology." *American Sociological Review, 71*(1), (Feb., 2006), pp. 1–15. Reprinted with permission.

[1]This was the original name and was changed to the American Sociological Association in the late 1950s.

[2]With some bemusement tinged with considerable irony, the *Guardian* reported on the 99th annual meeting of the ASA and subtitled the article, "US Sociologists Are Finally Challenging the Intellectual Stranglehold of Economists" (Steele 2004).

own breakaway organizations in the 1950s and 1960s. A segment that wanted sociologists to have more engagement with pressing social issues separated to form the Society for the Study of Social Problems. The discipline was caught short by the Watts Uprisings of 1965 and its cascading effects over the next three years through the urban disturbances of Detroit, MI and Newark, NJ. African American sociologists wanted more focus on issues of racial injustice and they broke away to form the Association of Black Sociologists. Similarly, sociologists in the emerging feminist movement demanded more focus on gender issues and spun at least partially away from the ASA to form Sociologists for Women in Society. The tale goes on and on: The symbolic interactionists broke to form The Society for the Study of Symbolic Interaction, and those who wanted to see more applications of social science knowledge formed the Society for Applied Sociology. Yet if there is a common thread that bonds most of the discipline together, it is based upon a general acknowledgment of the powerful role that social forces play in explaining human social behavior. This has been a consistent century-long counterpoint to the tendency to deploy either individual level or even smaller units of analysis (blood, genes, neurotransmitters) to account for scholastic achievement, crime rates, and even racism.

COMPARATIVE PERSPECTIVES ON THE SAME PHENOMENON, ROUTINE FEATURE OF OUR LIVES

There is nothing unusual or strange about the idea of social position determining what an individual sees. In the early twentieth century, Karl Mannheim's (1936) brilliant monograph spells out this tendency as one of the first principles of the sociology of knowledge. The obvious reason for different interpretations of what people see is that individuals bring very different personal and social histories, perspectives, sexual orientations, religious or secular views, and so forth.

Alfred Schütz (1955), the eminent phenomenologist, posits a fundamental domain assumption underlying human exchange inside a given group's boundaries, the so-called "assumption of the reciprocity of perspectives":

> I assume, and I assume that my fellow [hu]man assumes, that if [s]he stood where I stand, [s]he would see what I see. (p. 163)

When that assumption is routinely violated, there are limited choices—one of those being to form a new group of like-minded people. Under certain conditions, that can be a healthy development, a strategy to nurture and strengthen a fledgling perspective. But the danger is that this can result in a retreat from engagement with alternative perspectives. This article is about a particular version of like-mindedness and is divided into three sections. Part one documents a series of developments in which a wide range of seemingly unrelated inquiries have something vital in common—an attempt to explain human behavior or health conditions by looking only at data *inside* the body. I focus primarily on health and crime, because these are areas on the cutting edge of high technology application in molecular genetics—areas I have worked in for more than two decades (including membership on the National Advisory Council for Human Genome Research). Similar observations could be made about other arenas and research programs in those arenas. Indeed, part two describes the increasing challenge to sociology, a dramatic tilt in data collection, research agendas, research programs, and funding decisions that lean in the direction of increasing data and information on processes inside the body—while defunding or blocking access to research on forces outside the body. Part three suggests ways in which sociologists can meet this challenge by engaging in research on data collection at the very site of knowledge production to illuminate the social forces shaping the construction of knowledge claims.

PART I: DISCOVERY OF COMPETING PERSPECTIVES ON "BASIC PROCESSES"

During the mid-1970s, the National Academy of Sciences (NAS) convened a group of academic researchers (social as well as natural scientists) to address the state of knowledge about mind-altering substances. The multidisciplinary panel was composed of individuals with experience in research on mind-altering substances. Some had expertise with drugs like heroin and cocaine, others with psychotropic medicine, others with alcohol. When the topic turned to alcohol, the question was posed, "Why is the rate of alcoholism so high among Native Americans, Aborigines in Australia, and in Canada, First Nations' People?" According to the Indian Health Service, for example, the age-adjusted death rate from alcohol was more than seven times higher for Native Americans than for the general U.S. population (Beauvais 1998:255).

I along with my fellow social scientists thought the answer was obvious. These three broadly defined groups all experienced two centuries of displacement: They were sometimes forcibly and sometimes violently removed from their native soil, frequently shunted off to land where they had no knowledge of the local terrain. As a result of this displacement, their diets were dramatically changed, social organizations and economies destroyed, family structures disrupted, circumstances of work fundamentally altered or obliterated. And finally, members of each group (Native Americans, Aborigines, and First Nations' People) have been provided with easy access to cheap alcohol (Beauvais 1998; Beresford and Omaji 1996:1135; Spicer 1997). We thought, "That might drive some to drink!"

Our colleagues from the natural sciences (neurosciences and molecular genetics), looking at the same astronomically high rates of alcoholism, said that they were searching for neurotransmission patterns or specific genetic markers more likely to exist *in common* among Native Americans, Aborigines, and First Nations'

People. Indeed, one of the prevailing hypotheses was the claim of higher prevalence of "alcohol dehydrogenase polymorphisms in Native Americans" the ADH2*3 allele (Wall et al. 1997). Another claim is that Aborigines and Native Americans lack a protective gene mutation for the enzyme aldehyde dehydrogenase (Kibbey 2005).

All of us on the NAS panel were observing the same high rates of alcoholism among specific populations. The natural scientists—despite the overwhelming empirical evidence of social disruption—were committed to research they termed neuroadaptation at the molecular or cellular levels, seeking distinct neural circuits in the brain that explain the high rates of alcoholism in these populations. Instead, the social scientists were emphasizing the need to understand the role of forces outside the body for explaining the high rates of alcoholism among these three groups: social, historical, political, economic, and cultural forces. As early as 1835, Alexis de Tocqueville ([1835] 1966), while embracing the European perspective on the indigenous population of the United States as barbaric, nonetheless had this to say:

> When the Indians alone dwelt in the wilderness from which now they are driven, their needs were few. They made their weapons themselves, the water of the rivers was their only drink, and animals they hunted provided them with food and clothes. The Europeans introduced firearms, iron, and brandy among the indigenous populations of North America; they taught it [them] to substitute our cloth for the barbaric clothes which had previously satisfied Indian simplicity . . . [and] they no longer hunted for forest animals simply for food, but in order to obtain the only things they could barter with us. (p. 296)

This is the big picture and a far cry from genetic reductionism, where the disruption of Schütz's assumption of the reciprocity of perspectives could hardly be more complete, and the consequences of the victory of one perspective over another can hardly be overestimated. For example, the National Institute on Alcohol Abuse and Alcoholism (NIAAA) claims its mission is to "support and conduct biomedical and behavioral research on me causes, consequences, and treatment, and prevention of alcoholism and alcohol problems" (NIAAA 2005:2). However, the Strategic Plan of the NIAAA for 2001–2005 directs the institute to pursue the following seven goals:

1. Identify genes that are involved in alcohol-associated disorders.

2. Identify mechanisms associated with the neuroadaptations at the multiple levels of analysis (molecular, cellular, neural circuits, and behavior).

3. Identify additional science-based preventive interventions (e.g., drinking during pregnancy and college-age drinking).

4. Further delineate biological mechanisms involved in the biomedical consequences associated with excessive alcohol consumption.

5. Discover new medications that will diminish craving for alcohol, reduce the likelihood of post-treatment relapse, and accelerate recovery of alcohol-damaged organs.

6. Advance knowledge of the influence of environment on the expression of genes involved in alcohol-associated behavior, including the vulnerable adolescent years and in special populations.

7. Further elucidate the relationships between alcohol and violence.

Midanik (2004) points out that this list is decisively focused on processes inside the body. Indeed, even when the list finally concerns the influence of the environment (item no. 6), that influence is directed toward "the expression of genes." The NIAAA list also hints as to how and why sociological explanations of alcoholism began losing out to strong claimants pursuing "scientific investigations" of "basic processes occurring inside the body.

Indeed, on the very related matter of selective funding strategies that privilege research inside the body, the paradigmatic fight over how best to explain high rates of alcoholism described in the previous section has had direct consequences on what research gets funded. In 1990 at the NIAAA, 64 percent (n = 347) of all research grants (n = 539) went to biomedical/neuroscience investigators. In 2002, the number of grants for biomedical/neuroscience research increased to 494 (Midanik 2004:221), while the total number for epidemiology was 70.

The tendency to privilege internalist approaches to the explanations of complex social behaviors reached its zenith in the shifting approach by the National Institutes of Health (NIH) to the study of violence that was revealed in the early 1990s.

Basic Processes Versus the Sociocultural Explanation of Violence: The NIH Controversy

The following section is a partial transcript of the meeting of the National Mental Health Advisory Council on February 11, 1992. These are the unedited remarks of Frederick Goodwin, at that time the director of Alcohol, Drug Abuse, and Mental Health Administration (ADAMHA). After these remarks, Lewis Sullivan, the Secretary of Health and Human Services, then "demoted" Dr. Goodwin to the position of Director of the National Institute of Mental Health:

> If you look, for example, at male monkeys, especially in the wild, roughly half of them survive to adulthood. The other half die by violence. That is the natural way of it for males, to knock each other off and, in fact, there are some interesting evolutionary implications of that because the same hyper-aggressive monkeys who kill each other are also hyper-sexual, so they copulate more and therefore they reproduce more to offset the fact that half of them are dying.
>
> Now, one could say that if some of the loss of social structure in this society, and particularly within the high impact inner city areas, has removed some of the civilizing evolutionary things

that we have built up and that maybe it isn't just the careless use of the word when people call certain areas of certain cities jungles, that we may have gone back to what might be more natural, without all of the social controls that we have imposed upon ourselves as a civilization over thousands of years in our own evolution. This just reminds us that, although we look at individual factors and we look at biological differences and we look at genetic differences, the loss of structure in society is probably why we are dealing with this issue and why we are seeing the doubling incidence of violence among the young over the last 20 years.

Goodwin's remarks provoked a storm of controversy that, as noted, resulted in his so-called official demotion to being *merely* director of the National Institute of Mental Health.[3] But the controversy was beyond a single demotion, and it peaked in print and electronic media stories just as the first Bush administration (George H. W. Bush) was ending.

In late 1992, the Director of the NIH appointed a special panel to investigate the entire NIH portfolio on violence. I was among the more than two dozen appointees. During the first quarter of 1993, all agency heads at NIH were required to pull into a single portfolio any research funded in the recent period that dealt with violent behavior, including antisocial and aggressive behavior. Our task was to review the full range of studies in order to recommend where funding might best be directed to cover gaps in our knowledge about violence.

The vast majority (over 80 percent) of studies in the portfolio dealt with either the individual or smaller units of analysis (cells, neurotransmitters, genes). Yet the lack of balance in the research presented to the panel was so extreme that members from the natural sciences, psychiatry, and psychology felt the need to explain and justify this to the social scientists on the panel. The social scientists pointed out that we already know that violence (even variably defined) occurs in selected communities more than in others, and in selected social groupings more than in others. However, members of the biological sciences communicated one recurring theme—they were much more concerned with what they kept referring to as basic processes. They granted that the rest of us "non-scientists" might have a point—social, cultural, political, and economic forces might also explain varying levels of violence in a society. However, they were adamant in asserting that they were after more basic, and thus, more enduring truths about explanations of individual proclivities to violence. The biological scientists believed that if they could learn how to explain the mechanisms that control neurotransmission, then they would understand the more fundamental scientific problem. The rest could be addressed by "policy" and that was not their department, not as scientists *qua* scientists.

In the current version of what constitutes the parameters of science, any attempt to account for human behavior with a unit of analysis larger than the *individual* person is vulnerable to being called "political," "soft," humanistic, and not amenable to scientific investigation. In contrast, anything that coincides with the individual's body or that is a subset of that body (biochemistry, neurophysiology, molecular genetic, cellular) is regarded as at least an amenable candidate for scientific investigation.

Yet sociologists have a particularly important role to play in reshaping and redressing the imbalance in the portfolio and, ultimately, in conceiving the nature of the problem of "violence in society." When the unit of analysis is enlarged, there is the increasing adoption of a public health approach to studying violence that tries to take some of the conventional wisdom from studies of cardiovascular disease, cancer,

---

[3]Whether this was an actual demotion has long been contested, since a reorganization of the combined national institutes of drug administration (NIDA), alcohol (NIAAA), and mental health (NIMH) that was synthesized under the rubric of ADAMHA was in process during the previous year.

and infectious disease: i.e., the best way to prevent mortality and morbidity is through education, community-based prevention, and intervention strategies.

The official statistics indicate that the homicide rate among African Americans in key at-risk age groups is 12 times greater than that of whites (see Michigan national study 2005). Could whatever is meant by the term *basic processes* inside the body have any chance of explaining that level of difference? Could a scientist believe that the basic processes are so different between blacks and whites without proffering a biological theory of racial differences?

Whatever the domain assumptions, the picture fits well with the earlier account of the attempt to explain the high rate of alcoholism among Native Americans, namely, that the search for alcohol dehydrogenase polymorphisms occurs inside the body. An analysis of the role of displacement from native lands begins outside the body. As crude and rudimentary as it may sound, this distinction is replicated across many fields of inquiry, from cancer research to studies of educational achievement gaps, from high crime rates to hypertension and heart disease.

One-half of all cancers are diagnosed among people living in the industrialized world, though this group constitutes only one-fifth of the world's population (Steingraber 1997:59–60). The World Health Organization collected data on cancer rates from 70 countries and concluded that at least 80 percent of all cancer is attributable to environmental influences (Proctor 1995:54–74). Reporting problems and earlier deaths in the rest of the world may possibly explain some of these differences, but migrant studies are among the most powerfully persuasive devices that can be deployed to sharpen and isolate the environmental sources of the high incidence of cancer:

> Migrants to Australia, Canada, Israel and the United States all illustrate this pattern. Consider Jewish women who migrate from North Africa, where breast cancer is rare, to Israel, a nation with a high incidence. Initially, their breast cancer risk is one-half that of their Israeli counterparts. But . . . within thirty years, African-born and Israeli-born Jews show identical breast cancer rates. (Steingraber 1997:61–62)

In one of the most compelling environmental studies of cancer ever conducted, researchers found a statistically significant association between the use of agricultural chemicals and cancer mortality in 1,497 rural counties (Pickle et al. 1989).

In the United States, the rate of prostate cancer for African Americans is double that for white Americans. If we begin with these figures without any sense of history, sociology, or epidemiology, then it seems scientifically legitimate to ask, "Is 'race' as a biological concept playing a role?" Indeed, just as there are molecular geneticists searching for genes that predispose Aborigines and Native Americans to alcohol abuse by looking only inside the body, there are those looking for an answer to higher rates of prostate cancer among blacks—those searching for so-called candidate genes in this "special population."

However, given the data with which this article is introduced, a far more plausible explanation comes from an analysis of the sustained structural location of American blacks, derived from more than three and a half centuries with a predominant social location at the base of the U.S. economic structure (a higher proportion in poverty, and living closer to toxic waste sites; Bullard 1990; Sze 2004, forthcoming).

The story of four decades of research into the causes of cancer repeats with an even more dramatic challenge to sociology, a story that echoes those about hypertension and heart disease. What is at stake here is far more consequential than who gets funded. We have moved into new and challenging territory when the implications of where the explanation is located determines whether medicines will be developed for special populations versus a consideration of social interventions. To illustrate, the Food and Drug Administration (FDA) approved for the first time a drug aimed specifically at a racial group in the spring of 2005. In the rationale for the drug's development, and in the lead-up to the nature and character of the paradigmatic fight over this development, here is what the chief executive officer of that drug's manufacturing company had to say in Griffith's (2001) *Financial Times* article:

> Illnesses that seem identical in terms of symptoms may actually be a group of diseases with distinct genetic pathways. This would help explain blacks' far higher mortality rates for a host of conditions, including diabetes, cancer and stroke.
>
> Until now, these gaps have been attributed largely to racism in the healthcare sector and widespread poverty among African Americans. (p. 16)

The BiDil Story and the Medicalization of the Sources of Hypertension

In a classical piece of epidemiological research, Klag et al. (1991) show that, in general, the darker the skin color, the higher the rate of hypertension for American blacks. They conclude that the issue of race in relation to heart problems is not biological or genetic in *origin* but biological in *effect* due to stress-related outcomes of reduced access to valued social goods, such as employment, promotion, and housing stock. The effect was biological (e.g., hypertension) but the origin was social. But a competing perspective, now ratified by an extraordinary decision by the FDA, locates the problem primarily inside the body of African Americans. Patented and marketed to be specifically prescribed for blacks, isosorbide dinitrate hydralazine (BiDil) is a combination drug designed to restore low or depleted nitric oxide levels to the blood to treat or prevent cases of congestive heart failure. The manufacturer originally intended the drug for the general

population, and race was irrelevant. Early clinical studies revealed no compelling results, and an FDA advisory panel voted 9 to 3 against approval.

In a remarkable turn of events, however, BiDil was reborn as a racialized intervention. One of the investigators reviewed the data and found that African Americans in the original clinical trial seemed to show better outcomes than whites. Because the study was not designed to test that hypothesis, a new clinical trial would have to be approved. However, rather than setting up a study design to see whether BiDil worked better in one group than another, in March 2001 the FDA approved a full-scale clinical trial, the first prospective trial conducted exclusively in black men and women with heart failure.

In the early spring of 2005, anticipating FDA decision on approval in late spring, NitroMed (2005)—the company that developed BiDil—released a statement that was an attempt to provide a race-specific justification for approval of the drug:

> The African American community is affected at a greater rate by heart failure than that of the corresponding Caucasian population. African Americans between the ages of 45 and 64 are 2.5 times more likely to die from heart failure than Caucasians in the same age range.

The numbers are technically correct, but the age group 45 to 64 years only accounts for about 6 percent of heart failure mortality, while patients over 65 years of age constitute 93.7 percent of the mortality. Moreover, for the over 65 age group, the statistical differences in heart failure mortality between African Americans and Caucasians nearly disappear. Yet we have the FDA approving a new drug designed for African Americans, and we have a paradigmatic fight tilted dramatically to account for the sources of hypertension inside the body (see quote from *Financial Times* on page 6 of this article).

I reference that *Financial Times* quote again because it sharply identifies the nature of the contestation between where to best explain and how to intervene. Even more dramatic is this quotation from an article by Leroi (2005) summarizing the implications of DNA marker identification by race:

> In one promising test run, Neil Risch's group at Stanford University showed that African Americans with hypertension have a higher probability of African ancestry for two genomic regions—6q24 and 21q21—than their nonhypertensive relatives (Zhu et al. 2005). If this result is replicated it will no longer be possible to claim that racial disparity in the rates of disease is due entirely to socioeconomic factors or even the direct effect of racism itself. (p. 3)

Leroi (2005) and others working from this perspective conclude that, if African Americans with a particular genomic region marker "have a higher probability of hypertension" than those without that marker, then this is evidence that the marker explains the hypertension. This in turn leads to a discussion of the kinds of challenges facing sociology, not just in matters of trying to explain different health outcomes for different groups, but fending off the increasing attempts to give so-called scientific authority to explanations of phenomena as wide ranging as crime and violence on the one hand and academic achievement on the other.

Part II: What Is This Increasing Challenge to Sociology?

The challenge comprises four interrelated parts: 1) the tendency to prioritize and selectively fund so-called scientific work inside the body to explain complex social behavior and health outcomes; 2) the quick emergence and proliferation of national DNA databases; 3) the destruction of or blocked access to data on the social, economic, and political aspects of health, employment status, and social stratification; 4) the

attendant "molecularization of race" (Fullwiley 2005) in practical applications of human molecular genetics, from the delivery of pharmaceutical drugs to the attempt at identification of a person's race by "ancestral informative markers" in the DNA.

In 2003, the NIAAA discontinued the Alcohol and Alcohol Problems Science Database, a vital resource for social science researchers, clinicians and policy makers. This decision is part of an alarming overall strategy, the tip of an iceberg. As of January 7, 2005, the U.S. Commission on Civil Rights, by its own admission, purged 20 reports with vital social data from its Web site, such as the following 3 reports:

- Briefing on the Consequences of Government Race Data Collection on Civil Rights (May 2002);
- Native American Health Care Disparities Briefing Summary (February 2004); and
- Briefing on Tragedy Along Arizona-Mexico Border: Undocumented Immigrants Face Death in the Desert (August 2002).

Behavioral geneticists are quickly searching for genetic markers (and sometimes even coding regions) that they can associate with complex behavioral phenotypes, such as criminality, risk taking, violence, intelligence, alcoholism, manic depression, schizophrenia, and homosexuality. In the last decade, researchers have claimed links exist between DNA regions and cognitive ability in children (Chorney et al. 1998:159–66), crime (Jensen et al. 1998), violence (Caspi et al. 2002), and attention-deficit/hyperactivity disorder (Smalley et al. 2002).

New developments in population genetics now promise to explore the contributions of genetic differences to phenotypic differences between groups. The haplotype map, for example, is designed to look at sections of the DNA to find markers with the purpose of making such differentiations. These new molecular techniques allow researchers to correlate markers for racial background with behavioral outcomes, such as violence and impulsivity. Thus, these techniques are poised to usher in a whole new era of scientific justification for theories of racial and ethnic differences in social behaviors.

Social and cultural factors always influence human genetic research, beginning with the issue of why certain behaviors are chosen for genetic analysis. During the last decade, scientific and popular literature propagated overly simplistic genetic explanations to a variety of complex social behaviors, such as sexual preference, risk-seeking behavior, shyness, alcoholism, and even homelessness. There is a history of using genetic explanations to account for and justify differences in social stratification and the behavior of those at the bottom of the economic order (Black 2003; Kevles 1985; Reilly 1991). These converging preoccupations and tangled webs interlace crime and violence with race and genetic explanations.

For decades, social scientists have documented the substantial inequalities between school districts in the United States. In recent years, the increasing retreat of the white middle classes to private schools has exacerbated these differences in many urban areas (Kozol 1991). And even a century ago, the claim has been made that intelligence quotient (IQ) differences between both individuals and groups are better explained by genetics (Kamin 1974). However, previous claims about the genetic basis of IQ differences have used mainly correlational data or twin studies and adoption studies—all relying on data outside the body, and only then making an inference about genetic differences. With new computer chip technologies linked to DNA

profiling, behavioral geneticists now are able to focus on data that will permit them to better ask about patterns in the DNA.[4]

Why should sociologists be concerned about this? First, institutions are systematically destroying more and more databases of social factors and social processes.[5] This decreased access to social data is coupled with the simultaneous increase in DNA collection from ordinary citizens that has all the features of an inexorable technological juggernaut. The United Kingdom has been in the vanguard of these developments, but there is every indication that this will not be for long.[6] In April 2004, the UK Parliament passed a law permitting police to retain DNA samples from anyone, arrested for any reason, including people who are not charged with a crime. Anyone can have their DNA sample taken and stored. The UK database already contains 2.8 million DNA "fingerprints" taken from identified suspects, plus another 230,000 from unidentified samples collected from crime scenes (BJHC 2005). Samples are being added at the rate of between 10,000 and 20,000 per month.[7] The aim is to have on file a quarter of the adult population's DNA—a figure that exceeds 10 million, making it by far the largest DNA database in the world.

Ancestral Informative Markers: Identifying Race From Inside the Body via DNA

In the last decade, researchers using molecular genetic technologies have made remarkable claims in the scientific literature, including the

---

[4]For example, Chorney et al. (1998) claimed to find a DNA marker for insulin-like growth factor 2 (IGF2R) on chromosome 6 based on an analysis of 102 students. Actually, their study explained only 5 percent of the variance.

[5]In 1999 (the last year of the Bill Clinton administration) the Department of Labor published its extensive report on domestic violence against women. The National Council of Research on Women (2004) notes that the new recommissioned study on the same topic was due to be published in 2004 but is missing from the Web site of the Department of Labor.

[6]In April 2005, the Portuguese government announced its intention to collect DNA from all of its residents (Boavida 2005).

[7]This was before the bombings in London in early July 2005.

claim that it is possible to estimate a person's race by looking at specific markers in the DNA (Lowe et al. 2001; Shriver et al. 1997). The social implications reach far beyond personal recreational usage, where the individual submits a DNA sample and "discovers" the percentage of ancestry that comes from Europe, sub-Saharan Africa, or the Asian continent.[8] Companies are touting and marketing forensic applications, the direct consequence of a successful intervention in a sensational serial rape-murder case.[9]

Tang et al. (2005), make yet another claim about the capacity to use DNA to identify race, followed by an explicit challenge to the sociologists of race who maintain that "race is only a social construct":

> Genetic cluster analysis of the microsatellite markers produced four major clusters, which showed near-perfect correspondence with the self-reported race/ethnic categories. (p. 268)

On February 4, 2005, the Stanford University public information office released the following statement (Zhang 2005) to the press:

> A recent study conducted at the Stanford Medical School challenges the widely held belief that race is only a social construct and provides evidence that race has genetic implications. (p. 1)

The DNA data collection in the United States has been a fairly recent and quickly expanding venture. In 1994, the U.S. Congress passed the DNA Identification Act, authorizing the Federal Bureau of Investigation (FBI) to establish a national DNA database, the Combined DNA Index System (CODIS). Only since the mid-1980s have most states been collecting DNA samples and only from sexual offenders. But within a decade, all 50 states were contributing to CODIS with a capacity to interlink state databases and using DNA samples from a wide range of felons. At one time, the system had 9 states cross-linking approximately 100,000 offender profiles and 5,000 forensic profiles. In just three years, that number jumped to 32 states, the FBI, and the U.S. Army now linking approximately 400,000 offender profiles and 20,000 forensic profiles. States are now uploading an average of 3,000 offender profiles every month (Gavel 2000). Although searching within such a large pool of profiles may seem daunting, computer technology is increasingly efficient and extraordinarily fast. It takes less than a second—about 500 microseconds—to search a database of 100,000 profiles.

The further expansion of the databases is inevitable. The U.S. House of Representatives passed a bill (H.R. 3214 "Advancing Justice Through DNA Technology Act of 2003") that will expand the original CODIS to include persons merely indicted and not necessarily convicted. In 2004, California voters passed Proposition 69 that permits collection and storing of DNA for those *merely arrested* for certain crimes by 2008, thereby joining four other states collecting DNA on the same premise. The Violence Against Women Act of 2005 contains the following provision that DNA

---

[8]Many Web sites, such as AncestrybyDNA.com, provide information so that a person can apply for a kit to submit his or her DNA sample for the company to analyze and report the estimated proportion of a person's ancestry that is purportedly from one of several large continental groupings.

[9]In 2003, police in Baton Rouge, LA, were unsuccessful identifying a serial rapist-murderer, after interviewing over 1,000 white males who fit what one witness described as the likely suspect. A DNA sample was tested and analyzed by a company claiming it could discern that the suspect (based on DNA analysis) was 85 percent African ancestry (Touchette 2003). The prime suspect was apprehended and identified to be African American. Since then, the DNA testing company advertises its success on the Web and markets its expertise to police departments nationally.

samples can be obtained from people merely detained under federal authority:

> *Sec. 1004.* Authorization to Conduct DNA Sample Collection from Persons Arrested or Detained under Federal Authority.
>
> (a) In General-Section 3 of the DNA Analysis Backlog Elimination Act of 2000 (42 U.S.C. 14135a) is amended—(1) in subsection (a)
>
> (A) in paragraph (1), by striking 'The Director' and inserting the following:
>
> (A) The Attorney General may, as prescribed by the Attorney General in regulation, collect DNA samples from individuals who are *arrested or detained* under. (italics added)

As governments increase the number of profiles in the databases, researchers will increase proposals to provide DNA profiles of specific offender populations. Twenty states authorize the use of databanks for research on forensic techniques (Kimmelman 2000).

The emerging challenge to social theory will be substantial, precisely because the imprimatur of scientific authority tilts to so-called basic processes or to a parallel notion that locates the explanatory power to data collected inside the body. Of course one position is that collecting these data is valuable in that researchers can then assess empirically the relative explanatory power of competing explanations. The problem with this position is the role of the supercomputer in the generation of seductive but meaningless correlations to DNA markers. Although this matter would seem to be highly technical, it can be explained quite simply: Each human has 3 billion base pairs of DNA. Any two humans across the globe share 99.9 percent, or complete duplication, of their DNA sequences. However, that remaining 0.1 percent difference means that there are at least *3 million points of difference* between any two people, or any two groups of people. Current supercomputer technology can therefore find differences between *any* two groups of persons, whether or not those differences have any bearing on the manner of gene expression. A supercomputer can be programmed to find differences in the DNA sequences between any two arbitrarily and randomly selected groups of people. I have used the example of dividing an audience at a lecture into two groups, A and B, just by drawing an arbitrary line down the center of the audience. That would be trivial research that has little credibility and less chance of funding. However, if those two groups happen to coincide with socially significant categories (e.g., race, ethnicity, social class, or caste position), the demonstrated differences would feed easily into a competing explanation of the manifest differences between groups that necessarily resonate in (that) society.

Thus, the problems that need to be addressed are as follows:

1. Increasing pressure for national DNA databases;

2. Destruction of more and more databases about social categories;

3. A research agenda, waiting in the wings, to do single nucleotide polymorphisms (SNP) profiling;

4. Ever expanding and racially marked DNA databases, and the inevitable search for competing explanations of human behavior.

PART III: WHAT SOCIOLOGISTS CAN DO TO MEET THE COMING AND GROWING CHALLENGE

Sociologists can stand on the sidelines, watch the parade of reductionist science as it goes by, and point out that it is all "socially constructed." That will not be good enough to rain on this parade, because of the imprimatur of legitimacy increasingly afforded to the study of so-called basic processes inside the body. What can and should the discipline do?

Sociological Research and Sociological Work at the Site of "Rate Construction"

While this argument is indeed about social construction, sociologists need to spend more time showing how the rates got constructed.[10] How analysts theorize about social life has direct consequences. The sharply different approaches to the study of deviance, law, and the criminal justice system best illustrate these consequences. In the middle of the twentieth century, two competing schools of thought dominated research and theory in this area. Columbia University represented one orientation, where Robert Merton ([1949] 1990) and his students examined the relationship between the worlds of deviants and normals through an empirical strategy that relied heavily upon official statistics reported by police departments. Researchers assumed the collected FBI's Uniform Crime Reports accurately reflected deviant and criminal behavior. Those working in this tradition occasionally engaged in field site research, but the dominant tendency presumed there was not a large gap between official crime statistics and that of the phenomenal world of action, and that theorizing from these databases warranted little caution or concern.

The University of Chicago, which had a long and strong tradition of what they called "natural setting" research, represents the competing orientation. Unlike Columbia, the Chicago researchers were committed to close observation of the so-called hobo, gang, or prostitute. They spent years in what might now be described as an embedded strategy of data collection. Their practitioners literally went to those spaces that any common sense actor perceived to be the setting for deviance. According to the folklore, one of the most celebrated sociologists of the era got "caught with his pants down" in an up-close ethnography of prostitution; the university administration and the *Chicago Tribune* demanded that he be fired. This tale is a more colorful illustration of Chicago researchers' commitment to studying deviance in its natural setting. Still, researchers did not conduct their field work on white collar crime or in corporate settings. The accepted domain assumptions were to simply document the behaviors and practices of those already located in the existing categories.

In short, Chicago researchers and Columbia researchers approached the study of deviance in significantly different but fundamentally important ways. However, both schools conducted their work in a "taken-for-granted" empirical world.

Within this context, a third set of players challenged the epistemology of the whole playing field and ultimately shifted the focus of theory and research. Aaron Cicourel (1967) and Egon Bittner (1967) persuaded the police to let them ride with them on their routine rounds, permitting them to observe the wide discretion police used in their arrest procedures. Meanwhile, David Sudnow (1965) observed the actual processes of the Public Defender's office and recorded the ways prosecuting attorneys worked together to selectively secure guilty pleas from some individuals, while other individuals were able to bargain for better deals. Erving Goffman (1959) penetrated mental hospital wards and studied intake decision-making that blazed a trail for the next generation of mental health researchers. Yet deviance was merely the vehicle for obtaining a better understanding about how social institutions and organizations construct rates (and order). For example, Irving Zola (1966) sat in medical clinics, observing doctor–patient communication, the subject of his now classical study of how Jewish, Italian, and Irish patients present very different symptoms for the same physical condition, shaping how medical

---

[10]This segment is based on a short article previously published in *Social Problems* (Duster 2001).

doctors interpret, diagnose, and categorize (rate construction). This had obvious implications for how theorizing from "raw rates" could be completely distorted. Knowing that the Irish tend to be more stoic and the Italians more expressive in reporting the same symptoms has profound implications for developing a theory of ethnic differences in health and illness.

These researchers engaged in a methodology that seemed to parallel or complement the Chicago School, that is, field work in the natural setting. Yet the basic assumptions were very different, since Chicago researchers were trying to find out more about deviants' true characteristics. This newer approach began during the first decade of the new journal *Social Problems* and raised a very challenging question: "What are the social processes that account for why some get classified in a category and others do not, *even though both are engaged in the same or similar behavior?*"

When Kitsuse and Cicourel (1963) tried to publish their classic article on the uses and misuses of official statistics in social science, each major sociology journal (the *American Sociological Review,* the *American Journal of Sociology,* and *Social Forces)* rejected it—some reviewers explicitly argued that this was an attack on the citadel. Reviewers aligned with both traditions (Columbia and Chicago) worried that "if this were true (that official statistics grossly misrepresent social reality), we would have to go back to the drawing board and re-orient theory and research."[11] Howard Becker had just taken over the editorship of *Social Problems,* the breakaway journal of the *Society for the Study of Social Problems.* A different set of reviewers with a sharply different perspective urged publication. In the next few years, several published articles effectively challenged and

substantially replaced earlier schools. The 1960s exploded with more competing paradigms, from conflict theory to ethnomethodology to Marxist theory. Each had its own approach to the study of deviance and normality. But it was the professional skepticism regarding automatically accepting official statistics that had the most profound impact upon the developing epistemological crisis of the field.

The Importance of Data Collection at the Site of Knowledge Production

There are powerful organizational motives for police departments to demonstrate effectiveness in "solving crimes." It is a considerable embarrassment for a police department to have a long list of crimes on their books, for which no arrest has been made. No police chief wishes to face a city council with this problem. Thus, there are organizational imperatives for police departments to clean up the books by a procedure known as "cleared by arrest."

Few matters count as much as this one when it comes to reporting police activities to the public (Skolnick 2002; Skolnick and Fyfe 1993). To understand how arrest rates are influenced by this "cleared by arrest" procedure, it is vital to empirically ground this procedure by close observation.

Here is the pattern: Someone (P) is arrested and charged with committing a crime (x), such as burglary for example. There are several other burglaries in this police precinct. The arresting officers see a pattern to these burglaries and decide that the suspect is likely to have committed several on their unsolved burglary list. Thus, it sometimes happens that when P is arrested for just one of those burglaries, the police can clear by arrest the

---

[11]Kitsuse (1962) would also argue that the "social reaction" approach to deviance requires that the investigator go out into the field and study the social responses to deviance in its natural setting. So, while this approach affirms the "natural setting" methodology of the Chicago School, it asks the investigator to look at the social patterns in the discretions and strategies of sorting, naming, and classifying.

15–20 other burglaries with that single arrest. This can show up as a repeat offender in the statistics, though there may never be any follow-up empirical research to verify or corroborate that the police arrest record (rap sheet) accurately represents the burglaries now attributed to P.

But researchers can corroborate this activity as a pattern only by riding around in police cars or doing the equivalent close up observation of police work (Jackall 2005). And yet, if social theorists take the FBI Uniform Crime Reports as a reflection of the crime rate, with no observations as to how those rates were constructed, they will make the predictable "policy error" of assuming that there are only a small number of people who commit a large number of crimes. The resulting error in theorizing would be to then look for the kind of person who repeatedly engages in this behavior (as if it were not "cleared by arrest" that generated the long rap sheet). It is a very small step to search for explanations inside the body. In an earlier section, I mention the use of ancestral informative markers to attempt to identify a person's race. The U.S. prison population has undergone a dramatic shift in its racial composition in the last 30 years. The convergence of this social trend, along with the burgeoning redefinition of race as something determined by DNA patterns, will be a challenge to sociology at many levels, from the attempted reinscription of race as a biological or genetic category, to attempted explanation of a host of complex social behaviors. That challenge can only be met by doing what the social researchers of a previous generation did with police work, namely, going to the very site at which those data are generated.

To meet this challenge, social scientists will have to do the kind of research that documents how these categories are constructed. We need to treat so-called ancestral informative markers as the subject of close inquiry and observation. That means, rather than accepting or rejecting axiomatically, we need to penetrate the logic of this kind of work and determine just how subjects are sorted into categories that claim the DNA belongs to someone with "85 percent" African ancestry.[12]

In sum, if social construction is to be more than a comfortable shibboleth easily received by those who already accept its premises, it must be buttressed by investigations at key empirical sites that show the social forces at play in the construction. Otherwise, sociologists will be left watching the parade from the sidewalk, asserting to a resonant audience of like-minded social scientists that it is all "socially constructed." Meanwhile, incarceration rates continue to soar, DNA databases fill to the brim, and competing explanations have greater resonation.

REFERENCES

Beauvais, Fred. 1998. "American Indians and Alcohol." *Alcohol Health and Research World* 22(4):253–9.

Beresford, Quentin and Paul Omaji. 1996. *Rites of Passage: Aboriginal Youth, Crime and Justice.* Fremantle, Australia: Fremantle Arts Centre Press.

Bittner, Egon. 1967. "The Police on Skid-Row: A 'Study of Peace-Keeping.'" *American Sociological Review* 32:699–715.

BJHC. "Police Aim for DNA on 25% of UK Population." *BJHC,* February, volume 22, number 1, p. 10. Retrieved July 22, 2005 (http://www.bjhc.co.uk/news/1/2005/n502020.htm).

Black, Edwin. 2003. *War Against the Weak: Eugenics and America's Campaign to Create a Master Race.* New York: Four Walls Eight Windows.

Boavida, Maria João. 2005. "Portugal Plans a Forensic Genetic Database of Its Entire Population: 1st Part." *Newropeans Magazine,* April 8. Retrieved July 23, 2005 (http://www.newropeans-magazine.org/index.php?option=com_content&task=view&id=2059&Itemid=121).

---

[12]One important model is that of Fullwiley (2005), an anthropologist who enters the laboratories of these researchers to see how they constitute the "ancestral informative markers."

Bullard, Robert D. 1990. *Dumping in Dixie: Race, Class and Environmental Quality.* Boulder, CO: Westview Press.

Caspi, Avshalom, Joseph McClay, Terrie E. Moffitt, Jonathan Mill, Judy Martin, Ian W Craig, Alan Taylor, and Richie Poulton. 2002 "Role of Genotype in the Cycle of Violence in Maltreated Children." *Science* 297(5582):851–4.

Chorney, M. J., K. Chorney, N. Seese, M. J. Owen, J. Daniels, P. McGuffin, L. A. Thompson, D. K. Detterman, C. Benbow, D. Lubinski, T. Eley, and R. Plomin. 1998. "A Quantitative Trait Locus Associated With Cognitive Ability in Children." *Psychological Science* 9(3): 159–66.

Cicourel, Aaron V 1967. *The Social Organization of Juvenile Justice.* New York: Wiley.

Fullwiley, Duana. 2005. "The Biologistical Construction of Race: 'Admixture' Technology and the New Genetic Medicine." Department of Society, Human Development, and Health, Harvard University, Cambridge, MA. Unpublished manuscript.

Gavel, Doug. 2000. "Fighting Crime Through Science: Reno Lauds DNA Technology at KSG Talk." *Harvard Gazette,* November 30. Retrieved September 28, 2005 (http://www.news.harvard.edu/gazette/2000/11.30/05-crimefight.html).

Goffman, Erving. 1959. "The Moral Career of the Mental Patient." *Psychiatry* 22(2): 123–42.

Griffith, V 2001. "FDA Backs Ethnically Targeted Drug." *Financial Times,* March 9, p. 16.

Jackall, Robert. 2005. *Street Stories: The World of Private Detectives.* Cambridge, MA: Harvard University Press.

Jensen, Per, Kirsten Fenger, Tom G. Bolwig, and Sven Asger Sorensen. 1998. "Crime in Huntington's Disease: A Study of Registered Offences Among Patients, Relatives, and Controls." *Journal of Neurology, Neurosurgery, and Psychiatry* 65:467–71.

Kamin, Leon J. 1974. *The Science and Politics of I.Q.* New York: Humanities Press.

Kevles, Daniel. 1985. *In the Name of Eugenics: Genetics and the Uses of Human Heredity.* New York: Alfred A. Knopf.

Kibbey, Hal. 1995. "Genetic Influences on Alcohol Drinking and Alcoholism." *Research and Creative Activity* 17(3): 18–20. Retrieved December 20, 2005 (http://www.indiana.edu/~rcapub/v17n3/ p18.html).

Kimmelman, Jonathan. 2000. "Risking Ethical Insolvency: A Survey of Trends in Criminal DNA Databanking." *Journal of Law, Medicine and Ethic* 28:209–21.

Kitsuse, John I. 1962. "Societal Reaction to Deviant Behavior." *Social Problems* 9(3):247–56.

Kitsuse, John I. and Aaron V. Cicourel. 1963. "A Note on the Uses of Official Statistics." *Social Problems* 11(2): 131–9.

Klag, Michael J., P. K. Whelton, J. Coresh, C. E. Grim, L. H. Kuller. 1991. "Association of Skin Color With Blood Pressure in U.S. Blacks With Low Socioeconomic Status." *Journal of the American Medical Association* 265:599–602.

Kozol, Jonathan. 1991. *Savage Inequalities: Children in American Schools.* New York: Crown Publishers.

Leroi, Armand. 2005. "On Human Diversity: Why Has the Genetics Community Discarded So Many Phenotypes." *The Scientist* 19(20): 16–22.

Lowe, Alex L., Andrew Urquhart, Lindsey A. Foreman, and Ian Evert. 2001 "Inferring Ethnic Origin by Means of an STR Profile." *Forensic Science International* 119:17–22.

Mannheim, Karl. 1936. *Ideology and Utopia.* London: Routledge & Kegan Paul.

Merton, Robert K. [1949] 1990. *Social Theory and Social Structure.* New York: The Free Press of Simon and Schuster.

Michels, Robert. 1966. *Political Parties* (English translation) New York: Free Press.

Michigan National Study. 2005. *Age-Adjusted Homicide Death Rates by Race and Sex Michigan and United States Residents, 1980–2003.* Lansing, MI: Michigan Department of Community Health. Retrieved October 10, 2005 (http://www.mdch.state.mi.us/pha/osr/deaths/Homicdx.asp).

Midanik, Lorraine T. 2004. "Biomedicalization and Alcohol Studies: Implications for Policy." *Journal of Public Health Policy* 25(2):211–28.

Murray, Christopher J. L. and Alan D. Lopez, eds. 1996. *The Global Burden of Disease.* Cambridge, MA: Harvard University Press and the World Health Organization.

National Institute on Alcohol Abuse and Alcoholism. *NIAAA Strategic Plan 2001–2005.* Bethesda, MD: NIAAA. Retrieved September 20, 2005 (www.niaaa.nih.gov about/stratext-test.htm).

National Council for Research on Women. 2004. *Missing: Information About Women's Lives.* New York: National Council for Research on Women. Retrieved September 26, 2005 (http://www.ncrw.org/misinfo/report/htm).

National Mental Health Advisory Council. 1992. Transcript, February 11 meeting. Bethesda, MD: National Institute of Mental Health.

NitroMed. 2005. "FDA Accepts Nitromed's New Drug Application Resubmission for Bidil." February 3, news release. Retrieved June 28, 2005 (http://www.nitromed.com/02_03_05.asp).

Parsons, Talcott. [1937] 1968. *The Structure of Social Action.* New York: The Free Press of Macmillan Publishing.

Pickle L. W., T. J. Mason, and J. F. Fraumeni Jr. 1989. "The New United States Cancer Atlas." *Recent Results in Cancer Research.* 114:196–207.

Proctor, Robert N. 1995. *Cancer Wars: How Politics Shapes What We Know and Don't Know About Cancer.* New York: Basic Books.

Reilly, Philip R. 1991. *The Surgical Solution: A History of Involuntary Sterilization in the United States.* Baltimore, MD: Johns Hopkins University Press.

Rhoades, Lawrence J. 1981. *A History of the American Sociological Association 1905–1980.* Washington, DC: American Sociological Association. Retrieved September 26, 2005 (http://www.asanet.org/ index.ww).

Rosich, Katherine J. 2005. *A History of the American Sociological Association: 1981–2004.* Washington, DC: American Sociological Association. Retrieved September 26, 2005 (http://www.asanet.org/index .ww).

Schütz, Alfred. 1955. "Symbol, Reality, and Society." Pp. 135–203 in *Symbols and Society,* edited by L. Bryson, L. Finkelstein, H. Hoagland, and R. M. MacIver. New York: Harper.

Shriver, Mark D., Michael W. Smith, Li Jin, Amy Marcini, Joshua M. Akey, Ranjan Deka, and Robert E. Ferrell. 1997. "Ethnic-Affiliation Estimation by Use of Population-Specific DNA Markers." *American Journal of Human Genetics* 60:957–64.

Skolnick, Jerome H. 2002. "Corruption and the Blue Code of Silence." *Police Practice and Research* 3:7–19.

Skolnick, Jerome H. and James J. Fyfe. 1993. *Above the Law: Police and the Excessive Use of Force.* New York: Free Press.

Smalley, Susan L., Vlad Kustanovich, Sonia L. Minassian, Jennifer L. Stone, Matthew N. Ogdie, James J. McGough, James T. McCracken, I. Laurence MacPhie, Clyde Francks, Simon E. Fisher, Rita M. Cantor, Anthony P. Monaco, and Stanley F. Nelson. 2002. "Genetic Linkage of Attention-Deficit/Hyperactivity Disorder on Chromosome 16p13, in a Region Implicated in Autism." *American Journal of Human Genetics* 71(4):959–63.

Spicer, Paul. 1997. "Toward a (Dys)functional Anthropology of Drinking: Ambivalence and the American Indian Experience with Alcohol." *Medical Anthropology Quarterly* 11(3):306–23.

Steele, Jonathan. 2004. "US Sociologists Are Finally Challenging the Intellectual Stranglehold of Economists." *Guardian,* August 24, comment. Retrieved July 26, 2005 (*http://www.guardian*.co.uk/ comment/story/0,3604,1289361,00.html).

Steingraber, Sandra. 1997. *Living Downstream.* New York: Random House.

Sudnow, David. 1965. "Normal Crimes: Sociological Features of the Penal Code in a Public Defender Office." *Social Problems* 12:255–76.

Sze, Julie. 2004. "Gender, Asthma Politics, and Urban Environmental Justice Activism." Pp. 177–90 in *New Perspectives on Environmental Justice: Gender, Sexuality, and Activism,* edited by R. Stein. Piscataway, NJ: Rutgers University Press.

_____. Forthcoming. *Noxious New York: The Racial Politics of Urban Health and Environmental Justice.* Cambridge, MA: MIT Press.

Tang, Hua, Tom Quertermous, Beatriz Rodriguez, Sharon L. R. Kardia, Xiaofeng Zhu, Andrew Brown, James S. Pankow, Michael A. Province, Steven C. Hunt, Eric Boerwinkle, Nicholas J. Schork, and Neil J. Risch. 2005. "Genetic Structure, Self-Identified Race/Ethnicity, and Confounding in Case-Control Association Studies." *American Journal of Human Genetics* 76:268–75

Tocqueville, Alexis de. [1835] 1966. *Democracy in America,* edited by J. P. Mayer and M. Lerner, translated by G. Lawrence. New York: Harper and Row.

Touchette, Nancy. 2003. "Genome Test Nets Suspected Serial Killer." *Genome News Network* June 13, p. 1. Retrieved December 21, 2005 (http://www.genomenewsnet work.org/articles/06_03/serial.shtml).

U.S. Commission on Civil Rights. 2002. *Briefing on the Consequences of Government Race Data Collection on Civil Rights* (May). Washington, DC: U.S. Commission on Civil Rights.

_____. 2002. *Briefing on Tragedy Along Arizona-Mexico Border: Undocumented Immigrants Face Death in the Desert* (August). Washington, DC: U.S. Commission on Civil Rights.

_____. 2004. *Native American Health Care Disparities Briefing Summary* (February). Washington, DC: U.S. Commission on Civil Rights.

Wall, T. L., C. Garcia-Andrade, H. R. Thomasson, L. G. Carr, C. L. Ehlers. 1997. "Alcohol Dehydrogenase Polymorphisms in Native Americans: Identification of the ADH2*3 Allele." *Alcohol* 32(2): 129–32.

Zhang, Jessica. 2005. "New Study Links Race and DNA Material." *The Stanford Daily,* February 4, p. 1. Retrieved February 12, 2005 (http://daily.stanford .edu/daily/servlet/tempo?page=content&id=15971&re pository=0001_article).

Zhu, Xiaofeng, Amy Luke, Richard S. Cooper, Tom Quertermous, Craig Hanis, Tom Mosley, C. Charles Gu, Hua Tang, Dabeeru C. Rao, Neil Risch, and Alan Weder. 2005. "Admixture Mapping for Hypertension Loci with Genome-Scan Markers." *Nature Genetics* 37(2): 177–81.

Zola, Irving. 1966. "Culture and Symptoms: An Analysis of Patient's Presenting Complaints." *American Sociological Review* 31(5):615–30.

Great Divides

The Cultural, Cognitive, and Social Bases
of the Global Subordination of Women (2007)

Cynthia Fuchs Epstein

The world is made up of great divides—divides of nations, wealth, race, religion, education, class, gender, and sexuality—all constructs created by human agency. The conceptual boundaries that define these categories are always symbolic and may create physical and social boundaries as well (Gerson and Peiss 1985; Lamont and Molnar 2002). Today, as in the past, these constructs not only order social existence, but they also hold the capacity to create serious inequalities, generate conflicts, and promote human suffering. In this address, I argue that the boundary based on sex creates the most fundamental social divide—a divide that should be a root issue in all sociological analysis if scholars are to adequately understand the social dynamics of society and the influential role of stratification. The work of many sociologists contributes to this claim, although I can only refer to some of them in the context of a single article.

The conceptual boundaries that determine social categories are facing deconstruction throughout our profession. Once thought stable and real in the sense that they are descriptive of biological or inherited traits, social categories such as race and ethnicity are contested today by a number of scholars (Barth 1969; Brubaker 2004; Duster 2006; Telles 2004). Indeed, sociologists are questioning the underlying reasoning behind categorical distinctions, noting their arbitrariness, and further, the ways in which they tend to be "essentializing and naturalizing" (Brubaker 2004:9).[1] Yet, not many of these critical theorists have included *gender* in this kind of analysis.[2] Where they have, such work tends to be relegated to, if not ghettoized within, the field of "gender studies."[3]

Of course, the categories of race, ethnicity, and gender are real in the sense that—as W. I. Thomas put it in his oft-quoted observation—"if men *[sic]* define situations as real, they are real in their consequences" (cited in Merton [1949] 1963:421). Categorization on the basis of observable characteristics often serves as a

---

SOURCE: "Great Divides: The Cultural, Cognitive, and Social Bases of the Global Subordination of Women." *American Sociological Review*, 72(1), 1–22. Copyright © 2007. Reprinted with permission.

[1]Brubaker also cites the contributions of Rothbart and Taylor 1992; Hirshfield 1996; and Gil-White 1999 to this perspective.

[2]Duster (2006) does include gender.

[3]For example, see Epstein 1988; Lorber 1994; Connell 1987; Ridgeway 2006; Bussey and Bandura 1999; Tavris 1992.

mobilizing strategy for action against (or for) people assigned to the category and may even force them into a grouplike state (Bourdieu 1991; Brubaker 2004). Alternatively, categorization may create conformity to a stereotype—in the process known as "the self-fulfilling prophecy" (Merton [1949] 1963). But it is one thing for individuals to engage in categorical thinking, and another for social scientists to accept a category with its baggage of assumptions. Today, many social scientists use popular understandings of race, ethnicity, and gender as if they were descriptive of inherent or acquired stable traits, and they treat them as established variables that describe clusters of individuals who share common traits. In this manner, social scientists are no different from the lay public, who, in their everyday activities and thinking, act as if categories are reliable indicators of commonalities in a population.

The consequences of such categorization may be positive or negative for those in a given category. For example, people of color face far more suspicion from the police than do whites, and favored male professors benefit from the evaluation that they are smart and knowledgeable while comparatively, favored female professors tend to be evaluated as nice (Basow 1995). Yet, unlike the basis on which social *groups* may be defined, categories include individuals who may never know one another or have any interaction with each other. However, they may all share selected physical traits or relationships. Skin color, hair texture, genitals, place of birth, and genealogy are among the determinants of categories.

I consider *gender* to be the most basic and prevalent category in social life throughout the world, and in this address, I explore the life consequences that follow from this designation for the female half of humanity. Gender is, of course, based on biological sex, as determined by the identification of an individual at birth as female or male by a look at their genitals. This first glance sets up the most basic divide in all societies—it determines an individual's quality of life, position on the social hierarchy, and chance at survival. The glance marks individuals for life and is privileged over their unique intelligence, aptitudes, or desires. Of course, persons who are transgendered, transsexual, or hermaphrodites[4] do not fit this dichotomous separation, but there is little recognition of categories based on sex other than male and female in almost every society (Butler 1990; Lorber 1994, 1996).

SEX DIVISION AND SUBORDINATION

The sexual divide is the most persistent and arguably the deepest divide in the world today. Of course, it is only one of many great divides. Boundaries mark the territories of human relations. They are created by "cultural entrepreneurs"[5] who translate the concepts into practice—rulers behind the closed doors of palaces and executive offices; judges in courtrooms; priests, rabbis, and mullahs; leaders and members of unions and clubs; and teachers, parents, and the people in the street. The great divides of society are enforced by persuasion, barter, custom, force, and the threat of force (Epstein 1985). The extent to which boundaries are permeable and individuals can escape categorization, and thus, their assignment to particular social roles and statuses, is a function of a society's or an institution's stability and capacity to change. The ways in which boundaries may be transgressed make up the story of social change and its limits. They are the basis for human freedom.

Of all the socially created divides, the gender divide is the most basic and the one most resistant to social change. As I have suggested before

---

[4] I have used these commonly used terms, but alternative words such as "trans" and "intersex" are deemed more appropriate by some scholars and advocates.

[5] I offer this concept following Becker (1963) who writes of "moral entrepreneurs"; Brubaker (2004) who writes of "ethnopolitical entrepreneurs"; and Fine (1996) who writes of "reputational entrepreneurs."

(Epstein 1985, 1988, 1991b, 1992), dichotomous categories, such as those that distinguish between blacks and whites; free persons and slaves; and men and women, are always invidious. This dichotomous categorization is also particularly powerful in maintaining the advantage of the privileged category. With regard to the sex divide, the male sex is everywhere privileged—sometimes the gap is wide, sometimes narrow. Some individuals and small clusters of women may succeed in bypassing the negative consequences of categorization, and in some cases they may even do better educationally or financially than the men in their group. Among women, those from a privileged class, race, or nationality may do better than others. But worldwide, in every society, women as a category are subordinated to men.

I further suggest that the divide of biological sex constitutes a marker around which all major institutions of society are organized. All societal institutions assign roles based on the biological sex of their members. The divisions of labor in the family, local and global labor forces, political entities, most religious systems, and nation-states are all organized according to the sexual divide.

Cultural meanings are also attached to the categories of female and male, which include attributions of character and competence (Epstein 1988, see Ridgeway 2006 for a review). These situate individuals assigned to each category in particular social and symbolic roles. There is some overlap in the roles to which females and males are assigned, but in all societies sex status is the major determinant—it is the master status that determines the acquisition of most other statuses.

Of course, biological sex does prescribe humans' reproductive roles (e.g., child bearer, inseminator). But there is no biological necessity for a woman to become a mother, even though only women can become biological mothers, and a man may or may not choose to become a biological father. Therefore, we can conclude that *all* social statuses and the roles attached to them are *socially* prescribed. Further, norms prescribe (or proscribe) detailed behavior fixed to all social roles. And, because statuses are universally ranked, the statuses women are permitted to acquire usually are subordinate to men's statuses. Furthermore, women's roles are universally paired with roles assigned to men, in the family, in the workplace, and in the polity. Virtually no statuses are stand-alone positions in society; all are dependent on reciprocal activities of those who hold complementary statuses. These too are socially ranked and usually follow the invidious distinctions that "male" and "female" evoke. Almost no statuses are free from gender-typing.

These observations lead me to proposals that I believe are essential for comprehensive sociological analysis today, and to call for the elimination of the boundary that has separated so-called gender studies from mainstream sociology.[6]

Given the ubiquitous nature of sex-typing of social statuses, and social and symbolic behavior, I propose that the dynamics of gender segregation be recognized as a primary issue for sociological analysis and attention be paid to the mechanisms and processes of sex differentiation and their roles in group formation, group maintenance, and stratification.[7] I further suggest that

- Females' and males' actual and symbolic roles in the social structure are a seedbed for group formation and group boundary-maintenance.
- All societies and large institutions are rooted in the differentiation and subordination of females.
- The more group solidarities are in question in a society, the stronger the differentiation between males and females and the more severe is women's subjugation.

The enforcement of the distinction is achieved through cultural and ideological means that justify

---

[6]A number of sociologists have specifically called for a greater integration of feminist theory and studies within the mainstream of American sociology (e.g., Chafetz 1984, 1997; Laslett 1996; Stacey and Thorne 1985).

[7]I am not the first to make this plea (e.g., see Acker 1973; Blumberg 1978; Chafetz 1997).

the differentiation. This is despite the fact that, unlike every other dichotomous category of people, females and males are necessarily bound together, sharing the same domiciles and most often the same racial and social class statuses. Analyses of these relationships are difficult given the ways in which they are integrated with each other and the extent to which they are basic in all institutions.

There is, of course, variation in societies and the subgroups within them, and a continuum exists in the severity of female subordination. Indeed, subordination is not a static process and it varies from almost complete to very little. The process is dynamic in shape and degree. Women gain or lose equality depending on many elements—the state of an economy, the identity politics of groups or nations, the election of conservative or liberal governments, the need for women's labor in the public and private sectors, the extent of their education, the color of their skin,[8] the power of fundamentalist religious leaders in their societies, and their ability to collaborate in social movements. But even in the most egalitarian of societies, the invidious divide is always a lurking presence and it can easily become salient.

It is important to note that women's inequality is not simply another case of social inequality, a view I have held in the past (Epstein 1970). I am convinced that societies and strategic subgroups within them, such as political and work institutions, *maintain their boundaries*—their very social organization—through the use of invidious distinctions made

between males and females.[9] Everywhere, women's subordination is basic to maintaining the social cohesion and stratification systems of ruling and governing groups—male groups—on national and local levels, in the family, and in all other major institutions. Most dramatically, this process is at work today in the parts of the world where control of females' behavior, dress, and use of public space have been made representations of orthodoxies in confrontation with modernism, urbanism, and secular society. But even in the most egalitarian societies, such as the United States, women's autonomy over their bodies,[10] their time, and their ability to decide their destinies is constantly at risk when it intrudes on male power.

The gender divide is not determined by biological forces. *No society or subgroup leaves social sorting to natural processes.* It is through social and cultural mechanisms and their impact on cognitive processes that social sorting by sex occurs and is kept in place—by the exercise of force and the threat of force, by law, by persuasion, and by embedded cultural schemas that are internalized by individuals in all societies. Everywhere, local cultures support invidious distinctions by sex. As Jerome Bruner (1990) points out in his thoughtful book, *Acts of Meaning,* normatively oriented institutions—the law, educational institutions, and family structures—serve to enforce folk psychology, and folk psychology in turn serves to justify such enforcement. In this address, I shall explore some spheres in which the process of sex differentiation

---

[8]There is, of course, a growing body of scholarship on women of color. See, for example, Baca Zinn and Dill (1996); Collins (1998); and Hondagneu-Sotelo (2003).

[9]Martin (2004) and Lorber (1994) both consider gender to be a social institution.

[10]The most obvious example is the right to have an abortion, which through *Roe v. Wade* (1973) withdrew from the states the power to prohibit abortions during the first six months of pregnancy. In 1989, *Webster v. Reproductive Health Services* gave some of that power back. Since that time, President Bush and other legislators proposed a constitutional amendment banning abortions, giving fetuses more legal rights than women. This remains a deeply contested issue in American politics (Kaminer 1990). The National Women's Law Center has expressed concern that the current Supreme Court cannot be counted on to preserve women's "hard-won legal gains, especially in the areas of constitutional rights to privacy and equal protection" (2006). In many other places in the world women are not protected by their governments. In 2005, the World Health Organization found that domestic and sexual violence is widespread. Amnesty International reports tens of thousands of women are subjected to domestic violence, giving as examples Republic of Georgia and Bangladesh where, when women go to the authorities after being strangled, beaten, or stabbed, they are told to reconcile with their husbands (Lew and Moawad 2006).

and the invidious comparisons between the sexes are especially salient.

The Position of Women in the United States and in the Profession of Sociology

It is fitting that my presidential address to the 101st meeting of the American Sociological Association should begin with an analytic eye on our profession. I became the ninth woman president in the ASA's 101 years of existence. The first woman president, Dorothy Swaine Thomas, was elected in 1952, the second, Mirra Komarovsky, almost 20 years later—two women presidents in the first seven decades of the existence of the association. Seven others have been chosen in the 23 years since.[11]

We nine women are symbolic of the positive changes in the position of women in the United States. Our case is situated at the high end of the continuum of women's access to equality. Similarly, our profession has devoted much research attention to women's position in society, though the findings of scholars on the subject are often not integrated with the profession's major theoretical and empirical foci. Many radical voices in the discipline refer to "gender issues" only ritualistically. This is so even though sociological research on gender is one of the major examples of "public sociology" of the past 40 years.

When I was a sociology graduate student at Columbia University in the 1960s, there were no women on the sociology faculty, as was the case at most major universities. The entire bibliography on women in the workplace, assembled for my thesis (1968) on women's exclusion from the legal profession, was exhausted in a few pages. However, it included Betty Friedan's ([1963] 1983) *The Feminine Mystique,* with its attack on Talcott Parsons's (1954) perspective on the functions of the nuclear family and his observation that women's role assignment in the home had exceedingly positive functional significance in that it prevented competition with their husbands (p. 191).[12] She also attacked Freud's ([1905] 1975) theories that women's biology is their destiny, that their feelings of inferiority are due to "penis envy," and his contention "that the woman has no penis often produces in the male a lasting depreciation of the other sex" (Freud 1938:595, footnote 1).

Friedan contributed to both the knowledge base of the social sciences and to the status of women. I believe she did more than any other person in modern times to change popular perceptions of women and their place in the world. While not the first to identify the dimensions of women's inequality,[13] Friedan put theory into practice, building on the attention she received when *The Feminine Mystique* was published. At a moment made ripe by the sensibilities of the civil rights movement and the growing participation of women in the labor force, she took up a challenge posed to her by Pauli Murray, the African American lawyer and civil rights activist, to create "an NAACP for women."[14] With the encouragement and participation of a small but highly motivated group of women in government,

---

[11]Information from ASA: http://www.asanet.org/governance/pastpres.html. The current president, Frances Fox Piven, brings the number of women presidents to 10 in 102 years.

[12]It is curious that his further observation that the relationship was also "an important source of strain" (p. 191) has rarely been acknowledged, although Friedan did note this in *The Feminine Mystique.*

[13]These include (but of course, the list is incomplete) John Stuart Mill and Harriet Taylor, Mary Wollstonecraft, Elizabeth Cady Stanton, Lucretia Mott, Sojourner Truth, Charlotte Perkins Gilman, Emmeline Pankhurst, W.E.B. DuBois, Emma Goldman, and in the years just preceding Friedan's book, Simone de Beauvoir (1949), to whom she dedicated *The Feminine Mystique,* and Mirra Komarovsky (1946; [1953] 2004).

[14]I interviewed Friedan in 1999 about the origins of NOW for an article I was writing for *Dissent* (Epstein 1999a).

union offices, and professional life—white women, African American women, and women from Latin American backgrounds (a fact that has gone unnoticed far too long)—and with the participation of the third woman ASA president, Alice Rossi, Friedan founded the National Organization for Women in 1966. Working through NOW, Friedan set out to provide political support for implementation of Title VII of the Civil Rights Act of 1964, which prohibited discrimination on the basis of sex as well as race, color, religion, and national origin. The changes accomplished by the organizational work of Friedan, and a number of other activists[15] and scholars,[16] were nothing short of a social revolution. It is a revolution of interest to sociologists not only for its creation of women's rights in employment and education but because *it became a natural field experiment establishing that there was no natural order of things relegating women to "women's work" and men to "men's work."* Yet, like most revolutions it was limited in its accomplishment of its stated goals and its principles are constantly under attack.

But the revolution did motivate research. There has been an explosion of scholarship on the extent of sex divides on macro and micro levels. Social scientists have documented in hundreds of thousands of pages of research the existence and consequences of subtle and overt discrimination against women of all strata and nationalities and the institutionalization of sexism.

The number of studies of the differentiation of women's and girls' situations in social life has grown exponentially in the 40 years since the beginning of the second wave of the women's movement. This work has pointed to women's and girls' vulnerabilities in the home and the workplace; their lower pay and lesser ability to accumulate wealth; their exploitation in times of war and other group conflicts; and the conditions under which an ethos of hypermasculinity[17] in nations and subgroups controls women's lives. Some of the work of sociologists and of our colleagues in related disciplines has persuaded legislators and judges in many countries to acknowledge the inequalities and harsh treatment girls and women face. Pierre Sané, the Assistant Secretary General of UNESCO, has noted the synergy between social research and human rights activities, and he stresses in international meetings[18] that women's rights must be regarded as human rights and enforced by law.

Let us remember that the "woman question" as a serious point of inquiry for the social sciences is relatively new. In the past, wisdom on this subject came primarily from armchair ideologists, philosophers, legislators, judges, and religious leaders. With few exceptions,[19] these theorists asserted that women's subordinate position was for good reason—divine design, or for those not religiously inclined, *nature* mandated it. Today, a new species of theorists hold to this ideology—fundamentalist leaders in many nations, churches and religious sects in particular—but also scholars, some in the United States, in fields such as sociobiology and evolutionary psychology (e.g., Alexander 1979; Barash 1977; Trivers 1972; Wilson 1975). This

---

[15]One was Gloria Steinem, who worked with Friedan to establish the National Women's Political Caucus. Steinem became a notable public speaker on behalf of women's rights and established the national magazine *Ms.,* which reports on serious women's issues.

[16]Friedan recruited me as well in the formation of the New York City Chapter of NOW in 1966. Through her auspices I presented a paper on the negative social consequences for women of segregated help-wanted ads in newspapers at hearings of the EEOC in 1967 on Guidelines for Title VII of the Civil Rights Act and to establish guidelines for the Office of Federal Contract Compliance in 1968.

[17]For work on men see especially the work of Kimmel (1996); Connell (1987); Collinson, Knights, and Collinson (1990); and Collinson and Hearn (1994).

[18]The most recent was The International Forum on the Social Science-Policy Nexus in Buenos Aires, February 20 to 24, 2006.

[19]For example, John Stuart Mill (1869), *The Subjection of Women.*

was perhaps predictable, if my thesis is correct, because women had started to intrude into male ideological and physical turf in the academy and elsewhere in society, upsetting the practices of male affiliation. The prejudices that pass as everyday common sense also support this ideology, often with backing from sophisticated individuals responsible for making policies that affect girls and women.[20] They have been joined by some well-meaning women social scientists—a few possessing iconic status[21]—who have affirmed stereotypes about females' nature on the basis of poor or no data.[22]

FEMALE SUBORDINATION IN GLOBAL CONTEXT

The "woman question" is not just one among many raised by injustice, subordination, and differentiation. It is basic. The denigration and segregation of women is a major mechanism in reinforcing male bonds, protecting the institutions that favor them, and providing the basic work required for societies to function. To ignore this great social divide is to ignore a missing link in social analysis.

I will not illustrate my thesis about the persistence of the worldwide subordination of the female sex with pictures, graphs, or charts. Instead I call on readers' imaginations to picture some of the phenomena that illustrate my thesis. Imagine most women's lifetimes of everyday drudgery in households and factories; of struggles for survival without access to decent jobs. Imagine the horror of mass rapes by armed men in ethnic conflicts, and of rapes that occur inside the home by men who regard sexual access as their right.[23] Imagine also women's isolation and confinement behind walls and veils in many societies. Some examples are harder to imagine—for example, the 100 million women missing in the world, first brought to our attention by the economist Amartya Sen (1990), who alerted us to the bizarre sex ratios in South Asia, West Asia, and China. He pointed to the abandonment and systematic undernourishment of girls and women and to the poor medical care they receive in comparison to males. International human rights groups have alerted us to the selective destruction of female fetuses. It is estimated that in China and India alone, 10,000,000 females were aborted between 1978 and 1998 (Rao 2006). Also hidden are the child brides who live as servants in alien environments and who, should their husbands die, are abandoned to live in poverty and isolation. And there are the millions of girls and women lured or forced into sex work. In the Western world, only the occasional newspaper article brings to view the fact that African women face a 1 in 20 chance of dying during pregnancy (half a million die each year).[24]

---

[20]A pinpointed policy was enacted recently. Seeking to override a 1972 federal law barring sex discrimination in education (Title IX of the Civil Rights Act of 1964), the Bush administration is giving public school districts new latitude to expand the number of single-sex classes and single-sex schools (Schemo 2006). My own review of studies on the impact of segregated education shows no benefits (Epstein 1997; Epstein and Gambs 2001).

[21]Here I refer to a number of "standpoint" theorists such as Belenky et al. (1986), Smith (1990), Hartstock (1998), and of course Carol Gilligan (1982) whose initial study showing a difference in boys' and girls' moral values and moral development was based on eight girls and eight boys in a local school and 27 women considering whether to have an abortion. See also Helen Fisher (1982), an evolutionary anthropologist. These views typically assert that women are naturally more caring, more accommodating, and averse to conflict.

[22]See my analysis of this literature in Epstein (1988).

[23]For more horrors, see Parrot and Cummings (2006).

[24]Perhaps the best-known eye into this world is that of Nicholas Kristof, the *New York Times* writer, whose Op Ed articles chronicle the horrors faced by women in Africa and the inaction of Western societies to redress them (for example, the United States cut off funding to the United Nations Population Fund, an agency that has led the effort to reduce maternal deaths, because of false allegations it supports abortion) (Kristof 2006).

The persistent segregation of the workplace, in even the most sophisticated societies, in which girls and women labor in sex-labeled jobs that are tedious, mind numbing, and highly supervised, is out of view. Unseen too are the countless beatings, slights, and defamations women and girls endure from men, including intimates, every day all over the world.

Insistence and Persistence on "Natural Differences"

These patterns are largely explained in the world as consequences stemming from natural causes or God's will. Here, I limit analysis mainly to the view of *natural causation* as the *master narrative*—the narrative that attributes role division of the sexes to biology. Some believe that early socialization cements the distinction. It is clear that strong religious beliefs in the natural subordination of women determine the role women must play in societies.

Biological explanation is the master narrative holding that men and women are naturally different and have different intelligences, physical abilities, and emotional traits. This view asserts that men are naturally suited to dominance and women are naturally submissive. The narrative holds that women's different intellect or emotional makeup is inconsistent with the capacity to work at prestigious jobs, be effective scholars, and lead others. Popularized accounts of gender difference have generated large followings.[25]

But the set of assumptions about basic differences are discredited by a body of reliable research. Although there seems to be an industry of scholarship identifying sex differences, it is important to note that scholarship showing only tiny or fluctuating differences, or none at all, is rarely picked up by the popular press. Most media reports (e.g., Brooks 2006; Tierney 2006) invariably focus on sex differences, following the lead of many journals that report tiny differences in distributions of males and females as significant findings (Epstein 1991a, 1999b). Further, the media rarely reports the fact that a good proportion of the studies showing any differences are based on small numbers of college students persuaded to engage in experiments conducted in college laboratories and not in real-world situations. Or, in the case of studies indicating the hormonal relationship between men's aggression and women's presumed lack of it, a number of studies are based on the behavior of laboratory animals. Other studies compare test scores of students in college, rarely reporting variables such as the class, race, and ethnicity of the population being studied. Even in these settings, the systematic research of social scientists has proved that males and females show almost no difference or shifting minor differences in measures of cognitive abilities (Hyde 2005) and emotions.[26] And there may be more evidence for similarity than even the scholarly public has access to, because when studies find no differences, the results might not be published in scholarly publications. The Stanford University cognitive psychologist Barbara Tversky (personal communication) notes that when she has sought to publish the results of experiments on a variety of spatial tasks that show no gender differences, journal editors have demanded that she and her collaborators take them out because they are null findings. Even so, we can conclude that under conditions of equality, girls and women

---

[25]The works of John Gray (1992), the author of *Men Are From Mars, Women Are From Venus* and spinoff titles have sold over 30 million copies in the United States. See also Deborah Tannen's (1990) *You Just Don't Understand* on the presumed inability of men and women to understand each other on various dimensions, repudiated by the work of the linguistic scholar Elizabeth Aries (1996).

[26]There has been a recent flurry over reported differences in male and female brains (cf. Brizendine 2006; Bell et al. 2006) and reports of a 3 to 4 percentage difference in IQ. The brain studies are usually based on very small samples and the IQ studies on standardized tests in which the differences reported are at the very end of large distributions that essentially confirm male/female similarities (see Epstein 1988 for a further analysis).

perform and achieve at test levels that are the same as or similar to males—and, in many cases, they perform better.[27]

The American Psychological Association has reported officially that males and females are more alike than different when tested on most psychological variables. The APA's finding is based on Janet Hyde's 2005 analysis of 46 meta-analyses conducted recently in the United States. They conclude that gender roles and social context lead to the few differences. Further, they report that sex differences, though believed to be immutable, fluctuate with age and location.[28] Women manifest similar aggressive feelings although their expression of them is obliged to take different forms (Frodi, Macaulay, and Thome 1977). A 2006 report from the National Academy of Sciences found that after an exhaustive review of the scientific literature, including studies of brain structure and function, it could find no evidence of any significant biological factors causing the underrepresentation of women in science and mathematics.[29] Sociologists too have found women's aspirations are linked to their opportunities (Kaufman and Richardson 1982). I observe that like men, women want love, work, and recognition.

So, given similar traits, do women prefer dead-end and limited opportunity jobs; do they wish to work without pay in the home or to be always subject to the authority of men? In the past, some economists thought so. The Nobel Laureate Gary Becker (1981) proposed that women make rational choices to work in the home to free their husbands for paid labor. A number of other scholars follow the rational-choice model to explain women's poorer position in the labor force. Not only has the model proven faulty (England 1989, 1994), but history has proven such ideas wrong. The truth is that men have prevented the incursions of women into their spheres except when they needed women's labor power, such as in wartime, proving that women were indeed a reserve army of labor. As I found in my own research, when windows of opportunity presented themselves, women fought to join the paid labor force at every level, from manual craft work to the elite professions. Men resisted, seeking to preserve the boundaries of their work domains—from craft unionists to the top strata of medical, legal, and legislative practice (Chafe 1972; Epstein 1970, [1981] 1993; Frank 1980; Honey 1984; Kessler-Harris 1982; Lorber 1975, 1984; Milkman 1987; O'Farrell 1999; Rupp 1978).

Social and economic changes in other parts of the West, and in other parts of the world, provide natural field experiments to confirm this data from the United States. In the West, where women have always been employed in the unpaid, family workforce, a revolution in women's interest and participation in the paid workplace spiraled after the First World War. In the United States, from 1930 to 1970 the participation of

---

[27]A 2006 *New York Times* report shows that women are getting more B.A.s than are men in the United States. However, in the highest income families, men age 24 and below attend college as much as, or slightly more than their sisters, according to the American Council on Education. The article also reports that women are obtaining a disproportionate number of honors at elite institutions such as Harvard, the University of Wisconsin, UCLA, and some smaller schools such as Florida Atlanta University (Lewin 2006a). A comparison of female and male math scores varies with the test given. Females score somewhat lower on the SAT-M but differences do not exist on the American College Test (ACT) or on untimed versions of the SAT-M (Bailey n.d.).

[28]Girls even perform identically in math until high school when they are channeled on different tracks. In Great Britain, they do better than males, as noted in the ASA statement contesting the remarks of then Harvard President Lawrence Summers questioning the ability of females to engage in mathematics and scientific research (American Sociological Association 2005; see also Boaler and Sengupta-Irving 2006).

[29]The panel blamed environments that favor men, continuous questioning of women's abilities and commitment to an academic career, and a system that claims to reward based on merit but instead rewards traits that are socially less acceptable for women to possess (Fogg 2006).

married women ages 35 to 44 in the labor force moved from 10 percent to 46 percent and today it is 77 percent (Goldin 2006). The opening of elite colleges and universities to women students after the 1960s led progressively to their increased participation in employment in the professions and other top jobs. This was the direct result of a concerted effort to use the Civil Rights Act of 1964 to force the opening of these sectors. Ruth Bader Ginsburg and her associates in the Women's Rights Project of the ACLU fought and won important battles in the Supreme Court and Judge Constance Baker Motley, the first African American woman to become a federal judge, ruled that large law firms had to recruit women on the same basis as men to comply with the equal treatment promised by the Civil Rights Act.

Yet even as the ideology of equality became widespread and brought significant changes, the worldwide status of women remained subordinate to that of men. Stable governments and a new prosperity led to something of a revolution in women's statuses in the United States and other countries in the West, notably in Canada with its new charter prohibiting discrimination. There was also an increase in women's employment in the paid labor force in the 15 countries of the European Union, including those countries that traditionally were least likely to provide jobs for women, although the statistics do not reveal the quality of the jobs (Norris 2006). And, of course, women's movements have been instrumental in making poor conditions visible. In countries of the Middle East, the East, and the Global South, women are beginning to have representation in political spheres, the professions, and commerce,

although their percentage remains quite small. Women's lot rises or falls as a result of regime changes and economic changes and is always at severe risk.[30] But nowhere are substantial numbers of women in political control; nowhere do women have the opportunity to carry out national agendas giving women truly equal rights.[31]

Structural gains, accompanied by cultural gains, have been considerable in many places. Most governments have signed on to commitments to women's rights, although they are almost meaningless in many regimes that egregiously defy them in practice. And, of course, in many societies women have fewer rights than do men and find themselves worse off than they were a generation ago.[32]

In no society have women had clear access to the best jobs in the workplace, nor have they anywhere achieved economic parity with men. As Charles and Grusky (2004) document in their recent book, *Occupational Ghettos: The Worldwide Segregation of Women and Men*, sex segregation in employment persists all over the world, including in the United States and Canada. Women workers earn less than men even in the most gender-egalitarian societies. Charles and Grusky suggest that the disadvantage in employment is partly because women are clustered in "women's jobs"—jobs in the low-paid service economy or white-collar jobs that do not offer autonomy. These are typically occupational ghettos worldwide. While Charles and Grusky observe that women are crowded into the nonmanual sector, women increasingly do work in the globalized manufacturing economy—for example, in assembly line production that supplies the world

---

[30]Hartmann, Lovell, and Werschkul (2004) show how, in the recession of March to November 2001, there was sustained job loss for women for the first time in 40 years. The economic downturn affected women's employment, labor force participation, and wages 43 months after the start of the recession.

[31]In Scandinavian countries, women have achieved the most political representation: Finland (37.5 percent of parliament seats), Norway (36.4 percent of parliament seats), Sweden (45.3 percent of parliament seats), and Denmark (38 percent of parliament seats) (U.N. Common Database 2004; Dahlerup n.d.). Of course, women in some societies still do not have the right to vote, and in a few, like Kuwait, where they have just gotten the vote, it is unclear whether they have been able to exercise it independently.

[32]This is the case in Egypt, Iran, Iraq, Gaza, and Lebanon as fundamentalist groups have gained power, even in those regimes that are formally secular.

with components for computers or in the clothing sweatshops in Chinatowns in the United States and around the world (Bose and Acosta-Belén 1995; Zimmerman, Litt, and Bose 2006; see also Bao 2001; Lee 1998; Salzinger 2003).

Many women in newly industrializing countries experienced a benefit from employment created by transnational corporations in the 1980s and '90s. They received income and independence from their families, but they remained in sex-segregated, low-wage work, subject to cutbacks when corporations sought cheaper labor markets. As to their suitability for heavy labor, it is common to see (as I have personally witnessed) women hauling rocks and stones in building sites in India and other places. Throughout the world, where water is a scarce commodity it is women who carry heavy buckets and vessels of water, usually on foot and over long distances, because this has been designated as a woman's job and men regard it as a disgrace to help them. Apparently, in much of the world, the guiding principle of essentialism labels as women's jobs those that are not physically easier, necessarily, but rather those that are avoided by men, pay little, and are under the supervision of men.

Of course, women have moved into some male-labeled jobs. As I noted in my book on the consequences of sex boundaries, *Deceptive Distinctions* (1988), the amazing decades of the 1970s and '80s showed that women could do work—men's work—that no one, including themselves, thought they could and they developed interests no one thought they had, and numbers of men welcomed them, or at least tolerated them.

My research shows that women may cross gender barriers into the elite professions that retain their male definition, such as medicine and law (Epstein [1981] 1993), when there is legal support giving them access to training and equal recruitment in combination with a shortage of personnel. Women made their most dramatic gains during a time of rapid economic growth in the Western world.

I first started research on women in the legal profession in the 1960s, when women constituted only 3 percent of practitioners (Epstein [1981] 1993). When I last assessed their achievements (Epstein 2001), women composed about 30 percent of practicing lawyers and about half of all law students. The same striking changes were happening in medicine (they are now almost half of all medical students [Magrane, Lang, and Alexander 2005]), and women were moving into legal and medical specialties once thought to be beyond their interests or aptitudes, such as corporate law and surgery. Yet, even with such advances they face multiple glass ceilings (Epstein et al. 1995). Only small percentages have attained high rank.[33] And it should come as no surprise that men of high rank,[34] the popular media (Belkin 2003), and right-wing commentators (Brooks 2006; Tierney 2006) insist that it is women's own choice to limit their aspirations and even to drop out of the labor force. But this has not been women's pattern. Most educated women have continuous work histories. It is true, however, that many women's ambitions to reach the very top of their professions are undermined. For one thing, they generally face male hostility when they cross conventional boundaries and perform "men's work."[35] For another, they face inhospitable environments in male-dominated

---

[33]The current figure for women partners in large law firms (those with more than 250 lawyers) in the United States is 17 percent, although women are one-half of the recruits in these firms (National Association for Law Placement cited in O'Brien 2006; Nicholson 2006).

[34]A national survey of 1,500 professors (as yet unpublished) at all kinds of institutions in the United States conducted by Neil Gross of Harvard and Solon Simmons of George Mason University shows that most professors don't agree that discrimination—intentional or otherwise—is the main reason that men hold so many more positions than do women in the sciences (Jaschik 2006).

[35]In studies of jobs dominated by men that are seen as requiring traits that distinguish men as superior to women in intellect or strength, it is reported that men's pride is punctured if women perform them (see Chetkovich 1997 on firefighters; Collinson, Knights, and Collinson 1990 on managers).

work settings in which coworkers not only are wary of women's ability but visibly disapprove of their presumed neglect of their families. Women generally face unrelieved burdens of care work in the United States, with few social supports (Coser 1974; Gornick 2003; Williams 2000). And they face norms that this work demands their *personal* attention—a *female's attention.*

Even in the most egalitarian societies, a myriad of subtle prejudices and practices are used by men in gatekeeping positions to limit women's access to the better, male-labeled jobs and ladders of success, for example, partnership tracks in large law firms (Epstein et al. 1995). Alternative routes for women, "Mommy tracks" have been institutionalized—touted as a benefit—but usually result in stalled careers (Bergmann and Helburn 2002). Husbands who wish to limit their own work hours to assist working wives usually encounter severe discrimination as well. Individual men who are seen as undermining the system of male advantage find themselves disciplined and face discrimination (Epstein et al. 1999; Williams 2000). In the United States this may lead to the loss of a promotion or a job. In other places in the world, the consequences are even more dire.[36]

In the current "best of all worlds," ideologies of difference and, to use Charles Tilly's (1998) concept, "exploitation and opportunity hoarding" by men in control keep the top stratum of law and other professions virtually sex segregated. Gatekeepers today don't necessarily limit entry, as that would place them in violation of sex discrimination laws in the United States or put them in an uncomfortable position, given modern Western ideologies of equality. But powerful men move only a small percentage of the able women they hire (often hired in equal numbers with men) upward on the path toward leadership and decision making, especially in

professions and occupations experiencing slow growth. Most rationalize, with the approval of conventional wisdom, that women's own decisions determine their poor potential for achieving power.

Inequality in the workplace is created and reinforced by inequality in education. Newspaper headlines reported that more women than men get B.A.s in the United States today (Lewin 2006a), "leaving men in the dust." But a report a few days later noted that the increase is due to older women going back to school, and that women's degrees are in traditional women's fields (Lewin 2006b).

But women's performance and acceptance in the world of higher education in the United States is the good news! Consider the rest of the world. In many countries girls are denied *any* education. Consider, for example, the case of Afghanistan, where the Taliban still are attempting to resume power. In July 2006, they issued warnings to parents that girls going to school may get acid thrown in their faces or be murdered (Coghlan 2006).

Consider that in Southern Asia 23.5 million girls do not attend school and in Central and West Africa virtually half of all girls are also excluded (Villalobos 2006). While poverty contributes to poor educational opportunities for boys as well as girls in many parts of the world, girls' restrictions are far greater. Some fundamentalist societies permit women to get a higher education, but this is to prepare them for work in segregated conditions where they serve other women.

The sex segregation of labor as measured by sophisticated sociologists and economists does not even acknowledge women's labor *outside* the wage-earning structure. Women and girls labor behind the walls of their homes, producing goods that provide income for their families, income they have no control over. Thus, millions of girls and women are not even counted in the labor force, although they perform essential work in the economy (Bose, Feldberg, and Sokoloff 1987).[37]

---

[36]For example, when the magazine publisher Ali Mohaqeq returned to Afghanistan in 2004 after a long exile he was imprisoned for raising questions about women's rights in the new "democracy." Afghan courts claimed his offense was to contravene the teachings of Islam by printing essays that questioned legal discrimination against women (Witte 2005).

[37]Women have been unpaid workers on family farms or in small businesses, taking in boarders, and doing factory outwork (see Bose et al. 1987 for the United States; Bose and Acosta-Belén 1995 for Latin America; and Hsiung 1996 for Taiwan).

In addition, females can be regarded as a commodity themselves. They are computed as a means of barter in tribal families that give their girls (often before puberty) to men outside their tribe or clan who want wives to produce children and goods. Men also trade their daughters to men of other tribes as a form of compensation for the killing of a member of another tribe or other reasons.[38] Harmony is re-equilibrated through the bodies of females.

There is much more to report about the roles and position of women in the labor force worldwide—my life's work—but there are other spheres in which females everywhere are mired in subordinate roles. Chief among them are the family and the social and cultural structures that keep women both segregated and in a state of symbolic and actual "otherness," undermining their autonomy and dignity. Nearly everywhere, women are regarded as "others."[39]

Mechanisms Creating "Otherness"

To some extent, women are subject to the process of social speciation—a term that Kai Erikson (1996) introduced (modifying the concept of pseudospeciation offered by Erik Erikson) to refer to the fact that humans divide into various groups who regard themselves as "the foremost species" and then feel that others ought to be kept in their place by "conquest or the force of harsh custom" (Erikson 1996:52). Harsh customs and conquest certainly ensure the subordination of girls and women. I shall consider some of these below.

KIN STRUCTURES. In many societies brides are required to leave their birth homes and enter as virtual strangers into the homes of their husbands and their husbands' kin. Because of the practice of patrilocality they usually have few or no resources—human or monetary. Marrying very young, they enter these families with the lowest rank and no social supports. About one in seven girls in the developing world gets married before her 15th birthday according to the Population Council, an international research group (Bearak 2006). Local and international attempts to prevent this practice have been largely unsuccessful.[40]

In exploring the actual and symbolic segregation of women I have been inspired by the work of Mounira Charrad in her 2001 prize-winning book *States and Women's Rights: The Making of Postcolonial Tunisia, Algeria, and Morocco.* The work of Val Moghadam (2003) and Roger Friedland (2002) also informs this analysis. Writing of the relative status of women, Charrad points to the iron grip of patrilineal kin groups in North African societies. She notes how Islamic family law has legitimized the extended male-centered patrilineage that serves as the foundation of kin-based solidarities within tribal groups so that state politics and tribal politics converge. This supports the patriarchal power not only of husbands, but also of all male kin over women so that the clan defines its boundaries through a family law that rests on the exploitation of women. Her study shows how Islamic family law (Sharia) provides a meaningful symbol of national unity in the countries of the Maghreb. This has changed in Tunisia, but it remains the case for

---

[38]There are numerous references on the Web to the use of women given in marriage to another tribe or group in the reports of Amnesty International, for example in Papua New Guinea, Afghanistan, Pakistan, and Fiji.

[39]The characterization of women as "other" was most notably made by Simone de Beauvoir ([1949] 1993) in her book, *The Second Sex.*

[40]Struggles between human rights activists in and out of government and fundamentalist regimes have shifted upward and downward on such matters as raising the age of marriage of girls. For example, attempts by Afghanistan's King Abanullah in the 1920s to raise the age of marriage and institute education for girls enraged the patriarchal tribes who thwarted his regime. Fifty years later a socialist government enacted legislation to change family law to encourage women's employment, education, and choice of spouse. The regime failed in the early 1990s due to internal rivalries and a hostile international climate (Moghadam 2003:270) and the Taliban took power. In the early 1990s they exiled women to their homes, denied them access to education and opportunities to work for pay, and even denied them the right to look out of their windows.

other societies—Iraq, Saudi Arabia, Jordan, Kuwait, Afghanistan, southeastern Turkey, parts of Iran, and southern Egypt. As Moghadam (2003) points out, the gender dimension of the Afghan conflict is prototypical of other conflicts today. During periods of strife, segregation and subordination of women becomes a sign of cultural identity. We see it clearly in the ideologies of Hamas and Hezbollah, Iran, Chechnya, and other Islamic groups and societies, and in the ideologies of fundamentalist Christian and Jewish groups. Representations of women are deployed during processes of revolution and state building to preserve group boundaries within larger societies with competing ideologies, and when power is being reconstituted, linking women either to modernization and progress or to cultural rejuvenation and religious orthodoxy.

Few social scientists have paid attention to the role of kin structures and their accompanying conceptual structures in the minds of players in national and international politics, but I believe this negligence persists at our peril as we experience conflicts between kin-based collectivities in the world.

Of course, human sexuality has much to do with the cultural sex divide. The fact that men desire women sexually, and that women also desire men, means that they are destined to live together no matter what the culture and family structures in which they live. And sexuality could, and can, create equality through bonds of connection and affection. As William Goode (1959) points out in an important but perhaps forgotten paper, "The Theoretical Importance of Love," love is a universal emotion. As such it threatens social structures because the ties between men and women could be stronger than the bonds between men. Thus, everywhere the affiliations made possible by love are contained in various ways.

In societies in which marriage is embedded in a larger kin structure beyond the nuclear family, the practices and rules of domicile and the conventions around it have the potential to undermine the possibility of a truly affective marital tie, one that could integrate women in the society. A couple may face a wall of separation—apartheid in the home in separate parts of the compound or house. Or, they may be community-bound or homebound in fundamentalist religious groups within larger secular societies such as the United States (e.g., the Jewish Satmar community in New York [where women are not permitted to drive] [Winston 2005] or some Christian fundamentalist communities where women are required to home-school their children).

I shall now focus on some other symbolic uses of sex distinctions that facilitate the subordination of women.

HONOR. Females are designated as carriers of honor in many societies. Their "virtue" is a symbolic marker of men's group boundaries. As we know from Mary Douglas (1966) and others, we can think about any social practice in terms of purity and danger. In many societies, females are the designated carriers of boundary distinctions. Their conformity to norms is regarded as the representation of the dignity of the group, while males typically have much greater latitude to engage in deviant behavior. To achieve and maintain female purity, women's behavior is closely monitored and restricted. As Friedland (2002) writes, religious nationalists direct "their attention to the bodies of women—covering, separating and regulating" (p. 396) them, in order "to masculinize the public sphere, to contain the erotic energies of heterosexuality within the family seeking to masculinize collective representations, to make the state male, a virile collective subject, the public status of women's bodies is a critical site and source for religious nationalist political mobilization" (p. 401).

The idea that girls must remain virgins until they marry or their entire family will suffer dishonor is used as a mechanism for women's segregation and subordination all over the world. It is also used as justification for the murder of many young women by male family members claiming to cleanse the girls' supposed dishonor from the family.[41] In particular, we see this at play in parts of the Middle East and among some Muslim communities in the diaspora.

When a woman strays from her prescribed roles, seeks autonomy, or is believed to have had sex with a man outside of marriage, killing her is regarded as a reasonable response by her very own relatives, often a father or brother. In Iraq, at last count, since the beginning of the present war, there have been 2,000 honor killings (Tarabay 2006), and United Nations officials estimate 5,000 worldwide (BBC 2003). In the summer of 2006, the *New York Times* reported that in Turkey, a society becoming more religiously conservative, girls regarded as errant because they moved out of the control of their parents or chose a boyfriend, thus casting dishonor on the family, are put in situations in which they are expected and pressured to commit suicide. Suicide spares a family the obligation to murder her and face prosecution (Bilefsky 2006). Elsewhere, such murders are barely noted by the police.

Female circumcision is also intended to preserve women's honor. In many areas of the African continent, girls are subjected to genital cutting as a prelude to marriage and as a technique to keep them from having pleasure during sex, which, it is reasoned, may lead them to an independent choice of mate.

Conferring on women the symbolism of sexual purity as a basis of honor contributes to their vulnerability. In today's genocidal warfare, the mass rape of women by marauding forces is not just due to the sexual availability of conquered women. Rape is used as a mechanism of degradation. If the men involved in the Bosnian and Darfur massacres regarded rape as an atrocity and a *dishonor* to their cause, it could not have been used so successfully as a tool of war. Further, we know that the Bosnian and Sudanese rape victims, like women who have been raped in Pakistan, India, and other places, are regarded as defiled and are shunned, as are the babies born of such rapes.

CLOTHING AS A SYMBOLIC TOOL FOR DIFFERENTIATION. The chador and veil are tools men use to symbolize and maintain women's honor. Although men, with some exceptions,[42] wear Western dress in much of the world, women's clothing is used to symbolize their cultures' confrontations with modernity, in addition to clothing's symbolic roles. Presumably worn to assure modesty and to protect women's honor, the clothing prescribed, even cultural relativists must admit, serves to restrict women's mobility. Hot and uncomfortable, women cannot perform tasks that require speed and mobility, and it prevents women from using motorbikes and bicycles, the basic means of transportation in poor societies. Distinctive clothing is not restricted to the Third World. Fundamentalist groups in Europe and the United States also mandate clothing restrictions for women.[43]

Of course, clothing is used to differentiate women and men in all societies. In the past, Western women's clothing was also restrictive (e.g., long skirts and corsets) and today, as women

---

[41]A United Nations (2002) report found that there were legislative provisions "allowing for partial or complete defense" in the case of an honor killing in: Argentina, Bangladesh, Ecuador, Egypt, Guatemala, Iran, Israel, Jordan, Lebanon, Peru, Syria, Turkey, Venezuela, and the Palestinian National Authority (of course law does not equal practice). For example, in Pakistan and Jordan honor killings are outlawed but they occur nevertheless.

[42]In demonstrations in societies led by religious leaders, men typically wear Western-style shirts and trousers although their leaders typically choose clerics' robes and turbans. Leaders of countries outside the "Western" orbit often choose distinctive dress— robes, beards, open neck shirts, and other costumes for ceremonial occasions or to make political statements.

[43]Hella Winston (personal communication, September 30, 2006) told me that in the orthodox Jewish community of New Square in New York State, a recent edict by the rabbi reminded women they were to wear modest dress, specifying that "sleeves must be to the end of the bone, and [to] not wear narrow clothing or short clothing." They were not to ride bikes or speak loudly.

have moved toward greater equality, women and men are permitted to wear similar garb (such as jeans and T-shirts). Of course, fashion prescribes more sexually evocative (thus distinctive) clothing for women than it does for men.

TIME AND SPACE. How can we speak of the otherness and subordination of women without noting the power of the variables of time and space in the analysis? In every society the norms governing the use of time and space are gendered (Epstein and Kalleberg 2004). People internalize feelings about the proper use of time and space as a result of the normative structure. Worldwide, the boundaries of time and space are constructed to offer men freedom and to restrict women's choices. In most of the world, women rise earlier than do men and start food preparation; they eat at times men don't. Further, sex segregation of work in and outside the home means a couple's primary contact may be in the bedroom. If women intrude on men's space they may violate a taboo and be punished for it. Similarly, men who enter into women's spaces do so only at designated times and places. The taboo elements undermine the possibility of easy interaction, the opportunity to forge friendships, to connect, and to create similar competencies. In the Western world, working different shifts is common (Presser 2003), which also results in segregation of men and women.

There are rules in every society, some by law and others by custom, that specify when and where women may go, and whether they can make these journeys alone or must appear with a male relative. Some segregation is to protect men from women's temptations (e.g., Saudi Arabia, Iran, the Satmar sect in Monsey, NY) and some to protect women from men's sexual advances (e.g., Mexico, Tokyo, Mumbai). But the consequence is that men overwhelmingly are allotted more space and territorialize public space.

A common variable in the time prescription for women is surveillance; women are constrained to operate within what I am calling *role zones*. In

these, their time is accounted for and prescribed. They have less *free* time. In our own Western society, women note that the first thing to go when they attempt to work and have children is "free time." Free time is typically enjoyed by the powerful, and it gives them the opportunity to engage in the politics of social life. Most people who work at a subsistence level, refugees, and those who labor in jobs not protected by the authority of the dominant group, don't have free time either. Slave owners own the time of their slaves.

A THEORY OF FEMALE SUBORDINATION

All of this leads me to ask a basic sociological question. Why does the subordination of women and girls persist no matter how societies change in other ways? How does half the world's population manage to hold and retain power over the other half? And what are we to make of the women who comply?

The answers lie in many of the practices I have described and they remain persuasive with a global perspective. I propose an even more basic explanation for the persistence of inequality, and often a reversion to inequality, when equality seems to be possible or near attainment. In *Deceptive Distinctions* (1988) I proposed the theory that the division of labor in society assigns women the most important survival tasks—reproduction and gathering and preparation of food. All over the world, women do much of the reproductive work, ensuring the continuity of society. They do this both in physical terms and in symbolic terms. Physically, they do so through childbirth and child care. They do much of the daily work any social group needs for survival. For example, half of the world's food, and up to 80 percent in developing countries, is produced by women (Food and Agriculture Organization of the United Nations n.d.; Women's World Summit Foundation 2006). They also prepare the food at home, work in the supermarkets, behind the counters, and on the conveyor belts that package it. In their homes and in schools, they produce most preschool and primary school education. They take care of the elderly and infirm. They socialize their children in the social skills that make interpersonal communication possible. They are the support staffs for men. This is a good deal—no, a great deal—for the men.

Controlling women's labor and behavior is a mechanism for male governance and territoriality. Men's authority is held jealously. Men legitimate their behavior through ideological and theological constructs that justify their domination. Further, social institutions reinforce this.[44]

I shall review the mechanisms:

We know about the use and threat of force (Goode 1972).[45] We know as well about the role of law and justice systems that do not accord women the same rights to protection, property, wealth, or even education enjoyed by men. We know that men control and own guns and the means of transport, and they often lock women out of membership and leadership of trade unions, political parties, religious institutions, and other powerful organizations. We know too that huge numbers of men feel justified in threatening and punishing females who deviate from male-mandated rules in public and private spaces. That's the strong-arm stuff.

But everywhere, in the West as well as in the rest of the world, women's segregation and subjugation is also done *culturally* and through *cognitive* mechanisms that reinforce existing divisions of rights and labor and award men authority over women. Internalized cultural schemas reinforce men's views that their behavior is legitimate and persuade women that their lot is just. The media highlight the idea that women and men think differently and naturally gravitate to their social roles.[46] This is more than just "pluralistic ignorance" (Merton [1948] 1963). Bourdieu ([1979] 1984) reminds us that dominated groups often contribute to their own subordination because of perceptions shaped by the conditions of their existence—the dominant system made of binary oppositions. Using Eviatar Zerubavel's (1997) term, "mindscapes" set the stage for household authorities and heads of clans, tribes, and communities to separate and segregate women in the belief that the practice is inevitable and right. Such mindscapes also persuade the females in their midst to accept the legitimacy and inevitability of their subjection, and even to defend it, as we have seen lately in some academic discourses.

The mindscapes that legitimate women's segregation are the cognitive translations of ideologies that range the spectrum from radical fundamentalism to difference feminism; all are grounded in cultural-religious or pseudoscientific views that women have different emotions, brains, aptitudes, ways of thinking, conversing, and imagining. Such mind-sets are legitimated every day in conventional understandings expressed from the media, pulpits, boardrooms, and in departments of universities. Psychologists call them schemas (Brewer and Nakamura 1984)—culturally set definitions that people internalize. Gender operates as a cultural "superschema" (Roos and Gatta 2006)

---

[44]Where religious laws govern such areas of civic life as family relations, inheritance, and punishment for crimes, for example, they invariably institutionalize women's subordinate status.

[45]As one of many possible examples: When hundreds of women gathered in downtown Tehran on July 31, 2006 to protest institutionalized sex discrimination in Iran (in areas such as divorce, child custody, employment rights, age of adulthood, and court proceedings where a woman's testimony is viewed as half of a man's), 100 male and female police beat them. Reports also noted a tightening of the dress code and segregation on buses and in some public areas such as parks, sidewalks, and elevators. Another demonstration on March 8, 2006 was dispersed as police dumped garbage on the heads of participants (Stevens 2006).

[46]The recent book by Louann Brizendine (2006), which asserts that the female and male brains are completely different, offering such breezy accounts as "woman is weather, constantly changing and hard to predict" and "man is mountain," has been on the top 10 on the Amazon.com book list and led to her prominent placement on ABC's 20/20 and morning talk shows. Thanks to Troy Duster for passing this on.

that shapes interaction and cues stereotypes (Ridgeway 1997). Schemas that define femaleness and maleness are basic to all societies. Schemas also define insiders and outsiders and provide definitions of justice and equality.

In popular speech, philosophical musings, cultural expressions, and the banter of everyday conversation, people tend to accept the notion of difference. They accept its inevitability and are persuaded of the legitimacy of segregation, actual or symbolic. Thus, acceptance of difference perspectives—the idea that women often have little to offer to the group, may result in rules that forbid women from speaking in the company of men (in a society governed by the Taliban) or may result in senior academics' selective deafness to the contributions of a female colleague in a university committee room.

CONCLUSION

In conclusion I want to reiterate certain observations:

Intrinsic qualities are attributed to women that have little or nothing to do with their actual characteristics or behavior. Because those attributions are linked to assigned roles their legitimation is an ongoing project. Changing these ideas would create possibilities for changing the status quo and threaten the social institutions in which men have the greatest stake and in which some women believe they benefit.

Is women's situation different from that of men who, by fortune, color of skin, or accident of birth also suffer from exploitation by the powerful? I am claiming *yes,* because they carry not only the hardships—sometimes relative hardships—but the ideological and cognitive overlay that defines their

subordination as legitimate and normal. Sex and gender are the organizing markers in all societies. In no country, political group, or community are men defined as lesser human beings than their *female* counterparts. But almost everywhere women are so defined.

Why is this acceptable? And why does it persist?

So many resources are directed to legitimating females' lower place in society. So few men inside the power structure are interested in inviting them in. And so many women and girls accept the Orwellian notion that restriction is freedom, that suffering is pleasure, that silence is power.[47]

Of course this is not a static condition, nor, I hope, an inevitable one. Women in the Western world, and in various sectors of the rest of the world, have certainly moved upward in the continuum toward equality. Thirty-five years ago I noted how women in the legal profession in the United States were excluded from the informal networks that made inclusion and mobility possible. Now, noticeable numbers have ventured over the barriers. Similarly, there has been a large increase in the numbers of women who have entered the sciences,[48] business, medicine, and veterinary medicine (Cox and Alm 2005). This has changed relatively swiftly. Women didn't develop larger brains—nor did their reasoning jump from left brain to right brain or the reverse. Nor did they leave Venus for Mars. Rather, they learned that they could not be barred from higher education and they could get appropriate jobs when they graduated. The problem is no longer one of qualifications or entry but of promotion and inclusion into the informal networks leading to the top. But the obstacles are great.

In his review of cognitive sociological dynamics, DiMaggio (1997) reminds us of Merton's notion of "pluralistic ignorance," which

---

[47]For example, a recent poll cited in the *New York Times* (June 8, 2006) indicates that a majority of women in Muslim countries do not regard themselves as unequal (Andrews 2006). Of course, this attitude is widespread throughout the world, including Western societies.

[48]Comparing percentages of women attaining doctorates in the sciences from 1970–71 to 2001–2002 the increases were: Engineering .2–17.3; Physics 2.9–15.5; Computer Science 2.3–22.8; Mathematics 7.6–29.

is at work when people act with reference to shared collective opinions that are empirically incorrect. There would not be a firm basis for the subordinate condition of females were there not a widespread belief, rooted in folk culture, in their essential difference from males in ability and emotion. This has been proven time and time again in research in the "real" world of work and family institutions (e.g., Epstein et al. 1995) and laboratory observations (Berger, Cohen, and Zelditch 1966; Frodi et al. 1977; Ridgeway and Smith-Lovin 1999).

We know full well that there are stories and master social narratives accepted by untold millions of people that have no basis in what social scientists would regard as evidence. The best examples are the basic texts of the world's great religions. But there are also societywide beliefs of other kinds. Belief systems are powerful. And beliefs that are unprovable or proven untrue often capture the greatest number of believers. Sometimes, they are simply the best stories.

We in the social sciences have opened the gates to a better understanding of the processes by which subordinated groups suffer because the use of *categories* such as race and ethnicity rank human beings so as to subordinate, exclude, and exploit them (Tilly 1998). However, relatively few extend this insight to the category of gender or sex. The sexual divide so defines social life, and so many people in the world have a stake in upholding it, that it is the most resistant of all categories to change. Today, Hall and Lamont (forthcoming; Lamont 2005) are proposing that the most productive societies are those with porous boundaries between categories of people. Perhaps there is an important incentive in a wider understanding of this idea. Small groups of men may prosper by stifling women's potential, but prosperous nations benefit from women's full participation and productivity in societies. Societies might achieve still more if the gates were truly open.

Sociologists historically have been committed to social change to achieve greater equality in the world, in both public and private lives. But in this address I challenge our profession to take this responsibility in our scholarship and our professional lives; to observe, to reveal, and to strike down the conceptual and cultural walls that justify inequality on the basis of sex in all of society's institutions—to transgress this ever-present boundary—for the sake of knowledge and justice.

REFERENCES

Acker, Joan. 1973. "Women and Social Stratification: A Case of Institutional Sexism." Pp. 174–82 in *Changing Women in a Changing Society,* edited by Joan Huber. Chicago, IL: University of Chicago Press.

Alexander, Richard D. 1979. *Darwinism and Human Affairs.* Seattle, WA: University of Washington Press.

American Sociological Association. 2005. "ASA Council Statement on the Causes of Gender Differences in Science and Math Career Achievement" (February 28). Retrieved September 21, 2006 (http://www2.asanet .org/footnotes/mar05/indexthree.html).

Andrews, Helena. 2006. "Muslim Women Don't See Themselves as Oppressed, Survey Finds." *New York Times,* June 7, p. A9.

Aries, Elizabeth. 1996. *Men and Women in Interaction: Reconsidering the Differences.* New York: Oxford University Press.

Baca Zinn, Maxine and Bonnie Thornton Dill. 1996. "Theorizing Difference from Multiracial Feminism." *Feminist Studies* 22:321–31.

Bailey, Justin P. N.d. "Men Are From Earth, Women Are From Earth: Rethinking the Utility of the Mars/ Venus Analogy." Retrieved September 28, 2006 (www.framingham.edu/joct/pdf/J.Bailey.1. pdf).

Bao, Xiaolan. 2001. *Holding Up More Than Half the Sky: Chinese Women Garment Workers in New York City, 1948–92.* Urbana, IL and Chicago, IL: University of Illinois Press.

Barash, David P. 1977. *Sociobiology and Behavior.* New York: Elsevier.

Barth, Frederik. 1969. "Introduction." Pp. 9–38 in *Ethnic Groups and Boundaries: The Social Organization of Cultural Difference,* edited by Frederik Barth. London, England: Allen & Unwin.

Basow, Susan A. 1995. "Student Evaluation of College Professors: When Gender Matters." *Journal of Educational Psychology* 87:656–65.

BBC. 2003. "Speaking Out Over Jordan 'Honour Killings.'" Retrieved September 21, 2006 (http:// news.bbc.co .uk/2/hi/middle_east/2802305.stm).

Bearak, Barry. 2006. "The Bride Price." *New York Times Magazine,* July 9, p. 45.

Beauvoir, Simone de. [1949] 1993.*The Second Sex.* New York: Alfred A. Knopf.

Becker, Gary. 1981. *A Treatise on the Family.* Cambridge, MA: Harvard University Press.

Becker, Howard. 1963. *Outsiders: Studies in the Sociology of Deviance.* New York: The Free Press.

Belenky, Mary Field, Blythe Clinchy, Nancy Goldberger, and Jill Tarule. 1986. *Women's Ways of Knowing: The Development of Self, Voice, and Mind.* New York: Basic Books.

Belkin, Lisa. 2003. "The Opt-Out Revolution." *New York Times Magazine,* October 26, p. 42.

Bell, Emily C., Morgan C. Willson, Alan H. Wilman, Sanjay Dave, and Peter H. Silverstone. 2006. "Males and Females Differ in Brain Activation During Cognitive Tasks." *NeuroImage* 30:529–38.

Berger, Joseph, Bernard P. Cohen, and Morris Zelditch Jr. 1966. "Status Characteristics and Expectation States." Pp. 29–46 in *Sociological Theories in Progress,* vol. I, edited by Joseph Berger, Morris Zelditch Jr., and Bo Anderson. Boston, MA: Houghton Mifflin.

Bergmann, Barbara R. and Suzanne Helburn. 2002. *America's Child Care Problem: The Way Out.* New York: Palgrave, St. Martin's Press.

Bilefsky, Dan. 2006. "How to Avoid Honor Killing in Turkey? Honor Suicide." *New York Times,* July 16, section 1, p. 3.

Blumberg, Rae Lesser. 1978. *Stratification: Socioeconomic and Sexual Inequality.* Dubuque, IA: Brown.

Boaler, Jo and Tesha Sengupta-Irving. 2006. "Nature, Neglect & Nuance: Changing Accounts of Sex, Gender and Mathematics." Pp. 207–20 in *Gender and Education, International Handbook,* edited by C. Skelton and L. Smulyan. London, England: Sage.

Bose, Christine E. and Edna Acosta-Belén. 1995. *Women in the Latin American Development Process.* Philadelphia, PA: Temple University Press.

Bose, Christine E., Roslyn Feldberg, and Natalie Sokolof. 1987. *Hidden Aspects of Women's Work.* New York: Praeger.

Bourdieu, Pierre. [1979] 1984. *Distinctions: A Social Critique of the Judgment of Taste.* Cambridge, MA: Harvard University Press.

———. 1991. "Identity and Representation: Elements for a Critical Reflection on the Idea of Region." Pp. 220–28 in *The Logic of Practice,* edited by P. Bourdieu. Stanford, CA: Stanford University Press.

Brewer, William F. and Glenn Nakamura. 1984. "The Nature and Functions of Schemas." Pp. 119–60 in *Handbook of Social Cognition,* vol. 1, edited by R. S. Wyer and T. K. Srull. Hillsdale, NJ: Erlbaum.

Brizendine, Louann. 2006. *The Female Brain.* New York: Morgan Road Books.

Brooks, David. 2006. "The Gender Gap at School." *New York Times,* June 11, section 4, p. 12.

Brubaker, Rogers. 2004. *Ethnicity Without Groups.* Cambridge, MA: Harvard University Press.

Bruner, Jerome. 1990. *Acts of Meaning: Four Lectures on Mind and Culture.* Cambridge, MA: Harvard University Press.

Bussey, Kay and Albert Bandura. 1999. "Social Cognitive Theory of Gender Development and Differentiation." *Psychological Review* 106:676–713.

Butler, Judith. 1990. *Gender Trouble.* New York: Routledge.

Chafe, William H. 1972. *The American Woman: Her Changing Social, Economic and Political Roles: 1920–1970.* Oxford, England: Oxford University Press.

Chafetz, Janet Saltzman. 1984. *Sex and Advantage: A Comparative Macro-Structural Theory of Sex Stratification.* Totowa, NJ: Roman & Allanhyeld.

———. 1997. "Feminist Theory and Sociology: Underutilized Contribution for Mainstream Theory." *Annual Review of Sociology* 23:97–120.

Charles, Maria and David Grusky. 2004. *Occupational Ghettos: The Worldwide Segregation of Women and Men.* Stanford, CA: Stanford University Press.

Charrad, Mounira. 2001. *States and Women's Rights: The Making of Postcolonial Tunisia, Algeria, and Morocco.* Berkeley, CA: The University of California Press.

Chetkovich, Carol. 1997. *Real Heat: Gender and Race in the Urban Fire Service.* New York: Routledge.

Coghlan, Tom. 2006. "Taliban Use Beheadings and Beatings to Keep Afghanistan's Schools Closed." *The Independent,* July 11. Retrieved July 11, 2006 (http://news.independent.co.uk/world/asia/article1171369.ece).

Collins, Patricia Hill. 1998. *Fighting Words: Black Women and the Search for Justice.* Minneapolis, MN: University of Minnesota Press.

Collinson, David L. and Jeff Hearn. 1994. "Naming Men as Men: Implications for Work, Organization and Management." *Gender, Work and Organization* 1:2–22.

Collinson, David L., David Knights, and Margaret Collinson. 1990. *Managing to Discriminate.* London, England: Routledge.

Connell, R. W. 1987. *Gender and Power: Society, the Person and Sexual Politics.* Stanford, CA: Stanford University Press.

Coser, Rose Laub. 1974. "Stay Home Little Sheba: On Placement, Displacement and Social Change." *Social Problems* 22:470–80.

Cox, W. Michael and Richard Alm. 2005. "Scientists Are Made, Not Born." *New York Times,* February 25, p. A25.

Dahlerup, Drude. N.d. "The World of Quotas." *Women in Politics: Beyond Numbers.* International Institute for Democracy and Electoral Assistance. Retrieved September 21, 2006 (http://archive.idea.int/women/parl/ch4c.htm).

DiMaggio, Paul. 1997. "Culture and Cognition." *Annual Review of Sociology* 23:263–87.

Douglas, Mary. 1966. *Purity and Danger: An Analysis of Concepts of Pollution and Taboo.* London, England: Routledge & Keegan Paul.

Duster, Troy. 2006. "Comparative Perspectives and Competing Explanations: Taking on the Newly Configured Reductionist Challenge to Sociology." *American Sociological Review* 71:1–15.

England, Paula. 1989. "A Feminist Critique of Rational-Choice Theories: Implications for Sociology." *The American Sociologist* 20:14–28.

———. 1994. "Neoclassical Economists' Theories of Discrimination." Pp. 59–70 in *Equal Employment Opportunity,* edited by P. Burstein. New York: Aldine de Gruyter.

Epstein, Cynthia Fuchs. 1968. "Women and Professional Careers: The Case of Women Lawyers." Ph.D. Dissertation, Department of Sociology, Columbia University, New York.

———. 1970. *Woman's Place: Options and Limits in Professional Careers.* Berkeley, CA: University of California Press.

———. [1981] 1993. *Women in Law.* Urbana, IL: University of Illinois Press.

———. 1985. "Ideal Roles and Real Roles or the Fallacy of the Misplaced Dichotomy." Pp. 29–51 in *Research in Social Stratification and Mobility,* edited by Robert V. Robinson. Greenwich, CT: JAI Press Inc.

———. 1988. *Deceptive Distinctions.* New Haven, CT and New York: Yale University Press and Russell Sage Foundation.

———. 1991a. "What's Wrong and What's Right With the Research on Gender." *Sociological Viewpoints* 5:1–14.

———. 1991b. "The Difference Model: Enforcement and Reinforcement in the Law." Pp. 53–71 in *Social Roles and Social Institutions: Essays in Honor of Rose Laub Coser,* edited by J. Blau and N. Goodman. Boulder, CO: Westview.

———. 1992. "Tinkerbells and Pinups: The Construction and Reconstruction of Gender Boundaries at Work." Pp. 232–56 in *Cultivating Differences: Symbolic Boundaries and the Making of Inequality,* edited by M. Lamont and M. Fournier. Chicago, IL: University of Chicago Press.

———. 1997. "Multiple Myths and Outcomes of Sex Segregation." *New York Law School Journal of Human Rights* XIV: Part One, 185–210, Symposium.

———. 1999a. "The Major Myth of the Women's Movement." *Dissent* 46(4):83–86.

———. 1999b. "Similarity and Difference: The Sociology of Gender Distinctions." Pp. 45–61 in *Handbook of the Sociology of Gender,* edited by J. S. Chafetz. New York: Kluwer Academic/Plenum Publishers.

———. 2001. "Women in the Legal Profession at the Turn of the Twenty-First Century: Assessing Glass Ceilings and Open Doors." *Kansas Law Review* 49:733–60.

Epstein, Cynthia Fuchs and Deborah Gambs. 2001. "Sex Segregation in Education." Pp. 983–90 in *Encyclopedia of Gender,* vol. 2, edited by Judith Worell. Philadelphia, PA: Elselvier.

Epstein, Cynthia Fuchs and Arne Kalleberg, eds. 2004. *Fighting for Time: Shifting Boundaries of Work and Social Life.* New York: Russell Sage Foundation.

Epstein, Cynthia Fuchs, Robert Sauté, Bonnie Oglensky, and Martha Gever. 1995. "Glass Ceilings and Open Doors: The Mobility of Women in Large Corporate Law Firms." *Fordham Law Review* LXIV:291–449.

Epstein, Cynthia Fuchs, Carroll Seron, Bonnie Oglensky, and Robert Sauté. 1999. *The Part Time Paradox: Time Norms, Professional Life, Family and Gender.* New York and London: Routledge.

Erikson, Kai. 1996. "On Pseudospeciation and Social Speciation." Pp. 51–58 in *Genocide: War and Human Survival,* edited by C. Strozier and M. Flynn. Lanham, MD: Rowman & Littlefield.

Fine, Gary Alan. 1996. "Reputational Entrepreneurs and the Memory of Incompetence: Melting Supporters, Partisan Warriors, and Images of President Harding." *The American Journal of Sociology* 101:1159–93.

Fisher, Helen. 1982. *The Sex Contract: The Evolution of Human Behavior.* New York: William Morrow.

Fogg, Piper. 2006. "Panel Blames Bias for Gender Gap." *The Chronicle,* September 29. Retrieved October 24, 2006 (http://chronicle.com/ weekly/v53/i06/06a01301.htm).

Food and Agriculture Organization of the United Nations. N.d. "Gender and Food Security: Agriculture." Retrieved August 5, 2006 (http://www.fao.org/gender/en/agri-e.htm).

Frank, Marian. 1980. *The Life and Times of "Rosie the Riveter."* A study guide for the video *Rosie the Riveter,* Connie Field, director. Los Angeles, CA: Direct Cinema.

Freidan, Betty. [1963] 1983. *The Feminine Mystique.* New York: W. W. Norton.

Freud, Sigmund. 1938. *The Basic Writings of Sigmund Freud.* Translated by A. A. Brill. New York: Modern Library.

———. [1905] 1975. *Three Essays on the Theory of Sexuality.* New York: Basic Books.

Friedland, Roger. 2002. "Money, Sex and God: The Erotic Logic of Religious Nationalism." *Sociological Theory* 20:381–425.

Frodi, Ann, Jacqueline Macaulay, and Pauline Robert Thome. 1977. "Are Women Always Less Aggressive Than Men? A Review of the Experimental Literature." *Psychological Bulletin* 84:634–60.

Gerson, Judith and Kathy Peiss. 1985. "Boundaries, Negotiation and Consciousness: Reconceptualizing Gender Relations." *Social Problems* 32:317–31.

Gilligan, Carol. 1982. *In a Different Voice: Psychological Theory and Women's Development.* Cambridge, MA: Harvard University Press.

Gil-White, Francisco. 1999. "How Thick Is Blood? The Plot Thickens . . . : If Ethnic Actors Are Primordialists, What Remains of the Circumstantialist/Primordialist Controversy?" *Ethnic and Racial Studies* 22:789–820.

Goldin, Claudia. 2006. "The Quiet Revolution That Transformed Women's Employment, Education and Family." *American Economic Association Papers and Proceedings* 96:7–19.

Goode, William J. 1959. "The Theoretical Importance of Love." *American Sociological Review* 24:38–47.

———. 1972. "The Place of Force in Human Society." *American Sociological Review* 37:507–19.

Gornick, Janet. 2003. *Families that Work: Policies for Reconciling Parenthood and Employment.* New York: Russell Sage Foundation.

Gray, John. 1992. *Men Are From Mars, Women Are From Venus.* New York: HarperCollins.

Hall, Peter and Michele Lamont. Forthcoming. *Successful Societies* (working title).

Hartmann, Heidi, Vicky Lovell, and Misha Werschkul. 2004. "Women and the Economy: Recent Trends in Job Loss, Labor Force Participation and Wages." Briefing Paper, Institute for Women's Policy Research. IWPR Publication B235.

Hartstock, Nancy. 1998. *The Feminist Standpoint Revisited, and Other Essays.* Boulder, CO: Westview Press.

Hirschfeld, Lawrence A. 1996. *Race in the Making: Cognition, Culture and the Child's Construction of Human Kinds.* Cambridge, MA: MIT Press.

Hondagneu-Sotelo, Pierrette, ed. 2003. *Gender and U. S. Immigration: Contemporary Trends.* Berkeley, CA: University of California Press.

Honey, Maureen. 1984. *Creating Rosie the Riveter: Class, Gender and Propaganda During World War 2.* Boston, MA: University of Massachusetts Press.

Hsiung, Ping-Chun. 1996. *Living Rooms as Factories: Class, Gender and the Satellite Factory System in Taiwan.* Philadelphia, PA: Temple University Press.

Hyde, Janet Shibley. 2005. "The Gender Similarities Hypothesis." *American Psychologist* 60:581–92.

Jaschik, Scott. 2006. "Bias or Interest?" *Inside Higher Ed,* September 20. Retrieved September 28 (http://inside highered.com/layout/set/print/news/2006/09/20/ women).

Kaminer, Wendy. 1990. *A Fearful Freedom: Women's Flight from Equality.* Reading, MA: Addison-Wesley.

Kaufman, Debra R. and Barbara Richarson. 1982. *Achievement and Women: Challenging the Assumptions.* New York: The Free Press.

Kessler-Harris, Alice. 1982. *Women Have Always Worked: A Historical Overview.* Old Westbury, CT: Feminist Press.

Kimmel, Michael. 1996. *Manhood in America.* New York: The Free Press.

Komarovsky, Mirra. 1946. "Cultural Contradictions and Sex Roles." *The American Journal of Sociology* 52:184–89.

———. [1953] 2004. *Women in the Modern World: Their Education and Their Dilemmas.* Walnut Creek, CA: AltaMira Press.

Kristof, Nicholas. 2006. "Save My Wife." *New York Times,* September 17, opinion section, p. 15.

Lamont, Michele. 2005. "Bridging Boundaries: Inclusion as a Condition for Successful Societies." Presented at the Successful Societies Program of the Canadian Institute for Advanced Research, October, Montebello, Quebec, Canada.

Lamont, Michele and Virag Molnar. 2002. "The Study of Boundaries in the Social Sciences." *Annual Review of Sociology* 28:167–95.

Laslett, Barbara. 1996. *Gender and Scientific Authority.* Chicago, IL: University of Chicago Press.

Lee, Ching Kwan. 1998. *Gender and the South China Miracle: Two Worlds of Factory Women.* Berkeley, CA: University of California Press.

Lew, Irene and Nouhad Moawad. 2006. "Cheers & Jeers of the Week: Breast Cancer Strategies; Domestic Abuse Unnoticed." *Women's eNews,* September 30. Retrieved October 2, 2006 (http://www.womensenews.org/article.cfm/dyn/aid/2907/context/archive).

Lewin, Tamar. 2006a. "At Colleges, Women Are Leaving Men in the Dust." *New York Times,* July 9, p. A1.

———. 2006b. "A More Nuanced Look at Men, Women and College." *New York Times,* July 12, p. B8.

Lorber, Judith. 1975. "Women and Medical Sociology: Invisible Professionals and Ubiquitous Patients." Pp. 75–105 in *Another Voice,* edited by Marcia Millman and Rosabeth Moss Kanter. Garden City, NY: Doubleday/ Anchor.

———. 1984. *Women Physicians: Careers, Status, and Power.* New York: Tavistock Publications.

———. 1994. *Paradoxes of Gender.* New Haven, CT: Yale University Press.

———. 1996. "Beyond the Binaries: Depolarizing the Categories of Sex, Sexuality and Gender." *Sociological Inquiry* 66:143–59.

Magrane, Diane, Jonathan Lang, and Hershel Alexander. 2005. *Women in U.S. Academic Medicine: Statistics and Medical School Benchmarking.* Washington, DC: Association of American Medical Colleges.

Martin, Patricia Yancey. 2004. "Gender as Social Institution." *Social Forces* 82:1249–73.

Merton, Robert K. [1949] 1963. *Social Theory and Social Structure.* Glencoe, IL: The Free Press.

Milkman, Ruth. 1987. *Gender at Work: The Dynamics of Job Segregation by Sex During World War II.* Urbana, IL: University of Illinois Press.

Moghadam, Valentine. 2003. *Modernizing Women: Gender and Social Change in the Middle East.* 2d ed. London, England: Lynne Rienner.

O'Brien, Timothy. 2006. "Why Do So Few Women Reach the Top of Big Law Firms*?"* *New York Times,* March 19, p. B27.

O'Farrell, Brigid. 1999. "Women in Blue Collar and Related Occupations at the End of the Millenium." *Quarterly Review of Economics and Finance* 39:699–722.

National Women's Law Center. 2006. "New Report Analyzes What's at Stake for Women During Upcoming Supreme Court Term." Press Release. September 27. Retrieved October 2, 2006 (http://www.nwlc.org/details.cfm?id=2857 &section= newsroom).

Nicholson, Lisa H. 2006. "Women and the 'New' Corporate Governance: Making In-Roads to Corporate General Counsel Positions: It's Only a Matter of Time?" *Maryland Law Review* 65:625–65.

Norris, Floyd. 2006. "A Statistic That Shortens the Distance to Europe." *New York Times,* September 30, p. C3.

Parsons, Talcott. 1954. "The Kinship System of the Contemporary United States." Pp. 189–94 in *Essays in Sociological Theory.* Glencoe, IL: The Free Press.

Parrot, Andrew and Nina Cummings. 2006. *Forsaken Females: The Global Brutalization of Women.* Lanham, MD: Rowman & Littlefield.

Presser, Harriet. 2003. *Working in a 24/7 Economy: Challenges for American Families.* New York: Russell Sage Foundation.

Rao, Kavitha. 2006. "Missing Daughters on an Indian Mother's Mind." *Women's eNews,* March 16. Retrieved October 23, 2006 (http://www.womensenews.org/article.cfm?aid=2672).

Ridgeway, Cecelia L. 1997. "Interaction and the Conservation of Gender Inequality: Considering Employment." *American Sociological Review* 62:218–35.

———. 2006. "Gender as an Organizing Force in Social Relations: Implications for the Future of Inequality." Pp. 245–87 in *The Declining Significance of Gender?* edited by Francine D. Blau and Mary C. Brinton. New York: The Russell Sage Foundation.

Ridgeway, Cecelia L. and Lynn Smith-Lovin. 1999. "The Gender System and Interaction." *Annual Review of Sociology* 25:19–216.

Roos, Patricia and Mary L. Gatta. 2006. "Gender Inquiry in the Academy." Presented at the Annual Meeting of the American Sociological Association, August 14, Montreal, Canada.

Rothbart, Myron and Marjorie Taylor. 1992. "Category Labels and Social Reality: Do We View Social Categories as Natural Kinds?" Pp. 11–36 in *Language, Interaction and Social Cognition,* edited by Gun R. Semin and Klaus Fiedler. London, England: Sage.

Rupp, Leila. 1978. *Mobilizing Women for War: German and American Propaganda, 1939–1945.* Princeton, NJ: Princeton University Press.

Salzinger, Leslie. 2003. *Genders in Production: Making Workers in Mexico's Global Factories.* Berkeley, CA: University of California Press.

Schemo, Diana Jean. 2006. "Change in Federal Rules Backs Single-Sex Public Education." *New York Times,* October 25, p. A16.

Sen, Amartya. 1990. "More Than 100 Million Women Are Missing." *New York Review of Books,* 37(20). Retrieved January 25, 2006 (http://ucatlas.ucsc.edu/gender/Sen100M.html).

Smith, Dorothy. 1990. *The Conceptual Practices of Power: A Feminist Sociology of Knowledge.* Boston, MA: Northeastern University Press.

Stacey, Judith and Barrie Thorne. 1985. "The Missing Feminist Revolution in Sociology." *Social Problems* 32:301–16.

Stevens, Alison. 2006. "Iranian Women Protest in Shadow of Nuclear Face-off." *Women's eNews,* June 16. Retrieved September 28, 2006 (http://www.womensenews.org/article.cfm/dyn/aid/2780).

Tannen, Deborah. 1990. *You Just Don't Understand: Women and Men in Conversation.* New York: Morrow.

Tarabay, Jamie. 2006. "Activists Seek to Protect Iraqi Women From Honor Killings." *NPR Morning Edition,* May 18. Retrieved June 6, 2006 (http://www.npr.org/templates/story/story.php?storyId=5414315).

Tavris, Carol. 1992. *The Mismeasure of Woman: Why Women Are Not the Better Sex, the Inferior Sex, or the Opposite Sex.* New York: Touchstone.

Telles, Edward. 2004. *Race in Another America: The Significance of Skin Color in Brazil.* Princeton, NJ: Princeton University Press.

Tierney, John. 2006. "Academy of P.C. Sciences." *New York Times,* September 26, p. A23.

Tilly, Charles. 1998. *Durable Inequality.* Berkeley, CA: University of California Press.

Trivers, Robert L. 1972. "Parental Investment and Sexual Selection." Pp. 136–79 in *Sexual Selection and the Descent of Man, 1871–1971,* edited by B. Campbell. Chicago, IL: Aldine.

United Nations. 2002. *Working Towards the Elimination of Crimes Against Women Committed in the Name of Honor, Report of the Secretary General.* United Nations General Assembly, July 2. Retrieved October 23, 2006 (http://www.unhchr.ch/huridocda/huridoca.nsf/AllSymbols/985168F508EE799FC1256C52002AE5A9/%24File/N0246790.pdf).

U.N. Common Database. 2004. "Gender Equality: Indicator: Seats in Parliament Held by Women–2004." Retrieved September 21, 2006 (http://globalis.gvu.unu.edu/indicator.cfm?Indicator ID=63&country=IS#rowIS).

Villalobos, V. Munos. 2006. "Economic, Social and Cultural Rights: Girls' Right to Education." Report submitted by the Special Rapporteur on the right to education. United Nations Commission on Human Rights, Economic and Social Council. Retrieved September 28, 2006 (http://www.crin.org/docs/SR_Education_report.pdf).

Williams, Joan. 2000. *Unbending Gender: Why Family and Work Conflict and What to Do About It.* New York: Oxford University Press.

Wilson, Edward O. 1975. *Sociobiology: The New Synthesis.* Cambridge, MA: Belknap Press of Harvard University Press.

Winston, Hella. 2005. *Unchosen: The Hidden Lives of Hasidic Rebels.* Boston, MA: Beacon Press.

Witte, Griff. 2005. "Post-Taliban Free Speech Blocked by Courts, Clerics: Jailed Afghan Publisher Faces Possible Execution." *Washington Post,* December 11, p. A24.

Women's World Summit Foundation. 2006. "World Rural Women's Day: 15 October: Introduction." Retrieved September 28, 2006 (http://www.woman.ch/women/2-introduction.asp).

Zerubavel, Eviatar. 1997. *Social Mindscapes: An Invitation to Cognitive Sociology.* Cambridge, MA: Harvard University Press.

Zimmerman Mary K., Jacquelyn S. Litt, and Christine E. Bose. 2006. *Global Dimensions of Gender and Care Work.* Stanford, CA: Stanford University Press.

Reading

The Positive Functions of Poverty[1] (1975)

Herbert J. Gans

I

Over 20 years ago, Merton (1949, p. 71), analyzing the persistence of the urban political machine, wrote that because "we should ordinarily . . . expect persistent social patterns and social structures to perform positive functions which are at the time not adequately fulfilled by other existing patterns and structures . . . perhaps this publicly maligned organization is, under present conditions, satisfying basic latent functions." He pointed out how the machine provided central authority to get things done when a decentralized local government could not act, humanized the services of the impersonal bureaucracy for fearful citizens, offered concrete help (rather than law or justice) to the poor, and otherwise performed services needed or demanded by many people but considered unconventional or even illegal by formal public agencies.

This paper is not concerned with the political machine, however, but with poverty, a social phenomenon which is as maligned as and far more persistent than the machine. Consequently, there may be some merit in applying functional analysis to poverty, to ask whether it too has positive functions that explain its persistence. Since functional analysis has itself taken on a maligned status among some American sociologists, a secondary purpose of this paper is to ask whether it is still a useful approach.[2]

SOURCE: From Gans, H. The positive functions of poverty. *The American Journal of Sociology,* 78(2), pp. 275–289. Copyright © 1972, The University of Chicago Press. Reprinted with permission.

[1]Earlier versions of this paper were presented at a Vassar College conference on the war on poverty in 1964, at the 7th World Congress of Sociology in 1971, and in *Social Policy 2* (July–August 1971): 20–24. The present paper will appear in a forthcoming book on poverty and stratification, edited by S. M. Lipset and S. M. Miller, for the American Academy of Arts and Sciences. I am indebted to Peter Marris, Robert K. Merton, and S. M. Miller for helpful comments on earlier drafts of this paper.

[2]The paper also has the latent function, as S. M. Miller has suggested, of contributing to the long debate over the functional analysis of social stratification presented by Davis and Moore (1945).

II

Merton (1949, p. 50) denned functions as "those observed consequences which make for the adaptation or adjustment of a given system; and dysfunctions, those observed consequences which lessen the adaptation or adjustment of the system." This definition does not specify the nature or scope of the system, but elsewhere in his classic paper "Manifest and Latent Functions," Merton indicated that social system was not a synonym for society, and that systems vary in size, requiring a functional analysis "to consider a *range* of units for which the item (or social phenomenon H.G.) has designated consequences: individuals in diverse statuses, subgroups, the larger social system and cultural systems" (1949, p. 51).

In discussing the functions of poverty, I shall identify functions for *groups* and *aggregates;* specifically, interest groups, socioeconomic classes, and other population aggregates, for example, those with shared values or similar statuses. This definitional approach is based on the assumption that almost every social system—and of course every society—is composed of groups or aggregates with different interests and values, so that, as Merton put it (1949, p. 51), "items may be functional for some individuals and subgroups and dysfunctional for others." Indeed, frequently one group's functions are another group's dysfunctions.[3] For example, the political machine analyzed by Merton was functional for the working class and business interests of the city but dysfunctional for many middle class and reform interests. Consequently, functions are denned as those observed consequences which are positive *as judged by the values of the group under analysis;* dysfunctions, as those which are negative by these values.[4] Because functions benefit the group in question and dysfunctions hurt it, I shall also describe functions and dysfunctions in the language of economic planning and systems analysis as benefits and costs.[5]

Identifying functions and dysfunctions for groups and aggregates rather than systems reduces the possibility that what is functional for one group in a multigroup system will be seen as being functional for the whole system, making it more difficult, for example, to suggest that a given phenomenon is functional for a corporation or political regime when it may in fact only be functional for their officers or leaders. Also, this approach precludes reaching a priori conclusions about two other important empirical questions raised by Merton (1949, pp. 32–36), whether any

---

[3]Probably one of the few instances in which a phenomenon has the same function for two groups with different interests is when the survival of the system in which both participate is at stake. Thus, a wage increase can be functional for labor and dysfunctional for management (and consumers), but if the wage increase endangers the firm's survival, it is dysfunctional for labor as well. This assumes, however, that the firm's survival is valued by the workers, which may not always be the case, for example, when jobs are available elsewhere.

[4]Merton (1949, p. 50) originally described functions and dysfunctions in terms of encouraging or hindering adaptation or adjustment to a system, although subsequently he has written that "dysfunction refers to the particular inadequacies of a particular part of the system for a designated requirement" (1961, p. 732). Since adaptation and adjustment to a system can have conservative ideological implications, Merton's later formulation and my own definitional approach make it easier to use functional analysis as an ideologically neutral or at least ideologically variable method, insofar as the researcher can decide for himself whether he supports the values of the group under analysis.

[5]It should be noted, however, that there are no absolute benefits and costs just as there are no absolute functions and dysfunctions; not only are one group's benefits often another group's costs, but every group defines benefits by its own manifest and latent values, and a social scientist or planner who has determined that certain phenomena provide beneficial consequences for a group may find that the group thinks otherwise. For example, during the 1960s, advocates of racial integration discovered that a significant portion of the black community no longer considered it a benefit but saw it rather as a policy to assimilate blacks into white society and to decimate the political power of the black community.

phenomenon is ever functional or dysfunctional for an entire society, and, if functional, whether it is therefore indispensable to that society.

In a modern heterogeneous society, few phenomena are functional or dysfunctional for the society as a whole, and most result in benefits to some groups and costs to others. Given the level of differentiation in modern society, I am even skeptical whether one can empirically identify a social system called society. Society exists, of course, but it is closer to being a very large aggregate, and when sociologists talk about society as a system, they often really mean the nation, a system which, among other things, sets up boundaries and other distinguishing characteristics between societal aggregates.

I would also argue that no social phenomenon is indispensable; it may be too powerful or too highly valued to be eliminated, but in most instances, one can suggest what Merton calls "functional alternatives" or equivalents for a social phenomena, that is, other social patterns or policies which achieve the same functions but avoid the dysfunctions.

III

The conventional view of American poverty is so dedicated to identifying the dysfunctions of poverty, both for the poor and the nation, that at first glance it seems inconceivable to suggest that poverty could be functional for anyone. Of course, the slum lord and the loan shark are widely known to profit from the existence of poverty; but they are popularly viewed as evil men, and their activities are, at least in part, dysfunctional for the poor. However, what is less often recognized, at least in the conventional wisdom, is that poverty also makes possible the existence or expansion of "respectable" professions and occupations, for example, penology,

criminology, social work, and public health. More recently, the poor have provided jobs for professional and paraprofessional "poverty warriors," as well as journalists and social scientists, this author included, who have supplied the information demanded when public curiosity about the poor developed in the 1960s.

Clearly, then, poverty and the poor may well serve a number of functions for many nonpoor groups in American society, and I shall describe 15 sets of such functions—economic, social, cultural, and political—that seem to me most significant.

First, the existence of poverty makes sure that "dirty work" is done. Every economy has such work: physically dirty or dangerous, temporary, dead-end and underpaid, undignified, and menial jobs. These jobs can be filled by paying higher wages than for "clean" work, or by requiring people who have no other choice to do the dirty work and at low wages. In America, poverty functions to provide a low-wage labor pool that is willing—or, rather, unable to be unwilling—to perform dirty work at low cost. Indeed, this function is so important that in some Southern states, welfare payments have been cut off during the summer months when the poor are needed to work in the fields. Moreover, the debate about welfare—and about proposed substitutes such as the negative income tax and the Family Assistance Plan—has emphasized the impact of income grants on work incentive, with opponents often arguing that such grants would reduce the incentive of—actually, the pressure on—the poor to carry out the needed dirty work if the wages therefore are no larger than the income grant. Furthermore, many economic activities which involve dirty work depend heavily on the poor; restaurants, hospitals, parts of the garment industry, and industrial agriculture, among others, could not persist in their present form without their dependence on the substandard wages which they pay to their employees.

---

[6]Of course, the poor do not actually subsidize the affluent. Rather, by being forced to work for low wages, they enable the affluent to use the money saved in this fashion for other purposes. The concept of subsidy used here thus assumes belief in a "just wage."

Second, the poor subsidize, directly and indirectly, many activities that benefit the affluent.[6] For one thing, they have long supported both the consumption and investment activities of the private economy by virtue of the low wages which they receive. This was openly recognized at the beginning of the Industrial Revolution, when a French writer quoted by T. H. Marshall (forthcoming, p. 7) pointed out that "to assure and maintain the prosperities of our industries, it is necessary that the workers should never acquire wealth." Examples of this kind of subsidization abound even today; for example, domestics subsidize the upper middle and upper classes, making life easier for their employers and freeing affluent women for a variety of professional, cultural, civic, or social activities. In addition, as Barry Schwartz pointed out (personal communication), the low income of the poor enables the rich to divert a higher proportion of their income to savings and investment, and thus to fuel economic growth. This, in turn, can produce higher incomes for everybody, including the poor, although it does not necessarily improve the position of the poor in the socioeconomic hierarchy, since the benefits of economic growth are also distributed unequally.

At the same time, the poor subsidize the governmental economy. Because local property and sales taxes and the ungraduated income taxes levied by many states are regressive, the poor pay a higher percentage of their income in taxes than the rest of the population, thus subsidizing the many state and local governmental programs that serve more affluent taxpayers.[7] In addition, the poor support medical innovation as patients in teaching and research hospitals, and as guinea pigs in medical experiments, subsidizing the more affluent patients who alone can afford these innovations once they are incorporated into medical practice.

Third, poverty creates jobs for a number of occupations and professions which serve the poor, or shield the rest of the population from them. As already noted, penology would be miniscule without the poor, as would the police, since the poor provide the majority of their "clients." Other activities which flourish because of the existence of poverty are the numbers game, the sale of heroin and cheap wines and liquors, pentecostal ministers, faith healers, prostitutes, pawn shops, and the peacetime army, which recruits its enlisted men mainly from among the poor.

Fourth, the poor buy goods which others do not want and thus prolong their economic usefulness, such as day-old bread, fruit and vegetables which would otherwise have to be thrown out, second-hand clothes, and deteriorating automobiles and buildings. They also provide incomes for doctors, lawyers, teachers, and others who are too old, poorly trained, or incompetent to attract more affluent clients.

In addition, the poor perform a number of social and cultural functions:

Fifth, the poor can be identified and punished as alleged or real deviants in order to uphold the legitimacy of dominant norms (Macarov 1970, pp. 31–33). The defenders of the desirability of hard work, thrift, honesty, and monogamy need people who can be accused of being lazy, spendthrift, dishonest, and promiscuous to justify these norms; and as Erikson (1964) and others following Durkheim have pointed out, the norms themselves are best legitimated by discovering violations.

Whether the poor actually violate these norms more than affluent people is still open to question. The working poor work harder and longer than high-status job holders, and poor housewives must do more housework to keep

---

[7]Pechman (1969) and Herriott and Miller (1971) found that the poor pay a higher proportion of their income in taxes than any other part of the population: 50% among people earning $2,000 or less according to the latter study.

[8]Most official investigations of welfare cheating have concluded that less than 5% of recipients are on the rolls illegally, while it has been estimated that about a third of the population cheats in filing income tax returns.

their slum apartments clean than their middle-class peers in standard housing. The proportion of cheaters among welfare recipients is quite low and considerably lower than among income taxpayers.[8] Violent crime is higher among the poor, but the affluent commit a variety of white-collar crimes, and several studies of self-reported delinquency have concluded that middle-class youngsters are sometimes as delinquent as the poor. However, the poor are more likely to be caught when participating in deviant acts and, once caught, to be punished more often than middle-class transgressors. Moreover, they lack the political and cultural power to correct the stereotypes that affluent people hold of them, and thus continue to be thought of as lazy, spendthrift, etc., whatever the empirical evidence, by those who need living proof that deviance does not pay.[9] The actually or allegedly deviant poor have traditionally been described as undeserving and, in more recent terminology, culturally deprived or pathological.

Sixth, another group of poor, described as deserving because they are disabled or suffering from bad luck, provide the rest of the population with different emotional satisfactions; they evoke compassion, pity, and charity, thus allowing those who help them to feel that they are altruistic, moral, and practicing the Judeo-Christian ethic. The deserving poor also enable others to feel fortunate for being spared the deprivations that come with poverty.[10]

Seventh, as a converse of the fifth function described previously, the poor offer affluent people vicarious participation in the uninhibited sexual, alcoholic, and narcotic behavior in which many poor people are alleged to indulge, and which, being freed from the constraints of affluence and

respectability, they are often thought to enjoy more than the middle classes. One of the popular beliefs about welfare recipients is that many are on a permanent sex-filled vacation. Although it may be true that the poor are more given to uninhibited behavior, studies by Rainwater (1970) and other observers of the lower class indicate that such behavior is as often motivated by despair as by lack of inhibition, and that it results less in pleasure than in a compulsive escape from grim reality. However, whether the poor actually have more sex and enjoy it more than affluent people is irrelevant; as long as the latter believe it to be so, they can share it vicariously and perhaps enviously when instances are reported in fictional, journalistic, or sociological and anthropological formats.

Eighth, poverty helps to guarantee the status of those who are not poor. In a stratified society, where social mobility is an especially important goal and class boundaries are fuzzy, people need to know quite urgently where they stand. As a result, the poor function as a reliable and relatively permanent measuring rod for status comparison, particularly for the working class, which must find and maintain status distinctions between itself and the poor, much as the aristocracy must find ways of distinguishing itself from the *nouveau riche.*

Ninth, the poor also assist in the upward mobility of the nonpoor, for, as Goode has pointed out (1967, p. 5), "the privileged . . . try systematically to prevent the talent of the less privileged from being recognized or developed." By being denied educational opportunities or being stereotyped as stupid or unteachable, the poor thus enable others to obtain the better jobs. Also, an unknown number of people have moved themselves or their children up in the socioeconomic hierarchy through the incomes earned from the provision of

[9]Although this paper deals with the functions of poverty for other groups, poverty has often been described as a motivating or character-building device for the poor themselves; and economic conservatives have argued that by generating the incentive to work, poverty encourages the poor to escape poverty. For an argument that work incentive is more enhanced by income than lack of it, see Gans (1971, p. 96).

[10]One psychiatrist (Chernus 1967) has even proposed the fantastic hypothesis that the rich and the poor are engaged in a sado-masochistic relationship, the latter being supported financially by the former so that they can gratify their sadistic needs.

goods and services in the slums: by becoming policemen and teachers, owning "mom and pop" stores, or working in the various rackets that flourish in the slums.

In fact, members of almost every immigrant group have financed their upward mobility by providing retail goods and services, housing, entertainment, gambling, narcotics, etc., to later arrivals in America (or in the city), most recently to blacks, Mexicans, and Puerto Ricans. Other Americans, of both European and native origin, have financed their entry into the upper middle and upper classes by owning or managing the illegal institutions that serve the poor, as well as the legal but not respectable ones, such as slum housing.

Tenth, just as the poor contribute to the economic viability of a number of businesses and professions (see function 3 above), they also add to the social viability of noneconomic groups. For one thing, they help to keep the aristocracy busy, thus justifying its continued existence. "Society" uses the poor as clients of settlement houses and charity benefits; indeed, it must have the poor to practice its public-mindedness so as to demonstrate its superiority over the *nouveaux riches* who devote themselves to conspicuous consumption. The poor play a similar function for philanthropic enterprises at other levels of the socioeconomic hierarchy, including the mass of middle-class civic organizations and women's clubs engaged in volunteer work and fundraising in almost every American community. Doing good among the poor has traditionally helped the church to find a method of expressing religious sentiments in action; in recent years, militant church activity among and for the poor has enabled the church to hold on to its more liberal and radical members who might otherwise have dropped out of organized religion altogether.

Eleventh, the poor perform several cultural functions. They have played an unsung role in the creation of "civilization," having supplied the construction labor for many of the monuments which are often identified as the noblest expressions and examples of civilization, for example, the Egyptian pyramids, Greek temples, and medieval churches.[11] Moreover, they have helped to create a goodly share of the surplus capital that funds the artists and intellectuals who make culture, and particularly "high" culture, possible in the first place.

Twelfth, the "low" culture created for or by the poor is often adopted by the more affluent. The rich collect artifacts from extinct folk cultures (although not only from poor ones), and almost all Americans listen to the jazz, blues, spirituals, and country music which originated among the Southern poor—as well as rock, which was derived from similar sources. The protest of the poor sometimes becomes literature; in 1970, for example, poetry written by ghetto children became popular in sophisticated literary circles. The poor also serve as culture heroes and literary subjects, particularly, of course, for the Left, but the hobo, cowboy, hipster, and the mythical prostitute with a heart of gold have performed this function for a variety of groups.

Finally, the poor carry out a number of important political functions:

Thirteenth, the poor serve as symbolic constituencies and opponents for several political groups. For example, parts of the revolutionary Left could not exist without the poor, particularly now that the working class can no longer be perceived as the vanguard of the revolution. Conversely, political groups of conservative bent need the "welfare chiselers" and others who "live off the taxpayer's hard-earned money" in order to justify their demands for reductions in welfare payments and tax relief. Moreover, the role of the poor in upholding dominant norms (see function 5 above) also has a significant political function. An economy based on the ideology of laissez- faire

---

[11] Although this is not a contemporary function of poverty in America, it should be noted that today these monuments serve to attract and gratify American tourists.

requires a deprived population which is allegedly unwilling to work; not only does the alleged moral inferiority of the poor reduce the moral pressure on the present political economy to eliminate poverty, but redistributive alternatives can be made to look quite unattractive if those who will benefit from them most can be described as lazy, spendthrift, dishonest, and promiscuous. Thus, conservatives and classical liberals would find it difficult to justify many of their political beliefs without the poor; but then so would modern liberals and socialists who seek to eliminate poverty.

Fourteenth, the poor, being powerless, can be made to absorb the economic and political costs of change and growth in American society. During the 19th century, they did the backbreaking work that built the cities; today, they are pushed out of their neighborhoods to make room for "progress." Urban renewal projects to hold middle-class taxpayers and stores in the city and expressways to enable suburbanites to commute downtown have typically been located in poor neighborhoods, since no other group will allow itself to be displaced. For much the same reason, urban universities, hospitals, and civic centers also expand into land occupied by the poor. The major costs of the industrialization of agriculture in America have been borne by the poor, who are pushed off the land without recompense, just as in earlier centuries in Europe, they bore the brunt of the transformation of agrarian societies into industrial ones. The poor have also paid a large share of the human cost of the growth of American power overseas, for they have provided many of the foot soldiers for Vietnam and other wars.

Fifteenth, the poor have played an important role in shaping the American political process; because they vote and participate less than other groups, the political system has often been free to ignore them. This has not only made American politics more centrist than would otherwise be the case, but it has also added to the stability of the political process. If the 15% of the population below the federal "poverty line" participated

fully in the political process, they would almost certainly demand better jobs and higher incomes, which would require income redistribution and would thus generate further political conflict between the haves and the have-nots. Moreover, when the poor do participate, they often provide the Democrats with a captive constituency, for they can rarely support Republicans, lack parties of their own, and thus have no other place to go politically. This, in turn, has enabled the Democrats to count on the votes of the poor, allowing the party to be more responsive to voters who might otherwise switch to the Republicans, in recent years, for example, the white working class.

IV

I have described fifteen of the more important functions which the poor carry out in American society, enough to support the functionalist thesis that poverty survives in part because it is useful to a number of groups in society. This analysis is not intended to suggest that because it is functional, poverty *should* persist, or that it *must* persist. Whether it should persist is a normative question; whether it must, an analytic and empirical one, but the answer to both depends in part on whether the dysfunctions of poverty outweigh the functions. Obviously, poverty has many dysfunctions, mainly for the poor themselves but also for the more affluent. For example, their social order is upset by the pathology, crime, political protest, and disruption emanating from the poor, and the income of the affluent is affected by the taxes that must be levied to protect their social order. Whether the dysfunctions outweigh the functions is a question that clearly deserves study.

It is, however, possible to suggest alternatives for many of the functions of the poor. Thus, society's dirty work (function 1) could be done without poverty, some by automating it, the rest by paying the workers who do it decent wages, which would help considerably to cleanse that kind of work. Nor is it necessary for the poor to subsidize the activities they support through their low-wage jobs (function 2), for, like dirty work, many of these activities are essential enough to persist even if wages were raised. In both instances, however, costs would be driven up, resulting in higher prices to the customers and clients of dirty work and subsidized activity, with obvious dysfunctional consequences for more affluent people.

Alternative roles for the professionals who flourish because of the poor (function 3) are easy to suggest. Social workers could counsel the affluent, as most prefer to do anyway, and the police could devote themselves to traffic and organized crime. Fewer penologists would be employable, however, and pentecostal religion would probably not survive without the poor. Nor would parts of the second- and thirdhand market (function 4), although even affluent people sometimes buy used goods. Other roles would have to be found for badly trained or incompetent professionals now relegated to serving the poor, and someone else would have to pay their salaries.

Alternatives for the deviance-connected social functions (functions 5–7) can be found more easily and cheaply than for the economic functions. Other groups are already available to serve as deviants to uphold traditional morality, for example, entertainers, hippies, and most recently, adolescents in general. These same groups are also available as alleged or real orgiasts to provide vicarious participation in sexual fantasies. The blind and disabled function as objects of pity and charity, and the poor may therefore not even be needed for functions 5–7.

The status and mobility functions of the poor (functions 8 and 9) are far more difficult to substitute, however. In a hierarchical society, some people must be defined as inferior to everyone else with respect to a variety of attributes, and the poor perform this function more adequately than others. They could, however, perform it without being as poverty stricken as they are, and one can conceive of a stratification system in which the people below the federal "poverty line" would receive 75% of the median income rather than 40% or less, as is now the case—even though they would still be last in the pecking order.[12] Needless to say, such a reduction of economic inequality would also require income redistribution. Given the opposition to income redistribution among more affluent people, however, it seems unlikely that the status functions of poverty can be replaced, and they—together with the economic functions of the poor, which are equally expensive to replace—may turn out to be the major obstacles to the elimination of poverty.

The role of the poor in the upward mobility of other groups could be maintained without their being so low in income. However, if their incomes were raised above subsistence levels, they would begin to generate capital so that their own entrepreneurs could supply them with goods and services, thus competing with and perhaps rejecting "outside" suppliers. Indeed, this is already happening in a number of ghettoes, where blacks are replacing white storeowners.

Similarly, if the poor were more affluent, they would make less willing clients for upper- and middle-class philanthropic and religious groups (function 10), although as long as they are economically and otherwise unequal, this function need not disappear altogether. Moreover, some would still use the settlement houses and other philanthropic institutions to pursue individual upward mobility, as they do now.

The cultural functions (11 and 12) may not need to be replaced. In America, the labor unions have rarely allowed the poor to help build cultural monuments anyway, and there is

---

[12]In 1971, the median family income in the United States was about $10,000, and the federal poverty line for a family of four was set at just about $4,000. Of course, most of the poor were earning less than 40% of the median, and about a third of them, less than 20% of the median.

sufficient surplus capital from other sources to subsidize the unprofitable components of high culture. Similarly, other deviant groups are available to innovate in popular culture and supply new culture heroes, for example, the hippies and members of other countercultures.

Some of the political functions of the poor would, however, be as difficult to replace as their economic and status functions. Although the poor could probably continue to serve as symbolic constituencies and opponents (function 13) if their incomes were raised while they remained unequal in other respects, increases in income are generally accompanied by increases in power as well. Consequently, once they were no longer so poor, people would be likely to resist paying the costs of growth and change (function 14); and it is difficult to find alternative groups who can be displaced for urban renewal and technological "progress." Of course, it is possible to design city-rebuilding and highway projects which properly reimburse the displaced people, but such projects would then become considerably more expensive, thus raising the price for those now benefiting from urban renewal and expressways. Alternatively, many might never be built, thus reducing the comfort and convenience of those beneficiaries. Similarly, if the poor were subjected to less economic pressure, they would probably be less willing to serve in the army, except at considerably higher pay, in which case war would become yet more costly and thus less popular politically. Alternatively, more service-men would have to be recruited from the middle and upper classes, but in that case war would also become less popular.

The political stabilizing and "centering" role of the poor (function 15) probably cannot be substituted for at all, since no other group is willing to be disenfranchised or likely enough to remain apathetic so as to reduce the fragility of the political system. Moreover, if the poor were given higher incomes, they would probably become more active politically, thus adding their demands for more to those of other groups already putting pressure on the political allocators of resources. The poor might continue to remain loyal to the Democratic party, but like other moderate-income voters, they could also be attracted to the Republicans or to third parties. While improving the economic status of the presently poor would not necessarily drive the political system far to the left, it would enlarge the constituencies now demanding higher wages and more public funds. It is of course possible to add new powerless groups who do not vote or otherwise participate to the political mix and can thus serve as "ballast" in the polity, for example, by encouraging the import of new poor immigrants from Europe and elsewhere, except that the labor unions are probably strong enough to veto such a policy.

In sum, then, several of the most important functions of the poor cannot be replaced with alternatives, while some could be replaced, but almost always only at higher costs to other people, particularly more affluent ones. Consequently, *a junctional analysis must conclude that poverty persists not only because it satisfies a number of functions but also because many of the functional alternatives to poverty would be quite dysfunctional for the more affluent members of society.*[13]

V

I noted earlier that functional analysis had itself become a maligned phenomenon and that a secondary purpose of this paper was to demonstrate its continued usefulness. One reason for its presently low status is political; insofar as an analysis of functions, particularly latent functions, seems to justify what ought to be condemned, it appears to lend itself to the support of conservative ideological positions, although it can also have radical implications when

---

[13]Or as Stein (1971, p. 171) puts it: "If the non-poor make the rules . . . antipoverty efforts will only be made up to the point where the needs of the non-poor are satisfied, rather than the needs of the poor."

it subverts the conventional wisdom. Still, as Merton has pointed out (1949, p. 43; 1961, pp. 736–37), functional analysis per se is ideologically neutral, and "like other forms of sociological analysis, it can be infused with any of a wide range of sociological values" (1949, p. 40). This infusion depends, of course, on the purposes—and even the functions—of the functional analysis, for as Wirth (1936, p. xvii) suggested long ago, "every assertion of a 'fact' about the social world touches the interests of some individual or group," and even if functional analyses are conceived and conducted in a neutral manner, they are rarely interpreted in an ideological vacuum.

In one sense, my analysis is, however, neutral; if one makes no judgment as to whether poverty ought to be eliminated—and if one can subsequently avoid being accused of acquiescing in poverty—then the analysis suggests only that poverty exists because it is useful to many groups in society.[14] If one favors the elimination of poverty, however, then the analysis can have a variety of political implications, *depending in part on how completely it is carried out.*

If functional analysis only identifies the functions of social phenomena without mentioning their dysfunctions, then it may, intentionally or otherwise, agree with or support holders of conservative values. Thus, to say that the poor perform many functions for the rich might be interpreted or used to justify poverty, just as Davis and Moore's argument (1945) that social stratification is functional because it provides society with highly trained professionals could be taken to justify inequality.

Actually, the Davis and Moore analysis was conservative because it was incomplete; it did not identify the dysfunctions of inequality and failed to suggest functional alternatives, as Tumin (1953) and Schwartz (1955) have pointed out.[15] Once a functional analysis is made more complete by the addition of functional alternatives, however, it can take on a liberal and reform cast, because the alternatives often provide ameliorative policies that do not require any drastic change in the existing social order.

Even so, to make functional analysis complete requires yet another step, an examination of the functional alternatives themselves. My analysis suggests that the alternatives for poverty are themselves dysfunctional for the affluent population, and it ultimately comes to a conclusion which is not very different from that of radical sociologists. To wit: *that social phenomena which are functional for affluent groups and dysfunctional for poor ones persist; that when the elimination of such phenomena through functional alternatives generates dysfunctions for the affluent, they will continue to persist; and that phenomena like poverty can be eliminated only when they either become sufficiently dysfunctional for the affluent or when the poor can obtain enough power to change the system of social stratification.*[16]

---

[14]Of course, even in this case the analysis need not be purely neutral, but can be put to important policy uses, for example, by indicating more effectively than moral attacks on poverty the exact nature of the obstacles that must be overcome if poverty is to be eliminated. See also Merton (1961, pp. 709–12).

[15]Functional analysis can, of course, be conservative in value or have conservative implications for a number of other reasons, principally in its overt or covert comparison of the advantages of functions and disadvantages of dysfunctions, or in its attitudes toward the groups that are benefiting and paying the costs. Thus, a conservatively inclined policy researcher could conclude that the dysfunctions of poverty far outnumber the functions, but still decide that the needs of the poor are simply not as important or worthy as those of other groups, or of the country as a whole.

[16]On the possibility of radical functional analysis, see Merton (1949, pp. 40–43) and Gouldner (1970, p. 443). One difference between my analysis and the prevailing radical view is that most of the functions I have described are latent, whereas many radicals treat them, as manifest: recognized and intended by an unjust economic system to oppress the poor. Practically speaking, however, this difference may be unimportant, for if unintended and unrecognized functions were recognized, many affluent people might then decide that they ought to be intended as well, so as to forestall a more expensive antipoverty effort that might be dysfunctional for the affluent.

REFERENCES

Chernus, J. 1967. "Cities: A Study in Sadomasochism." *Medical Opinion and Review* (May): 104–9.

Davis, K., and W. E. Moore. 1945. "Some Principles of Stratification." *American Sociological Review* 10 (April): 242–49.

Erikson, K. T. 1964. "Notes on the Sociology of Deviance." In *The Other Side,* edited by Howard S. Becker. New York: Free Press.

Gans, H. J. 1971. "Three Ways to Solve the Welfare Problem." *New York Times Magazine,* March 7, pp. 26–27, 94–100.

Goode, W. J. 1967. "The Protection of the Inept." *American Sociological Review* 32 (February): 5–19.

Gouldner, A. 1970. *The Coming Crisis of Western Sociology.* New York: Basic.

Herriot, A., and H. P. Miller. 1971. "Who Paid the Taxes in 1968." Paper prepared for the National Industrial Conference Board.

Macarov, D. 1970. *Incentives to Work.* San Francisco: Jossey-Bass.

Marshall, T. H. Forthcoming. "Poverty and Inequality." Paper prepared for the American Academy of Arts and Sciences volume on poverty and stratification.

Merton, R. K. 1949. "Manifest and Latent Functions." In *Social Theory and Social Structure.* Glencoe, Il.: Free Press.

———. 1961. "Social Problems and Sociological Theory." In *Contemporary Social Problems,* edited by R. K. Merton and R. Nisbet. New York: Harcourt Brace.

Pechman, J. A. 1969. "The Rich, the Poor, and the Taxes They Pay." *Public Interest,* no. 17 (Fall): 21–43.

Rainwater, L. 1970. *Behind Ghetto Walls.* Chicago: Aldine.

Schwartz, R. 1955. "Functional Alternatives to Inequality." *American Sociological Review* 20 (August): 424–30.

Stein, B. 1971. *On Relief.* New York: Basic.

Tumin, M. B. 1953. "Some Principles of Stratification: A Critical Analysis." *American Sociological Review* 18 (August): 387–93.

Wirth, L. 1936. "Preface." In *Ideology and Utopia,* by Karl Mannheim. New York: Harcourt Brace.

Reading

Theodicy and Life Satisfaction Among Black and White Americans (2000)

Marc A. Musick

Social scientists have long been interested in the relationship between religion and individual well-being. Allport (1950) and others (e.g., Argyle and Beit-Hallahmi 1975) noted the importance of religion for adjustment and integration. More recently, Idler (1987) predicted that religion would have important consequences for well-being through four mechanisms: (1) religion provides a sense of comfort in times of trouble; (2) the integrative aspect of religion gives access to a large network of potential support providers; (3) religious norms discourage behaviors that might lead to health problems; and (4) religious beliefs furnish a cognitive framework through which people can better understand the meaning of pain, suffering, and death.

The theory underlying religion and well-being has not advanced greatly over the past century. Some of the more innovative work being done today extends the theoretical concepts used by

Durkheim ([1897] 1951) and Allport (1950). For instance, Ellison and George (1994) examined the impact of religion on social integration and support (see also Bradley 1995). Others examined the comfort dimension of religion showing how religion inhibits the translation of stressful conditions, such as ill health, into worse mental functioning (e.g., Idler 1995; Johnson and Spilka 1991; Koenig *et al.* 1993). A number of others investigated the impact of religious prohibitions of unhealthy or deviant behavior on physical health (Gardner and Lyon 1982; Phillips and Snowdon 1983; Payne *et al.* 1991). In sum, most of the extant research on religion and well-being can be traced to Durkheim's assertion of the importance of religion for well-being.

As the literature on religion and well-being grows, one facet seems to receive less attention than the others: studies that examine the impact of theodicy (i.e., religious beliefs related to the meaning of suffering) on well-being seem to be in short supply. Given the potential importance of such beliefs for well-being (Idler 1987), more evidence is needed to determine whether this is indeed a plausible line of inquiry. Several authors have purported to examine the effects of theodicy but fall short because they rely on a proxy measure—denominational affiliation (e.g., Ferraro and Albrecht-Jensen 1991; Musick 1996).

The purpose of this paper is to further the study of religion and well-being by focusing on the effects of specific theodicy beliefs in addition to the more traditional indicators of religious activity. Further, I will argue that the effects of these beliefs are not the same across all social contexts; rather, personal characteristics (i.e., race) and social factors moderate the relationship such that the effects of theodicy are stronger for some groups than for others.

THEORETICAL OVERVIEW

Sin and Evil in Christian Theodicy

Sociological writings on theodicy are certainly not new. Weber (1946) discussed at length both the meaning of theodicy and its implications. He emphasized that one function of religion was not to do away with life's problems but to help explain them. Berger (1967) draws heavily upon Weber's work to develop his ideas about theodicy. In proposing a definition of theodicy, Berger explains:

> The anomic phenomena must not only be lived through, they must also be explained—to wit, explained in terms of the nomos established in the society in question. An explanation of these phenomena in terms of religious legitimations, of whatever degree of theoretical sophistication, may be called a theodicy (p. 53).

Because individuals experience problems and traumas, they must have a system of belief that accounts for those experiences. As Berger goes on to argue, there can be any number of plausible theodicies. However, all of the possibilities share the single purpose of providing meaning. In this vein, Berger notes:

> If theodicy answers, in whatever manner, this question of meaning, it serves a most important purpose for the suffering individual, even if it does not involve a promise that the eventual outcome of his suffering is happiness in this world or the next. It would, for this reason, be misleading to consider theodicies only in terms of their 'redemptive' potential. Indeed, some theodicies carry no promise of 'redemption' at all-except for the redeeming assurance of meaning itself (p. 58),

Although theodicies need not necessarily hold redemptive value, many nevertheless do. Given that a vast majority of Americans belong to the Christian faith (Roof and McKinney 1987), I focus here upon the implications of Christian theodicy. According to Stark (1972), the two core beliefs in Christian theology are mankind's fall from grace and the promise of redemption. More specifically, became of original sin and mankind's fall from grace due to sin, all of humanity is cut off from God and redemption. However, because of the sacrifice of Jesus Christ, the possibility of redemption remains.

Taking these two core elements of Christian belief and setting them beside the definition of theodicy given by Berger, it appears that the *sin* aspect is that which is most appropriately termed Christian theodicy (see also Berger 1967). This aspect of the Christian belief system is its theodicy because it *explains* why bad things happen. That is, the presence of sin in the world and in mankind is the explanation for the problems that befall individuals and societies.

The redemptive portion of Christian beliefs does not explain why bad things happen, they merely suggest that for the true believer, eventual bliss will come. In the hypothesized relationship between religion and health, this redemptive aspect of the Christian core belief dyad may best be referred to as part of the comfort aspect of religion (Glock, Ringer, and Babbie 1967). If one thinks of religious beliefs in terms of their importance for coping, then it is important to keep the two elements separate. The theodicy, or explanatory, component provides individuals with a framework whereby they may understand and find meaning in a problematic life circumstance. Once the problem is understood, the religious adherent may then draw upon the comforting power of religious belief to provide hope (Koenig 1994). Indeed, it is religion's ability to provide meaning and hope for the future, even in the face of current life adversity, that may have such powerful effects for well-being.

It is the combination, meaning and comfort, which sets religion apart from other social institutions. To take the example of the social cohesiveness hypothesis (Idler 1987) one can imagine any number of groups other than religious bodies which could provide access to supportive others. However, these groups will lack the underlying foundation of belief that gives religion such power in people's lives.

Theodicy and Life Satisfaction

Although the Christian belief system places the concept of sin at the core of its explanation for suffering, individual adherents can vary by the importance they place on sin as being responsible for the suffering of humanity. It stands to reason that people who voice a theodicy that emphasizes evil and sin will not be as satisfied as those who see the world in more benevolent terms. Why would this be true?

People who see the world in terms of evil and sin will tend to devalue the material world. Adherents to these sorts of religious beliefs tend to be members of religious groups that are best classified as what Weber (1946) terms, "otherworldly" religions. They are also those most likely to follow the Bible's assertion that Christians should resist the world: "Love not the world, neither the things that are in the world. If any man love the world, the love of the Father is not in him" (I John 2:15). For those who follow this belief system, only elements of the sacred and redemption will be valued.

It is possible that this devaluation of the material world leads one to be less satisfied with it. Several researchers (e.g., Campbell *et al.* 1976; George 1981) have noted that perceptions of satisfaction are based on cognitive assessments of life situations rather than affective ones. These cognitive assessments tend to be stable over time and are rooted in comparisons to external elements. In thinking about theodicies of evil and life satisfaction, we could regard the external referent as the world as it should be. In other words, compared to the ideal world where there is no evil and sin (e.g., heaven), the material world simply is not good enough in the eyes of these believers. For that reason, dissatisfaction is likely to result.

Some contemporary Christian literature takes this rejection of the world one step further. According to one author, the powers of Satan are at work in the world to destroy Christianity (Marrs 1988). The language used in these writings is akin to language that might be used to describe warfare. Consequently, from this perspective, Christians are, in the words of Ellison and Musick, "persecuted soldiers of the

Lord, valiantly struggling against ungodly forces in an unsympathetic, even hostile, world" (1993: 382). Living in a world characterized by this level of hostility and chaos is not conducive to feelings of satisfaction. Rather, satisfaction will come only with redemption in the afterlife.

Race and Sin Theodicies

Recent research has emphasized the importance of separating Whites from Blacks when examining the relationship between religious factors and well-being. Studies of religion and health that have done so have shown differential effects by racial group (e.g., Ellison 1995; Ferraro and Koch 1994; Musick *et al.* 1998). Consequently, it may be possible that the effects of theodicy on life satisfaction may differ between Blacks and Whites. There are several possible reasons for these potential differences. First, as Taylor *et al.* (1996) recently showed, Blacks report greater levels of religious activity and attachment than Whites (see also Levin, Taylor, and Chatters 1994). Moreover, there is some suggestion that the content and function of Black religious services tends to vary from those of Whites (Gilkes 1980; Griffith, English, and Mayfield 1980).

Second, the Black church has historically been one of the most influential institutions in the lives of African Americans (Chatters and Taylor 1994; Lincoln and Mamiya 1990); thus, their experience in the church and their relationship to it and other parishioners tends to be different than those relationships for Whites. Indeed, for Blacks living in certain areas of the country (e.g., rural South), the church is a "semi-involuntary" institution (Ellison and Sherkat 1995; Nelsen and Nelsen 1975). In other words, all or most Blacks living in these areas will be attached to the church and will see it as an essential part of their social and personal lives.

Third, given greater levels of deprivation in terms of health and other resources among African Americans (Mutran 1985; Manuel 1988), the Black church serves an important role

in providing an outlet for the attainment of personal and social resources among its members. For example, Blacks often use the church as a source of social support (Taylor and Chatters 1986, 1988), social status (Moore 1991), racial identity (Moore 1991), and self-esteem (Hughes and Demo 1989). In sum, for the reasons listed above, examining the individual consequences of religion without separating respondents by race may hide important distinctions between racial groups.

The reasons outlined above for dividing the analyses by race could plausibly be applied to any study of religion and well-being. However, in considering the relationship of sin theodicies to well-being, we must take special consideration of the important role of religious belief in the lives of African Americans. According to Cooper-Lewter and Mitchell (1986), it is impossible to understand the current experience of African-American religionists without understanding their belief in the world as being a fundamentally good place. These authors argue that without such, a conception, African Americans could never have survived the bondage of slavery or the century and a half of travails that followed emancipation. As these authors note, "Even the worst inhumane treatment never convinced most slaves to accept Calvinist theories of total human depravity. They often sang of sinners, but they never expressed a loss of hope" (1986: 69). The key to our understanding the possible differential impact of a sin theodicy between the races lies in the latter statement made by Cooper-Lewter and Mitchell. On the one hand, African Americans can believe in the basic sinfulness of mankind and the world, but on the other, they never lose the hope that comes with believing in a fundamentally good God who can, and does, bestow blessings on his people. So, although a given African American may acknowledge a sin theodicy, the effects of holding that theodicy will not be as great as that for Whites due to the religious belief system in which that sin theodicy is set.

Moderating Factors of the Relationship Between Theodicy and Well-Being

As stated previously, we should not expect that the effects of a sin theodicy on life satisfaction will be the same across all individuals but rather should vary by other factors. The first such factor is the degree to which the believer is integrated into the church. As noted previously, uncertainty of belief is an ever-present menace in pluralistic society. One reliable way to maintain beliefs is to interact with others who share those beliefs. Not only does frequent interaction with fellow adherents shield believers from temptations or from ideas that challenge their own, but as Berger and Luckmann (1966) argued, interaction through verbal and non-verbal means reinforces those shared beliefs (see also White 1968). It follows that the situation of non-integrated believers is precarious: Not only are they embedded in a world which they are supposed to reject, but they must also face challenges to their beliefs without the support of others of a like faith. In short, I expect that the negative effects of a sin theodicy will be greater for believers who are less integrated into their religious community.

The second factor that should moderate the effect of sin theodicies on life satisfaction is the presence of other stressful circumstances. Simply stated, persons who face other stressors (e.g., financial problems, loss of a loved one) may be more vulnerable to the effects of the sin theodicy. This line of thinking is consonant with the vulnerability hypothesis in stress research: The effects of certain risk factors on psychiatric morbidity are heightened among persons who are experiencing some form of chronic stress (Kessler, Price, and Wortman 1985; George 1992). The primary explanation for this effect is that chronic stressors tend to drain psychological and social resources that might otherwise be used to cope with a specific risk factor. If holding a sin theodicy is a risk factor for dissatisfaction, then we would also expect that experiencing stressful situations makes one more

vulnerable to the effects of that theodicy. It might also be the case that stressful circumstances serve as a validation of one's negative view of the world. In sum, I expect that the effects of holding a sin theodicy will be strongest among those who experience other forms of stress.

Given the arguments presented above, I offer the following hypotheses.

Hypothesis 1: Theodicies that place more emphasis on sin and evil are associated with less life satisfaction.

Hypothesis 2: The negative effects of holding a sin theodicy on life satisfaction are stronger among Whites than Blacks.

Hypothesis 3: The effects of holding a sin theodicy vary by levels of interaction with fellow believers such that the negative effect is strongest among those who interact less frequently.

Hypothesis 4: The effects of holding a sin theodicy vary by levels of stress such that the negative effect is strongest among people experiencing stressful circumstances.

METHODS

Data for the study come from the General Social Survey (Davis and Smith 1991) distributed by The Roper Center for Public Opinion Research. The survey, which has been collected on a yearly basis from 1972 to 1994 (with the exception of years 1979, 1981, and 1992), has been used in numerous previous studies and has been shown to be both reliable and representative of the adult population of the United States. The GSS is an independently drawn sample of persons eighteen years or older who are English speaking and live in the United States in non-institutionalized settings. I use data from 1987 (N = 1,819) because it contains all of the variables needed for my analyses as well as an oversample of Blacks. Missing cases for independent variables were imputed using the mean value for ordinal and continuous variables and the mode for dichotomous ones; however, no imputation was made for the dependent variable.[1] Due to these missing cases, the sample size used in the final analyses is 537 for Blacks and 1,215 for Whites. All respondents who reported their race as other than White or Black were excluded from the analyses.

Measurement

The hypothesized relationships are tested using multivariate ordinary least squares regression. Life satisfaction is measured using an index composed of several items asking about satisfaction with different domains of life (e.g., family life, friendships). Theodicy is measured using a two-item index first created by Ellison and Musick (1995) termed "Ubiquity of Sin." The two moderating factors—interaction with the religious group and stressful circumstances—are measured using frequency of church attendance and two stressors: financial problems and life events. Because there will be some overlap with theodicy and religious affiliation, I control for whether the respondent reports belonging to a conservative Christian denomination, which is most likely to advocate theodicies about sin and evil. It may also be the case that any relationship we observe between sin theodicies and life satisfaction is due to distrust of others. That is, persons who see the world in terms of evil fundamentally distrust others, and as such, have low levels of life satisfaction. To adjust for this possibility, I include a three-item measure of distrust in the multivariate models. Finally, the models are adjusted for several other sociodemographic factors that are commonly shown to affect individual well-being (e.g., gender, education).

Dependent Variable

Life Satisfaction. ($\alpha = .71$) Life satisfaction is measured using a five-item index that gauges satisfaction in different life domains. Respondents are asked how much satisfaction they receive from their city, hobbies, family life, friendships, and health. Higher scores on the index indicate more satisfaction.

Independent Variables

Ubiquity of Sin. ($\alpha = .63$; $r = .46$) The measure of theodicy I use is the "Ubiquity of Sin" scale used previously by Ellison and Musick (1995). The scale indicates the degree to which respondents feel that the world and the people in it are evil or sinful. For each of the items in the measure, respondents were asked to place themselves on a seven point scale between two beliefs about the world. For the first question, the two beliefs presented are "the world is basically filled with evil and sin," and "there is much goodness in the world that hints at God's goodness." The two statements that make up the second question are "human nature is basically good" and "human nature is fundamentally perverse and corrupt." The overall index is coded such that higher values indicate a belief that the world is filled with sin and is basically corrupt.

Church Attendance. The measure of church attendance approximates the "associational" or formal type of religious participation (Lenski 1963). The eight response categories are: (0) never; (1) less than once per year; (2) about once or twice per year; (3) several times per year; (4) about once a month; (5) two or three times per month; (6) nearly every week; (7) every week; and (8) several times per week.

Conservative Protestant Denomination. I use the scheme of Roof and McKinney (1987) to classify denominations into conservative versus non-conservative groups. The denominations which fall into the conservative portion under this method include: Southern Baptist, Independent

---

[1]Most of the variables with imputed values were missing 2% or less of their cases. However, approximately 8% of the cases were missing for income and traumatic episodes. I constructed dummy variables to indicate those people who were missing on each item and included them in the final analyses. However, because they had no significant impact on the model, I dropped them from the analyses.

Baptist, National Baptist Convention (Black respondents only), Evangelical Congregational, Assemblies of God, Brethren, Church of Christ (except United Church of Christ), Churches of God, Church of God in Christ, Evangelical, Evangelical Reformed, Full Gospel, Foursquare Gospel, Holiness, Nazarene, Missouri Synod Lutheran, Pentecostals, Sanctified, Sanctification, Seventh-Day Adventist, and other small evangelical and fundamentalist groups.

Stressors. The first stressor is a measure of the number of *life events* (e.g., death, divorce, disabilities) the respondent experienced during the previous year.[2] The original responses on this item ranged from one to four; however, because of skewness towards the lower end of the distribution, the variable was recoded to reflect one or more events versus none. The second stressor, *financial strain,* gauges whether respondents' financial situation had been getting better, worse, or stayed the same during the past few years. The item is coded such that respondents who report their finances as getting worse receive a score of one, and all others receive a zero.

Interpersonal Distrust ($\alpha = .64$). This three-item summated scale is coded such that higher scores indicate greater distrust (Demaris and Yang 1994). Data for the three items were gathered using the following questions: (1) "Do you think most people would try to take advantage of you if they got a chance, or would they try to be fair?"; (2) "Would you say that most of the time people try to be helpful, or that they are mostly just looking out for themselves?"; and (3) "Generally speaking, would you say that most people can be trusted or that you can't be too careful in dealing with people?"

Sociodemographics. The four sociodemographic items included are gender (0) = male, (1) = female, age (in years), education (in years of schooling), and family income (20 categories ranging from under $1,000 to $60,000 and over).

RESULTS

Descriptive Statistics and Bivariate Associations

Table 1 reports mean levels of the variables used in the analyses, by race. According to this table, a majority of respondents in both races are female and the mean age is about forty-four years. White respondents tend to have both higher levels of education and family income than Blacks. In terms of the religion variables, Blacks report higher levels of ubiquity of sin, and church attendance, and are more likely to be affiliated with a conservative Protestant denomination. Blacks also report more life events and distrust than Whites.

Table 2 displays the unadjusted correlations between all of the variables in the analysis, by race. Correlations for Blacks are above the diagonal and those for Whites are below. Among Blacks there are several significant correlations. Life satisfaction is positively associated with education, family income, and church attendance but is negatively correlated with distrust and both stressors. Ubiquity of sin is negatively associated with education and family income but is positively associated with distrust.

---

[2]The point that is being made in the analyses with regard to the stressful situations is that respondents faced with such a situation, will fare worse than those who do not face such problems. Although the traumatic events measure may appear inadequate at tapping these ongoing problems, I do not believe this is the case. The measure itself does tap a specific event bounded in time (e.g. death of spouse or divorce), but it also serves as a proxy for ongoing difficulties. For example, one who has been divorced within the past year may still be going through readjustment problems in terms of relocating, claiming custody of children, or adjusting to new friendship dynamics among friends. Similarly, a job loss or spousal death, while both bounded in time, may have stressful repercussions that last for years.

Among White respondents, the pattern of association is similar to that for Blacks; however, due to the larger sample size, more of the correlations are significant for Whites. There are a few notable exceptions. Among Whites, the association between ubiquity of sin and life satisfaction is negative and significant. Conservative Protestants tend to report higher levels

TABLE 1 Descriptive Statistics of Variables Used in the Analyses, by Race (Unadjusted Least Squares Means Estimates)

Variable	Range	Mean and Standard Deviation		Difference[a]
		Blacks	Whites	
Sociodemographics				
Female	0–1	.62	.56	*
		(—)	(—)	
Age	18–89	43.15	45.90	**
		(17.68)	(17.61)	
Education	0–20	11.65	12.68	***
		(3.46)	(3.10)	
Family Income	1–20	10.53	13.57	***
		(4.98)	(4.74)	
Religion Variables				
Ubiquity of Sin	1–7	3.67	3.06	***
		(1.61)	(.137)	
Church Attendance	0–8	4.59	3.93	***
		(2.31)	(2.60)	
Conservative Protestant	0–1	.60	.23	***
		(—)	(—)	
Other Variables				
Financial Strain	0–1	.19	.19	*
		(—)	(—)	
Life Events	0–1	.41	.34	**
		(—)	(—)	
Interpersonal Distrust	0–3	2.09	1.24	***
		(.99)	(1.10)	

NOTES: [a] Asterisks indicate a significant difference between means. *$p < .05$; ** $p < .01$; ***$p < .001$.

of ubiquity of sin and lower levels of life satisfaction. This finding supports the contention of others that a measure of denominational affiliation can serve as a proxy for some religious beliefs (e.g., Ferraro and Albrecht-Jensen 1991). However, given the low magnitude of the correlation among both Whites and Blacks, it is clear that denomination serves as a poor proxy for theodicy beliefs.

Regression Models for Black Respondents

Table 3 reports the multivariate regression models for life satisfaction and all of the independent covariates among Black respondents. The first model in this table reports the baseline model whereas the second includes three cross-product interaction terms. According to the coefficients in the first column, income and church attendance are positive predictors of life satisfaction. In contrast, Blacks reporting some financial strain or one or more stressful life events have lower levels of satisfaction. Most notable, however, is the fact that ubiquity of sin has no effect on life satisfaction among Blacks.

The second model in Table 3 includes all of the independent covariates in addition to three cross-product interaction terms. Recall that I expect that the effects of ubiquity of sin are strongest among those reporting low church attendance and more financial strain and stressful life events. Given that none of the interaction effects are significant, these hypotheses are not supported for Blacks.

Regression Models for White Respondents

Table 4 displays the results of the regression of life satisfaction on ubiquity of sin and the other covariates for White respondents. According to the results in the first model, holding a sin theodicy is associated with lower levels of life satisfaction. Other significant predictors in this model include education, family income, financial strain, life events, and distrust. Among the other religion variables, only service attendance has an effect on life satisfaction. Consistent with earlier studies of religion and well-being, higher levels of attendance predict greater satisfaction.

The second model in Table 4 includes the hypothesized moderating effects between ubiquity of sin, church attendance, financial strain, and life events.[3] First, the interaction effect between ubiquity of sin and church attendance is positive and significant. The positive sign indicates that the negative effect of ubiquity of sin is strongest among those who attend church least often. The anticipated effect for the next two interaction terms is that the negative effect of ubiquity of sin is strongest among those reporting more stressful circumstances. The significant negative coefficient for the life events measure supports this speculation. An F-test calculated to determine whether the addition of the cross-product terms significantly added to the explained variance in the model indicates that the change in explained variance is significant ($F = 5.23; p < .01$).

Because cross-product regression coefficients are often difficult to interpret, it is sometimes useful to specify the interaction effect in other ways. Table 5 reports the adjusted mean levels of satisfaction by levels of the interaction terms. In these models, ubiquity of sin and attendance are split at their means. Note also that the mean levels shown in Table 5 are adjusted for all of the other independent covariates included in the previous models. For the interaction between church attendance and ubiquity of sin, the results indicate that among low attendees, higher levels of ubiquity of sin beliefs are associated with significantly less life satisfaction; however, for high attendees (attend once a month or more),

---

[3]In analyses not shown here, I tested each of the interaction effects in a model that included only that term and the main effects. The results for the interaction effects in these models were very similar to those reported here in terms of both magnitude and significance level.

TABLE 2 Unadjusted Correlations Between Variables, by Race (Blacks Above Diagonal, Whites Below)[a]

Variables	v1	v2	v3	v4	v5	v6	v7	v8	v9	v10	v11	v12	v13
v1: Life Satisfaction	—	.02	-.06	.16	.17	-.08	.13	.01	.06	.04	-.16	-.14	-.17
v2: Female	.04	—	.05	-.07	-.24	-.01	.20	-.05	.26	.01	.02	.01	.02
v3: Age	.05	.06	—	-.45	-.08	-.03	.17	.02	.30	.03	.02	.05	-.08
v4: Education	.08	-.05	-.33	—	.28	-.13	-.01	-.09	-.19	.02	-.01	-.10	-.12
v5: Family Income	.23	-.12	-.17	.40	—	-.11	-.10	-.08	-.13	-.04	-.07	-.18	-.10
v6: Ubiquity of Sin	-.19	-.05	-.06	-.16	-.12	—	.03	.07	.04	-.06	.01	.04	.24
v7: Church Attendance	.16	.11	.15	.04	.03	.03	—	.09	.46	.21	-.01	.00	.07
v8: Conservative Protestant	-.07	.01	.01	-.15	-.05	.11	.07	—	.06	.04	-.02	.02	.04
v9: Prayer	.07	.24	.23	-.11	-.14	.01	.49	.11	—	.23	-.07	.03	.00
v10: Belief in Afterlife	.08	.06	-.05	.03	.05	-.04	.26	.14	.28	—	-.02	-.04	-.07
v11: Financial Strain	-.13	.02	.03	-.05	-.16	.05	-.00	.01	.06	.00	—	.08	-.01
v12: Life Events	-.09	.03	.11	-.15	-.12	.02	.01	.03	.02	-.01	.10	—	.03
v13: Interpersonal Distrust	-.26	-.01	-.18	-.19	-.16	.26	-.14	.12	-.04	-.02	.10	.02	—

NOTES: [a]Coefficients in bold type are significant at *p* <.05.

TABLE 3 Estimated Net Effects of Ubiquity of Sin and Other Covariates on Life Satisfaction Among Black Respondents (OLS Regression Estimates; $n = 537$)

	Model 1[a]	Model 2
Sociodemographics		
Female	.081/.039	.083/.040
Age	−.002/−.042	−.002/−.042
Education	−025/.085	.024/.085
Family Income	.025/.127**	.025/.124**
Religion Variables		
Ubiquity of Sin	−.019/−.030	−.037/−.059
Church Attendance	.058/.133**	.084/.194
Conservative Protestant	.047/.023	.047/.023
Other Variables		
Financial Strain	−.356/−.139***	−.692/−.270**
Life Events	−.189/−.093*	−.224/−.110
Interpersonal Distrust	−.130/−.129**	−.131/−.130**
Interaction Effects		
Ubiquity of Sin		
x Church Attendance	—	−.006/−.057
x Financial Strain	—	.089/.143
x Life Events	—	.011/.023
Intercept	4.923	4.890
Adjusted R^2	.099	.098

NOTES: [a]Unstandardized Coefficient/Standardized Coefficient. *$p < .05$; **$p < .01$; ***$p < .001$.

TABLE 4 Estimated Net Effects of Ubiquity of Sin and Other Covariates on Life Satisfaction Among White Respondents (OLS Regression Estimates; *n* = 1,215)

	Model 1[a]	Model 2
Sociodemographics		
Female	.066/.036	.062/.034
Age	.001/.013	.001/.011
Education	−.020/−.068*	−.022/-.073*
Family Income	.037/.194***	.037/.194***
Religion Variables		
Ubiquity of Sin	−.086/−.129***	−.051/−.077*
Church Attendance	.049/.138***	−.005/−.015
Conservative Protestant	−.084/−.039	−.087/−.040
Other Variables		
Financial Strain	−.161/−.068*	−.067/−.029
Life Events	−.125/-.065*	.197/.102
Interpersonal Distrust	−.140/−.168***	−.140/−.169***
Interaction Effects		
Ubiquity of Sin		
x Church Attendance	—	.016/.162*
x Financial Strain	—	−.027/−.041
x Life Events	—	−.100/−.185**
Intercept	5.640	5.777
Adjusted R^2	.140	.149

NOTES: [a]Unstandardized Coefficient/Standardized Coefficient. *p < .05; **p < .01; ***p < .001.

TABLE 5 Moderated Effects of Ubiquity of Sin on Life Satisfaction Among White Respondents (Adjusted Least Squares Means)

	Low Ubiquity of Sin	*High Ubiquity of Sin*	*Difference*[a]
Church attendance			
< once a month	5.65	5.41	***
> once a month	5.76	5.69	
Financial strain			
Finances did not worsen	5.70	5.60	
Finances worsened	5.65	5.27	**
Stressful life events			
No events	5.69	5.65	
1+ events	5.71	5.31	***

NOTES: [a]Asterisks indicate a significant differences in mean level of life satisfaction between levels of ubiquity of sin.** $p < .01$;***$p < .001$.

ubiquity of sin has no effect, on life satisfaction. The hypothesized interaction between stress and ubiquity of sin also gained support from these analyses. That is, higher levels of ubiquity of sin result in lower life satisfaction only among respondents who reported either having financial problems or one or more stressful life events. Note, however, that although the pattern of effect of the ubiquity of sin/financial strain test follows the hypothesized direction, it does not provide support for the hypothesis because the cross-product term in the regression model is not significant,

Black–White Differences in the Effects of Ubiquity of Sin

The second hypothesis speculated that the effects of ubiquity of sin would be stronger for Whites than for Blacks. Recall from Tables 3 and 4 that the negative effect of ubiquity of sin is indeed stronger for Whites (b = −.086; $p < .001$) than for Blacks (b = −.019; n.s.). In order to determine whether this difference is significant, I computed a two-tailed t-test based on the difference in coefficients for ubiquity of sin in the baseline model.[4] This computation yielded a t-score of 2.00 indicating that the difference in coefficients is significant at $p < .05$. Jaccard, Turrisi, and Wan (1990) proposed an alternative for testing differences in coefficients across models.[5] Using the equation proposed by Jaccard and his colleagues yields a t-score of 5.51 ($p < .001$). In sum, the effects of holding a sin theodicy on life satisfaction are significantly greater for Whites than for Blacks.

DISCUSSION

The major hypothesis in this paper argues that respondents who emphasize a sin theodicy have

[4]The equation for testing differences in coefficients between models is:

$$\frac{b_{1b} - b_{1w}}{\left[(SE_{1b})^2 + (SE_{1w})^2 \right]^{1/2}}$$

lower levels of life satisfaction compared to those who see humanity and the world in more positive terms. This expectation is supported in the White subsample: Respondents who tend to view the world more in terms of sin and evil report lower levels of life satisfaction. This effect remained net of a number of other variables, including church attendance, religious affiliation, and distrust of others.

The second hypothesis predicts that the effects of holding a sin theodicy on life satisfaction are stronger for Whites than for Blacks. The results provide support for this hypothesis. Indeed, not only is the effect of holding a sin theodicy stronger for Whites, but such an effect does not even appear for Blacks. This finding provides further support for the notion that when examining the linkages between religion and various measures of health and well-being, researchers should split the sample along racial lines before testing proposed effects.

The third and fourth hypotheses predict that the effects of holding a sin theodicy would vary by levels of church attendance and stressful circumstances. These hypotheses receive support in the White subsample. In the regression models and in the means models, the results indicate that those respondents who are less integrated into the church group (i.e., attend church less frequently) do indeed suffer more from higher levels of ubiquity of sin beliefs than those who are more integrated. This should be true if integration in the church group acts as a barrier against outside ideas and serves to reinforce beliefs held in common by the group.

The other hypothesized interaction effect is between stressful situations and ubiquity of sin beliefs. In this instance, I expected that because the additional stressors would make respondents more vulnerable to the effects of holding a theodicy emphasizing evil and sin, the effects of that measure would be strongest among those who report facing stressful circumstances. This

hypothesis receives support in the White subsample, but only for the life events measure.

Note that service attendance, net of the other religion variables, was a strong positive predictor of life satisfaction in both subsamples. This finding is meaningful because it highlights the dual nature of religion's effect on well-being. That is, on one hand, religion serves an integrative component which boosts levels of life satisfaction for congregants. On the other, certain religious beliefs are associated with lower life satisfaction. The lesson is that the relationship between religion and health is somewhat complex: individuals can attend church frequently, but the positive effects of such attendance can be offset by a conservative theodicy. Indeed, as shown in Table 5, the mean level of life satisfaction for those Whites reporting high levels of service attendance and ubiquity of sin beliefs are almost identical to the mean for Whites who attend services less often but also report low levels of ubiquity of sin beliefs.

Study Limitations

Due to the data used in this study, the analyses have certain limitations. One such limitation is the cross-sectional nature of the General Social Survey. Because the variables were measured contemporaneously, it is difficult to ascertain the causal ordering between the variables. However, as Bern (1970) noted in describing the hierarchy of belief structure, religious beliefs are usually of the first-order variety. That is, they occupy a place in our belief hierarchy that occurs just above our zero-order beliefs or those which "are the 'nonconscious' axioms upon which our other beliefs are built" (p. 6). Religious beliefs, being of the first order, will tend to precede all of our other higher order beliefs. It stands to reason, then, that outcomes such as life satisfaction, being somewhat

---

[5]The equation for testing differences in coefficients across models from Jaccard *et al.* (1990: 49) is:

$$\frac{b_{1b} - b_{1w}}{\left\{ (SSE_b + SSE_w) / [(n_b + n_w) - 4] \left(\Sigma X_{1b}^2 + \sigma X_{1w}^2 \right) / \left(\Sigma X_{1b}^2 \Sigma X_{1w}^2 \right) \right\}^{1/2}}$$

Where SSE_b is the sum of squares error for Blacks and SSE_w is the sum of squares error for Whites.

more transient in nature, will be a higher order of belief. Consequently, they will be affected by a lower order belief (e.g., a religious one) but not the opposite. So, although I cannot ascertain the causal ordering of these variables given the cross-sectional data, there is ample warrant to believe that theodicy will precede life satisfaction and not the converse. Nevertheless, the study would have profited from panel data which would allow testing the effects of the theodicy on changes in well-being over time. Future research should again test for these effects using such data.

Future Directions

Recently, the John Templeton Foundation in collaboration with the National Institute for Healthcare Research (Larson, Swyers, and McCullough 1997) issued a report on spirituality and health that arose out of a conference on the topic. Citing the growing amount of studies linking religion and spirituality to positive health outcomes, the authors of the report issued several mandates to researchers regarding future examination of the subject. One of these mandates is to "Elucidate not only the potential salutory [sic] clinical effects of religion and spirituality, but also the potential negative effects" (p. 8). The purpose of this study is not specifically to uncover "negative" effects of religion on well-being; however, in considering the effects of theodicy, such a perspective is necessary. Given the findings of this study and the theory on which it is based (see also Ellis 1962, 1980), researchers of religion and health should make efforts to uncover the possibility of negative effects.

There are a number of areas in which investigators might look for such relationships. For example, a number of authors have argued that the church often provides support for individual members. However, it might also be the case that certain church groups place excessive demands on members, either in terms of conforming to behavioral norms or to acting on behalf of the church. These demands may in turn have negative repercussions for health and well-being (Krause and Ellison 1999). Another possibility for

negative effects lies with certain types of religious coping (Pargament et al. 1999) or beliefs that might constrain religious individuals from acting in ways that are conducive to well-being. In terms of the latter, one could think of the authoritarian personality. Adorno and his colleagues (1950) argued that the ability to remain flexible and open to new experiences would foster successful adaptation and be conducive to better mental health. In contrast, as Batson and Vintis note:

> The closed-minded individual blocks out new information, refusing to adjust his or her view of reality in its light. Over time, such closed-mindedness can leave the individual living in a reality of illusion that is quite divorced from his or her experience (1982: 220).

Batson and Ventis go on to cite a number of studies that have shown that individuals who hold more conservative or orthodox religious beliefs tend to have more rigid and authoritarian personalities (see also Lenski 1963). In sum, while the integrative and comfort aspects of religion can have benefits for the individual, other aspects of the religious experience may have very different effects. A recent working group on religion and spirituality assembled by the National Institute on Aging and the Fetzer Foundation have made efforts to elaborate some of these possible pathways (Idler et al. 1998). Yet, much work in this area remains. Without such efforts, researchers will never have a full understanding of the effects of religion for individual health and well-being.

These findings also point to other avenues along which future research should proceed. First, future studies should not rely on denomination as a proxy for theodicies and other beliefs. While I find that White conservative Protestants are more likely to hold theodicy beliefs emphasizing sin and evil, the correlation is modest ($r = .11$). Among Black respondents, die correlation is insignificant. As such, whenever possible, researchers should not rely on denomination as a proxy for complex belief structures.

Finally, these analyses provide further evidence for the importance of considering the possibility that the effects of religion on well-being may vary by other factors. For instance, I find that stress moderates the relationship between religion and well-being. Others (e.g., Idler 1995) have argued that health problems might moderate this relationship in terms of the comfort hypothesis. In this line of inquiry, the researchers expected that the comfort religion provides would be most needed, and therefore most useful, for those experiencing some difficulty. One author (Musick 1996) found that the effects of religious activity were indeed stronger for those with physical limitations or health problems than for those without. In sum, researchers need to consider the possibility that other factors, such as stress, may moderate the effect of religion on well-being.

REFERENCES

Adorno, T. W., E. Frenkel-Brunswik, D. J. Levimon, and R. N. Sanford. 1950. *The authoritarian personality.* New York: Norton.

Allport. G. W. 1950. *The individual and his religion.* New York: Macmillan.

Argyle, M., and B. Beit-Hallahmi. 1975. *The social psychology of religion.* London: Routledge.

Batson, C. D., and W. L. Vintis. 1982. *The religious experience: A social-psychological perspective.* New York: Oxford University Press.

Bern, D. J. 1970. *Beliefs, attitudes, and human affairs.* Belmont, CA: Brooks/Cole Publishing Company.

Berger, P. L. 1967. *The sacred* canopy: Elements *of a sociological theory of religion.* New York: Doubleday.

_____. 1979. The *heretical imperative: Contemporary possibilities of religious affirmation.* Garden City, NY: Anchor Books.

Berger, P. B., and T. Luckmann. 1966. *The social construction of reality A treatise in the sociology of knowledge.* New York: Doubleday.

Bradley. D. E. 1995. Religious involvement and social resources: Evidence from the dataset "Americans' Changing Lives." Journal *for the Scientific Study of Religion* 34: 259–267.

Campbell, A., P. E. Converse, and W. L. Rogers. 1976. *The quality of American life. Perceptions, evaluations, and satisfactions.* New York: Russell Sage Foundation.

Chatters, L. M., and R. J. Taylor. 1994. Religious involvement among older African Americans. In Religion *in aging and health,* edited by J. S. Levin, 196–230. Thousand Oaks, CA: Sage Publications.

Cooper-Lewter, N.C., and H. H. Mitchell. 1986. *Soul theology: The heart of American Black culture.* San Francisco: Harper and Row.

Davis, J. A., and T. W. Smith. 1991. General *Social Surveys, 1972–1991.* Chicago, IL: National Opinion Research Center.

Demaris, A., and R. Yang. 1994. Race, alienation, and interpersonal mistrust. *Sociological Spectrum* 14:327–349.

Durkheim, E. [1897]1951. *Suicide: A study in sociology.* New York: Free Press.

Ellis, A. 1962. *Reason and emotion* in *psychotherapy.* Lyle Stuart.

_____. 1980. Psychotherapy and atheistic values: A response to A. E. Bergin's "Psychotherapy and religious values." *Journal of Consulting and Clinical Psychology* 48: 635–39.

Ellison, C. G. 1995. Race, religious involvement, and depressive symptomatology in a southeastern US community. *Social Science and Medicine* 40: 1561–1572.

Ellison, C. G., and L. K. George. 1994. Religious involvement. social ties, and social support in a southeastern community. *Journal for the Scientific Study of Religion* 33: 46–61.

Ellison, C G., and M. A. Musick. 1993. Southern intolerance: A fundamentalist effect? *Social Forces* 72: 379–98.

_____. 1995. Conservative Protestantism and public opinion toward science. Review *of Religious* Research 36: 245–62.

Ellison, C. G., and D. E. Sherkat. 1995. The "semi-involuntary institution" revisited: Regional variations in church participation among Black Americans. *Social Forces* 73: 1415–37.

Ferraro, K. F., and C. M. Albrecht-Jensen. 1991. Does religion influence adult health? *Journal for the Scientific Study of Religion* 30:193–202.

Ferraro, K. F., and J. R. Koch. 1994. Religion and health among Black and White adults: Examining social support and consolidation. *Journal for the Scientific Study of Religion* 33: 362–75.

Gardner, J. W., and J. L. Lyon. 1982. Cancer m Utah Mormon women by church activity level. *American Journal of Epidemiology* 116: 258–65.

George, L. K. 1981. Subjective well-being: Conceptual and methodological issues. *Annual Review of Gerontology and Geriatrics* 2: 345–382.

George, L. K. 1992. Social factors and the onset and outcome of depression. In *Aging, health behaviors, and health outcomes,* edited by K. Warner Senate, J. S. House, and D. G. Blazer, 137–159. Hillsdale, NJ: Lawrence Erlbaum Associates.

Gilkes, C. T. 1980. The Black church as a therapeutic community: Suggested areas for research into the Black religious experience. *The Journal of the Interdenominational Theological Center* 8: 29–44.

Griffith, E., T. English, and V. Mayfield. 1980. Possession, prayer, and testimony: Therapeutic aspects of the Wednesday night meeting in a Black church. *Psychiatry* 43: 120–28.

Glock, C. Y., B. B. Ringer, and E. R. Babbie. 1967. *To comfort and to challenge: A dilemma of the contemporary church.* Berkeley: University of California Press.

Hughes, M., and D. H. Demo. 1989. Self-perceptions of Black Americans: Self-esteem and personal efficacy. American *Journal of Sociology* 95: 132–59.

Idler, E. 1987. Religious involvement and the health of the elderly: Some hypotheses and an initial test. *Social Forces* 66: 226–38.

———. 1995. Religion, health, and nonphysical senses of self. *Social Forces* 74: 683–704.

Idler, E., M. Ory, C. Ellison, K. Pargament, L. George, L. Powell, N. Krause, D. Williams, J. Levin, and L. Underwood-Gordon. 1998. *National Institute on Aging/Fetzer Institute Working Group Brief Measure of Religiousness and Spirituality: Conceptual Development.* Unpublished manuscript.

Jaccard, J, R. Turrisi, and C. K. Wan. 1990. *Interaction effects in multiple regression.* Newbury Park, CA: Sage Publications.

Johnson, S. C, and B. Spilka. 1991. Coping with breast cancer: The roles of clergy and faith. *Journal of Religion and Health* 30: 21–33.

Jonas, H. 1963. *The Gnostic religion: The message of the alien God and the Beginnings of Christianity.* Boston. MA: Beacon Press.

Kessler, R. C, R. H. Price, and C. B. Wortman 1985 Social factors in psychopathology: Stress, social support, and coping processes. ANNUAL *Review of Psychology* 36: 351–72.

Koenig, H. G. 1994. AGING *and God: Spiritual pathways to mental health in midlife and later years.* New York: The Haworth Pastoral Press.

Koenig, H. G., H. J. Cohen, D. G. Blazer, C. Pieper, K. G. Meador, F. Shelp, V. Goli, and B. DiPasquale. 1993. Religious coping and depression among elderly, hospitalized medically ill men. *American Journal of Psychiatry* 149: 1693–700.

Krause, N., and C. G. Ellison. 1999. Church-based support, negative interaction, and psychological well-being: Findings from a national sample of Presbyterians. *Journal for the Scientific Study of Religion* 37: 725–41.

Larson, D. B, J. P. Swyers, and M. E. McCullough. 1997. *Scientific research on spmtuality and health: A consensus report.* Washington, DC: National Institute for Healthcare Research.

Lenski, G. 1963. *The religious factor: A sociological study of religion's impact on politics, economics, and family life.* Garden City, NY: Doubleday and Company.

Levin, J. S., R. J. Taylor, and L. M. Chatters. 1994. Race and gender differences in religiosity among older adults: Findings from four national surveys. *Journal of Gerontology. Social Sciences* 49: S137–45.

Levin, J. S., and H. Y. Vanderpool. 1987. Is frequent religious attendance really conducive to better health: Toward an epidemiology of religion. *Social Science and Medicine* 24: 589–600.

Lin, N., and W. M. Ensel. 1989. Life stress and health: Stressors and resources. *American Sociological Review* 54: 382–89.

Lincoln, C. E., and L. H. Mamiya. 1990. *The Black church in the African-American experience.* Durham, NC: Duke University Press.

Manuel, R. C. 1988. The demography of older Blacks in the United States. In *The Black American elderly: Research on physical and psychosocial health,* edited by J. S. Jackson, 25–49. New York: Springer Publishing Company.

Moore, T. 1991. The African-American church: A source of empowerment, mutual help, and social change. *Prevention in Human Services* 10: 147–67.

Musick, M. A. 1996. Religion and subjective health among Black and White elders. *Journal of Health and Social Behavior* 37: 221–37.

Musick, M. A., H. G. Koenig, J. C. Hays, and H. J. Cohen. 1998. Religious activity and depression among community-dwelling elderly persons with cancer: The moderating effects of race. *Journal of Gerontology: Social Sciences* 53B: S218-S227.

Mutran, E. 1985. Intergenerational family support among Blacks and Whites responses to culture or to socioeconomic differences. *Journal of Gerontology* 40: 382–89.

Nelsen, H. M., and A. Kusener Nelsen 1975. *Black church in the sixties.* Lexington: The University Press of Kentucky.

Pargament, K. L, B. W. Smith, H. G. Koenig, and L. Perez. 1999. Patterns of positive and negative religious coping with major life stressors. *Journal for the Scientific Study of Religion* 37: 710–24.

Payne, I. R, A. E. Bergin, K. A. Bielerna, and P. H. Jenkins. 1991. Review of religion and mental health: Prevention arid enhancement of psychosocial functioning. *Prevention in Human Services* 9: 11–40.

Phillips, R. L., and D. A. Snowdon. 1983. Association of meat and coffee use with cancers of the large bowel, breast, and prostate among Seventh Day Adventists: Preliminary results. Cancer *Research* 43: 2403s-2403s.

Roof, W. C., and W. McKinney. 1987. *American mainline religion: Its changing shape and future.* New Brunswick, NJ: Rutgers University Press.

Stark, W. 1972. *The sociology of religion: A study of Christendom. Vol 5: Types of religious culture.* London: Routledge and Kegan Paul.

Taylor, R. I., L. M. Chatters, R. Jayakody, and J. S. Levin. 1996. Black and White differences in religious participation: A multi-sample comparison. *Journal for the Scientific Study of Religion* 35: 403–10.

Weber, M 1946. Part III: Religion. *In From Max Weber. Essays in sociology,* edited by H. H. Gerth and C. Wright Mills, 267–359. New York: Oxford University Press.

White, R. H. 1963. Toward a theory of religious influence. *Pacific Sociological Review* 11: 23–28

Section II

RESEARCH DESIGN

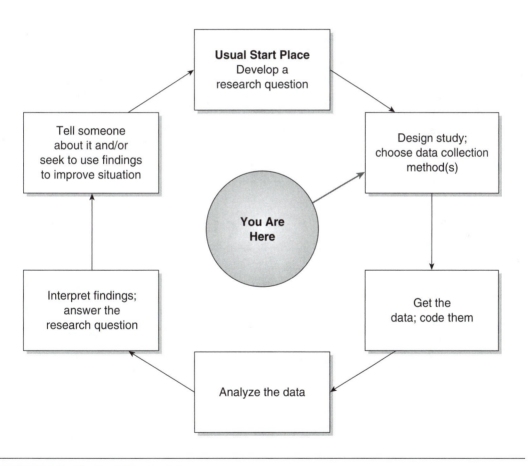

FIGURE 2.1   The Road Map (again)

After developing and explaining our research question, the next step is to figure out how we are going to answer the question given the complex mess of actions, interactions, data sources, motivations, etc., we call reality. This step is called **research design**. Research design is the point where researchers define the scope of the research—the limits and content of the data investigated. The research design is a detailed plan that specifies the kind of data needed (measurement), the strategy for collecting the data (the research method), the subjects (sampling, if needed), and the research site (when and where to get the data).

When we write about our work, we usually present the research as if it flowed exactly as in the map in Figure 2.2. That is, we start with the stuff in the first box and move along carefully to the last box. But here's the part you should know if you wish to get good grades: The figure is a lot neater than reality. We often actually start with

an interest in particular data, or an opportunity to conduct a particular kind of data collection, and we work the rest of the design around that. Even so, you will need a good plan to get from the research question to the answer.

We design our research plan around our specific research questions. Once we are clear on what we want to learn and our concepts are carefully defined, we look for specific indicators we can measure to reflect or capture these concepts. That is, we decide exactly what measures we will use to represent each concept. For example, if the concept is inebriation, we might count the number of alcoholic drinks consumed in an evening, or one's blood alcohol level, or one's ability to speak clearly. Whichever one (or combination of the above) we choose as our measure, that becomes the working definition of that variable for the research project.

Following Sherlock Holmes or any good detective, choosing the best technique for

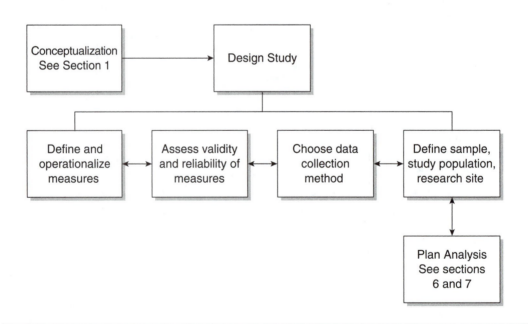

FIGURE 2.2 Research Design Detail Map

gathering evidence depends to a great extent on knowing what kind of information we are supposed to be looking for. As we break down abstract ideas into empirically observable attributes and events, we are able to find ways of measuring our concepts in spite of the complexity of social relations. Thus, if we were studying reckless behavior, including drunk driving, we might measure inebriation as the blood alcohol levels at which subjects decided that they were too drunk to drive. If, instead, we were interested in small group interactions, we might measure inebriation as the point at which one's friends report that one has had enough. The two measures are very different from each other and we need to choose deliberately between them *according to the needs of our research.*

FROM IDEAS TO MEASURABLE INDICATORS

As discussed in the previous section, conceptualization consists of defining and specifying the ideas that our variables have to represent. The next task is to figure out how to measure these variables. The first stage in the design process, **operationalization**, does just that. Operationalization is the bridge that carries us from concepts to measures. It converts information (things we observe) into data (things we can record and analyze). There is an intricate relationship between operationalization and measurement since the attributes we identify when we operationalize a concept determine to a great extent the levels of measurements we shall employ.

As Ellen Wratten discusses in her analysis of the various approaches to studying urban poverty, measurements are not without controversy. The operationalization of ideas varies depending on our theoretical positions, our assumptions, and even on our values and ideologies. Hence, as Wratten shows, the field of **development economics** had defined poverty in terms of income. This operationalization might seem straightforward

enough, but such an approach contains assumptions about life, work, and the very reasons that we would measure economic data in the first place. While the *concept* of poverty was tied to other concepts, such as "human welfare," the operationalization of poverty left those other considerations out. Further, the use of "income" as a measure of one's economic resources and socioeconomic status really works only under the conditions of an industrial society in which most people have defined "jobs." Worldwide, people rely on a variety of exchanges and nonmarket behaviors to "make a living." Viewed from a broader perspective, then, income as a measure of social deprivation became increasingly untenable because of both the imprecise measurements of income and the **spurious** relationship between income and quality of life. In response, many international institutions have adopted a different **paradigm** that accounts for poverty by examining social indicators that provide a more encompassing picture of social deprivation. In Bhutan, for example, one of the factors currently accounting for social development is the rate of happiness.

There is an interesting irony about how our knowledge affects the measurements we select. Although it is generally the case that the more we know about a topic, the more easily we can identify the many meanings embedded in its conceptualization, it is also true that the more we think we know about a topic, the less precise our measures might be. Because we are confident in our prior knowledge, we may be less critical of our initial ideas and therefore less likely to recognize their limitations.

In short, one consideration to bear in mind is that although the idea of measurement may seem mechanical, it is fraught with opportunities for confusion and contention because theoretical constructs shape our perspectives on reality. Thus, we as researchers need to identify our assumptions clearly when designing our measures.

Box 2.1 Max Weber (1864–1920)

Weber is considered one of the early pillars of the social sciences. A prolific writer, he made several major methodological contributions to the social sciences. Concepts such as "bureaucracy," "power," "charisma," and "social status," to name a few, are still routinely perceived and measured in the form in which they had been defined by Weber. In addition, he made essential contributions to the field of comparative and historical sociology with his work on economics and society. Perhaps his most notable book, *The Protestant Ethic and the Spirit of Capitalism* (1905), argued for the importance of ideas and beliefs over material conditions in creating subsequent economic success, challenging sociologists to attend as much to the qualitative dimensions of economic life as to the numbers.

VALIDITY AND RELIABILITY: GETTING IT RIGHT

Researchers have developed two key criteria with which to evaluate our designs. These are **validity** and **reliability**. The former calls attention to, among other things, the need for accuracy of measurements. In essence, it asks whether we are really measuring what we think we are measuring, or merely discussing something sort of similar. This question has two essential dimensions: Do the measurements we construct accurately reflect the contextual meaning of our variables? And have we accounted for everything? To put it simply, when we identify **indicators** to measure ideas, we need to show that they truly reflect the meaning of an idea in its proper time and context. (Are we placing enough limits on our measures?) And we need to show that these indicators account for all the definitional dimensions of variables. (Are we placing too many limits on our measures?)

Reliability, on the other hand, relates more closely to consistency and repeatability. The reliability question asks whether the data we're collecting mean the same thing each time we get it, across different times and places. If a question is vague, or if it relies on situational knowledge, then the answers we get will depend on what respondents think we're talking about at that moment. To continue our earlier example, the question "Do you drink?" might mean one thing to a casual social drinker, another to a recovering alcoholic, a third thing to someone who's religion forbids alcohol, and something else entirely to a teenager with a fake ID. Depending on whom we ask, the pattern of our answers can vary dramatically. In contrast, the more precise, less conversational "Have you consumed at least one alcoholic drink within the past 30 days?" is extremely reliable.

When designing studies that rely on **self-reports**, we have to bear in mind that subjects won't always be able to tell us what we want to know. This is not about honesty, but rather a matter of awareness. Certain kinds of questions require a deep level of self-awareness that we generally don't possess. For example, the question "How do advertisements affect your purchasing decisions" seems simple enough, but advertising actually works because it affects us at both the conscious and unconscious levels. So we can't answer that. Some questions require speculation about things we can't know, such as "Is there tension between the immigrant workers and the native-born workers at your job?" If there is obvious tension, the subjects may be able to answer. If the tension is relatively hidden, then they won't. And, of course, some topics are sensitive, and some people would rather make up an answer than share the real details. Money, for example, is often too sensitive a matter. All of these types of questions are inherently unreliable.

It is all too easy to concentrate our attention on only one or two indicators of any complex matter, thereby overlooking the bigger picture. This is one of the principal concerns of the Grzywacz and Carlson review of the ways in which we study the balance between work and family. As their study illustrates, the academic literature on this topic has been very active in recent decades. However, the authors show that most of the measures of "balance" have either lacked validity—because they were really measuring some other concept such as "equality" rather than balance—or they have lacked reliability—because they were inconsistently applied, yielding different results with each study.

Grzywacz and Carlson demonstrate that we need to think in terms of multidimensional measurements to understand the complexity that governs the balance between work demands and family responsibilities. They therefore identify several relevant dimensions of "balance" that are often overlooked, including different measures of stress and satisfaction in both home and work environments. With these, the authors recommend a "comprehensive" approach to measurement wherein researchers can identify and measure each of the major components of their concept independently, and then characterize the variety of ways that each component affects the larger concept. That is, the different measures can't be considered just good or bad for work–family balance. Some things have positive effects on some aspects of the concept and negative consequences for other aspects. Thus, by measuring several different attributes and different effects of both family and work, they achieve a valid and reliable measure of work–family balance.

DATA COLLECTION OVERVIEW

Validity and reliability are commonly perceived to go hand in hand. Nonetheless, we should keep in mind that certain data collection strategies tend to be stronger in one than in the other. Deep, contextually sensitive studies may be highly valid, but the findings may not reliably reflect different contexts, while a more generalizable approach with a broader range of data may sacrifice some validity in exchange for great reliability. The next stage of design, **data collection**, must therefore recognize the trade-off between breadth and depth as well as cost versus efficiency.

Qualitative research can take the context of a study into account, which typically strengthens the validity of the measures. This is the case because qualitative studies tend to emphasize more in-depth analysis of specific situations and populations. This type of research also prides itself on its ability to decipher hidden meanings and latent structures in addition to the obvious observations. Yet this emphasis on context may actually reduce the reliability of qualitative results. Comparable studies in different times and places may yield different findings. **Quantitative research**, on the other hand, assembles large populations, and these methods more often than not follow standard procedures that can be consistently replicated. Such studies look for **generalizable** measures that retain their meanings even outside of their original settings. This work is highly reliable, though it may lose some depth in exchange for such consistency.

Quantitative data collection strategies entail measuring whatever we're interested in on some scale that can be represented numerically. You may have answered, or written, a **survey** with *fixed format* answer categories, for example. Surveys typically involve many short-answer questions in which answers may be selected from a set of choices, usually labeled as numbers. Each question represents one variable, and each answer is one value in a database. The database may then be analyzed using any statistical software package.

With **secondary analysis** the researcher performs new statistical analyses on data previously collected for other purposes. There is so much information already out there that an enterprising researcher does not actually need to collect new data in order to do new research.

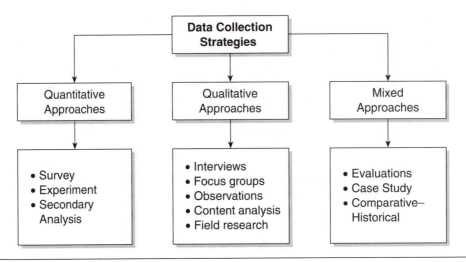

FIGURE 2.3 Data Collection Detail Map

And much of these data are compiled over far more time and distance than any one of us could manage. Data are collected about nations, communities, and continents, as well as birth and death rates, the spread of illnesses, and rates of accidents and injuries. All of this can be recorded numerically and analyzed statistically.

There are also limitations to using secondary analysis. We cannot always find data that are conceptualized or operationalized exactly as we would have wanted them to be. We can, however, assess the validity and reliability of secondary data by carefully reading the methodological notes in these studies before we use the data. Secondary analysis is discussed further in Section VI.

Experimental research often makes use of numeric outcome measures, such as one's response time or measurable physiological changes. Experiments may also be conducted with groups of subjects, in which case one may use measures such as the percentage of subjects who respond in a particular way. Experiments tend to be very focused on a single relationship (like, "a change in X causes a change in Y"), and very controlled. Experiments are often

conducted in a laboratory setting where the researcher can control for the effects of any other variable by isolating the study from its environment, and subjects are typically chosen to limit the amount of variability among them. These artificial conditions improve the reliability of the findings, since the results pretty much have to be caused by the experiment itself. But experimental results are not always the most valid measures of how people behave under natural conditions.

Qualitative data collection strategies focus on the particular qualities of events and circumstances that cannot be reduced to numbers. **Interviews**, for example, might record subjects' recollections of certain events, in their own words, with an emphasis on how they feel about those events now. Whatever meaning can be found in actual words, distinct from what can be put on a scale from good to bad, is qualitative. Consider the description: "After my morning of capturing bees, I spent the afternoon in the peach stand out on the highway, selling T. Ray's peaches. It was the loneliest summer job a girl could have, stuck in a roadside hut with three walls and a flat tin roof."[1] Clearly, there is much more information contained in such a description than in a quantitative scale ("degree of loneliness 1 . . . 5"). Other qualitative data collection techniques include participant and nonparticipant **observations**, **content analysis** of text or imagery from various cultural artifacts, and combinations of techniques, such as **focus group interviews** and **ethnographies**. These are discussed in more detail in Section V.

Qualitative data collection strategies are often, though not always, associated with **fieldwork**. Getting out into the research setting, such as the community under study, the homes of our informants, or the public hearings or private meetings where our issues are discussed, provides us with a deeper and more tangible feel for the social context in which our topic plays out. We can interview bartenders or shopkeepers anywhere, but imagine how much more we can learn by speaking to them in their bars or shops. Rather than reducing the data to simple codes or patterns, we explore and elaborate on the data with rich narrative descriptions of the physical layout and emotional ambiance of the research setting.

Mixed methods are discussed in detail in Section VIII. As the term implies, mixed method studies draw on combinations of the techniques discussed so far. **Case studies,** for example, generally entail extensive fieldwork at a single study site, possibly conducting observations and interviews, often backed by quantitative measures such as survey or secondary data analysis. This approach is particularly appropriate for exploratory questions and situations where a great many variables might have different kinds of effects. **Comparative historical** research, by contrast, rarely involves fieldwork or observations. Yet, as there are many different kinds of historical records available, but rarely as much of it as you want, a researcher seeking historical data must be prepared to work with an assortment of data gathering, coding, and analysis techniques.

Evaluation Research may be thought of as a particular kind of case study, typically one that is concerned with the impact of a specific program or policy change. The question underlying most evaluations is whether or not the study subject is having the desired effect or meeting its goals. But program goals are often defined rather vaguely, and the question of success may be very open to interpretation. As well, evaluation research is generally **longitudinal**, since some change has to be demonstrated over time. The evaluation researcher, then, must creatively combine techniques and data sources to come up with a definitive answer.

SAMPLING

Whether you are choosing a neighborhood for field research, a set of television ads for content analysis, or a pool of subjects for survey research, you must address how to get the *right* neighborhood, ads, or people. This is the problem of sampling, the three key components of which are (1) defining your study population; (2) defining a subset of that population that is **representative** of it; and (3) getting the cases. A sample is the right sample if it validly represents the larger study population.

We call a sample **biased** if there is something about the cases you chose that is different from the population that they are supposed to represent. In medical research, for example, clinical drug trials are intended to indicate drug safety for everyone who might use the medicines. But many studies limit trial access to healthy men of a particular age range who are not taking any other medicines. This makes the study easier, but it tells us nothing about the health risks to older populations, pregnant women, or teenagers on psychiatric medicines. In popular use, a bias is a kind of prejudice. But for research

---

[1]Sue Monk Kidd, *The Secret Life of Bees,* p. 15.

purposes, it is any leaning or tendency among a set of cases that makes it unique.

There are a large number of sampling strategies to choose from, depending on the size and accessibility of your population. Remember that the goal is to draw a sample that can stand in for the study population. If your population is very large and well defined, such as all residents of the state of Nebraska, every school child in southern Italy, or every undergraduate at your college, then the best approach is usually a **random** sample. The crucial attribute of a random sample is that the population can be more or less listed, by name, or address or e-mail or something. Then you can use a random number generator, or a big hat, to select some percentage of them for inclusion in your study. Having a truly random process literally means that every case in the population has an equal chance of being selected, and that neither anything that you do nor anything that you want will bias the selection.

Random sampling strategies are not always feasible. Many populations are small, or hidden, or hard to define. They may be defined by some hidden characteristic, such as a shared childhood experience or stigmatized condition. You could not, for example, use random sampling to select an adult group of formerly convicted juvenile criminal offenders. Your study population may also be a minority group in a larger population, such as college-educated first-generation immigrants in New York City who have had to change their careers in order to find work. Such populations are neither large nor well defined. You must seek them out through one of the targeted, or **purposive,** sampling strategies.

Random sampling needs to be contrasted with haphazard sampling. The typical haphazard approach is to walk up to strangers in a mall or bus station and ask them to participate in your survey. This approach introduces numerous sampling biases that make it unrepresentative of almost any population. For one thing, the pools of people available at one mall versus another are likely to be different in ways that would affect your results. You would certainly have an easier time getting people who are shopping alone rather than in groups, which introduces additional biases. Regardless of your intentions, you will have an easier time approaching people who are similar to yourself, and therefore undersample people who are different. At the same time, and for the same reasons, the less someone is like you, the less likely they are to agree to participate, further biasing your sample. Haphazard sampling is low in both reliability and validity, containing numerous hidden biases. To put that in less technical terms: It's a bad idea. Just because you don't know who your subjects are, that doesn't make them a random set.

In our next selection, Katherine Irwin uses a combination of sampling strategies to compare adolescents' experiences of violence across different socioeconomic settings. She begins by noting that the leading theories of adolescent violence attribute violent behaviors and encounters to neighborhood factors. Some of these factors are perceived as cultural, including the idea that in places where jobs and other paths to upward mobility are scarce, toughness can help one not only to get by but also to prove one's worth. Other factors are economic, as much of the increase in youth violence during the 1990s corresponded to the spread of illegal drug markets and the use of teens in the drug business. Yet, while so much of the research in this area assumes that youth violence occurs as it does because of the neighborhoods, almost no comparable research has occurred in more economically advantaged neighborhoods. Not only is this a conspicuous failure to empirically test the neighborhood effects, but, as Irwin shows, it allows people in "better" neighborhoods to define the violence that they see as somehow imported by youths from other areas.

The first level of Irwin's study, then, is a stratified sample of neighborhoods, each of

TABLE 2.1 Popular Sampling Strategies

Strategies	Description	Advantages	Disadvantage
Random			
Simple Random	Everyone in the population has an equal chance of being selected.	It is economical and very representative.	Must have some sort of population list available.
Systematic	Involves using a simple formula, such as "every fifth person" to select your cases.	It is practical and easy to use.	It may compromise the representativeness of the sample.
Stratified	Divide the population into groups that are likely to be different, and then select cases at random from within each group.	It reflects the diversity of the population.	The choice of groups affects the outcomes; must be carefully considered with respect to the research question.
Multistage Cluster	A sample of groups is drawn and then each group is subsampled.	Do not need to be able to define the entire population.	Relatively complex.
Nonrandom			
Snowball	Each member of the sampled is selected by reference from a previous participant.	It is very useful when we do not know our population well.	It can be used only with people. There might be some selection bias.
Quota	Divide the population according to groups and then pick equal numbers from each group using the same selection strategy.	It works well for diverse populations where the groups are of unequal size.	Time consuming, potentially expensive. Nonrandom criteria for selecting cases within each group.
Deviant	Select cases/individuals outside the norm.	Identifies uncommon and/or hidden cases.	Must identify what counts as the norm.

which represents a characteristic that is seen as crucial to the popular models of youth violence. Each neighborhood is then treated as its own social world. Within each, she uses targeted sampling strategies, such as snowball sampling, to collect a sample pool of families with shared experiences and backgrounds. Due to their social ties and similarities, it would be difficult to generalize from a single one of these targeted samples to a wider population. But as each cluster represents only their social spaces, this similarity becomes a strength of the design. The author is then able to find the patterns of data that characterize each group and compare them.

There are several benefits to this approach. For one thing, this comparative research improves our understanding of neighborhood effects, by treating the neighborhoods as a variable rather than just background. Further, Irwin is able to relate the types of violent encounters that are more or less likely to occur in each setting to the residents' perceptions of these events. Since each group has a different understanding of the nature and causes of the violence around them, each has adopted different coping strategies. These strategies themselves have consequences. Completing the picture, Irwin notes that both residents and researchers tend to view the different consequences as characteristics of the neighborhoods, as though they reflected different values. Instead, as Irwin finds, most of the adolescents prefer to avoid violence, or take steps to minimize its impact. Given their perceptions of their circumstances, they all enact these same goals in very different ways.

CONCLUSION

Measurement in social research consists of defining theoretical concepts and identifying empirical indicators that would guide our search for evidence to support our assertions. There are many design strategies in social science research, each with its own strengths and limitations. Researchers choose a particular design or a combination of two or more strategies, according to the content of their research topic. The underlying question of any research design is, "What is the best way to answer my research question?" The design should provide a map from the question to the data collection to the analysis, ending with the answer. The more detail you can put into your design before you begin your research, the fewer unpleasant surprises will await you.

DISCUSSION QUESTIONS

1. Why does the way you measure almost anything (e.g., wealth, attitudes, actions, dreams, memories, family size, spending) so affect what you find? Do you consider this a threat to the validity of social research?

2. Give *three* different measures of *each* of the following concepts. Explain the ideas behind what each measure would capture.

   a. a "happy family"
   b. a "good city"
   c. a "good friend"

3. How does the definition of, and research on, work–family balance affect the way social scientists might influence management practice in the workplace?

WEB RESOURCES

The following links can provide you with more detailed information on the topics discussed in this section. You may also go to www.sagepub.com/lunestudy where you will find additional resources and hot-links to these sources.

Yale's Center for Comparative Research: http://www.yale.edu/ccr
UCLA Center for Comparative History: http://www.sscnet.ucla.edu/issr/cstch
Social Science Research Council: http://www.ssrc.org

Conceptualizing Urban Poverty (1995)

Ellen Wratten

I. INTRODUCTION

The purpose of this paper[1] is to review the different ways in which urban poverty has been understood, and to assess the implications of such an understanding for the measurement of poverty and the design of antipoverty programmes.

For economic and demographic reasons, during the 1980s and 1990s poverty has become increasingly concentrated in urban settlements. Economic crisis and structural adjustment policies introduced in the Third World have had a disproportionate impact on the urban poor, due to rising food prices, declining real wages and redundancy in the formal labour market, and reduced public expenditure on basic services and infrastructure.[2] As a result of rapid urbanization, within the next two decades the proportion of the world's population living in towns and cities is set to overtake the proportion living in rural areas for the first time.[3] Thus, the numbers of urban people in poverty are likely to be g rowing at a faster rate—and in parts of the world are already greater in absolute terms[4]—than the numbers of poor rural people. Whereas in 1980 there were twice as many poor rural households as poor urban ones, by the year 2000 more than half of the absolute poor will live in towns and cities.[5] While the global demographic shift to urban areas is undisputed, predictions about the urbanization of poverty are based on a multitude of controversial assumptions regarding the definition of urban areas, the nature of poverty and our capacity to measure it. Analysis of the problems of the "urban poor" often glosses over, or disregards, these important facts. Rarely is the meaning of poverty (and the criteria used to identify the poor) made explicit, or the usefulness of urban poverty as a distinct conceptual category challenged.

SOURCE: *From* "Conceptualizing Urban Poverty" by Ellen Wratten in *Environment and Urbanization* 7(11). Copyright © 1995. Reprinted with permission.

[1] An earlier version of this paper was presented at the CROP International Workshop on Urban Poverty in Bergen, Norway, 6–9 October 1994. I am grateful to Christine Whitehead for her helpful comments on the manuscript. Any errors remain my own.

[2] Moser, Caroline O N, Alicia J Herbert and Roza E Makonnen (1993), "Urban poverty in the context of structural adjustment: recent evidence and policy responses," TWU Discussion Paper No 4, Urban Development Division, World Bank, Washington DC, May; also, World Bank (1991), *Urban Policy and Economic Development: An Agenda for the 1990s,* World Bank Policy Paper, Washington, DC.

[3] According to "best estimates," the percentage of the world's population living in urban areas was 29.3 per cent in 1950, 37.7 per cent in 1975 and 43.1 per cent in 1990. It is predicted to pass the 50 per cent level at some point between 2003 and 2020—the date being dependent on the rate at which countries urbanize which, in turn, for all but the most urbanized countries, is strongly associated with the strength of their economic performance; personal communication with David Satterthwaite, Human Settlements Programme, IIED.

[4] Over half of the population of the following regions already live in urban areas: Northern and Western Europe; North, Central and South America and the Caribbean; the Middle East and North Africa; Southern Africa; Western Asia; and Australasia.

[5] Beall, Jo (1993), "The gender dimensions of urbanization and urban poverty," paper prepared for the Division for the Advancement of Women, United Nations Office in Vienna, and presented at the Seminar on Women in Urban Areas, Vienna, 8–12 November.

This paper explores three issues. It first examines how, and by whom, poverty has been defined and measured, contrasting conventional economic and participatory anthropological approaches. Second, it questions the extent to which "urban poverty" differs conceptually fro m poverty in general. How far is analysis of the urban–rural divide helpful in understanding the underlying causes of poverty? Finally, the paper reviews the principal ways in which urban poverty has been understood in the South and the North, and the policy prescriptions which flow fro m such an understanding. It concludes by identifying the linkages between alternative definitions of poverty, different urban anti-poverty policy approaches, and the choice of measurement techniques.

II. Defining and Measuring Poverty

What is poverty and who should define it? Most definitions associate poverty with a "lack" or "deficiency" of the necessities required for human survival and welfare. However, there is no consensus about what basic human needs are or how they can be identified. Two main approaches are discussed here: conventional economic defi-nitions which use income, consumption, or a range of other social indicators to classify poor groups against a common index of material wel-fare; and alternative interpretations developed largely by rural anthropologists and social plan-ners working with poor rural communities in the Third World, which allow for local variation in the meaning of poverty, and expand the defini-tion to encompass perceptions of non-material deprivation and social differentiation.

III. Conventional Definitions

a. Definitions Based on Income or Consumption

Few economists would argue that human welfare can be adequately described by income alone. Yet, in practice, income (or consumption) is the most frequently used proxy for welfare. The justification is that (in market-based economies) lack of income is highly correlated with other causes of poverty and is a predictor of future problems of deprivation.

Underlying the economists' concept of poverty is the idea of merit goods: goods that society agrees are necessary, and is prepared to ensure that members of society can achieve. This is less problematic in the North, where poverty is generally a minority problem, than in the South, where it can be argued that the majority fail to achieve the minimum acceptable standard of living and that society lacks the capacity to make good the deficit.

Income is defined as command over resources over time or as the level of consumption that can be afforded while retaining capital intact.[6] People are classified as poor when their income (or consumption) is less than that required to meet certain defined needs. For example, the World Bank's World Development Report[7] uses two income cut-off points or poverty lines: those with an income per capita of below US$370 per year (at 1985 purchasing power parity) are deemed poor, while those with less than US $275 per year are extremely poor.[8] In 1994, 1,390 million people were estimated to fall into the "poor" category.[9] Within countries, income and consumption data have been used by the Bank to distinguish different

[6]Piachaud, David (1993), "The definition and measurement of poverty and inequality" in Barr, Nicholas and David Whynes (edi-tors), Current Issues in the Economics of Welfare, Macmillan, Basingstoke and London, pages 105–129.

[7]World Bank (1990), World Development Report 1990 , Oxford University Press, Oxford and New York.

[8]In comparison, the USA's official poverty threshold for a family of three was US$8,277 in 1984 (see Portes, Alejandro, Manuel Castells and Lauren A Benton (editors) (1989), The Informal Economy: Studies in Advanced and Less Developed Countries, Johns Hopkins University Press, Baltimore and London, page 128.

[9]van der Hoeven, Rolph and Richard Anker (editors) (1994), Poverty Monitoring: An International Concern, UNICEF publica-tion, St Martin's Press, Basingstoke and London.

groups such as the "new poor" (the direct victims of structural adjustment), the "borderline poor" (those on the brink of the poverty line, who are pushed under it by austerity measures) and the "chronic poor," who were extremely poor even before adjustment began. In addition to calculating the headcount index (the proportion of the population below the poverty line), the Bank assesses the severity of poverty by calculating the poverty gap index (the ratio of the gap between the poverty line and the mean income of the poor expressed as a ratio to the poverty line).

Income-defined poverty lines are problematic for a number of reasons. Income is a useful indicator if we want to identify which people are likely to lack the resources to achieve a socially acceptable standard of living. However, it does not measure accurately their capacity to achieve access (which may be influenced by other factors such as education, information, legal rights, illness, threatened domestic violence or insecurity).

Incomes are commonly analyzed at the household level. Yet, individual members of a household do not have equal command over resources, and those with low entitlement to consume resources (due, for example, to their age, gender or social status) may be hidden within relatively prosperous households.[10] Moreover, adjustments have to be made in order to compare households of different size. Which is poorer: a family with two adults and five children living on US$2,500 per year, or a single adult with an annual income of just US$400? Using the World Bank criterion of US$370 per capita, all seven members of the larger family would be classified as poor, whereas the single adult would not. Per capita incomes take no account of the economies of scale which benefit the larger household (such as savings on cooking fuel by preparing food in bulk) or the particular needs of people of different ages or different gender roles.[11] Nor is it easy to value home production or earnings from self-employment, which are generally assumed to be important income sources for the "urban poor."

Needs are equally difficult to define in a standardized way. The items which people regard as essential are influenced by culture and personal preference, and vary from individual to individual. Warm clothing and heating may be required to keep an old person alive in a London winter but these would be unlikely priorities in Mombasa.

Both needs and living costs may vary considerably between rural and urban areas, and between urban settlements of different sizes. Certain basic items—including fuel, freshwater and building materials—have to be purchased in most urban areas, but can be obtained free (apart from the opportunity costs of time and labour spent in collection), or are much cheaper, in many rural areas in the South. Rural dwellers can, in addition, obtain some of their food free from common lands, forests, rivers, lakes or coastal waters—although subsistence agriculture is widespread in urban areas, rent is often payable for the land used. Dietary preferences are likely to vary according to location: in cities there is greater availability of imported foods, promoted through advertising; different working patterns (including, in many countries, higher female participation in the paid labour force), which makes it convenient to purchase prepared meals and snacks; less space at home in which to cook and entertain friends and relatives, reinforcing the need to purchase prepared foods from outside; and possibly, some variation in calorific requirements. It has been estimated that urban food costs are generally 10–15 per cent higher than those in rural areas.[12]

Typically, housing costs are far higher in cities and are a major expense of urban households. In larger cities, people who work in or close to the centre face a trade-off between living in cheaper housing on the periphery and the high monetary and time costs of transport from the suburbs. The

---

[10]Sen, A K (1981), *Poverty and Famines: An Essay on Entitlement and Deprivation,* Clarendon Press, Oxford.

[11]Moser, Caroline O N (1993), *Gender Planning and Development: Theory, Practice and Training,* Routledge, London and New York.

[12]Ravallion, Martin (1992), *Poverty Comparisons: A Guide to Concepts and Methods,* Living Standards Measurement Study Working Paper No 88, World Bank, Washington, DC.

poor tend to pay proportionately more for their housing than the better-off, since the unit cost of renting small areas of accommodation in overcrowded, unserviced and dangerous neighbourhoods near the centre can exceed the costs of renting the same amount of accommodation in a higher-quality area (the problem for the poor is that accommodation in up-market areas is available in larger, non-divisible units or in locations inaccessible to those relying on their feet or public transport to move around).

In recognition of these differences, it is common to use separate cut-off levels for urban and rural poverty. However, this is a crude refinement, and cannot capture accurately the diversity of needs and entitlements coexisting within urban and rural populations.

b. Absolute and Relative Definitions of Poverty

If poverty is defined in absolute terms, needs are considered to be fixed at a level which provides for subsistence, basic household equipment, and expenditure on essential services such as water, sanitation, health, education and transport. The absolute definition is in common use by the World Bank and governments. However, it does not describe the extent of income inequality within society nor the fact that needs are socially determined and change over time. The absolute definition has to be adjusted periodically to take account of technological developments such as improved methods of sanitation.

The concept of relative poverty is more flexible, and allows for minimum needs to be revised as standards of living in society alter. It reflects the view that poverty imposes withdrawal or exclusion fro m active membership of society: people are relatively deprived if they cannot obtain "...*the conditions of life—that is the diets, amenities, standards and services—which allow them to play the roles, participate in the relationships and follow the customary behaviour which is expected of them by virtue of their membership of society.*"[13] Under this definition, there could in theory be a higher incidence of poverty in London, New York or Tokyo than in Delhi, Lusaka or Rio de Janeiro. In contrast, very few of the destitute and homeless people living on the streets of London could scrape under the World Bank's absolute poverty line, which is set well below the minimal social security benefit level for UK citizens.

c. Definitions Based on Social Indicators

Because many aspects of well-being cannot be captured adequately by income or consumption-based measures, supplementary social indicators are sometimes used to define poverty, such as life expectancy, infant mortality, nutrition, the proportion of the household budget spent on food, literacy, school enrollment rates, access to health clinics or drinking water. Again, the idea is to have a standard scale so that different population groups may be compared. Such indicators are often used to contrast the welfare of rural and urban populations since they avoid the problem of rural–urban price differences.

Where a range of indicators are used to describe poverty, as in the World Bank's *World Development Report*,[14] the different variables may tell conflicting stories about the pattern of deprivation. Thus, in practice, income and consumption measures remain the key way in which poverty is defined, despite the grave deficiencies of using any single indicator of well-being.

To overcome this, composite poverty indices have been developed which combine several weighted variables. For example, the UNDP's Human Development Index aggregates income, literacy and life expectancy into a single measure

---

[13]Townsend, Peter (1993), *The International Analysis of Poverty,* Harvester Wheatsheaf, Hemel Hempstead, page 36.

[14]See reference 7.

of the standard of living with a scale of values ranging from zero to one, along which countries can be ranked.[15] Other examples include the Physical Quality of Life Index,[16] the Food Security Index and the Relative Welfare Index.[17] Such measures are arbitrary and "*aggregate what we should wish to disaggregate.*"[18] They inevitably miss out important aspects of well-being, since a limited number of variables can be brought into the calculation. Moreover, they view poverty from the perspective of external professionals rather than from that of the poor.

Box 1 Defining poverty using social indicators: examples from Tanzania

Two recent studies of poverty in Tanzania used different social indicators to identify the poorest groups. In Sender and Smith's research[a] in Tanga region, an index of material well-being was compiled by listing 14 different possessions (such as a metal roof, a bicycle and a coat) and counting the number of items that each surveyed household owned. Out of 100 households, just over half (53) had scores of 0–2, and only 15 had scores of over 10. The possessions scores showed strong correlation with access to the major means of production, work in the formal sector, female education and child mortality.

Households with scores of 10–14 held six times the land acreage of households with scores of one or zero, were far less likely to sell (and far more likely to buy) land, were 30 times more likely to contain an enumerated sector employee, were twice as likely to have at least one literate family member, and their children were ten times less likely to die.

In Mbeya District, Tanzania, the Health and Nutrition District Support (HANDS) Project[b] used nutritional status among children under the age of five to define urban and peri-urban poverty. Child malnutrition was found to be associated statistically with mothers who had no education and no monthly salary, families who had to sell maize from the last harvest, and families with poor housing and lack of assets.

Both research studies found correlation between their chosen indicators and other aspects of poverty, such as landholding and access to education and health services. However, this is not necessarily the case. Ownership of possessions may be a matter of taste rather than a sign of constrained opportunity.

As Piachaud points out, people who do not buy meat may be wealthy vegetarians (see debate in Townsend,[c] Chapter 6). Similarly, small children may become malnourished for reasons other than a lack of material resources. Children over the age of one, left in the care of siblings while their parents work, are particularly at risk because of insufficiently frequent

(Continued)

---

[15]For a discussion of the method used to compile the Human Development Index, see Kanbur, Ravi (1994), "Poverty and development: the Human Development Report (1990), and the World Development Report (1990)" in van der Hoeven and Anker (1994), see reference 9, pages 84–94.

[16]Morris, M D (1979), *Measuring the Condition of the World's Poor: The Physical Quality of Life Index,* Frank Cass, London.

[17]Jazairy, Idriss, Mohiuddin Alamgir and Theresa Panuccio (1992), *The State of World Rural Poverty,* IT Publications, London.

[18]Streeten, Paul (1994), "Poverty concepts and measurement" in van der Hoeven and Anker (1994), see reference 9, pages 15–30.

(Continued)

feeding. Malnutrition may be more the result of the unequal gender division of labour and long working hours of mothers in Tanzania than of low income levels *per se* (see Wratten[d]).

Notes

a. Sender, John and Sheila Smith (1990), *Poverty, Class and Gender in Rural Africa: A Tanzanian Case Study*, Routledge, London.

b. Mbeya Health and Nutrition District Support (HANDS) (1992), "Malnutrition in Mbeya town. Report of a nutrition and socioeconomic survey," HANDS Project, Mbeya, Tanzania, June–July.

c. Townsend, Peter (1993), *The International Analysis of Poverty*, Harvester Wheatsheaf, Hemel Hempstead.

d. Wratten, Ellen (1993), "Poverty in Tanzania," report prepared for the Overseas Development Administration, London, February.

IV. PARTICIPATORY DEFINITIONS

Standardized definitions are useful to policy makers because they provide a uniform scale against which comparisons can be made of the incidence of poverty in different sub-populations (urban and rural; urban populations living in different parts of the city; male- and female- headed households; old and young, etc.) or of the same population over time. Comparative data are essential in order to target resources to the poorest groups. However, the standard of living of an individual or a household is a multi-dimensional concept involving, in principle, every aspect of direct consumption as well as non-consumption activities and services.[19] The quantification of poverty invariably restricts the number of criteria used to describe it, so that the data provide only a partial picture of the reality of being poor. Attempts to use universal indicators (such as an income defined poverty line) can also be counter-productive in masking the structural causes of poverty.[20]

Equally important, the use of a common index implies an external decision about who is poor. As Rahnema states: *"There may be as many poor and as many perceptions of poverty as there are human beings."*[21] Any poverty line is inherently a subjective judgement about what is an acceptable minimum standard of living in a particular society. While it is possible to set an income-defined poverty line in a participatory way by asking survey respondents what they consider to be the minimal income level necessary to make ends meet and averaging the results, the requirement to judge each person using the same standard means that their individual definition of their own needs is subordinated. The "poor" are labelled as poor by outsiders, not according to their own criteria.

Anthropological studies of poverty have shown that people's own conceptions of disadvantage often differ markedly from those of professional "experts." Great value may be attached to qualitative dimensions such as independence,

[19]Sen, A K (1987), *The Standard of Living,* Cambridge University Press, Cambridge.

[20]Francis, Paul A (1991), "Poverty in Bangladesh: profile and policy implications," report prepared for the Overseas Development Administration, May.

[21]Rahnema, Majid (1992), "Poverty" in Sachs, Wolfgang (editor), *The Development Dictionary: A Guide to Knowledge as Power,* Zed Books, London and New Jersey, pages 158–176.

security, self-respect, identity, close and nonexploitative social relationships, decision-making freedom, and legal and political rights. This has led Francis and others to argue that to obtain an adequate definition of poverty requires involvement of the "poor" themselves.[22]

The genesis of gender planning during the 1980s has focused attention on the different poverty outcomes deriving from the socially constructed roles and responsibilities of women and men, and the gender relations between them. Socially constructed roles also constrain the opportunities of other population sub-groups—such as the young and old, ethnic minorities and majorities, recent rural migrants and established urban residents, and different social classes—and their experience and perceptions of poverty are differentiated accordingly.[23]

From the 1970s, the conventional view that poverty can be defined in terms of income has been further challenged on the grounds that the environmental consequences of economic growth result in reduced human welfare, and that "traditional" frugal and self-reliant lifestyles are not inferior.[24]

a. Vulnerability and Entitlement

Participatory investigations have highlighted two concepts—vulnerability and entitlement—which add rigour to the conceptualization of poverty and greatly extend our understanding of the process by which people become and remain poor.

BOX 2 PARTICIPATORY ASSESSMENT OF POVERTY: AN EXAMPLE FROM PAKISTAN

A participatory poverty research study was undertaken recently in Pakistan, where people in ten low-income communities were asked about their perceptions of poverty. Poor households were identified by respondents as those with no adult males and a large number of dependents; widows, especially those with young children; sick or disabled adults unable to engage in paid work; households with a large number of unmarried daughters (dowry costs are considerable for poor families and were identified as a major factor in perpetuating poverty); households where men are unemployed or engaged in irregular and poorly paid casual work; and households with debt bondage to landowners, employers, commission agents or informal money lenders. Powerlessness, helplessness, insecurity, absence of choice and lack of faith in official mechanisms and poverty alleviation programmes were common themes raised by respondents. Although using a different methodology, the findings of the study corresponded with those of a quantitative poverty assessment undertaken simultaneously by the World Bank in Pakistan. The results are therefore complementary, with the qualitative research adding in-depth insights into the nature of poverty in different localities, while the quantitative poverty assessment shows the extent of poverty throughout the country.

SOURCE: Beall, Jo et al. (1993), "Social safety nets and social networks: their role in poverty alleviation in Pakistan," report prepared for the Overseas Development Administration, two volumes, Development Planning Unit, University College London.

---

[22]See reference 20.

[23]See reference 5.

[24]The Ecologist (1993), *Whose Common Future? Reclaiming the Commons*, Earthscan, London.

Vulnerability is not synonymous with poverty, but means defencelessness, insecurity and exposure to risk, shocks and stress. It is linked with assets, such as human investment in health and education, productive assets including houses and domestic equipment, access to community infrastructure, stores of money, jewelery and gold, and claims on other households, patrons, the government and the international community for resources in times of need. While poverty (measured by income) can be reduced by borrowing, such debt makes the poor more vulnerable. Chambers points out that poor people have a horror of debt, and are more aware than professionals of the trade-offs between poverty and vulnerability.[25] Failure to distinguish between the two concepts is harmful because it prevents disaggregation of the experience of poverty and maintains stereotypes about the undifferentiated mass of the poor. An understanding of how people deplete household assets or resources is helpful in explaining how the well-being of urban households can decline, even when there are improvements in labour market or production opportunities.[26]

Entitlement refers to the complex ways in which individuals or households command resources.[27] These ways vary between people and over time, in response to shocks and long-term trends. They may include wage labour, sale of assets, own production, reduced consumption and public provision of goods and services. Although the concept of entitlement was originally applied in the rural sector to the study of famine and hunger, it is useful in explaining how poverty affects different people—even within the same household—in different ways. This disaggregation is central to the analysis of household survival strategies during periods of stress, and their implications for the

work burdens of women, men and children and intra-household re source allocation.[28]

Participatory investigation is useful in identifying what increases the risk of poverty and the underlying reasons why people remain in poverty. It allows different types of poverty to be distinguished by drawing on the life experience of poor people. An in-depth understanding of the process by which people become deprived is not an inferior substitute for a large-scale exercise to quantify poverty: it is a pre requisite to devising antipoverty programmes which address root causes of poverty and meet people's perceived needs. Not least, concentrating on poor people's priorities challenges a dominant view of the poor as passive or irresponsible, and the patronizing assumption of experts that poor people are there to be planned for.

V. The Concept of Urban Poverty: An Historical Perspective

The urban poverty debate is conducted on different planes in the Southern and Northern world. Historically, the development literature has focused on inequalities between poor rural and better-off urban populations, and the linkages between urbanization, the spread of capitalism and poverty. By contrast, poverty analysis in the North has been concerned with the problems of inner-city or peripheral urban social housing estates, or with regional and sectoral unemployment and income inequality. Far less attention has been paid to the urban–rural divide.

In the colonial period, it was widely assumed that poverty in the South could be solved through urbanization and the transfer of labour from low-productivity subsistence agriculture to

[25]Chambers, Robert (editor) (1989), special issue on "Vulnerability: how the poor cope," *IDS Bulletin* Vol 20, No 2.

[26]See reference 5.

[27]See reference 10.

[28]Moser, Caroline O N (1993), "Women, gender and urban development: challenges for the 1990s," paper prepared for the Final Workshop of the Ford Foundation Research Project on Urban Research in the Developing World: Towards an Agenda for the 1990s, Cairo, 14–18 February.

high-productivity modern industry.[29] Development planners started to question the assumptions of this two-sector growth model during the 1970s. After decades of modernization policies, the benefits of growth had not trickled down to the rural areas where the mass of the population still lived. Lipton's influential "urban bias" thesis blamed rural poverty on inequitable government taxation and expenditure policies which favoured city élites: rather than solving the problem of poverty, urban centres were depriving rural areas of infrastructure and resources.[30]

Urban bias became a mainstream view among development agencies in the 1970s and 1980s. In many Third World countries, poverty alleviation strategies (including sectoral strategies for primary health care, water supply and education) were reoriented to improve living conditions in rural areas. From the mid-1980s, structural adjustment policies have reinforced these efforts by removing subsidies given to urban consumers and raising prices to market levels to favour rural producers.

However, recent research in the 1980s and 1990s has revealed great diversity in the extent and depth of poverty within the urban sector in the Third World. This has supported a backlash, with some writers counter-arguing that the depth of poverty is worse in deprived city slums than in rural communities.[31] The availability of disaggregated urban poverty data, coupled with the recognition that urban growth is inevitable (and attributable more to the increase in the existing urban population than to a preventable process of rural–urban migration) is finally pushing urban poverty up the development agenda. The World Bank's latest policy paper for the urban sector acknowledges that ". . . *by the late 1980s, urban per capita incomes in some countries had reverted to 1970 levels and in some countries to 1960 levels.*"[32]

The urban bias of the 1980s' economic crisis is revealed in ECLA estimates for urban and rural poverty in ten Latin American countries. While the proportion of Latin America's rural households living in poverty remained static or declined between 1981 and 1986, the proportion of poor urban households increased. In the late 1980s, the percentage of rural households in poverty was higher than the corresponding percentage of urban households. However, Table 1 shows that in terms of the absolute numbers of people involved, urban poverty was a greater problem in seven of these countries. For all ten countries, whereas in 1980, 48 per cent of the poor (53 million persons) lived in urban areas, in 1986 this had risen to 58 per cent (80 million people).[33] The narrowing of the rural–urban differential is also recorded in Costa Rica and

[29]Lewis, Oscar (1958), *Five Families,* Random House, New York.

[30]The urban bias argument has classical roots and can be traced back to Adam Smith's *The Wealth of Nations* (1776). Michael Lipton's thesis—see Lipton, Michael (1976), *Why Poor People Stay Poor—Urban Bias in World Development,* Temple Smith, London—has been developed by Bates, Robert H (1981), *Markets and States in Tropical Africa,* University of California Press, Berkeley to construct a theory of "urban bias" for tropical Africa. For further discussion of the urban bias debate, see Moore, M and J Harriss (editors) (1984), *Development and the Rural-Urban Divide,* Frank Cass, London.

[31]Harpham, Trudy, Tim Lusty and Patrick Vaughan (editors) (1988), *In the Shadow of the City: Community Health and the Urban Poor,* Oxford University Press, Oxford and New York; also Amis, Philip and Peter Lloyd (editors) (1990), *Housing Africa's Urban Poor,* Manchester University Press, Manchester and New York.

[32]See reference 2, World Bank (1991), pages 45–46; also, according to the Bank's calculations, in 1988 there were some 330 million urban poor, comprising about 25 per cent of the total urban population. While this estimate gives recognition to the widespread extent of urban poverty, it implies that three-quarters of the South's urban population were not "poor." This assumption ignores the relative deprivation of urban communities in developing countries, including the lack of access to basic services and environmental hazards suffered by the majority of city residents.

[33]Feres, Juan Carlos and Arturo León (1990), "The magnitude of poverty in Latin America," *CEPAL Review* Vol 41, August, pages 133–151.

[34]Rottenberg, Simon (1993), *Costa Rica and Uruguay: The Political Economy of Poverty, Equity and Growth,* a World Bank comparative study, Oxford University Press, New York.

Uruguay.[34] African data indicate a real decline in urban wages since the early 1970s, with a halving of real income levels in many cases and a general deterioration in urban employment security and benefits such as employer housing. The urban–rural income differential has sharply reduced and, in some nations (Tanzania, Uganda and Ghana), has actually been reversed.[35] Falling urban living standards and a narrowing gap between poverty in rural and urban areas is also documented in Bangladesh.[36]

In industrial Europe and North America, the majority of the population (and also most of the poor) have lived in towns and cities since the early twentieth century. Consequently, a longer tradition of poverty research in urban areas exists

TABLE 1 The rural–urban distribution of poverty in ten Latin American countries, 1986–88

Country	Urban population as a percentage of the total 1986–88[b]	Percentage of households in poverty 1988[a]		Ratio of poor urban: poor rural population households[c]
		Urban	Rural	
Argentina	86	12	17	4.34: 1
Venezuela	83	25	34	3.59: 1
Uruguay	85	14	23	3.45: 1
Colombia	69	36	42	1.91: 1
Brazil	75	34	60	1.70: 1
Peru	69	45	64	1.57: 1
Mexico	71	23[d]	43[d]	1.31: 1
Panama	54	30	43	0.82: 1
Costa Rica	45	21	28	0.61: 1
Guatemala	33	54	75	0.34: 1

SOURCES: a. ECLA estimates quoted in Feres, Juan Carlos and Arturo León (1990), "The magnitude of poverty in Latin America," *CEPAL Review* Vol 41, August, page 143.
b. World Bank (1990), *World Development Report 1990,* Oxford University Press, Oxford and New York, Table 31, pages 238–239.
c. Author's calculation.
d. ECLA estimates for Mexico are based on 1984 data.

[35]Weeks, J (1986), " Vulnerable segments of the labour market: urban areas of the African region," paper for the ILO, mimeo, cited in Amis, Philip (1990), "Key themes in contemporary African urbanization" in Amis, Philip and Peter Lloyd (editors), *Housing Africa's Urban Poor,* Manchester University Press, Manchester and New York, pages 1–34.

[36]See reference 20.

[37]Rowntree, B Seebohm (1901), *Poverty: A Study of Town Life,* Macmillan, London.

(see, for example, Rowntree[37]). Perhaps because urban images have been influential in shaping perceptions of poverty, "urban poverty" is seldom regarded by Northern researchers to be conceptually distinct from poverty in general. In the UK and USA, the term "urban poverty" is often used specifically to refer to concentrations of deprivation in inner-city areas or peripheral social housing estates. However, Mangen's comparative study of social deprivation in inner cities suggests that this is not the case in mainland Europe, where inner-city poverty is viewed as *"a component of the overarching issue of marginalization"* rather than as a separate issue.[38]

VI. IS A DISTINCTION BETWEEN URBAN AND RURAL POVERTY USEFUL?

Conceptualizing urban poverty as a separate category from rural poverty is problematic for two reasons. First, the definition of the categories is arbitrary. And second, a dualistic spatial classification may have the undesirable effect of straight-jacketing discussion about the structural causes of poverty and diverting attention from national and international level (rather than city level) solutions.

If "poverty" is hard to define, then "urban" is just as difficult. There are no common criteria for deciding whether a settlement is a town or a rural village. The yardsticks include inconsistent population thresholds (settlements with over 1,000 people qualify as towns in Canada, but the lower limit is 2,000 in Kenya, 10,000 in Jordan, and 50,000 in Japan); the density of residential building; the type and level of public services provided; the proportion of the population engaged in non-agricultural work; and officially designated localities.[39] Villages can be reclassified as urban areas when they reach a given threshold size, without any change in the lifestyles of the people who live there.

Furthermore, there is great heterogeneity in the nature of urban areas, their functions and the lifestyles of their people. Only one-third of the urban population in the Third World lives in cities with one million or more inhabitants.[40] Do the people of a small Mexican town have more in common with the inhabitants of Mexico City (population 15 million in the 1991 census) than with those in surrounding villages? In China (which has an enormous impact on global urbanization statistics due to its population size), vast tracts of countryside are included in the catchment area of cities in order to provide reservoirs and hydroelectric power supplies for urban dwellers. Should peri-urban areas be classified as urban, rural, or neither category?

A strong case can be made for treating the urban–rural divide as a continuum rather than as a rigid dichotomy. First, human settlements clearly comprise a wide spectrum which cannot easily be reduced to two categories. The cut-off point for any such division is bound to be chosen arbitrarily. More over, there are linkages between the functions of cities, small towns and rural areas, which imply that the problems of one "sector" cannot be treated in isolation from the other. Interdependence between town and countryside exists in areas such as rural–urban migration and population growth, seasonal labour, the markets for food, industrial goods and services, water supply and demand, facilities for education, health care and recreation, flows of remittance income and family support networks. Individuals may cross back and forth between the sectors during their lives and extensive trading arrangements exist between the two. Intervention in one part of the system will have a range of repercussions,

[38]Mangen, Steen (1993), "Marginalization and inner-city Europe," Cross-National Research Papers, 2nd series, No 7 "Dualistic Europe," page 60.

[39]UNCHS (Habitat) (1987), *Global Report on Human Settlements 1986,* Oxford University Press, Oxford and New York.

[40]Hardoy, Jorge E, Diana Mitlin and David Satterthwaite (1992), *Environmental Problems in Third World Cities,* Earthscan, London, page 31.

affecting other parts of the "same sector" as well the "other sector."[41]

Second, concentrating on whether urban poverty is worse or more extensive than rural poverty diverts attention from structural determinants which affect the life chances of the poor in both sectors. These are likely to include the distribution of land, assets and human capital; socially constructed constraints to opportunity based on class, gender, race, age and disability; government social and macro-economic policies; external shocks such as famine and war; and external relationships which shape exchange rates, the terms of trade, economic sanctions (for example, during and after the Gulf War), debt repayments and the scope for domestic economic policies. Many of these fundamental causal factors cannot be tackled adequately by urban level interventions alone.

Third, the acknowledgement of diversity in life-chances within urban settlements means that we have to disaggregate within the city in order to analyze and explain poverty. Once the city is studied as a series of interrelated but heterogeneous neighbourhoods or districts, the dichotomous categories of urban and rural become less relevant. It may be more useful to focus on different spatial categories such as inner-city, suburb and peri-urban, or other types of categories such as tenure type, household type, social class, race, age, gender or level of education.

Bearing in mind these caveats, certain characteristics of poverty are closely identified with urbanization. These attributes of urban poverty can be grouped into four interrelated areas

Urban environmental and health risks. The special environmental and health problems faced by the urban poor result from the spatial juxtaposition of industrial and residential functions; competition for land, high living densities and overcrowded housing in hazardous areas; the speed of urban growth and the inadequate pace at which clean water supply, sanitation and solid waste disposal services are expanded; and risks of traffic congestion and the inability to implement effective controls over pollution and accident prevention.

Urban settlements develop in order to group capitalist enterprises in a cost-effective spatial configuration.[42] Many people are attracted to cities mainly by the opportunities for work. However, the externalities of urban production are borne disproportionately by the poor. Cheap housing areas and heavy industry both tend to be located on lower-cost land in cities and, in the absence of effective planning controls, this proximity can cause special environmental problems. The Bhopal industrial catastrophe in India, which killed over 3,000 people, seriously injured 100,000 and caused 200,000 to be evacuated would not have affected so many people had the factory been situated in a sparsely populated rural area or a non-residential planning zone. For people with very low earning levels, living on cheap land adjacent to economic opportunities is a rational choice, despite the risk. Yet, such disasters have enormous implications for the vulnerability of the poor, who may lose their homes, belongings, source of income and previous social networks if relocated.[43]

---

[41]This argument has parallels with the debate over the usefulness of the formal and informal sector concepts in the analysis of employment and production (see Bromley, Richard (editor) (1978), "The urban informal sector: critical perspectives," *World Development* No 6, Vol 9/10, pages 1031–1198). Multiple criteria have been used to define the informal sector, and activities fall into different sectors depending on which is used. Moreover, there are complex inter-relationships between producers and consumers across the formal–informal spectrum, involving the articulation of different modes of production through subcontracting, and the same individual may be involved in both sectors simultaneously (see Portes, Castells and Benton (1989), reference 8).

[42]Harvey, David (1975), *Social Justice and the City,* Edward Arnold, London.

[43]See reference 40.

BOX 3 URBAN POLLUTION AND POVERTY: THE EXAMPLE OF ALEXANDRIA, EGYPT

Alexandria, the second city of Egypt, contains 40 per cent of Egypt's heavy industry. In the 1980s, the city's sewage was pumped, untreated, through a series of short outflows running from the beaches into the Mediterranean Sea and into the freshwater Lake Maryut. Over half of the wastewater came from industrial sources, creating serious problems of heavy metal pollution and causing contamination of fish. Infections relating to untreated sewage were common. One consultancy report referred euphemistically to "identifiable floatables"—raw faeces visible in the seawater. While this affected both rich and poor sea bathers, the poor were worse affected as they could not escape to less polluted private beaches outside the city and had no alternative source of bathing water. Air pollution from the government-owned asbestos plant was a further major health hazard for residents of the surrounding poor neighbourhood.

SOURCE: Wratten, Ellen (1985), Unpublished background research for the Alexandria Comprehensive Plan Implementation Strategy, Governorate of Alexandria, Egypt.

Hardoy, Cairncross and Satterthwaite estimate that at least 600 million of the urban residents of the Third World live in what might be termed life and death-threatening homes and neighbourhoods.[44] Risks include typhoid, diarrhoeal diseases, cholera, and intestinal worms from contaminated water and food; diseases associated with poor drainage and garbage collection such as malaria; disease vectors associated with overcrowded, poor quality housing and insufficient water for domestic hygiene such as lice, fleas, scabies, rats and cockroaches; tuberculosis, influenza and meningitis, associated with overcrowding and poor ventilation; high lead blood levels which retard children's mental development; respiratory infections related to poor ventilation and open fires ; landslides, flooding and earthquake damage on marginal sites; injury in fire and domestic accidents—particularly affecting children who have no safe play areas; and lack of mobility for disabled people in overcrowded neighbourhoods with poor accessibility.[45]

The quality of the environment has been deteriorating in many Third World cities during the last decade. For example, trend data for Chawama, Lusaka for the period 1978–88 show that the proportion of the population with access to piped water has declined from 99 per cent to 83 per cent, while the proportion with collected rubbish has dropped by two-thirds, from 11 per cent to just 4 per cent.[46] At the household level, this has increased the amount of time women and children must spend fetching water daily.

Vulnerability arising from commercial exchange. In general, cities are characterized by a greater degree of commercialization than rural areas:

[44]Hardoy, Jorge E, Sandy Cairncross and David Satterthwaite (editors) (1990), *The Poor Die Young: Housing and Health in Third World Cities,* Earthscan, London.

[45]See reference 31, Harpham, Lusty and Vaughan (1988); also Surjadi, Charles (1993), "Respiratory diseases of mothers and children and environmental factors among households in Jakarta," *Environment and Urbanization* Vol 5, No 2, pages 78–86; and Tabizbadeh, I, ARossi-Espagnet and R Maxwell (1989), *Spotlight on the Cities: Improving Urban Health in Developing Countries,* WHO, Geneva.

[46]Moser, Caroline O N et al. (1994), "Poverty and vulnerability in Chawama, Lusaka, Zambia, 1978–1992," research project on Urban Poverty and Social Policy in the Context of Adjustment, draft paper, TWURD, Urban Development Division, World Bank, Washington, DC, May.

production tends to be more highly specialized and people are reliant on market exchange to buy basic goods and services and to earn money. Obviously, subsistence production (including agriculture) and unpaid productive and domestic work do exist in cities,[47] and commoditization is also a feature of rural areas in many parts of the world.[48] Nevertheless, commercial exchange is more ubiquitous in the urban context. It affects all three aspects of the "trinity of deprivation" identified by Mangen as crucial determinants of poverty in European inner-city areas: the local economy, housing and education.[49]

Urban households require money in order to buy basic items such as water, food and rent, which might be free (or at least cheaper) in rural areas, and to pay for goods and services which might not be available in rural areas but are normally consumed in the city (such as electricity and hospital fees). This increases pressure to earn a money income. Like landless rural labourers, the main asset the urban poor can sell in order to command income is their own labour, and the choice of work open to them is constrained by a lack of formal educational qualifications. With limited choice, the experience of employment in the urban context ". . . is often not a form of

independent existence at all, but an outcome of a comprehensive dependency relationship with an employer who is also a social superior."[50]

Those without savings or saleable capital assets are extremely vulnerable to changes in the demand for labour and the price of basic goods. Low-grade formal-sector jobs are increasingly insecure due to subcontracting and accompanying casualization.[51] In African cities, retrenchment of low-grade civil service jobs and public sector wage freezes have occurred at the same time as removal of government subsidies on food and the introduction of user charges for education and health services. Consequently, there has been an expansion in working hours, particularly among women in the unregulated informal sector.[52] Earnings in the urban informal sector are typically irregular and often low. Research has shown that illness-induced loss of employment is disproportionately borne by the poorest households and, in the absence of sickness insurance, re p resents a major risk to the ability to command re sources.[53] Unemployment is another important source of vulnerability: even a few days without work can represent a serious financial blow.

The commoditization of housing is now widespread in cities and even small towns in

---

[47]In Tanzania, the economic crisis has increased the incentive for city residents to engage in subsistence agriculture. During the 1980s, real urban wages fell sharply. The minimum wage earner was able to buy only 1.3 kilos of maize flour with a day's wages in 1990, compared to 2.9 kilos in 1989 and 8 kilos in 1982–84. In Dar es Salaam, a study by Lugalla (Lugalla, Joe L P (1989), "The state, law and urban poverty in Tanzania," *Law and Politics in Africa, Asia and Latin America* Vol 22, No 2, pages 131–157) found that 85 per cent of households were cultivating land, 17 per cent raised poultry and 17 per cent kept dairy cattle. Extensive urban agriculture has been documented in China, India, Kenya, Mexico and Taiwan: see Freeman, D B (1991), *City of Farmers,* McGill/Queens University Press, Montreal; also Smit, J and J Nasr (1992), "Urban agriculture for sustainable cities: using wastes and idle land and water bodies as resources," *Environment and Urbanization* Vol 4, No 2, pages 141–52; and Hardoy, Mitlin and Satterthwaite (1992), see reference 40.

[48]Marsden, Terry et al. (1993), *Constructing the Countryside,* UCL Press, London.

[49]See reference 38.

[50]Pryer, Jane and Nigel Crook (1988), *Cities of Hunger: Urban Malnutrition in Developing Countries,* Oxfam, Oxford.

[51]Rakodi, Carole (1993), "Planning for whom?" in Devas, Nick and Carole Rakodi (editors), *Managing Fast-growing Cities: New Approaches to Urban Planning and Management in the Developing World,* Longman, Harlow, pages 207–235.

[52]Wratten, Ellen (1993), "Poverty in Tanzania," report prepared for the Overseas Development Administration, London, February.

[53]Corbett, Jane (1989), "Poverty and sickness: the high costs of ill-health," *IDABulletin* Vol 20, No 2, pages 58–62; also Harriss, John (1989), "Urban poverty and urban poverty alleviation," *Cities,* August; Pryer, Jane (1989), "When breadwinners fall ill: preliminary findings from a case study in Bangladesh," *IDS Bulletin* Vol 20, No 2, pages 49–57; and Pryer, Jane (1993), "The impact of adult ill-health on household income and nutrition in Khulna, Bangladesh," *Environment and Urbanization* Vol 5, No 2, pages 35–49.

certain Third World countries.[54] Between one-third and two-thirds of the residents of cities in the South are housed in sub-standard or illegal accommodation. In the 1960s, low-income urban residents built their own housing on vacant land but in 1990s their children are increasingly renting accommodation within the same squatter settlements. Due to intense competition for land, real rents tend to rise sharply in rapidly growing cities. Renting creates an additional set of dependency relationships between tenant and landlord, particularly where rooms in a house are sub-let by an owner-occupier. In many cities, the poor are vulnerable to eviction at short notice, with possible loss of their possessions. In Nairobi, for example, fires have been used to clear rented housing in central squatter areas, in order to allow redevelopment of commercially valuable land. The decline in home ownership—from 60 per cent to 37 per cent in Chawama, Lusaka over the period 1978–92[55]—reduces the chances for the poor to hold an appreciating asset, and increases urban vulnerability.

Education is a major item of household expenditure for urban households in many countries. In the Third World, economic crisis has led to increased user charges for school fees, books and uniforms. Evidence from Ecuador suggests that the simultaneous intensification of women's work, resulting from cuts in real urban wages and community services, has led to girls being taken out of school in order to look after their younger siblings, thus reducing the chances of the next generation to escape poverty.[56]

A number of authors have contended that the instability associated with the commoditization process reinforces inequality. Adelman and Morris, in a comparative review of poverty in the mid-nineteenth century, suggest that commercialization tends to increase poverty among the poorest members of the population.[57] If commercialization is concentrated within cities, this may lead to a greater widening of intra-urban income differentials.

Social diversity, fragmentation and crime. Cities are heterogeneous "melting pots." They attract rural migrants and refugees with different ethnic, cultural and linguistic origins. Poor urban neighbourhoods contain a diversity of household types. The proportion of female-headed households is often higher than in surrounding rural areas: in Latin America there are greater opportunities for women's work in cities,[58] while in parts of Africa customary law excludes women from owning rural land in their own right, and the city offers a means for their independent survival after marital separation.[59] Due to the socially constructed gender division of labour and high dependency ratios, these households tend to have fewer income-earning opportunities and are generally poorer than male-headed and jointly headed

[54]See reference 31, Amis and Lloyd (1990); also see reference 46; Gilbert, Alan and Ann Varley (1991), *Landlord and Tenant: Housing the Poor in Urban Mexico,* Routledge, London; and Wratten, Ellen (forthcoming), "Self-help housing, the World Bank and the urban poor: a study of the impact of multilateral lending on government policy and the housing allocation process in Kenya," PhD dissertation, University of Cambridge.

[55]See reference 46.

[56]Moser, Caroline O N (1989), "The impact of recession and adjustment policies at the micro level: low-income women and their households in Guayaquil, Ecuador" in *The Invisible Adjustment: Poor Women and the Economic Crisis,* UNICEF, Santiago, Chile.

[57]Adelman, Irma and Cynthia Taft Morris (1978), "Growth and impoverishment in the middle of the nineteenth century," *World Development* Vol 6, No 3, pages 245–273.

[58]Brydon, Lynne and Sylvia Chant (1989), *Women in the Third World: Gender Issues in Rural and Urban Areas,* Edward Elgar, Aldershot.

[59]Schlyter, Ann (1988), *Women Householders and Housing Strategies: The Case of George,* Zambia, National Council for Building Research, Gävle, Sweden; also Schlyter, Ann (1989), *Women Householders and Housing Strategies: The Case of Harare, Zimbabwe,* National Council for Building Research, Gävle, Sweden.

households (though not all female-headed households are poor). Typically, women have lower levels of education (a rational response by poor families wishing to maximize earnings is to send sons rather than daughters to school), long working hours (including domestic work such as water collection and fuel-gathering), responsibility for child care as well as productive and community management roles, poorer diets and more restricted physical mobility than men. The growing phenomenon of urban "street" children—either unaccompanied by adults or, more commonly, living with their families at night and working on the streets by day—is also strongly associated with poverty and family breakdown.[60]

Social diversity is likely to create new tensions and survival strategies. Relationships in the urban context may be more impersonal. Lifestyles, kinship and neighbourhood support networks are different from those in rural areas, though links with a rural extended family can remain an important part of an urban household's survival strategy. In Latin America, urban social movements, based on the recognition of collective class interests, are important means by which the poor lobby for land rights and infrastructure.[61] Community-based organizations also provide a means of saving and arranging income-earning opportunities.

The extent of relative poverty is at its most conspicuous where the rich and the poor live side by side. Cities contain wealthy, poor and inbetween neighbourhoods, often in close proximity. A single bus journey in Nairobi can take one from the shanty of Mathare Valley, through the modern city centre, to lush tree-lined roads and the irrigated lawns of guarded mansions. The temptation and opportunities for crime may be greater in cities, but the poor rather than the well-off are most often the victims. Fear of personal safety—real or imagined—restricts mobility after nightfall in low-income areas.

The vandalism of community infrastructure by alienated youth is costly to the poor and leads to scarce resources being spent on measures to improve security. For example, in Lusaka, parent–teacher associations raised funds to build perimeter walls around school grounds rather than spend the money on books and equipment.[62] Drug and alcohol abuse, AIDS, domestic violence, female depression and family breakdown, while not exclusive to urban areas, have all been associated with urban poverty.

Vulnerability arising from the intervention of the state and police. Finally, the urban poor are likely to have more contact with state agents and the police than their rural counterparts. While government policies can have an important positive impact on poverty alleviation, many poor people experience the state in negative ways—as an oppressive bureaucracy which attempts to regulate their activities without understanding their needs,[63] or as corrupt policemen, demanding money in order to turn a blind eye to illicit income-generating activities such as brewing or prostitution[64]—rather than as servants of the public.

[60]Boyden, Jo (1991), *Children of the Cities,* Zed Books, London; also Dimenstein, Gilberto (1991), *Brazil: War on Children,* Latin America Bureau, London; and Patel, Sheela (1990), "Streetchildren, hotel boys and children of pavement dwellers and construction workers in Bombay: how they meet their daily needs," *Environment and Urbanization* Vol 2, No 2, pages 9–26.

[61]Castells, Manuel (1983), *The City and Grass Roots: A Cross-cultural Theory of Urban Social Movements,* Edward Arnold, London; also Gilbert, Alan and Peter Ward (1984), "Community action by the urban poor: democratic involvement, community self-help or a means of social control," *World Development* Vol 12, No 8; and Friedmann, J (1989), "The Latin American *barrio* movement as a social movement: contribution to a debate," *International Journal of Urban and Regional Research* Vol 13, No 3, pages 501–510.

[62]See reference 46.

[63]de Soto, Hernando (1992), "Combating urban poverty in Latin America: the Peruvian case" in Netherlands Ministry of Foreign Affairs, *Urban Poverty Alleviation in Latin America,* Development Cooperation Information Department, Ministry of Foreign Affairs, The Hague, pages 31–38.

[64]Nelson, Nici (1988), "How women and men get by: the sexual division of labour in a Nairobi squatter settlement" in Gugler, Joseph (editor), *The Urbanization of the Third World,* Oxford University Press, Oxford, pages 183–203.

Policing in poor areas is particularly problematic when it is associated with racial antagonism, and has provoked riots in inner-city areas in the USA, France and Britain in recent years.

Rakodi asserts that ". . . planners have little understanding about how the poor survive.[65] As a result, urban plans and policies generally have little relevance to the situation which the poor face and may well make it far worse." One way this can impact badly on the poor is where a rigid constraint is placed on the supply of serviced land and housing. Residents of squatter settlements live in terror of official clearances in which they may lose their few capital assets and personal possessions. In Brazil, where the state pursued a policy of eradicating favelas (squatter settlements) in the1960s and 1970s, Portes comments that subsequent government neglect was "not an unwelcome event."[66] Lee-Smith argues that it is in the interests of the ruling élite to continue to prevent easy access to land by the urban poor because control of land provides a source of cash income and political support.[67] This is likely to reinforce the official ideology of maintaining high building standards and ensuring that petty commodity production, including building, remains in the informal sector.

Castells argues that the state plays a central role in mediating class interests in urban areas by subsidizing the cost of reproducing labour.[68] Where governments have intervened in favour of the poor, the withdrawal of this assistance may be devastating. The removal of state subsidies on basic foodstuffs has greatly increased the vulnerability of the urban poor in Africa, causing rapid price rises and falling real incomes. In Zambia, for example, the majority of low-income households in Lusaka changed their diets following government auctioning of foreign exchange from 1985, substituting mealie-meal for protein, while the poorest cut down their consumption of mealie-meal. Extensive rioting broke out in the Copperbelt towns in December 1986 following an attempted doubling of the price of mealie-meal by the government. As a result of devaluation and removal of price controls, the official price of mealie-meal increased seven-fold between 1985 and 1989.[69] The price has continued to spiral steeply since 1989, trebling in 1992–93.[70]

The importance of these four, interlinked features of urban poverty–environmental and health risks, vulnerability arising from commoditization, social fragmentation and crime, and negative contact with the state and police—is not that they are only found in the poor parts of towns and cities. None of them are associated exclusively with the urban sector: they may be found to some degree in rural areas, and not every town will exhibit all the features. However, it is significant that in poor neighbourhoods in the city, these characteristics may be uniquely combined in ways that intensify the insecurity and life-threatening health risks experienced with poverty, and influence the coping strategies adopted by the poor at the household and community levels.[71]

[65]See reference 51.

[66]Portes, Alejandro (1979), "Housing policy, urban poverty and the state: the *favelas* of Rio de Janeiro, 1972–1976," *Latin American Research Review* Vol XIV, No 2, pages 3–24.

[67]Lee-Smith, Diana (1990), "Squatter landlords in Nairobi: a case study of Korogocho" in Amis, Philip and Peter Lloyd (editors), *Housing Africa's Urban Poor,* Manchester University Press, Manchester and New York, pages 175–189.

[68]Castells, Manuel (1977), *The Urban Question,* Edward Arnold, London.

[69]Kalinda, Beatrice and Maria Floro (1992), "Zambia in the 1980s: a review of national and urban-level economic reforms," INURD Working Paper No 18, Urban Development Division, World Bank, Washington, DC.

[70]Wratten, Ellen (1993), "Zambia peri-urban self-help project," report prepared for the Overseas Development Administration, London, October.

[71]Edwards, J (1989), "Positive discrimination as a strategy against exclusion: the case of the inner-cities," *Policy and Politics* Vol 17, pages 11–24.

The effects of poverty at the urban level are therefore likely to be different, even if the basic underlying causes are common.

Is there a conceptual difference between urban and rural poverty? Urban poverty, as experienced in New York ghettos or Nairobi's squatter settlements, certainly feels qualitatively different. Yet, location within the city is not a sufficient predictor of poverty: *"Inner-city and marginalization are not coterminous. Mere location within the core does not marginalize, since not all the heterogeneity of communities housed there conforms to this label, neither are political responses to them uniform since plainly some are regarded as the deserving poor. There have to be other factors attached to individuals and groups for the marginalization process to congeal"*[72]

The social constructs of race, class, gender and age affect poverty in both urban and rural contexts, as do national and international policies and external shocks. It is also important to remember that a key distinguishing feature of rural poverty—accessibility—can also be a problem for people living in poor urban communities. While there may be a greater volume and quality of community services in cities, the urban poor are invariably denied access to them: isolation is determined by political clout as well as spatial location.

To get a complete picture of poverty, we need methods of analysis which examine these similar features as well as the differences. Rural and urban human settlements are linked economic and social systems, and it is unhelpful to restrict our vision to only one part of the system or to use poverty data to set one arbitrarily defined part against another.

VII. Why Are the Poor Poor? Alternative Perceptions and Their Policy Implications

The analysis of poverty has been dominated by two broadly opposed perspectives, each of which leads to an alternative set of policy prescriptions. On the one hand, poverty is attributed to the personal failings of the individuals concerned, which leads to self-perpetuating cycles of social pathology. On the other hand, it is viewed as the inevitable outcome of an unfairly structured political and economic system which discriminates against disadvantaged groups. The former perspective is intellectually rooted in laissez-faire individualism and the legitimisation of racial discrimination.[73] It tends to lead to free-market economic policies coupled with residual social policies which focus on the psychological rehabilitation of the poor.[74] The alternative radical view draws from Marxist theory and is closely associated with the developmentalist or basic needs tradition. Policy prescriptions involve a more interventionist role for the state in promoting equity, analysis of poverty as a social construct rather than an individual problem, and the redistribution of assets and decision-making power at international, national, regional, community, household and intra-household levels.

a. Low- and middle-income societies

In the Third World country literature (much of which has been written by Northern researchers), these two views are typified by the "culture of poverty" thesis of Oscar Lewis, in which the poor

---

[72]See reference 38.

[73]See reference 13.

[74]Hardiman, Margaret and James Midgley (1989), *The Social Dimensions of Development,* 2nd edition, Gower, London.

are assumed to be marginal to urban development due to innate and culturally determined personal characteristics and resulting deviant behaviour;[75] and the alternative "marginalization" thesis, which ascribes a more positive role to the activities of poor urban communities and emphasizes the structural barriers which exclude their participation in formal economic, political and social institutions.[76] Oscar Lewis's anthropological studies of poor families in Mexico City and San Juan, Puerto Rico led him to the conclusion that those trapped in poverty had characteristically different behaviour patterns and values from the dominant society and culture. He argued that: *"The culture of poverty is both an adaptation and a reaction of the poor to their marginal position in a class-stratified, highly individuated, capitalistic society. It represents an effort to cope with feelings of hopelessness and despair which develop from the realization of the improbability of achieving success in terms of the values and goals of the larger society."*[77] The hypothesis of the separate "sub-culture" was used to explain the perpetuation of their poverty from generation to generation. Children born into poor families grew up with a weak family structure, ineffective interpersonal relations, a present-time orientation and unrestrained spending patterns. This environment engendered values such as helplessness, dependence, a sense of inferiority, resignation and fatalism. Such children would be less interested in education, the value of work or self-improvement. They would have a low ability to plan ahead or to identify and react to changing opportunities.

These adaptive responses to economic deprivation and social marginality would, in turn, make the disadvantaged position of the poor yet more entrenched. Characteristics such as male machismo, sexual promiscuity, teenage pregnancy, illegitimacy and female-headed households, a rigid division of family responsibilities between men and women, alcohol and drug abuse, and poor educational performance serve as "own goals," preventing the poor from rising out of their situation and precluding economic, social and political integration into the mainstream culture.[78] Lewis further claimed that the basic attitudes and values of the debilitating sub-culture are absorbed *". . . by the time slum children are age six or seven,"* thus ensuring that the traits causing poverty are passed on to the next generation.[79] Appropriate remedies would include removing children from their home environment in order to rehabilitate them and encourage a change in their values.

Lewis' work has provoked widespread debate and criticism. Concern has been expressed with the research methods used, the lack of representativeness of the families studied, and the ethnocentricity with which Lewis judged other people's lives. Valentine argued strongly that the lifestyle of the poor is not based on deviant values but is instead a rational response to having insufficient money.[80] Perlman's classic study of urban poverty in Rio de Janeiro provided empirical evidence to challenge Lewis'

---

[75]See reference 29; also Lewis, Oscar (1961), *The Children of Sanchez: Autobiography of a Mexican Family,* Penguin, Harmondsworth and Vintage Books, New York; and Lewis, Oscar (1965), *La Vida: A Puerto Rican Family in the Culture of Poverty—San Juan and New York,* Random House, New York.

[76]Perlman, Janice E (1976), *The Myth of Marginality: Urban Poverty and Politics in Rio de Janeiro,* University of California Press, Berkeley and London; also Moser, Caroline O N and David Satterthwaite (1985), "Characteristics and sociology of poor urban communities," mimeo, London.

[77]See reference 75, Lewis (1965), page xiv.

[78]Burton, C Emory (1992), *The Poverty Debate: Politics and the Poor in America,* Greenwood Press, Westport, Connecticut and London.

[79]Lewis, Oscar (1966), "The culture of poverty," *Scientific American* Vol 215, No 4, pages 19–25.

[80]Valentine, Charles A (1968), *Culture of Poverty: Critique and Counterproposals,* University of Chicago Press, Chicago and London.

TABLE 2 Urban poverty: meaning, measurement and policy implications

Meaning of Urban poverty	Implications for Measurement	Implications for Urban Poverty Programmes
Conventional economic definition: poverty is a lack of income (or consumption), defined in absolute or relative terms.	Quantitative approach, using a common scale of measurement (usually a poverty line based on household budget surveys); measurement of the extent of poverty (number affected) and the depth of poverty (how far incomes are below the poverty line).	Focus on redistribution at the macro level. Increase urban productivity and incomes through job creation; deal with residual poverty through transfer payments, social safety nets, subsidies on basic items.
Participatory social development definition: poverty is multi-faceted and its definition varies between individuals.	Qualitative analysis of the processes underlying poverty and the ways in which poverty affects different subgroups among "the poor" (such as young and old people, women and men, different household types, castes and ethnic groups). Uses a range of "bottom-up" participatory methods such as focus groups, life histories, wealth-ranking and mapping to examine people's perceptions of poverty, vulnerability, and intra-household and community level entitlements.	Focus on micro-level support to enable individuals to participate socially and economically and strengthen their ability to stay out of poverty. May include community-level interventions to strengthen health, education, communications, credit for small enterprises, people's capacity to make decisions affecting their own lives, political participation and legal literacy; decentralization of decision-making to local levels (the poor know best how to use resources in their own neighbourhoods); and the differentiation of special needs of particular groups among "the poor."
Integrated development approach: causes of poverty are interlinked (environment, housing, health, income generation, education, etc.) and must be tackled in a coordinated way.	Quantitative and qualitative assessments are complementary. Quantification includes social indicators such as life expectancy, incidence of disease, education levels, as well as income and expenditure. Need to understand the spatial distribution of poverty at the citywide level in order to target resources at the poorest groups; within poor areas, need to understand priorities of different sub-groups.	Holistic, integrated approach to urban development and poverty alleviation—redistribute resources to provide for basic needs of the poor, coordinating interventions in primary health care, water and sanitation, pollution control, housing, income generation, education, crime control, domestic violence, leisure facilities. Acknowledge linkages between national economic and social policies and poverty in urban and rural areas.

stereotype.[81] Far from being marginal to urban development, the poor made an important contribution to the city's informal economy. They did not have the attitudes and behaviours supposedly associated with marginal groups, were socially well organized and cohesive, culturally optimistic, aspired to improve their houses and their children's education, and were neither politically apathetic nor radical. Poverty resulted from discriminatory structures which denied the non-privileged the means to realize their aspirations. Moser and Satterthwaite reinforced this view.[82] They pointed out that although squatter settlements are built in peripheral areas, where there is less competition for land from high-income groups, squatters are usually established urban residents who are well integrated into the city economy. In fact, squatter settlements are highly heterogeneous and contain middle-income as well as low-income residents.

The dispute over the validity of the culture of poverty hypothesis, and the shift towards a structural explanation of poverty, reflects wider shifts in development thinking. In the 1970s, modernization theory—which prescribed a blueprint development strategy based on rapid economic growth and accorded a residual role for social policy[83]—was challenged by dependency theorists who claimed that urban and rural poverty in the Third World was intrinsically linked to the process of capital accumulation in the North, and by proponents of basic needs strategies who called for a redefinition of the goals of development to emphasize equity and democracy as well as growth.[84] In the 1980s, the growth models re-emerged in new forms, with pressure from the World Bank and bilateral development agencies for macro-economic reforms which would facilitate private sector development.

This approach is mirrored by the World Bank's latest policy paper for the urban sector, which attributes the causes of urban poverty largely to "... *structural constraints and inefficiencies in the urban economy including excessive protection of capital-intensive industry, ineffective public policies and weak public institutions,*" and argues that "... *poverty reduction is possible in part through improving productivity at the individual, household, firm, and urban levels.*"[85] The previous emphasis on housing and infrastructure projects (outlined by the World Bank Task Force on Poverty[86]) has given way to interventions designed to strengthen citywide economic management, deregulation of the private sector, increased social sector expenditure for human resource development of the urban poor by providing basic services in education, health, nutrition, family planning and vocational training, and support for the voluntary sector.

There is now widespread recognition that structural adjustment programmes have exacerbated poverty, particularly among lower middle-class and low-income groups in cities.[87] In 1987, UNICEF called for greater targeting of public expenditure to benefit the poorest groups, and compensatory measures to lessen the impact

---

[82]See reference 76, Moser and Satterthwaite (1985).

[83]See reference 74.

[84]Streeten, Paul (editor) (1978), special issue on "Poverty and inequality," *World Development* Vol 6, No 3; also Streeten, Paul (1981), *First Things First: Meeting Basic Human Needs in Developing Countries,* World Bank publication, Oxford University Press, New York and Oxford; and Wisner, Ben (1988), *Power and Need in Africa: Basic Needs and Development Policies,* Earthscan, London.

[85]See reference 2, World Bank (1991), page 45.

[86]World Bank Task Force on Poverty (1983), *Focus on Poverty,* World Bank, Washington, DC.

[87]See reference 2, World Bank (1991).

on their health and productivity.[88] These measures included public works employment schemes and nutrition interventions such as selective food subsidies and direct feeding for the most vulnerable. However, UNICEF have since expressed concern that adjustment programmes need to focus on the structural aspects of poverty:

> ... restructuring the economy in order to reach a reasonable growth path should not be the only major objective of adjustment programmes but also a speedy elimination of structural poverty... compensatory programmes and the establishment of the safety nets which often accompany structural adjustment programmes can...—in high income countries— contribute to reducing poverty. In general, however, these programmes do not... attack the root causes of structural poverty.[89]

Safety nets (including food for work schemes and transfer payments to those below the poverty line) are unlikely to be an effective or sustainable solution to urban poverty in the poorest countries where a majority of the population are living below the subsistence income level. In Zambia, for example, where 80 per cent of the national population and 40 per cent of the urban population fall beneath the official poverty line, food for work projects in Lusaka's squatter compounds have benefited as few as 5 per cent of eligible households, and their continuation is dependent on foreign food aid.[90]

The structural approach to poverty demands more radical redistributive measures (such as land and tax reform, changes in the legal rights of women, and the coordinated provision of infrastructure and basic services to all parts of the city), in order to increase there sources of the poor and improve their long-term ability to earn a decent livelihood, and increase popular participation in decision-making. It also stresses the links between poverty in Third World cities and unequal global trading relationships, requiring change in the international economic order (particularly a moratorium on debt repayments and the curbing of multinational corporate power).[91]

In an interesting work bridging the analysis of poverty in the North and the South, Townsend proposes a structural theory of poverty based on three elements: the economic and social influence of global institutions and transnational corporations; analysis of the ways in which human needs are socially created—by the state in defining the rights and obligations of "citizenship," and by other sub-national associations such as communities, families and commercial organizations; and by gender preference, which is "... *a prime determinant of the construction of society and hence of unequal privilege and the unequal distribution of income and other resources in society.*"[92] The policy implications of this theory are a restructuring of world trade and international action to regulate and change the pattern of ownership of transnational corporations; a more positive approach to social planning, with the coordination of social and economic policies, and a creative or preventative role for social policy rather than a casualty treatment role; a fairer distribution of wealth (rather than an emphasis on social security transfer income) and withdrawal

---

[88]Cornia, Giovanni A, Richard Jolly and Frances Stewart (1987), *Adjustment with a Human Face: Protecting the Vulnerable and Promoting Growth,* Oxford University Press for UNICEF, Oxford.

[89]See reference 9, page 122.

[90]See reference 70.

[91]Hoogvelt, Anke M M (1982), *The Third World in Global Development,* Macmillan, London; also Hayter, Teresa (1981), *The Creation of World Poverty,* Pluto Press, London.

[92]See reference 13, chapter 5.

of the right to inherit vast wealth; the introduction of maximum as well as minimum wages and the extension of wages to women in unpaid work; and the enlargement of the rights of citizens to participate in community institutions.

b. Industrial Societies

The idea that the poor are to blame for their poverty is a recurrent theme in social policy in the North. In Britain, it is enshrined in the concept of the "deserving" and "undeserving" poor which is used to justify the differential treatment of those deemed to have brought their condition on themselves through socially irresponsible behaviour (such as teenage girls who have become pregnant "just so as to qualify for social housing"[93]) and innocent, "decent" and hard-working citizens who have fallen on hard times (such as war widows with young children).

This view is mirrored by Jenks, writing about poverty in the USA: "*A growing fraction of the population is poor because they have violated rules that most Americans regard as reasonable.*"[94] The culture of poverty was debated extensively in the USA and UK in the 1960s and 1970s, but in the 1980s and 1990s discussion has shifted to the notion of "underclass." This concept parallels the culture of poverty but is narrower in focus. It is applied to those trapped in the geographic and social isolation of the ghetto rather than to the majority of the "deserving" or "respectable" poor.

According to Wilson, there are three aspects to the creation of a ghetto underclass: concentration, social isolation and spatial mismatch.[95] Urban poverty in the USA has become increasingly concentrated among ethnic minorities in the poorest neighbourhoods of major cities. Of the 2.4 million ghetto poor, 65 per cent are black and 22 per cent are Hispanic.[96] As middle-class families have moved out of the inner-city, a distinct local social milieu has been created where teenage pregnancies, school drop-outs, crime, violence and welfare dependency are normal behaviour rather than a disgrace. Simultaneously, industrial transformation has resulted in job losses in inner-city areas, leaving the urban underclass with few opportunities. The physical isolation of the ghetto poor has been reinforced by highway and housing projects which have segregated the black population and isolated them from employment outside the inner-city.

Thus, the underclass hypothesis emphasizes that marginalization is the outcome of an interaction between personal and group cultural characteristics and a complex web of demographic and economic changes, and government policy, which combine to create a poverty trap for ghetto residents.[97] The poor are both the victims of the system which binds them in the ghetto and a cause—through the criminal and antisocial activities that some of them are alleged to engage in—of the deteriorating quality of life in their neighbourhoods.

The concepts of universal basic needs and social exclusion have also been important in framing alternative approaches to poverty in the twentieth century. Neo-Keynesian analysis views the problem as one of cyclical macro-economic

---

[93]A view epitomized in the speech by Peter Lilley, Secretary of State for Social Security, to the British Conservative Party conference in October 1993.

[94]Jenks, Christopher (1991), "Is the American underclass growing?" in Jenks, Christopher and Paul E Peterson (editors), *The Urban Underclass,* The Brookings Institution, Washington, DC, pages 28–100.

[95]Wilson, W J (1987), *The Truly Disadvantaged: The Inner-city, the Underclass and Public Policy,* University of Chicago Press, Chicago.

[96]Wilson, W J (1991), "Studying inner-city social dislocations: the challenge of public agenda research," *American Sociological Review* Vol 53, pages 1–14.

[97]See reference 95.

demand management, and stresses job creation through reflation of the economy and training of the unemployed. In Britain, nationalization of industry, greater state control of employment, regional assistance,[98] the strengthening of the town and country planning system and nationalization of the right to develop land, the opening of universal access to education and health services, and legislation to diminish racial and gender discrimination between 1945 and 1979 fitted with a structural understanding of the causes of poverty. However, this was mixed with subsistence-level, means-tested social security benefits which echo the idea that the long-term unemployed should not enjoy the same entitlement to income as those in work.

In continental Europe, unemployment benefits are set at a more generous level based on average wages and reflecting the concept of equal citizenship. The French second-generation national assistance scheme (the *revenu minimum d'insertion*) and its counterpart programme operating in many of the Spanish regions attempts permanent rehabilitation of the poor through job retraining. Mangen found the underclass concept was not applied widely to inner-city areas in mainland Europe.[99] While interpretations of poverty varied between the European countries studied, the central notion was found to be "social exclusion superimposed on material and cultural deprivation." For example van Parijs distinguishes between "outsiders" who are permanently excluded from a job, wage and welfare benefits including future

pension rights, and "insiders" who have secure jobs.[100] European policy responses typically include employment, training and education programmes coupled with physical regeneration strategies for deprived inner-city areas and "problem" housing estates, which aim to remove marginalized people permanently from poverty and "reinsert" them into society.

In contrast, the current emphasis of employment policy in Britain and the USA reflects a concern with the welfare dependency of the poor, with short-term "work experience" being offered rather than training schemes which lead to permanent jobs and van Parijs' "insider" benefits. "Workfare" schemes have been introduced in the USA under the Family Support Act 1988, whereby welfare-dependent mothers are required to undertake low-paid community service work rather than receive benefits. Wilson has proposed universal child care to allow poor working parents access to education, training and employment.[101] Again, state child care provision is far more extensive in continental Europe than in either the UK or USA, where private provision is the main form.

Urban poverty alleviation strategies are different in the South and the North, not only because state resources vary but also because the conceptualization of urban poverty differs. In the North, where urban poverty is not generally treated as a separate category, the emphasis of policy has been on national and regional interventions, with selective assistance at intra-city level to targeted deprived areas or groups. In

---

[98]Regional policy has had mixed results. Doreen Massey's research suggests that changes in the local gender division of labour was more important than government incentives in attracting new industries to the assisted regions. Following male redundancy, women no longer had to provide round-the-clock domestic services for husbands and sons on shift work, and became freer to take up paid employment themselves (LSE Gender Institute public lecture, 1992).

[99] See reference 38.

[100]Van Parijs, Philippe (1992), "Introduction: competing justifications of basic income" in Van Parijs, Philippe (editor), *Arguing for Basic Income: Ethical Foundations for a Radical Reform*, Verso, London and New York, pages 3–43; also Van Parijs, Philippe (1995), *Real Freedom for All: What (If Anything) Can Justify Capitalism?*, Clarendon Press, Oxford.

[101]See reference 95.

the South, where urban poverty has been neglected until recently, policies have focused on raising incomes and improving access to services in the rural sector. Given the interrelated determinants of urban and rural poverty, what is required is an integrated approach which simultaneously addresses ways of increasing the opportunities and reducing the inequalities of people in both sectors. As Stren states, writing about the urban crisis in Africa:

> It is not a question of determining whether the rural sector or the urban sector is the most important; an understanding of their symbiotic relationship is required. . . .One cannot let the urban system crumble to the point that it cannot support rural development, while channelling all available funds into the rural sector. . . (page 2)

> [But nevertheless] It is now widely appreciated that rural conditions are even worse than urban conditions, and this is the root cause of the urban management problem. (page 305)[102]

The magnitude of poverty is such that its solution is unlikely to involve any one agency acting alone. But governments do have the responsibility, jointly and severally, of setting a policy context within which discriminatory social and economic structures are removed. Moreover, urban policy must be defined less narrowly than a preoccupation with the provision of infrastructure or economic management to raise productivity, and give equal emphasis to social and political structures which influence people's well-being and the ways in which they a reaffected by adversity.

VIII. Conclusions: The Linkage Between Definitions, Policy and the Measurement of Urban Poverty

Perceptions about the nature of poverty, and the policy responses which follow from these perceptions, are central in deciding how best to study, measure and analyze the phenomenon. Different kinds of information are demanded by different approaches. For example, if poverty is understood as the product of a deviant subculture, then priority might be given to identifying and collecting information about behavioural problems such as family instability, alcoholism and drug abuse. Alternatively, if anti-poverty policies are designed to deal with structural causes, information would be required about not only access to employment, housing and educational opportunities at the city level but also social and institutional structures which discriminate against the poor at international and national levels.[103]

The first section of this paper identified two principal ways in which poverty has been defined: conventional definitions which use income or other social indicators as a proxy for welfare, and participatory definitions which allow for flexibility in local perceptions of poverty and view it in non-material as well as physical terms. The conventional approach lends itself to quantitative measurement and allows individuals or households to be ranked along a common, externally defined scale which serves as a surrogate measure of poverty. This is useful in so far as it is necessary to understand general patterns of deprivation and to compare different groups or countries in order to target

---

[102]Stren, Richard E and Rodney R White (editors) (1989), *African Cities in Crisis: Managing Rapid Urban Growth,* Westview Press, Boulder, Colorado and London.

[103]Hirschfield, Alexander (1993), "Indices of deprivation: study approaches, data sources and analytical techniques," mimeo, Department of Civic Design, University of Liverpool.

resources in the most effective way.[104] Comparative measurement is essential in designing and monitoring redistributive policies and social safety nets.

However, if we accept that poverty is an inherently subjective concept, then such measurements can only give us an accurate picture of its incidence if everyone holds an identical view of what poverty is—which, as we have shown, they do not. The contribution of the anthropological approaches to poverty measurement is that they recognize the diversity of perceptions of poverty and enable us to build up an understanding of its many dimensions for particular poor groups. This type of analysis is extremely important in designing "enabling" strategies which help to overcome the structural constraints to economic, social and political participation by the poor. In order to "help the poor to help themselves"—the mainstream of current anti-poverty thinking in the Third World and an idea which is superseding the welfare state approach in some Northern countries—we need to understand the nature of entitlements and vulnerability at a disaggregated level.

Recent work in developing participatory rural research in the South has much to offer the analysis of poverty in the urban context in both the South and the North.[105] The use of multiple measures to observe any phenomenon, including poverty, is in theory superior to the use of just one or two measures. Yet, there are drawbacks. Participatory analysis requires greater time input (from ordinary people as well as professionals) and, while it can further the objective of involving the poor in decision-making, it is by nature a highly localized exercise and tends to lead to micro-level solutions rather than challenge the broader national and international structures which shape poverty.

Statistics about the incidence of "urban poverty" and "rural poverty" a re frequently used as ammunition to capture resources by those on either side of the urban–rural divide. This paper has challenged the usefulness of treating urban poverty as a separate conceptual category. Any such classification is intrinsically arbitrary. More importantly, from a structural perspective, the determinants of urban and rural poverty are interlinked and have to be tackled in tandem.

Within cities, certain of the problems associated with poverty—poor environmental conditions, vulnerability arising from commercialization, social stress and conflict with state authority—occur in unique combination and defy solution by vertical sectoral interventions. An integrated strategy, which aims to deal with social, economic, political and environmental problems in a coordinated way, offers more hope. The integrated development approach requires both quantitative poverty indicators—to "best guess" the distribution and depth of deprivation within cities and countries—and qualitative analysis of social structures and the process by which poverty affects different groups. As a tool to guide the planning and monitoring of policy, both quantitative and qualitative approaches to measurement therefore have a place. Neither is sufficient alone.

---

[104]The cost-effectiveness of expenditure has to be considered as well as equity in determining the best use of resources to combat poverty. For example, would preventive measures directed at the general population (such as mass immunization or the provision of universal, good quality child care) reduce poverty more than selective interventions targeted at the very poor? The trade-off between such choices is political as well as economic, since popular support for anti-poverty policies may be dependent on how the benefits are distributed.

[105]For an account of the application of rural PRA methodologies in urban participatory poverty assessments, see Norton, Andy (1994), "Observations on urban applications of PRA methods from Ghana and Zambia: participatory poverty assessments," *RRA Notes* No 21, special issue on Participatory Tools and Methods in Urban Areas, pages 55–56.

Conceptualizing Work–Family Balance

Implications for Practice and Research (2007)

Joseph G. Grzywacz and Dawn S. Carlson

The idea of work–family balance has generated substantial interest in the academic, applied, and popular press. Academicians argue that work–family balance contributes to individual well-being and that it is a lynchpin for a healthy and well-functioning society (Halpern, 2005). Applied professionals in business and policy arenas struggle to find solutions to the "challenge" workers face in combining their work and family lives. Work–family balance, or more aptly difficulty achieving balance, is highlighted in popular periodicals such as *Fortune, Wall Street Journal,* and *Newsweek* (Caminiti, 2005; Chao, 2005; Dwyer, 2005), and bookstores are replete with books providing tips and suggestions for individuals and couples to achieve work–family balance.

Interest in work–family balance is well deserved. In nearly two thirds of couples with children younger than 18, both partners are employed (Bureau of Labor Statistics, 2006), 35% of workers currently provide care for an aging parent or family member and the proportion of workers providing eldercare will likely increase (Bond, Thompson, Galinsky, & Prottas, 2002), and 60% of working adults report difficulty balancing work and family (Keene & Quadagno, 2004). Evidence also suggests that the absence of work–family balance, typically defined in terms of elevated work–family conflict, may undermine individual health and

well-being (Frone, 2000; Frone, Russell, & Cooper, 1997; Grzywacz & Bass, 2003; Major, Klein, & Ehrhart, 2002), and organizational performance (Allen, Herst, Bruck, & Sutton, 2000; Kossek & Ozeki, 1998). Indeed, some suggest that the ability to balance work and family is one of the primary social challenges of our era (Halpern, 2005).

Work–family balance is at the core of issues central to human resource development (HRD). Indicators of balance have been associated with greater employee commitment, job satisfaction (Allen et al., 2000; Kossek & Ozeki, 1999), and organizational citizenship behavior (Bragger, Rodriguez-Srednicki, Kutcher, Indovino, & Rosner, 2005). The absence of balance, notably high levels of work–family conflict, has been linked to greater turnover intention (Allen et al., 2000; Kossek & Ozeki, 1999) and greater sickness absence (Jansen et al., 2006). In addition, work–family balance has been linked, albeit modestly, to employee performance (Allen et al., 2000; Kossek & Ozeki, 1999). This evidence indicates that, implicitly or explicitly, work–family balance is at the core of HRD's major functions and that it may be a powerful leverage point for promoting individual and organizational effectiveness. Indeed, a recent report by a consortium of Fortune 100 companies concluded that organizational strategies that help employees better balance their work and family lives are simply good business (Corporate Voices for Working Families, 2005).

Unfortunately, the ability to capitalize on work–family balance as a leverage point for HRD practice is impaired because theorizing and conceptualizations of the construct have not kept pace with interest. The "balance" metaphor is widely used but rarely defined in specific terms (Greenhaus & Allen, 2006). When scholars do define balance, the definition is rarely situated in theory. The first notable exception was Marks and MacDermid's (1996) handling of "role balance," which was offered as an alternative to the dominant view that individuals prioritize roles hierarchically for organizing and managing multiple responsibilities (Lobel, 1991; Thoits, 1995). Most recently, Greenhaus and Allen (2006) articulated a thoughtful analysis of the balance construct. In this article, we develop a conceptually based definition of work–family balance that parallels but narrows previous handlings of the concept. Following this development, we turn to practical issues surrounding our view of work–family balance: issues related to measurement as well as issues related to HRD research and practice. We conclude our article with directions for future research.

WORK–FAMILY BALANCE: BACKGROUND AND CONCEPTUALIZATION

Work–family balance is inconsistently defined despite widespread academic and applied interest. Historically, and most frequently, researchers view work–family balance as the absence of work–family conflict, or the frequency and intensity in which work interferes with family or family interferes with work. Greenhaus, Collins, and Shaw (2003), drawing on role balance theory (Marks & MacDermid, 1996) and previous nominal definitions (Clark, 2000; Kirchmeyer, 2000), defined work–family balance as "the extent to which individuals are equally engaged in and equally satisfied with work and family

roles" (p. 513). Voydanoff (2005) drew on person–environment fit theory and suggested that work–family balance is "a global assessment that work resources meet family demands, and family resources meet work demands such that participation is effective in both domains" (p. 825). Most recently, Greenhaus and Allen (2006) defined work–family balance as "the extent to which an individual's effectiveness and satisfaction in work and family roles are compatible with the individual's life priorities." Although helpful, some of these definitions do not adequately capture adults' commonsense representations of work–family balance. Role balance, as conceptualized by Marks and MacDermid (1996), was offered as an organizational strategy rather than as a characterization of an adult's work and family life per se. We see little evidence in the literature suggesting that people seek "equality" or even "near equality" in their work and family lives as suggested by Greenhaus et al. (2003). Indeed, role balance theory suggests that people seek full and meaningful experiences in their work and family lives (Marks, Huston, Johnson, & MacDermid, 2001; Marks & MacDermid, 1996). It is important to note that role balance theory makes no prescription for equality, in part because it is questionable whether work- and family-related activities have comparable worth and that they can be effectively monitored (S. M. MacDermid, personal communication, April 5, 2006; S. R. Marks, personal communication, April 6, 2006). There is also little empirical evidence suggesting that working adults think of balance as a transaction between work-related resources and family-related demands, or vice versa, as conceptualized by Voydanoff (2005).

Greenhaus and Allen's (2006) definition of work–family balance is compelling; however, it overemphasizes individual satisfaction in work and family. Satisfaction within and across life domains is important, but defining balance in terms of satisfaction is conceptually problematic. The primary problem is that defining balance in terms of satisfaction isolates individuals in their workand family-related activities from the organizations and families in which these activities are performed. The fundamental issue raised here is whether work–family balance is a psychological or social construct. By claiming that work–family balance is "inherently in the eye of the beholder," Greenhaus and Allen situate balance as a psychological construct. However, is work and family balanced if an individual is satisfied and feels "effective" in both domains but this satisfaction and appraisal of effectiveness is at the expense of another (e.g., a working wife who picks up the slack at home as her husband climbs the corporate ladder)? Decontextualized views of balance focused on introspective, and to a certain degree hedonistic, elements of daily work and family life such as satisfaction do not adequately capture the fundamental meaning of work–family balance.

Defining balance in terms of satisfaction also raises practical problems. Developing effective and sustainable interventions to enhance satisfaction within and across domains is challenging because it, like other concepts that have little observable meaning outside of the individual, is inherently retrospective and under constant reconstruction based on recent and accumulated experiences (Gergen, 1973; Spence, 1944). If work–family balance is, in fact, in the eye of the beholder, an extreme view would argue that there is little that can be done to create systematic strategies to help individual workers balance work and family, because the experience of work–family balance is inherently idiosyncratic. Even more concerning, is the potential for reducing work–family balance down to an individual-level problem. Viewing work–family balance as an individual-level problem borders on victim blaming because individuals shoulder the burden of the work–family challenge; yet the challenge itself is the consequence of demographic transitions in the workforce and the American family, and transitions in how work is performed (Bianchi, Casper, & King, 2005). Of course, work–family balance is likely shaped by both individual and contextual factors, thereby

necessitating a view of the construct that is not exclusively psychological. This is not to say that the psychological perspective should be abandoned; rather, alternative perspectives are needed, and we propose that a social perspective of work–family balance is valuable.

We define work–family balance as accomplishment of role-related expectations that are negotiated and shared between an individual and his or her role-related partners in the work and family domains. Several features of this definition warrant specific comment. First, our focus on accomplishing role-related activities across roles and life domains is consistent with role balance theory (Marks & MacDermid, 1996) and the argument that full engagement in both work and family is both viable and fulfilling. It is also consistent with emerging developmental theory, suggesting that successfully managing multiple responsibilities is a developmental task for contemporary adults (Lachman & Boone-James, 1997). Next, by focusing on accomplishment of role-related activities as opposed to satisfaction with life roles, work–family balance is viewed as a social rather than a psychological construct and it takes on meaning outside of the individual. Giving work–family balance meaning outside the individual has significant implications for validating measures and for designing studies to test and refine theories of work–family balance. Further, by uncoupling accomplishment of role-related expectations (what Greenhaus and Allen have referred to as "effectiveness") and satisfaction, researchers can build additional layers of theory around the balance construct. Researchers could, for example, elaborate the individual and contextual circumstances shaping how and for whom accomplishment of role-related expectations leads to satisfaction across the work and family domains. This type of layering is essential for developing rich theories of work and family (MacDermid, Roy, & Zvonkovic, 2005) and for informing the design and implementation of effective interventions within organizations. Finally, our definition focuses on accomplishing role-related expectations that are socially negotiated and shared. This focus is consistent with long-standing views that individuals both "take" and actively "make" roles (Kahn, Wolfe, Quinn, Snoek, & Rosenthal, 1964; Thomas & Biddle, 1966), but it is also consistent with the view that "work" and "family" are shorthand labels for a myriad of ongoing and spontaneous daily interactions that individuals have with other people (Darrah, 2005). Focusing on the inherently interactional aspects of daily work and family life is essential for accurately characterizing work–family balance.

IMPLICATIONS FOR HRD RESEARCH AND PRACTICE

Our conceptualization of work–family balance has several implications for HRD research and practice, some of which are reviewed next. We begin with measurement, because high-quality measures are essential to theory enriching as well as practical research. Measurement is equally important in practice because, if it is to become a leverage point for HRD managers, valid measures are needed to monitor the effectiveness of programs targeting balance.

Measurement

Documenting levels of work–family balance is a necessity for both researchers and practitioners, in part because "what gets measured gets done." Unfortunately, an instrument for assessing work–family balance, as it is conceptualized here has not been published. Developing and validating a measure of work–family balance is a critical element for advancing research in this arena, but it is not the focus of this article. Nonetheless, we feel compelled to point out some key factors that should be considered in developing a balance scale based on our definition. First, the items should emphasize accomplishment of work and family role-related expectations rather than satisfaction with work and family roles. Second, because we focus on work–family balance, items should focus on accomplishment of expectations in these domains only (vis-à-vis work–life balance). Further, to the extent possible, items should focus on general relationships that accompany a role (e.g., important others at home) rather than specific relationships (e.g., spouse) so that the instrument will have broad utility. Finally, items in the measure need to capture the extent to which individuals are accomplishing socially negotiated role-related expectations. An example item might be, "It is clear to me, based on feedback from coworkers and family members, that I am accomplishing both my work and family responsibilities."

Until such an instrument is developed and published, HRD professionals and practicing managers have two primary alternatives for assessing work–family balance in their organizations. The first alternative is the use of overall appraisals of work–family balance that have been used in previous studies, such as, "How successful do you feel at balancing your paid work and your family life?" (Keene & Quadagno, 2004). Although it focuses on individuals' role-related activities across life domains and is therefore useful for descriptive purposes, this approach to measuring work–family balance has several problems. The primary concern is whether a single item elicits an accurate summary of individuals' performance in complex life domains like work or family. Both "work" and "family" involve multiple roles and responsibilities thereby necessitating gross generalization on the part of individuals asked to summarize performance within and across domains. It is questionable how well individuals perform such complex cognitive tasks (MacDermid, 2005). Furthermore this and other items emphasize affective elements of work and family (e.g., how successful do you feel...) raising questions about the degree to which performance in work and family are accurately appraised. The validity of global, single-item approaches is further undermined by the fact that work- and family-related role configurations can vary substantially from person to person, and it is simply unknown if individuals use comparable notions of "success" and "balance" when responding to single-item questions.

A compelling second alternative is to measure components of work–family balance, namely, work–family enrichment and work–family conflict (Frone, 2003). Work–family conflict captures the degree to which the responsibilities of work are incompatible with family life or vice versa (Greenhaus & Beutell, 1985), whereas enrichment refers to the extent to which individuals' involvement in one domain benefits their participation in another life domain (Greenhaus & Powell, 2006). Frone (2003) argued that work–family balance results from high levels of work–family enrichment and low levels of work–family conflict, suggesting that work–family balance may be a "formative" rather than "reflective" latent construct (Edwards & Bagozzi, 2000). Likewise, Greenhaus and Allen's (2006) model also suggests that balance is a formative latent construct. Consistent with these views, rather than conceptualizing conflict and enrichment as observable consequences of work–family balance, we submit that they give meaning and form to individuals' evaluations of how well they are meeting shared and negotiated role-related responsibilities, thereby serving as useful indicators of work–family balance as it is conceptualized here.

This second approach, which we characterize as a "components approach" because it uses work–family conflict and work–family enrichment scales to measure work–family balance, offers HRD researchers and practitioners several advantages. First, validated measures of work–family conflict (Carlson, Kacmar, & Williams, 2000; Netemeyer, Boles, & McMurrian, 1996) and work–family enrichment (Carlson, Kacmar, Wayne, & Grzywacz, 2006) exist. These measures capture a variety of types of work–family conflict and enrichment, and they capture both directions of the linkage (i.e., work-to-family and family-to-work). Although criticisms have been leveled about typical

measures of work–family experiences (MacDermid, 2005), the existence of comprehensive measures helps ensure adequate coverage of the experiences that contribute to work–family balance and lessens the necessity of individuals to summarize abstract concepts. Next, in contrast to monolithic measures, a components approach enables greater precision and clarity in delineating antecedents of work–family balance (Edwards, 2001). It is highly unlikely that work–family conflict and work–family enrichment have identical antecedents (Frone, 2003; Grzywacz & Butler, 2005). Likewise, it is highly plausible that work–family conflict and work–family enrichment may have different consequences (Wayne, Musisca, & Fleeson, 2004), or that unique combinations of conflict and enrichment may be pivotal in understanding salient outcomes like employee health (Grzywacz & Bass, 2003). By studying the constituent elements, researchers can develop a comprehensive understanding of how to promote work–family balance and how to use it as a strategic tool for accomplishing desired organizational goals. Although some eschew the approach of measuring work–family balance via conflict and enrichment (Greenhaus & Allen, 2006), others argue that it is a viable and useful strategy (Tetrick & Buffardi, 2006). Until there is a well-established direct measure of the construct, we advocate that HRD researchers study work–family balance by measuring experiences of work–family conflict and work–family enrichment.

To illustrate the value of a components approach to measuring work–family balance, we analyzed data from the 1997 National Study of the Changing Workforce (Bond, Galinsky, & Swanberg, 1998). We examined a general measure of balance as well as the four components of balance (work-to-family conflict [WFC], family-to-work conflict [FWC], work-to-family enrichment [WFE], family-to-work enrichment [FWE]) in relation to three work-related outcomes (job satisfaction, attitude toward employer, and job stress) and three nonwork-related outcomes (family satisfaction, marital satisfaction, and overall stress). These results comparing the percentage of variance explained across the two methods are reported in Table 1. The components approach consistently explains more variance in work and nonwork outcomes than does the general measure of balance. For example, when predicting the dependent variable job stress, the single item measure of balance explained 18% of the variance. However, when the four components of balance were examined in relation to job stress, 45% of the variance was explained. In the case of each of the six dependent variables, the four components of balance explained more of the variance in the dependent variable than did the global balance measure alone.

Research

Our conceptualization of work–family balance and recommendations for measuring balance via a components approach has important implications for HRD research. One salient implication is the need for a definitive strategy for modeling the four components of balance (i.e., WFC, FWC, WFE, FWE). Based on our conceptualization, we submit that work–family balance meets the basic criteria for a direct formative latent construct (Edwards & Bagozzi, 2000). That is, work–family balance has low to moderate correlations with work–family conflict (−.5 and −.3 for WFC and FWC, respectively) and work–family enrichment (.4 and .3 for WFE and FWE, respectively; Butler, Grzywacz, Bass, & Linney, 2005), suggesting that work–family balance is distinct from conflict and enrichment. In addition, evidence suggests that work–family conflict and enrichment precede and contribute to appraisals of work–family balance (Butler et al., 2005), suggesting that a temporal association consistent with a formative latent construct is plausible. Although there are other analysis strategies, such as Edwards' (1995) polynomial regression approach (see Tetrick & Buffardi, 2006), we suggest that researchers begin by modeling work–family balance as a direct formative latent construct (Edwards & Bagozzi, 2000) because it is most consistent with the conceptual definition offered in this article.

Researchers will need to expand their repertoire of potential antecedents of work–family balance, particularly if they are using a components

TABLE 1 Explained Variance of Work and Family Outcomes Through Different Conceptualizations of Work–Family Balance

	Explained Variance	
Work-related outcomes	*General Measure of Balance*	*Four Components of Balance*
Job satisfaction	.04	.10
Attitude toward employer	.01	.04
Job stress	.18	.45
Family-related outcomes		
Family satisfaction	.08	.12
Marital satisfaction	.05	.07
Overall stress	.11	.23

NOTE: Estimates based on data from the 1997 National Study of the Changing Workforce (Bond, Galinsky, & Swanberg, 1998).

approach for measuring balance. Work–family research to date has identified a plethora of potential antecedents of work–family conflict (for recent reviews, see Eby, Casper, Lockwood, Bordeaux, & Brinley, 2005; Frone, 2003; Parasuraman & Greenhaus, 2002). Although this research identifies some of the "barriers" to work–family balance, it says little about the factors that enable work–family balance. Consistent with the enabling factors and barriers metaphors for work–family balance, evidence suggests that the negative and positive experiences that shape individuals' appraisals of balance (i.e., work-family conflict and work-family enrichment) have unique individual and contextual antecedents. Extraversion, for example, has been associated with greater work–family enrichment but was unassociated with work–family conflict (Grzywacz & Marks, 2000; Wayne et al., 2004), whereas neuroticism was more strongly associated with work–family conflict than indicators of work–family enrichment. Likewise, contextual variables at work and in the family have different relations with work–family conflict and enrichment. In the workplace, decision latitude was positively related to enrichment but not related to conflict (Grzywacz & Marks, 2000). On the other hand, pressures such as psychological demands and unscheduled extra work hours have been found to be strongly related to conflict and not related to enrichment (Grzywacz & Marks, 2000; Voydanoff, 2004). Collectively, this information suggests that researchers interested in identifying the antecedents of balance to inform HRD practices will need to consider individual and contextual antecedents that serve as barriers to work–family balance, as well as those that enable balance.

An implication of greater relevance to intervention researchers interested in documenting the value of work–family balance to HRD is the need to think multidimensionally in evaluating strategies for promoting work–family balance. Underlying this issue is the possibility that some antecedents may affect work–family balance in different yet competing ways. This possibility is illustrated by research suggesting that work–family conflict and work–family enrichment occasionally share antecedents that have similar rather than opposite effects. For example, Wayne et al. (2004) suggested that limiting work hours may benefit workers' level of work–family balance because fewer work hours was associated with less work–family conflict. However, fewer work hours was also associated with less work–family enrichment. Similarly, Grzywacz and Butler (2005) found that substantively complex jobs and those that demand a variety of skills may contribute to work–family enrichment (presumably because individuals are acquiring skills than can be applied outside the workplace), but they also may contribute to work–family conflict (presumably because substantively complex jobs are inherently more demanding). The results of these studies suggest that organizational interventions designed to help workers balance work and family, like curbing work hours or enriching jobs with greater complexity or task diversity, may not produce the desired effect. In essence, the intervention would have the potential of both enabling work–family balance (e.g., cutting back on work may help meet family-related expectations) and concurrently serving as a barrier to balance (e.g., it may be difficult to meet work-related expectations if hours are cut). Researchers need to consider the possible competing effects of different antecedents of balance and target those antecedents that have mutually reinforcing effects on work–family balance via multiple mechanisms (e.g., worker control; Grzywacz & Butler, 2005). If an intervention focuses on an antecedent that can exert competing effects on balance, then the researcher needs to be prepared with adequate methods to evaluate the strategy.

The implications outlined in this section hold regardless of whether researchers use a components or a direct approach to measuring balance. If researchers reject the components approach, they will need to overcome the absence of a conceptually based measure of work–family balance. So, although the nature of the measurement problem changes, the need for basic research as to how best configure a measurement model remains. If researchers favor a direct measurement approach of work–family balance, they will need to supplement their conceptual and empirical models of work–family balance with a broader array of antecedents: Existing literature can offer insight into the individual and contextual factors that undermine balance (via work–family conflict), but it offers little insight into those factors that help people effectively meet their daily work- and family-related responsibilities. Finally, intervention researchers in any domain and focused on any outcome need to consider the potential unanticipated consequences of their intervention and they need to determine if the probability and significance of these consequences is problematic (Stokols, Grzywacz, McMahan, & Phillips, 2003).

Practice

The view of work–family balance offered in this article has implications for HRD and management practitioners, many of which parallel the implications for researchers. If HRD embraces work–family balance as a leverage point for practice, professionals will need to make informed decisions about how they will monitor work–family balance in their organizations. General indicators are simple and useful for describing and documenting continuity and change in work–family balance. Unfortunately, as previously described, it is not clear how well general indicators effectively assess work–family balance. Moreover, to the extent that work–family balance is a multifaceted construct as we and others have argued (Frone, 2003; Greenhaus & Allen, 2006; Tetrick & Buffardi, 2006), it is difficult to interpret descriptions of, particularly changes in, work–family balance. If balance reflects the combination of several experiences, how are practitioners to interpret their data? If practitioners monitor components of balance, as we suggest, interpretation is clearer, but the primary disadvantage is the relative inability to summarize work–family balance among workers.

The conceptualization of balance in this article has important implications for practitioners interested in promoting balance as a means to achieving other valued outcomes like greater employee commitment and organizational citizenship behaviors. Our definition of balance guides practitioners' attention to potential targets for change within the organization. If work–family balance is shaped by socially negotiated role expectations, HRD practitioners should use their skills in managing organizational change to identify explicit and implicit expectations placed on workers that are unnecessary, or create new resources that help workers satisfy the expectations of their career. This is the basic framework outlined in the dual-agenda approach (Rapoport, Bailyn, Fletcher, & Pruitt, 2002). Rapoport et al. (2002) suggested that organizations frequently adhere to taken-for-granted policies and practices, such as mandatory early morning or late afternoon business meetings or a reactionary project management culture, that undermine organizational performance and interfere with workers' ability to balance work and family. Practitioners seeking to promote work–family balance should consider these types of work processes as high-priority targets for change.

Practitioners also need to be careful when selecting potential targets for promoting work–family balance. For example, as previously discussed, curbing work hours may not yield meaningful improvements in work–family balance, because gains to work–family balance resulting from (presumably) greater ability to satisfy family-related expectations may be attenuated by greater difficulty meeting work-related expectations. Practitioners therefore need to think systemically when identifying potential targets for improving work–family balance. If they select a target that has the potential for competing effects on work–family balance, like curbing hours, then the overall intervention needs to include secondary and tertiary elements (like reducing work load, staff expansion, etc.) to circumvent potential negative consequences of the intervention.

However, individuals also play a role in shaping their work–family balance because they participate (actively or passively) in the social negotiation of role-related expectations. This suggests that practitioners responsible for promoting work–family balance should devise multilevel interventions. Working at multiple levels within the organization is consistent with standard HRD practice as well as other organizational functions like health promotion/wellness (McLeroy, Bibeau, Steckler, & Glanz, 1988; Stokols, 1996), and they would likely be effective for promoting work–family balance. The basic approach involves creating coordinated activities at the individual and organizational level that are mutually supportive. Recognizing that worker control or authority is a strong candidate for promoting work–family balance (Grzywacz & Butler, 2005), an HRD-led multilevel intervention might include implementation of schedule flexibility, redesign of workflow procedures to accommodate flexible work arrangements, time management seminars, and structured protocols for remediation of inappropriate personal use of the flexible work arrangements. This coordinates both organization-level (i.e., implementation of schedule flexibility, workflow redesign) and individual-level elements (i.e., time management, personal-level remediation) that are focused on enabling workers to allocate their time effectively, thereby fostering greater levels of control and work–family balance. Practitioners are encouraged to explore and evaluate comparable multilevel strategies in their organizations.

The current conceptualization of work–family balance also has strategic implications for HRD and management practice. Most important, practitioners should be cautious in making claims about the virtues of what accomplishment of work- and family-related role responsibilities (i.e., work–family balance) will yield. Arguably, promoting work–family balance likely yields a variety of benefits for organizations (Corporate Voices for Working Families, 2005), yet it is not a panacea. The role of work–family balance in employee health provides a cogent example. There is good theoretical reason to believe that work–family balance may contribute to well-being (Marks & MacDermid, 1996; Thoits, 1983), or the subjective side of employee health (Keyes, 2002), but the evidence linking work–family balance to morbidity is less clear. Although studies have linked indicators of balance to psychiatric and physical morbidity (Frone, 2000; Frone et al., 1997; Grzywacz & Bass, 2003), they did not account for the reciprocal relationship between subjective well-being and objective morbidity, thereby confounding the interpretation of observed associations (Grzywacz & Keyes, 2005). Ultimately, the significance of work–family balance to well-being and morbidity is an empirical question; however, in the meantime, HRD and management professionals should not base the value of programs designed to promote work–family balance on health cost containment. Instead, base the value of work–family balance on enhancements to employee well-being and the added value it provides to organizations (Harter, Schmidt, & Keyes, 2002; Keyes & Grzywacz, 2005).

CONCLUSIONS AND SUMMARY

The goal of this article was to refine previous conceptualizations of work–family balance to provide a definition that could guide research as well as HRD and management practice. We define work–family balance as accomplishment of role-related expectations that are negotiated and shared between an individual and his or her role-related partners in the work and family domains. This definition focuses on accomplishing role-related responsibilities at work and in the family, it is theoretically based in role theory, and it emphasizes the inherently social nature of individuals' role-related responsibilities.

The definition of work–family balance proposed in this article overcomes key limitations of previous definitions. First, whereas previous definitions combined both accomplishment and satisfaction in work and family, our definition has a purer focus on accomplishment of role-related responsibilities. This refinement makes the construct clearer and easier to interpret, and it will contribute to richer theories of work and family. Next, the proposed definition moves the construct out of the "eye of the beholder" into the social domain. This feature of the definition has important implications for validating the construct and for identifying the organizational circumstances that contribute to work–family balance. Further, shifting work–family balance from a psychological to a social construct minimizes the potential of reducing work–family balance to an individual problem resulting from poor choices.

We maintain that HRD professionals and practicing managers should operationalize work–family balance using a components approach until a validated measure of the construct is created. The components approach helps ensure adequate coverage of possible universe of the experiences that contribute to work–family balance. Nevertheless, the final selection of a work–family balance measure should be shaped by the goal of the research being conducted. If, for example, the purpose of the research is to monitor overall levels of work–family balance within an organization, then a well-crafted global measure would likely be sufficient. On the other hand, if the goal is to determine how to improve work–life balance because it is impacting important organizational outcomes, then using the components approach would likely be best because it would provide more refined insight into the manifestation of work–family balance as well as potential unanticipated consequences of promoting work–family balance.

Work–family balance is an omnipresent factor in contemporary organizations and society. Unfortunately, theoretical and conceptual development of work–family balance has not kept pace with popular interest. In this article, we offer a refined, focused, and theoretically based definition of work–family balance. Substantial research needs to be done to fully develop a complete understanding of this important construct; yet, with a solid conceptualization in place, HRD professionals have a foundation upon which to begin creating strategies that contribute to organizational goals by helping workers achieve work–family balance.

REFERENCES

Allen, T. D., Herst, D. E., Bruck, C. S., & Sutton, M. (2000). Consequences associated with work-to-family conflict: A review and agenda for future research. *Journal of Occupational Health Psychology, 5,* 278–308.

Bianchi, S. M., Casper, L. M., & King, R. B. (2005). Complex connections: A multidisciplinary look at work, family, health, and well-being research. In S. M. Bianchi, L. M. Casper, & R. B. King (Eds.), *Work, family, health and well-being* (pp. 1–17). Mahwah, NJ: Lawrence Erlbaum Associates.

Bond, J. T., Galinsky, E., & Swanberg, J. E. (1998). *The National Study of the Changing Workforce.* New York: Families and Work Institute.

Bond, J. T., Thompson, C., Galinsky, E., & Prottas, D. (2002). *Highlights of the National Study of the Changing Workforce: Executive Summary.* Retrieved May 24, 2006, from http://www.familiesandwork.org/summary/nscw2002.pdf

Bragger, J. D., Rodriguez-Srednicki, O., Kutcher, E. J., Indovino, L., & Rosner, E. (2005). Work–family conflict, work–family culture, and organizational citizenship behavior among teachers. *Journal of Business and Psychology, 20,* 303–324.

Bureau of Labor Statistics. (2006). *Families with own children: Employment status of parents by age of youngest child and family type, 2004–05 annual averages* (Table 4). Retrieved May 24, 2006, from http://www.bls.gov.news.release/famee.t04.htm

Butler, A. B., Grzywacz, J. G., Bass, B. L., & Linney, K. D. (2005, November). *Predicting work–family balance from work–family conflict and facilitation among couples.* Poster presented at the 67th Annual Conference of the National Council on Family Relations. Phoenix, AZ.

Caminiti, S. (2005, September 19). Work-life: What happens when employees enjoy flexible work arrangements? They are happier and more productive (Supplement). *Fortune,* pp. S2–S7.

Carlson, D. S., Kacmar, K. M., Wayne, J. H., & Grzywacz, J. G. (2006). Measuring the positive side of the work–family interface: Development and validation of a work–family enrichment scale. *Journal of Vocational Behavior, 68,* 131–164.

Carlson, D. S., Kacmar, K. M., & Williams, L. J. (2000). Construction and validation of a multidimensional measure of work–family conflict. *Journal of Vocational Behavior, 56,* 249–276.

Chao, L. (2005, November 29). What GenXers need to be happy at work. *The Wall Street Journal,* p. B6.

Clark, S. C. (2000). Work/family border theory: A new theory of work/family balance. *Human Relations, 53,* 747–770.

Corporate Voices for Working Families. (2005). *Business impacts of flexibility: An imperative for expansion.* Boston: WFD Consulting.

Darrah, C. N. (2005). Anthropology and the workplace–workforce mismatch. In S. M. Bianchi, L. M. Casper, & R. B. King (Eds), *Work, family, health and well-being* (pp. 201–214). Mahwah, NJ: Lawrence Earlbaum Associates.

Dwyer, K. P. (2005, December 4). Still searching for equilibrium in the work-life balancing act. *New York Times,* section 10, pp. 1, 3.

Eby, L. T., Casper, W. J., Lockwood, A., Bordeaux, C., & Brinley, A. (2005). Work and family research in IO/OB: Content analysis and review of the literature (1980–2002). *Journal of Vocational Behavior, 66,* 127–197.

Edwards, J. R. (1995). Alternatives to difference scores as dependent variables in the study of congruence in organizational research. *Organizational Behavior and Human Decision Processes, 64,* 307–324.

Edwards, J. R. (2001). Multidimensional constructs in organizational behavior research: An integrative analytic framework. *Organizational Research Methods, 4,* 144–192.

Edwards, J. R., & Bagozzi, R. P. (2000). On the nature and direction of relationships between constructs and measures. *Psychological Methods, 5,* 155–174.

Frone, M. R. (2000). Work–family conflict and employee psychiatric disorders: The National Comorbidity Survey. *Journal of Applied Psychology, 85,* 888–895.

Frone, M. R. (2003). Work–family balance. In J. C. Quick & L. E. Tetrick (Eds.), *Handbook of occupational health psychology* (pp. 143–162). Washington, DC: American Psychological Association.

Frone, M. R., Russell, M., & Cooper, M. L. (1997). Relation of work–family conflict to health outcomes: A four-year longitudinal study of employed parents. *Journal of Occupational and Organizational Psychology, 70,* 325–335.

Gergen, K. J. (1973). Social psychology as history. *Journal of Personality and Social Psychology, 26,* 309–320.

Greenhaus, J. H., & Allen, T. D. (2006, March). *Work–family balance: Exploration of a concept.* Paper presented at the Families and Work Conference, Provo, UT.

Greenhaus, J. H., & Beutell, N. J. (1985). Sources of conflict between work and family roles. *Academy of Management Review, 10,* 76–88.

Greenhaus, J. H., Collins, K. M., & Shaw, J. D. (2003). The relation between work–family balance and quality of life. *Journal of Vocational Behavior, 63,* 510–531.

Greenhaus, J. H., & Powell, G. N. (2006). When work and family are allies: A theory of work–family enrichment. *Academy of Management Review, 31,* 72–92.

Grzywacz, J. G., & Bass, B. L. (2003). Work, family, and mental health: Testing different models of work–family fit. *Journal of Marriage and Family, 65,* 248–261.

Grzywacz, J. G., & Butler, A. B. (2005). The impact of job characteristics on work-to-family facilitation: Testing a theory and distinguishing a construct. *Journal of Occupational Health Psychology, 10,* 97–109.

Grzywacz, J. G., & Keyes, C. L. M. (2005, November). *Work–family balance and health: Broadening the conceptualization of health.* Paper presented at the 67th Annual Conference of the National Council on Family Relations. Phoenix, AZ.

Grzywacz, J. G., & Marks, N. F. (2000). Reconceptualizing the work–family interface: An ecological perspective on the correlates of positive and negative spillover between work and family. *Journal of Occupational Health Psychology, 5,* 111–126.

Halpern, D. F. (2005). Psychology at the intersection of work and family: Recommendations for employers, working families, and policymakers. *American Psychologist, 60,* 397–409.

Harter, J. K., Schmidt, F. L., & Keyes, C. L. M. (2002). Well-being in the workplace and its relationship to business outcomes: A review of the gallup studies. In C. L. M. Keyes & J. Haidt (Eds.), *Flourishing: Positive psychology and the life well-lived* (pp. 205–224). Washington, DC: American Psychological Association.

Jansen, N. W., H., Kant, I. J., van Amelsvoort, L. G. P. M., Kristensen, T. S., Swaen, G. M. H., & Nijhuis, F. J. N. (2006). Work–family conflict as a risk factor for sickness absence. *Journal of Occupational and Environmental Medicine, 63,* 488–494.

Kahn, R. L., Wolfe, D. M., Quinn, R. P., Snoek, J. D., & Rosenthal, R. A. (1964). *Organizational stress: Studies in role conflict and ambiguity.* New York: Wiley.

Keene, J. R., & Quadagno, J. (2004). Predictors of perceived work–family balance: Gender difference or gender similarity. *Sociological Perspectives, 47,* 1–23.

Keyes, C. L., & Grzywacz, J. G. (2005). Health as a complete state: The added value in work performance and health-care costs. *Journal of Occupational and Environmental Medicine, 47,* 523–532.

Keyes, C. L. (2002). The mental health continuum: From languishing to flourishing in life. *Journal of Health and Social Behavior, 43,* 207–222.

Kirchmeyer, C. (2000). Work-life initiatives: Greed or benevolence regarding workers' time? In C. L. Cooper & D. M. Rousseau (Eds.), *Trends in organizational behavior* (Vol. 7, pp. 79–93). Chichester, UK: Wiley.

Kossek, E. E., & Ozeki, C. (1998). Work–family conflict, policies, and the job-life satisfaction relationship: A review and directions for organizational behavior-human resources research. *Journal of Applied Psychology, 83,* 139–149.

Kossek, E. E., & Ozeki, C. (1999). Bridging the work–family policy and productivity gap: A literature review. *Community Work & Family, 2,* 139–149.

Lachman, M. E., & Boone-James, J. (1997). Charting the course of midlife development: An overview. In M. E. Lachman & J. Boone-James (Eds.), *Multiple paths of midlife development* (pp. 1–20). Chicago: The University of Chicago Press.

Lobel, S. A. (1991). Allocation of investment in work and family roles: Alternative theories and implications for research. *Academy of Management Review, 16,* 507–521.

MacDermid, S. M. (2005). (Re)Considering conflict between work and family. In E. E. Kossek & S. Lambert (Eds.), *Work and family integration in organizations: New directions for theory and practice* (pp. 19–40). Mahwah, NJ: Lawrence Erlbaum Associates.

MacDermid, S. M., Roy, K., & Zvonkovic, A. (2005). Don't stop at the borders: Dynamic and contextual approaches to theorizing about work and family. In V. L. Bengtson, A. C. Acock, K. R. Allen, P. Dilworth-Anderson, & D. M. Klein (Eds.), *Sourcebook on family theory and research methods* (pp. 493–516). Thousand Oaks, CA : Sage.

Major, V. S., Klein, K. J., & Ehrhart, M. G. (2002). Work time, work interference with family, and psychological distress. *Journal of Applied Psychology, 87,* 427–436.

Marks, S. R., Huston, T. L., Johnson, E. M., & MacDermid, S. M. (2001). Role balance among White married couples. *Journal of Marriage and Family, 63,* 1083–1098.

Marks, S. R., & MacDermid, S. M. (1996). Multiple roles and the self: A theory of role balance. *Journal of Marriage and the Family, 58,* 417–432.

McLeroy, K. R., Bibeau, D., Steckler, A., & Glanz, K. (1988). An ecological perspective on health promotion programs. *Health Education Quarterly, 15,* 351–377.

Netemeyer, R. G., Boles, J. S., & McMurrian, R. (1996). Development and validation of work–family conflict scales and family–work conflict scales. *Journal of Applied Psychology, 81,* 400–410.

Parasuraman, S., & Greenhaus, J. H. (2002). Toward reducing some critical gaps in work–family research. *Human Resource Management Review, 12,* 299–312.

Rapoport, R., Bailyn, L., Fletcher, J. K., & Pruitt, B. H. (2002). *Beyond work–family balance: Advancing gender equity and workplace performance.* San Francisco, CA: Jossey-Bass.

Spence, K. W. (1944). The nature of theory construction in contemporary psychology. *Psychological Review, 51,* 47–68.

Stokols, D. (1996). Translating social ecological theory into guidelines for community health promotion. *American Journal of Health Promotion, 10,* 282–298.

Stokols, D., Grzywacz, J. G., McMahan, S., & Phillips, K. (2003). Increasing the health promotive capacity of human environments. *American Journal of Health Promotion, 18,* 4–13.

Tetrick, L. E., & Buffardi, L. C. (2006). Measurement issues in research on the work–home interface. In F. Jones, R. J. Burke, & M. Westman (Eds.), *Work-life balance: A psychological perspective* (pp. 90–114). Hove, UK: Psychology Press.

Thoits, P. A. (1983). Multiple identities and psychological well-being: A reformulation and test of the social isolation hypothesis. *American Sociological Review, 48,* 174–187.

Thoits, P. A. (1995). Identity-relevant events and psychological symptoms: A cautionary tale. *Journal of Health and Social Behavior, 36,* 72–82.

Thomas, E. J., & Biddle, B. J. (1966). Basic concepts for classifying the phenomena of role. In B. J. Biddle & E. J. Thomas (Eds.), *Role theory: Concepts and research* (pp. 23–63). New York: Wiley.

Voydanoff, P. (2005). Toward a conceptualization of perceived work–family fit and balance: A demands and resources approach. *Journal of Marriage and Family, 67,* 822–836.

Wayne, J. H., Musisca, N., & Fleeson, W. (2004). Considering the role of personality in the work–family experience: Relationships of the big five to work–family conflict and facilitation. *Journal of Vocational Behavior, 64,* 108–130.

THE VIOLENCE OF ADOLESCENT LIFE

Experiencing and Managing Everyday Threats (2004)

Katherine Irwin

By the mid-1990s, the grim statistics regarding adolescent violence gained national attention. At the same time that the United States witnessed relatively stable crime rates, the juvenile arrest rates for violent offenses exploded between the early 1980s and mid-1990s, leading some to call this era the "epidemic of youth violence" (Cook & Laub, 1998).

Among the more shocking statistics were the tripling of homicide-victimization rates for Black youths between the ages of 13 and 17 years (Cook & Laub, 1998), an approximately 70% increase in youth arrest rates for violent offenses, and a nearly 300% growth in youth homicide arrest rates from 1983 to 1994 (Snyder & Sickmund, 1999). Although some researchers painted a stark picture of the early 2000s should these rates have continued (see Snyder, Sickmund, & Poe-Yamagata, 1996), arrest statistics revealed a significant waning in violence rates by 1999 (see Blumstein & Wallman, 2000). Thus, the dramatic increase in youth violence looked more like a momentary escalation than the establishment of a new, more violent type of adolescence in America.

This article examines the violence epidemic from the perspective of youths living in five different Denver, Colorado, neighborhoods from 1994 to 1996. During a qualitative study of 43 youths, the statistics regarding the violence epidemic seemed to emerge as a palpable threat as the majority of youths interviewed expressed concerns about and attempted to manage pervasive violence. More interesting, although concerns about violence were common, adolescents' accounts suggested that individuals had different experiences with violence. Corresponding with differences in violent experiences, youths also used different management strategies, which, in some cases, potentially increased the violence problem for themselves and others. As an exploration of inner-city youths' experiences with violence during the 2 years preceding the peak in the violence epidemic, this article attempts to bridge the gap between the statistics and theories regarding youth violence, and the reality of violence for a range of youths. In fact, as an examination of youths' everyday experiences with and attempts to manage violence, this article offers an interactional perspective of youth violence that builds on and expands some of the dominant theories used to explain youth violence in the 1990s and early 2000s.

Two perspectives of the violence epidemic prevailed in the late 1990s and early 2000s, including the illicit economy explanation (Blumstein, 1995; Blumstein & Cork, 1996; Blumstein & Wallman, 2000) and street culture explanations (Anderson, 1999; Bourgois, 1995, 1996). The illicit economy perspective suggests that the introduction of crack markets in inner cities encouraged a dramatic increase in youth homicide rates in many urban centers in the 1980s and early 1990s. As the escalating juvenile drug arrest rates from 1985 to 1992 indicate (Blumstein, 1995; Blumstein & Cork, 1996), juveniles served as "front-line" drug dealers in these new crack markets. To regulate this unstable industry, young drug dealers increasingly used guns to resolve disputes and protect themselves. The deadly use of guns, according to Blumstein (1995), was diffused from young drug dealers to their non-drug-dealing friends rather quickly because juveniles are "tightly networked with other young people in their neighborhoods" and with whom they "attend the same schools or . . . walk the same streets" (p. 30). Thus, we see that gun-related violence, and concomitant increase in gun-related homicides, began within the drug trade and was diffused to other youths living in the same neighborhoods or attending the same schools (see also, Blumstein & Cork, 1996).

The street culture perspective departs from the illicit economic explanation provided by Blumstein by locating violence within poor, inner-city, neighborhood cultures (rather than within underground economies). Several structural conditions (joblessness, rampant drug sales and use, lack of public services, global economic shifts, and racism) plagued poor inner-city neighborhoods and denied individuals, usually men of color, legitimate means to achieve positive identities. As particular populations became more estranged from legitimate resources—as some have argued was the case in the 1980s and early 1990s (Wilson, 1996)—men were caught in a bind. They were culturally expected to take on traditional masculine roles but had no resources to adopt legitimate male identities (Anderson, 1999; Bourgois, 1995). The solution came by creating and participating in an alternative and violent street culture—a system of values and norms that Anderson (1999) called "the code of the streets." The street culture offered men the chance to establish dominance, power, respect, and status through the use or threat of violence (see Decker & VanWinkle, 1996) against other men and often against women in the form of partner abuse and rape (Bourgois, 1996).

These analyses paint a particular image of the context of violence. By focusing almost exclusively on poor neighborhoods that are (for one reason or another) prone to drug use, drug sales, and oppositional street cultures, these perspectives suggest that poor or "disadvantaged communities" play an important role in the violence epidemic— perhaps an even more important role than resource-rich communities. Within the illicit economy perspective, we see that neighborhoods have two functions in the youth violence epidemic. First, poor neighborhoods are places where crack markets are likely to flourish. Second, neighborhoods are locations where young drug dealers "diffuse" such violent norms as gun use.

What is missing in these analyses are explanations of the experiences of juveniles across a range of neighborhoods and contexts. Working with Blumstein's diffusion hypothesis (Blumstein, 1995; Blumstein & Cork, 1996), youths interact within tightly woven networks. As Warr (2002) noted, adolescent peer groups comprise moral universes that are created through interaction in multiple locations, such as schools, parks, recreation centers, and popular "hangouts." Little is known, however, about the role of these contexts and violence. Therefore, explanations of youth violence have focused rather exclusively on disadvantaged communities and ignored the ways that violent norms can become diffused across multiple neighborhoods and social contexts.

This article fills this gap in our understanding of juvenile violence by examining the everyday experiences of juveniles living in neighborhoods ranging in disadvantage, violent crime, and poverty rates. The youths in the current study not only lived in different neighborhoods but also attended different schools, belonged to different peer groups, confronted different violent "risk factors" (see Hawkins et al., 1998; Lipsey & Derzon, 1998), and had different violent experiences. By examining the dimensions of youths' experiences and attempts to cope with the threat of violence, this article highlights the ways that youths interact within and across different contexts. It demonstrates how Denver adolescents' social networks and contexts predict their everyday experiences of violence. In addition, the current study closely examines the ways that proviolence norms can become diffused across multiple contexts and, thus, add more detail to the image of youth violence provided by the illicit market and street culture perspectives.

To examine how adolescents experienced and managed violence in their everyday lives, this article first discusses how the current study was designed, adolescents were selected, and violence was measured. Next, a typology is employed to describe the different dimensions of teens' experiences with, fears of, and attempts to manage violence. Because not all teens in the current study experienced violence similarly, three groups are identified: a high-risk group, whose members confronted violence regularly; a moderate-risk group, whose members confronted violence occasionally; and a low-risk group, whose members never reported experiencing violence. In addition to noting the differences among these groups in terms of their direct experiences with violence, this article outlines the types of violence prevention strategies used by adolescents. The discussion of this article examines how these different experiences with and attempts to manage violence may theoretically increase opportunities for violence. Specifically, it is argued that the threat of violence was diffused across multiple contexts and encouraged protective interaction patterns among youths.

Building on the illicit economy and street culture perspectives, a hypothesis is offered that these protective interaction patterns not only place some individuals at greater risk for violence but also help sustain violence rates. The article concludes by outlining a new agenda for violence research and prevention that targets exclusionary interaction patterns leaving some youths with very few choices but to become violent.

METHOD

Study Design and Neighborhood Selection

These data presented here are derived from a 2-year qualitative study of adolescents and parents living in five Denver neighborhoods. From 1994 to 1996, a team of University of Colorado researchers conducted face-to-face, in-depth interviews with 43 adolescents (ages 10 to 20 years) and 42 parents to assess individuals' perceptions regarding the role of neighborhood, family, peers, and school in adolescent development. The original design of the current study was to examine the way that neighborhood contexts influenced adolescents' transition into adulthood.[1]

At the onset, the current study was designed to focus on the experiences of families in different types of neighborhoods. The five neighborhoods in the current study ranged in disadvantage measures—measures used to indicate the ability of neighborhoods to control criminal, delinquent, and problem behavior (Bursik & Grasmick, 1993; Sampson, 1985;

Simcha-Fagan & Schwartz, 1986). Theoretically, neighborhoods with greater cohesion would have lower crime, high-school dropout, teen pregnancy, drug use, and violence rates and, thus, would present fewer contextual challenges to adolescent development. Components of the disadvantage measures were compiled from the 1990 census and included poverty (percentage of neighborhood families living in poverty), mobility (percentage of neighborhood families living in a different location in 1985), household structure (percentage of single-parent households), and racial mix. These measures were combined into a variable called neighborhood disadvantage, in which a high disadvantage score indicated that the neighborhood had high poverty, resident turnover, single-parent household, and racial/ethnic heterogeneity rates. After this statistic was compiled for several neighborhoods in Denver, a collection of high-, medium-, and low-disadvantage neighborhoods were selected to be included in the current study.

Two neighborhoods in the current study, South Creston and Westside, represented advantaged neighborhoods (low resident turnover, single-parent household, poverty, and heterogeneity rates).[2] These neighborhoods were predominantly White, middle-class communities in which residents shared a common sense of community pride. According to the neighborhood effects literature, such characteristics predict that neighbors will be able to exert informal social control over the neighborhood that, in turn, reduces the delinquency rates among neighborhood adolescents. Northside and Martin Park were the most disadvantaged neighborhoods in the current study (high resident turnover, single-parent

---

[1]This qualitative study is a smaller part of the MacArthur Research Program on Successful Adolescent Development in which a collection of urban neighborhoods are quantitatively and qualitatively assessed to determine the role of neighborhood in adolescent development (see Elliott et al., 1996). Although a team of researchers collected this data, the sole author analyzed and wrote up the findings. Thus, the Methods section discusses the efforts of the research team, while the remainder of the article discusses the analysis and hypotheses of the sole author.

[2]To preserve the confidentiality of study participants, the names of people, neighborhoods, streets, parks, and businesses are pseudonyms.

household, poverty, and heterogeneity rates). Northside was a middle-class neighborhood containing a densely populated, racially diverse, and low-income housing development called Allenspark. During the current study, it became clear that Allenspark represented a highly disadvantaged neighborhood within a larger advantaged to moderately advantaged neighborhood. One neighborhood, Parkview, represented a moderately disadvantaged neighborhood and had medium poverty, mobility, and single-parent household rates. Parkview was, however, racially and ethnically heterogeneous.

Interviews

To recruit interviewees, researchers contacted neighborhood boards, attended neighborhood meetings, and went door-to-door to describe the research and inquire whether parents or adolescents were interested in participating in the current study. Researchers also employed snowball sampling techniques (Biernacki & Waldorf, 1981) by asking participants to refer other neighborhood youths and parents to the current study. Interviews were tape-recorded and conducted in participants' homes or in local coffee shops and restaurants and lasted anywhere from 1 to 2 hr. During the interviews, researchers asked adolescents and parents to describe how neighborhoods, schools, families, and peer groups can help or get in the way of adolescents' "chances for success" (i.e., chances for successful transition into adulthood). In addition, researchers also used open-ended interview guides that directed interviewers through a list of subjects to discuss with interviewees and included such topics as definitions of and experiences within neighborhoods, school experiences, family contexts and parenting practices, and adolescents' career and family aspirations.

Analysis

Once tape-recorded interviews were transcribed, researchers coded the interviews for common themes. During the coding of initial interviews, researchers noted that violence was mentioned during many adolescent interviews, even though the original design of the current study was not to investigate neighborhood violence. Because the topic emerged early in the current study, violence was added to the list of codes and probed for during later interviews. This emergent analysis method closely resembled the constant comparative analysis techniques articulated by Glaser and Strauss (1967).

The groups discussed in this article (high, medium, and low risk for violence) reflect adolescents' reports regarding their violent experiences. Individuals described being victims and perpetrators of violence. In addition, a number of youths in the current study described witnessing violence. Thus, the term *violent experiences* is used to represent perpetration, victimization, as well as witnessing violence. Because parents were often unaware of their children's exposure to violence, the 42 parent interviews were analyzed to provide more information about the adolescents' family and neighborhood contexts.[3]

---

[3]Because the original design of the research was not to investigate violence in the lives of Denver adolescents, this study confronts some limitations. First, the types of violence mentioned by adolescents are limited. Researchers never asked about sexual, family, or dating violence, and given their personal nature, these topics were unlikely to be mentioned by interviewees. Thus, this study is limited to analyzing the types of violence that adolescents were most willing to describe. Second, because questions about violent experiences were not asked during every interview, violence might be under reported. In fact, if individuals did not mention violence during their interviews, researchers occasionally failed to bring it up. The timing of the interviews presents another study limitation. Conducted soon after the summer dubbed by the media as the "summer of violence," individuals' concerns tended to reflect the media's reports of gang shootings, deadly fights with weapons, and to a lesser extent, kidnappings. Had the interviews been conducted after the 1999 Columbine High School shootings, the types of violence mentioned during interviews might have differed dramatically.

EXPERIENCING VIOLENCE

The most common forms of violence that individuals mentioned were fistfights, fights or threats with weapons (guns, knives, or bats), and drive-by shootings. Analysis of the adolescent interviews revealed that most youths in the current study feared these sorts of conflicts. Despite this pervasive fear, adolescents had vastly different violent experiences. Some individuals worried about local news stories of violence (see Barzagan, 1994; Chiricos, Eschholz, & Gertz, 1997; Chiricos, Padgett, & Gertz, 2000; O'Keefe & Reid-Nash, 1987) and secondhand stories of victimization (see Lavrakas, 1982) but reported facing very little violence in their own lives. Other adolescents described experiencing violence regularly and worried that they, similar to their friends and siblings, might be hit, shot, or stabbed while walking in their neighborhoods or spending time with friends at local hangouts.

To capture the range of these adolescents' experiences, the current study explored the accounts of individuals in three different groups: high, medium, and low risk. The high-risk group comprised adolescents who noted experiencing violence regularly (an average of twice a month), and the moderate-risk group included youths who reported experiencing violence occasionally (a few times a year). The low-risk group was made up of individuals who did not mention experiencing violence.

High-Risk Group

Approximately one fourth of the adolescents interviewed ($n = 11$) reported confronting violence regularly. While going to school, walking in their neighborhoods, and hanging out with friends, they expected to confront violence. Their expectations often came to brutal fruition, forcing them to negotiate frequent conflicts. Benny, a 14-year-old Latino living in Allenspark, illustrates the experiences within this group.

Benny's family moved into Allenspark 2 years before the interview. According to Benny, the move was bittersweet. Benny and his older brother were initially happy to live in a neighborhood that housed a collection of teens. In fact, the two boys quickly found themselves in the center of a large group of friends who attended the same school. Benny soon grew leery of his new lifestyle. He complained that there was much more violence among youths in his new neighborhood and, although he did not mind the fistfights occurring in Allenspark (usually fights between Latino and Vietnamese American youths), he feared occasions when outsiders entered the neighborhood carrying weapons. He described this type of violence:

> The kids are the worst. There's gangs, like the NSMs [North Side Mafia] and the Untouchables and stuff. The westsiders [teens from the west side of Denver] will come over here and they'd start shooting. They just start shooting at each other. And we have to hear it all the time—all the gunshots and everything. . . . One week it'll just be crazy and the next week it'll be calm. Sometimes there'll be good times where everybody just has a good time without anything happening. But then there's other times. It's mostly people that come from out of Allenspark that start the trouble. When they start shooting you have to run.

Such incidents as shootings and fights with weapons, according to Benny, were rare. The everyday kinds of violence, such as fistfights with peers in school or the neighborhood, tended to be less extreme. Benny, like most individuals in this group, described fistfights as unavoidable, and in fact, some teens boasted that fighting was an important part of maintaining status. For example, Benny explained, "There's a lot of Vietnamese that live here. And then they'll start talking stuff to everybody. They'll start talking stuff. You have to fight 'em. But after you knock a couple of them out, then they leave you alone."

Benny's story illustrates the experiences of individuals living in high-violence neighborhoods. Some adolescents who lived in more advantaged, less-violent neighborhoods also reported experiencing violence regularly. Many of these youths described their neighborhoods as quiet, peaceful areas of the city. They also noted that they did not spend much time in their own community. Instead, they usually hung out with friends in public parks and parking lots of stores and restaurants. It was in these venues that they were most likely to experience violence.

Hector, a 16-year-old Latino living in Parkview, reported experiencing very little violence in his neighborhood, however he often confronted violence while spending time with school friends. He described how fights were likely to start:

> Right there by Fatso's [a local fast-food restaurant] that's where, oh, I can't even explain how many fights happen there. I've gotten in fights at those places, different places. Well, I'm not the kind that just fights over a word. But, it's that they keep on saying stuff, and I'll tell 'em "Shut up," and whatever. But, it's like I won't up there and hit them. Once they hit me, THAT's when I'll fight.

Hector noted that these fights often included weapons. He explained, "When we start fighting, then his friends want to jump in, then it turns into a battle. That's when they start whipping out bats and knives and all that." Although not afraid of knives and bats, Hector expressed concern about guns. Not only had he been grazed by a stray bullet on one occasion but also he witnessed a fatal shooting a year before the interview. He described the event:

> We were just standing against the wall and some guys, they just drove up and shot some dude. I was right there on his side. It happened over there by High Park. There's like this park and there's this wall. We were just kicking it right there on that wall. And all you heard is just a loud bang and the guy hit the wall and came back forward.

While boasting that he would not avoid bats or knives, Hector claimed that he would run if a gun

were brandished, even if it meant leaving a friend to fight alone. He explained that "well, it's better if one goes down than both of us."

As Benny's and Hector's narratives suggest, teens in this group were surrounded by violence. They were usually enmeshed in a group of peers who engaged in and were targets of regular fistfights. Occasionally, they experienced more serious conflicts, such as drive-by shootings or fights with weapons. Some teens were introduced to these violent social networks in their neighborhoods. Other individuals who lived in peaceful communities, such as Hector, were introduced to violence while hanging out with school friends.

Moderate-Risk Teens

One third ($n = 15$) of the adolescents in the current study reported confronting violence a few times a year. Similar to high-risk youths, individuals in the moderate-risk group experienced fistfights as well as fights with weapons. Some adolescents in this group lived in peaceful communities but faced numerous conflicts at school. Other youths told us that they liked the quiet atmosphere at school but worried about being hassled, threatened, or challenged to fight while walking in their neighborhoods.

Eduardo, a 16-year-old Latino, provides an example of individuals in this group. Eduardo lived in a less densely populated section of Northside located several blocks from the Allenspark apartment complex. In the following, Eduardo compared his section of Northside to Allenspark:

> Well this part of the neighborhood here, it's pretty decent—it's a nice area to grow up in. The houses are really nice. In this part of the town, there's not really too much violence, whereas you get closer to Allen Lane and down in that area, that's where you kind of run into some problems. But here, in this area, it's more calm, and kind of relaxed, and not too much violence goes on around here. I think maybe just living in that part of town would cause a little more fear

in a person. There's always the possibility of getting in a fight because you don't know if some people are crazy. You can get hurt whether it be in a fight or whether somebody be drunk and slam into you. I know a lot of people who that has happened to, and I just don't want that to happen to me.

Although living in a peaceful section of Northside, Eduardo attended the same school as Benny and other Allenspark teens. At school, Eduardo befriended several teens who fought regularly. After school, Eduardo participated in youth group activities organized through his parents' church or played basketball with his next-door neighbor. When spending time with his neighbor or members of his church group, Eduardo rarely confronted violence. When hanging out with his school friends, he occasionally witnessed fistfights.

Other youths in the moderate-risk group described their neighborhoods as places riddled with violence. Phan, a 16-year-old Vietnamese American living a few apartments away from Benny, corroborated accounts of violence in Allenspark, especially between Asian and Latino teens. Despite his efforts to avoid teens who fought regularly, he was occasionally targeted. He described his first fight:

I sit there with my friend. I look at [this person from the neighborhood] and I think he's drunk or something. And he go by me and he saw his brother over there and [his brother] just tell him to hit me. After that, his brother came by and he knock me down. This is my first time fighting. I never fight. When he knocked me down, they say something to me and let me go.

After this incident, Phan spent as little time as possible in Allenspark. This was not a hardship for Phan or his best friend, who lived nearby. They walked to and from school, attended classes, and met for lunch to study together every day. In the evening, after finishing their homework and household chores, they played basketball at a local recreation center. A recreation coordinator supervised the activities in the center and strictly forbade fighting. This safe routine was occasionally disrupted, however, when they or their friends were targeted and threatened in the neighborhood.

As these narratives illustrate, the teens in the moderate-risk group managed to dodge regular violent confrontations one way or another. For some youths, such as Phan, sidestepping neighborhood antagonisms required constant vigilance and careful orchestration. These data also demonstrate that the neighborhood was not the only force introducing violence to adolescents' lives. Teens such as Eduardo, who reported living in tranquil communities, should—according to common wisdom—have been able to avoid violence. Eduardo, who attended school with a number of violent teens, illustrated how school and peer factors can overcome the advantages of growing up in a peaceful community.

Low-Risk Group

Approximately 40% (*n* = 17) of the adolescent sample reported experiencing no violence. The vast majority of these individuals lived in South Creston and Westside, the two advantaged communities in the current study. Despite their lack of experience with violence, most individuals worried about gangs, weapons, and kidnappings. In many cases, their fears stemmed from a few highly publicized, yet isolated, events near their neighborhoods and schools.

Cory, a 12-year-old White South Creston resident, exemplifies the experiences of many individuals in this group. Although describing his neighborhood and school as "safe" places, he had heard stories about dangerous schoolmates and neighbors that worried him. He described the source of his school concerns by saying "There's one kid that used to go to our school who was in a gang. He was expelled for bringing a gun to school or something, a weapon—some sort of weapon. It was last year. It's like the first time it's ever happened at our school." Later in the interview, Cory noted that he feared students wearing gang colors. When we asked Cory what he would say to individuals moving into South Creston, he touched on his neighborhood anxieties:

> The kids around the neighborhood are nice. I'd just tell them to look out for the bad people. I'd just tell them how nice the neighborhood is and that they made a good decision to move into the house. There's a lot of things to do. It's fun to live here. Well, I don't feel comfortable in the dark. Some people have been kidnapped, and I don't want to be either.

Although never directly experiencing violence, Cory acknowledged that his neighborhood and school were not immune to weapons, gangs, and kidnappings. Regarding school violence, most members of the low-risk group were similar to Cory. They could recount occasions when fights occurred or weapons were brought to school. Individuals' knowledge of these events, however, was gleaned from secondhand stories. Evan, a 17-year-old White teen living in Westside, described why he was unlikely to witness school violence:

> All my classes since my freshman year have been accelerated classes. So in the accelerated classes, it is not the type of kids that would be carrying weapons. So you don't really see or talk to those type of kids. I know that a kid—a gun dropped out of his pocket in some class. You just hear about stuff like that.

Another source of information, and consequently worries, about violence for members of this group was the media. In 1993, 1 year before the current study, Denver experienced "the summer of violence," which was, according to local news reporters, a wave of gang and youth violence that swept through the city. Some of the publicized incidents occurred in North Creston, a predominantly African American, low-income neighborhood abutting South Creston. Stories about gang-related shootings and kidnappings received sensational attention and became part of a common lore about neighborhood violence.

Sophia, a White 16-year-old living in South Creston, described the coverage of one incident: "So a drug dealer was killed there. The shooting went on like way out in North Creston, and there's a lot of stuff in the newspaper about how awful Creston is and everything, but everything happened down past Division Street, which is technically not our neighborhood."

Although most South Creston residents interviewed noted that the violence occurred outside of their community, most individuals felt that these incidents encroached on their sense of safety.

Cory's and Evan's narratives highlight some of the reasons that adolescents were protected from violence. Low-risk individuals lived in peaceful neighborhoods segregated from more violent areas of the city. These youths were also separated from violence in school through a sort of "tracking" process (Kelly, 1974; Oakes, 1985) whereby delinquent or at-risk students tend to be enrolled in the less advanced and noncollege track classes. This suggests that although low-risk youths often attended the same schools as teens from more dangerous areas of the city, they were unlikely to interact with violent youths in their classes.

MANAGING VIOLENCE

Although juveniles in the current study had different experiences with violence, most worried about and attempted to manage violence. Adolescents' violence prevention strategies differed. For example, members of the high-risk group were not necessarily attempting to avoid violence. As Benny and Hector explained, the willingness and ability to fight were considered necessary tools for maintaining respect. Fights with guns, however, were problematic and became the focus of their violence prevention strategies. Teens in the moderate risk category, in contrast, usually avoided fisticuffs as well as fights with weapons. Low-risk youths held more vague and abstract concerns and were not necessarily focused on one type of violence over another. Therefore, kidnappers, gun-toting schoolmates, and strangers in the neighborhood garnered similar responses from members of this group.

In general, individuals described three types of management strategies: turning to friends, avoiding places, and avoiding people. Although these strategies are described as being distinct, individuals combined different approaches at different times in their everyday lives. In addition, individuals in the varying risk groups relied on and employed these strategies in different ways.

Turning to Friends

Most individuals in the moderate and high-risk groups turned to friends to manage violence. In fact, no adolescent in the low-risk group discussed friends as a source of violence prevention. For individuals in the high- and moderate-risk groups, peers (especially older teens and gang members) were viewed as street-savvy individuals who knew when conflicts were likely to occur and who could identify dangerous individuals. They also possessed valuable information about how to talk, act, and dress to avoid inviting trouble.

For example, most adolescents in the current study noted that there were historic rivalries among Denver youth groups. As Benny described, some of these schisms were race based (Vietnamese American vs. Latino youths, for example). Other conflicts were geographic. Latino and Latina youths living on the west side of Denver, called "westsiders," disliked Latinos and Latinas from north Denver, called "northsiders." As in many other U.S. cities, animosities also existed among urban gangs. Managing violence, and especially avoiding deadly encounters, for members of high- and moderate-risk groups meant understanding these historic antagonisms. Most felt that this information allowed them to predict, prepare for, or avoid dangerous confrontations.

In addition to providing useful information, friendships with violent youths helped individuals

to construct themselves as friendly agents in their communities and schools. Anna, a 13-year-old Latina living in Allenspark, discussed the importance of amicability when interacting with peers:

> Like, if you were to wear a northside shirt and go to the westside, some people who think that they're all bad would start stuff. But, really, if you're cool with everybody, then they're cool with you. I have friends that are eastsiders. I do know westsiders. But, I hang around with the northsiders. . . . If you're cool with everybody you get respect.

High-risk adolescents relied on friends in a different way than members of the moderate-risk group. For example, moderate-risk adolescents attempted to "be cool" with everyone. High-risk teens wanted to do more than be cool: They wanted to use their friendships for protection. Members of the high-risk group reported that it was important to have friends who were willing to fight with or for them. This became one motivation to join gangs. For some youths, joining a gang meant having partners who "watched their backs" and looked out for them. For example, Linda, a 16-year-old Parkview Latina, explained how she confided in a gang member when someone at school threatened to kill her:

> I got so scared. I didn't know what to do. I ran in the house and called my friend Daryl and I was really crying and [said] "I don't know what to do." And Daryl's all, "What's his number? What's his number?" And I gave it to him. Since that day, that same guy will leave me alone because Daryl went up to him and told him he better leave me alone or else something is going to happen to him and his family.

This strategy produced mixed results. Finding friends who were willing to fight for them obligated individuals to return the favor and, thus, ensured that they would confront future violence. Hector recounted his experience as an unwilling participant in a fight:

> They'll come [and] they will be wearing a westside hat, and [my friends] will say, "what's that all

about?" They will just start fighting, over just a HAT. Well, actually, I have gotten into a fight because of a hat. Because my partner, he started fighting with them, and then more people jumped in, and you have to get his back. Just don't run away.

Anderson (1999) and Bourgois (1995) argued that, in neighborhoods plagued by social problems (i.e., joblessness, racism, drug dealing and use), individuals often earn and maintain status by fighting. As we see here, youths using friends for protection were unwittingly drawn into their friends' contests for respect and quickly found themselves fighting regularly.

Avoiding Places

Similar to geographic restrictive practices outlined by Furstenberg, Cook, Eccles, Elder, and Sameroff (1999), many youths in the current study avoided locations where violence was likely to occur (see also, Ferraro, 1995; Liska, Sanchirico, & Reed, 1988; Pain, 1997). Members of all groups used this strategy, however because individuals had different violent experiences, the consequences of this strategy varied. For example, youths in the high-risk group reported pervasive violence. Therefore, avoiding violent places dramatically changed their interactions in the world, and for some youths, it meant rarely leaving their homes.

Anita, a 16-year-old Latina from Parkview who reported confronting violence regularly, stopped attending school, hanging out in her neighborhood, and spending time with friends. She initiated this strategy after two events: the birth of her daughter and witnessing the nearly fatal shooting of her boyfriend. She reported, "We mostly stay home because of what happened. We don't go anywhere no more." Anita explained that her old life was too risky for her and her newborn and said, "I don't really do things that much, because I have a baby. And they [her friends] think of me like I'm tied down and that I can't do things with them. But, it's just that I don't want to."

Where Anita became housebound, other adolescents noted less dramatic uses of this strategy. For example, Benny remained in his apartment when violence was likely to occur and explained, "Some of my friends that are in gangs, they tell me to stay inside or don't leave. If something is going to happen, they will let us know." Individuals in the moderate-risk group steered clear of the dangerous areas in their neighborhoods or schools. Avoiding unsafe areas, however, did not mean staying in the house. Like Phan, many teens living in violent communities found safe places to spend time, such as recreation centers.

Members of the low-risk group also avoided places. This strategy, however, was not a hardship for them. Low-risk youths were likely to see particular neighborhoods, areas of their schools, or teen hangouts as dangerous places. Instead of venturing into these locations, they usually stayed in their own resource-rich communities. South Creston adolescents noted that they rarely journeyed into nearby North Creston. Similarly, one Westside teen reported walking several blocks out of his way to school to avoid traveling through a dangerous neighborhood. As parents and youths from South Creston and Westside reported, these advantaged communities contained ample recreational opportunities for local youths. Therefore, being bound to the neighborhood did not limit their activities or their ability to access the many nearby resources.

Avoiding People

Where some individuals, usually from the high- and moderate-risk groups, befriended violence-savvy youths, other adolescents avoided potentially violent people. This was the most common strategy reported by low-risk adolescents. Perceiving that they could encounter violent individuals almost anywhere, these juveniles carefully looked for threatening signs among adolescents at school and in their neighborhoods. As no one in the low-risk group experienced violence, their perceptions of threatening characters evolved from stereotypes, hearsay, and media stories. The most common construction of a dangerous teen was a Latino or African American gang member from a lower class neighborhood. Thomas, a 16-year-old White Westside resident, described his feelings about African American students and school violence:

> The students are kind of a problem. If you are walking through the hall and bump into somebody, totally accidental, the hall is crowded. "Oops." And all of a sudden the guy turns around [and says], "What the hell do you think you're doing?" "Sorry man." "Man, if you ever hit me like that again, I swear to God I'm going to kill you." I don't mean to sound mean to anybody, but it tends to be more in the Black community. They all want equal rights and all this other stuff. But, all of a sudden they turn around, like pushing people around, and threatening people, and stuff like that.

Holly, a 17-year-old White Westside resident, also believed that African American students were potentially violent. In fact, she noted that violence segregated particular peer groups at school. She said,

> There's a lot of racial segregation. The ones that hang out with us, they don't care. Their mind is more free and they don't really care if you're a different color. But, if we were to walk into a Black person's party, they would have a fit! They would probably give you crap. And you would leave because you don't want to be around people like that, because they have guns. You don't know who has guns. I'm sure a lot of them have guns, and it is easy for them to get guns.

Although having no firsthand knowledge of weapon distribution among students, Holly guessed that African Americans had access to guns. Thomas attributed contests of respect common within disadvantaged neighborhoods to undesirable behaviors among Black students. Low-risk teens' accounts might be considered misinterpretations of a different peer-based moral universe (Warr, 2002). Although a seemingly innocent problem, the implications are that low-risk teens avoided and negatively labeled (Becker, 1963) other students.

In addition to identifying and avoiding potentially violent students, several individuals scanned their neighborhoods for troublemakers. Perceptions of dangerous individuals in the neighborhood approximated the stereotypes circulating within school. For example, Westside teens reported that the neighborhood seemed safer in the summer. When asked why, one youth told us that during the summer there were fewer "minority" kids walking through the neighborhood on their way to school. Charles, a 15-year-old White Westside resident, stated,

> It's a real nice neighborhood over here. But, they bus those kids from the bad neighborhoods over. They just kind of like make it real bad. If they miss the bus, they stick around for awhile. I usually know the kids that live around here by the way they act. Kids around here are really nice. [The other kids] are usually Hispanic or Black. My friend who moved away said that a lot of them carry big screwdrivers and stuff, like weapons.

Where low-risk youths avoided dangerous students, they called the police on suspicious characters in the neighborhood. The well-publicized shootings in North Creston inspired the formation of a South Creston neighborhood watch group made up of residents who patrolled the streets watching out for trouble. Terry, a 17-year-old White South Creston resident, described the neighborhood watch group's activities:

> At the end of last summer, it was really active because that was the "summer of violence" and crime. I haven't heard much about it lately, though, except that they supposedly have a group that walks around every night with flashlights and phones, and, if anything goes on, they call the police.

Two South Creston adults stated that they closely monitored strangers in the neighborhood. When asked who was most likely to start trouble in the neighborhood, these parents noted watching out for Black youths from North Creston during their neighborhood walks. Therefore, in school potential troublemakers were informally shut out of nonviolent groups. In neighborhoods, however, labeling was more formal and potentially resulted in questioning by the police and removal from the neighborhood.

DISCUSSION

As hundreds of violence prevention programs are designed and implemented throughout the nation, we see that youths were busy designing and using their own strategies to cope with violence. The types of everyday management strategies varied according to the amount of violence that youths reported experiencing. The individuals in the low-risk group might be viewed as being "protected" from violence in that they lived in resource-rich, low-crime communities in which neighbors effectively organized themselves against outside threats to their safety. The narratives of these youths also suggested that they were unlikely to confront violence at school as they usually attended "accelerated" classes—courses that tended to exclude teens who regularly experienced violence. Youths in the low-risk group attempted to maintain their safety by avoiding unsafe areas, including other, less-peaceful communities. Their fears of violence also encouraged them to informally or formally exclude potential troublemakers from their peer groups and their neighborhoods. Thus, the image of protected, low-risk teens emerges within the current study as individuals who were raised with several advantages and who maintained these privileges by keeping away from risky places and keeping risky people out of their social circles.

The current study also reveals the experiences of teens who were not necessarily raised in advantaged communities and who—through a network of peer, school, and neighborhood influences—found themselves confronting violence occasionally or regularly. In contrast to low-risk and protected teens, most individuals in this group managed violence by forging ties with other teens: usually the individuals classified as "troublemakers" by the low-risk teens. By becoming friendly with more violence-savvy youths, individuals in the high and moderate-risk groups initiated their own collection of "protective factors," including learning when and where violence was likely to occur, who was likely to be violent, and how to avoid being targeted by other teens. Some youths felt that the best form of protection against deadly conflicts was to join a social group whose members would fight with and for them (i.e., gangs or other violent peer groups).

These everyday violence management strategies employed by Denver teens are problematic in at least two ways. First, these data suggest that these management strategies may be adversely affecting individuals in the current study. In particular, individuals who join violent groups for protection might increase their chances of meeting a violent demise. For instance, having delinquent friends is one of the strongest predictors of juvenile delinquency, including violence (Elliott, 1994; Elliott, Huizinga, & Ageton, 1985; Matsueda & Heimer, 1987; Tittle, Burke, & Jackson, 1986; Warr & Stafford, 1991). Although there is little data available regarding acquaintanceships (as opposed to friendships) among peers (see Warr, 1996), delinquent opportunity theory (Cloward & Ohlin, 1960) suggests that being acquainted with violent individuals, as opposed to being a member of a violent peer group, might increase juveniles' chances of experiencing violence. In this way, turning to friends who are enmeshed in violence might be putting individuals at risk for experiencing violence themselves.

Second, these management strategies may adversely influence violence rates. More specifically, these findings highlight the way that violence rates can escalate to epidemic proportions. Combining the illicit economy and street culture explanations (Anderson, 1999; Blumstein, 1995; Blumstein & Cork, 1996; Bourgois, 1995), we see how economic and cultural forces increased violence rates during the 1980s and early 1990s. According to the illicit economy perspective, the structural changes in underground economies (i.e., introduction of new crack markets) influenced a spike in violence rates. The spike occurred when young crack dealers eventually diffused the reliance on guns to their school and neighborhood friends. The street culture perspective indirectly suggests that youths entrenched in a violent street ethos were happy to pick up on gun use to establish strong identities— something that they could not obtain through legitimate means. Thus, we see that particular structural conditions can encourage violence rate increases in drug markets. These violence rates are then sustained through cultural norms and diffusion.

The data presented in this article add to the illicit economy and cultural explanations by offering another hypothesis regarding the way that violence rates can be sustained. More specifically, these findings demonstrate how initial violence peaks within disadvantaged communities can instigate a pattern of interactions across multiple contexts. These "across-context" interaction patterns may theoretically sustain violence rates. The process generally begins as a response to increasing threats of violence and ends with a set of violence management techniques that leave many youths with few choices but to become violent.

The findings from the fear-of-crime literature suggests that individuals routinely respond to fears of victimization by employing different management techniques, such as carrying weapons (Arria, Wood, & Anthony, 1995; Bankston & Thompson, 1989) and avoiding dangerous situations or locations (Ferraro, 1995; Liska et al., 1988; Pain, 1997). Thus, given the increasing threat of violence, real or perceived, individuals will respond to manage violence in everyday contexts. The general increase in violence rates in the early 1990s (the years just before the current study), suggest that the threat of violence was fairly intense for youths.

As rates of violence increase, these threats are also likely to increase. These violent threats, in turn, encourage a pattern of informal protective interactions across several groups, institutions, and contexts. These protective interactions can potentially encourage violence in two ways. First, these interactions may motivate some youths to become violent. As a case in point, low-risk teens' favorite responses to secondary threats were avoiding risky places and people. Those who lived in nonviolent communities vigilantly patrolled their neighborhoods and avoided potential troublemakers. This predicts that if an individual confronting many violent risk factors were to enter nonviolent neighborhoods they will be shunned and reminded that they "do not belong." Certainly this informal and formal chiding provide additional motivations to put on the tough and threatening personas that Anderson (1999) and Bourgois (1995) described. Therefore, individuals living in or near areas where "street ethics" reign had few choices but to join in or isolate themselves.

Second, these interaction patterns may strengthen violence-prone social networks. As Warr (2002) argued, "The fact that adolescents often face the threat of violence at school and elsewhere suggests a mechanism that may encourage group formation in daily life" (p. 83). Youths in the high-risk group were likely to find protection in violent social networks and unlikely to join nonviolent groups whose members offered them no protection against the acrimonious world they regularly confronted. Thus, as Warr (2002) predicted, threats are likely to ensure that individuals confronting multiple violence risks will learn the proviolence norms circulating in the most vicious social circles.

When the threat of violence reaches a particular level, the interaction patterns initiated across multiple contexts can increase the numbers of individuals who are likely to become violent. Thus, through a collection of structural (drug market), cultural (street culture), and interaction patterns (everyday threats) we see how initial violence peaks inside illicit markets can set off cultural and interaction patterns that lock individuals into a cycle of violence.

More than offering a vision of the way that structural, cultural, and interaction patterns combine to increase violence rates, these data point to a new violence research and prevention agenda. Specifically, the current study suggests that exclusionary interaction patterns across multiple contexts may leave many youths with few opportunities but to become violent. Thus, a new agenda for researchers, practitioners, and stakeholders is to address the patterns of exclusion cutting across multiple contexts. Because gangs are often viewed as a particularly violent type of peer group, gang research provides a concrete example of the way that a multiple context research agenda might be employed. To date, most gang research has been comparative, meaning that researchers have tended to consider two or more gangs from different neighborhoods and, in some cases, different cities. The approach advocated here would not only compare gangs in one context to gangs in another but would delineate the way that gangs (or other violent youth groups) form within a larger peer context. The central goal of this research, therefore, will be to examine the way that systems of exclusion segregate peer groups based on race, ethnicity, area of residence, and socioeconomic status. Without addressing these across-context exclusionary mechanisms research will, at best, fail to show the way that multiple social groups are complicit in social problems and, at worst, continue the perception that violence is a problem isolated to one type of social group (i.e., poor gang members of color living in disadvantaged communities).

Because the current study focused on the connections among different social contexts, it also sheds light on current trends in the field of violence prevention and intervention. In contrast to the "nothing works" era in criminal justice programs during the 1970s and 1980s (Martinson, 1974; Regnery, 1985; Sechrest, White, & Brown, 1979), in the 1990s several researchers argued that some programs work to reduce violence (Gendreau & Ross, 1980; Hawkins et al., 1995; Lipsey & Wilson, 1997; Sherman et al., 1997). The preferred or model programs identified in this literature have been proven effective in reducing violent behavior or the behaviors correlated with violence during research trials. The findings from the current study suggest that not all preferred programs may, in fact, reduce violence rates. The vast majority of outcome evaluation studies has measured success by examining whether the individuals exposed to these programs are less violent than individuals who do not receive the programs. Although some studies have determined whether programs reduce violence rates in one city or neighborhood (Jones & Offord, 1989; Schinke, Orlandi, & Cole, 1992), these large-scale evaluations tend to be extremely costly and, consequently, rare.

Because this research examines the across-context interaction patterns, it suggests that creating changes within individuals may not be enough to stem escalations in violence rates. For example, the question remains whether decreasing violence in one neighborhood may inadvertently lead to an explosion of deadly conflicts in another. Similarly, it is unknown whether steering one adolescent away from a delinquent pathway may propel several youths down a violent road. Therefore, the measure of success for policy makers and practitioners would be to decrease social exclusion and marginalization of youths confronting the brunt of large-scale social problems (joblessness, rampant drug sales and use, lack of public services, global economic shifts, and racism).

Working with this premise, the most promising programs for stemming violence rates might be those that specifically target fear-based segregation among groups. This calls for a shift in violence prevention programming from targeting one group of youths, such as those considered at risk for violence, to targeting a large cross-section of youths. It also calls for a shift in ways of measuring program effectiveness from locating changes within individuals to changes within a larger social system. The ultimate goal of system changes is to open avenues for meaningful participation in legitimate society for excluded youths.

REFERENCES

Anderson, E. (1999). *Code of the street: Decency, violence, and the moral life of the inner city.* New York: Norton.

Arria, A. M., Wood, N. P., & Anthony, J. C. (1995). Prevalence of carrying a weapon and related behaviors in urban schoolchildren, 1989 to 1993. *Archives of Pediatric Adolescent Medicine, 149,* 1345–1450.

Bankston, W. B., & Thompson, C. Y. (1989). Carrying firearms for protection: A causal model. *Sociological Inquiry, 59,* 75–87.

Barzagan, M. (1994). The effects of health, environmental, and socio-psychological variables on fear of crime and its consequences among urban Black elderly individuals. *International Journal of Aging and Human Development, 38,* 99–115.

Becker, H. (1963). *Outsiders: Studies in the sociology of deviance.* London: Free Press.

Biernacki, P., & Waldorf, D. (1981). Snowball sampling: Problems and techniques of chain referral sampling. *Sociological Methods and Research, 10,* 141–163.

Blumstein, A. (1995). Youth violence, guns, and the illicit-drug industry. *The Journal of Criminal Law and Criminology, 86,* 10–36.

Blumstein, A., & Cork, D. (1996). Linking gun availability to youth gun violence. *Law and Contemporary Problems, 59,* 5–24.

Blumstein, A., & Wallman, J. (2000). *The crime drop in America.* New York: Cambridge University Press.

Bourgois, P. (1996). In search of masculinity: Violence, respect and sexuality among Puerto Rican crack dealers in East Harlem. *British Journal of Criminology, 36,* 412–427.

Bourgois, P. I. (1995). *In search of respect: Selling crack in El Barrio.* New York: Cambridge University Press.

Bursik, R. J., & Grasmick, H. G. (1993). *Neighborhoods and crime: The dimensions of effective community control.* New York: Lexington.

Chiricos, T., Eschholz, S., & Gertz, M. (1997). Crime, news, and fear of crime: Toward an identification of audience effects. *Social Problems, 44,* 342–357.

Chiricos, T., Padgett, K., & Gertz, M. (2000). Fear, TV news, and the reality of crime. *Criminology, 38,* 755–786.

Cloward, R., & Ohlin, L. (1960). *Delinquency and opportunity.* New York: Free Press.

Cook, P. J., & Laub, J. H. (1998). The unprecedented epidemic in youth violence. In M. Tonry & M. H. Moore (Eds.), *Youth violence. Crime and justice: A review of research* (pp. 27–64). Chicago: University of Chicago Press.

Decker, S., & VanWinkle, B. (1996). *Life in the gang: Family, friends and violence.* New York: Cambridge University Press.

Elliott, D. S. (1994). Serious violent offenders—Onset, developmental course, and termination. The American Society of Criminology 1993 presidential address. *Criminology, 32,* 1–21.

Elliott, D. S., Huizinga, D., & Ageton, S. S. (1985). *Explaining delinquency and drug use.* Beverly Hills, CA: Sage.

Elliott, D. S., Wilson, W. J., Huizinga, D., Sampson, R. J., Elliott, A., & Rankin, B. (1996). The effects of neighborhood disadvantage on adolescent development. *Journal of Research in Crime and Delinquency, 33,* 389–426.

Ferraro, K. F. (1995). *Fear of crime: Interpreting victimization risk.* Albany: State University of New York Press.

Furstenberg, F. F., Jr., Cook, T. D., Eccles, J., Elder, G. H., Jr., & Sameroff, A. (1999). *Managing to make it: Urban families and adolescent success.* Chicago: University of Chicago Press.

Gendreau, P., & Ross, R. R. (1980). *Effective correctional treatment.* Toronto, Canada: Butterworths.

Glaser, B., & Strauss, A. L. (1967). *The discovery of grounded theory: Strategies for qualitative research.* Chicago: Aldine.

Hawkins, J. D., Herrenkohl, T. L., Farrington, D. P., Brewer, D., Catalano, R. F., & Harachi, T.W. (1998). A review of predictors of youth violence. In R. Loeber & D. P. Farrington (Eds.), *Serious and violent juvenile offenders: Risk factors and successful interventions* (pp. 106–146). Thousand Oaks, CA: Sage.

Jones, M. B., & Offord, D. R. (1989). Reduction of antisocial behavior in poor children by nonschool skill-development. *Journal of Child Psychology and Psychiatry, 30,* 737–750.

Kelly, D. H. (1974). Track position and delinquent involvement: A preliminary analysis. *Sociology and Social Research, 58,* 380–386.

Lavrakas, P. J. (1982). Fear of crime and behavioral restrictions in urban and suburban neighborhoods. *Population and Environment, 5,* 242–264.

Lipsey, M.W., & Derzon, J. H. (1998). Predictors of violent and serious delinquency in adolescence and early adulthood: A synthesis of longitudinal research. In

R. Loeber & D. P. Farrington (Eds.), *Serious and violent juvenile offenders: Risk factors and successful interventions* (pp. 86–105). Thousand Oaks, CA: Sage.

Lipsey, M.W., &Wilson, D. B. (1997). *Effective interventions for serious juvenile offenders: A synthesis of research.* Nashville, TN: Vanderbilt University.

Liska, A. E., Sanchirico, A., & Reed, M. D. (1988). Fear of crime and constrained behavior: Specifying and estimating a reciprocal effects model. *Social Forces, 66*, 827–837.

Martinson, R. (1974, spring). What works? Questions and answers about prison reform. *Public Interest, 35*, 22–54.

Matsueda, R. L., & Heimer, K. (1987). Race, family structure, and delinquency: A test of differential association and social control theories. *American Sociological Review, 52*, 826-840.

Oakes, J. (1985). *Keeping track: How schools structure inequality.* New Haven, CT: Yale University Press.

O'Keefe, G. J., & Reid-Nash, K. (1987). Crime news and real-world blues: The effects of the media on social reality. *Communication Research, 14*, 147–163.

Pain, R. H. (1997). "Old age" and ageism in urban research: The case of fear of crime. *International Journal of Urban and Regional Research, 21*, 117–128.

Regnery, A. S. (1985). Getting away with murder. *Policy Review, 34*, 1–4.

Sampson, R. J. (1985). Neighborhood and crime: The structural determinants of personal victimization. *Journal of Research in Crime and Delinquency, 22*, 7–40.

Schinke, S. P., Orlandi, M. A., & Cole, K. C. (1992).Boys & Girls Clubs in public housing developments: Prevention services for youth at risk. *Journal of Community Psychology* (OSAP Special Issue), 118–128.

Sechrest, L., White, S., & Brown, E. (1979). *Rehabilitation of criminal offenders: Problems and prospects.* Washington, DC: National Academy of Sciences.

Sherman, L.W., Gottfredson, D. C., MacKenzie, D., Eck, J., Reuter, P., & Bushway, S. (1997). *Preventing crime: What works, what doesn't, what's promising: A report to the U.S. Congress.* College Park: University of Maryland.

Simcha-Fagan, O., & Schwartz, J. E. (1986). Neighborhood and delinquency: An assessment of contextual effects. *Criminology, 24*, 667–703.

Snyder, H. N., & Sickmund, M. (1999). *Juvenile offenders and victims: 1999 national report* (NCJ 178257).Washington, DC: U.S. Department of Justice, Office of Justice Programs, Office of Juvenile Justice and Delinquency Prevention.

Snyder, H. N., Sickmund, M., & Poe-Yamagata, E. (1996). *Juvenile offenders and victims: 1996 update on violence.* Washington, DC: Office of Juvenile Justice and Delinquency Prevention.

Tittle, C. R., Burke, M. J., & Jackson, E. F. (1986). Modeling Sutherland's theory of differential association: Toward an empirical clarification. *Social Forces, 65*, 405–432.

Warr, M. (1996). Organization and instigation in delinquent groups. *Criminology, 34*, 11–37.

Warr, M. (2002). *Companions in crime: The social aspects of criminal conduct.* Cambridge, UK: Cambridge University Press.

Warr, M., & Stafford, M. (1991). The influence of delinquent peers: What they think or what they do? *Criminology, 29*, 851–866.

Wilson, W. J. (1996). *When work disappears: The world of the new urban poor.* New York: Knopf.

Section III

ETHICS IN SOCIAL RESEARCH

W e're now going to take a little parallel trip alongside our map of the research process to discuss ethical concerns. The reason that this subject isn't on the main map is that ethics isn't something you do once along the way. It's part of the background to every step in the process.

ASA PROFESSIONAL CODE OF ETHICS

Students sometimes wonder why we would teach about our professional code of ethics in an undergraduate course. Some might feel these codes are for committed professionals only, not for students, whose work doesn't *really* count. On the other hand, some might feel that such codes are pleasant abstractions, or just advice, much as someone used to remind you to look both ways before you cross a street. But the reality is that all of us, whatever our purposes, must always consider all of the ways in which our research could affect others.

The first reading in this section is not a research article; it is the American Sociological Association's Code of Ethics. The ethics code is the principal document that defines our professional obligations as researchers, scholars, teachers, and members of the sociological community.

Why the ethics code? The answer is probably a lot more interesting than you would at first think. Scholars have done some frightening things to research **subjects** in the name of "science." We've violated confidentiality, we've been deceptive in hurtful ways, and we've been unforthcoming about the benefits and gains to the research subjects. We've exposed research subjects to threats from law enforcement and brought to light information that threatened their jobs and families. Even as student researchers, you must be mindful of causing harm to research subjects, to your reputation, and to your institution (e.g., department, college, university). In this short introduction we try to give some context and relevance to the ethics code, and guide you to avoiding errors that others have made. Let's start with the four questions:

1. When do we notice behaviors, and what does that have to do with ethics?

2. What is a professional?

3. What does it mean to be ethical in one's research?

4. Who benefits from ethical research practices?

We consider each in turn.

When Do We Notice Behaviors?

Emile Durkheim (1858–1917), one of the great founders of sociology, observed that we usually notice rules of behavior—**norms**—when they are violated. Try standing in the front of an elevator while facing all of the people rather than facing the elevator door. Bingo. You've now violated a norm of elevator riding you've perhaps never noticed but long obeyed. And others have noticed you doing it. Ethical research practices are a norm for our profession, though we rarely discuss them until they are violated.

When professional or other groups set out codes of behaviors, they are usually seeking to write down what they hold to be the standards for their members. Because sociologists study professionalism and professional organizations, there's more than a touch of didactic self-reflection in the ASA's Code of Ethics. The "Introduction" to the code states, "These principles and standards . . . constitute normative statements for sociologists and provide guidance on issues that sociologists may encounter in their professional work."

And, as Durkheim would tell us, we ordinarily would be socialized into following these principles and standards, so we would consult them only when we question someone's or some organization's actions. But that would be a waste because the code embodies a set of useful guidelines that will enhance your professional life, your career, your interactions with others, and, err, your ethics. Of course, we should also remember that as with the law, ignorance of the code is not an excuse for violating it. It is our responsibility to know and follow the code.

What Is a Professional?

The second question is more complicated. The word *professional* is used in many ways, few of them relevant to serious sociology. For example, "professional baseball player" distinguishes people who make money playing baseball from those of us who play for fun. Professional dishwasher, similarly, means someone who may work at a restaurant and is paid for his or her work. But that professional dishwasher may be no better at washing dishes than you are. When we use the term the "first profession" we are referring to prostitution. There again, earning money for a task does not necessarily imply having greater skill, commitment, or enthusiasm than others. Last, "professional dress" generally means business-like attire, although it might be a white lab coat, a miner's light and helmet, or a swimsuit.

None of these definitions really covers what sociologists study about professions. In sociology, the term *profession* is much more precise than it is in general conversation. It encompasses several elements: A unique and esoteric body of knowledge; control over professional entrance and education; autonomy; altruism and social responsibility; community; and ethics. Professional training occurs in specialized programs. Members of the profession control who enters the training or not, and who receives certification. The profession regulates itself and its schools.

Every profession has a professional code of conduct whether it's fully spelled out or not. Professionals are supposed to use their skills for the benefit of society and of their clients or patients. We realize this is sometimes hard to believe in the current environment, but it underlies what it is to be a professional. A businessperson can develop a better paint or software program, patent it, and make a lot of money. But if a doctor developed a better way of conducting an operation, he or she would be obliged to share that information with the profession and the world. If a biologist found an organism that affects plant growth (good or bad), her or his obligation would be to publish that finding. Similarly, if you go to a doctor who does not like you, he or she must treat you at least enough that you can make it to a hospital or another doctor. Here is a typical statement from a medical society:

> Principle of primacy of patient welfare. This principle is based on a dedication to serving the interest of the patient. Altruism contributes to the trust

that is central to the physician–patient relationship. Market forces, societal pressures, and administrative exigencies must not compromise this principle.

So, the job of the American Sociological Association's Code of Ethics is to set out the rules for sociologists in their professional lives. Also, because some outrageous personal behaviors would reflect badly on the profession as a whole, there are even statements about how sociologists should act in their personal lives. These rules reflect the principles of professionalism enumerated above.

The profession polices its own members for adherence to professional standards and evidence of *competence, integrity, scientific and professional responsibility, rights and dignity,* and *service to the public,* as described in the following pages.

Sociologists should not tolerate incompetent colleagues working under the banner of sociology. Hence there are requirements for education, ongoing education, and the need to consult others when you do not have the expertise to tackle a project. Similarly, you are not permitted to "go beyond" your expertise or the findings of your research. If you studied the relationship between earnings and education in some community, that does not give you the authority to speak professionally about water pollution.

Integrity is required of professionals when they discuss their research, when dealing with each other, and when holding information that has been promised to be confidential. We make assumptions about the way data are collected and analyzed. Those assumptions hold that we are honestly informed of the research process and results. Transparency—of notes, data, and analytic methods—is the requirement of science and helps in that process. Intentional deceit may cloud transparency, at least for a short while. In part, we have the need for "reproducibility" to control for any deception, but also for honest methodological, historical, or factual differences. There are many valid reasons for different findings, but misrepresentation of information is not among them.

The element of responsibility combines several of the aspects of professionalism raised above. We are required to be respectful of other sociologists, but we are also required to maintain a commitment to the truth. If we know a colleague is engaging in unethical conduct, we are obliged to bring that behavior to the attention of other colleagues and of a professional ethics council.

As members of the society, and as students of social life, sociologists are particularly expected to respect and even to promote the rights and dignity of other people. At the very least, we hold one another accountable *not* to engage in or tolerate discrimination based on race, age, gender, ethnicity, national orientation, sexual identity, disability, and the like.

Finally, the profession and its members must seek to apply the knowledge of sociology for the public good. That does not mean that we all have to agree on what that good is. But whatever we feel it (the public good) is, we must pursue it in good faith.

What Does It Mean to Be Ethical in One's Research?

The ethics code says a lot about how we as researchers should treat our research subjects. If we promise **anonymity** (i.e., that we don't know who the subject is), we must ensure we design the research so we don't know who the subject is. If we promise **confidentiality** (i.e., we know who the subject is but we will never tell), we must keep our word. And keeping our word means designing forms where the name is removed, securing information in locked drawers, encoding names, and so on. Sometimes that means refusing to name our subjects publicly, even when subpoenaed to do so.

If we ask people to participate, we must be very clear about the dangers, benefits, and demands of the research. At the very least, we usually take up the subjects' time. And, if we ask them to participate in a focus group, for example, there is a real danger that something unpleasant will be said by another participant or (unintentionally, we hope) by the moderator. Even a questionnaire may elicit memories and self doubts. Consider the innocent-sounding demographic question:

Do you live alone or with others?

What if the respondent had recently undergone a divorce or the death of a spouse? What if the respondent were depressed over her or his lonely existence? Who are we to force a respondent to confront such issues? Similarly, consider:

How many children to you have?

One of us asked that question during an interview on the very day that the **respondent**'s son had died 14 years ago. By the end of the interview, both of us were in tears. (And the interview was on a seemingly benign topic—something like housing preferences.)

Are you in a relationship? Or, How good or bad is your relationship?

No comment needed.

The ultimate principle is the same as in medicine: "First, do no harm." Or, perhaps more realistically stated, "Do everything in your power to avoid causing harm." As researchers, we must be careful not to expose information about our subjects provided in confidence. We must even be certain not to collect information we don't need. (Why risk possible exposure and why take up their time and our time?) As discussed, we must be exquisitely sensitive to the subjects' feelings, hopes, and beliefs. That includes, of course, ensuring voluntary participation where it is possible, and even reminding subjects that their participation is voluntary. There can be no penalty to voluntary subjects if they refuse to participate at any point in the research.

The types of damage we can do are often related to the forms of research we are conducting. If we are engaged in fieldwork (say, participant observation of a group of political activists), we can create problems by exposing the names of members, in addition to creating other financial, legal, political, and social problems. When we use anonymous questionnaires, we can still create financial, legal, political, and social problems for the group, even if we don't know individual members.

Consider what could happen if we did a study of alcohol consumption on your campus. Suppose also that the study was anonymous (we did not know any of the students' names) but of course we knew the name of the school. What if we found and reported that 60% of the students drank heavily on weekends, and that 30% drank during the week? What if we reported that an unspecified sports team or debating club actively encouraged underage drinking? Do you think the value of your degree would be affected? Would parents, deans, or disciplinary rules be affected? Would any of our subjects come under greater administrative surveillance? In short, could we pretend that we hadn't hurt anyone just because we didn't use names?

Insider–Outsider Relations. Another ethical issue arises when an "insider," say, a member of a sorority, writes about her experiences and group. Many, if not all, of those interactions and observations were made in a context where the participants assumed confidentiality. What right does the researcher have to expose actions and statements made under those assumptions? We could say that the researcher should first obtain permission from any and all participants. But is it enough to do that post hoc? And what if some say OK but others object? Perhaps people would not have acted in certain ways, would not have said things, if they knew they would be open to public scrutiny.

On the other hand, what if the actions in the "secret society" violated the norms and laws of our society? Let's say some people were getting seriously hurt. Do researchers have an obligation to expose such actions? Do not scientists have obligations to study and understand such behaviors? As with all of these ethical issues, the answers are never easy, but there are ways of examining the questions that help guide us. The ethics codes and the writings of fellow scholars are often our best way-finders.

Researcher Subjectivity. The methods of social research help practitioners conduct careful and systematic observations. Statements of theoretical positions provide context and often implicit views on the nature of society and the "nature of human nature." The (hopefully) complete transparency of presentation and the clarity of the methods help readers understand and evaluate the researchers' actions, tools, and underlying assumptions. The entire process is, nevertheless, a very human endeavor; **subjectivity**—the researchers' own views and biases—do not magically disappear. We use the conventions of research and research reporting to minimize and illuminate any personal influence, but ultimately it is incumbent on the researcher and the consumer to be hyper vigilant in action and interpretation.

Often, the researchers' political or theoretic positions are well known in advance. Researchers will sometimes issue clear statements about their values vis-à-vis the research issues. In these cases, the researchers will often discuss the protections they are taking against the influence of their beliefs. Readers are then able to evaluate very carefully the methods and evidence in relation to any bias in method or interpretation. Often, such tension makes for the most exciting research and debate.

Institutional Review Boards. One of the organizational bodies that guides and polices researchers is the **Institutional Review Board** (IRB), a group of faculty, researchers, and ethicists who review every research proposal before it can be executed, especially those with any human subjects. Most colleges and research centers have IRBs. Their job is to help ensure that researchers

- provide full disclosure (informing the subjects of what will happen to them, to their information, to the reports that may be issued)—often called **informed consent**
- present questions that are clear and understandable
- provide protection for the data collected
- are knowledgeable about ethics and protection of subjects
- protect against any other dangers
- inform the IRB of any ethics lapses

In addition, IRBs serve another function: They help protect the university or institution from being sued by subjects who may have been harmed by the research. That is, if the IRB helps researchers to do a better job of protecting the subjects—in design of the study, in keeping data, in question wording, and so forth—then the institution is less likely to be sued by a research subject.

Who Benefits From Ethical Research Practices?

Following ethical guidelines helps all of us. Honest. If a researcher fails to keep information confidential, the breach of trust damages the research subject . . . and all of us. Consider:

- It tarnishes or destroys the reputation of the researcher, and significantly lowers the probability of further funding.
- It affects the reputation and funding of researchers and the institution where she or he works. And there may be dramatic financial penalties.
- Perhaps more important, however, is that it harms the ability of all scholars to conduct research. If people believe their information won't be confidential, then they will refuse to speak with us, or at least be less honest than they were before.
- Last, and probably most important, society is hurt by the inability to learn and act on what we gain from research. Think of the many research projects and their policy implications. Here are just a few of the millions of examples. Without research on human subjects, we would be unable to:
  - explain the importance of vaccinations
  - design immigration policy that is most responsive to the needs of employers, immigrants, their families, and the society
  - convince people to go for HIV testing
  - design programs for people with defined social needs, such as the elderly or infirm, to evaluate and address their needs and the needs of their loved ones
  - improve the way we teach students in elementary or high schools

POLITICS

The ASA Code of Ethics identifies a wide assortment of things that researchers can do that cause harm to others through their carelessness or bad judgment. Often, however, unprofessional conduct occurs in response to outside pressures, frequently from those who are funding the research and who have their own interests or agendas.

We can distinguish between the normal daily "politics" that occurs when people who have influence over you want something from you, and "Politics," the professional world of governance and law. Examples of the first would include getting research support and assistance from a charity that you admire, and then discovering a discrediting secret about the group. Ethically, you cannot suppress or ignore data that is relevant to your work. But politically, if you reveal what you've found, the organization is likely to withdraw its support and possibly prevent you from concluding your work.

Politics-with-a-capital-P can have much greater consequences. In the next selection, Mark Solovey resurrects a little-known era of the cold war research effort, called "Project Camelot," when various branches of the U.S. government funded social scientists *IF* their work promoted specific political agendas.

Recall that researchers are not without values, and that those values may be reflected in our choice of research questions. But that does *not* mean our personal preferences can determine or even color our answers. There is nothing inherently wrong with a researcher who is, for example, opposed to Communism and doing research on Communism. It becomes a problem, however, when a government influences the nature or direction of the work, or the dissemination of its findings, to create a desired outcome, just as it would be wrong for individual researchers to alter their findings to bolster their particular ideology.

Solovey refers to the dramatic changes in the relationship between government and social science

research as an "epistemological revolution," meaning a significant shift in the way we think about the "production" and use of knowledge. For many in the period of Project Camelot, it was something of a shock to consider knowledge itself as a kind of tool or, worse, a weapon. The study of revolutions, for example, may be highly revealing about how people experience or respond to oppression, how they act collectively, how governments respond when their power is threatened, and how societies undergo massive and often unexpected shifts. Yet, with a slight change in focus, these academic questions can become servants to political programs to create or suppress revolutions in other nations.

As with other ethical violations, the failure to ensure political neutrality in the way we conduct research hurts all of us. How, for example, can we ask members of a disadvantaged group to participate in our research if we, as a profession, are viewed as handmaidens to the elite powers of our society? How can we seek international cooperation for social science research if each nation has to treat each foreign scientist as a potential spy? How can we present data that either support or critique things that are happening in our own societies if we are assumed to be motivated by our ideologies rather than by our findings? Moreover, research subjects are not passive objects. Referring to the history of ethical violations in research involving African Americans, sociologist Harlon Dalton noted that "the deep-seated suspicion and mistrust many of us feel whenever whites express a sudden interest in our well-being hampers our progress in dealing with AIDS" (1989:211).

This epistemological debate has recently resurfaced, particularly among anthropologists. Amid concerns that anthropologists have assisted the Pentagon in the production of a Human Terrain System (HTS) through which researchers in Iraq have potentially exposed subjects to military action from U.S. armed forces,[1] professional organizations such as The Network of Concerned Anthropologists are seeking to strengthen guidelines and restrictions against work that "contribute

---

[1]http://www.aaanet.org/pdf/EB_Resolution_110807.pdf

to counter-insurgency operations in Iraq or in related theaters in the 'war on terror.'"[2] In the midst of these events, U.S. Secretary of Defense Robert Gates recently announced a proposal for Project Minerva, a new Pentagon initiative to support social science research. Unlike Project Camelot and the HTS, the Minerva project promises to operate with "complete openness and rigid adherence to academic freedom and integrity."[3]

Sociologists and other social scientists routinely contribute to political debates, testify before Congress and other legislative bodies, and file briefs before the U.S. Supreme Court. It is deemed (by our professional associations and by most social scientists) entirely appropriate for those who study society, policy, program effectiveness, economies, and governance to participate in the public discourse around those matters. Indeed, it's not clear why we would study them at all if our findings did not contribute to helping society. Professional ethics help ensure that academic research respects and protects the people we study, is trustworthy and transparent,

and is focused on the pursuit of knowledge rather than on supporting a desired outcome.

CONCLUSION

We hope we have demonstrated that ethical and professional codes are more than a stodgy list of dos and don'ts. They guide important decisions that help researchers, research subjects, our institutions, and, indeed, all of society.

In the ethics code that follows this introduction, readers will see the ways in which these principles and goals are spelled out. It codifies the specific actions and responsibilities of sociologists. In addition to treatment of data and research findings, there are many sections on interactions with students, colleagues, employees, public media, and research subjects. It also covers authorship, conflicts of interest, publications, and contractual responsibilities. You may even find it a useful guide for other areas of your life.

DISCUSSION QUESTIONS

1. Discuss when might it be appropriate, if ever, to violate your promise of confidentiality?

2. When you present yourself to the group you are going to study (via fieldwork/qualitative methods), you have options as to how much of your study's purpose you wish to convey to them. What are some of the ethical issues you face? Hint: Consider what you are going to do with your findings; who will see them? Also consider your relationships with the people you've studied; and, of course, your ethical obligations.

3. You are on an institutional review board. A project is presented to you that involves the experimenter pretending he or she is having a seizure. Collaborators in the same public area are going to record the actions of the bystanders. What are your concerns as a member of the IRB? Would you allow the study to be conducted?

WEB RESOURCES

The following links can provide you with more detailed information on the topics discussed in this section. You may also go to www.sagepub.com/lunestudy where you will find additional resources and hot-links to these sources.

The ASA Code of Ethics is available for free at http://www.asanet.org/cs/root/leftnav/ethics/ethics

Also available on the ASA's Web site are the rules of the ASA's professional ethics body—the Committee on Professional Ethics (COPE): http://www.asanet.org/cs/root/leftnav/ethics/cope_policies_and_procedures

[2]http://concerned.anthropologists.googlepages.com/internationalpledge

[3]http://www.insidehighered.com/news/2008/04/16/minerva

Code of Ethics Policies and Procedures of the ASA Committee on Professional Ethics (1997)

American Sociological Association

INTRODUCTION

The American Sociological Association's (ASA's) Code of Ethics sets forth the principles and ethical standards that underlie sociologists' professional responsibilities and conduct. These principles and standards should be used as guidelines when examining everyday professional activities. They constitute normative statements for sociologists and provide guidance on issues that sociologists may encounter in their professional work.

ASA's Code of Ethics consists of an Introduction, a Preamble, five General Principles, and specific Ethical Standards. This Code is also accompanied by the Rules and Procedures of the ASA Committee on Professional Ethics which describe the procedures for filing, investigating, and resolving complaints of unethical conduct.

The Preamble and General Principles of the Code are aspirational goals to guide sociologists toward the highest ideals of sociology. Although the Preamble and General Principles are not enforceable rules, they should be considered by sociologists in arriving at an ethical course of action and may be considered by ethics bodies in interpreting the Ethical Standards.

The Ethical Standards set forth enforceable rules for conduct by sociologists. Most of the Ethical Standards are written broadly in order to apply to sociologists in varied roles, and the application of an Ethical Standard may vary depending on the context. The Ethical Standards are not exhaustive. Any conduct that is not specifically addressed by this Code of Ethics is not necessarily ethical or unethical.

Membership in the ASA commits members to adhere to the ASA Code of Ethics and to the Policies and Procedures of the ASA Committee on Professional Ethics. Members are advised of this obligation upon joining the Association and that violations of the Code may lead to the imposition of sanctions, including termination of membership. ASA members subject to the Code of Ethics may be reviewed under these Ethical Standards only if the activity is part of or affects their work-related functions, or if the activity is sociological in nature. Personal activities having no connection to or effect on sociologists' performance of their professional roles are not subject to the Code of Ethics.

PREAMBLE

This Code of Ethics articulates a common set of values upon which sociologists build their professional and scientific work. The Code is intended to provide both the general principles and the rules to cover professional situations encountered by sociologists. It has as its primary goal the welfare and protection of the individuals and groups with whom sociologists work. It is the individual responsibility of each sociologist to aspire to the highest possible standards of conduct in research, teaching, practice, and service.

The development of a dynamic set of ethical standards for a sociologist's work-related conduct requires a personal commitment to a lifelong effort to act ethically; to encourage ethical behavior by students, supervisors, supervisees, employers, employees, and colleagues; and to consult with others as needed concerning ethical problems. Each sociologist supplements, but does not violate, the values and rules specified in the Code of Ethics based on guidance drawn from personal values, culture, and experience.

General Principles

The following General Principles are aspirational and serve as a guide for sociologists in determining ethical courses of action in various contexts. They exemplify the highest ideals of professional conduct.

Principle A: Professional Competence

Sociologists strive to maintain the highest levels of competence in their work; they recognize the limitations of their expertise; and they undertake only those tasks for which they are qualified by education, training, or experience. They recognize the need for ongoing education in order to remain professionally competent; and they utilize the appropriate scientific, professional, technical, and administrative resources needed to ensure competence in their professional activities. They consult with other professionals when necessary for the benefit of their students, research participants, and clients.

Principle B: Integrity

Sociologists are honest, fair, and respectful of others in their professional activities—in research, teaching, practice, and service. Sociologists do not knowingly act in ways that jeopardize either their own or others'

professional welfare. Sociologists conduct their affairs in ways that inspire trust and confidence; they do not knowingly make statements that are false, misleading, or deceptive.

Principle C: Professional and Scientific Responsibility

Sociologists adhere to the highest scientific and professional standards and accept responsibility for their work. Sociologists understand that they form a community and show respect for other sociologists even when they disagree on theoretical, methodological, or personal approaches to professional activities. Sociologists value the public trust in sociology and are concerned about their ethical behavior and that of other sociologists that might compromise that trust. While endeavoring always to be collegial, sociologists must never let the desire to be collegial outweigh their shared responsibility for ethical behavior. When appropriate, they consult with colleagues in order to prevent or avoid unethical conduct.

Principle D: Respect for People's Rights, Dignity, and Diversity

Sociologists respect the rights, dignity, and worth of all people. They strive to eliminate bias in their professional activities, and they do not tolerate any forms of discrimination based on age; gender; race; ethnicity; national origin; religion; sexual orientation; disability; health conditions; or marital, domestic, or parental status. They are sensitive to cultural, individual, and role differences in serving, teaching, and studying groups of people with distinctive characteristics. In all of their work-related activities, sociologists acknowledge the rights of others to hold values, attitudes, and opinions that differ from their own.

Principle E: Social Responsibility

Sociologists are aware of their professional and scientific responsibility to the communities and societies in which they live and work. They apply and make public their knowledge in order to contribute to the public good. When undertaking research, they strive to advance the science of sociology and to serve the public good.

ETHICAL STANDARDS

1. Professional and Scientific Standards

Sociologists adhere to the highest possible technical standards that are reasonable and responsible in their research, teaching, practice, and service activities. They rely on scientifically and professionally derived knowledge; act with honesty and integrity; and avoid untrue, deceptive, or undocumented statements in undertaking work-related functions or activities.

2. Competence

(a) Sociologists conduct research, teach, practice, and provide service only within the boundaries of their competence, based on their education, training, supervised experience, or appropriate professional experience.

(b) Sociologists conduct research, teach, practice, and provide service in new areas or involving new techniques only after they have taken reasonable steps to ensure the competence of their work in these areas.

(c) Sociologists who engage in research, teaching, practice, or service maintain awareness of current scientific and professional information in their fields of activity and undertake continuing efforts to maintain competence in the skills they use.

(d) Sociologists refrain from undertaking an activity when their personal circumstances may interfere with their professional work or lead to harm for a student, supervisee, human subject, client, colleague, or other person to whom they have a scientific, teaching, consulting, or other professional obligation.

3. Representation and Misuse of Expertise

(a) In research, teaching, practice, service, or other situations where sociologists render professional judgments or present their expertise, they accurately and fairly represent their areas and degrees of expertise.

(b) Sociologists do not accept grants, contracts, consultation, or work assignments from individual or organizational clients or sponsors that appear likely to require violation of the standards in this Code of Ethics. Sociologists dissociate themselves from such activities when they discover a violation and are unable to achieve its correction.

(c) Because sociologists' scientific and professional judgments and actions may affect the lives of others, they are alert to and guard against personal, financial, social, organizational, or political factors that might lead to misuse of their knowledge, expertise, or influence.

(d) If sociologists learn of misuse or misrepresentation of their work, they take reasonable steps to correct or minimize the misuse or misrepresentation.

4. Delegation and Supervision

(a) Sociologists provide proper training and supervision to their students, supervisees, or employees and take reasonable steps to see that such persons perform services responsibly, competently, and ethically.

(b) Sociologists delegate to their students, supervisees, or employees only those responsibilities that such persons, based on their education, training, or experience, can reasonably be expected to perform either independently or with the level of supervision provided.

5. Nondiscrimination

Sociologists do not engage in discrimination in their work based on age; gender; race; ethnicity; national origin; religion; sexual orientation; disability; health conditions; marital, domestic, or parental status; or any other applicable basis proscribed by law.

6. Non-exploitation

(a) Whether for personal, economic, or professional advantage, sociologists do not exploit persons over whom they have direct or indirect supervisory, evaluative, or other authority such as students, supervisees, employees, or research participants.

(b) Sociologists do not directly supervise or exercise evaluative authority over any person with whom they have a sexual relationship, including students, supervisees, employees, or research participants.

7. Harassment

Sociologists do not engage in harassment of any person, including students, supervisees, employees, or research participants. Harassment consists of a single intense and severe act or of multiple persistent or pervasive acts which are demeaning, abusive, offensive, or create a hostile professional or workplace environment. Sexual harassment may include sexual solicitation, physical advance, or verbal or non-verbal conduct that is sexual in nature. Racial harassment may include unnecessary, exaggerated, or unwarranted attention or attack, whether verbal or non-verbal, because of a person's race or ethnicity.

8. Employment Decisions

Sociologists have an obligation to adhere to the highest ethical standards when participating in employment related decisions, when seeking employment, or when planning to resign from a position.

8.01 Fair Employment Practices

(a) When participating in employment-related decisions, sociologists make every effort to ensure equal opportunity and fair treatment to all full- and part-time employees. They do not discriminate in hiring, promotion, salary, treatment, or any other conditions of employment or career development on the basis of age; gender; race; ethnicity; national origin; religion; sexual orientation; disability; health conditions; marital, domestic, or parental status; or any other applicable basis proscribed by law.

(b) When participating in employment-related decisions, sociologists specify the requirements for hiring, promotion, tenure, and termination and communicate these requirements thoroughly to full- and part-time employees and prospective employees.

(c) When participating in employment-related decisions, sociologists have the responsibility to be informed of fair employment codes, to communicate this information to employees, and to help create an atmosphere upholding fair employment practices for full- and part-time employees.

(d) When participating in employment-related decisions, sociologists inform prospective full- and part-time employees of any constraints on research and publication and negotiate clear understandings about any conditions that may limit research and scholarly activity.

8.02 Responsibilities of Employees

(a) When seeking employment, sociologists provide prospective employers with accurate and complete information on their professional qualifications and experiences.

(b) When leaving a position, permanently or temporarily, sociologists provide their employers with adequate notice and take reasonable steps to reduce negative effects of leaving.

9. Conflicts of Interest

Sociologists maintain the highest degree of integrity in their professional work and avoid conflicts of interest and the appearance of conflict. Conflicts of interest arise when sociologists' personal or financial interests prevent them from performing their professional work in an unbiased manner. In research, teaching, practice, and service, sociologists are alert to situations that might cause a conflict of interest and take appropriate action to prevent conflict or disclose it to appropriate parties.

9.01 Adherence to Professional Standards

Irrespective of their personal or financial interests or those of their employers or clients, sociologists adhere to professional and scientific standards in (1) the collection, analysis, or interpretation of data; (2) the reporting of research; (3) the teaching, professional presentation, or public dissemination of sociological knowledge; and (4) the identification or implementation of appropriate contractual, consulting, or service activities.

9.02 Disclosure

Sociologists disclose relevant sources of financial support and relevant personal or professional relationships that may have the appearance of or potential for a conflict of interest to an employer or client, to the sponsors of their professional work, or in public speeches and writing.

9.03 Avoidance of Personal Gain

(a) Under all circumstances, sociologists do not use or otherwise seek to gain from information or material received in a confidential context (e.g., knowledge obtained from reviewing a manuscript or serving on a proposal review panel), unless they have authorization to do so or until that information is otherwise made publicly available.

(b) Under all circumstances, sociologists do not seek to gain from information or material in an employment or client relationship without permission of the employer or client.

9.04 Decisionmaking in the Workplace

In their workplace, sociologists take appropriate steps to avoid conflicts of interest or the appearance of conflicts and carefully scrutinize *potentially biasing* affiliations or relationships. In research, teaching, practice, or service, such potentially biasing affiliations or relationships include, but are not limited to, situations involving family, business, or close personal friendships or those with whom sociologists have had strong conflict or disagreement.

9.05 Decisionmaking Outside of the Workplace

In professional activities outside of their workplace, sociologists in *all* circumstances abstain from engaging in deliberations and decisions that allocate or withhold benefits or rewards from individuals or institutions if they have *biasing* affiliations or relationships. These biasing affiliations or relationships are: 1) current employment or being considered for employment at an organization or institution that could be construed as benefiting from the decision; 2) current officer or board member of an organization or institution that could be construed as benefiting from the decision; 3) current employment or being considered for employment at the same organization or institution where an individual could benefit from the decision; 4) a spouse, domestic partner, or known relative who as an individual could benefit from the decision; or 5) a current business or professional partner, research collaborator, employee, supervisee, or student who as an individual could benefit from the decision.

10. Public Communications

Sociologists adhere to the highest professional standards in public communications about their professional services, credentials and expertise, work products, or publications, whether these communications are from themselves or from others.

10.01 Public Communications

(a) Sociologists take steps to ensure the accuracy of all public communications. Such public communications include, but are not limited to, directory listings; personal resumes or curriculum vitae; advertising; brochures or printed matter; interviews or comments to the media; statements in legal proceedings; lectures and public oral presentations; or other published materials.

(b) Sociologists do not make public statements that are false, deceptive, misleading, or fraudulent, either because of what they state, convey, or suggest or because of what they omit, concerning their research, practice, or other work activities or those of persons or organizations with which they are affiliated. Such activities include, but are not limited to, false or deceptive statements concerning sociologists' (1) training, experience, or competence; (2) academic degrees; (3) credentials; (4) institutional or association affiliations; (5) services; (6) fees; or (7) publications or research findings. Sociologists do not make false or deceptive statements concerning the scientific basis for, results of, or degree of success from their professional services.

(c) When sociologists provide professional advice or comment by means of public lectures, demonstrations, radio or television programs, prerecorded tapes, printed articles, mailed material, or other media, they take reasonable precautions to ensure that (1) the statements are based on appropriate research, literature, and practice; and (2) the statements are otherwise consistent with this Code of Ethics.

10.02 Statements by Others

(a) Sociologists who engage or employ others to create or place public statements that promote their work products, professional services, or other activities retain responsibility for such statements.

(b) Sociologists make reasonable efforts to prevent others whom they do not directly engage, employ, or supervise (such as employers, publishers, sponsors, organizational clients, members of the media) from making deceptive statements concerning their professional research, teaching, or practice activities.

(c) In working with the press, radio, television, or other communications media or in advertising in the media, sociologists are cognizant of potential conflicts of interest or appearances of such conflicts (e.g., they do not provide compensation to employees of the media), and they adhere to the highest standards of professional honesty (e.g., they acknowledge paid advertising).

11. Confidentiality

Sociologists have an obligation to ensure that confidential information is protected. They do so to ensure the integrity of research and the open communication with research participants and to protect sensitive information obtained in research, teaching, practice, and service. When gathering confidential information, sociologists should take into account the long-term uses of the information, including its potential placement in public archives or the examination of the information by other researchers or practitioners.

11.01 Maintaining Confidentiality

(a) Sociologists take reasonable precautions to protect the confidentiality rights of research participants, students, employees, clients, or others.

(b) Confidential information provided by research participants, students, employees, clients, or others is treated as such by sociologists even if there is no legal protection or privilege to do so. Sociologists have an obligation to protect confidential information and not allow information gained in confidence from being used in ways that would unfairly compromise research participants, students, employees, clients, or others.

(c) Information provided under an understanding of confidentiality is treated as such even after the death of those providing that information.

(d) Sociologists maintain the integrity of confidential deliberations, activities, or roles, including, where applicable, that of professional committees, review panels, or advisory groups (e.g., the ASA Committee on Professional Ethics).

(e) Sociologists, to the extent possible, protect the confidentiality of student records, performance data, and personal information, whether verbal or written, given in the context of academic consultation, supervision, or advising.

(f) The obligation to maintain confidentiality extends to members of research or training teams and collaborating organizations who have access to the information. To ensure that access to confidential information is restricted, it is the responsibility of researchers, administrators, and principal investigators to instruct staff to take the steps necessary to protect confidentiality.

(g) When using private information about individuals collected by other persons or institutions, sociologists protect the confidentiality of individually identifiable information. Information is private when an individual can reasonably expect that the information will not be made public with personal identifiers (e.g., medical or employment records).

11.02 Limits of Confidentiality

(a) Sociologists inform themselves fully about all laws and rules which may limit or alter guarantees of confidentiality. They determine their ability to guarantee absolute confidentiality and, as appropriate, inform research participants, students, employees, clients, or others of any limitations to this guarantee at the outset, consistent with ethical standards set forth in 11.02(b).

(b) Sociologists may confront unanticipated circumstances where they become aware of information that is clearly health- or life-threatening to research participants, students, employees, clients, or others. In these cases, sociologists balance the importance of guarantees of confidentiality with other principles in this Code of Ethics, standards of conduct, and applicable law.

(c) Confidentiality is not required with respect to observations in public places, activities conducted in public, or other settings where no rules of privacy are provided by law or custom. Similarly, confidentiality is not required in the case of information available from public records.

11.03 Discussing Confidentiality and Its Limits

(a) When sociologists establish a scientific or professional relationship with persons, they discuss (1) the relevant limitations on confidentiality, and (2) the foreseeable uses of the information generated through their professional work.

(b) Unless it is not feasible or is counter-productive, the discussion of confidentiality occurs at the outset of the relationship and thereafter as new circumstances may warrant.

11.04 Anticipation of Possible Uses of Information

(a) When research requires maintaining personal identifiers in databases or systems of records, sociologists delete such identifiers before the information is made publicly available.

(b) When confidential information concerning research participants, clients, or other recipients of service is entered into databases or systems of records available to persons without the prior consent of the relevant parties, sociologists protect anonymity by not including personal identifiers or by employing other techniques that mask or control disclosure of individual identities.

(c) When deletion of personal identifiers is not feasible, sociologists take reasonable steps to determine that appropriate consent of personally-identifiable individuals has been obtained before they transfer such data to others or review such data collected by others.

11.05 Electronic Transmission of Confidential Information

Sociologists use extreme care in delivering or transferring any confidential data, information, or communication over public computer networks. Sociologists are attentive to the problems of maintaining confidentiality and control over sensitive material and data when use of technological innovations, such as public computer networks, may open their professional and scientific communication to unauthorized persons.

11.06 Anonymity of Sources

(a) Sociologists do not disclose in their writings, lectures, or other public media confidential, personally identifiable information concerning their research participants, students, individual or organizational clients, or other recipients of their service which is obtained during the course of their work, unless consent from individuals or their legal representatives has been obtained.

(b) When confidential information is used in scientific and professional presentations, sociologists disguise the identity of research participants, students, individual or organizational clients, or other recipients of their service.

11.07 Minimizing Intrusions on Privacy

(a) To minimize intrusions on privacy, sociologists include in written and oral reports, consultations, and public communications only information germane to the purpose for which the communication is made.

(b) Sociologists discuss confidential information or evaluative data concerning research participants, students, supervisees, employees, and individual or organizational clients only for appropriate scientific or professional purposes and only with persons clearly concerned with such matters.

11.08 Preservation of Confidential Information

(a) Sociologists take reasonable steps to ensure that records, data, or information are preserved in a confidential manner consistent with the requirements of this Code of Ethics,

recognizing that ownership of records, data, or information may also be governed by law or institutional principles.

(b) Sociologists plan so that confidentiality of records, data, or information is protected in the event of the sociologist's death, incapacity, or withdrawal from the position or practice.

(c) When sociologists transfer confidential records, data, or information to other persons or organizations, they obtain assurances that the recipients of the records, data, or information will employ measures to protect confidentiality at least equal to those originally pledged.

12. Informed Consent

Informed consent is a basic ethical tenet of scientific research on human populations. Sociologists do not involve a human being as a subject in research without the informed consent of the subject or the subject's legally authorized representative, except as otherwise specified in this Code. Sociologists recognize the possibility of undue influence or subtle pressures on subjects that may derive from researchers' expertise or authority, and they take this into account in designing informed consent procedures.

12.01 Scope of Informed Consent

(a) Sociologists conducting research obtain consent from research participants or their legally authorized representatives (1) when data are collected from research participants through any form of communication, interaction, or intervention; or (2) when behavior of research participants occurs in a private context where an individual can reasonably expect that no observation or reporting is taking place.

(b) Despite the paramount importance of consent, sociologists may seek waivers of this standard when (1) the research involves no more than minimal risk for research participants, and (2) the research could not practically be carried out were informed consent to be required. Sociologists recognize that waivers of consent require approval from institutional review boards or, in the absence of such boards, from another authoritative body with expertise on the ethics of research. Under such circumstances, the confidentiality of any personally identifiable information must be maintained unless otherwise set forth in 11.02(b).

(c) Sociologists may conduct research in public places or use publicly-available information about individuals (e.g., naturalistic observations in public places, analysis of public records, or archival research) without obtaining consent. If, under such circumstances, sociologists have any doubt whatsoever about the need for informed consent, they consult with institutional review boards or, in the absence of such boards, with another authoritative body with expertise on the ethics of research before proceeding with such research.

(d) In undertaking research with vulnerable populations (e.g., youth, recent immigrant populations, the mentally ill), sociologists take special care to ensure that the voluntary nature of the research is understood and that consent is not coerced. In all other respects, sociologists adhere to the principles set forth in 12.01(a)-(c).

(e) Sociologists are familiar with and conform to applicable state and federal regulations and, where applicable, institutional review board requirements for obtaining informed consent for research.

12.02 Informed Consent Process

(a) When informed consent is required, sociologists enter into an agreement with research participants or their legal representatives that clarifies the nature of the research and the responsibilities of the investigator prior to conducting the research.

(b) When informed consent is required, sociologists use language that is understandable to and respectful of research participants or their legal representatives.

(c) When informed consent is required, sociologists provide research participants or their legal representatives with the opportunity to ask questions about any aspect of the research, at any time during or after their participation in the research.

(d) When informed consent is required, sociologists inform research participants or their legal representatives of the nature of the research; they indicate to participants that their participation or continued participation is voluntary; they inform participants of significant factors that may be expected to influence their willingness to participate (e.g., possible risks and benefits of their participation); and they explain other aspects of the research and respond to questions from prospective participants. Also, if relevant, sociologists explain that refusal to participate or withdrawal from participation in the research involves no penalty, and they explain any foreseeable consequences of declining or withdrawing. Sociologists explicitly discuss confidentiality and, if applicable, the extent to which confidentiality may be limited as set forth in 11.02(b).

(e) When informed consent is required, sociologists keep records regarding said consent. They recognize that consent is a process that involves oral and/or written consent.

(f) Sociologists honor all commitments they have made to research participants as part of the informed consent process except where unanticipated circumstances demand otherwise as set forth in 11.02(b).

12.03 Informed Consent of Students and Subordinates

When undertaking research at their own institutions or organizations with research participants who are students or subordinates, sociologists take special care to protect the prospective subjects from adverse consequences of declining or withdrawing from participation.

12.04 Informed Consent with Children

(a) In undertaking research with children, sociologists obtain the consent of children to participate, to the extent that they are capable of providing such consent, except under circumstances where consent may not be required as set forth in 12.01(b).

(b) In undertaking research with children, sociologists obtain the consent of a parent or a legally authorized guardian. Sociologists may seek waivers of parental or guardian consent when (1) the research involves no more than minimal risk for the research participants, and (2) the research could not practically be carried out were consent to be required, or (3) the consent of a parent or guardian is not a reasonable requirement to protect the child (e.g., neglected or abused children).

(c) Sociologists recognize that waivers of consent from a child and a parent or guardian require approval from institutional review boards or, in the absence of such boards, from another authoritative body with expertise on the ethics of research. Under such circumstances, the confidentiality of any personally identifiable information must be maintained unless otherwise set forth in 11.02(b).

12.05 Use of Deception in Research

(a) Sociologists do not use deceptive techniques (1) unless they have determined that their use will not be harmful to research participants; is justified by the study's prospective scientific, educational, or applied value; and that equally effective alternative procedures that do not use deception are not feasible; and (2) unless they have obtained the approval of institutional review boards or, in the absence of such boards, with another authoritative body with expertise on the ethics of research.

(b) Sociologists never deceive research participants about significant aspects of the research that would affect their willingness to participate, such as physical risks, discomfort, or unpleasant emotional experiences.

(c) When deception is an integral feature of the design and conduct of research, sociologists attempt to correct any misconception that

research participants may have no later than at the conclusion of the research.

(d) On rare occasions, sociologists may need to conceal their identities in order to undertake research that could not practically be carried out were they to be known as researchers. Under such circumstances, sociologists undertake the research if it involves no more than minimal risk for the research participants and if they have obtained approval to proceed in this manner from an institutional review board or, in the absence of such boards, from another authoritative body with expertise on the ethics of research. Under such circumstances, confidentiality must be maintained unless otherwise set forth in 11.02(b).

12.06 Use of Recording Technology

Sociologists obtain informed consent from research participants, students, employees, clients, or others prior to videotaping, filming, or recording them in any form, unless these activities involve simply naturalistic observations in public places and it is not anticipated that the recording will be used in a manner that could cause personal identification or harm.

13. Research Planning, Implementation, and Dissemination

Sociologists have an obligation to promote the integrity of research and to ensure that they comply with the ethical tenets of science in the planning, implementation, and dissemination of research. They do so in order to advance knowledge, to minimize the possibility that results will be misleading, and to protect the rights of research participants.

13.01 Planning and Implementation

(a) In planning and implementing research, sociologists minimize the possibility that results will be misleading.

(b) Sociologists take steps to implement protections for the rights and welfare of research participants and other persons affected by the research.

(c) In their research, sociologists do not encourage activities or themselves behave in ways that are health- or life-threatening to research participants or others.

(d) In planning and implementing research, sociologists consult those with expertise concerning any special population under investigation or likely to be affected.

(e) In planning and implementing research, sociologists consider its ethical acceptability as set forth in the Code of Ethics. If the best ethical practice is unclear, sociologists consult with institutional review boards or, in the absence of such review processes, with another authoritative body with expertise on the ethics of research.

(f) Sociologists are responsible for the ethical conduct of research conducted by them or by others under their supervision or authority.

13.02 Unanticipated Research Opportunities

If during the course of teaching, practice, service, or non-professional activities, sociologists determine that they wish to undertake research that was not previously anticipated, they make known their intentions and take steps to ensure that the research can be undertaken consonant with ethical principles, especially those relating to confidentiality and informed consent. Under such circumstances, sociologists seek the approval of institutional review boards or, in the absence of such review processes, another authoritative body with expertise on the ethics of research.

13.03 Offering Inducements for Research Participants

Sociologists do not offer excessive or inappropriate financial or other inducements to obtain the participation of research participants, particularly when it might coerce participation.

Sociologists may provide incentives to the extent that resources are available and appropriate.

13.04 Reporting on Research

(a) Sociologists disseminate their research findings except where unanticipated circumstances (e.g., the health of the researcher) or proprietary agreements with employers, contractors, or clients preclude such dissemination.

(b) Sociologists do not fabricate data or falsify results in their publications or presentations.

(c) In presenting their work, sociologists report their findings fully and do not omit relevant data. They report results whether they support or contradict the expected outcomes.

(d) Sociologists take particular care to state all relevant qualifications on the findings and interpretation of their research. Sociologists also disclose underlying assumptions, theories, methods, measures, and research designs that might bear upon findings and interpretations of their work.

(e) Consistent with the spirit of full disclosure of methods and analyses, once findings are publicly disseminated, sociologists permit their open assessment and verification by other responsible researchers with appropriate safeguards, where applicable, to protect the anonymity of research participants.

(f) If sociologists discover significant errors in their publication or presentation of data, they take reasonable steps to correct such errors in a correction, a retraction, published errata, or other public fora as appropriate.

(g) Sociologists report sources of financial support in their written papers and note any special relations to any sponsor. In special circumstances, sociologists may withhold the names of specific sponsors if they provide an adequate and full description of the nature and interest of the sponsor.

(h) Sociologists take special care to report accurately the results of others' scholarship by using correct information and citations when presenting the work of others in publications, teaching, practice, and service settings.

13.05 Data Sharing

(a) Sociologists share data and pertinent documentation as a regular practice. Sociologists make their data available after completion of the project or its major publications, except where proprietary agreements with employers, contractors, or clients preclude such accessibility or when it is impossible to share data and protect the confidentiality of the data or the anonymity of research participants (e.g., raw field notes or detailed information from ethnographic interviews).

(b) Sociologists anticipate data sharing as an integral part of a research plan whenever data sharing is feasible.

(c) Sociologists share data in a form that is consonant with research participants' interests and protect the confidentiality of the information they have been given. They maintain the confidentiality of data, whether legally required or not; remove personal identifiers before data are shared; and, if necessary, use other disclosure avoidance techniques.

(d) Sociologists who do not otherwise place data in public archives keep data available and retain documentation relating to the research for a reasonable period of time after publication or dissemination of results.

(e) Sociologists may ask persons who request their data for further analysis to bear the associated incremental costs, if necessary.

(f) Sociologists who use data from others for further analyses explicitly acknowledge the contribution of the initial researchers.

14. Plagiarism

(a) In publications, presentations, teaching, practice, and service, sociologists explicitly identify, credit, and reference the author when they take data or material verbatim from another person's written work, whether it is published, unpublished, or electronically available.

(b) In their publications, presentations, teaching, practice, and service, sociologists provide acknowledgment of and reference to the use of others' work, even if the work is not quoted verbatim or paraphrased, and they do not present others' work as their own whether it is published, unpublished, or electronically available.

15. Authorship Credit

(a) Sociologists take responsibility and credit, including authorship credit, only for work they have actually performed or to which they have contributed.

(b) Sociologists ensure that principal authorship and other publication credits are based on the relative scientific or professional contributions of the individuals involved, regardless of their status. In claiming or determining the ordering of authorship, sociologists seek to reflect accurately the contributions of main participants in the research and writing process.

(c) A student is usually listed as principal author on any multiple-authored publication that substantially derives from the student's dissertation or thesis.

16. Publication Process

Sociologists adhere to the highest ethical standards when participating in publication and review processes when they are authors or editors.

16.01 Submission of Manuscripts for Publication

(a) In cases of multiple authorship, sociologists confer with all other authors prior to submitting work for publication and establish mutually acceptable agreements regarding submission.

(b) In submitting a manuscript to a professional journal, book series, or edited book, sociologists grant that publication first claim to publication except where explicit policies allow multiple submissions. Sociologists do not submit a manuscript to a second publication until after an official decision has been received from the first publication or until the manuscript is withdrawn. Sociologists submitting a manuscript for publication in a journal, book series, or edited book can withdraw a manuscript from consideration up until an official acceptance is made.

(c) Sociologists may submit a book manuscript to multiple publishers. However, once sociologists have signed a contract, they cannot withdraw a manuscript from publication unless there is reasonable cause to do so.

16.02 Duplicate Publication of Data

When sociologists publish data or findings that they have previously published elsewhere, they accompany these publications by proper acknowledgment.

16.03 Responsibilities of Editors

(a) When serving as editors of journals or book series, sociologists are fair in the application of standards and operate without personal or ideological favoritism or malice. As editors, sociologists are cognizant of any potential conflicts of interest.

(b) When serving as editors of journals or book series, sociologists ensure the confidential nature of the review process and supervise editorial office staff, including students, in accordance with practices that maintain confidentiality.

(c) When serving as editors of journals or book series, sociologists are bound to publish all manuscripts accepted for publication unless major errors or ethical violations are discovered after acceptance (e.g., plagiarism or scientific misconduct).

(d) When serving as editors of journals or book series, sociologists ensure the anonymity of reviewers unless they otherwise receive permission from reviewers to reveal their identity. Editors ensure that their staff conform to this practice.

(e) When serving as journal editors, sociologists ensure the anonymity of authors unless and until a manuscript is accepted for publication

or unless the established practices of the journal are known to be otherwise.

(f) When serving as journal editors, sociologists take steps to provide for the timely review of all manuscripts and respond promptly to inquiries about the status of the review.

17. Responsibilities of Reviewers

(a) In reviewing material submitted for publication, grant support, or other evaluation purposes, sociologists respect the confidentiality of the process and the proprietary rights in such information of those who submitted it.

(b) Sociologists disclose conflicts of interest or decline requests for reviews of the work of others where conflicts of interest are involved.

(c) Sociologists decline requests for reviews of the work of others when they believe that the review process may be biased or when they have questions about the integrity of the process.

(d) If asked to review a manuscript, book, or proposal they have previously reviewed, sociologists make it known to the person making the request (e.g., editor, program officer) unless it is clear that they are being asked to provide a reappraisal.

18. Education, Teaching, and Training

As teachers, supervisors, and trainers, sociologists follow the highest ethical standards in order to ensure the quality of sociological education and the integrity of the teacher-student relationship.

18.01 Administration of Education Programs

(a) Sociologists who are responsible for education and training programs seek to ensure that the programs are competently designed, provide the proper experiences, and meet all goals for which claims are made by the program.

(b) Sociologists responsible for education and training programs seek to ensure that there is an accurate description of the program content, training goals and objectives, and requirements that must be met for satisfactory completion of the program.

(c) Sociologists responsible for education and training programs take steps to ensure that graduate assistants and temporary instructors have the substantive knowledge required to teach courses and the teaching skills needed to facilitate student learning.

(d) Sociologists responsible for education and training programs have an obligation to ensure that ethics are taught to their graduate students as part of their professional preparation.

18.02 Teaching and Training

(a) Sociologists conscientiously perform their teaching responsibilities. They have appropriate skills and knowledge or are receiving appropriate training.

(b) Sociologists provide accurate information at the outset about their courses, particularly regarding the subject matter to be covered, bases for evaluation, and the nature of course experiences.

(c) Sociologists make decisions concerning textbooks, course content, course requirements, and grading solely on the basis of educational criteria without regard for financial or other incentives.

(d) Sociologists provide proper training and supervision to their teaching assistants and other teaching trainees and take reasonable steps to ensure that such persons perform these teaching responsibilities responsibly, competently, and ethically.

(e) Sociologists do not permit personal animosities or intellectual differences with colleagues to foreclose students' or supervisees' access to these colleagues or to interfere with student or supervisee learning, academic progress, or professional development.

19. Contractual and Consulting Services

(a) Sociologists undertake grants, contracts, or consultation only when they are knowledgeable about the substance, methods, and techniques they plan to use or have a plan for incorporating appropriate expertise.

(b) In undertaking grants, contracts, or consultation, sociologists base the results of their professional work on appropriate information and techniques.

(c) When financial support for a project has been accepted under a grant, contract, or consultation, sociologists make reasonable efforts to complete the proposed work on schedule.

(d) In undertaking grants, contracts, or consultation, sociologists accurately document and appropriately retain their professional and scientific work.

(e) In establishing a contractual arrangement for research, consultation, or other services, sociologists clarify, to the extent feasible at the outset, the nature of the relationship with the individual, organizational, or institutional client. This clarification includes, as appropriate, the nature of the services to be performed, the probable uses of the services provided, possibilities for the sociologist's future use of the work for scholarly or publication purposes, the timetable for delivery of those services, and compensation and billing arrangements.

20. Adherence to the Code of Ethics

Sociologists have an obligation to confront, address, and attempt to resolve ethical issues according to this Code of Ethics.

20.01 Familiarity with the Code of Ethics

Sociologists have an obligation to be familiar with this Code of Ethics, other applicable ethics codes, and their application to sociologists' work. Lack of awareness or misunderstanding of an ethical standard is not, in itself, a defense to a charge of unethical conduct.

20.02 Confronting Ethical Issues

(a) When sociologists are uncertain whether a particular situation or course of action would violate the Code of Ethics, they consult with other sociologists knowledgeable about ethical issues, with the ASA's Committee on Professional

Ethics, or with other organizational entities such as institutional review boards.

(b) When sociologists take actions or are confronted with choices where there is a conflict between ethical standards enunciated in the Code of Ethics and laws or legal requirements, they make known their commitment to the Code and take steps to resolve the conflict in a responsible manner by consulting with colleagues, professional organizations, or the ASA's Committee on Professional Ethics.

20.03 Fair Treatment of Parties in Ethical Disputes

(a) Sociologists do not discriminate against a person on the basis of his or her having made an ethical complaint.

(b) Sociologists do not discriminate against a person based on his or her having been the subject of an ethical complaint. This does not preclude taking action based upon the outcome of an ethical complaint.

20.04 Reporting Ethical Violations of Others

When sociologists have substantial reason to believe that there may have been an ethical violation by another sociologist, they attempt to resolve the issue by bringing it to the attention of that individual if an informal resolution appears appropriate or possible, or they seek advice about whether or how to proceed based on this belief, assuming that such activity does not violate any confidentiality rights. Such action might include referral to the ASA's Committee on Professional Ethics.

20.05 Cooperating with Ethics Committees

Sociologists cooperate in ethics investigations, proceedings, and resulting requirements of the American Sociological Association. In doing so, they make reasonable efforts to resolve any issues of confidentiality. Failure to cooperate may be an ethics violation.

20.06 Improper Complaints

Sociologists do not file or encourage the filing of ethics complaints that are frivolous and are intended to harm the alleged violator rather than to protect the integrity of the discipline and the public.

NOTE: This revised edition of the American Sociological Association's Code of Ethics builds on the 1989 edition of the Code and the 1992 version of the American Psychological Association's Ethical Principles of Psychologists and Code of Conduct.

Reading

Policies and Procedures (1997)

Committee on Professional Ethics

American Sociological Association

INTRODUCTION

These Policies and Procedures describe the responsibilities of the Committee on Professional Ethics (COPE) of the American Sociological Association (ASA), the general operating rules of COPE, and the policies and procedures related to the submission and resolution of complaints of violations of the ASA Code of Ethics.

Part I. Responsibilities and Authority of COPE

1. Responsibilities

COPE has been established by the Council of the ASA in order to promote ethical conduct by sociologists at the highest professional level through development and sponsorship of educational activities for ASA members and other sociologists, investigation of complaints concerning the ethical conduct of members of the ASA, and imposition of sanctions when a violation of the Code has occurred.

2. Authority of COPE

COPE is authorized to:

(a) Publicize the Code of Ethics to the members of the ASA and other interested persons.

(b) Educate the members of the ASA and other interested persons concerning the ethical obligations of sociologists under the Code of Ethics through articles, seminars, lectures, casebooks, or other materials.

(c) Recommend to the ASA Council changes in the Code of Ethics and these Policies and Procedures.

(d) Provide to individual members of the ASA on an informal and confidential basis advice regarding their ethical obligations under the Code of Ethics.

(e) Seek to resolve allegations of unethical conduct of members of the ASA informally through mediation or other means.

(f) Investigate allegations of unethical conduct of members of the ASA, determine violations of the Code of Ethics, and, where appropriate, impose sanctions.

(g) Adopt such rules and procedures governing the conduct of all matters within its jurisdiction as

are consistent with the Constitution and By-Laws of the Association, the Code of Ethics, and these Policies and Procedures.

3. Responsibilities of the Executive Office

(a) Works with COPE in the administration of 2(a)-(g).

(b) Reports to COPE on an annual basis the number and types of complaints received, the number recommended for informal resolution, and any other pertinent information regarding the involvement of the Executive Office in ethics inquiries.

Part II. Operating Rules of COPE

1. Membership

The members of COPE shall be appointed in accordance with the By-Laws of the Association. After the end of his/her term of office, a member of COPE may continue to participate in the investigation of a matter to which he/she was previously assigned, and such member may participate in reaching the findings and recommendation of the Investigation Panel with respect to that matter.

2. Officers

The Chair and Co-Chair of COPE shall be appointed at the Council meeting held during the Annual Meeting of the Association and shall serve a term of one (1) year beginning on January 1 of the next calendar year. Prior to the Annual Meeting, COPE shall deliver to the Council its recommendations for the Chair and Co-Chair for the succeeding year. The Chair shall have primary responsibility for carrying out the mandate of COPE. The Co-Chair shall have the authority to perform all of the duties of the Chair when the latter is unavailable or unable to perform them and shall perform other tasks as delegated by the Chair.

3. Meetings

A regular meeting of COPE shall be held annually in connection with the Annual Meeting of the Association. Additional meetings may be held, upon the call of the Chair, from time to time in person or by telephone conference call.

4. Quorum and Voting

A quorum for the transaction of business at any meeting of COPE shall consist of a majority of the members then in office. All decisions shall be by majority vote of the members present at a meeting.

5. Voting by Mail

Any action of COPE which could be taken at a meeting may be taken upon the affirmative vote, in writing or by electronic communication, of a majority of members then in office.

6. Conflicts of Interest

No member of COPE shall participate in the deliberations or decision of any matter with respect to which the member has a conflict of interest as outlined in the Code of Ethics.

PART III. ENFORCEMENT OF THE CODE OF ETHICS

1. Jurisdiction

(a) COPE shall have jurisdiction to receive and determine any timely complaint of the violation of the ASA Code of Ethics by a current member of the ASA in any category of membership whatsoever. In the event that a complainee resigns from the ASA subsequent to the filing of a complaint against him or her, COPE shall have discretion to resolve the complaint as if the complainee were still a member.

(b) In the event that a complaint alleges conduct which is, or may be, the subject of other legal or institutional proceedings, COPE may, in its discretion, defer further proceedings with respect to the complaint until the conclusion of the other legal or institutional proceedings.

2. Filing of Complaint

(a) Any member or non-member of the ASA who perceives that an ASA member has violated an ethical standard may file a complaint with COPE.

(b) A complaint may be initiated by COPE on its own behalf.

(c) Initial telephone contact with the Executive Officer or his/her designee is encouraged to clarify whether concerns about a possible ethical violation are covered by the Code. If it appears that a potential complaint may be covered by the Code, a copy of the Code and a complaint form shall be sent to the potential complainant. Informal dispute resolution and use of other venues of investigation will be encouraged.

(d) A complaint may not be accepted or initiated if it is received more than 18 months after the alleged conduct either occurred or was discovered. A complaint received after the 18-month time limit set forth in this paragraph shall not be accepted unless the Chair of COPE determines that there is good cause for the complaint not to have been filed within the 18-month time limit. No complaint will be considered if it is received more than five years after the alleged conduct occurred or was discovered.

(e) A complaint shall include the name and address of the complainant; the name and address of the complainee; the provisions of the Code of Ethics alleged to have been violated; a statement that other legal or institutional proceedings involving the alleged conduct have not been initiated or, if initiated, the status of such proceedings; a full statement of conduct alleged to have violated the Code of Ethics, including the sources of all information on which the allegations are based; copies of any documents supporting the allegations; and, if necessary, a request that the 18-month time limit be waived. Anonymous complaints shall not be accepted. If material in the public domain is provided anonymously, COPE may choose to use such material in support of its own complaint.

3. Preliminary Screening of Complaint

(a) The Executive Officer or his/her designee shall screen each complaint to determine whether the complainee is a member of the ASA and whether the alleged conduct is covered by the Code. If the complaint does not include the information required by 2(e), the Executive Officer or his/her designee shall so inform the complainant, who will be given the opportunity to provide additional information. If no response is received from the complainant within thirty (30) days, the matter will be closed and the complainant so notified. (b) If the complaint is complete as set forth in 2(e), the Executive Officer or his/her designee shall notify the Chair of COPE and provide relevant materials regarding the complaint. The Chair of COPE and the Executive Officer or his/her designee shall evaluate whether there is cause for action by COPE. Cause for action shall exist when the complainee's alleged actions and/or omissions, if proved, would in the judgment of the Chair of COPE and the Executive Officer or his/her designee constitute a breach of ethics. For purposes of determining whether cause for action exists, incredible, speculative, and/or internally inconsistent allegations may be disregarded. If cause for action exists, a formal case is initiated, as set forth in 4(a). If cause for action does not exist, the complaint will be dismissed at this stage and the complainant so notified.

4. Notice of Complaint and Informal Resolution

(a) If cause for action is found, the Executive Officer or his/her designee shall provide a copy of the complaint and all supporting materials, and a copy of the Code of Ethics and these Policies and Procedures, to the complainee and encourage a settlement through informal means. If a method of informal dispute settlement is not otherwise available to the complainant and complainee, a mediator who is not a member of COPE may be recommended by the Executive Officer or his/her designee. Mediation services will in most cases be by written correspondence or telephone. If informal dispute resolution is declined, the members of COPE shall not be informed which party declined.

(b) Any person appointed to serve as a mediator shall agree to maintain the confidentiality of the proceedings as set forth in the Code of Ethics and these Policies and Procedures. The mediator shall report to the Executive Officer or his/her designee only whether or not a matter has been resolved to the satisfaction of the parties.

5. Response to Complaint

If either or both the complainant and complainee decline informal dispute settlement or if informal dispute settlement fails to resolve the complaint, the Executive Officer or his/her designee shall notify the complainee that the case will go forward in accordance with these Policies and Procedures. Complainee shall have thirty (30) days after receipt of this notice to respond in writing to the complaint. An extension may be granted by the Executive Officer if good cause is shown, but the extension shall not exceed ninety (90) days.

6. Initial Determination of the Chair

The complaint and response shall be submitted to the Chair of COPE for an initial determination whether there is sufficient evidence to proceed with the case. The Chair may, in his/her discretion, request additional information from the complainant and/or any other appropriate source before making the initial determination, provided, however, that the Chair shall not rely on such additional information unless it has been shared with the complainee and the complainee has been afforded an opportunity to respond. If the Chair shall decide that there is insufficient evidence to proceed, the matter shall be closed and the complainant and complainee notified in writing.

7. Investigation and Recommendation

If the Chair determines that there is sufficient evidence to proceed with the complaint, he/she shall appoint an Investigation Panel composed of the Chair or Co-Chair and two members of COPE to investigate the complaint. The Panel may communicate with the complainant, complainee, witnesses, or other sources of information necessary to carry out its functions. The Panel shall conduct as much of its business as is practical through written correspondence or verbal communication. Although complainants and complainees have the right to consult with attorneys concerning all phases of the ethics process, the complainant must file and the complainee must respond to charges of unethical conduct personally and not through legal counsel or another third party, unless the complainant or complainee provides good cause as to why he or she cannot respond personally. The Panel shall submit a written report of its findings and any recommendation for sanction to the full Committee within ninety (90) days, unless a longer period is necessary in the opinion of the Chair or Co-Chair. A copy of the Panel's findings and recommendation shall be provided to the complainant and complainee, who may submit a response in writing within a time frame of not more than thirty (30) days.

8. Determination of Violation

COPE shall determine whether a violation of the Code of Ethics has occurred on the basis of the complaint, the response, any other information provided to the Investigation Panel, the recommendation and findings of the Panel, and the responses of the parties thereto, provided, however, that COPE may hear the testimony of witnesses where in its view it is essential to the fairness of the proceeding. COPE may return any matter to the Investigation Panel for further investigation. Upon completion of its review, COPE shall issue a determination of whether one or more violations of the Code of Ethics have occurred, including a summary of the factual basis for this determination, and of the appropriate sanction.

9. Sanctions

In any case in which it has determined that a violation of the Code of Ethics has occurred, COPE may impose no sanction or one or more of the following, as appropriate:

(a) *Private Reprimand.* In cases where there has been an ethics violation but the violation did not cause serious personal and/or professional harm, an educative letter concerning the violation, including any stipulated conditions of redress, may be sent to the complainee. Failure to comply with stipulated conditions of redress in a reprimand may result in the imposition of a more severe sanction.

(b) *Public Reprimand.* Where COPE determines that the seriousness of the violation warrants more than a private reprimand, it may direct that a copy of the letter of reprimand be made public in an appropriate manner.

(c) *Denial of Privileges.* In appropriate cases, COPE may determine that a complainee shall be denied one or more of the privileges of ASA membership and/or the opportunity to participate in ASA-sponsored activities including but not limited to appointment to the editorial boards of any ASA publications, election or appointment to any ASA offices and committees, receipt of any ASA awards, publishing in or serving as an editor of one or more ASA-sponsored journals, presenting a paper or otherwise participating at one or more meetings sponsored by the ASA, or receiving research or scholarship assistance from any program sponsored by the ASA.

(d) *Termination of Membership.* In cases where there has been an ethics violation and the violation caused serious personal and/or professional harm, the ASA membership of the complainee may be terminated for a period to be determined by COPE. Eligibility to renew membership at the expiration of this period may be automatic or may be conditioned on a future determination by COPE that eligibility is appropriate.

10. Notice of Determination

The Chair of COPE shall notify the complainant and complainee of the decision of COPE. If a sanction is imposed under 9(c) or 9(d), COPE shall instruct the Executive Officer to take the appropriate actions called for under COPE's determination, except that such notice shall be postponed if an appeal is filed as set forth in paragraph 11.

11. Appeal of Termination

A complainee who is found by COPE to have violated the Code of Ethics and who receives a sanction under 9(b) through 9(d) may appeal this determination by filing a Notice of Appeal and Statement of Reasons no later than thirty (30) days after receipt of the Notice of Determination. If an appeal is filed, the President of the ASA shall appoint a three-member Appeal Panel of past members of COPE to review all information considered by COPE and, within ninety (90) days, make a decision to uphold or reverse the determination. The Appeal Panel may set aside COPE's determination that a violation has occurred or it may determine that the sanction imposed by COPE is not appropriate and impose a less severe sanction. The decision of the Appeal Panel shall constitute the final decision of the ASA with respect to all matters subject to this paragraph.

12. Confidentiality

(a) The filing of a complaint against an ASA member and all proceedings held under this Part III shall be kept confidential by COPE, the Investigation Panel, the Appeal Panel, and the President of the ASA prior to a final determination of the matter, except that information regarding complaints may be shared with the Executive Officer, any staff designated by the Executive Officer to assist COPE, and ASA legal counsel. Determinations of violations of the Code of Ethics by COPE or by an Appeal Panel shall be kept confidential, except in the case of termination of membership, or unless disclosure of the determination to the public is imposed as part of another sanction. The name of each individual whose membership is terminated and a brief statement of the reason for termination shall be reported annually to the ASA Council and in the official newsletter of the ASA.

(b) The Committee may disclose such information when compelled by a valid subpoena or by a final court order.

(c) Notwithstanding the foregoing, COPE may publish reports of its determinations in order to educate the membership about the requirements of the Code of Ethics but will not make the identity of the parties public unless otherwise provided for in Part III, section 12(b).

(d) Initiation of legal action against the ASA or its officers or employees shall constitute a waiver of confidentiality by the person initiating such action.

(e) Records relating to the investigation of complaints of violations of the Code, whether or not COPE determined that a violation occurred, shall be maintained in a secure place indefinitely. These records should always remain confidential, unless otherwise provided for in 12(b) and 12(d). Permission to use these materials for research and educational purposes may be granted by the Executive Officer within the first fifty (50) years of the closing of the complaint, as long as the materials do not identify the individuals involved. After fifty (50) years, these materials are available for research or educational purposes without special approval as long as the commitment to confidentiality is honored and the materials do not identify the individuals involved.

NOTE: These Policies and Procedures replace Section V of the 1989 edition of the American Sociological Association's Code of Ethics.

Reading

Project Camelot and the 1960s Epistemological Revolution

Rethinking the Politics–Patronage–Social Science Nexus (2001)

Mark Solovey

The influence of political decisions and climates on social research is not new, but the fact that this can no longer be ignored is. Camelot, a proposed international social science research project sponsored by the Army Research Office of the United States Department of Defense, was the turning point.[1]

Anthropologist Ralph L. Beals, 1969

Project Camelot, a 1960s military-sponsored study of the revolutionary process, had a curiously brief existence, yet it also left an important legacy. Camelot's projected cost of six million US dollars would have made it the largest social science project in US history, but international complaints about this study's imperialistic implications led in mid-1965 to its cancellation, before Camelot had even moved beyond the planning stage. Camelot's full importance became manifest only in the following years, as this study became the focal point of an extensive controversy about the relationship between American

---

SOURCE: From "Project Camelot and the 1960s Epistemological Revolution: Rethinking the Politics-Patronage-Social Science Nexus." By Solovey, M. in *Social Studies of Science, Vol. 31*, No. 2, Science in the Cold War (Apr., 2001), pp. 171–206. Copyright © 2001. Reprinted with permission of Sage Publications, Ltd.

1. Ralph L. Beals, Politics of Social Research: An Inquiry Into the Ethics and Responsibilities of Social Scientists (Chicago, IL: Aldine Publishing Company, 1969), 4.

politics, military patronage, and American social science.[2]

Camelot thus became an important episode in the long-standing (and still ongoing) debate about the nature of the social science enterprise. Ever since the emergence of professional social science in the United States during the late 19th and early 20th centuries, scholars, patrons and consumers of social research have argued about the relationships between inquiry and politics, research and reform, scholarship and ideology.[3] From the 1940s until the early 1960s especially, the dominant sentiment held that the social sciences were junior partners to the natural sciences.[4] This position implied that the former needed to follow in the footsteps of the latter, which, by further implication, required a clear-cut, impermeable boundary between science and politics. But as the decade of the 1960s unfolded, the social sciences became major participants in what historian Peter Novick has called 'the epistemological revolution that began in the 1960s.'[5]

At the heart of this revolution, according to Novick, was a multi-faceted scholarly challenge to the dominant post-WWII model of social science inquiry based upon an idealized positivist and empiricist image of the natural sciences—an image that posited an objective, value-neutral scholarly enterprise whose intellectual practices and products were well insulated from 'extra-scientific' or 'external' social influences. Novick suggests, for example, that currents in the history and philosophy of science, including Thomas Kuhn's work on scientific revolutions, sometimes helped to undermine commitments to mainstream academic paradigms that looked to the natural sciences for guidance. Elsewhere, scholarly interest in literary theory and hermeneutics drew attention to the problems involved in interpreting the meaning of human action, problems whose proper study seemed to require tools of analysis that the natural sciences could not provide. Focusing on these and other scholarly developments, Novick argues that

. . . although the highly charged political atmosphere of the period sometimes raised the stakes of controversies about objectivity in the social sciences, it was for the most part 'strictly academic' considerations which initiated debates, and contributed the categories in which heterodox views were advanced.[6]

[2]Good sources from the 1960s on Project Camelot include: US Congress, House, Committee on Foreign Affairs, Subcommittee on International Organizations and Movements, Behavioral Sciences and the National Security, Report No. 4, together with Part 9 of Winning the Cold War: The US Ideological Offensive, hearings [hereafter, BSNS], 89th Congress, 1st session (1965); US Congress, House, Committee on Science and Astronautics, Subcommittee on Science, Research, and Development, Technical Information for Congress, Report, Serial A, Chapter 6, 'Congressional Response to Project Camelot,' 92nd Congress, 1st session (25 April 1969, revised 15 May 1971); Irving Louis Horowitz (ed.), The Rise and Fall of Project Camelot: Studies in the Relationship Between Social Science and Practical Politics (Cambridge, MA: MIT Press, 1967). The best historical study of Project Camelot places it in the context of the growing authority of psychological experts in the nation's cultural and political life during the early Cold War decades: Ellen Herman, The Romance of American Psychology: Political Culture in the Age of Experts (Los Angeles & Berkeley: University of California Press, 1995), Chapters 5 & 6; also Herman, 'The Career of Cold War Psychology,' Radical History Review, No. 63 (Fall 1995), 5285.

[3]There is a large literature about the emergence of professional social science. The most comprehensive study, whose footnotes provide a useful guide to the literature, is Dorothy Ross, The Origins of American Social Science (Cambridge & New York: Cambridge University Press, 1991).

[4]For a useful overview, though it does not aim for historical sophistication, see Daniel Bell, 'The Social Sciences since the Second World War,' in Encyclopedia Britannica, The Great Ideas Today (Chicago, IL: The University of Chicago Press, 1979), 139–81.

[5]Peter Novick, That Noble Dream: The 'Objectivity Question' and the American Historical Profession (Cambridge: Cambridge University Press, 1988), 546.

[6]Ibid., 546–63, at 546.

Without denying the importance of these 'academic' contributions, I suggest that this historical interpretation needs to be revised, for as the Camelot controversy reveals, political developments and political concerns had a central place in the 1960s challenge to scientific objectivity, and to related ideals like value-neutrality and professional autonomy in American social science.

My analysis of the Camelot controversy highlights the importance of the politics–patronage–social science nexus in the epistemological revolution. I want to make three main points. First, far from being an internal scholarly affair, the 1960s challenge to the then-dominant view of the social sciences, which suggested that they should follow the lead of the natural sciences, became by mid-decade a national political affair. In this turn of events, the Camelot controversy played a key role by making the intellectual status and political import of the social sciences the subject of a wide-ranging national controversy, thus accomplishing what scholars critical of orthodox social science had by themselves not done. Second, this public context inspired changes in the parameters of discussion, as scholars (together with politicians, and sometimes other observers) now focused on the importance of Cold War politics and military patronage in shaping (and perhaps distorting) American social science. Third, in the wake of Camelot, critical consideration of the politics–patronage–social science nexus helped to strengthen opposition to the orthodox understanding of social science as an objective, value-neutral scholarly enterprise immune to extra-scientific (and especially political or ideological) influences.

At the outset I should note that although the ways in which the particular disciplines participated in, and were affected by, the epistemological revolution varied significantly—a point emphasized by Novick—this paper largely puts aside questions about variation across the

disciplines. This is because my main focus is on salient changes in the politics–patronage–social science nexus during the 1960s that were not limited to a single discipline, and on efforts to criticize and analyse this nexus (and thus to rethink the nature of American social science) in a global manner.

MILITARY PATRONAGE AND THE QUEST FOR SCIENTIFIC LEGITIMACY IN THE EARLY POST-WWII PERIOD

Since the problems concerning Project Camelot and the politics–patronage–social science nexus were rooted in developments since the 1940s, it is important to begin by considering the creation of a post-war partnership between the social sciences and the military. In the early post-WWII years, social scientists faced widespread scepticism about their political significance and scientific credentials. In this context, the development of a partnership with the military helped social scientists in their quest for public respectability and scientific legitimacy. Although, in retrospect, it seems clear that military support left a deep imprint on the institutional conditions, intellectual orientation and political significance of academic social research, the threats of political subordination and loss of intellectual independence seemed at the time to be manageable; it seemed, to many key players at least, that social research carried out with military funding could contribute to important Cold War goals without losing its objectivity and other 'scientific' characteristics. In fact, the military took a special interest in social research that appeared to be rigorously scientific—meaning, much like natural science research.

Following World War II, a new politics of American science presented a number of difficulties for social scientists as they sought funding and public support.[7] Although social scientists had participated extensively in the

Allied war effort, their contributions were overshadowed by the remarkable achievements of natural scientists, especially physical scientists whose work led to the atom bomb, radar, and other weapons used against the Axis powers. By the end of the war, preparations to establish adequate post-war support for American science concentrated on the natural sciences as well.[8]

The early history of the US National Science Foundation made the peripheral status and questionable scientific credentials of the social sciences painfully evident. In an effort to create a comprehensive, post-war federal science agency, the question of whether or not the social sciences should even be included generated extensive controversy, as a variety of critics doubted that the social science were more than distant cousins of the natural sciences. After more than half a decade of national debate on this and other matters, a 1950 legislative act created the National Science Foundation, or 'NSF.' Permissive wording in NSF's charter left the support of the social sciences up in the air, a matter to be (re)considered by the

Foundation's predominantly natural-science leaders. Though this agency was much smaller than originally envisioned, its legislative history still demonstrated just how far the social sciences were from the centre of national concern. Subsequently, NSF's hesitating, cautious entry into the social sciences helped to confirm their marginal position.[9]

So did the overwhelming natural-science bias in post-war military science programmes. These sprang up during the late 1940s to fill the gap created by the delay in NSF's establishment.[10] The case of the Office of Naval Research (ONR) is revealing. By the end of the first post-war decade, ONR had become the most important federal patron of academic science: but, from the social sciences, only psychology received substantial support from ONR.[11]

Social scientists also had to confront the fact that physical scientists dominated the key federal wartime and post-war science advisory posts. In NSF's origins, it became clear that few if any natural scientists were committed to the notion that the social sciences deserved comparable

---

[7]The literature on social science during World War II is large. Useful works include: Virginia Yans-McLaughlin, 'Science, Democracy, and Ethics: Mobilizing Culture and Personality for World War II,' History of Anthropology, Vol. 4 (1986), 184–217; James H. Capshew, Psychologists on the March: Science, Practice, and Professional Identity in America, 1929–1969 (Cambridge & New York: Cambridge University Press, 1999), Chapters 2–7; Peter Buck, 'Adjusting to Military Life: The Social Sciences Go to War, 1941–1950,' in Merritt Roe Smith (ed.), Military Enterprise and Technological Change: Perspectives on the American Experience (Cambridge, MA: MIT Press, 1985), 203–52; Herman, Romance of American Psychology, op. cit. note 2, Chapters 2–4.

[8]On the ascendancy of the physical sciences in post-war science policy, see Daniel Kevles, The Physicists: The History of a Scientific Community in Modern America (New York: Alfred A.Knopf, 1978), Chapters 21–23; Daniel Lee Kleinman, Politics on the Endless Frontier: Postwar Research Policy in the United States (Durham, NC; Duke University Press, 1995), Chapter 3; Silvan S. Schweber, 'The Mutual Embrace of Science and the Military: ONR and the Growth of Physics in the United States after World War II,' in Everett Mendelsohn, Merritt Roe Smith and Peter Weingart (eds.), Science, Technology and the Military, Sociology of the Sciences Yearbook No. 12 (Dordrecht & Boston, MA: Kluwer Academic Publishers, 1988), 1–45; Paul Hoch, 'The Crystallization of a Strategic Alliance: The American Physics Elite and the Military in the 1940s,' ibid., 87–116.

[9]Samuel Z. Klausner and Victor M. Lidz (eds.), The Nationalization of the Social Sciences (Philadelphia: University of Pennsylvania Press, 1986); Otto N. Larsen, Milestones & Millstones: Social Science at the National Science Foundation, 1945–1991 (New Brunswick, NJ: Transaction Publishers, 1992), Chapter 1; Roberta Balstad Miller, 'The Social Sciences and the Politics of Science: The 1940s,' American Sociologist, Vol. 17 (1982), 205–09. On NSF's social science programme in the 1950s, see Daniel Lee Kleinman and Mark Solovey, 'Hot Science/Cold War: The National Science Foundation After World War II,' Radical History Review, No. 63 (Fall 1995), 110–39; Larsen, Milestones & Millstones, op. cit., Chapter 3.

[10]Kleinman, Politics on the Endless Frontier, op. cit. note 8, 147–50.

[11]John G. Darley, 'Psychology and the Office of Naval Research: A Decade of Development,' American Psychologist, Vol. 12 (1957), 305–23; Lyle H. Lanier, 'The Psychological and Social Sciences in the National Military Establishment,' ibid., Vol. 4 (1949), 127–47, esp. 137–38.

public support, recognition or influence. By occupying top positions in such important settings as the Office of Scientific Research and Development, the National Academy of Sciences (NAS), NSF, and the President's Science Advisory Committee, these same natural scientists of the Manhattan Project generation exercised substantial influence over the nation's scientific development.[12] Within this élite circle, social scientists were notable mainly by their absence.

Considerable scepticism about the intellectual foundations and political meaning of social science, and sometimes hostility from conservative politicians in the Congress, caused further problems. Conservative political opponents, who associated social science with New Deal liberalism, racial equality and—worst of all—Marxist socialism and communism, joined forces with sceptical natural scientists to prevent social science from obtaining a major presence in the new National Science Foundation: at one point it looked as if conservatives had managed to exclude what they saw as partisan (and thus unscientific) social disciplines altogether.[13] The power of conservative politicians only increased as the Cold War became an ongoing international emergency, supporting the growth of rampant domestic anti-communism. Through the mid-1950s, individual social scientists, social science organizations and their patrons, especially the large private foundations, became frequent targets of university, state and national investigations into subversive, un-American activities.[14]

Under these conditions, the establishment of amiable relations with the military became particularly appealing. Beginning with its first serious involvement with the social sciences during World War I, the military demonstrated a special interest in psychological expertise.[15] During World War II and the Cold War, the expertise of psychologists, psychiatrists, and professionals in related areas seemed especially relevant to military and intelligence operations. Psychologists proclaimed that their work was perhaps even more valuable than military hardware in winning the allegiances of foreign governments and peoples. This viewpoint gained substantial support among American foreign policy experts who were interested in the 'Communist Mind' and concerned about communist efforts to control the psyches of peoples in nations around the world, including the United States. As suggested by Cold War rhetoric on both sides of the Iron Curtain, this conflict was not only about economics, politics and military might, but also about competing worldviews and ideologies. From this perspective, the major stakes included the hearts and minds of individuals, subjects about which psychologists presumably knew more than anybody else did. Not surprisingly, throughout this period psychology's most important extra-university patron was the military.[16]

---

[12]Kevles, The Physicists, op. cit. note 8, Chapters 19–23.

[13]Miller, 'Social Sciences,' op. cit. note 9.

[14]On the difficulties social scientists and their patrons encountered during the McCarthy era, see Harry Alpert, 'Congressmen, Social Scientists, and Attitudes Toward Federal Support of Social Science Research,' American Sociological Review, Vol. 23 (1958), 682–86; Ellen W. Schrecker, No Ivory Tower: McCarthyism and the Universities (New York: Oxford University Press, 1986); Paul F. Lazarsfeld and Wagner Thielens, Jr, The Academic Mind: Social Scientists in a Time of Crisis (Glencoe, IL: The Free Press, 1958); David W. Southern, Gunnar Myrdal and Black-White Relations: The Use and Abuse of An American Dilemma, 1944–1969 (Baton Rouge: Louisiana State University Press, 1987), 172–75.

[15]Daniel J. Kevles, 'Testing the Army's Intelligence: Psychologists and the Military in World War I,' Journal of American History, Vol. 55 (1968), 565–81; Franz Samelson, 'World War I Intelligence Testing and the Development of Psychology,' Journal of the History of the Behavioral Sciences, Vol. 13 (1977), 274–82; John Carson, 'Army Alpha, Army Brass, and the Search for Army Intelligence,' Isis, Vol. 84, No. 2 (June 1993), 278–309.

[16]Capshew, Psychologists on the March, op. cit. note 7, Chapters 2–7; Herman, Romance of American Psychology, op. cit. note 2, Chapters 2–6; John Marks, The Search for the 'Manchurian Candidate' (New York: W.W. Norton & Co., 1979).

In an impressive range of cases, the military stimulated the growth of other social sciences as well. Political studies on nuclear strategy, including such central Cold War doctrines as deterrence and mutual assured destruction, received the Department of Defense (DOD)'s attention.[17] The RAND Corporation, the most famous of the military think tanks, facilitated research on nuclear strategy, as well as on operations research and systems theory—research which drew from a number of social science disciplines, but especially economics.[18] Economists interested in game theory also worked at RAND, while enjoying support from other DOD science programmes as well.[19] The large private foundations—Carnegie, Rockefeller and Ford—together with national security agencies, pushed for and financed the development of the Harvard and Columbia Russian studies programmes, MIT's Center for International Studies and, more generally, the proliferation of area studies programmes throughout American higher education.[20] In these settings, social scientists from varied disciplinary backgrounds pursued investigations in such cutting-edge fields as modernization and development studies,[21] which together with social systems analysis later became part of Project Camelot. The rapid growth of communications studies also depended heavily on military and intelligence agencies for support.[22]

While this discussion is not meant to be comprehensive, it does indicate that military funding and related programmes of patronage provided valuable sustenance for many prominent developments in post-war social science. Based on recent scholarly contributions and his own extensive work on this topic, Christopher Simpson has concluded that 'military, intelligence, and propaganda agencies provided by far the largest part of the funds for large research projects in the social sciences in the United States from World War II until well into the 1960s.'[23]

---

[17]Deborah Welch Larson, 'Deterrence Theory and the Cold War,' Radical History Review, No. 63 (Fall 1995), 86–109.

[18]Stephen P. Waring, 'Cold Calculus: The Cold War and Operations Research,' Radical History Review, No. 63 (Fall 1995), 28–51; Thomas P. Hughes, Rescuing Prometheus (New York: Pantheon, 1998); Michael A. Fortun & Silvan S. Schweber, 'Scientists and the Legacy of World War II: The Case of Operations Research (OR),' Social Studies of Science, Vol. 23, No. 4 (November 1993), 595–642; Philip Mirowski, 'Cyborg Agonistes: Economics Meets Operations Research in Mid-Century,' ibid., Vol. 29, No. 5 (October 1999), 685–718.

[19]Robert J. Leonard, 'War as a "Simple Economic Problem": The Rise of an Economics of Defense,' in Craufurd D. Goodwin (ed.), Economics and National Security: A History of Their Interaction, Annual Supplement to the History of Political Economy, Vol. 23 (Durham, NC: Duke University Press, 1991), 261–83; Michael A. Bernstein, 'American Economics and the National Security State, 1941–1953,' Radical History Review, No. 63 (Fall 1995), 8–26; William Poundstone, Prisoner's Dilemma (New York: Doubleday, 1992); E. Roy Weintraub (ed.), Toward a History of Game Theory, Annual Supplement to the History of Political Economy, Vol. 24 (Durham, NC: Duke University Press, 1992); Sharon Ghamari-Tabrizi, 'Simulating the Unthinkable: Gaming Future War in the 1950s and 1960s,' Social Studies of Science, Vol. 30, No. 2 (April 2000), 163–223.

[20]Sigmund Diamond, Compromised Campus: The Collaboration of Universities with the Intelligence Community, 1945–1955 (New York: Oxford University Press, 1992); Robert A. McCaughey, International Studies and Academic Enterprise: A Chapter in the Enclosure of American Learning (New York: Columbia University Press, 1984).

[21]Irene L. Gendzier, Managing Political Change: Social Scientists and the Third World (Boulder, CO: Westview Press, 1995); Gendzier, 'Play It Again Sam: The Practice and Apology of Development,' in Christopher Simpson (ed.), Universities and Empire: Money and Politics in the Social Sciences during the Cold War (New York: The New Press, 1998), 195–231; Immanuel Wallerstein, 'The Unintended Consequences of Cold War Area Studies,' in Noam Chomsky (ed.), The Cold War & the University: Toward an Intellectual History of the Postwar Years (New York: The New Press, 1997), 195–231; Bruce Cumings, 'Boundary Displacement: Area Studies and International Studies During and After the Cold War,' in Simpson (ed.), Universities & Empire, op. cit., 159–88.

[22]Christopher Simpson, Science of Coercion: Communication Research and Psychological Warfare, 1945–1960 (New York: Oxford University Press, 1994).

[23]Christopher Simpson, 'Universities, Empire, and the Production of Knowledge: An Introduction,' in Simpson (ed.), Universities & Empire, op. cit. note 21, xi–xxxiv, at xii.

The general goal of the military's growing commitment to the social sciences was eminently practical, involving DOD's immense managerial tasks. Charles Bray served as a member of the Smithsonian Institution's Research Group in Psychology and the Social Sciences, which under military contract carried out social science planning studies. The title of Bray's 1962 published account in the *American Psychologist*, 'Toward a Technology of Human Behavior for Defense Use,' underscored the military's practical interests in the social sciences. DOD's basic aim in sponsoring social research was, in Bray's words, 'to lay the basis for an overall increase in the sophistication and inventiveness with which Defense management meets [problems related to] the expansion of military operations . . . into new social settings.' Just as research in the natural sciences and engineering had improved DOD's 'sophistication and inventiveness about the production of physical objects,' research in the social sciences would presumably improve the military's 'sophistication and inventiveness about people.'[24]

In speaking of a 'technology of human behavior,' Bray drew upon a pervasive post-war rhetoric that portrayed social science as a junior—but rapidly maturing—colleague to natural science within a unified scientific enterprise. Disciplinary histories suggest that a pronounced emphasis on proper methodology during these years was often considered by social scientists to be the key to making social inquiry truly 'scientific.'[25]

This position resonated with cultural programmes for a modern, secular society that took as their basis a cosmopolitan, universalized vision of scientific inquiry.[26] The social science emphasis on scientific unity through methodology also served at the National Science Foundation and elsewhere as a strategy for strengthening the shaky scientific status of social inquiry.

In the case of military science programmes, a dominant orientation toward the physical sciences meant that social scientists, if they did not want to be viewed as imposters, had to display their scientific stripes prominently. Consistently, social scientists as individuals and members of advisory committees emphasized that social research that had much in common with natural science inquiry was the type that had the greatest potential benefit to the military. The point that social science comprised a vital component of the sciences rather than the humanities came through again and again in their writings.[27] This message also stood out in the first report on the social sciences from the physical-sciences-dominated President's Science Advisory Committee (PSAC). According to this landmark 1962 statement:

> Progress in behavioral science has come about by using the scientific processes of observing, experimenting, and extensively following up and correcting working hypotheses. Indeed, all the general attitudes and strategies of physical and biological science have found a place in behavioral science.[28]

---

[24]Charles Bray, 'Toward a Technology of Human Behavior for Defense Use,' American Psychologist, *Vol.* 17 (1962), 527–41, at 528.

[25]Bell, 'The Social Sciences,' op. cit. note 4. Examples of disciplinary histories that point to a heightened post-war emphasis on proper methodology include: David M. Ricci, Tragedy of Political Science: Politics, Scholarship, and Democracy (New Haven, CT: Yale University Press, 1984), Chapter 5; Jennifer Platt, A History of Sociological Research Methods in America, 1920–1960 (New York: Cambridge University Press, 1996).

[26]David Hollinger, 'Science as a Weapon in Kulturkämpfe in the United States During and After World War II,' Isis, Vol. 86, No. 3 (September 1995), 440–54.

[27]See the various task committee reports and the final report of the Smithsonian's Research Group in Psychology and the Social Sciences, Record Unit 179, Records 1957–1963, Archives and Special Collections of the Smithsonian Institution, Washington, DC.

[28]The Behavioral Sciences Sub-panel of the President's Science Advisory Committee, 'Strengthening the Behavioral Sciences,' Science, Vol. 136 (20 April 1962), 233–41, at 238.

PSAC's use of the term 'behavioral science(s)' rather than the more traditional 'social science(s)' was revealing, as it reflected the improved status of the social disciplines within the national science establishment. Since social science had been associated with supposedly un-American programmes of social reform (and sounded suspiciously like socialism), leading scholars and their patrons often looked for other words to signify a stronger commitment to a hard-core type of science. During the 1950s, the Ford Foundation helped to propagate this message through its Behavioral Sciences Program.[29]

The hard-core, technocratic orientation of military-sponsored social research faithfully mirrored the 'behavioral sciences' rhetoric. Recent scholarship on social science and its ties to the national security state suggests that such research typically aimed to facilitate prediction and control, qualities often considered, at least since the time of the 17th-century Scientific Revolution, to be hallmarks of 'science.' During World War II, psychologists, anthropologists, and other scholars working in the field of culture and personality studies, all sought to predict national behaviour as part of wartime operations.[30] In the case of communications studies, scholars with close ties to psychological warfare programmes contributed to building, as Christopher Simpson has aptly put it, a 'science of coercion.' Its scholarly products would enable American political leaders to control beliefs and attitudes within target populations, both domestic and foreign.[31] Similarly, the field of modernization studies had a decidedly manipulative bent. Based upon the notion that underdeveloped countries were especially vulnerable to Communist penetration, scholars set out to identify the key variables and stages in the process of development, with the hope that the resulting knowledge would enable US leaders to direct this process in a manner favourable to American interests.[32]

Military social research efforts typically deployed 'hard' scientific methodologies as well. This meant a marked preference for quantitative analysis as opposed to historical, qualitative, and other forms of social research that seemed 'soft' by comparison. Charles Bray emphasized that behavioural technology was 'based on controlled observation, and, preferably . . . expressed in formulas, tables, and graphs. That is to say, it is not only tested but it is quantitative information that is needed.'[33] To take just one specific, salient case, in the early development of operations research and systems analysis, mathematicians, engineers and physical scientists led the way. As the historian of technology Thomas Hughes has pointed out, 'from operations research, systems analysis borrowed holistic, transdisciplinary characteristics and the reliance on natural scientists and scientifically trained engineers and their

[29]Bernard Berelson, 'Behavioral Sciences,' in David L. Sills (ed.), International Encyclopedia of the Social Sciences, Vol. 2 (New York: Free Press, 1968), 41–45.

[30]Yans-McLaughlin, 'Science, Democracy & Ethics,' op. cit. note 7.

[31]Simpson, Science of Coercion, op. cit. note 22.

[32]Gendzier, Managing Political Change, op. cit. note 21; Michael E. Latham, 'Ideology, Social Science, and Destiny: Modernization and the Kennedy-Era Alliance for Progress,' Diplomatic History, Vol. 22 (1998), 199–229. Studies of the impact of World War II and the Cold War on the goals and orientations of the social sciences are part of a much larger literature on Cold War American science, and this theme runs throughout the essays in the present volume. See the classic article by Paul Forman, 'Behind Quantum Electronics: National Security as Basis for Physical Research in the United States, 1940–1960,' Historical Studies in the Physical Sciences, Vol. 18, Part 1 (1987), 149–229, and the useful historiographic essay by Stuart W. Leslie, 'Science and Politics in Cold War America,' in Margaret C. Jacob (ed.), The Politics of Western Science, 1640–1990 (Atlantic Highlands, NJ: Humanities Press, 1994), 199–233.

[33]Bray, 'Toward a Technology of Human Behavior,' op. cit. note 24, 528–29.

methods.'[34] In order for social scientists to become participants, they had to display certain skills and methods of analysis. Competence in mathematics and quantitative cost-benefit analysis helped economists, in particular, to gain credibility. So much so that during the early 1960s, the new Secretary of Defense Robert McNamara recruited systems experts, many with backgrounds in economics, to help place the management of military affairs on a rational, scientific basis.[35]

On top of this, military support during the early post-war period promised to leave scholarly objectivity, autonomy and independence intact. In the 1940s and 1950s, authors from the natural and social sciences, as well as from the history, philosophy, and sociology of science, commonly distinguished between science and politics, research and reform, scholarship and ideology. Though nuanced differences of opinion and some strongly contrary perspectives persisted, the dominant sentiment held that patrons and their beneficiaries should not confuse the two sides in these pairs. Classic cases of the Soviet State corrupting genetics, and of the Nazi State destroying parts of its scientific community, provided frequently repeated lessons about what could go wrong.[36] Of course, military support raised the spectre of State domination of science

at home as well,[37] but many observers at the time found that certain features of post-war American science seemed to militate against this possibility. These features included the military's extensive reliance on universities as sites of research and training; its regular use of university scholars as advisors; the existence of pluralistic sources of public and private support; and the cultivation of a 'basic' science component within military research programmes. Scientists pointed, for example, to the Office of Naval Research as a major patron that respected the special needs of science.[38] These circumstances help to explain the fact that, as historian Allan Needell has observed, 'the potential impact of such support [from military and intelligence agencies]—direct or indirect—on the quality and independence of research and on the teaching of these subjects remained largely unevaluated,' at least until the 1960s.[39] In short, the theory and practice of science suggested that academic researchers could feed at the public trough without becoming subordinate to political power.

So President Eisenhower's famous warning that dependence on the federal patron could harm American science came, especially as far as the social sciences were concerned, at an

[35]James A. Smith, The Idea Brokers: Think Tanks and the Rise of the New Policy Elite (New York: Free Press, 1991), 135–40.

[36]David A. Hollinger, 'The Defense of Democracy and Robert K. Merton's Formulation of the Scientific Ethos,' Knowledge and Society: Studies in the Sociology of Culture, Past and Present, Vol. 4 (1983), 1–15; Hollinger, 'Science as a Weapon,' op. cit. note 26; Everett Mendelsohn, 'Robert K. Merton: The Celebration and Defense of Science,' Science in Context, Vol. 3 (1989), 269–89.

[37]Jessica Wang, American Science in an Age of Anxiety: Scientists, Anticommunism, and the Cold War (Chapel Hill: University of North Carolina Press, 1999).

[38]From psychology, John G. Darley emphasized that 'ONR's program emerged from the research interests of civilian scientists': see Darley, 'Psychology and the ONR,' op. cit. note 11, 319. On ONR more generally, see Anon., 'The Scientists,' Fortune Magazine (October 1948), 106–12, 166, 168, 170, 173–74, 176; Harvey M. Sapolsky, 'Academic Science and the Military: The Years Since the Second World War,' in Nathan Reingold (ed.), The Sciences in the American Context: New Perspectives (Washington, DC: Smithsonian Institution Press, 1979), 379–99.

[39]Allan A. Needell, '"Truth Is Our Weapon": Project TROY, Political Warfare, and Government-Academic Relations in the National Security State,' Diplomatic History, Vol. 17 (1993), 399–420, at 418.

[34]Hughes, Rescuing Prometheus, op. cit. note 18, 164. See also: Leonard, 'War as a "Simple Economic Problem,"' op. cit. note 19, 269–79; Fortun & Schweber, 'Scientists and the Legacy of WWII,' op. cit. note 18, 627; Angela M. O'Rand,'Mathematizing Social Science in the 1950s: The Early Development and Diffusion of Game Theory,' in Weintraub (ed.), Toward a History of Game Theory, op. cit. note 19, 177–204.

awkward moment. In his 1961 Farewell Presidential Address, Eisenhower noted that with the passage of time, the threat of political subordination had grown stronger. As scientific research became increasingly costly, more of it was conducted directly and indirectly for the American government, contributing to the growth of what Eisenhower called the 'military–industrial complex,' and what later commentators referred to as the 'military–industrial–academic complex.' In this situation, there was a great danger that government contracts would become 'virtually a substitute for intellectual curiosity.' 'The prospect of domination of the nation's scholars by Federal employment, project allocations, and the power of money is,' cautioned the ex-military general, 'ever present.'[40]

The soon-to-be ex-President made his dire remarks following the success of social scientists in obtaining at least a small space and moderate scientific credentials within the expanding federal science system. This had not been easy, for they first had to demonstrate their true 'scientific' colours and practical worth to more powerful players whose main concerns often lay elsewhere. A growing partnership with the military indicated that social scientists had made some progress; they had acquired a measure of respect from a patron that stood for American might and national vigour. Additionally, they had done so while apparently retaining—and even strengthening—the institutional conditions, social relations, methodological practices, epistemological goals and habits of mind commonly associated with rigorous scientific inquiry. Thus social scientists and the military seemed to be working together on projects of common interest, without contaminating social inquiry with unscientific ideology or values. The politics–patronage–social science nexus seemed to be working well.

MOVING TOWARD THE POLITICAL CENTRE STAGE: PLANNING FOR PROJECT CAMELOT

Whereas the social sciences had been a prime target of conservative political attacks during the first post-war decade, the public status of these disciplines rose dramatically during the liberal Democratic administrations of John F. Kennedy and Lyndon B. Johnson. In the history of American social science, these years were truly remarkable, as scholars from all of the major disciplines—psychology, sociology, political science, economics, anthropology—helped to shape major domestic and foreign policy initiatives. Kennedy himself had a well-known enthusiasm for scholars who could straddle the worlds of academia and politics comfortably, the so-called 'action intellectuals' or 'policy scientists.' Though he was not so popular with this group as Kennedy had been, Johnson, as the nation's new leader following Kennedy's assassination in late 1963, came to depend even more heavily upon advisory groups and individuals with extensive academic connections.[41] Within the social sciences, no study reflected their rapidly rising (and soon to be widely challenged) position better than Project Camelot. Rooted deeply in the post-war partnership with the military, Camelot promised to provide American social scientists with abundant resources and opportunities to fulfil the twin goals of producing first-rate science and solving important political problems.

[40]Dwight D. Eisenhower, 'Farewell Radio and Television Address to the American People,' in Public Papers of the Presidents of the United States, 1960–61 (Washington, DC: US GPO, 1961), 1035–40, quotes at 1038, 1039.

[41]Gene M. Lyons, The Uneasy Partnership: Social Science and the Federal Government in the Twentieth Century (New York: Russell Sage Foundation, 1969), Chapters 5–7; Robert C. Wood, Whatever Possessed the President? Academic Experts and Presidential Policy, 1960–1988 (Amherst: University of Massachusetts Press, 1993), Chapters 2–3; Smith, The Idea Brokers, op. cit. note 35, Chapters 6–7.

During his 1960 presidential campaign, Kennedy promised to correct what he took to be a flawed national defence policy. The Eisenhower administration's emphasis on preparation for full-scale nuclear war and the threat of massive retaliation seemed inadequate in light of changing Cold War politics. Soon after assuming the presidential office, Kennedy delivered a message to the Congress outlining the need for new military capabilities to meet novel foreign policy challenges. Only two months before, Soviet leader Nikita Krushchev had announced that his country would support 'national liberation wars,' a policy soon adopted by Communist China, as indicated in the *Peking People's Daily:* 'The Communists of all countries . . . must . . . resolutely support wars of national liberation.' To combat this style of communist aggression, Kennedy called upon the American military to strengthen its ability to identify pockets of Communist-supported revolutionary activity, and respond with conventional and counter-insurgency forces.[42]

Against this background, DOD's internal and external social research programmes underwent an impressive expansion. Between 1960 and 1966, the annual budget of DOD's Research, Development, Test and Evaluation programme in counter-insurgency alone grew from $10 million to $160 million. Of the latter figure, $6 million went to social science research, or 'non-material research' as it was sometimes referred to by military personnel.[43] From 1961 to 1964, DOD support for research in the psychological sciences rose from $17.2 million to $31.1 million, while its support for research in the social sciences (not including psychology) increased from $0.2 million to $5.7 million.[44]

The immediate impetus for Project Camelot came in 1964, when DOD's Director of Defense Research and Engineering asked the Defense Science Board (a high-level military science advisory group) to study existing research programmes 'relating to ethnic and other motivational factors involved in the causation and conduct of small wars.' The resulting report, after noting various deficiencies in DOD's behavioural sciences programme, identified a need to improve 'the knowledge and understanding in depth of the internal cultural, economic and political conditions that generate conflicts between national groups.' Better understanding required greater emphasis on the collection of primary data in overseas areas. The Defense Science Board also criticized DOD's failure to 'organize appropriate multidisciplinary programs and to use the techniques of such related fields as operations research.' In response to such criticisms, the Army began to develop an ambitious research programme, known as Project Camelot, to study revolutionary movements and counter-insurgency tactics.[45]

Camelot's detailed planning lay in the hands of the Special Operations Research Office (SORO). Created in 1956, SORO was a military-supported, quasi-independent research institute, located on the campus of American University in Washington, DC, that served as the main centre for Army-contract research in the behavioural sciences. Over half of SORO's personnel produced handbooks on countries throughout the world, providing information on social structures, political and economic systems, and revolutionary potential. One such handbook had the not-too-subtle title 'How Americans Serving Abroad Can Help the Free World Win the Battle of Ideas in the Cold War.' SORO also established a Counter-insurgency Information Analysis Center for the purpose of storing and transmitting information that SORO collected and produced.

---

[42]Kruschev and China paper quoted in BSNS, 71. Kennedy's address is also discussed in this document.

[43]BSNS, 72.

[44]'Congressional Response to Project Camelot,' op. cit. note 2, 128–29.

[45]DSB report quoted in BSNS, 3R.

Though initially SORO's activities involved little field research, SORO soon became a major centre for this type of inquiry as well.[46]

A SORO description of Project Camelot explained its integrated scientific and political objectives. First, Camelot would 'devise procedures for assessing the potential for internal war within national societies.' Second, this study would 'identify with increased degrees of confidence those actions which a government might take to relieve conditions which are assessed as giving rise to a potential for internal war.' Third, Camelot would 'assess the feasibility of prescribing the characteristics of a system for obtaining and using the essential information needed for doing the above two things.'[47]

A vast geographical scope accompanied Camelot's ambitious aims. According to SORO documents, survey research and field studies would be conducted in the following countries: Bolivia, Colombia, Ecuador, Paraguay, Peru, Venezuela, Iran and Thailand. Fieldwork would be complemented by comparative historical studies of Argentina, Bolivia, Brazil, Colombia, Cuba, the Dominican Republic, El Salvador, Guatemala, Mexico, Paraguay, Peru, Venezuela, Egypt, Iran, Turkey, Korea, Indonesia, Malaysia, Thailand, France, Greece and Nigeria.[48]

In putting together the intellectual and human resources for this grand undertaking, SORO counted upon a pool of élite academics. As SORO's Director Theodore R. Vallance proudly indicated, his research institute cultivated 'good working relationships with the topflight behavioral scientists in most of the major institutions around the country.'[49] In the case at hand, 33 consultants hailed from such prestigious institutions as California-Berkeley, MIT, Johns Hopkins, Princeton, Columbia, Michigan, Pittsburgh, Virginia and Stanford.

As for the study's Director, the military chose Rex D. Hopper, a most suitable candidate. Head of the sociology programme at Brooklyn College, Hopper specialized in Latin American area studies, travelling to that region on numerous occasions to lecture and conduct research. He also had a deep interest in revolution and its scientific management. As early as 1950, he had begun to design a developmental model of revolutionary movements. A generalized description of the revolutionary process, Hopper emphasized, 'is a necessary prerequisite to any attempt at control.'[50]

Camelot incorporated many features characteristic of military-sponsored work that made it attractive to leading scholars. To begin with, Camelot offered the opportunity to do sophisticated scientific work, including the construction of social systems models for entire societies, and studies in nation-building. Both areas of research had been receiving substantial support from leading private and public patrons of post-WWII academic social science. In addition, the military discussed this study in the terms of 'basic science.' Of course, Camelot was not undirected research stemming solely from intellectual curiosity. But neither did the official viewpoint depict Camelot as an applied, technical task. Instead, the picture presented by DOD suggested that the two sides, academic and military, were working in a mutually supportive relationship, to develop social research with substantial scholarly importance and policy

---

[46]BSNS, 28–30.

[47]See Document 1 in Horowitz (ed.), Rise & Fall of Project Camelot, op. cit. note 2, 47–49. Documents 1, 2 and 3 in this volume come from SORO documents about Project Camelot from December of 1964. Document 4 comes from a public description of Camelot released by SORO in July of 1965, at about the time when Camelot was cancelled.

[48]Document 3 in Horowitz (ed.), Rise & Fall of Project Camelot, op. cit. note 2, 57–58.

[49]BSNS, 61–62, at 61.

[50]Rex D. Hopper, 'The Revolutionary Process: A Frame of Reference for the Study of Revolutionary Movements,' Social Forces, Vol. 28 (1950), 270–79, at 270. On Hopper's background, see Herman, Romance of American Psychology, op. cit. note 2, 146–47.

payoffs.[51] Perhaps as a sign of respect for Camelot's scholarly status, this study, despite its obvious foreign policy concerns, was not even classified.

Furthermore, since counter-insurgency research brought together investigators from a broad range of social science disciplines, scholars in search of policy-relevant knowledge would not be hindered by common disciplinary constraints. As Seymour Deitchman, Special Assistant for Counter-insurgency, explained, all of the major social disciplines were needed to understand the very real-world matters of concern:

> The [cold] war itself revolves around the allegiance and support of the local population. The Defense Department has therefore recognized that part of its research and development efforts to support counterinsurgency operations must be oriented toward the people, United States and foreign, involved in this type of war; and the DOD has called on the types of scientists—anthropologists, psychologists, sociologists, political scientists, economists—whose professional orientation to human behavior would enable them to make useful contributions in this area.[52]

SORO itself, added director Vallance, had over one hundred social researchers with diverse disciplinary backgrounds.[53] Like much of the work done at MIT's Center for International Studies, RAND, and other military-funded research centres, Camelot would pursue interdisciplinary work matched to current policy needs.

The project's name resonated with the Kennedy and Johnson administrations' growing confidence in social engineering as the key to social harmony, 'Camelot,' explained Vallance, referred to the Arthurian legend about 'the development of a stable society with domestic tranquility and peace and justice for all. This is an objective that seemed to, if we were going to have a code label, connote the right sort of things.'[54] After Kennedy's death, 'Camelot' had also become associated with his legendary idealism and youthful vigour.

Last but not least, the anticipation of bountiful funding suggested Camelot's great importance, as well as its obvious attraction to action intellectuals. Camelot's unprecedentedly large budget would be as much as $6 million, to be distributed over a four-year period. Moreover, director Vallance referred to Camelot as a pilot or 'feasibility' study. If all went well, bigger projects would follow.[55] Presumably, Camelot would provide valuable data and an important learning environment for researchers working on future studies. The final stage of this effort, noted Army Chief of Research and Development William W. Dick, Jr, would be the production of 'a single model which could be used to estimate the internal war potential of a developing nation.'[56]

No wonder that one participant suggested that Camelot would serve as the Manhattan Project for the social sciences. Another Camelot participant heard—perhaps only a rumour—that Camelot, or a follow-up study, might eventually receive as much as $50 million annually. Writing a few years later, the anthropologist Ralph Beals speculated in a similar vein that . . .

> . . . the full implementation of the Camelot proposal would have required the involvement of social scientists on a scale comparable to the involvement of physical scientists and engineers with putting a man on the moon.[57]

---

[51]BSNS, 30–32. On Camelot as basic science, also see notes 75–76 below, and the corresponding text [p. 18].

[52]Deitchman, in ibid., 72.

[53]Vallance, in ibid., 22.

[54]Ibid., 20.

[55]Ibid., 5.

[56]Dick, in ibid., 31.

[57]Comment about Manhattan Project noted by Ralph Beals in Politics of Social Research, op. cit. note 1, 6; Beals' own quotation is at 7. Comment about possibility of $50m a year is noted by Marshall Sahlins in 'The Established Order: Do Not Fold, Spindle, or Mutilate,' in Horowitz (ed.), Rise & Fall of Project Camelot, op. cit. note 2, 71–79, at 71.

So, whether they were under the military's enlightened scientific guidance, or whether they were providing scientific guidance to the military as it ventured into new and dangerous terrain, the social sciences were moving toward the political centre stage, apparently destined for greatness.

THE POLITICS–PATRONAGE–SOCIAL SCIENCE NEXUS UNDER SCRUTINY

On the road to Camelot, however, something went very wrong. In 1965, US troop commitments to the Vietnam War rose dramatically, triggering a corresponding increase in domestic anti-war sentiment and protests. As a result, during the second half of the 1960s, relations between the national-security state and academia became embedded in divisive arguments about the nature of American society and its rôle on the world stage. Of special relevance, universities themselves became major centres of political debate and social activism in the anti-war movement. Campus protests against the so-called Establishment identified scholars and their academic institutions as integral components of the American war machine. According to a growing number of distressed voices, American scientists and other parts of the academy had sold their souls to the forces of evil, now disguised in official double-speak as the benevolent protector of the free world.[58]

In this context, Project Camelot became a main event, serving as the first major focal point of national discussion about the use and abuse of social science by the State. If social scientists were working for the military (or for the government more generally), was their work going to be influenced by current policy objectives? If so, was social science destined to serve power? Or could social scientists, even while dependent on powerful patrons for support, maintain a fair measure of freedom and critical perspective in designing, conducting and interpreting research? As many commentators now saw it, contrary to the pervasive post-WWII rhetoric about increasing scientific rigour and objectivity in the social or behavioural sciences, the politics–patronage–social science nexus had undermined claims about the ideological and political purity of American social science. Thus in the glare of the public spotlight, post-war efforts that appealed to a unified, objective scientific enterprise as a means of managing the political meaning and intellectual status of the social sciences began to unravel rapidly.

Since Camelot served as a catalyst, not the original spark, in a debate with deep roots in the scholarly community, it is important first to note some of the emerging academic concerns about mainstream social science that had by the early 1960s been gaining strength. Although it would be impossible to do justice here to the full range of these concerns, brief mention of some of the more relevant ones helps to set the stage for the Camelot controversy.

One source of frustration within a variety of fields of study involved certain pervasive social-science assumptions about human beings and society that contradicted commonsense notions about the willful nature of human action and the value of personal autonomy. Within psychology, for instance, practitioners who were unhappy with the mechanistic and deterministic models offered by the dominant behaviourist and psychoanalytic schools, championed a new approach called 'humanistic psychology.' One of their leaders, Abraham Maslow, represented

---

[58]Roger L. Geiger, Research and Relevant Knowledge: American Research Universities Since World War II (New York: Oxford University Press, 1993), 237–42; Kevles, The Physicists, op. cit. note 8, 401–09; Stuart W. Leslie, The Cold War and American Science: The Military-Industrial-Academic Complex at MIT and Stanford (New York: Columbia University Press, 1993), Chapter 9; on American intellectuals and the Vietnam War more generally, see Robert R. Tomes, Apocalypse Then: American Intellectuals and the Vietnam War: 1954–1975 (New York: New York University Press, 1998). On intellectuals in the 1960s, see Howard Brick, Age of Contradiction: American Thought and Culture in the 1960s (Ithaca and London: Cornell University Press, pbk edn, 2000; originally published by Twayne, 1998).

many of them in his insistence that an adequate psychology required careful attention to such basic human traits as freedom, morality and spiritual growth.[59]

Critics were also uneasy about the mainstream's commitment to value-neutrality, and to related professional ideals that suggested scholars needed to remain objective (and thus disinterested) when it came to questions about political and moral ends. Along with humanistic psychologists, vocal scholars in sociology and political science found the notion that research could, and should only, be concerned with means and not ends problematic. The extent of this concern became clearer in the debate over the socalled end-of-ideology thesis. Put forth in the 1950s by prominent intellectuals like the sociologist Daniel Bell and the political scientist Seymour Martin Lipset, this thesis said that the development of social and political thought within the United States was converging on a remarkably widespread agreement over fundamental aims. Thus the nation could now focus on the best ways of achieving such aims. But the debate over this thesis revealed that, in fact, there remained substantial scholarly interest in discussing the ends of social life, as well as a desire shared by many scholars to address the matter of fundamental principles directly in their writings.[60]

In 1964, in a remarkable effort to synthesize such challenges to the social science mainstream, Floyd W. Matson, who at the end of the 1960s became president of the newly-formed professional association for humanistic psychologists, proposed that it was time to rethink the nature of the social sciences. Trying to discern what a variety of unorthodox scholarly trends added up to, Matson concluded that the mainstream had produced a 'broken image' of human nature. This image diminished human beings by offering them an impoverished understanding of themselves and society. Furthermore, this image lent itself to a manipulative orientation that saw human beings as objects to be studied, observed, analysed, and ultimately controlled by supposedly objective scientific experts. This broken image, Matson argued, was due in no small part to the long history of unsuccessful efforts to apply the viewpoint of Newtonian physical science to the study of human beings.[61]

The case of Project Camelot took these concerns about deficiencies in mainstream scholarship, concerns that had mainly been confined to scholarly discussion, placed them in the national spotlight, and thus transformed the character of that discussion. The public setting involved a wider range of participants. It also gave discontented scholars a broader public audience and greater visibility within the academy, as social scientists now testified before Congress about the connections among national politics, military patronage and the academy; politicians considered proposals to restructure those connections; and the national press offered frequent coverage of the many complex issues. There thus emerged a widespread controversy about the relationship between social science and the national-security state, and especially about the implications of military patronage for the social science enterprise.

The turmoil began in a location geographically distant from the United States, but well within the scope of American foreign policy interests. In April of 1965, Hugo Nutini, a Chilean-born assistant professor of anthropology at the University of Pittsburgh, went to Chile,

[59]Maslow's ideas are discussed in Roy Jose DeCarvalho, The Founders of Humanistic Psychology (New York: Praeger, 1991), passim.

[60]Job L. Dittberner, The End of Ideology and American Social Thought, 1930–1960 (Ann Arbor, MI: UMI Research Press, 1979), Chapters 3–6; Chaim Waxman (ed.), The End of Ideology (New York: Simon & Schuster, 1969).

[61]Floyd W. Matson, The Broken Image: Man, Science and Society (New York: George Braziller, 1964), remains a readable, provocative interpretation of 20th-century developments from a wide range of fields in the physical, biological and social sciences, as well as philosophy, that called into question mechanistic, deterministic approaches in the social sciences.

apparently on a recruiting mission. He met with Chilean scholars and Alvaro Bunster, the Secretary-General of the University of Chile, to discuss what Nutini characterized as a social science project involving top US scholars from a variety of disciplines. When asked about the project's sources of support, Nutini, who had been involved in Camelot's planning, replied that funds came from the civilian National Science Foundation and various universities.[62]

Bunster was suspicious, however, in part because this study had a code name. After reading a project outline, he became convinced that Camelot was 'political in nature,' and that it posed 'a grave threat' to his nation's sovereignty. At about that same time, Johan Galtung, a Norwegian social scientist who had already declined to participate in Camelot after his concerns about its unsavoury political aspects had not been satisfactorily addressed, shared what he knew with Chilean scholars. Troubled, they then confronted Nutini, who responded by denying that he had had knowledge that he had been working for nefarious ends, and promised to sever his connections with the study.

But Chilean intellectuals and nationalists in the Chilean government were still worried about the political implications of Project Camelot. Their fears were probably heightened by the fact that American troops had recently been stationed in the Dominican Republic amidst a political crisis, suggesting that Camelot, though its planning documents did not list Chile as a country of study, might be part of American preparations to intervene in Chilean affairs. In August, a member of the Chilean Senate named Aniceto Rodriguez denounced Nutini as a 'degraded Chilean who disowned his country to become a Yankee spy.' The Chilean government subsequently banned Nutini from returning to his homeland. In December, the Chilean Select Chamber of Deputies unanimously approved an extensive report portraying Project Camelot as 'an attempt against the dignity, sovereignty, and independence of states and peoples and against the right of the latter to self-determination.'[63]

Elsewhere, anti-American voices used Camelot as a case in point about American imperialistic ambitions. According to Radio Moscow, Camelot revealed that the Pentagon was 'plotting to subjugate Latin America.' From the Soviet Union, Tass regarded this study as a 'vivid illustration of the growing efforts of the Pentagon to take into its own hands the conduct of U.S. foreign policy.' Havana Radio in Cuba and Politica, a Soviet-subsidized magazine published in Mexico City, both warned that such studies were part of a sinister plot to thwart national wars of liberation and overthrow duly elected governments.[64]

Within the United States, international outcry from abroad triggered a series of communications involving the US ambassador to Chile, the State Department, the military, and the White House, leading in July of 1965 to Camelot's cancellation. The cancellation of many other studies in various countries followed. In the coming years, the

---

[62]Material in this paragraph and the next comes from the following sources: George E. Lowe, 'The Camelot Affair,' Bulletin of the Atomic Scientists, Vol. 22, No. 4 (May 1966), 44–48, quote from Gaining at 45; Johan Galtung, 'After Camelot,' in Horowitz (ed.), Rise & Fall of Project Camelot, op. cit. note 2, 281–312. A Chilean news magazine, Ercilla, said that Nutini identified (apparently incorrectly) distinguished social scientists including Kingsley Davis, Seymour Lipset and Robert Merton as the study's directors. See Kalman H. Silvert, 'American Academic Ethics and Social Research Abroad: The Lesson of Project Camelot,' in Horowitz (ed.), ibid., 80–106, at 85.

[63]Quoted in 'Congressional Response to Project Camelot,' op. cit. note 2, 133, footnote 18. Also see the critical response of Jorge Montes from the Chilean Chamber of Deputies, in 'A Communist Commentary on Camelot,' in Horowitz (ed.), Rise & Fall of Project Camelot, op. cit. note 2, 232–36.

[64]All quoted in William Giandoni (Latin American Editor of Copley News Service), 'Hemisphere Report: Communists Assail "Operation Camelot,"' p. 3, Box 43, Folder 1, Fred Harris Papers [hereafter, Harris Papers], Carl Albert Center, University of Oklahoma, Norman, Oklahoma.

conduct of social research by American scholars in many Latin American countries became difficult, and sometimes impossible.[65]

If foreign critics saw Camelot as a thoroughly political endeavour, so did a post-mortem investigation by the US Congress, though with a big difference, as the viewpoint here was favourable toward military-sponsored social science. The congressional Subcommittee on International Organizations and Movements, which had already been studying the role of ideological factors in American foreign policy, placed Camelot squarely in relationship to American foreign policy objectives. Florida Democrat Dante B. Fascell, the head of the subcommittee, assured the military that it could 'get all the money' for such research that it wanted 'without much question,' because this research obviously strengthened 'national security.' In the subcommittee's final report, the military's growing commitment to the development and use of the social sciences to further US interests also received firm support. Not incidentally, this report employed military imagery in describing the social sciences as 'one of the vital tools in the arsenal of the free societies.' Other subcommittee publication titles highlighted the close alliance between social science and Cold War objectives. The transcript of the subcommittee's 1965 hearings on Project Camelot, together with its final report, was printed under the title *Behavioral Sciences and the National Security,* one of many publications in a series on *Winning the Cold War: The US Ideological Offensive.*[66]

For social scientists who believed in the value of military-sponsored research, the subcommittee's assessment was excellent news. Sociologist Robert A. Nisbet remarked that he could 'think of nothing more edifying for social scientists than a reading of this two-hundred-page document; edifying and flattering.'[67] (Yet there was a touch of sarcasm in this comment since Nisbet, as noted below, was critical of Project Camelot.) Ithiel de Sola Pool, a political scientist and a major figure at MIT's Center for International Studies, had long been involved in research related to foreign policy. The public clamour over the defunct study gave him a chance to expand on, as he put it a bit awkwardly, 'The Necessity for Social Scientists Doing Research for Governments.' 'The social sciences,' Pool proposed, had assumed the responsibility of training the 'mandarins of the twentieth century.' Previously this had been the task of the humanities. But in the modern world Pool saw that 'the only hope for humane government in the future is through the extensive use of the social sciences by government.'[68]

But growing turmoil within the government and larger society about the course of American foreign policy in Vietnam and elsewhere also prompted more caustic comments about Camelot's political or ideological meaning. Senator William J. Fulbright, a Democrat from Arkansas and former university president at the University of Arkansas, was well known for creating a major international scholarly exchange programme bearing his name. He took a great interest in higher education, and worried extensively about its military connections. According to his scathing assessment, beneath the 'jargon of "science"' in Project Camelot lay

[65]Silvert, 'American Academic Ethics,' op. cit. note 62, 80. Yet it should be noted that the military continued to sponsor much social science, including studies along the lines of Project Camelot, often as classified research: see Herman, Romance of American Psychology, op. cit. note 2, 168–70.

[66]Fascell's remarks, and Final Report, in BSNS, 53, 5R.

[67]Robert A. Nisbet, 'Project Camelot: An Autopsy,' in Philip Rieff (ed.), On Intellectuals: Theoretical Studies/Case Studies (New York: Anchor Books, 1970), 307–39, at 313.

[68]Ithiel de Sola Pool, 'The Necessity for Social Scientists Doing Research for Governments,' in Horowitz (ed.), Rise & Fall of Project Camelot, op. cit. note 2, 267–80, quotes at 267, 268.

a reactionary, backward-looking policy opposed to change.

> Implicit in Camelot, as in the concept of 'counterinsurgency,' is an assumption that revolutionary movements are dangerous to the interests of the United States and that the United States must be prepared to assist, if not actually to participate in, measures to repress them.[69]

While the movement of the social sciences toward the political centre stage had much to recommend it according to Pool and the Subcommittee on International Organizations and Movements, Camelot looked troublesome to Senator Fulbright and foreign critics like Galtung because Camelot, its scientific pretensions notwithstanding, had obvious ties to deeply controversial political objectives.

Meanwhile, as Seymour Deitchman later wrote, the press had a 'a field day,' bringing 'DOD's supposed misbehavior to public account.'[70] For example, one article discussing military patronage in The Nation, a weekly magazine, despaired that 'federal research money has for a long while been a barb sunk deep in the soft flesh of the universities . . . they no longer struggle.'[71]

In this charged national context, American scholars wrote extensively about the politics–patronage–social science nexus, exposing the underlying assumptions about social stability and revolutionary activities, the conservative political values, and the managerial mind-set implicit in Project Camelot, and in military-funded studies more globally. A close look at the language used by scholars and military personnel associated with counter-insurgency research helped to reveal Camelot's negative stance toward revolution and in favour of social stability. Counter-insurgency specialists, as pointed out by the anthropologist Marshall Sahlins, characterized Camelot as a study within the field of 'epidemiology.' They identified revolutionary developments as 'antisystem activities' and 'destabilizing processes.' In considering nations caught up in such developments, these specialists used medical metaphors to support a diagnosis of 'social pathology,' while they proposed that revolution spread through a process of 'contagion.' Counter-insurgency experts went on to recommend a type of social engineering as appropriate treatment, something called 'insurgency prophylaxis,' which would be administered by the United States Army. Presumably, social scientists would prescribe and help administer this treatment. In this view of things, social scientists and the military performed the humanitarian tasks normally assigned to doctors. Their patients, however, were social movements or entire countries, not individuals. Clearly, Cold War priorities guided social science judgements about what constituted 'national sickness,' and what should be done in order to restore afflicted nations to 'good health.'[72]

To show that Camelot was committed to the concern for social stability embedded in official US policies toward the so-called Third World, it helped to imagine how the study of revolution could assume a different orientation. This was the tack taken by Herbert Blumer, a founding figure of symbolic interactionism within sociology. Blumer proposed that one could ask, though Camelot planners did not,

> . . . how insurgency could be encouraged and promoted . . . how agitation could be organized and facilitated, how passions could be aroused and

---

[69]Fulbright quoted in John Walsh, 'Social Sciences: Cancellation of Camelot After Row in Chile Brings Research Under Scrutiny,' Science, Vol. 149 (10 September 1965), 1211–13; also see William J. Fulbright, 'America in an Age of Revolution,' in Horowitz (ed), Rise & Fall of Project Camelot, op. cit. note 2, 196–202.

[70]Seymour Deitchman, The Best-Laid Schemes: A Tale of Social Research and Bureaucracy (Cambridge, MA: MIT Press, 1976), 169–89, at 169.

[71]Anon., 'Angled Money,' The Nation (22 August 1966), 140.

[72]Sahlins, 'The Established Order,' op. cit. note 57, 77–79.

dissidence mobilized for action, how weak and vulnerable points in the social structure could be detected and exploited, and how control by a dominant elite could be undermined.[73]

Others placed the conservative political bias in social research in the historical context of American imperialism. Before social scientists had made their presence known in Central America, American business, often with protection from the American military, had descended upon that region. Foreigners, explained Robert Nisbet, now had good reason to infer that the 'American research industry' was entering its 'imperialist phase.' If so, American scholars, like American capitalists, were hardly welcome: 'the rape of national dignity by American academic enterprise is as repugnant to foreign feeling as rape by American business or government.'[74]

Against this background, the fact that DOD described Project Camelot as a basic science project, rather than a political one, seemed peculiar as well as troubling. One DOD paper said that

> Project Camelot will employ a scientific approach, that is to say, it is an objective, fact-finding study concerned with what is and not with what ought to be. It will not formulate value statements concerning the adoption of any particular policy but will provide a possible basis for policy.[75]

SORO's director Theodore Vallance claimed that it was 'an objective, nonnormative study concerned with what is or might be and not with

what ought to be.' But even Vallance acknowledged at another point that this study had two different supporting arguments, one political and the other scientific.[76] Yet the line of analysis articulated by Fulbright, Sahlins and others made the case that a political orientation pervaded this study's conceptualization from the start. Indeed, the boundary between politics and social science seemed to have disappeared.

Just as problematic, scholars associated with Camelot were not necessarily aware that they were engaged in such a thoroughly value-laden investigation, with only a thinly-veiled ideological bent favouring the suppression of revolutionary developments. Many of them had studied and worked for the past couple of decades in professional contexts that placed great weight on a purportedly objective, value-neutral, apolitical form of scholarly inquiry modelled after an idealized image of the natural sciences. Military research programmes had reinforced this self-understanding. So these scholars might easily fail to see that their work supported the established order and its underlying conservative principles. Herbert Kelman, chair of the Doctoral Program in Social Psychology at the University of Michigan, suggested that the reason for this blindspot was not hard to grasp:

> One can easily fail to notice the role of value preferences when he works within the frame of reference of the status quo, since its value assumptions are so much second nature to members of the society that they perceive them as part of objective reality.[77]

---

[73]Herbert Blumer, 'Threats from Agency-Determined Research: The Case of Camelot,' in Horowitz (ed.), Rise & Fall of Project Camelot, op. cit. note 2, 153–74, at 161.

[74]Nisbet, 'Project Camelot: An Autopsy,' op. cit. note 67, at 338, 323. Nisbet, it should be emphasized, was no critic of scholarly collaboration with the military in general. Assuming that the behavioural sciences were, as many of their practitioners claimed, 'non-ideological' and 'objective,' he saw nothing 'intrinsically wrong with their conclusions being used by, or given to, the Army' (316). But even this favourable predisposition toward military social science did not get in the way of his seeing that Project Camelot did not fit such a description.

[75]Document Number 4 in Horowitz (ed.), Rise & Fall of Project Camelot, op. cit. note 2, 62 (emphasis in original).

[76]Theodore Vallance, 'Project Camelot: An Interim Postlude,' in Horowitz (ed.), ibid., 203–10, at 204 (emphasis in original).

[77]Herbert Kelman, A Time to Speak: On Human Values and Social Research (San Francisco, CA: Jossey-Bass, 1968), 5.

Sociologist Irving Louis Horowitz agreed, as he testified before Congress, wrote extensively on the politics and ethics of social research, and probably did more than any other social scientist to draw attention to the wide range of worrisome issues concerning military patronage of academic social research. Like Kelman, Horowitz surmised that many social scientists had adopted the values of the 'Establishment' to such an extent that it seemed to them as if these values had disappeared. But the truth was quite different; in their effort to avoid normative commitments, they accepted as beyond challenge the prevailing social arrangements, power structures and cultural norms. As a result, their research and conclusions about social reality supported the status quo.[78]

In these political and scholarly commentaries, the power of the military patron to shape the course of research in directions congenial to official Cold War policy goals occupied a prominent place. While the danger that patrons would impose their interests on scholarly research had often seemed manageable during the 1940s and 1950s, the case of Camelot encouraged an alternative, darker conclusion. Scholars, of course, did not have to accept military money. But once they did, it seemed unlikely that they would (or could) pursue work that challenged military operations and American foreign policy aims. 'The Army,' asserted Irving Horowitz in a discussion of the compromised rôle of social scientists, was '"hiring help" . . . not openly and honestly submitting a problem to the higher professional and scientific authority of social science.'[79]

As a result, social scientists working under military contract would be led to accept the premises, at least in the context of their research, that revolution was harmful and established governments allied with the United States were to be preferred. As 'research that is tied to foreign policy or military operations is, of necessity, conceived within the framework of existing policy,' observed Herbert Kelman, ' . . . it does not fulfill the function of providing new frameworks that would not normally emerge out of the policy-making apparatus itself.'[80] Similarly, Herbert Blumer recognized that 'in responding to the practical interest and policy orientation of the [funding] agency,' research takes on an ' "ideological" slant.'[81]

Moreover, the professional social scientist in this situation could easily end up in the role of a social-control-minded technician or engineer. After first accepting the sponsor's objectives as a given, a researcher typically focused solely on determining the best means to achieve them. As Pio E. Uliassi has it, since 'sponsored work must be roughly consonant with the basic values and outlooks of its sponsors,' the social scientist tends to adopt 'an "engineering" conception of his role.'[82] Such a limited vision of the scholar's role led self-identified 'responsible, non-ideological experts' to confine themselves to offering 'advice on tactical questions,' added the linguist and outspoken critic of American foreign policy, Noam Chomsky. Meanwhile, it was other so-called 'irresponsible "ideological types"' who raised a storm about 'principles . . . moral issues and human rights.'[83]

[78]Irving Louis Horowitz, 'Social Science Objectivity and Value Neutrality: Historical Problems and Projections,' in Horowitz, Professing Sociology: Studies in the Life Cycle of Social Science (Chicago, IL: Aldine Publishing Co., 1969), 30–45.

[79]I.L. Horowitz, 'The Life and Death of Project Camelot,' in Horowitz, Professing Sociology, ibid., 287–304, at 300.

[80]Herbert C. Kelman, 'The Use of University Resources in Foreign Policy Research,' p. 5 Box 42, Folder 18, Harris Papers.

[81]Blumer, 'Threats,' op. cit. note 73, 159.

[82]Pio E. Uliassi, 'Government Sponsored Research in International and Foreign Affairs,' in Irving Louis Horowitz (ed.), The Use and Abuse of Social Science: Behavioral Research and Policy Making (New Brunswick, NJ: Transaction Books, 2nd ed., 1975), 287–320, at 313.

[83]Noam Chomsky, 'The Responsibility of Intellectuals,' in Chomsky, American Power and the New Mandarins (New York: Pantheon, 1969), 256–90, at 269.

Actions taken by the Executive Branch shortly after Camelot's cancellation only strengthened political and scholarly concerns about the subordination of social science to the State, a resulting technocratic orientation, and a more general intellectual myopia. After the blow-up in Chile over Camelot, the State Department initiated correspondence with the White House about the problems of keeping publicly-funded social research from provoking foreign hostility. Subsequently, a letter from President Johnson to Secretary of State Dean Rusk—the letter was initially drafted by the State Department—outlined the need for a review process to prevent future social science projects from damaging the image of the United States. Previously, each agency had been responsible for reviewing projects according to its own criteria, though an effort to improve coordination on a voluntary basis had been made in 1964, when the Council on Foreign Affairs Research (FAR) was established to coordinate and plan research on foreign areas for some two dozen agencies. To meet the President's request, FAR received orders to establish a set of review procedures. In order to avoid meddling in the affairs of agencies that had ostensibly academic purposes, the new review procedures only pertained to research projects with obvious ties to national foreign policy objectives, and that thus might elicit international protest.[84]

Despite this important limitation, the federal checkpoint to prevent future social science fiascos came under fire from those who worried that the Establishment was showing no respect for scholarly freedom. Alfred de Grazia, editor of the American Behavioral Scientist, had previously been a member of Project Camelot's design team. As he saw things, State Department officials had no reason to be proud of what they were doing. The new review procedures would probably impede the advance of the social sciences and, what was worse, might therefore harm the national defence effort.[85] Though Irving Horowitz was critical of Project Camelot, he found it appalling that Camelot had been terminated due to foreign policy considerations, a result that represented, in his words, 'a decisive setback for social science research.' Since the new review procedures were concerned not with scholarly merit but international sensitivities, Horowitz found these invidious as well.[86]

Such worries about the limitations on scholarly autonomy also surfaced inside the prestigious National Academy of Sciences (NAS). During NAS's first century, its interest in the social sciences had been limited to anthropology and psychology. But in the early 1960s, the Academy created a Division of Behavioral Sciences so as to bring in representatives from other social disciplines whose work, as the 'behavioral sciences' label implied, was sufficiently 'scientific,' and thus would command the respect of the Academy's natural-science leaders. Regarding the new review process, the Division of Behavioral Sciences' executive committee complained that by sponsoring the directive from President Johnson, the State Department had 'aimed a dagger at the independent integrity of the behavioral sciences.'[87] A declassified document

[84]Testimony of Thomas L. Hughes, Director of Intelligence and Research, State Department, in US Congress, Senate, Committee on Government Operations, Subcommittee on Government Research, Federal Support of International Social Science and Behavioral Research, Hearings [hereafter, FSISSBR], 89th Congress, 2nd session (1966), 3–4. Johnson's letter is reprinted in BSNS, 107.

[85]Alfred de Grazia is quoted at length in Gideon Sjoberg, 'Project Camelot: Selected Reactions and Personal Reflections,' in Sjoberg (ed.), Ethics, Politics, and Social Research (Cambridge, MA: Schenkman Publishing Co., 1967), 141–61, at 143–45.

[86]Horowitz, 'Life & Death of Project Camelot,' op. cit. note 79, 302.

[87]Minutes, Second Meeting, Advisory Committee on Government Programs in the Behavioral Sciences (10 December 1965), Central Policy File Series, Folder: Behavioral Sciences 1965 Committee on Government Programs in Behavioral Sciences: Advisory Meetings: Minutes: December, National Academy of Sciences Archives [hereafter, NAS Archives], Washington, DC.

in NAS archives indicates that due to heightened national security regulations, preserving the independence of academic social science became, following Camelot's demise, even more difficult. In August of 1965, Harold Brown, the Director of Defense Research and Engineering, presented new security guidelines in a memorandum to the assistant secretaries of the Army, Navy and Air Force, and the director of the Advanced Research Projects Agency. These guidelines are worth quoting at some length because of their wide scope:

> Sensitive aspects of work having primary interest to the US Government (as opposed to a foreign government) must be treated in such a way that offense to foreign governments and propaganda advantage to the communist apparatus are avoided. This means that task statements, contracts, working papers, reports, etc. which refer to US assistance or potential US assistance to foreign countries in the internal defense area; or which express US concern over internal violence or revolution, whether communist inspired or not; or which refer to the development or examination of US policies for the purpose of influencing allied policies or actions; or which could imply US interference or intervention in the internal affairs of a foreign government, will have to be classified and marked as not for disclosure to foreign nationals except where a specific and well-considered exception is made.[88]

There is a glaring irony in this move to beef up security: though concerns about military influence on the social sciences had originally erupted over Project Camelot, an unclassified study, the official response resulted in further subordination of social science to non-academic authorities.

If military funding by itself might take the social sciences down a conservative political path, alarmed observers recognized that the extensive imposition of secrecy by federal authorities only raised the likelihood that the critical capacities of scholars would be compromised. Regarding the struggle between the scholar's professional interest in publishing in the open literature and the government's interest in keeping privileged information secret, Irving Horowitz surmised that the latter often won, mainly due to the imbalance in power between buyer and seller. Because classified research placed severe limits on the open discussion and evaluation of scholarly ideas, the heightened security measures were especially problematic.[89]

One could pursue the extensive public controversy over Camelot and these subsequent developments further, but the analysis so far already shows how deeply this controversy challenged conventional notions about the relations among national politics, military patronage, and American social science. Alarmed participants from the scholarly and political communities feared that military patronage was turning social scientists into servants of established interests, with questionable implications for social science scholarship. Often starting from the same basic premise put forth by foreign critics (namely, that social research was a tool of American imperialism), American commentators argued that military patronage deeply influenced the shape of academic social science; that researchers working with military funds were compromising their scholarly freedom, objectivity and integrity; and that the social sciences were in grave danger of becoming technocratic servants to the powers that be. In sum, the road to Camelot, rather than leading to a peaceful and just society guided by impartial, objective behavioural scientists, had thrust action-oriented scholars into the public spotlight where the mantle of objectivity, value-neutrality and professional autonomy received a barrage of stinging criticism.

---

[88]Memorandum for the Assistant Secretary of the Army (Research and Development), the Assistant Secretary of the Navy (Research and Development), the Assistant Secretary of the Air Force (Research and Development), and the Director, Advanced Research Projects Agency (18 August 1965), Central Policy File Series, Folder: Behavioral Science 1965 Committee on Government Programs in Behavioral Science: Advisory General, NAS Archives.

[89]Irving Horowitz, 'Social Science and Public Policy: Implications of Modern Research,' in Horowitz (ed.), Rise & Fall of Project Camelot, op. cit. note 2, 339–76, esp. 347–60.

BROADER IMPLICATIONS FOR THE SOCIAL SCIENCE ENTERPRISE: PATRONAGE, IDEOLOGY, VALUE-NEUTRALITY

The controversy over Camelot quickly became entangled with other national problems that drew further critical attention to the politics–patronage–social science nexus. Not only did this controversy lead almost immediately, in 1965, to heightened security requirements for federally sponsored social research; in the coming years, previously hidden or little-discussed arrangements linking social science to the national-security state and the Vietnam War were also subjected to public scrutiny. For example, it became well known that a group of Michigan State social scientists had received CIA funds to support their work with police forces in the South Vietnam government.[90] At the same time, the emergence of widespread public criticism of various domestic programmes, especially the War on Poverty and related social welfare initiatives, substantially broadened the discussion about the political and ideological dimensions of American social science, and the institutional arrangements that brought social science experts to bear on national policy.[91]

Given this complicated picture, it is perhaps impossible to isolate and pin down with great precision the broader implications of the Camelot controversy; nevertheless, it is possible to identify certain salient issues in this controversy that became part of important efforts to rethink and reform the social science enterprise. A brief look at three areas– patronage, ideology, and value-neutrality—reveals more fully Camelot's legacy, and the centrality of political issues in the evolution of unorthodox epistemological positions.

Concerned participants in the Camelot controversy feared, as we have seen, that social science had become (or was rapidly becoming) subservient to political power. The problem seemed especially deep in the case of foreign area research, which in 1966 alone received almost $36 million from the military and other governmental sources of support.[92] That same year, the year after Camelot's cancellation, the Senate Subcommittee on Government Research held hearings on social research on foreign areas. Subcommittee chairman Fred R. Harris, a Democrat from Oklahoma, drew attention to the militarization, or what he called the 'over-militarization,' of social science.[93] Elsewhere, Noam Chomsky warned his readers about the problem of counter-insurgency or counter-revolutionary subordination in American scholarship. Just as American intellectuals during the Cold War often pointed to the overwhelming pressures on scholars in communist countries to support the Party line, Chomsky pointed to the integration of American scholars into the State apparatus as the basis for an uncritical commitment to the US government's anti-revolutionary outlook.[94] From this viewpoint, the question for the social sciences was how they could be restored to good health.

One widespread response focused on the corrosive impact of patronage, and especially the

[90]Irving Louis Horowitz, 'Michigan State and the CIA: A Dilemma for Social Scientists,' Bulletin of the Atomic Scientists, Vol. 22, No. 7 (September 1966), 26–29; Warren Hinckley, 'The University on the Make,' Ramparts, Vol. 4 (April 1966), 11–22.

[91]Daniel Patrick Moynihan, Maximum Feasible Misunderstanding (New York: Free Press, 1970); Henry J. Aaron, Politics and the Professors: The Great Society in Perspective (Washington, DC: Brookings Institution, 1978).

[92]Elizabeth T. Crawford and Gene M. Lyons, 'Foreign Area Research: A Background Statement,' in Foreign Area Research: A Conference Report (January 1967), from the Advisory Committee on Government Programs in the Behavioral Sciences, Division of Behavioral Science, National Academy of Science-National Research Council, 4–12, at 5.

[93]FSISSBR: Senator Harris discusses his concerns throughout the subcommittee's published hearings.

[94]Noam Chomsky, 'Objectivity and Liberal Scholarship,' in Chomsky, American Power & the New Mandarins, op. cit. note 83, 23–129.

partnership with the military. Regarding this topic, the Camelot controversy, by generating concern about the harmful impact of military patronage on the critical capacities of social scientists, proved to be of singular importance. Though the initial 1965 congressional investigation by the House Subcommittee on International Organization and Movements issued a decidedly favourable report on military social science programmes, that same report noted the danger, previously pointed to in Eisenhower's farewell address, that greatly increased federal support for American science would undermine the independence of the academic enterprise.[95] The following year, in 1966, the work of Senator Harris's Subcommittee revealed that fear about the 'overmilitarization' of the social sciences had spread within the political and scholarly communities.[96]

In this context, the idea of strengthening scholarly integrity by severing ties with national-security agencies received extensive consideration. Decades before, the famous anthropologist Franz Boas had bemoaned the participation of his academic colleagues as spies in World War I.[97] Now, in the wake of Project Camelot, leaders of the American Anthropological Association (AAA) warned the public of a similar problem on the op-ed pages of the *New York Times:*

> Attempts to utilize scientific research programs . . . to cloak activities with non-scholarly or non-scientific purposes seriously threaten the integrity of the discipline and the execution of legitimate scientific research. The criteria of legitimate scientific research activities include full disclosure of sponsorship, of sources of funds, and of the purposes of the research, and public reporting of results, subject to the proper protection of the personal privacy of those studied or assisting the research. The gathering of information and data which can never be made available to the public does not constitute scientific research and should not be so represented.[98]

The anthropologist Ralph Beals subsequently undertook, on behalf of the AAA, an extensive study of politics and ethics in social research, finding that the problems of clandestine research were, indeed, pervasive. He estimated that the CIA employed perhaps as many as 1000 social scientists. Intelligence operations more generally employed an unknown number. Pointing out that 'virtually all such work is classified and its quality cannot be judged,' Beals concluded that

> . . . such activities contribute nothing to the development of the social sciences. Far worse, to the extent that social scientists or persons posing as social scientists use their titles, positions, or research activities to conceal secret intelligence activities, the future of social research is threatened.[99]

Some people suggested that new federal arrangements were therefore needed to support social science in a manner that did not constrain research in undesirable ways, or force scholarly thinking into an uncritical mould. With this in mind, the Senate Subcommittee on Government Research emerged as an advocate for a new, civilian social science agency. The idea for such a separate agency had first arisen during the 1940s' National Science Foundation legislative debate, but as national science policy concentrated at that time on the natural sciences, this proposal had received little attention. By the

[95]BSNS, 6R.

[96]FSISSBR.

[97]Franz Boas, Letter to the Editor of The Nation (20 December 1919), reprinted in Simpson (ed.), Universities & Empire, op. cit. note 21, 1–2.

[98]Stephen Boggs (for the Executive Board, AAA), Letter to the Editor of the New York Times (7 June 1966), reproduced in FSISSBR, 75.

[99]Beals, Politics of Social Research, op. cit. note 1, 96–97, and other documents regarding these concerns of anthropologists in Beals' Appendix B.

mid-1960s, the scene had changed notably, as growing concern about the ill effects of military patronage combined with strong support within the Johnson administration for using the social sciences to improve domestic affairs. Under these conditions, Senator Harris concluded—though wrongly as it turned out—that a National Social Science Foundation would be viable. He argued that such an agency should encourage social scientists to pursue work on controversial matters that challenged current political policies or widespread social practices and beliefs.[100]

In the following decades, the possibility that patronage could shape the social sciences (and science more generally) became a widely debated and contentious matter, continuing to challenge the claims of those who maintained that the funding of social science research did not mean that such research was directed by extra-scientific social interests. A small sub-field of scholarly study focused on the influence of philanthropic support in the development of American social science.[101] This literature was complemented by studies that focused on, as one author put it, 'government influence on the social science paradigm.'[102] Then there was a much larger body of scholarship arguing that patronage was a key factor shaping the context, conduct and content of science.[103]

Second, Camelot's legacy underscored the problem of ideology in social science, a problem that scientific leaders and other observers of the scientific scene in the post-WWII years had tried

to resolve by banishing ideology (along with politics) from legitimate scientific inquiry. As a highly visible and extensively discussed example of a large-scale social science project that would incorporate cutting-edge research and theory and yet was riddled with a conservative bias, Camelot helped to alert the scholarly imagination to the possibility that ideology, together with subjective, social commitments that lay beyond empirical demonstration might, in fact, be frequently present in American social science.

Because of Camelot's particular concern with revolutionary movements in developing countries, this study had special relevance for the ideological underpinnings of the field of foreign area studies, where research on modernization had been enthusiastically pursued. Before the mid-1960s, the presence of ideology in development studies had not been recognized by the mainstream as a problem. Social scientists had proceeded with confidence, assuming that their studies offered an objective, rational and scientific (as opposed to a subjective, emotional and ideological) analysis of the major problems confronting developing nations. These scholars then discussed how these problems could be overcome with expert-guided development pursued within a framework of social stability (and thus these countries could avoid the dangers of revolution and communist penetration). The uproar over Camelot helped to call into question this confidence, as critics began to emphasize that such scholarship was grounded

---

[100]Fred R. Harris, 'National Social Science Foundation: Proposed Congressional Mandate for the Social Sciences,' American Psychologist, *Vol. 22* (1967), 904–10; Harris, 'The Case for a National Social Science Foundation,' Science, Vol. 157 (4 August 1967), 507–09.

[101]Robert Arnove (ed.). Philanthropy and Cultural Imperialism: The Foundations at Home and Abroad (Boston, MA: G.K. Hall, 1980). In the 1980s, British sociologist Martin Bulmer and Canadian sociologist Donald Fisher carried on an extended argument about the critical case of the Rockefeller Foundation's influence on American social science. See the commentary with relevant references to their works by Salma Ahmad, 'American Foundations and the Development of the Social Sciences Between the Wars: Comment on the Debate Between Martin Bulmer and Donald Fisher,' Sociology, Vol. 25 (1991), 511–20. For a more recent discussion of patronage and American social science, see Piatt, A History, op. cit. note 25, Chapter 5, 'Funding and Research Methods,' 142–99.

[102]Michael Useem, 'Government Influence on the Social Science Paradigm,' Sociological Quarterly, Vol. 17 (1976), 146–61.

[103]See, for example: Bruce T. Moran (ed.), Patronage and Institutions: Science, Technology, and Medicine at the European Court, 1500–1750 (Woodbridge, Suffolk & Rochester, NY: Boydell Press, 1991); Jacob (ed.), Politics of Western Science, op. cit. note 32; Mendelsohn, Smith & Weingart (eds.), Science, Technology & the Military, op. cit. note 8.

in a value-laden vision that took an idealized picture of the history of the United States, and then presented it inappropriately as a model for 'Third World,' 'underdeveloped,' 'developing,' or, in the most explicitly pejorative language, 'backward' nations.[104]

This challenge to the post-war social science orthodoxy contributed to an emerging crisis within area studies. As political scientist Irene Gendzier puts it, through the Camelot controversy, 'the alleged neutrality of social science research was exploded before the evidence of complicity between well-known scholars of development and political change, and the policy planners in charge of the military operations in Southeast Asia.' As concerns about the moral and cognitive basis of development studies mounted, proponents of new opposing scholarly paradigms proposed that power inequalities led to the dependence of developing nations on (rather than their independence from) the United States and other dominant powers.[105]

In another assault on the mainstream's commitment to the separation of social science from ideology, critics took aim at the extensive bodies of research incorporating functionalist and social systems theories. Prominent scholars like Harvard sociologist Talcott Parsons had promoted these theories as part of a comprehensive scientific edifice for understanding and predicting the interactions of various components or subsystems of a society. This work tended to emphasize the functional integration of these components, noting how a social system maintained itself, and thus did not disintegrate. Project Camelot's design plans had drawn upon these ideas for obvious reasons: American counter-insurgency policy during the 1960s

included programmes for development in a manner intended to reinforce social stability. As governmental policies lost more and more public support, this concern with stability came under fire as a social science prop for the embattled status quo. Again, Camelot served as a case in point, as Marshall Sahlins observed that 'what had been for some time a cultural common-law marriage between scientific functionalism and the natural interest of a leading world power in the status quo became under the aegis of Project Camelot an explicit and legitimate union.'[106] For Irving Horowitz, Camelot provided 'the final proof, if such were necessary, that the functionalist credo of order, stability, pattern maintenance, stress management, and so forth indeed reveals strong conservative drives.'[107]

Lying just beyond the problem of ideology in social research was a third piece of Camelot's legacy that challenged the dominant post-war emphasis on the value-neutral rôle of the social scientist. The case of Camelot suggested to many observers that a conservative bias in social science reflected a particularly narrow conception of the scholar as a handmaiden to power, a conception now seen to be firmly rooted in this same conservative bias. The labels 'action-intellectual' or 'policy scientist' implied that social scientists, who in the earlier post-war years had often been marginal to high-level scientific and political discussions, were now well inside the corridors of power. Nevertheless, the scholar entered only as a servant of power, an advisor to those who had real power. Since, as Camelot's critics observed, this advisory rôle did not encourage debate over fundamental principles, social scientists often took a managerial, technocratic view of social problems. This point

[104]Gendzier, Managing Political Change, op. cit. note 21; Robert A. Packenham, Liberal America and the Third World: Political Development Ideas in Foreign Aid and Social Science (Princeton, NJ: Princeton University Press, 1973).

[105]Gendzier, Managing Political Change, op. cit. note 21, 9.

[106]Sahlins, 'The Established Order,' op. cit. note 57, 78.

[107]Horowitz, 'Life & Death,' op. cit. note 79, 304.

also surfaced in the related debate over the end of ideology. But by the mid-1960s, growing frustrations with major domestic and foreign policies helped to draw attention to the support provided by social scientists to these same policies, rendering the claims of political impartiality (and thus value-neutrality) suspect.

Perhaps, then, it was time to reject the value-neutral stance as deceitful, and even socially naïve. Robert Boguslaw, a scientist and former member of Camelot's design team, wrote extensively about the rise of systems analysis in the social sciences. In his view, if the social sciences were to make the most of their opportunities to influence the larger society, these disciplines had to adopt a new conception of the scholar's rôle:

> As social science begins to emerge from the morass of inconsequentiality in which so much of it has for so long been embedded, its obligation to develop more sophisticated methods for normative analysis becomes urgent. It can no longer afford to relegate this subject to the obscurity of philosophy texts or to the sporadic emotional outbursts of its practitioners. In the absence of progress in normative analysis, the efforts of social scientists and the content of social science are guided by the subtle controls implicit in a 'value-free ideology.'[108]

In thinking about the broader problems raised by Camelot, Boguslaw recommended that scholars (re)turn to 'normative analysis,' welcoming a moral perspective in social science inquiry, rather than denying that one existed or trying to excise it, as orthodox practitioners wanted to do.

Reorienting the social scientist toward normative inquiry could, additionally, help to curb the much-criticized tendency of social scientists to adopt a dehumanizing managerial

outlook. Social scientists needed to think hard about the moral implications of their work, or else they would probably end up reinforcing the dehumanizing tendencies of modern society, argued Herbert Kelman. Counter-insurgency research, with its emphasis on producing knowledge that would facilitate the control of other nations and their peoples, represented in Kelman's analysis a good example of this worrisome streak in modern scholarship. As an antidote, Kelman called on social scientists to make the support of human freedom and dignity an explicit professional goal.[109]

In these various ways, Camelot's implications nurtured continuing doubts about the validity, and even the desirability, of the objective social science model: Camelot contributed to the efforts to reconsider the impact of the role of patronage and its 'extra-scientific' social interests on the content of social science, the place of ideology in social research, and the value-neutral conception of the social scientist's social role.

The overall impact was summed up well by two social scientists who, in the late 1960s, undertook extensive studies of American politics and American social science. The sociologist Gene Lyons was the author of a book about what he called 'The Uneasy Partnership' between the social sciences and the federal government in the 20th century. As Lyons saw it, one of the most troubling aspects of the Camelot controversy was the realization on the part of many scholars of 'the extent to which they were accepting and supporting the premises of official policy when they undertook military-sponsored research, no matter how basic the investigation.'[110] Thus no matter how hard they tried in their own work to be objective, no matter how rigorous their scientific methodology, no matter how impartial

---

[108]Robert Boguslaw, 'Ethics and the Social Scientist,' in Horowitz (ed.), Rise & Fall of Project Camelot, op. cit. note 2, 107–27, at 118.

[109]Herbert Kelman, 'The Social Consequences of Social Research,' in Kelman, A Time to Speak, op. cit. note 77, 34–57.

[110]Lyons, Uneasy Partnership, op. cit. note 41, 169.

their professional outlook, their work was still likely to be shaped by patronage relations that infused their research with a political bias.

To return to the quotation with which I opened this paper: in the book based upon his study about social science and ethics for the American Anthropological Association, Ralph Beals remarked that Camelot was surely not the first instance of 'the influence of political decisions and climates on social research.' But what was new was the 'fact' that this political influence could 'no longer be ignored'; and Beals continued:

> Camelot, a proposed international social science research project sponsored by the Army Research Office of the United States Department of Defense, was the turning point.[111]

CONCLUSION

This paper has examined the fascinating story of Project Camelot, from its roots in the post-war partnership between American social science and the military, its immediate origins in DOD's counter-insurgency mission of the 1960s, its cancellation in July 1965 at a time of rising anti-Establishment sentiment and activity, the widespread controversy that followed, and some of the broader implications of this controversy that supported continued challenges to scientific objectivity and related ideals, such as value-neutrality and professional autonomy.

In the early post-WWII period, military funding seemed to be helping social scientists in their quest for public respect and scientific legitimacy. But the Camelot controversy contributed to a darker interpretation, according to which the politics–patronage–social science nexus had undermined orthodox claims about the separation of social science from politics and ideology. It seemed that Camelot, and military-sponsored social research more generally, supported official US interest in preserving an unjust world order with the help of expert-guided management of social change and the suppression of revolutionary developments, if those threatened official goals. Social scientists, far from being impartial, objective scientists, seemed to be servants of power who were wedded to a conservative technocratic viewpoint that disguised their true political character. While the 'strictly academic' criticisms of the mainstream that Novick discusses had already been making some impact, the Camelot controversy, I have argued, thrust such concerns into the national spotlight, transforming the discussion by opening it up to a much broader array of participants, and bringing the politics–patronage–social science nexus into the centre of consideration.

Project Camelot's planners talked about designing a social systems model that could help diagnose social pathology, and assist in indicating an appropriate remedy. In the end, however, critics found that it was the social science enterprise that was sick. Efforts to restore it to good health suggested that it was first necessary to rethink such key issues as the rôle of patronage, the presence of ideology, and the ideal of value-neutrality in American social science.

---

[111]Beals, Politics of Social Research, op. cit. note 1, 4.

[112]BSNS, 62.

Section IV

QUANTITATIVE DATA COLLECTION

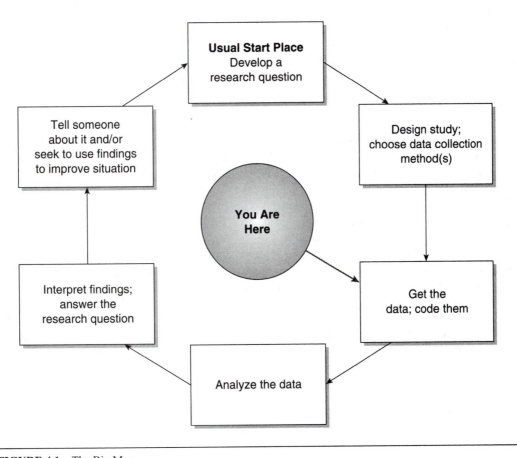

FIGURE 4.1 The Big Map

We divide the many data collection options into three sets of approaches: quantitative, qualitative, and mixed. This chapter examines the first. As Peter Blau summarized it, "quantitative sociology is . . . the analysis of the implications of the numbers and distributions of people for their social relations."[1] It is not the analysis of numbers that counts, but the implications those numbers have for the social life that they represent. Quantitative data collection methods are those techniques that meaningfully represent dimensions of social life in numeric terms.

One of the advantages of gathering large amounts of data in the social sciences is that having more data tends to yield reliable research findings. This works because a very large sample of cases is more likely to be **representative** of the population from which it is drawn, meaning that there is as much variation in whatever we're measuring in the sample as there is in the whole group that it represents. If, for example, you ask ten of your friends what recent movies they liked most, we can learn something about your friends, but that won't tell us much about other people. But if we could ask 10,000 moviegoers from around the nation, then we could draw general inferences about what is popular in this culture at this time. The results may not reflect the same movies that your friends like best, and they probably won't be the very best movies in any dramatic or artistic sense (since those probably appeal more strongly to smaller audiences), but they will very likely be quite similar to the movies that were most popular last year. Hence, the quantitative approach has proven to be valuable not only in the social sciences but also for market research, policy analysis, evaluations, and public opinion research, to name a few applications. Of course, findings from a large sample of a subset of the population can't be generalized to the population as a whole. If you interviewed, say, a hundred of your movie-going friends in an especially devout young people's church group, the findings would probably not apply to even most young people, much less to the entire population.

QUANTITATIVE CODING

But wait. Movies aren't quantitative, and there is no natural numeric measure for how much you like something. As it turns out, however, this isn't important. Almost anything can be **coded** numerically. For example, if I ask 300 subjects to name five recent films that they liked a lot, then I can add one point to each film for each person who mentions it. Then I can declare the films with the most points (the most mentions) to be the most popular. In this case, the coding scheme is to assign each film a number of "popularity" points that equals the number of mentions it got. Or I could try to be a little more complicated by asking everyone to name their top five films, and number them 5 (best) down to 1. Again, add all the points to see which films get the most. This is a different coding scheme. The numbers can go higher even with fewer mentions since we're adding values for the relative strength of the evaluations. If you have ever indicated your level of pain on a scale from ☺ to ☹, you have coded complex feelings as a simple numeric. (Hospitals use these emoticons during patient intake.)

As powerful as our statistical techniques are, we must also guard against **false precision**. False precision occurs when you use a computer program or other system to make a precise calculation using data that are not that precise. (In computer science, this is called GIGO—"garbage in, garbage out.") This can occur through careless coding, as when researchers treat **ordinal** data as though they were **interval** data. If, for example, you code approval of something on a 1–5 scale, the answer 4 ("approve") shows more approval than the answer 1 ("strongly disapprove"), but it doesn't show four times more approval. Those

---

[1]Blau, 1977:26.

numbers are just categories in order (hence, ordinal), not real numbers.

False precision and related errors also occur when crucial qualifiers are overlooked. A frequent example of that may be found in popular reports on medical research. Journalists often attempt to simplify the technical language of research reports and consolidate the findings into just the key points that consumers would need. But researchers often use precise technical language because that language limits the kinds of claims one can make about the results. When a researcher studies a small convenience sample from an accessible population, the work may be highly valid but difficult to generalize to a larger population. A program that increases AIDS awareness 50% among college students in a nursing concentration is a good program, but it would be highly inaccurate to say simply that the program can increase AIDS awareness by 50%, period. Careful specification of all of the limitations in the research design is essential to the accuracy of the conclusions.

A related problem occurs when results are presented as a percentage change in something. Consider a clinical trial of a new treatment for a rare, but life-threatening condition. If the old treatment was 3% effective and the new treatment is 4% effective, then one could say that the new drug is 33% more likely to save your life. That's because the 4% success rate is one third more than the old 3%. But reporting it that way might easily imply that the new treatment will save 33% of the population, whereas the reality is that we still anticipate a 96% failure rate. The more people skim the numbers, the more misinformed they are likely to become.

In the first selection for this topic, Ronald Inglehart uses survey data to measure the impact of socioeconomic conditions on deeply held individual values. To get at such subtleties, Inglehart constructed several **indexes** for different dimensions of the underlying value systems that are most common in different countries at varying times. Specifically, he is coding multiple

dimensions of value systems across many cultures. He uses survey **instruments** (a fancy word for *questionnaires* or for a list of questions for interviews, called *interview schedules*) containing more than 300 items each. Each survey instrument is slightly modified for each of the nations where the survey is administered. He also codes many other kinds of data to analyze in relation to his data on values, which allows him to conclude that economic conditions play such a large role in individual value formation.

Relying on both theory and prior empirical research, Inglehart defines two value spectrums—two dimensions of human values—one ranging from *traditional to secular-rational,* and one ranging from *focus on survival to focus on self-expression.* (The explanations and justifications for these two indexes are in the article.) These concepts are defined using dozens of different indicators (or attributes), each of which is measured independently. Then, by examining the patterns of association among the different indicators, including changes across nations and across decades, Inglehart is able to conclude that "the two dimensions explain fully 71 percent of the cross-cultural variation among those ten items." In short, he has taken several very complex concepts, broken them down into a large number of small measures (indicators), and then discovered which few of these individual measures together define a regular and consistent pattern that best represents his larger concepts. After decades of research and hundreds of thousands of individual data points, he can now do what this paper claims—map global human values.

The tables in this article present the *factor loadings* for each of the variables that make up the major indexes. The correlations among the different factors are also presented. The use and meaning of this level of analysis is beyond the scope of this book, so we are going to skip over that part. But it is worth spending a few minutes looking at the "Cultural Map of the World in 2000," which orders the nations of this study according to their collective score on the traditional/secular and survival/expression scales. Notice which nations are more similar to each other. Inglehart has labeled some of these groupings, such as "English speaking" or "Ex-communist" nations. Do you think these labels explain the similarities in the patterns of values among each nation's citizens?

Although his interest lies in democracy, the researcher is not measuring whether people vote or if a free press is protected or any other democratic institutional mechanisms. These would be characteristics of a nation, not of its citizens, and so would not be measured by a survey. Nor is he asking people how they feel about democracy itself. And he certainly isn't trying to obtain his measure of the relationship between values and economics by asking people whether they feel that economic systems affect their values. Instead, he is asking about the values that lie at the foundation of democracies, such as the belief in individual expression or a tolerance for diversity. The research subjects provide the individual answers. It is the researcher's job to (1) record the data in numeric form; (2) analyze the patterns of association that exist within these numbers; and (3) translate those findings back into knowledge about people. The main tasks for the quantitative researcher, then, are to code the data for analysis, and then decode it in order to explain its meaning.

There are three basic and popular quantitative data collection strategies: surveys, experiments, and secondary analysis. For clarity, we discuss secondary analysis in Section VI.

SURVEYS

The most familiar quantitative data collection tool in the social sciences is the survey. The popularity of survey research dates back to the early 20th century, while the philosophical foundations of this methodology rest on the older **positivist** premise that social sciences should be based on verifiable facts. (There are many forms of knowledge other than those that are popularly perceived as "facts," including both knowledgeable and arbitrary conjecture, inference from comparable cases, faith, and inference from logic.) In the United States, perhaps one of the earliest expositions of the survey methodology was our national census, the first of which was undertaken in 1790. In the early part of the 20th century, social reformers who were interested in democratizing policy research surveyed individuals to make popular opinion count. According to Stephen Turner, reformers inspired the adoption of survey techniques among philanthropies and scholars interested in the study of social problems who were able to use the technique to study the lives of their subjects almost firsthand.[2] Another influential movement behind the general acceptance of this method was the early community research studies, starting around the 1920s, which used surveys to quickly acquire a series of "snapshots" of life in a community. By this time, research methods books already included chapters about survey methodology.[3]

There are different opinions among social scientists with respect to the size and format of questionnaires. Nonetheless, some rules of thumb are generally observed. Questionnaires should be as short and as simple as possible. Each question should measure exactly one thing (which is critical when you are trying to understand the answers). This last guideline is extremely important, but it can require a good deal of work. If a complex concept is made up of several different elements, then that concept is measured using a **composite variable**, and each element is considered one **dimension** of the variable. The composite variable is measured by including separate questions for each dimension and then calculating a **scale variable** that puts

[2]See Turner, 2007, pp. 121–22.

[3]See Platt, 1998.

the pieces together somehow. Therefore, you need at least one question per indicator. (For example, if you were measuring the concept of "ability to play baseball" you would have individual indicators for batting, throwing, catching, running, etc.) The number of indicators identified during the measurement and operationalization phase determines the number of questions in a questionnaire.

Another important design guideline is to avoid questions that would be at all confusing to your respondents or that attempt to measure more than one variable (the so-called double-barreled questions). Clear instructions are helpful to both the researcher and the subject. It is often useful to start the questionnaire with a short statement of research purpose and with simple, non-threatening questions to get the subjects started. **Closed-ended** (fixed answer options) questions are easier to tabulate than open-ended ones, but it is often helpful to include an **open-ended** question or two at the end to solicit additional comments that you might not have anticipated.

Generally speaking, the return rates or completion rates reflect the effectiveness of our preparation. If we conduct a survey and few subjects are willing to complete it, this indicates a faulty **sampling frame**, unattractive questionnaire design, or both. In addition, one obvious but often forgotten consideration is that surveys are what we could call a one-shot methodology. By this we mean that researchers have one chance to administer the survey to each individual. If we want them to cooperate, we have to make sure our questionnaire is inviting, easy to follow, and does not burden anyone who has volunteered for the study. Finally, questionnaire design and development is time consuming and requires a sizeable investment of resources.

In addition to writing the survey carefully, the researcher must choose an appropriate method for administering the survey to **respondents**. There are a variety of media available to conduct surveys. Until recently, perhaps the most popular was the "in-person" encounter between the researcher and the research subjects, either face to face or by telephone. Another popular medium

is the self-administered mail survey. In this option, surveys are mass mailed to eligible subjects who then return them on their own. Although the return rate with this type of approach is not always high, mail surveys are popular today because they are more cost effective, less intrusive, and researchers have the ability to reach a wide population. Researchers may also use available technologies such as computer-assisted telephone interviewer (CATI) and interactive voice response (IVR) self-administered surveys, whether conducted by telephone or Web-based platforms, and Web-based surveys. CATI and some IVR surveys involve automated programs phoning people at home and "asking" the questions. Web surveys, in which subjects receive an e-mail directing them to the survey Web site, are coming to replace most other automated methods. Technology-based survey options are widely used in customer and employee satisfaction studies and market research; they tend to be short and often require anonymity.

Survey Design

Whichever survey strategy one chooses, it is imperative that the researcher undertakes a number of preparatory steps before the survey is implemented. These steps must include the survey design, question coding, validity checking, reliability checking, adopting a sampling strategy, and pretesting the survey instrument. As Eve Waltermaurer demonstrates in the next selection, our ability to address our research questions meaningfully depends on how we ask the questions.

Preparation and pretesting are essential, because at this early stage the questionnaire is revised and amended as many times as necessary before it is implemented in the field. Since one of the strengths of a survey is its reliability, discovering inconsistencies or inadequacies in questionnaires as late as the implementation phase could prove disastrous for any study, since the questionnaire cannot be amended once it rolls out.

At the root of any survey is the questionnaire itself, also known as the **data collection instrument**. The questionnaire is a document that contains all the questions necessary to collect data and measure the **indicators** identified in our measurements. In the case of measuring interpersonal violence (IPV), early research revealed that there were more dimensions of IPV than had been previously realized. This exploratory work, while highly valuable, used survey instruments that recorded only a limited range of violent acts. Thus, Waltermaurer argues, researchers need to replace those surveys with newer ones now in development, and those newer ones must be extensively tested and validated before they are adopted for widespread use.

There are two interesting things to note about Waltermaurer's case. First, she is not claiming that the earlier research instruments were wrong. They accurately measured all of the dimensions of interpersonal violence that were recognized at the time. As this research progressed, however, the definition of the concept changed. We would be negligent in our work if we failed to update our instruments to follow modifications in our research conceptualizations. The second point is to note that many of the modifications in the conceptualization of IPV came from qualitative research. Thus, in this case, qualitative explorations of a concept challenged and refined our measures, thereby improving the validity of the quantitative research that followed.

These last two points highlight another element of preparation: Reading the previous literature is not just about benefiting from the work and insights of others. As the field changes, new insights and new data will be reflected only in the most recent publications. If you read only the classics, you will miss those vital details.[4] A thorough review of the previous research is a requirement for any research project, and researchers who fail that step will be quickly exposed as foolish and slapdash.

Researchers must remain aware of the shortcomings of survey research. For one, this methodology is most useful in dealing with contemporary social issues, not historical ones. Inglehart's data can go back only as far as the first time they administered the survey. It would not be valid to ask respondents about values that they used to hold. Since survey research tends to produce large amounts of data, we must be well versed in database design and statistical manipulation to analyze these data. And, as we have just seen, researchers must be aware that survey research into complex social issues may lack validity unless adequate safeguards are taken.

EXPERIMENTS

Quantitative research and analysis can literally measure the strength of an association between two variables. That is, with proper sampling, data collection, and coding we can say that a specific percentage of the variability of something that we're measuring depends on the values of something else that we're measuring. Whether we are talking about the relationship between height and weight, or years of schooling and attitudes about smoking, we can represent consistent patterns of behavior *almost* as though they were chemical properties. Of course, as we mentioned in the first section, the social world is constantly changing. Sociologists qualify their mathematical predictions with the Latin phrase *ceteris paribus,* which means "all else being equal," or, roughly, as long as nothing else changes. It's a great system with only one limitation: Other things are not equal. So how can we measure the effect of one thing on another without interference from any of these other things?

Experimental research provides an answer. Sometimes we can conduct research in a lab where we have control over just about everything that could affect the study. (This is called a

---

[4]All three of us have read student literature reviews that referred to "recent changes" with reference to 40-year-old articles.

"controlled environment.") Other times, we can even conduct an experiment in the field when nature or circumstance has provided us with a naturally occurring change isolated from other factors. (This is a "natural experiment.") For example, the classic "blind taste test" experiment asks subjects to taste and evaluate several different wines, or soft drinks, or chilies, without knowing anything about the price, label, or cook, or anything else that might cause them to favor one over another. In wine tasting, some inexpensive wines have beat out expensive wines in blind competitions. But this happens less often when tasters can see the labels, indicating that their expectations affect their judgment.

In general, there are two ways to control for the effects of outside variables. The first is to measure them and include them in your calculations. In survey research, for example, you can control for age by recording all of your subjects' ages and testing whether other relationships we find vary according to age. The second is to prevent them from varying, at least during the time of the research. Conducting studies in labs of, say, opinions about clothes isolates subjects from the influence of other people's opinions, just as conducting medical research in a lab controls for the effects of everyday life stressors (work, family, news) by isolating the subject from all of those things. The ultimate goal of an experiment is to measure the effect of some variable X on some outcome Y ceteris paribus, by controlling for the possible effects of just about anything that isn't X or Y—where you do make sure everything else stays the same (all else being equal).

We also need to control for the effect of the experiment itself. We want to know what effect a change in variable X has on variable Y, but we are really changing both X and the environment in which X and Y meet. For example, watching scary movies in a theater might lead me to have nightmares at home, but will watching scary movies in a classroom lead to nightmares in a sleep lab? A drug might lower your blood pressure, but having blood pressure monitors strapped to your arm for a few hours might raise it again. So

a classic experimental design will have two groups—the **experimental group** for whom the variable X changes and the **control group** for whom it does not. All else is kept the same between them. The important results, then, will not be the change in the values of Y, but rather the extent to which Y changed more in one group than in the other. This group comparison is the basis for most natural experiments, in which something happens in the world that directly affects some people (the test group) but not others (the control group). Such studies are often called "quasi-experimental design," since there is no laboratory control of other environmental variables.

Many controlled experiments are conducted outside of the laboratory. For example, myriad studies of hiring discrimination have been conducted using carefully designed "almost twin" résumés. The researchers send out almost identical résumés—same schools, same levels of experience and awards—with only the gender or ethnicity of the "candidates" varying from one application to the next. Then, the researchers evaluate the number of job offers to see if the one difference (gender or ethnicity) influences the responses. (It does.)

In our next reading, Foschi and Buchan measured the influence of gender and ethnicity on people's *perceptions* of competence. Subjects were asked to collaborate with unknown partners to complete given tasks. Thus, the outcome data, Y, were the subjects' evaluations of their partners' competence and their willingness to alter their own answers to test questions based on their partners' answers. The researchers controlled the interactions among the participants and the nature of the tasks in order to remove the influence of the very things they appeared to be asking about: task competence. What remained as their X variable were the sorts of outside factors that bias people's opinions: the status markers (gender and ethnicity) of the partners. The primary measure of the effect of X on Y was the question of whether the subjects were more or less likely to take advice from their partners depending on the gender or ethnicity of the partners. All else being equal, if such status markers did not influence people's perceptions of other people's competence, then the pattern of results would be consistent regardless of the partners' characteristics. Of course, this didn't happen.

Similar experiments have been conducted using teams of house buyers, credit card applicants, and even fancy car buyers. In circumstances in which outcomes are supposed to be based on credit scores, incomes, or other simple economic data, researchers have created identical sets of applications for different potential customers, differing only by gender or ethnicity. It is commonplace that the ethnic minorities will be shown inferior houses, or that their credit will be deemed insufficient even as their matched white customers will be approved for whatever it is they are seeking. (Hidden camera news teams and government investigators use similar techniques to demonstrate discrimination at car rental agencies and real estate offices.)

CONCLUSION

Quantitative data collection methods have helped sociologists and others understand many of the essential issues of society. These are invaluable tools of the discipline. While they can be misused and badly used, in the hands of careful researchers they help to build theory, inform policy, guide more targeted research, address social ills, and expose aspects of our world that were previously unknown. Of course, like all powerful tools and techniques, these methods can also be used in deceptive marketing and political manipulation. That is why, in addition to the use of these methods in research, the more we understand about these methods, the more we can be informed citizens, consumers, and societal participants.

DISCUSSION QUESTIONS

1. You've developed a questionnaire on binge drinking that you wish to administer to students on your campus. You don't have enough money to send it to everyone. What would you consider in selecting a sample? Which approach would likely yield better representativeness: distributing your survey to each of the students in a sample of classes, or mass mailing the survey to every student on campus along with a prepaid return envelope for them to return the completed form?

2. You learn of an experiment in which students are given different sizes of bowls of soup—but all of the bowls were very, very large. Students with the bigger bowls generally ate more than students with the smaller bowls. The students know they are being observed by the researchers. Why might you question the results of this study? Think about internal and external validity. What might limit the generalizability of this experiment?

WEB RESOURCES

The following links can provide you with more detailed information on the topics discussed in this section. You may also go to www.sagepub.com/lunestudy where you will find additional resources and hot-links to these sources.

Princeton University Survey Research Center: http://www.princeton.edu/~psrc
Pew Research Center: http://people-press.org
U.S. Census: http://www.census.gov
American Association of Public Opinion Research: http://www.aapor.org
The General Social Survey: http://www.norc.org/GSS+Website
European Public Opinion: http://ec.europa.eu/public_opinion/index_en.htm

Mapping Global Values (2006)

Ronald Inglehart

INTRODUCTION

The world now contains nearly 200 independent countries, and the beliefs and values of their publics differ greatly, in thousands of different ways. Yet, among the many dimensions of cross-cultural variation, two are particularly important. Each dimension reflects one of the two waves of economic development that have transformed the world economically, socially and politically in modern times: the transition from agrarian society to industrial society that emerged two hundred years ago and is now transforming China, India, Indonesia and many other countries; and the transition from industrial society to the post-industrial or knowledge society that began to emerge fifty years ago and is now reshaping the socioeconomic systems of the U.S., Canada, Western Europe, Japan, Australia and other economically advanced societies.

These processes of economic and technological change have given rise to two key dimensions of cross-cultural variation: (1) a *Traditional/Secular-Rational* dimension that reflects the contrast between the relatively religious and traditional values that generally prevail in agrarian societies, and the relatively secular, bureaucratic and rational values that generally prevail in urban, industrialized societies; and (2) a *Survival/Self-expression* dimension that also taps a wide range of beliefs and values, reflecting an inter-generational shift from an emphasis on economic and physical security above all, towards increasing emphasis on self-expression, subjective well-being, and quality of life concerns.

These dimensions are robust aspects of cross-cultural variation, and they make it possible to map the position of any society on a two-dimensional map that reflects their relative positions at any given time. But gradual shifts are occurring along these dimensions, transforming many aspects of society. One of the most important of these changes is the fact that the shift toward increasing emphasis on Self-expression values makes democratic political institutions increasingly likely to emerge and flourish.

Our analysis is based on a body of survey evidence that represents 85 percent of the world's population. Data from four waves of the Values Surveys, carried out from 1981 to 2001, indicate that major cultural changes are occurring, *and* that a society's religious tradition, colonial history, and other major historical factors, give rise to distinctive cultural traditions that continue to influence a society's value system despite the forces of modernization.

MODERNIZATION AND CULTURAL CHANGE

In the nineteenth and early twentieth centuries, modernization theorists from Karl Marx to Max

Weber analyzed the emerging industrial society and tried to predict its future. Their analyses of cultural change emphasized the rise of rationality and the decline of religion, and they assumed that these developments would continue in linear fashion, with the future being a continuation of the same trends that were occurring during the 19th century. From today's perspective, it is clear that modernization is more complex than these early views anticipated. The numbers of industrial workers ceased growing decades ago in economically advanced societies, and virtually no one any longer expects a proletarian revolution. Moreover, it is increasingly evident that religion has not vanished as predicted. Furthermore, it is apparent that modernization can not be equated with Westernization, as early analyses assumed. Non-Western societies in East Asia have surpassed their Western role models in key aspects of modernization such as rates of economic growth and high life expectancy, and few observers today attribute moral superiority to the West.

Although, today, few people accept the original Marxist version of modernization theory, one of its core concepts still seems valid: the insight that, once industrialization begins, it produces pervasive social and cultural consequences, from rising educational levels to changing gender roles.

This article maps cross-cultural variation using data from the World Values Surveys and European Values Surveys, which have measured the beliefs and values of most of the world's people. These surveys offer an unprecedentedly rich source of insight into the relationships between economic development and social and political change. They show that, even during the relatively brief time since the first wave of the Values Surveys was carried out in 1981, substantial changes have occurred in the values and beliefs of the publics of these societies. These changes are closely linked with the economic changes experienced by a given society. As we will demonstrate, economic development is associated with predictable changes away from absolute norms and values, toward a syndrome of increasingly rational, tolerant, trusting, and post-industrial values. But we find evidence of both massive cultural change *and* the persistence of traditional values.

Throughout most of history, survival has been uncertain for most people. But the remarkable economic growth of the era following World War II, together with the rise of the welfare state, brought fundamentally new conditions in advanced industrial societies. The postwar birth cohorts of these countries grew up under conditions of prosperity that were unprecedented in human history, and the welfare state reinforced the feeling that survival was secure, producing an intergenerational value change that is gradually transforming the politics and cultural norms of advanced industrial societies. The best documented aspect of this change is the shift from Materialist to Postmaterialist priorities. A massive body of evidence gathered from 1970 to the present demonstrates that an intergenerational shift from Materialist to Postmaterialist priorities is transforming the behavior and goals of the people of advanced industrial societies (Inglehart, 1997; Inglehart and Welzel, 2005). But recent research demonstrates that this trend is only one aspect of an even broader cultural shift from Survival values to Self-expression values.

Economic development and cultural change move in two major phases, each of which gives rise to a major dimension of cross-national value differences. Factor analysis of national-level data from the 43 societies studied in the 1990 World Values Survey found that two main dimensions accounted for well over half of the cross-national variance in more than a score of variables tapping basic values across a wide range of domains, ranging from politics to economic life and sexual behavior (Inglehart, 1997). These dimensions of cross-cultural variation are robust; when the 1990–1991 factor analysis was replicated with the data from the 1995–1998 surveys, the same two dimensions of cross-cultural variation emerged—even though the new analysis was based on 23 additional countries not included in the earlier study (Inglehart and Baker, 2000).

The same two dimensions also emerged in analysis of data from the 2000–2001 surveys—although numerous additional countries were again added to the pool, including eight predominantly Islamic societies—a cultural region that had been relatively neglected in previous surveys (Inglehart and Welzel, 2005). Each dimension taps a major axis of cross-cultural variation involving many different values. Table 1 shows the results of this most recent set of analyses, based on data from more than 70 societies, aggregated to the national level. Although each of the two main dimensions is linked closely with scores of values, for technical reasons, our indices were constructed by using only five key indicators for each of the two dimensions.

TABLE 1 Two Dimensions of Cross-Cultural Variation

First Factor (46%)	Factor Loadings
TRADITIONAL VALUES emphasize the following:	
God is very important in respondent's life	.91
It is more important for a child to learn obedience and religious faith than independence and determination [Autonomy index]	.88
Abortion is never justifiable	.82
Respondent has strong sense of national pride	.81
Respondent favors more respect for authority	.73

(SECULAR-RATIONAL VALUES emphasize the opposite)

Second Factor (25%)	
SURVIVAL VALUES emphasize the following:	
Respondent gives priority to economic and physical security over self-expression and quality of life [4-item Materialist/Postmaterialist Values Index]	.87
Respondent describes self as not very happy	.81
Homosexuality is never justifiable	.77
Respondent has not and would not sign a petition	.74
You have to be very careful about trusting people	.46

(SELF-EXPRESSION VALUES emphasize the opposite)

NOTE: The original polarities vary; the above statements show how each item relates to the given factor. (Factors = 2, varimax rotation, listwise deletion).

SOURCE: World Values Survey data from more than 200 surveys carried out in four waves in 78 societies.

Human values are structured in a surprisingly coherent way: the two dimensions explain fully 71 percent of the cross-cultural variation among these ten items. More impressive still is the fact that each of these two dimensions taps a broad range of other attitudes, extending over a number of seemingly diverse domains. Table 2 shows the correlations of 24 additional variables that are relatively strongly linked with the first dimension, showing correlations above the .40 level.

TABLE 2 Correlates of Traditional vs. Secular-rational Values

TRADITIONAL values emphasize the following:	*Correlation with Traditional/ Secular Rational Values*
Religion is very important in respondent's life	.89
Respondent believes in Heaven	.88
One of respondent's main goals in life has been to make his/her parents proud	.81
Respondent believes in Hell	.76
Respondent attends church regularly	.75
Respondent has a great deal of confidence in the country's churches	.72
Respondent gets comfort and strength from religion	.71
Respondent describes self as "a religious person"	.66
Euthanasia is never justifiable	.65
Work is very important in respondent's life	.63
There should be stricter limits on selling foreign goods here	.61
Suicide is never justifiable	.60
Parents' duty is to do their best for their children even at the expense of their own well-being	.57
Respondent seldom or never discusses politics	.57
Respondent places self on Right side of a Left-Right scale	.57
Divorce is never justifiable	.56
There are absolutely clear guidelines about good and evil	.56
Expressing one's own preferences clearly is more important than understanding others' preferences	.56
My country's environmental problems can be solved without any international agreements to handle them	.53

TRADITIONAL values emphasize the following:	Correlation with Traditional/ Secular Rational Values
If a woman earns more money than her husband, it's almost certain to cause problems	.49
One must always love and respect one's parents regardless of their behavior	.45
Family is very important in respondent's life	.43
Relatively favorable to having the army rule the country	.41
Respondent favors having a relatively large number of children	.40
(SECULAR-RATIONAL values emphasize the opposite)	

NOTES: The number in the right-hand column shows how strongly each variable is correlated with the Traditional/Secular-rational Values Index. The original polarities vary; the above statements show how each item relates to the Traditional/Secular-rational Values Index.

SOURCE: Nation-level data from 65 societies surveyed in the 1990 and 1996 World Values Surveys

The *Traditional/Secular-Rational* dimension reflects the contrast between the relatively religious and traditional values that generally prevail in agrarian societies, and the relatively secular, bureaucratic and rational values that generally prevail in urban, industrialized societies. Traditional societies emphasize the importance of religion, deference to authority, parent–child ties and two-parent traditional families, and absolute moral standards; they reject divorce, abortion, euthanasia, and suicide, and tend to be patriotic and nationalistic. In contrast, societies with secular-rational values display the opposite preferences on all of these topics.

Table 3 shows 31 additional variables that are closely linked with the *Survival/Self-expression'* dimension, which also taps a wide range of beliefs and values. A central component involves the polarization between Materialist and Post-materialist values that reflects an intergenerational shift from an emphasis on economic and physical security above all, towards increasing emphasis on self-expression, subjective well-being, and quality of life concerns. Societies that

rank high on Survival values tend to emphasize materialist orientations and traditional gender roles; they are relatively intolerant of foreigners, gays and lesbians and other out-groups, show relatively low levels of subjective well-being, rank relatively low on interpersonal trust, and emphasize hard work, rather than imagination or tolerance, as important things to teach a child. Societies that emphasize Self-expression values, display the opposite preferences on all these topics.

These two dimensions are remarkably robust. If we compare the results from the two most recent waves of the Values Surveys, we find a .92 correlation between the positions of given countries on the Traditional/ Secularrational values dimension from one wave of the surveys to the next. With the Survival/Self-expression dimension, the positions of given countries are even more stable: their positions in the earlier wave show a .95 correlation with their positions five years later. Although major changes are occurring along these dimensions, the relative positions of given countries are highly stable. If one compares the map based on the 1990 surveys with the map based on the 1995 surveys or the 2000 surveys, they initially seem to be the same map, showing given clusters of countries (such as Protestant Europe, the English-speaking countries, the Latin American societies, the Confucian societies) in the same relative position—although each successive wave of surveys was not only carried out roughly five years later than the previous one, but included many countries not covered in previous surveys.

TABLE 3 Correlates of Survival vs. Self-expression Values

SURVIVAL values emphasize the following:	*Correlation with Survival/ Self-expression Values*
Men make better political leaders than women	.86
Respondent is dissatisfied with financial situation of his/her household	.83
A woman has to have children in order to be fulfilled	.83
Respondent rejects foreigners, homosexuals and people with AIDS as neighbors	.81
Respondent favors more emphasis on the development of technology	.78
Respondent has not recycled things to protect the environment	.78
Respondent has not attended a meeting or signed a petition to protect the environment	.75
When seeking a job, a good income and safe job are more important than a feeling of accomplishment and working with people you like	.74
Respondent is relatively favorable to state ownership of business and industry	.74
A child needs a home with both a father and mother to grow up happily	.73
Respondent does not describe own health as very good	.73
One must always love and respect one's parents regardless of their behavior	.71
When jobs are scarce, men have more right to a job than women	.69
Prostitution is never justifiable	.69
Government should take more responsibility to ensure that everyone is provided for	.68
Respondent does not have much free choice or control over his/her life	.67
A university education is more important for a boy than for a girl	.67
Respondent does not favor less emphasis on money and material possessions	.66

SURVIVAL values emphasize the following:	*Correlation with Survival/ Self-expression Values*
Respondent rejects people with criminal records as neighbors	.66
Respondent rejects heavy drinkers as neighbors	.65
Hard work is one of the most important things to teach a child	.64
Imagination is *not* one of the most important things to teach a child	.62
Tolerance and respect for others are *not* the most important things to teach a child	.62
Scientific discoveries will help, rather than harm, humanity	.60
Leisure is not very important in life	.60
Friends are not very important in life	.58
Having a strong leader who does not have to bother with parliament and elections would be a good form of government	.56
Respondent has not and would not take part in a boycott	.56
Government ownership of business and industry should be increased	.55
Democracy is not necessarily the best form of government	.45
Respondent opposes sending economic aid to poorer countries	.42

(SELF-EXPRESSION values emphasize the opposite)

NOTES: The number in the right-hand column shows how strongly each variable is correlated with the Survival/Self-expression Values Index. The original polarities vary; the above statements show how each item relates to the Traditional/Secular-rational Values Index.

SOURCE: Nation-level data from Sixty-five societies surveyed in the 1990 and 1996 World Values Surveys.

Figure 1 shows a two-dimensional cultural map on which the value systems of 80 societies are depicted, using the most recent data available for each country (mostly from the 2000 wave but in some cases from the 1995 wave). The vertical dimension represents the Traditional/ Secular-rational dimension, and the horizontal dimension reflects the Survival/Self-expression values dimension. Both dimensions are strongly linked with economic development, with the value systems of rich countries differing systematically from those of poor countries. Thus, Germany, France, Britain, Italy, Japan, Sweden, the U.S. and all other societies with a 1995 annual per capita GNP over $15,000 rank relatively high on both dimensions: without exception, they fall in a broad zone near the upper right-hand corner.

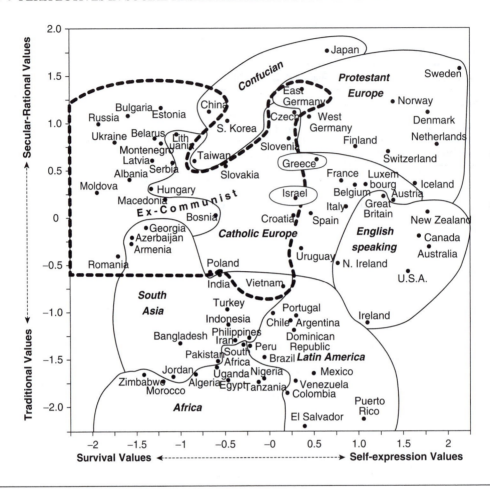

FIGURE 1   Cultural Map of the World in 2000

Conversely, every one of the societies with per capita GNPs below $2,000 falls into a cluster at the lower left of the map; India, Bangladesh, Pakistan, Nigeria, Zimbabwe, Morocco, Brazil and Peru all fall into this economic zone, which cuts across the African, South Asian, ex-Communist, and Orthodox cultural zones. The remaining societies fall into intermediate cultural-economic zones. Economic development seems to pull societies in a common direction regardless of their cultural heritage.

ECONOMIC DEVELOPMENT INTERACTS WITH A SOCIETY'S CULTURAL HERITAGE

Nevertheless, two centuries after the industrial revolution began, distinctive cultural zones persist. Different societies follow different trajectories, even when they are subjected to the same forces of economic development, because situation-specific factors, such as a society's cultural heritage, *also* shape how a particular society develops. Huntington (1996) has emphasized the role of religion in shaping the world's eight major civilizations: Western Christianity, Orthodox, Islam, Confucian, Japanese, Hindu, African, and Latin American. Despite the forces of modernization, these zones were shaped by religious traditions that are still powerful today.

Economic development is strongly associated with both dimensions of cultural change. But a society's cultural heritage also plays a role. Thus, all eleven Latin American societies fall into a coherent cluster, showing relatively similar values: they rank high on traditional religious values, but are characterized by stronger emphasis on Self-expression values than their economic levels would predict. Economic factors are important, but they are only part of the story; such factors as their common Iberian colonial heritage seem to have left an impact that persists centuries later.

Similarly, despite their wide geographic dispersion, the English-speaking countries constitute a compact cultural zone. In the same way, the historically Roman Catholic societies of Western Europe (e.g., Italy, Portugal, Spain, France, Belgium and Austria) display relatively traditional values when compared with Confucian or ex-Communist societies with the same proportion of industrial workers. And, virtually all of the historically Protestant societies (e.g., West Germany, Denmark, Norway, Sweden, Finland and Iceland) rank higher on both the Traditional Secular Rational dimension and the Survival/Self-expression dimension than do the historically Roman Catholic societies. All four of the Confucian-influenced societies (China, Taiwan, South Korea and Japan) have relatively secular values, constituting a Confucian cultural zone, despite substantial differences in wealth. As Huntington claimed, the Orthodox societies constitute another distinct cultural zone.

A society's religious and colonial heritage seem to have had an enduring impact on the contemporary value systems of the 80 societies. But a society's culture reflects its entire historical heritage. A central historical event of the twentieth century was the rise and fall of a Communist empire that once ruled one-third of the world's population. Communism left a clear imprint on the value systems of those who lived under it. East Germany remains culturally close to West Germany despite four decades of Communist rule, but its value system has been drawn toward the Communist zone. And, although China is a member of the Confucian zone, it also falls within a broad Communist-influenced zone. Similarly, Azerbaijan, though part of an Islamic cluster, also falls within the Communist superzone that dominated it for decades. Changes in GNP and occupational structure have important influences on prevailing worldviews, but traditional cultural influences persist.

The ex-Communist societies of Central and Eastern Europe all fall into the upper left-hand quadrant of our cultural map, ranking high on the Traditional/Secular-rational dimension (toward the secular pole), but low on the Survival/Self-expression dimension (falling near the survival-oriented pole). A broken line encircles all of the societies that have experienced Communist rule, and, although they overlap with several different cultural traditions, they form a reasonably coherent group. Although by no means the poorest countries in the world, many Central and Eastern Europe societies have recently experienced the collapse of Communism, shattering their economic, political and social systems and bringing a pervasive sense of insecurity. Thus, Russia, Ukraine, Bulgaria, Romania and Moldova rank lowest of any countries on earth on the Survival/Self-expression dimension, exhibiting lower levels of subjective well-being than much poorer countries such as India, Bangladesh, Zimbabwe, Uganda and Pakistan. People who have experienced stable poverty throughout their lives tend to emphasize survival values, but those who have experienced the collapse of their social system (and may, as in Russia, currently have living standards and life expectancies far below where they were 15 years ago) experience a sense of unpredictability and insecurity that leads them to emphasize Survival values even more heavily than those who are accustomed to an even lower standard of living.

Not surprisingly, Communist rule seems conducive to the emergence of a relatively secular-rational culture: the ex-Communist countries in general, and those that were members of the Soviet Union in particular (and thus experienced communist rule for seven decades, rather then merely four decades), rank higher on secular-rational values than non-Communist countries. And, to an equally striking extent, ex-Communist countries in general, and former Soviet countries in particular, tend to emphasize survival values far more heavily than societies that have not experienced Communist rule.

Thus, as Inglehart and Baker (2000) demonstrate with multiple regression analysis, even when we control for level of economic development and other factors, a history of Communist rule continues to account for a significant share of the cross-cultural variance in basic values (with seven decades of Communist rule having more impact than four decades). But, by comparison with societies historically shaped by a Roman Catholic or Protestant cultural tradition, an Orthodox tradition seems to reduce emphasis on Self-expression values.

A society's position on the Survival/Self-expression values dimension has important political implications; as we will see, it is strongly linked with its level of democracy.

INDIVIDUALISM, AUTONOMY AND SELF-EXPRESSION VALUES

As Tables 1, 2 and 3 demonstrated, the two main dimensions of cross-cultural variation tap a wide range of beliefs and attitudes. But their ramifications go farther still; the Survival/Self-expression values dimension taps a concept of major interest to psychologists, although they refer to it as individualism.

The broad distinction between individualism and collectivism is a central theme in psychological research on cross-cultural differences. Hofstede (1980) defined *individualism* as a focus on rights above duties, a concern for oneself and immediate family, an emphasis on personal autonomy and self-fulfillment, and a basing of identity on one's personal accomplishments. Hofstede developed a survey instrument that measured individualism/collectivism among IBM employees in more than 40 societies. More recently, individualism has been measured cross-nationally by Triandis (1989, 2001, and 2003). Schwartz (1992, 1994, and 2003) measured the related concept of autonomy/embeddedness among students and teachers in scores of countries. As we will demonstrate, individualism-collectivism as measured by Hofstede and Triandis, and autonomy/ embeddness as measured by Schwartz, seem to tap the same dimension of cross-cultural variation as Survival/Self-expression values; they all reflect the extent to which a given society emphasizes autonomous human choice.

Individualism/collectivism, autonomy/ embeddedness and Survival/Self-expression values are all linked with the process of human development, which moves toward diminishing constraints on human choice (Inglehart and Welzel, 2005). Self-expression values are defined in very similar terms to Hofstede's emphasis on personal autonomy and self-fulfillment as core elements of individualism. Similarly, Schwartz's emphasis on intellectual autonomy and affective autonomy captures core elements of Self-expression values. All of these variables reflect a common theme: an emphasis on free choice.

The core principle of collectivism is that groups bind and mutually obligate individuals. In collectivist societies, social units have a common fate and common goals; the personal is simply a component of the social, making the in-group crucial. Collectivism implies that group membership is a central aspect of identity, and sacrificing individual goals for the common good is strongly emphasized. Collectivism further implies that fulfillment comes from carrying out externally defined obligations, making people focus on meeting others' expectations. Accordingly, emotional self-restraint is valued to ensure harmony, even at the cost of one's own happiness. In collectivist societies, social context is prominent in people's perceptions and causal reasoning, and meaning is contextualized. Finally, collectivism implies that important group memberships are seen as fixed facts of life, toward which people have no choice; they must accommodate. Boundaries between in-groups and outgroups are stable, relatively impermeable, and important; exchanges are based on mutual obligations and patriarchal ties.

Today, empirical measures of individualism, autonomy and self-expression values are available from many societies, and it turns out that they all tap a common dimension of cross-cultural variation, reflecting an emphasis on autonomous human choice. The mean national scores on these three variables show are closely correlated, with an average strength of $r = .66$. As Table 4 demonstrates, factor analysis of the mean national scores from many countries reveals that individualism, autonomy and self-expression values all tap a single underlying dimension, which accounts for fully 78 percent of the cross-national variance.

High levels of individualism go with high levels of autonomy and high levels of self-expression

TABLE 4 Self-expression Values and Individualism and Autonomy Scales Tap a Common Dimension

The Individualism/Autonomy/Self-expression Dimension: Emphasis on Autonomous Choice	
(Principal Component Analysis)	*Variance explained 78%*
Inglehart, Survival vs. Self-expression values	.91
Hofstede, Individualism vs. Collectivism rankings	.87
Schwartz, Autonomy vs. Embeddedness (mean of student/teacher samples)	.87

values. Hofstede's, Schwartz's, Triandis' and Inglehart's measures all tap cross-cultural variation in a common aspect of human psychology: the drive toward broader human choice. As the Values Surveys demonstrate, they also measure something that extends far beyond whether given cultures have an individualistic or collective outlook. Societies that rank high on Self-expression tend to emphasize individual autonomy and the quality of life, rather than economic and physical security. Their publics have relatively low levels of confidence in technology and scientific discoveries as the

solution to human problems, and they are relatively likely to act to protect the environment. These societies also rank relatively high on gender equality, tolerance of gays, lesbians, foreigners and other outgroups; they show relatively high levels of subjective well-being, and interpersonal trust, and they emphasize imagination and tolerance, as important things to teach a child.

But individualism, autonomy and self-expression are not static characteristics of societies. They change with the course of socioeconomic development. As we have seen, socioeconomic development brings rising levels of existential security (especially in its post-industrial phase), which leads to an increasing emphasis on individualism, autonomy and self-expression. Birch and Cobb (1981) view this process as reflecting an evolutionary trend towards the "liberation of life." Inglehart and Welzel (2005) describe it as a process of human development in which the most distinctively human ability—the ability to make autonomous choices, instead of following biologically and socially predetermined behavior—becomes an increasingly central feature of modern societies. As we will see, this syndrome of individualism, autonomy, and self-expression is conducive to the emergence and survival of democratic institutions.

The common dimension underlying individualism, autonomy and self-expression is remarkably robust. It emerges even when one uses different measurement approaches, different types of samples, and different time periods. Hofstede found it in the late 1960s and early 1970s, when analyzing the values of a cross-national sample of IBM employees. Schwartz measured it in surveys of students and teachers carried out from 1988 to 2002; and Inglehart first found it in an analysis of representative national samples of the publics of 43 societies surveyed in 1989-91, with the same dimension emerging in successive cross-national surveys in 1995 and in 2000. This dimension seems to be an enduring feature of cross-cultural variation, to such an extent that one might almost conclude that it is difficult to *avoid* finding it if one measures the basic values of a broad range of societies.

INDIVIDUALISM, AUTONOMY AND SELF-EXPRESSION AS EVOLVING PHENOMENA

Most cultural-psychological theories have treated the individualism-collectivism polarity as a static attribute of given cultures, overlooking the possibility that individualist and collectivist orientations reflect a society's socioeconomic conditions at a given time. Our theory holds that the extent to which Self-expression values (or individualism) prevail over Survival values (or collectivism) reflects a society's level of development; as external constraints on human choice recede, people (and societies) place increasing emphasis on Self-expression values or individualism. This pattern is not culture-specific. It is universal.

The most fundamental external constraint on human choice is the extent to which physical survival is secure or insecure. Throughout most of history, survival has been precarious for most people. Most children did not survive to adulthood, and malnutrition and associated diseases were the leading cause of death. This is remote from the experience of Western publics today, but existential insecurity is still the dominant reality in most of the world. Under such conditions, Survival values take top priority. Survival is such a fundamental goal that, if it seems uncertain, one's entire life strategy is shaped by that fact. Low levels of socioeconomic development not only impose material constraints on people's choices; they also are linked with low levels of education and information. This intellectual poverty imposes cognitive constraints on people's choices. Finally, in the absence of the welfare state, strong group obligations are the only form of social insurance, imposing social constraints on people's choices.

In recent history, a growing number of societies have attained unprecedented levels of economic development. Diminishing material, cognitive and social constraints on human choice are bringing a shift from emphasis on Survival values to emphasis on Self-expression values, and from a collective focus to an individual one.

People's sense of human autonomy becomes stronger as objective existential constraints on human choice recede. As will be seen, this has important societal consequences. Mass emphasis on human choice tends to favor the political system that provides the widest room for choice: democracy.

ECONOMIC DEVELOPMENT AND CULTURAL CHANGE

Because our two main dimensions of cross-cultural variation—Traditional/ Secular-rational values and Survival/Self-expression values—are linked with economic development, we find pervasive differences between the world-views of people in rich and poor societies. Moreover, time series evidence shows that, with economic development, societies tend to move from the values prevailing in low-income societies toward greater emphasis on Secular-rational and Self-expression values (Inglehart and Baker, 2000; Inglehart and Welzel, 2005).

These changes largely reflect a process of intergenerational value change. Throughout advanced industrial societies, the young emphasize self-expression values and secular-rational values more strongly than the old. Cohort analysis indicates that the distinctive values of younger cohorts are stable characteristics that persist as they age. Consequently, as younger birth cohorts replace older ones in the adult population, the society's prevailing values change in a roughly predictable direction.

The unprecedented level of economic development during the past several decades, coupled with the emergence of the welfare state in advanced societies, means that an increasing share of the population has grown up taking survival for granted. Thus, priorities have shifted from an overwhelming emphasis on economic and physical security toward an increasing emphasis on subjective well-being, self-expression and quality of life. Inglehart and Welzel (2005) demonstrate that orientations have shifted from Traditional toward Secular-rational values, and from Survival values toward Self-expression values in almost all advanced industrial societies that have experienced economic growth.

THE SOCIETAL IMPACT OF CHANGING VALUES

Evidence from the Values Surveys demonstrates that people's orientations concerning religion, politics, gender roles, work motivations, and sexual norms are evolving—along with their attitudes toward child-rearing, their tolerance of foreigners, gays and lesbians, and their attitudes toward science and technology (Inglehart and Norris, 2003; Inglehart and Welzel, 2005). Figure 2 provides one example, showing the percentage of respondents saying that homosexuality is "Never" justifiable. The respondents were shown a ten-point scale, on which point 1 means that homosexuality is never justifiable, and point 10 means that it is always justifiable, with the eight intermediate points indicating intermediate positions. As this figure demonstrates, in 1981 about half of those surveyed in five Western countries took the extreme negative position, placing themselves at point 1 on the scale (the publics of developing countries being even less tolerant of homosexuality).

However, attitudes changed substantially in subsequent years. By the 2000 survey, only about 25 percent of the West Europeans, and 32 percent of the Americans took this position. Although attitudes toward homosexuality show a .86 stability correlation across the two most recent waves of the WVS, sizeable changes are occurring; most countries were changing, but their relative positions remained surprisingly stable, reflecting an underlying component of continuity within given generations. Thus, change is occurring largely through intergenerational population replacement. The cumulative effect of changing attitudes in this field has led to recent societal-level changes, such as the legalization of same-sex marriages in some countries and certain cities in the U.S. This, in turn, mobilized a strong reaction by people with traditional values and referenda seeking to ban same-sex marriage, giving rise to widespread belief that the U.S.

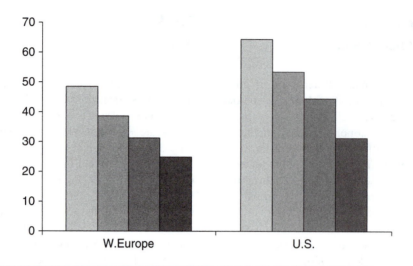

FIGURE 2   Changes in the percentage saying that homosexuality is never justifiable, in Britain, France, Germany Italy, and the U.S., from 1981 to 2000

public in general is becoming increasingly hostile to gays and lesbians; the opposite is true.

The basic values of individuals are changing, and these changes have a major impact on a wide range of important societal-level phenomena. They are reshaping the extent to which given societies have objective gender equality in political, social and economic life, as well as human fertility rates, the role of religion, legislation concerning the rights of gays and lesbians, and environmental protection laws. Changing individual-level values also seem to have a major influence on the extent to which a society has good governance, and the emergence and flourishing of democratic institutions.

SELF-EXPRESSION VALUES AND DEMOCRACY

A society's position on the survival/self-expression index is strongly correlated with its level of democracy, as indicated by its scores on the Freedom House ratings of political rights and civil liberties. This relationship is remarkably powerful, and it is clearly not a methodological artifact, since the two variables are measured at

different levels and come from entirely different sources. Virtually all of the societies that rank high on Survival/Self-expression values are stable democracies. Virtually all of the societies that rank low on this dimension have authoritarian governments. We find a correlation of .83 between Survival/Self-expression values and democracy; this is significant at a very high level, and seems to reflect a causal linkage (Inglehart and Welzel, 2005, articles 7 and 8).

The Freedom House measures are limited by the fact that they only measure the extent to which civil and political liberties are institutionalized, which does not necessarily reflect the extent to which these liberties are actually respected by political elites. Some very important recent literature has emphasized the importance of the distinction between formal democracy and genuine liberal democracy (Ottaway, 2003; O'Donnell, Vargas Cullel and Iazzetta , 2004). In order to tap the latter, we need a measure of "effective democracy" which reflects not only the extent to which formal civil and political liberties are institutionalized, but also measures the extent to which these liberties are actually *practiced*, thus indicating how much free choice people really have in their lives. To construct such an index of effective democracy, we multiply the Freedom House measures of civil and political rights by the World Bank's anti-corruption scores (Kaufman, Kraay and Mastruzzi, 2003), which we see as an indicator of "elite integrity," or the extent to which state power actually follows legal norms (see Inglehart and Welzel, 2005 for a more detailed discussion of this index). When we examine the linkage between this measure of genuine democracy and mass self-expression values, we find an amazingly strong correlation of $r = .90$ across 73 nations. This reflects a powerful cross-level linkage, connecting mass values that emphasize free choice, and the extent to which societal institutions actually provide free choice.

Figure 3 depicts the relationship between this index of effective democracy and mass self-expression values. The extent to which self-expression values are present in a society explains over 80 percent of the cross-national variance in the extent to which liberal democracy is actually practiced. These findings suggest that the importance of the linkage between individual-level values and democratic institutions has been underestimated. Mass preferences play a crucial role in the emergence of genuine democracy (Inglehart and Welzel, 2005).

The linkage between mass self-expression values and democratic institutions is remarkably strong and consistent, having only a few outliers: such countries as China, Iran and Vietnam show lower levels of democracy than their publics' values would predict. These countries have authoritarian regimes that are under growing

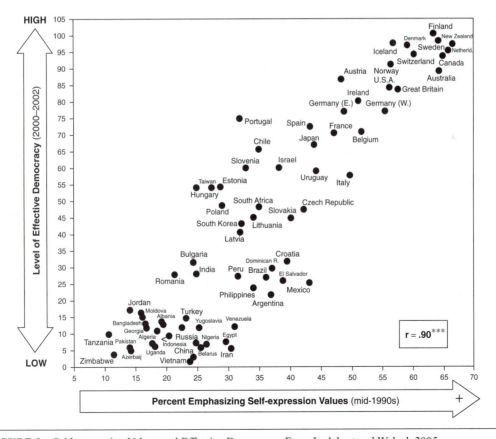

FIGURE 3 Self-expression Values and Effective Democracy. From Inglehart and Welzel, 2005

societal pressure to liberalize, and we expect that they will liberalize within the next 15 to 20 years. Authoritarian rulers of some Asian societies have argued that the distinctive "Asian values" of these societies make them unsuitable for democracy (Lee and Zakaria, 1994; Thompson, 2000). But, in fact, the position of most Asian countries on Figure 3 is about what their level of socio-economic development would predict. Japan ranks with the established Western democracies, both on the Self-expression values dimension, and on its level of democracy. The positions of Taiwan and South Korea on both dimensions is similar to those of other relatively new democracies such as Hungary or Poland. The publics of Confucian societies are more supportive of democracy than is generally believed.

Which comes first—a democratic political culture or democratic institutions? The extent to which people emphasize Self-expression values is closely linked with the flourishing of democratic institutions. But what causes what?

I have argued that economic development interacts with a society's cultural heritage, so that high levels of development (linked with the rise of the knowledge society) bring growing emphasis on Self-expression values, which produce strong mass demands for liberalization and democratic institutions. The reverse interpretation would be that democratic institutions give rise to the self-expression values that are so closely linked with them. In other words, democracy makes people healthy, happy, non-sexist, tolerant and trusting, and instills Post-materialist values. This interpretation is appealing, and, if it were true, it would provide a powerful argument for democracy, implying that we have a quick fix for most of the world's problems: adopt democratic institutions and live happily ever after.

Unfortunately, the experience of the Soviet Union's successor states does not support this interpretation. Since their dramatic move toward democracy in 1991, they have not become healthier, happier, more trusting, more tolerant or more Post-materialist: most of them have moved in exactly the opposite direction. The fact that their people are living in economic and physical insecurity seems to have more impact than the fact that their leaders are chosen by reasonably free elections. Moreover, the World Values Survey demonstrate that growing emphasis on Self-expression values emerged through a process of inter-generational change within the authoritarian Communist regimes; democratic regimes do not necessarily produce self-expression values, and self-expression values can emerge even within authoritarian regimes if they produce rising levels of existential security.

Democratic institutions do not automatically produce a culture that emphasizes Self-expression values. Instead, it seems that economic development gradually leads to social and cultural changes that make democratic institutions more likely to survive and flourish. That would help explain why mass democracy did not emerge until a relatively recent point in history, and why, even now, it is most likely to be found in economically more developed countries—in particular, those that emphasize self-expression values over survival values.

During the past few decades, most industrialized societies have moved toward increasing emphasis on Self-expression values, in an intergenerational cultural shift linked with economic development. In the long run, the process of intergenerational population replacement tends to make these values more widespread. The flourishing of democratic institutions is also contingent on economic development and political stability, but, other things being equal, the inter-generational shift toward increasing emphasis on Self-expression values produces growing mass pressures in favor of democracy.

CONCLUSION

Modernization is not linear. It goes through various phases, each of which brings distinctive changes in people's worldviews. The Industrial Revolution was linked with a shift from traditional to Secular-rational values, bringing the secularization of authority. In the post-industrial phase of modernization, another cultural change becomes dominant: a shift from survival values to self-expression values, which brings increasing emancipation *from* authority. Rising Self-expression values makes democracy increasingly likely to emerge—indeed, beyond a certain point it becomes increasingly difficult to *avoid* democratization.

Cross-cultural variation is surprisingly coherent, and a wide range of attitudes (reflecting people's beliefs and values in such different life domains as the family, work, religion, environment, politics and sexual behavior) reflect just two major underlying dimensions: one that taps the polarization between *traditional values* and *secular-rational* values, and a second dimension that taps the polarization between *survival values* and *self-expression values*. The world's societies cluster into relatively homogenous cultural zones, reflecting their historical heritage, and these cultural zones persist robustly over time.

Although the desire for freedom is a universal human aspiration, it does not take top priority when people grow up with the feeling that survival is uncertain. But, when survival seems secure, increasing emphasis on self-expression values makes the emergence of democracy increasingly likely where it does not yet exist, and makes democracy increasingly *effective* where it already exists. Conversely, adopting democratic institutions does not automatically make self-expression values people's top priority. These values emerge when socioeconomic development gives rise to a subjective sense of existential security. This can occur under *either* democratic or authoritarian institutions, and, when it does, it generates mass demands for democracy.

We find that when socioeconomic development reaches the post-industrial phase, it produces a rising emphasis on "self-expression values." These values give high priority to the civil and political liberties that are central to democracy, so the cultural shift from emphasis on Survival values to Self-expression values is inherently conducive to democracy. The powerful correlation shown in Figure 3 reflects a causal process in which economic development gives rise to increasing emphasis on self-expression values, which in turn lead to the emergence and flourishing of democratic institutions. Demonstrating that the rise of self-expression values is conducive to democracy, rather than the other way around, requires a complex empirical analysis that I will not present here since it appears in Inglehart and Welzel (2005).

Analysis of data from scores of societies reveals two major dimensions of cross-cultural variation: a Traditional/Secular-rational values dimension and a Survival/Self-expression values dimension. These dimensions are deep-rooted aspects of cross-cultural variation, and they make it possible to map the position of any society on a two-dimensional map that reflects their relative positions. Despite their relative stability, gradual shifts are occurring along these dimensions, and they are transforming many aspects of society. One particularly important change stems from the fact that the shift from Survival values toward Self-expression values, makes democratic political institutions increasingly likely to emerge and flourish.

REFERENCES

Birch, Charles and John B. Cobb Jr.

1981 *The Liberation of Life: From the Cell to the Community.* Cambridge: Cambridge University Press.

Hofstede, Geert

1980 *Culture's Consequences: Intentional Differences in Work-related Values.* Beverly Hills, CA: Sage.

Huntington, Samuel P.

1996 *The Clash of Civilizations and the Remaking of World Order.* New York: Simon & Schuster.

Inglehart, Ronald

1997 *Modernization and Postmodernization: Cultural, Economic and Political Change in 43 Societies.* Princeton: Princeton University Press.

Inglehart, Ronald and Wayne Baker

2000 "Modernization, Cultural Change and the Persistence of Traditional Values." *American Sociological Review (February)*:19–51.

Inglehart, Ronald and Christian Welzel

2005 *Modernization, Cultural Change and Democracy.* New York and Cambridge: Cambridge University Press.

Kaufmann, Daniel, Aart Kraay and Massimo Mastruzzi

2003 "Governance Matters III: Governance Indicators for 1996-2002." *World Bank Policy Research Department Working Paper No. 2195*, Washington, D.C.: World Bank.

Lee, Kuan Yew and Fareed Zakaria

1994 "Culture Is Destiny: A Conversation with Lee Kuan Yew." *Foreign Affairs* 73 (2): 109-26.

Norris, Pippa and Ronald Inglehart

2004 *Sacred and Secular: Religion and Politics Worldwide.* New York and Cambridge: Cambridge University Press.

O'Donnell, Guillermo, Jorge Vargas Cullel and Osvaldo Miguel Iazzetta (eds.)

2004 *The Quality of Democracy: Theory and Applications.* Notre Dame: University of Notre Dame Press.

Ottaway, Marina

2003 *Democracy Challenged: The Rise of Semi-Authoritarianism.* Washington, D.C.: Carnegie Endowment for International Peace.

Schwartz, Shlalom H.

1992 "Universals in the Content and Structure of Values: Theoretical Advances and Empirical Tests in 20 Countries." In Mark P. Zanna (ed.): *Advances in Social Psychology.* New York: Academic Press. 1-65.

"Beyond Individualism/Collectivism: New Cultural Dimensions of Values." In U. Kim, H.C. Triandis, C. Kagitcibasi, S.C.

Choi, and G. Yoon (eds.), *Individualism and Collectivism: Theory, Method and Applications.* Newbury Park, CA: Sage. 85-119.

2003 "Mapping and Interpreting Cultural Differences around the World." In Henk Vinken, Joseph Soeters, and Peter Ester (eds.), *Comparing Cultures, Dimensions of Culture in a Comparative Perspective.* Leiden, The Netherlands: Brill.

Thompson, John B.

2000 "The Survival of Asian Values as 'Zivilisationskritik.'" *Theory and Society 29*: 651-86.

Triandis, Harry C.

1989 "The Self and Social Behavior in Differing Cultural Contexts." *Psychological Review* 96: 506-20.

1995 *Individualism and Collectivism.* Boulder, CO: Westview Press.

2001 Individualism and Collectivism. In D. Matsumoto (ed.) *Handbook of Cross-Cultural Psychology.* New York: Oxford University Press.

2003 "Dimensions of Culture Beyond Hofstede." In Henk Vinken, Joseph Soeters, and Peter Ester (eds.), *Comparing Cultures, Dimensions of Culture in a Comparative Perspective.* Leiden, The Netherlands: Brill.

Weber, Max

1904 *The Protestant Ethic and the Spirit of Capitalism.* [original, 1904-1905; English translation, 1958]. New York: Charles Scribner's Sons.

Reading

Measuring Intimate Partner Violence (IPV)

You May Only Get What You Ask For (2005)

Eve Waltermaurer

Whether approached as a social problem, a public health concern, a medical condition, or a criminal victimization, intimate partner violence (IPV) is a challenging phenomenon to measure. Over the past 20 years, rather than refining one instrument, multiple tools for measuring IPV have emerged. IPV researchers have relied on a combination of experience, intuition, and statistical skill, and still, for good reason, IPV remains a very difficult experience to

SOURCE: From "Measuring Intimate Partner Violence (IPV): You May Only Get What You Ask For" by Waltermaurer, E., in *Journal of Interpersonal Violence,* Vol. 20, No. 4, April 2005, 501–506. Used with permission of Sage Publications.

empirically define. Although the limitations to the measurement of IPV result in limitations to responding to IPV, it is through the increased understanding of the complexity of IPV that researchers have learned to respect the individuality of IPV victims despite the commonality of their experiences.

This article will describe the considerations and advances in the development of instruments for measuring IPV and also provide some suggestions as to how, over the next 20 years, those interested in improving the validity of IPV research could apply what we have learned thus far. Accuracy in identifying IPV victimization or risk extends beyond instrumentation. Other potential biases or differences in IPV measurement have been found to result from study design differences, interviewer effects (Bachman & Saltzman, 1995; Gelles, 2000; McNutt & Lee, 2000; Schwartz, 2000; Tjaden & Thoennes, 1998), and enrollment criteria (Armstrong et al., 2001; Bohannon, Dosser, & Lindley, 1995; Schafer, Caetano, & Clark, 1998; Szinovacz, 1983; Waltermaurer, Ortega, & McNutt, 2003), to name few. Although these are all important considerations, this article will look solely at the development and interpretation of instruments designed to measure IPV. It will not systematically compare the various IPV instruments but rather identify the primary domains that are germane to the understanding and application of the various IPV instruments.

IPV INSTRUMENTATION ISSUES: LOOKING BACK

The Definition of IPV

The early days of IPV research saw two methods of IPV measurement. In households, families were assessed for their conflict responses characterized by the Conflict Tactics Scale (CTS; Straus, 1979), and in shelters, battered women provided qualitative reports of their experiences (Dobash & Dobash, 1979).

While setting a standard that was then duplicated considerably by subsequent researchers, the groundbreaking IPV research focused almost singularly on acts of physical violence. However, even when restricted to acts of physical violence, the presence of IPV victimization was not easily assigned. It was clear from these earliest measures that the type of physical abuse and the frequency of abuse would differentiate one individual's IPV experience from another's.

Over time, rather than resolving this complication, IPV researchers instead progressed to understanding that there was more than physical IPV. IPV instruments were developed in response that included sexual abuse, emotional abuse, and psychological abuse (for examples, see Brown, Lent, Brett, Sas, & Pederson, 1996; Lewis, 1985; McFarlane, Parker, Soeken, & Bullock, 1992; Shepard & Campbell, 1992; Tolman, 1989). This evolution of the characterization of IPV led to numerous dissimilarities in IPV measurements, as some still included only physical violence whereas others considered some combination of physical, sexual, emotional, and psychological abuse. Nonetheless, even with the inclusion of the differing types of abuse, refined definitions of IPV needed to consider frequency and severity based on an intuitive identification of which physical, emotional, and sexual acts were most severe and what frequency denoted regular abuse. The options of how to quantify this now multilevel measurement have resulted in almost as many definitions of IPV as there are IPV researchers.

Simultaneously, other researchers followed the path set out by Dobash and Dobash by applying more of a qualitative approach in their identification of abuse by ascertaining victims' descriptions of behaviors and self-reports of perceived severity of experiences (e.g., Hamby, Poindexter, & Gray-Little, 1996; Smith, Earp, & Devellis, 1995; Waltermaurer et al., 2003). This process of self-identification revealed that, in some cases, acts that were considered abusive by the individual were not always available on the IPV instrument. For example, unless the participant is asked about experiences in an open-ended manner, someone who may have been thrown across a room or thrown down onto the cement but experienced no other act of abuse could come up negative in an IPV instrument that does not list these conditions (Hamby et al., 1996). As it became clear that individuals may identify abuse that the researcher could miss, it has also slowly been noted in IPV research that an experience defined as severe IPV in a screening instrument may not always be considered severe by the victim (Smith, Smith, & Earp, 1999; Waltermaurer et al., 2003).

The Definition of the IPV Perpetrator

When first measured, the only potential IPV perpetrator considered was the spouse and possibly a cohabiting partner (Gelles, 1974; Hudson & McIntosh, 1981; Lewis, 1985). This earlier body of work was done at a time when nonspousal relationships among adults were more rare and issues surrounding IPV, such as the stigmatization of divorce (Dobash & Dobash, 1979), were more relevant. As we modernized as a nation, so too did the identification of who the potential IPV abuser may be so that today, in many instruments, the potential abuser may be a spouse or ex-spouse, current or former boyfriend or girlfriend, or heterosexual or same-sex partner.

However, as most IPV researchers have met the challenge of changing times, not all have considered when asking respondents to identify their perpetrator that the definition of the IPV perpetrator has been further obfuscated by the widespread prevalence of divorce, separation, and multiple partnering. Although a respondent can conceivably be in a nonabusive relationship but may be victimized by a past partner or abused by both a past and present partner within the same time period, at this point it is rare that an IPV instrument provides this level of detail concerning the victim/perpetrator relationship.

Time Period of Victimization

The decision to select a specific time frame provides a researcher the opportunity to decide if his or her interests are toward understanding the life cycle of abuse or toward understanding immediate risk. A review of IPV instruments reveals numerous possible time frames for victimization, including the past 6 months (Tolman, 1989), the past year (Campbell, 1995; McFarlane et al., 1992; Straus, 1979; Straus, Hamby, Boney-McCoy, & Sugarman, 1996), as an adult (Briere & Runtz, 1988), the past 12 months of most recent adult relationship (Hegarty, Sheehan, & Schonfeld, 1999), lifetime (McFarlane et al., 1992), or no time frame but referencing a present partner (Brown et al., 1996; Lewis, 1985). Aside from the comparability complications resulting from different time frames for different instruments, these varying periods have apparently confused the definition of IPV for different studies as a measure of incidence or prevalence (Brownridge & Halli, 1999). This issue is further complicated by some researchers' decisions to count the number of IPV victims, whereas others count the number of IPV victimizations.

IPV Instrumentation Issues: Looking Forward

Between the years of 1979 and 2003, at least 33 different screening instruments have been designed and applied to specifically measure IPV. The very fact that so many different tools have been developed reflects both a liability and an advancement in the field of IPV research. These multiple instruments serve as a liability in that the varying definitions of IPV and the abuser limit our ability to compare IPV over time and across populations. However, these different instruments also reflect the growing understanding by IPV researchers with regard to this dynamic experience. These multiple tools can be used in our favor if applied accurately. What follows are a few suggestions that may assist this process.

First, each IPV instrument should be assessed for validity and reliability. These assessments should be done in multiple geographic areas and among multiple subpopulations. In addition to assessing the reliability within each instrument, it is important that the reliability between instruments is measured as well. By understanding the comparability across measures, we can overcome the hurdle created by having multiple instruments. For those instruments that have been found to be reliable, it is important that IPV researchers understand that by changing these instruments in terms of question inclusion or time frame, they are infringing on the efficacy of these instruments.

Choosing or creating a specific IPV instrument needs to be a purposeful process. When choosing the appropriate instrument, the IPV researcher needs to be thoughtful of his or her goals, as the various time frames and means of ascertaining IPV identify different types of abuse and different types of risk. Although it is certainly commendable to use multiple instruments for one group of respondents, the IPV researcher must understand that divergences from different measures may not mean that one instrument is better but rather that each instrument may be revealing different stories. Similarly, adding a perceived measure of abuse in conjunction with a list of abuse experiences may appear to provide conflicting information with regard to severity but in actuality serves to introduce a greater understanding of each respondent's individual IPV experience. To observe the change in IPV over time, it is clear that we must work toward developing some consistency in our measures; however, measurement consistency should never take precedence over adjusting and adapting to our growing understanding of IPV.

REFERENCES

Armstrong, T., Heideman, G., Corcoran, K., Fisher, B., Medina, K., & Schafer, J. (2001). Disagreement about the occurrence of male-to-female intimate partner violence: A qualitative study. *Family and Community Health, 24*(1), 55-75.

Bachman, R., & Saltzman, L. (1995). *Violence against women: Estimates from the redesigned survey* [Special report]. Washington, DC: Bureau of Justice Statistics.

Bohannon, J., Dosser, D., & Lindley, S. (1995). Using couple data to determine domestic violence rates: An attempt to replicate previous work. *Violence and Victims, 10*(2), 133-141.

Briere, J., & Runtz, M. (1988). Multivariate correlates of childhood psychological and physical maltreatment among university women. *Child Abuse and Neglect, 12*, 331-341.

Brown, J., Lent, B., Brett, P., Sas, G., & Pederson, L. (1996). Development of the Woman Abuse Screening Tool for use in family practice. *Family Medicine, 28*, 422-428.

Brownridge, D. ,& Halli, S. (1999). Measuring family violence: The conceptualization and utilization of prevalence and incidence rates. *Journal of Family Violence, 14*(4), 333-350.

Campbell, J. (1995). *Assessing dangerousness*. Newbury Park, CA: Sage.

Dobash, R.E., & Dobash, R.(1979).*Violence against wives*. New York: Free Press/Macmillan.

Gelles, R. (1974). The violent home: A study of physical aggression between husbands and wives. Newbury Park, CA: Sage.

Gelles, R. (2000). Estimating the incidence and prevalence of violence against women, national data systems and sources. *Violence Against Women, 17*, 784-804.

Hamby, S., Poindexter, V., & Gray-Little, B. (1996). Four measures in partner violence: Construct similarity and classification differences. *Journal of Marriage and the Family, 58*, 127-139.

Hegarty, K., Sheehan, M., & Schonfeld, C. (1999). A multi-dimensional definition of partner abuse: Development and preliminary validation of the Composite Abuse Scale. *Journal of Family Violence, 14*(4), 399–415.

Hudson, W., & McIntosh, S. (1981). The assessment of spouse abuse: Two quantifiable dimensions. *Journal of Marriage and the Family, 43*(4), 873-885.

Lewis, B. (1985). The Wife Abuse Inventory: A screening device for the identification of abused women. *Social Work, 30*(1), 32-35.

McFarlane, J., Parker, B., Soeken, K., & Bullock, L. (1992). Assessing for abuse during pregnancy. *Journal of the American Medical Association, 267*, 3176-3178.

McNutt, L. A., & Lee, R. (2000). Intimate partner violence prevalence estimation using telephone surveys: Understanding the effect of nonresponse bias. *American Journal of Epidemiology, 152*(5), 438-441.

Schafer, J., Caetano, R., & Clark, C. (1998). Rates of intimate partner violence in the United States. *American Journal of Public Health, 88*(11), 1702-1704.

Schwartz, M. (2000). Methodological issues in the use of survey data for measuring and characterizing violence against women. *Violence Against Women, 6*(8), 815-838.

Shepard, M., & Campbell, J. (1992). The Abusive Behavior Inventory: A measure of psychological and physical abuse. *Journal of Interpersonal Violence, 7*, 219-306.

Smith, P., Earp, J., & Devellis, R. (1995). Measuring battering: Development of the Woman's Experience with Battering (WEB) Scale. *Women's Health: Research on Gender, Behavior and Policy, 1*, 273–288.

Smith, P., Smith, J., & Earp, J. (1999). Beyond the measurement trap. *Psychology of Women Quarterly, 23*, 177–193.

Straus, M. (1979). Measuring intrafamily conflict and violence: The Conflict Tactics (CT) Scales. *Journal of Marriage and the Family, 41*, 75–88.

Straus, M., Hamby, S., Boney-McCoy, S., & Sugarman, D. (1996). The Revised Conflict Tactics Scales (CTS2) development and preliminary psychometric data. *Journal of Family Issues, 17*(3), 283–316.

Szinovacz, M. (1983). Using couple data as a methodological tool: The case of marital violence. *Journal of Marriage and the Family, 45*(3), 633–644.

Tjaden, P., & Thoennes, N. (1998, November). *Prevalence, incidence, and consequences of violence against women: Findings from the National Violence Against Women Survey*. National Institute of Justice, Centers for Disease Control and Prevention Research in Brief.

Tolman, R. (1989). The development of a measure of psychological maltreatment of women by their male partners. *Violence and Victims, 4*(3), 159–177.

Waltermaurer, E., Ortega, V., & McNutt, L. A. (2003). Issues in estimating the prevalence of intimate partner violence: Assessing the impact of abuse status on participation bias. *Journal of Interpersonal Violence, 18*(9), 959–974.

Reading

Ethnicity, Gender, and Perceptions of Task Competence (1990)*

Martha Foschi and Shari Buchan

INTRODUCTION

A substantial body of research investigates social psychological aspects of ethnic relations in Canada. The range of topics includes self-identity, interpersonal liking, social distance, attributions, biased evaluations, and stereotypes. Definitions of "ethnic group" vary, and use one or more of the following categories: nationality, race, religion, language, and culture. (For an examination of the notion of "ethnicity" see Isajiw, 1985.) In Canada, interethnic relations involve Native Indian peoples, English and French Canadian groups, and immigrants from virtually every part of the world. Clearly, historical developments as well as regional representation must be taken into account in order to understand these relations. For example, English Canadians' perceptions of French Canadians in contemporary Quebec differ from those recorded in the sixties,

SOURCE: From "Ethnicity, Gender, and Perceptions of Task Competence" by Foschi, M. & Buchan, S., in *Canadian Journal of Sociology, 15*.1:1-18. Copyright © 1990. Reprinted with permission.

*This project was supported by a Secretary of State (Multiculturalism Directorate) research grant to the senior author. We gratefully acknowledge this support. We also thank Sabrina Freeman for her many contributions at various stages of the project, Thelma S. Cook and Neil Guppy for their comments on an earlier draft, and Richard Floyd, Junko Takagi, and Sam Vovnik for their assistance with data collection. Please address all correspondence and offprint requests to Professor Martha Foschi, Department of Anthropology and Sociology, University of British Columbia, Vancouver, B.C. V6T 2B2.

and the experiences associated with being Chinese in British Columbia are not the same as those of being Chinese in Prince Edward Island. (For literature reviews of the social psychology of ethnic relations in Canada as well as examples of research see Gardner and Kalin, 1981; Bienvenue and Goldstein, 1985; Earn and Towson, 1986.)

A group of studies within this literature has focussed on ethnicity as a cue to task competence. The studies involve a wide variety of situations, from solving anagrams to being considered suitable for a job. We define "perceived task competence" as including all of these contexts, as long as the participants value doing well at the task in question. In our opinion, such perceptions are the key to understanding ethnic relations. The topic is also important for practical reasons: in work settings, for example, considering members of a given ethnic group to be likeable, or trustworthy, or to have a sense of humour does not have the same consequences as labelling them "intelligent," "smart," or "capable." Whereas the traits in the first set may very well be important for employment and job advancement, those in the second are necessary conditions.

Both surveys and experiments have been done on this topic, and a variety of ethnic groups has been studied. The research stems from several theoretical traditions, representing both psychological and sociological approaches. Due to space limitations, we only mention the most relevant studies. These include work on the content of ethnic stereotypes (Gardner et al., 1970; Aboud and Taylor, 1971; Mackie, 1974; Driedger and Clifton, 1984; Lambert et al., 1986), biased evaluations of performances (Labovitz, 1974) and self-attributions of success and failure (Fry and Ghosh, 1980). Several experiments have investigated speech cues as a basis for competence judgments, including the "matched guise technique" studies (Lambert et al., 1960, 1966) and the work on evaluative judgments of job candidates (Kalin and Rayko, 1978; Kalin et al., 1980). In spite of their theoretical and methodological differences, each of the above studies shows evidence of an order of perceived task competence based on ethnicity, with either English Canadians or White Canadians (depending on the groups being investigated) at the top of the ranking. (Several of the earlier findings involving French Canadian and English Canadian subjects reflect conditions that have now changed; see, for example, Lambert et al., 1960, 1966; Gardner et al., 1970; Aboud and Taylor, 1971. Nevertheless, that work is essential to understanding the relationship between ethnicity and perceived competence in its historical context.)

Although assignment of traits and evaluative judgments provide important data, the crucial test of ethnicity as a cue to competence is whether these variables translate into behaviours. Our search identified only four studies reporting behavioural measures. Clifton (1981) investigated academic performance as a function of teachers' expectations for French-speaking and German-speaking high school students in Ontario. Official records of grades provided an indirect measure of academic achievement, and findings indicate that past performance had a stronger effect than ethnicity. Cook (1975) studied greater Vancouver elementary school boys participating in a game in groups of four (two White and two Native Indian). Her results show that the former initiated more acts and were more influential than the latter. Tuzlak and Moore's (1984) experiment involved same-sex dyads performing a collective task. Subjects were White undergraduates in Toronto, assigned at random to work with either a White or a Black

---

[1]By adopting the terms 'White' and 'East Indian' we follow common usage in the ethnicity literature. These terms also appear frequently in everyday language to refer to the broad categories our procedures were designed to bring to mind (see Methods section below).

partner. Findings showed clear effects of race on influence patterns. Finally, Henry and Ginzberg (1985) report two related studies of ethnic discrimination in employment practices in the Toronto area. In response to job advertisements appearing in local newspapers, subjects posed as applicants with similar resumés, and either phoned or applied in person. "Job seekers" were Black West Indian, Indo-Pakistani, or White. Predictably, more interviews and job offers were received by the White group.

It is clear from this overview that much has yet to be learned about the effects of ethnicity on perceptions of competence and ensuing behaviours. More subject and more target groups, from different regions and sectors of the population, need to be studied. In this paper we present the results from an experiment on perceptions of competence of White and East Indian[1] partners of both sexes. The study is formulated within the context of status generalization theory. The theory is especially useful for our purposes because of its emphasis on linking perceptions to behavioural measures, and because its concepts encompass ethnicity as well as gender[2] as status categories. The theoretical context also facilitates comparison of our findings with other studies, both inside and outside Canada.

THEORETICAL AND EMPIRICAL BACKGROUND

Status generalization theory is part of a research program on expectations, performances, and evaluations in task groups. Empirical tests show strong support for the various theories comprising the program, and an applied branch establishes its practical utility. (For recent reviews of the program see Berger et al., 1985 and Webster

and Foschi, 1988.) A central concept in this research tradition is that of a status characteristic, or valued attribute implying task competence. Such characteristics may be specific or diffuse, depending on the range of their perceived relevance. For example, the ability to solve geometric puzzles is commonly seen as applicable to only a few situations and is therefore specific. On the other hand, social class, sex, and ethnicity tend to be used to infer a person's level in a wide variety of abilities, and are thus examples of diffuse characteristics. Status characteristics generate performance expectations which, in turn, determine the power and prestige hierarchy of a group. This hierarchy is defined as a set of interrelated behaviours, namely, the unequal distribution in the offer and acceptance of opportunities to perform, the type of evaluation received (positive or negative), and the rates of exerted influence.

"Status generalization" refers to the process through which a characteristic not directly relevant to success at a group's task is nevertheless used to assign task competence. An example would be the importing of gender-based expectations from the larger society to the task-related discussions of a jury or of a fund-raising group, and the use of these expectations to decide, in each case, that men have better ideas than women regarding the task at hand. Status generalization effects from a variety of characteristics, both specific and diffuse, have been demonstrated. As to the effects of ethnicity as a diffuse status characteristic, a large portion of the research on this topic has been carried out by E.G. Cohen and associates. Their work has involved a series of interventions designed to create equal classroom interaction among various ethnic groups; Cook (1975) (mentioned earlier) is part of this series. Other studies investigating status

---

[2]As generally agreed in the social psychological literature, we use the term 'sex' to refer to biological differences between males and females, and 'gender' to cultural aspects of these differences. Thus, beliefs about the relative competence of men and women are social products and therefore a gender issue, whereas what activates these beliefs is usually nothing more than the perception of sex differences among the performers. When the evidence available involves only such perceptions, we use 'sex' rather than 'gender.'

generalization effects of ethnicity include Webster and Driskell (1978, Whites and Blacks in the US), Yuchtman-Yaar and Semyonov (1979, European-American and Asian-African Jews in Israel), Tuzlak and Moore (1984, described above), and Riches and Foddy (1989, Anglo-Australians and Greek-Australians). (For a review of work on ethnicity as a diffuse status characteristic see Cohen, 1982.) The present study is the first to use status generalization theory to study White East Indian relations.

Results from various Canadian studies suggest that "White" and "East Indian" can be thought of as states of a diffuse status characteristic. Thus several surveys (Goldstein, 1978; Li, 1979; Driedger and Mezoff, 1981; Clifton and Perry, 1985; Robson and Breems, 1985) have shown the low ranking received by East Indians in social distance measures and, overall, the negative attitudes held towards them. More specifically, of the studies on ethnicity and perceived competence reviewed above, the three which include East Indians (Fry and Ghosh, 1980; Kalin et al., 1980; Henry and Ginzberg, 1985) report that this group is seen as having less competence than the White comparison group(s). In sum, previous research indicates that East Indians occupy a relatively low position among ethnic groups in Canada, a status they share with various other groups making up the so-called "visible minorities." (For historical accounts of the East Asian experience in Canada, from early immigration to more recent tensions, see Krauter and Davis, 1978: Chapter 6; Buchignani et al., 1985.)

The largest concentrations of East Indians in Canada are found in the Toronto and Vancouver metropolitan areas. In both places they constitute visible minorities in terms of physical appearance, including dress style. They are also quite visible in terms of media coverage: national as well as local (Vancouver and Toronto) news coverage, particularly about Sikhs' protests against the Indian government, has been frequent and detailed. Negative attitudes and hostile acts directed towards East Indians in Vancouver in the early 1980s are well documented in Robson and Breems (1985; see also Buchignani et al., 1985: 209–217).

Our study has undergraduates at the University of British Columbia as subjects. The work on ethnicity and status generalization described above includes a variety of populations; those studies in which subjects are undergraduates (Webster and Driskell, 1978; Tuzlak and Moore, 1984) show that they are not immune to the status distinctions based on ethnicity occurring in the surrounding community. (Further, other work in this research tradition shows similar effects among undergraduates from other status distinctions, such as gender and level of education.) Accordingly, we expected this to be also the case in our study, particularly since a large proportion of UBC undergraduates are from the metropolitan Vancouver area.

We thus hypothesized status generalization effects in White East Indian interactions. That is, we predicted different perceptions of competence and resulting behaviours for White subjects performing a task with a partner, depending on whether the partner was White or East Indian. In the former case, equal performance expectations for self and other would be formed whereas in the latter case, self would feel more competent than the partner. These expectations would, in turn, be reflected in the behavioural measure, rejection of influence from the partner.

In order to assess the generality of this hypothesis, we tested it with both male and female dyads.[3] Status generalization theory assumes that equal expectations for self and partner would be formed in the two types of dyads, given that sex is not a differentiating factor. However, the theory leaves the door open for other factors to affect expectations. Only four studies present data that can be used to investigate this assumption: Tuzlak and Moore (1984) and Foschi et al. (1985) found no significant differences between the two types of dyads (although some of the differences are worth noting); on the other hand, findings from Ridgeway (1982) and Foschi and Freeman (1987) indicate that, under certain conditions, differences between male and female dyads occur in response to other elements in the situation (such as source of expectations and organizational authority). We thus collected auxiliary data on several variables to investigate these possibilities.

METHOD

Subjects

Subjects were forty-four male and forty-six female undergraduates, recruited from first and second year arts and sciences courses at the University of British Columbia. Average age was 18.87 for the men and 18.54 for the women; standard deviations were 1.09 and 1.05, respectively. Participation was voluntary and the chance of winning one of four $50 prizes was used as an incentive.

All subjects were White. Suitability to this criterion was determined from the surname on the recruitment form, and confirmed through visual cues upon the person's arrival in the laboratory. Questions about ethnicity were not included in that instrument in order to avoid suspicion. In an attempt to make our sample more homogeneous, scheduling priority was given to subjects with Anglo-Saxon surnames; however, some names with no clearly identifiable (to us) nationality or ethnicity were also included. Persons with obviously French, Italian, Greek, and Asian surnames were excluded—again in order to increase similarity. At the time of the experiment, there were about 16,000 full-time undergraduates at the university, 52 percent of whom were male. The university does not keep statistics by student's ethnicity, but we estimate that about 50 percent of the undergraduates would fall under the definition of "White" used here. Our sample of volunteers reflected the composition of the undergraduate population in these two respects.

Subjects participated in same-sex dyads and were assigned at random to one of two ethnicity conditions. In all ninety experimental sessions, the partner was a confederate of the same sex as the subject.

Procedures and Materials

For comparability, procedures were a variant of the standardized experimental situation developed for status generalization studies (Berger et al., 1977: 43–48). Each session was conducted by one of two White female graduate students of similar age. Consistency in appearance and delivery of instructions was maintained throughout the study.

The two participants were seated at stations separated by an opaque partition, and were not allowed to meet or talk with each other. Each person completed a demographic form and these were then exchanged. The demographic forms were used, in conjunction with the recruitment forms, to equate subject and partner in sex, age bracket (17 to 22), marital status (single), level of schooling (undergraduate), and place of residence (B.C.). The partner's demographic form also contained cues to his/her ethnicity through name, country of birth, and language(s), in four different versions: Doug Edwards, Canada, English (Condition 1); Mandip Sidhu, India, English, and Punjabi (Condition 2); Diane Edwards, Canada, English (Condition 3); Satinder Sidhu, India, English and Punjabi (Condition 4). Thus (1) and (3) constituted the "White partner" conditions, and (2) and (4), the "East Indian partner" conditions. (For other studies in which ethnicity is manipulated only through written cues see Labovitz, 1974 and Orpen, 1981; for an example of a status generalization experiment using only verbal cues, see Moore, 1968.)

---

[3]Gender effects in mixed-sex dyads are well known and beyond the scope of this project. For the same reasons, we did not investigate the effects of differentiating subjects along more than one diffuse status characteristic. See Berger et al. (1985) and Webster and Foschi (1988) for reviews of work on both topics.

The stated purpose of the study was to investigate performance on a "contrast sensitivity" task in two simulated work environments: an individual setting and a team setting. The instructions were written to motivate the subjects to do well (that is, to be task oriented) and to inform them that the partner was of the same year (either first or second) and faculty (either Arts or Science) at the university. The ability was said to be of considerable importance and now included in major aptitude tests. At the same time, it was mentioned that "no significant relationship has so far been found between it and sex, age, education, mathematical ability, or artistic skills" (a statement included in order to control for expectations based on these variables). Nothing was said about ethnicity, but the possibility of an association between it and the task was left open by indicating that "life experiences and patterns of socialization may be correlated with contrast sensitivity."

The task is a reliable instrument which, for comparability across experiments, has been extensively used in expectation states studies. It consists of several trials, each involving a different slide showing two rectangles. Each rectangle is covered to about the same extent by white and black areas. The subject must decide, within a limited time, which of the two figures has the highest proportion of white. There is in fact no correct answer.

During the first part of the study participants worked individually on the task, making decisions on twenty slides (no scores were given), and then completed a written questionnaire. Next they were asked to work on the same task as a team. In all cases, it was mentioned that the team had been randomly assigned to participate under conditions of limited information about the partner and of restricted communication between partners. The instructions reinforced the collective orientation by indicating that a team would be awarded points only for those trials in which both persons were correct. Each participant's station was equipped with a response terminal connected to a common main panel (in an adjoining room) from which the experimenter manipulated the feedback. After making an initial choice on a slide, the subject received controlled feedback regarding the partner's choice; next the subject made a final decision. On twenty of twenty-five trials, the partner was said to disagree with the subject's initial choice. Rejection of influence was measured by the proportion of times a subject rejected the partner's decision (that is, made a "self" or "s-response") when making a final choice.

At the conclusion of these trials, the subject completed a second questionnaire designed to check on the various manipulations and to assess any misunderstandings and/or suspicions. Next, the person was individually interviewed to check further on these items and then debriefed. Special care was taken to explain the purpose of the study. If a subject asked whether his/her results indicated the presence of prejudice, one of two answers were given, depending on the person's level of rejection of influence. Although presented in more detail, the responses were basically either: "No, it does not appear that you have been influenced by your partner's ethnicity" or "It is quite common to rush to conclusions when one has limited information. It appears that this is what you did today." In both cases we mentioned that perhaps he/she could use the experience as a reminder of the mistakes one often makes in such situations.

RESULTS

Examination of the questionnaire and post-experimental interview data resulted in the exclusion of thirteen subjects, or 14.4 percent of the total number of participants. Rejection rules were conservative, formulated beforehand and based on objective criteria, and this percentage is similar to the figures reported in comparable experiments (see, in particular, Tuzlak and Moore, 1984). Subjects were excluded from analysis on the basis of suspicion, not understanding the instructions, or lacking task/or collective orientation; there is no evident pattern in the distribution of these subjects across conditions and/or basis for exclusion. Only the data from the seventy-seven retained subjects are presented in what follows.

Ethnicity Manipulation

In addition to surnames and visual cues, ethnicity was checked through several questionnaire items. Due to the sensitivity of the issue, questions were cautiously phrased and dealt only with the most basic information. Sixty-seven subjects (87 percent) were native Canadians, the rest had been born in Australia, England, New Zealand, Scotland, Sweden, the US, or Yugoslavia. Since language of partner was part of the ethnicity manipulation, we also collected information on the languages the subjects themselves could read, speak, and/or write. Thirty-six (47 percent) indicated English only, and thirty-two (41 percent) listed English and various levels of proficiency in French. The remaining nine (12 percent) gave German, Italian, Serbo-Croatian, or Spanish as an additional language. There were no noticeable differences across conditions in the distributions of place of birth and/or languages.

When asked about "the partner's ethnic background," subjects in conditions (1) and (3) fell in two groups: twenty thought that this background was similar to theirs, and eighteen said that they did not know. There were no sex differences in these distributions. All thirty-nine subjects in conditions (2) and (4) thought that the partner was of a different ethnicity. Since the information we provided about the partner was not as distinctive in the White as in the East Indian case, the large proportion of "don't knows" in the former is to be expected and does not detract from the formation of two different ethnicity conditions.

Other Manipulations

All subjects remembered correctly the partner's sex. All but one identified this person as of the same age bracket, and all but two indicated similarity in level of education. (The three exceptions checked "don't know.") Data on task importance and on extent of task and collective orientations indicate that the instructions had been effective. There were no significant differences among conditions regarding these variables, or in the distribution of four causal attribution factors (ability, effort, chance, and task difficulty).

Dependent Variable

Tables 1 and 2 present the results on rejection of influence. Mann-Whitney U tests on the proportion of s-responses (p(s)) are used for comparability with the majority of expectation states studies involving predictions about pairs of conditions.[4] The tests show that the hypothesis regarding the effects of ethnicity is supported for men but not for women, and that the prediction of no differences between same-sex dyads receives support for the White but not for the East Indian partner. Further analysis and interpretation of these findings now follows.

Discussion

Conditions (1) and (2) show the predicted effects of status generalization: male subjects accepted significantly less influence from an East Indian partner than from a White one. Although the p(s) value for condition (2) is lower than the values obtained in comparable conditions in expectation states research, variations due to special design features and population characteristics are to be

---

[4]Furthermore, since they are sensitive to the shape of the distributions, Mann-Whitney U tests are particularly appropriate for the analysis of our results: the p(s) distribution from condition (2) is clearly different from each of the other three, notably in having thirteen of its subjects grouped in the upper values (.60 to .75).

TABLE 1 Rejection of Influence by Condition

	Proportion of s-responses	
Condition	$\bar{X}$	*s.d.*
(1) White, male partner	0.539	0.096
N = 18		
(2) East Indian, male partner	0.598	0.132
N = 20		
3) White, female partner	0.543	0.117
N = 20		
(4) East Indian, female partner	0.532	0.144
N = 19		

expected and are of secondary importance to the findings obtained within a given experiment.[5] A comparison with Tuzlak and Moore (1984) is nevertheless pertinent because of that study's key similarities and differences with ours. Their experiment involved White subjects interacting with either a White or a Black partner, in a situation in which visual cues were provided. (The effects of sex of dyad and confidence of partner were also studied.) The comparison of interest here is between the White and the Black partner conditions, where the partner was confident and both participants were male. The p(s) values obtained (.681 and .596, respectively) show a more marked ethnicity effect than ours, thus suggesting two factors for further consideration: choice of ethnic groups and type of cues.

Among the studies reviewed earlier, a very limited number (Driedger and Mezzoff, 1981; Henry and Ginzberg, 1985; Robson and Breems, 1985) examine the relative positions of East Indians and Blacks. The three studies suggest that the status of Blacks is marginally higher than that of East Indians, although only Henry and Ginzberg's research deals specifically with the

---

[5]As mentioned above, subjects in this experiment were told that self and partner were of the same sex, and similar in age and level of education. This was done in order to make the situation less "abstract" and thus to decrease the possibility of suspicion. Equating characteristics have been shown to dampen the effect of differentiating information (for example, see Webster and Driskell, 1978). But subjects in our experiment were instructed that there was no significant association between contrast sensitivity and any of those three, and questionnaire data indicate that the instructions were effective: only two subjects—in condition (2)—associated contrast sensitivity with age, two—in condition (4)—linked it to level of education, and none related it to sex differences. This suggests that the stated absence of a significant relationship between contrast sensitivity and other attributes, rather than equating, kept the p(s) values relatively low. Another possibility is the following: in the process of creating two work contexts ("individual" and "team") we may have given the subjects the opportunity to realize how difficult the task really was. Other status generalization experiments (e.g., Tuzlak and Moore, 1984) include only the "team" phase.

TABLE 2 Mann-Whitney U tests* on the Proportions of S-Responses

Conditions compared	U	Z	p	
(1) and (2)	118.0	−1.812	0.034	1-tailed
(3) and (4)	193.0	−0.084	0.472	
(1) and (3)	175.0	−0.146	0.883	2-tailed
(2) and (4)	135.0	−1.545	0.119	

Note: *adjusted for ties

issue of perceived competence. These findings thus point to type of cues rather than to ethnic group as a likely factor in our case. As mentioned earlier, other studies have relied only on verbal cues and still successfully activated status differences. However, visual cues may be particularly important in the case of ethnicity, as Rosenholtz and Cohen (1985) point out. If this is the case, our use of minimal cues may have worked against confirmation of the status generalization hypothesis, and in that respect our study constitutes a stricter test.[6]

The results from conditions (1) and (3) are also as expected: when subjects are similar in ethnicity, equal expectations result. But the findings from the females with an East Indian partner—condition (4)—are not in line with the predictions: these subjects do not differ significantly from the females with a White partner—condition (3), and instead do differ considerably from males with an East Indian partner—condition (2). Notice that the comparison between conditions (2) and (4) in

Table 2 shows the result from a two-tailed test. As indicated in the previous section, male and female subjects were similar in various respects, ranging from age to pattern of attributions. The auxiliary data rule out several other possible explanations: As mentioned earlier, there are no significant differences among the four conditions regarding the additional manipulations (such as importance attached to task), and no pattern was evident in the distribution of excluded subjects. A trial-by-trial analysis of the p(s) values showed notable similarities in terms of stability and primacy/recency effects, particularly among conditions (2), (3), and (4).

Sex differences such as the one observed here invite rushed conclusions. We could, for example, interpret the findings as indicating that women are less prejudiced than men. Thus we could argue that firsthand experience with discrimination makes women more fair in interpersonal relations. Or it could be that the East Indian female was seen as an exception. Although both are possible occurrences, there is

[6]The same conclusion may be reached from another aspect of the study. Thus, we could consider the possibility that 'East Indian' evoked no clear image in the subjects' minds. Still, all subjects in condition (2) thought that the partner differed from them in ethnicity. That results would be obtained on just those grounds makes them even more crucial.

no evidence from the questionnaire and interview data pointing in either direction.[7]

AN EXPLANATION

We did find, however, that men and women differed with respect to the number and type of characteristics they related to contrast sensitivity. The instructions had indicated no significant relationship between it and sex, age, education, mathematical ability, or artistic skills. But the possibility was left open for an association with ethnicity through life experiences and socialization. We used the two questionnaires to check on the effectiveness of these instructions and to obtain a measure of status generalization. In each case we asked the subjects whether they thought contrast sensitivity was related to any of the following: sex, age, educational level, mathematical skill, artistic talent, intelligence, reasoning ability, socialization, and life experiences. As an alternative, subjects could also check "it is not yet known." Results regarding these nine attributes were first averaged per subject over the two measures,[8] and then averaged over subjects. Findings are presented in Table 3, and show that men associated contrast sensitivity with more characteristics than women. The low averages for both sexes reflect that there was a fixed set from which to choose, that five of the nine characteristics had been exempted by the instructions, and that checking "it is not yet known" was a reasonable alternative.

A closer examination of the responses showed that, in all conditions, most subjects linked contrast sensitivity to reasoning ability (a result that also serves as a check that the task was seen as requiring competence). The pattern of sex differences is due largely to the responses to two items—artistic talent and mathematical skill—that the experimenter had identified as not significantly related to contrast sensitivity. In particular, most men in condition (2) disregarded this statement while most women in condition (4) accepted it. Furthermore, responses indicating "it is not yet known" also show a sex difference. More women (six per condition) than men (three per condition) checked this answer in the first questionnaire. The second questionnaire elicited similar results.

These findings are of interest because of their internal consistency and the unobstrusive nature of the measures. The pattern appearing in Table 3 suggests an interaction between sex of subject and type of decision to be made. Subjects in this experiment were required to make relative assessments of task competence on the basis of limited and indirect information. When this indicated equality between the partners, the decision should have been less controversial and therefore easier to make than when the information pointed to inequality. Thus the comparison of interest is between men and women with an East Indian partner, and a Mann-Whitney U test (one-tailed, adjusted for ties) for conditions (2) and (4) in Table 3 shows a significant difference (U: 111.5, z: –2.206, p:

---

[7]As it is usually done in status generalization studies (see, for example, Moore, 1968), we tried to elicit subjects' reactions to the "White" and "East Indian" categories and to their relationship to contrast sensitivity. Thus we invited written comments at the end of the second questionnaire, and probed the subjects during the post-experimental interview. This kind of information is of course difficult to obtain, and even more so in the case of ethnicity, since most people would consider it poor manners to give public indications of ethnic prejudice. Only one subject made a comment along these lines, and it was guarded: "I would have trusted my partner's answers more if he had been born in Canada." On the other hand, five men and three women indicated an explicit dissociation between ethnicity and contrast sensitivity. None of them was excluded, however, since the statements were about "ethnicity," not "Whites" and "East Indians," and in addition could have been made for self-enhancement.

[8]Subjects did not have the first questionnaire available to them while answering the second. Responses in the two instruments coincide in 660 of 693 cases (77 subjects times 9 items), or 95.2 percent. There are no noticeable variations across conditions.

0.013). None of the other three relevant comparisons result in such a difference.

Since both sexes indicated similar levels of task and collective orientation, what these auxiliary data point to are different approaches to forming expectations. By describing contrast sensitivity as not significantly related to several attributes, the instructions did not encourage status generalization. Yet most men did not accept that the ability could be unrelated to so many characteristics, and thus kept the door open for contrast sensitivity to be connected to ethnicity by making their own associations between that ability and several others. Most women, on the other hand, interpreted the instructions more literally, placing emphasis on their cautious wording. The sex difference regarding the "it is not yet known option" is also in line with this.

In a related study, Foschi and Freeman (1987) found significant differences in influence rates between male and female dyads. The study was an expectation states experiment not involving ethnicity, but with subjects from the same population as the present one. The authors review research on gender and the social psychology of experimentation, and interpret their own results in terms of sex differences in acceptance of the experimenter's instructions. These differences, in turn, are seen as a function of subjects' perceived ability to evaluate relative to the experimenter (see Foddy, 1988 for an elaboration of this notion). The same interpretation may be applied here. The fact that in the present case the two experimenters were of the same sex (female) strengthens the explanation. No pattern of differences between experimenters could be detected from any measure. As in the Foschi and Freeman experiment, the results point to women's lower status relative to men in the larger society and in this university context in particular.[9] By showing the strength of sex as a diffuse status characteristic even in same-sex dyads, the findings from the two studies also point to the need to refine the status generalization assumption about such dyads.

We note that our explanation does not directly connect rejection of influence results, contrast sensitivity, and ethnicity. The latter was not included among the attributes that subjects could

TABLE 3 Task Ability as Related to Other Characteristics, by Condition

Condition	Number of responses associating contrast sensitivity to other characteristics	
	$\bar{X}$	s.d.
(1) White, male partner	1.583	1.179
N = 18		
(2) East Indian, male partner	1.850	1.299
N = 20		
(3) White, female partner	1.275	1.175
N = 20		
(4) East Indian, female partner	1.000	0.866
N = 19		

check because we thought this would be a reactive measure. Although evidence for it is indirect, the explanation is worth considering for several reasons. First, it is the only one supported by this study's data: of a variety of auxiliary measures taken, only associations with contrast sensitivity show sex differences. The data on these associations are internally consistent and theoretically interpretable. Second, previous research on status generalization and on ethnicity in Canada ruled out possible alternative explanations, as did the highly structured nature of the experimental situation. The ethnicity manipulation worked as intended, and their own status relative to the experimenter's was one of the few items of information available to the subjects. No evidence was found for the possibilities that the women were less prejudiced than the men or that the East Indian woman was seen as an exception. Finally, the proposed explanation is consistent with previous work on gender as a diffuse status characteristic and its effects even in same-sex dyads.

SUMMARY AND CONCLUSIONS

This study involved White undergraduates at the University of British Columbia, working on a collective task with a partner of the same sex. The partner was described as either White or East Indian. The experimental setting replicated features of everyday work contexts, such as receiving instructions from a superior, making decisions about task competence on the basis of limited information, and working as a team but with restricted interaction. Manipulation checks indicated that the subjects valued the task, were motivated to do it well, and felt involved in a team effort. The study showed the effects of two diffuse status characteristics—ethnicity and gender—on perceived competence.

It was predicted that the subjects would accept more influence from the White than from the East Indian partner. This prediction was supported for the men. The results are of interest because this is the first time that White East Indian interactions have been investigated within status generalization theory. It is also worth noting that significant behavioural differences were obtained with minimal (verbal only) cues and with experimental instructions that did not encourage status generalization.

Females did not differentiate between the White and the East Indian partner. Post-experimental questionnaires indicate that women followed instructions more closely than men, particularly in the East Indian partner conditions: the experimenter's description of the task as unrelated to several attributes was accepted more by women than by men. This, in turn, is linked to sex differences in perceived ability to evaluate relative to the experimenter, and provides an explanation of why women treated both the White and the East Indian partner as equals. Reasons for favoring this explanation over several others are discussed. Further, the theoretical implications of these findings are noted. Status generalization theory, as initially formulated, assumes no differences between same-sex dyads. However, there have been very few studies investigating this issue. The present experiment provides evidence for the refinement of that assumption, by pointing out that if the situation contains other status elements that could be used to form expectations, the effects of these elements need to be included.

The inference of competence on the basis of ethnicity is a sensitive issue to study. In Canada, the

[9]This explanation is also consistent with the interpretation of sex differences in male and female task dyads presented in Ridgeway (1988). She argues that sex of organizational authority affects how males and females behave in such dyads. In the current case, the research was referred to as a faculty member's project (sex unspecified, but presumably male). At the University of British Columbia, as at most universities, sex of organizational authority is distinctly male: most professors are men and most research projects are conducted by men.

official policy of multiculturalism is taught in schools and emphasized daily through various media. As a result, the overall level of prejudice is probably lower than in most other countries. But another (unintended) consequence of this policy is that people are quite reluctant to talk about perceptions based on ethnicity. Thus, the prejudice and stereotyping that remain take subtle forms. In this study we took a corresponding cautious approach to activating ethnicity in terms of the cues provided. We also emphasized behavioural measures, on the assumption that they are more accurate indicators than verbal responses. Our study can thus be seen as an initial step: in the future it would be worthwhile to conduct a series of experiments with more cues about ethnicity and with more direct questions about it, to establish where reactivity would start. This would also provide a larger picture of ethnicity effects in Canada.

The study may also be seen within the context of the role of legislation in intergroup relations. In addition to the Multiculturalism Act, Canada has progressive employment equity legislation. But as important as legislation is, it reflects ideals rather than reality. In general, laws are an effective but slow way of changing that reality. Besides, legislation cannot cover the entire repertoire of workplace interactions involving ethnicity. For example, a person may be hired but still treated in day-to-day evaluations as having inferior competence; as in the present experiment, most jobs include tasks where that is possible because there are no objective evaluation criteria. Studies such as the present one serve to document the extent of the gap between legislation and perceptions. Recent immigration trends are also relevant here. These show that a large number of newcomers belong to visible minorities. Since these are precisely the groups reported to be experiencing the most difficulties in the workplace, it is particularly important to understand and document how these groups fare in terms of perceptions of competence. As noted earlier, status generalization research offers singular theoretical and methodological strengths for the study of this issue.

Finally, the research presented here also relates to the larger question of how status-based inequalities are maintained. As noted earlier, our interpretation in terms of subjects' perceived ability to evaluate relative to the experimenter does not rule out the possibility that women discriminate less than men on the basis of status characteristics. That is, women in this experiment could have followed instructions more closely than men because they thought that that was the fair thing to do, and because they cared more than men about being fair in a situation involving status characteristics. In future experiments it would be interesting to investigate the extent to which a given status order is accepted by both high- and low- status members. In the interest of generalizing the findings, it would be a good idea to explore this issue with other status characteristics, such as social class and level of education.

REFERENCES

Aboud, Frances E. and Donald M. Taylor

1971 "Ethnic and role stereotypes: Their relative importance in person perception." *Journal of Social Psychology* 85: 17-27.

Berger, Joseph, M. Hamit Fisek, Robert Z. Norman, and Morris Zelditch, Jr.

1977 *Status Characteristics and Social Interaction: An Expectation-States Approach.* New York: Elsevier.

Berger, Joseph, David G. Wagner, and Morris Zelditch, Jr.

1985 "Introduction: Expectation states theory—Review and assessment." In Joseph Berger and Morris Zelditch, Jr., eds., *Status, Rewards and Influence: How Expectations Organize Behavior*, pp. 1-72. San Francisco: Jossey-Bass.

Bienvenue, Rita M. and Jay E. Goldstein, eds.

1985 *Ethnicity and Ethnic Relations in Canada: A Book of Readings.* Toronto: Butterworths, 2nd ed.

Buchignani, Norman, Doreen M. Indra, and Ram Srivastiva

1985 *Continuous Journey: A Social History of South Asians in Canada. Toronto:* McClelland and Stewart. Clifton, Rodney A.

1981 "Ethnicity, teachers' expectations, and the academic achievement process in Canada." *Sociology of Education* 54: 291–301.

Clifton, Rodney A. and Raymond Perry

1985 "Has ethnic prejudice increased in Winnipeg schools? A comparison of Bogardus social distance scales in 1971 and 1981." *Canadian Ethnic Studies* 17: 72–80.

Cohen, Elizabeth G.

1982 "Expectation states and interracial interaction in school settings." *Annual Review of Sociology* 8: 209–235.

Cook, Thelma S.

1975 "Producing equal status interaction between Indian and White boys in British Columbia: An application of expectation training." Ph.D. Dissertation, School of Education, Stanford University.

Driedger, Leo and Rodney A. Clifton

1984 "Ethnic stereotypes: Images of ethnocentrism, reciprocity or dissimilarity?" *Canadian Review of Sociology and Anthropology* 21: 287–301.

Driedger, Leo and Richard A. Mezoff

1981 "Ethnic prejudice and discrimination in Winnipeg high schools." *Canadian Journal of Sociology* 6: 1–17.

Earn, Brian and Shelagh Towson, eds.

1986 *Readings in Social Psychology: Classic and Canadian Contributions.* Peterborough, Ontario: Broadview Press.

Foddy, Margaret

1988 "Paths of relevance and evaluative competence." In Murray Webster, Jr. and Martha Foschi, eds., *Status Generalization: New Theory and Research,* pp. 232–247 and 501. Stanford: Stanford University Press.

Foschi, Martha and Sabrina Freeman

1987 "Inferior performance, standards, and influence in same-sex dyads." Paper presented at the Annual Meeting of the American Sociological Association, Washington, D.C.

Foschi, Martha, G. Keith Warriner, and Stephen D. Hart

1985 "Standards, expectations, and interpersonal influence." *Social Psychology Quarterly* 48: 108–117.

Fry, P.S. and R. Ghosh

1980 "Attributions of success and failure: Comparison of cultural differences between Asian and Caucasian children." *Journal of Cross-Cultural Psychology* 11: 343–353.

Gardner, Robert C. and Rudolf Kalin, eds.

1981 *A Canadian Social Psychology of Ethnic Relations.* Toronto: Methuen.

Gardner, R.C., D.M. Taylor, and H.J. Feenstra

1970 "Ethnic stereotypes: Attitudes or beliefs?" *Canadian Journal of Psychology* 24: 321–334.

Goldstein, Jay

1978 "The prestige of Canadian ethnic groups: Some new evidence." *Canadian Ethnic Studies* 10: 84–96.

Henry, Frances and Effie Ginzberg

1985 *Who Gets the Work: A Test of Racial Discrimination in Employment.* Toronto: The Urban Alliance on Race Relations and The Social Planning Council of Metropolitan Toronto.

Isajiw, Wsevolod W.

1985 "Definitions of ethnicity." In Rita M. Bienvenue and Jay E. Goldstein, eds., *Ethnicity and Ethnic Relations in Canada: A Book of Readings,* pp. 5–17. Toronto: Butterworths, 2nd ed.

Kalin, Rudolf and Donald S. Rayko

1978 "Discrimination in evaluative judgments against foreign-accented job candidates." *Psychological Reports* 43: 1203–1209.

Kalin, R., D.S. Rayko, and N. Love

1980 "The perception and evaluation of job candidates with four different ethnic accents." In Howard Giles, W. Peter Robinson, and Philip Smith, eds., *Language: Social Psychological Perspectives,* pp. 197–202. Oxford: Pergamon Press.

Krauter, Joseph F. and Morris Davis

1978 *Minority Canadians: Ethnic Groups.* Toronto: Methuen. Labovitz, Sanford

1974 "Some evidence of Canadian ethnic, racial, and sexual antagonism." *Canadian Review of Sociology and Anthropology* 11: 247–254.

Lambert, Wallace E., Hannah Frankel, and G. Richard Tucker

1966 "Judging personality through speech: A French-Canadian example." *Journal of Communication* 16: 305–321.

Lambert, W.E., R.C. Hodgson, R.C. Gardner, and S. Fillenbaum

1960 "Evaluational reactions to spoken languages." *Journal of Abnormal and Social Psychology* 60: 44–51.

Lambert, Wallace E., Lambros Mermigis, and Donald M. Taylor

1986 "Greek Canadians' attitudes toward own group and other Canadian ethnic groups: A test of the multiculturalism hypothesis." *Canadian Journal of Behavioural Science* 18: 35–51.

Li, Peter S.

1979 "Prejudice against Asians in a Canadian city." *Canadian Ethnic Studies* 11: 70–77.

Mackie, Marlene

1974 "Ethnic stereotypes and prejudice—Alberta Indians, Hutterites, and Ukrainians." *Canadian Ethnic Studies* 6: 39–52.

Moore, James C., Jr.

1968 "Status and influence in small group interactions." *Sociometry* 31: 47–63.

Open, Christopher

1981 "Causal attributions for the success and failure of Black and White managers." *Journal of Occupational Behavior* 2: 81–87.

Riches, Phoebe and Margaret Foddy

1989 "Ethnic accent as a status cue." *Social Psychology Quarterly* 52:197–206.

Ridgeway, Cecilia L.

1982 "Status in groups: The importance of motivation." *American Sociological Review* 47: 76–88.

1988 "Gender differences in task groups: A status and legitimacy account." In Murray Webster, Jr. and Martha Foschi, eds., *Status Generalization: New Theory and Research,* pp. 188-206 and 495–497. Stanford: Stanford University Press.

Robson, R.A.H. and Brad Breems

1985 *Ethnic Conflict in Vancouver.* Vancouver: B.C. Civil Liberties Association.

Rosenholtz, Susan J. and Elizabeth G. Cohen

1985 "Activating ethnic status." In Joseph Berger and Morris Zelditch, Jr., eds., *Status, Rewards, and Influence: How Expectations Organize Behavior,* pp. 430–444. San Francisco: Jossey-Bass.

Tuzlak, Aysan and James C. Moore, Jr.

1984 "Status, demeanor and influence: An empirical reassessment." *Social Psychology Quarterly* 47: 178–183.

Webster, Murray, Jr. and James E. Driskell, Jr.

1978 "Status generalization: A review and some new data." *American Sociological Review* 43: 220–236.

Webster, Murray, Jr. and Martha Foschi

1988 "Overview of status generalization." In Murray Webster, Jr. and Martha Foschi, eds., *Status Generalization: New Theory and Research,* pp. 1–20 and 477–478. Stanford: Stanford University Press.

Yuchtman-Yaar, Ephraim and Moshe Semyonov

1979 "Ethnic inequality in Israeli schools and sports: An expectation-states approach." *American Journal of Sociology* 85: 576–590.

Section V

QUALITATIVE DATA COLLECTION

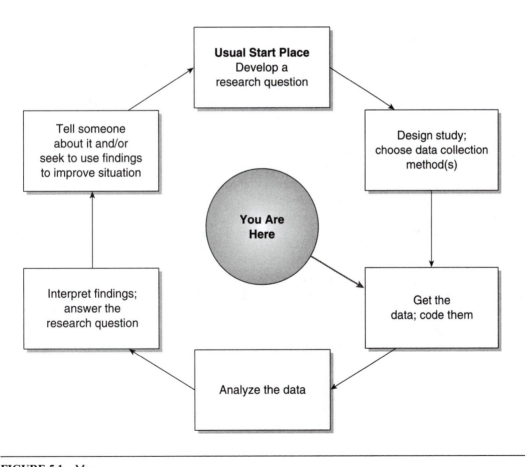

FIGURE 5.1 Map

As we discussed in Section IV, one of the great strengths of quantitative data collection methods is that they are reliable. That is, the pattern of results that is yielded by these research methods tends to remain consistent and predictable across different studies. By reducing complex social phenomena to patterns of concise and focused measures, preferably under controlled circumstances in which the time and place of the study have little to no impact, we are able to get a close reading of attitudes, opinions, and recent behaviors. Following the **positivist paradigm**, certain quantitative data collection methods seek to measure patterns of data that are so consistent within a given society that they might seem almost like behavioral laws.

Nonetheless, context matters. The observable fact that people's feelings and behaviors change as they move through different parts of their lives and interact with different people means that these things have no single, "true" meaning. It means that we need methods of measuring phenomena as they occur, in the social world. This is the principle assumption of the **naturalist paradigm**. It may be useful, for example, to know what people *think* they would do in some stressful situation, but that doesn't mean that they would actually do it. A naturalist approach to research, therefore, requires different methods than a positivist approach.

There are two key issues in selecting a naturalist approach over a positivist one. First, there are limits to **self-report** data. People don't always know enough about their motivations or feelings to really tell us what we want to know or to anticipate what they would do. So a survey of simple questions can measure how one feels at the moment that the question is asked, not in a "real" situation. There is also something inherently artificial about research itself that also threatens the validity of our findings. Asking questions leads respondents to think about things in particular ways, which means that they will think differently about them as a direct result of the research itself. There is a self-consciousness

to that, and therefore a difference between how people think about something when we call their attention to it and how they think about it the rest of the time. The farther we remove the respondents from the contexts of their daily lives, the more we need to worry about such effects. Observable actions in their normal contexts are less conscious, and therefore reveal different things. Each kind of measure has its place, and each has its limitations.

The second issue is depth. There are things that we want to know that are qualities of thought and action, feeling and impression. *What* people think can be quantified. *Why* they think that is more naturally a matter of deeper qualities. In such circumstances we might allow, and even go beyond the kind of self-consciousness that we were just concerned with, to really challenge respondents to explain themselves and their responses. (By challenge, we don't mean attack, but rather to stay on a single topic longer while we probe its meaning more fully.)

In this section we will explore three qualitative data collection methods: interviews, focus groups, and observations. Two of them, interviews and focus groups, are designed to allow for the deep exploration of meanings and ideas. Observation research techniques, on the other hand, are intended to be much more **unobtrusive**, and therefore more naturalistic. Content analysis will be covered in Section VII.

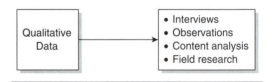

FIGURE 5.2   Qualitative Methods

INTERVIEWS

An interview is a conversation with a purpose. The essence of it is that the researcher asks a lot of questions and the interview **subject**—the respondent—answers. But that description alone would be misleading. For one thing, interviews tend to be more about discovery than about the recording of facts. Often, the conversation between the researcher and the subject will lead to answers that even the subject was not aware of initially. While some interviews can be highly **structured**, following a strict script of particular questions, most tend to be **semistructured** or **unstructured**. In an unstructured interview, the researcher begins with a set of topics or issues that must be covered, but allows the interview subjects to lead the conversation in whatever direction makes the most sense to them. One can then record 10, 20, or 100 interviews on the same topic and each one will be a unique experience.

In our first reading for this section, Cecilia Menjívar's study of the role of religion in the lives of Salvadorans in the United States, the author conducted more than 100 interviews with subjects in two different churches across three cities. No individual interview subject could address the central question on the relationship between the churches and the community. But collectively they provided a pattern of responses that allows the researcher to examine similarities and differences across the different settings. When Menjívar concludes, for example, that the Catholic Church plays a significantly different role in the lives of Salvadorans as immigrants than do the Evangelical churches, and that these roles are rooted in different concepts of the relationship between religion and politics, this conclusion is not a summary of the beliefs of her subjects on this question. It is an analysis of the pattern of responses given by each subject to the question of the role of religion in their own lives.

Note that in the examples that Menjívar provides of their responses, the individual subjects have their own ways of defining the role of the church in their lives. They each have their own language, their own stories of pivotal events in their own lives, and their own explanations for what they view as appropriate or desirable church-led activities. From this mosaic of different voices,

the author weaves a coherent narrative that addresses her research questions in the language of sociology. There is a difference, therefore, between what we ask and what we discover.

Before introducing the data, the author establishes some background on the lives of immigrants generally and Salvadoran immigrants in particular, along with the state of our understanding of the role of religion in immigrants' lives. This establishes the context of what she wishes to study. (See "Reviewing the Literature" in Section I.) The interview process, then, becomes a guided conversation on topics of interest to the researcher, but in the language and perspectives of each subject. It is the research participants, and not the interviewer, who choose which stories best exemplify the role of their church in the community. But it is the researcher who frames these stories, in this case using Max Weber's notions of sense making and uprootedness.

FOCUS GROUPS

Like interviews, **focus group** discussions involve respondents answering questions posed by researchers. In this case, however, the conversation involves a group of subjects together, generally one that was brought together due to some shared experience or background. Like interviews, focus groups yield deeper discussions and open-ended stories related to the topic of interest that may be coded and analyzed in depth. The unique element of the focus group, however, is the group dynamic. Here, rather than simply recording what people have to say about a topic, the researcher primarily attends to how group members respond to each other's responses. Among other things, the researcher might want to distinguish among the comments that most groups members agree with, and those that they fight over. It is often worth noting the direction of the conversation. Did the group move from a range of ideas toward *consensus* around a particular idea or perspective? Did group members begin with compatible positions and fall into disagreement? Did one idea or contribution suddenly draw the group from disagreement into agreement? When that happens, we refer to it as *resonance,* and take it as an indication that certain ideas have more power than others in the group's thinking.

Focus groups are most often associated with forms of marketing, such as advertising and politics. In marketing research, the goal is to find words and ideas that are capable of persuading large numbers of people. Generally, in social research, our goals are different. We seek a better understanding of how people think about various issues. This is not often something that we can learn just by asking. (Try it: Think about a song or television show that you used to like but aren't interested in anymore. Can you really explain why you once felt the way you did and why that changed? Can you put into words the feelings that you no longer feel?) Interestingly, if you were in a conversation with other people who had different tastes than your own, chances are good that as the conversation developed, you would find ways to explain your thoughts to the group. Having an audience, and having the desire to communicate clearly to them, requires different conversational strategies than a one-on-one discussion. In this way, a focus group can often yield much richer data on justifications, explanations, and thought processes than other techniques.

In our next reading, Alan Lewis takes full advantage of this kind of interaction to explore his research on how "morality" affects investment decisions. His questions for this focus group subjects center on the investment decisions themselves. His data collection, on the other hand, centers on statements of motivation. These motivations are first divided into ethical/nonethical categories, and further analyzed terms of the specific goals and justifications offered. These, in turn, are compared to the theoretically derived categories of "economically rational behavior" and "green" behavior.

Most of the investors in Lewis's study offer relatively straightforward explanations for their investment decisions. But, beyond those, many of the subjects exhibit concern for how their decisions sound to others. And so, through the process of the group discussion, they tend to justify or qualify their positions. As Lewis notes, "Ethical investors were reluctant to agree to any characterization, direct or implied, that could impute 'economically rational' interests to themselves" (p. 336). Yet, "even 'standard' (nonethical) investors are faintly embarrassed by the notion that they invest primarily, for income and capital growth. 'Precaution,' 'foresight,' avoiding being a 'burden to others' in old age and the motive to bequeath are frequently mentioned by ethical and nonethical investors alike" (p. 339).

Box 5.1 Robert K. Merton (1910–2003)

When National Public Radio announced the passing of Robert K. Merton on Sunday, February 23, 2003, they referred to him as "Mr. Sociology." This is a small recognition for a man who over much of the twentieth century dominated the social sciences in the United States. Merton's many accolades are too numerous to list here. Suffice it to say that he was a key player in the development of the Columbia School of Sociology and that university's Bureau of Applied Social Research. He was closely associated with the diffusion of structural-functionalism as one of the discipline's dominant paradigms.

With regard to methodology, Merton made at least four pathbreaking contributions. The first was the development of the focus group as a strategy to collect information in group settings, which Merton introduced to measure the impact of radio propaganda during the final years of World War II. Today, versions of this process have been institutionalized into market and political research as well as social research. Merton's second contribution was to focus our analysis on a middle level—between the individual and the society as a whole. This allowed him to pay close attention to mechanisms in society operating at the group or smaller organizational level (the middle level of analysis). Correspondingly, Merton was also associated with the promotion of "middle range theories," a theoretical device that calls for an explanation of measurable evidence, as opposed to grand or macro theories. Finally, Merton made significant contributions to the sociology of knowledge and the sociology of science, a field close to his heart. As part of this research, he developed the concept of serendipity to illustrate how major scientific discoveries sometimes happened by chance while we research something else, if our minds are open to the unexpected and unexplained.

FIELDWORK

In Section II we introduced the idea of fieldwork, or field research, and discussed the challenges associated with **gaining entry** to a field site. Suppose you have chosen your site and negotiated entry. Now what? How do you choose your own role in the field? Data collection in the field may be considered along a continuum from the least intrusive observations—where the researcher stays out of the way and takes notes—to the most involved ethnographic studies involving combinations of interviews, observations, and the analysis of social artifacts (e.g., looking through people's garbage).

Observational studies are the most *naturalist* of our methods, and the most anthropological. The goal of these techniques is for researchers to immerse themselves in a social setting, **blending in** as much as possible, and to notice what happens, when it happens, and how it happens. Preferably, your presence as the researcher should have little effect on the setting, and so the behaviors that you observe and record can be assumed to be a valid reflection of what "normally" happens in this setting.

Consider the topic of group relations in a work place. If the formal job descriptions for the staff in some office included cooperating with one another, then staff would have an incentive to emphasize how much they cooperate if they were asked. They would also have a great incentive to act in a cooperative manner in the presence of their bosses. But if you could be a "fly on the wall" in some office, observing without judgment or impact on the setting, you might well find that there are measurable patterns to the kinds of cooperation that occur or don't. Some individuals might not be very helpful. Some will be very cooperative with some people but not others, or great early in the morning but terrible by late afternoon. Some staff members may be relatively ostracized and receive little cooperation from anyone. Further, if you were to repeat such observations across many different types of offices, you might find consistent patterns within these data; that regardless of the unique and highly personal dynamics that can occur anywhere, certain characteristics tend to be associated with effectively soliciting cooperation or failing to do so. In highly gendered occupations, for example, members of the minority gender might have the most trouble. Under conditions of high stress and tight resources, on the other hand, staff might keep careful track of who has helped them in the past before deciding how much help to offer to others.

Observations may be either **participatory** or **nonparticipatory**. In either case, observation research should not be confused with going undercover or intruding on people's privacy. Even in the hypothetical office study above, the researcher might not tell the observed subjects that he or she is interested in cooperation, but they would still have to know that a researcher is present. A participant observer might volunteer to work part-time in the office, performing some identifiable task while also asking research questions about all of the other stuff that goes on there. A researcher with experience writing grant applications, for example, might volunteer to help a small nonprofit organization get outside funding. In exchange for this help, the researcher would be allowed to conduct research from "inside" the organization.

Nonparticipant observation is extremely difficult to do within a private setting, such as an organization. But it can be one of the richest, most creative approaches to research in a public setting, and few research projects have done more with observational studies than the "Mass-Observation Project." Launched in England in the 1930s, and cut short by World War II, the Project simply envisioned the observation of everything by everyone and anyone. In a direct and deliberate challenge to the academic assumptions that only certain subjects were worthy of serious study, and that only trained professionals could do it, Mass-Observation sought to document and analyze the ordinary details of ordinary, everyday life.[1] To assist in this, they recruited the best available experts in the topic—ordinary people.

The next reading is from Mass-Observation's analysis of *The Pub and the People*. Using both trained ethnographers and local volunteers, combining long "native" experience within the working-class neighborhood that they're studying with a fresh "outsider" perspective, the researchers offer a detailed and nuanced examination of the people of "Worktown," their habits, interests, values, and concerns as seen through the shared social world of the pub. Why pubs? "Of the social institutions that mould men's lives between home and work in an industrial town, such as Worktown, the pub has more buildings, holds more people, takes more of their time and money, than church, cinema, dance-hall, and political organizations put together" (p. 17).

Through casual observations, the researchers and their team reveal the complexity of the role of the pub in the lives of the people they are studying, which of course reveals much about the complexity of their lives. What goes on in a pub?

> It is no more true to say that people go to public houses to drink than it is to say that they go to private homes to eat and sleep. . . . These things are often connected with pubs: weddings and funerals; quarrels and fights; bowls, fishing and picnics; trade unions; secret societies, Oddfellows, Buffs; religious processions; sex; getting jobs; crime and prostitution; dog shows; pigeon flying. People sell and buy: bootlaces, hot pies, black puddings, embrocation. (pp. 19–20, grammar altered for clarity)

ENTERING A FIELD SITE

If our research involves fieldwork, then the researcher faces an additional set of challenges. Numerous questions arise: Where to go? How to gain access? How to present oneself in the field? How and when to exit the field?

Sociologists give names to some of the strategies used to negotiate these challenges. **Gaining entry**, for example, often requires (1) conducting enough nonparticipant observation of the site to develop a rough mapping of the informal social structure at work there; (2) identifying **gatekeepers** who can ease our entry or bar our way; and (3) choosing **key informants** who can guide us through the site with insider's knowledge. Presenting ourselves in the field requires us to take on recognizable social roles within the community or setting, including the role of "researcher." As researchers, we must be honest about who we are and why we are there.

---

[1]In their Introduction to the study excerpted here, one of the project originators acknowledges that they were drawing in part on the model of "The Chicago School" ethnographies of the same time period.

But we must also develop other relations with people in that setting, and hopefully establish a kind of "rapport" with them that will encourage them to cooperate with our work.

Mitch Duneier's ethnography, *Sidewalk,* documents both the lives of sidewalk booksellers in New York City and the complex, shifting relations that the author experienced hanging out with and studying his subjects. Uniquely, as our next selection shows, Duneier also asked his key informant, Hakim Hasan to write an afterword to the study. Although Hasan is not an ethnographer or a sociologist—he's a street-side dealer in used books—his essay describes from the subject's perspective all of the steps that the researcher must undergo in order to enter a community and find his or her place within it. Complementing Duneier's self-awareness as an outsider trying to fit into a small world bounded by significant differences of class, race, and even religion, Hasan describes his own changing feelings about becoming someone else's research project. His reflections provide a crucial and often overlooked dimension of the process of doing research among those whom we often call our "human subjects."

CONCLUSION

The excerpt from Mass-Observation presented here captures only the nonparticipant observation portion of the study. The complete project of *The Pub and the People* is a detailed, multiple-method ethnography. Researchers participated in regular activities in the community, spoke with residents about themselves and those activities, and read the newspapers and local flyers, ads, and other writings. Where the observations provide descriptive material about people's lives that the researchers can analyze and interpret, the complete ethnography incorporates the residents' own interpretations. In both cases, as with both the interview and focus group techniques presented here, the data collection methods follow a naturalist paradigm. Researchers seek to maximize the validity of their data by recording the words and behaviors of their subjects in "real" contexts. Such techniques allow a kind of collaboration between the researcher and the subjects in the act of giving meaning to the data. We use these approaches to get past the *what* of our topics and into the *why*.

DISCUSSION QUESTIONS

1. Why is it so important to be careful of what you record in your field notes? What are the dangers of others seeing those notes? Hint: Consider: friends and family, law enforcement officials, lawyers, and public health officials.

2. What is the one special advantage of focus group research that is not available from other forms of interviewing? How would you deal with the effect of your presence in a group you wish to study?

WEB RESOURCES

The following links can provide you with more detailed information on the topics discussed in this section. You may also go to www.sagepub.com/lunestudy where you will find additional resources and hot-links to these sources.

Berkeley Center for Urban Ethnography: http://cue.berkeley.edu
University of Michigan Survey Research Center: http://www.isr.umich.edu/home/centers
The Focus Group Center: http://www.mnav.com/qualitative_research.htm
Case Western Applied Social Research: http://msass.case.edu/faculty/jfloersch/qualitativemethods.html

Religion and Immigration in Comparative Perspective

Catholic and Evangelical Salvadorans in San Francisco, Washington, D.C., and Phoenix (2004)

*Cecilia Menjívar**

In this article I examine religious institutions in the lives of Salvadoran immigrants, focusing on how they view their participation in the church and the role the church plays in their lives. Religious rituals infuse important events in the immigrants' lives with transcendental meaning, but religious institutions also respond in practical terms to the immigrants' needs and afflictions. Thus, religion is highly significant for immigrants—past and present, an idea that lies at the core of the sociological study of immigration and religion (Warner 1998:15). Consequently, religious participation was a major theme in sociological studies of turn-of-the-last

century immigration, when the church occupied a prominent place in the lives of immigrants through the provision of an intricate welfare system to serve the needs of many newcomers. The massive migration of Catholics, Jews, and German Lutherans contributed to increase the sociological relevance of religious identity itself (Warner 1993:1058).

This earlier research interest gave way to new foci in studies of post-1965 immigration. These have concentrated on the ever-increasing diversity that "new" immigrants have brought to American soil, their participation in the labor force, the sociodemographic composition of the

SOURCE: "Religion and Immigration in Comparative Perspective: Catholic and Evangelical Salvadorans in San Francisco, Washington, D.C., and Phoenix" by Menjívar, C., in *Sociology of Religion 64*(1):21–45. Copyright © 2003. Reprinted with permission of the Association for the Study of Religion.

*Direct correspondence to: Cecilia Menjívar, School of Justice Studies, Arizona State University, Tempe, AZ 85287–0403, e-mail: menjivar@asu.edu. Several individuals and institutions assisted me at different stages in the making of this article. I held a Chancellor's Post-doctoral Fellowship at the University of California, Berkeley, a grant from the Pews Charitable Trusts to Anna Peterson, Manuel Vasquez, and Phillip Williams supported research in Washington, D.C., and I received grants from the Center for Urban Inquiry and the Dean's Incentive Grant at Arizona State University. Research assistants for this project were: Carmen Albertos, Carlos Ramírez, Eugene Arène, Cindy Bejarano, Michelle Moran-Taylor, Eddie Portillos and Emily Skop. I presented earlier versions of this article at the Center for Comparative immigration Studies, University of California-San Diego, and at Arizona State University. Helen Rose Ebaugh, Victor Agadjanian, those who attended my semina at UC-San Diego and at Arizona State University, and three anonymous reviewers provided me with excellent comments and suggestions. And Mary Fran Draisker, as usual, prepared the different versions of the manuscript. Copyright © 2003 EBSCO Publishing.

[1]There have been several explanations for the paucity of studies of religion among recent immigrants, which Ebaugh and Chafetz (2000:15) discuss at length.

flows, the effects of immigration policy on the immigrants' lives, family and gender relations, and social networks among these immigrants (Menjívar 1999).[1] These new foci do not mean that religion is no longer important for immigrants. Religious institutions have remained central in immigrant life, as reflected in a recent resurgence of studies of immigrant religious communities (Kim 1991; Kim 1994; Warner and Wittner 1998; Menjívar 1999; Ebaugh and Chafetz 2000; Levitt 2001). As Herberg (1960) observed in *Protestant, Catholic, Jew,* religion is a fundamental category of identity and association in society through which immigrants can find a place in American life. Thus, religion still provides an important lens to understand immigrant life as well as the place of immigrants in the receiving society.

Following the tradition of recent scholarship on religion and immigration (cf. Warner and Wittner 1998; Ebaugh and Chafetz 2000), the present study focuses on "what immigrants do together religiously in the United States" (Warner 1998:5), what they do for and within their congregations. Sociologically this is important, as through this lens we can examine how immigrant communities are developing and, thus, we can avoid a focus simply on individual action and perception. Recognizing the importance of a comparative perspective that the work of Ebaugh and Chafetz (2000) has revealed, this study compares the same immigrant group in three different locations and within these sites in two different types of congregations. This approach permits us to hold constant certain factors and examine the effects of those that vary; it also allows us to bridge insights gained from recent scholarship in the field of religion and immigration with those from immigration research more generally.

Immigration research has pointed to the context of reception—shaped by immigration policies, the local labor market and the organization of the receiving community—as key in understanding processes of immigrant incorporation (Portes and Zhou 1993; Portes and Rumbaut 1996; Menjívar 2000). And Rollwagen (1975) criticized the assumption that cities are similar and thus the city in which immigrants settle has no impact on their lives. Based on these analytical insights, in this study I examine the role of religious institutions in the lives of Salvadoran immigrants in three cities—San Francisco, Washington, D.C. and Phoenix—a comparison that offers a unique opportunity to look at the same immigrant group in dissimilar local contexts to disentangle the effects that receiving communities may have on the role of religious institutions in immigrant life.

Although the immigration policies that Salvadorans have encountered do not differ by location, and local economies have tended to offer them similar opportunities, local community dynamics differ across destination points. San Francisco is a well-established receiving area for Salvadorans and the city with the longest continuous history of Salvadoran migration to the United States (Menjívar 2000). Washington, D.C. is a relatively new destination point, with the overwhelming majority of Salvadorans having arrived in the past two decades. Yet Washington is the only U.S. city where Salvadorans comprise the majority of the Latino population. Finally, Phoenix differs from the other two cities in that it is one of the newest points of destination for Salvadorans—the majority having arrived either directly from El Salvador or from California in the 1990s—and they constitute a minority of the Latino population. These diverse configurations could result in different perceptions by location that Salvadoran immigrants may have about their participation in religious institutions and about the church in their lives.

Within the broader comparison of the three receiving points, I examine two churches—Catholic and Evangelical—and their doctrines and organizational structures. In making this comparison I do not mean to convey a monolithic image of either Catholic or Evangelical churches, as there exist variations of each.[2] The common thread among the Evangelical churches in this study is that they ground their approach on biblical authority and emphasize personal choice and individual strategies for any projects they undertake. Whereas the teachings and institutional structures of churches are different, in the end both Catholic and Evangelical help the immigrants to achieve their goals (be they basic survival, socioeconomic advancement in the United States, or connections to their home communities) and to cope (materially and spiritually) with the difficulties in their lives. An important question that emerges is whether these religious institutions impact differently the long-term objectives of the immigrants in the host society. Although I do not have longitudinal data to assess the effects of the different paths that Catholics and Evangelicals follow, based on the comparative analysis of this study I will, in the last section of this article, point to some possible outcomes. All the churches in this study have high proportions of immigrants and they tend to respond to the immigrants' needs, therefore their approach may only be representative of those congregations with immigrant concentrations.

The Salvadoran case is particularly suitable for examining the questions posed in this study. Religious congregations—Catholic and Evangelical, as well as other denominations—have been pivotal before, during, and after the twelve-year civil war in El Salvador (approximately 1979 to 1991), during which thousands of Salvadorans fled. In the United States, the Catholic Church—along with mainline Protestant denominations—has filled the vacuum of government assistance for these *de facto* refugees and has been actively involved in improving their lives. These churches have offered Salvadoran immigrants the assistance and protection that the U.S. government has

refused to extend them. They created sanctuaries throughout the country to protect them from deportation to life-threatening conditions in their homeland, have provided settlement assistance, championed the legal struggle that eventually granted Temporary Protected Status to Salvadorans and an opportunity to resubmit asylum applications *(American Baptist Churches v. Thornburgh* court decision passed in 1990), and issued pastoral calls to remind Catholics to welcome immigrants into their communities. Evangelical churches did not create a similar infrastructure of support and they lacked the infrastructure that permits the Catholic Church to coordinate efforts at the national, and even international, levels. Nonetheless, their role in the immigrants' lives has been central. In this case, newcomers themselves have established churches and have opened up their new temples to welcome their brothers and sisters in need. Thus, given the involvement of religious workers in the Salvadorans' lives, it is likely that these immigrants' views of religious institutions will differ from those of other contemporary immigrants. The Salvadorans' experience is perhaps more similar to that of turn-of-the-last century immigrants who arrived at a time when no government resettlement programs were available and it was the church that provided institutional assistance for immigrants in need. From this vantage point, the Salvadoran case provides a good opportunity for close examination of how religious institutions still impact immigrants' lives and their prospects in the host society.

IMMIGRANTS, RELIGION, AND THE HOST SOCIETY

According to Max Weber, religion creates a "meaningful cosmos of a world experienced as

---

[2]Recently a small, but growing, literature has explored the complexities in Evangelicalism, which tempers the stark contrast between political activism among Catholics and Evangelicals. This new literature steers away from portraying Evangelicalism as uniformly conservative in its political and social views, and focuses on how Evangelical churches have been a force behind social change. Brusco's work (1995) on Evangelicalism altering women's position in Colombia and Smith and Haas's (1997) analysis of the participation of Evangelicals in revolutionary politics in Nicaragua illustrate this more nuanced view.

specifically senseless" (Gerth and Mills 1946:218), a view especially applicable to immigrants' lives. Immigration involves crossing not only territorial borders, but also the physical, social, cultural, and psychological borders that shape and define relations, systems of meaning, membership, and worldviews of everyday experiences (Berger and Luckmann 1966; Berger 1967). In fact, Smith (1978) argued that immigration itself is often a "theologizing experience" because religion provides an ethical slant and the resources that nourish the immigrants' outlook as they react to the confusion and alienation that result from their uprooting.

Religion offers important psychological comfort to immigrants, however, it also plays an important institutional role—providing an anchorage for people undergoing the process of resettlement in a foreign land (Gleason 1992:168). Immigrants are not only already familiar with the churches they come to join or found, but also the church is perhaps one of the most supportive and welcoming institutions for immigrants, particularly for those who face extremely difficult circumstances. Many churches offer the newcomers material and financial support, as well as legal counsel, access to medical care and housing, a lobby for less stringent immigration policies, and a welcome from the non-immigrant members. To reach out to newcomers, churches also incorporate popular religious practices that are culturally essential for the immigrants. Immigrants create new religious spaces, new churches and congregations—such as storefront Evangelical congregations—and bring new expressions of the faith to long-established churches. Thus, in efforts to become relevant to the newcomers, established churches—like the Catholic and other mainline congregations—do not remain static. Responding to needs of the new flock, churches themselves are changing and new ones are being created, so that in the interaction between new immigrants and the receiving society's religious spaces transformation occurs both ways.

Given the importance of religious institutions and practices in the lives of immigrants—past and present—scholars have examined religious participation in terms of its contribution (or lack thereof) to assimilation, as well as to the ability of immigrants to maintain ties to their communities of origin. Some researchers have sought to clarify the role of religious institutions in the integration of immigrants, as well as the effects of religious affiliation on immigrants' socioeconomic success and political integration (Gleason 1968; Nelli 1970; Litt 1970). Others have focused on the role of the ethnic parish in helping newcomers retain their cultural heritage in their adopted country (Dolan 1975; Gleason 1968) and in holding immigrant groups together (Tomasi 1970). Whereas some scholars have argued that a church with close ties to the home country may hinder immigrants' assimilation (Mullins 1987) and that some religious doctrines may slow down integration or Americanization (Barnouw 1937; Mol 1961), others such as W. I. Thomas (Janowitz 1966), have noted that institutions like the church, rather than isolating newcomers from American life, actually provide the organizational vehicles that allow them to participate in it. Some have even argued that a powerful religious conviction may be a valued asset for adjustment and may serve to prevent "personal disorganization" (Mol 1961:11).

Generally, the broader context where immigrants arrive is crucial for their initial adaptation and eventual incorporation into the host society. Immigration policies define who stands within and outside the law and dictate rights to the labor market and, thus, determine whether immigrants will become full members of society or become some of its most destitute members. The local economy determines whether immigrants have access to and the kinds of jobs available and, thus, impacts the immigrants' short- and long-term opportunities. The immediate community links the micro-level worlds of everyday life to broader forces (Menjívar 2000). At this level religious communities have played a key role, as they mediate the effects of broader structures on the lives of the immigrants. Together these factors of the context of reception shape the immigrants' lives, the resources available to them and, generally, their structure of opportunities.

Although the context of reception is crucial, immigrants have always maintained ties with their communities of origin while simultaneously attempting to become part of the host society. With modern innovations in transportation and communication technology and the increasing global economic interdependence of contemporary capitalism, many of today's immigrants can more easily remain active in their homeland communities (Menjívar 1999). Immigrant churches have always played an important role in linking the immigrants' communities of origin with the new communities they enter. And recently, researchers have noted the important place of religious institutional ties for contemporary immigrants to remain connected to their origin countries (Levitt 2001; Warner and Wittner 1998; Menjívar 1999).[3] Thus, religious institutions are important not only in helping immigrants adjust in the receiving society, but also in creating spaces for them to remain actively connected to their homelands.

SOURCES OF DATA

The data for this study were gathered from 1989 through 2000. In San Francisco I undertook ethnographic fieldwork in the Salvadoran community from late 1989 to 1994, conducting 50 in-depth interviews and a survey of 150 respondents. At first I did not select congregations in this city, because the main research objective was not to study religion in the immigrants' lives. However, and importantly, in their stories my informants often made references to churches,

priests and pastors. Thus, in an inductive manner, my original conversations and observations in this site led me to contact, and then interview, two Catholic priests and one Evangelical pastor (and to spend time in their congregations). Then I went back to speak with my informants (since it was an ongoing ethnography) about the place of the church in their lives. The research objective in Washington, D.C. was to document the relationship between Salvadorans and their churches. Thus, data from this site come from qualitative observations and 25 intensive interviews and a survey of 87 respondents conducted from 1996 to 1997, in two Catholic congregations with a large Latino membership (many of them Salvadorans) and two Evangelical congregations (one having an almost all-Salvadoran membership), which generated particularly rich data.[4] And the data from Phoenix come from qualitative field research conducted between 1998 and 2000, where 25 Salvadoran immigrants were interviewed. Similar to the study in San Francisco, the aim of the research in Phoenix was to understand the social aspects of general patterns of immigration. However, in contrast to the field research in San Francisco (but similar to that in Washington), from the beginning of the fieldwork I included a focus on religion and the church and one of my research assistants and I spent a full summer doing fieldwork in two Catholic and two Evangelical congregations, Thus, informants in San Francisco were located through a variety of channels (such as churches, language schools, immigrant assistance programs, health clinics, and local businesses); in Washington, study participants were contacted through the congregations studied; and in Phoenix through a combination of both.[5]

---

[3]In the interest of space I cannot cite individually the chapters in the Warner and Wittner (1998) volume, but would like to point out that it is a helpful resource, as each chapter is dedicated to a new immigrant congregation.

[4]I have used the data from the surveys conducted in two of the research sites mainly to establish the comparability of these locations, for they were designed to compose a sociodemographic profile of the study participants.

[5]By not focusing solely on religious congregations in San Francisco and Phoenix I was able to avoid "sampling on the dependent variable" (e.g., focusing only on immigrants who participate in a congregation), and to verify that the results from Washington (where sampling was done in congregations) were not an exaggerated portrayal of how Salvadorans perceive the church in their lives.

In all three sites I asked the same basic questions about the role of religion in the immigrants' lives and about their view of the church; in Washington and Phoenix I expanded on these questions. In the three locations (in Washington and Phoenix with help from research assistants), I conducted participant observation in Evangelical and Catholic churches—as well as in the neighborhoods and communities where the immigrants lived—and spoke informally with many more individuals than those actually interviewed. In all locations I contacted (in addition to religious leaders) community workers, language instructors, staff of community clinics and social service agencies, merchants, restaurant owners, and operators of small stores that also serve as courier agencies. Although in all three sites I tried to ensure that study participants would represent different sectors of the Salvadoran population by contacting them in diverse places, the small number of informants in each site and the absence of strict randomization procedures in selecting them preclude my generalizing from these observations to all Salvadoran immigrants in those locations or elsewhere in the United States. But, in the tradition of qualitative research, these observations illuminate important linkages among local institutions, the broader contexts of reception, and the immigrants' lives.

The local contexts of the three locations differ, but there are key similarities among the informants that strengthen the comparative angle. The study participants had been residing in the three cities for no more than five years and had to be at least eighteen years of age at the time they left El Salvador. The educational attainment of the immigrants varied within each site, but not much across locales. For instance, in an almost all-Salvadoran Evangelical church in Washington, some immigrants had barely completed their elementary schooling, whereas in a different Evangelical church in the same city, there was a sizable concentration of white-collar workers. In Phoenix, there were business owners as well as immigrants with little more than the clothes on their back. But the majority

in all three cities had finished ninth grade and a few had a number of years of higher education. The types of work they performed in the three sites were remarkably similar, with more variations within sites than among them. The majority of these immigrants were primarily involved in low-paying (sometimes temporary and/or part-time) jobs in service industries, often stitching together several part-time jobs to earn no more than poverty wages. Women worked as hotel chambermaids, housekeepers, babysitters, factory and fast-food workers, and nursing home aids. The men held jobs as gardeners, construction workers, dishwashers or servers in restaurants, and as helpers in small businesses. In all three cities the study participants tended to live in unsafe neighborhoods with the usual host of problems (such as drugs and gangs), and in dilapidated housing that was not necessarily inexpensive. Most of the study participants in the three cities were either undocumented or in the process of regularizing their status. Thus, the socioeconomic standing of the immigrants in the three cities was comparable.

THE CHURCH AND THE IMMIGRANTS' PARTICIPATION IN THE RECEIVING COMMUNITIES

Many Salvadoran immigrants in the different locales have received support from Catholic and Evangelical churches. Regardless of the specific location, Salvadorans in all three cities have similar views of their participation in the church and of the role the church plays in their lives. In the words of Isabel, a Catholic in Washington, D.C., "[our] faith is very important because without it it's very difficult to survive here. . . . One finds many barriers in this country, enormous barriers . . . the language, customs, legal barriers. So our faith keeps us going. The church helps us get through all this." Marcela, in San Francisco, was concerned that she was probably sinning because she was attending both a Southern Baptist and a Catholic church, but she had found in both congregations the support she had not found in her own family. In Phoenix, Manuel, who confessed not to be religious at all, explained: "I am like the majority of human beings, we only remember the church when we have a rope around our neck. When I was coining here [during the trip] I used to pray, Oh God, let all this turn out well. I'll go to church if I make it alive. And when things are fine, I sometimes thank God. But it's not with the same fervor as when I'm asking Him for help. When you're in need, you pray, you even go to mass and talk to the priest (laughs), even if normally you're not religious, like me."

Although Salvadoran immigrants have obtained substantial help from different churches and their perceptions of the church in their lives are fairly consistent in all three cities, differences in the approaches that the Catholic and the Evangelical churches take to providing such assistance and the resources they offer emerged as more significant for the immigrants in this study. Not only do their teachings differ, but so do other institutional aspects—such as structure, size and composition—that accentuate the dissimilar ways in which they assist immigrants. For example, one of the Evangelical churches in Washington had approximately 400 members, but it later split into two. One Sunday mass I attended at a Catholic church in that city had more people than the services in two Evangelical churches combined.[6] The ethnic composition of the congregations also differed, with more diverse groups congregating in the Catholic than in some of the Evangelical churches. Due to the similarities in the views of immigrants across locales, in the following sections I will focus the comparison on the two churches and how their approaches are expressed in dissimilar institutional arrangements.

In the Catholic congregations, the "communitarian ethic" invoked by religious leaders and the membership guides efforts to reach out to and unite a large and ethnically diverse membership—not only Latinos of different nationalities but Catholic immigrants from around the world. In the Evangelical congregations (usually founded by new immigrants themselves), a focus on individual salvation leads efforts to bring the benefits of conversion to its smaller and more ethnically homogeneous flock—usually comprised of Salvadorans and other Latino groups.

The Catholic Churches

The Catholic Church's long history of assisting immigrants has continued to the present, as the experience of Salvadoran immigrants in the past two decades attests. In assisting contemporary immigrants and advocating for their rights, it is noteworthy that religious workers often have challenged U.S. immigration policies, a stance firmly rooted in religious teachings (Bau 1985; Wiltfang and McAdam 1991). This church has created centers that channel a wide range of assistance to immigrants, Catholic or not, in San Francisco and in Washington, D.C., offering immigration workshops to assist people with filling out immigration forms, with the complex process of applying and reapplying for Temporary Protected Status, and with the submission of political asylum applications. Given how recently Salvadorans have arrived in Phoenix, the Catholic Church does not provide specific services to them, but has set up campaigns to help Latino immigrants prepare applications for permanent residence and for naturalization. The church also keeps immigrants informed (sometimes in announcements at Sunday mass) of the latest developments in the often-confusing immigration laws that govern their lives, and is ready to lobby on their behalf. The Catholic Church's

---

[6]It is difficult to estimate the size of the Catholic congregations, for many people do not register in the parish. The priests would calculate an approximate number by extrapolating from the number of people in the churches' committees and church groups, as well as those who had requested sacraments.

actions in support of the immigrants have also taken place nationally, at the higher levels of leadership. Church officials have openly criticized policies that negatively affect the lives of immigrants, such as the *Illegal Immigration Reform and Immigrant Responsibility Act* and the *Welfare Reform Act of 1996,* and the Bishops Conference in 2000 made a pastoral call to respect immigrants' rights as human rights. Priests and Catholic workers do not hesitate to explain that they view these actions as their mission—"representing the voice of the voiceless," as a religious worker in Phoenix put it.

Catholic leaders bring the teachings closer to the members' lives in different ways. In homilies, prayer groups or informal conversations, priests in all three locations draw parallels between the lives of the immigrants and that of Christ—who, like themselves, faced poverty and exclusion. In Bible-reading groups in all three cities, the participants read and reflect on the relevance of scripture for their own immediate problems. In Washington, after reading and explaining that David had problems with his children, but that one of them built a great temple, the moderator of the group adapted this passage to something closer to the immigrants' world: communication between parents and children to avoid drug use and early pregnancies.

The Catholic leadership also summons the immigrants to address the social problems they face, inviting them to reflect from a spiritual perspective about the political and economic forces that affect their lives. In a Sunday mass devoted to the day of *El Salvador del Mundo* (The Savior of the World, the patron saint of El Salvador), a Salvadoran priest in Washington—standing between the Salvadoran flag and an image of Christ the Savior—delivered a homily charged with sociopolitical content. A few days later, President Clinton was to sign the welfare reform bill into law, so the priest took this opportunity to speak to the congregation in the manner that religious leaders have been long advocating in Latin America: a combination of spiritual formation with social action and reflection. In the priest's words:

> Although we're celebrating the day of *El Salvador del Mundo* and we're rejoicing in this festivity, it's been a tough week for us. President Clinton will sign the law of social [welfare] reform, and when this law passes, there will be great hunger and poverty in our streets. The Catholic Church categorically opposes the passage of this law [with a closed fist hitting the podium] the way it's written. Our Cardinal wrote to the President because this law will affect all immigrants, legal and illegal, the women, the poor. . . . What do we say to all this? Jesus provides us with examples of compassion, of love. For instance, one day the disciples wanted to get rid of all the poor people because Jesus was tired, but Jesus had a mandate for them: feed them. The disciples had to respond to these people. Jesus did not let them abandon the hungry. Jesus doesn't abandon us, but politicians do. Politicians want your vote, Jesus doesn't. He's with us, in the Eucharist, accessible to all. Jesus gives us an example of conscientization. Our Lord calls us to respond, to help others, to have compassion for our neighbors, and importantly, to do something, to act.

The call to action in this priest's words has found expression in the Church's community work. In addition to introspective teachings that invite parishioners to reflect on their conditions, Catholic leaders have been involved in providing their parishioners with tools for social mobilization and community action. In all three cities, they not only have denounced unfavorable policies but also have participated in openly opposing them. During the Mount Pleasant riots in Washington, D.C. in 1991, when a largely Latino crowd clashed with the police to protest police brutality, a Catholic priest and other church leaders tried to ease the tensions by organizing community meetings in the basement of one of the largest churches in the area. These meetings led to the formation of an inter-faith coalition that now works on different issues of concern to the Hispanic community, including police abuse, political leadership, and immigration issues.

Catholic workers in San Francisco have been involved in broad coalition building so that the immigrants can "find a voice to be able to make changes in their conditions," as a young priest put it. In Phoenix, Catholic workers have to "organize and work fast" as one leader said, because so many Latinos of different nationalities have moved to the city recently and the church is doing what it can to accommodate them. And a Salvadoran priest in Washington pointed out that social justice was an integral part of his work: "We need to develop a new faith, one that responds to the needs of our people here. And, inevitably, this will have to be linked to issues of social justice. No doubt about that."

The Congregation—"A Dios Rogando y con el Mazo Dando (Praying to God but at the Same Time, Working)"

The Catholic Church's institutional actions on behalf of immigrants are crucial, but so are the immigrants' understandings of such actions and their perception of them. Immigrants in the three locales were well aware of the church leadership's response to the problems they faced and of the church's help to deal with these issues efficiently. When asked if they thought the church responded in concrete *ways* to the needs of the community, more than half answered affirmatively. In Phoenix, Alberto—who explained that he had "no religion" but believed in God, went to mass on holidays, and had received help from the church with preparing immigration-related paperwork—said that he saw the work of the church in his everyday life: "I had never seen this, I had never imagined that the church could help so much. Here [in Phoenix] I have seen with my own eyes what the church can do." Informants in the three cities indicated that their church not only had assisted them with immigration-related issues, but that it had also implemented initiatives to deal with the problems of gangs and drugs in their neighborhoods (among their most serious concerns).

Informants who participated in Bible-reading groups were quick to observe the importance of these reflections for their daily lives. Blanca, in Washington, often reflected on biblical readings when she felt she could not go on anymore, particularly when she had to get up at three to start working at four in the morning. She pointed out that her faith had helped her to work on changing the conditions in the environment around her, such as improving her deteriorating neighborhood. Through church initiatives to work with youth groups and to write to President Clinton to alert him to the deleterious effects of new immigration laws and welfare reforms, she believed she could act to change the conditions in which she, as well as other immigrants she cared about, lived. In her words: "We must do something about this, but at the same time, pray. These two things go together. If we only do one of them, [shaking her head] we better don't do anything at all. As the saying goes, *A Dios rogando y con el mazo dando* [Praying to God but at the same time, working]."

Underscoring the importance of the church in the immigrants' lives, informants in all three locations expected the church to help them, and believed that this was the church's mission. In Phoenix, Claudia thought that the church should be involved in social projects, such as creating alternative activities to bring youngsters from the streets, food collections, and legal assistance. She believed that the church has credibility and that if it undertakes a project, many people will be involved, both as providers and as receivers. Mario, in San Francisco, explained: "Because the church is a mother, right? The Holy Mother Church, as we call it when we pray, you know? I think one expects good things to come from it. We want the church to protect us and to guide us here, in a place where we face many difficulties. Wouldn't you also go to your mom for something like that? Well, same thing with the church." Some informants also emphasized that it was the church's responsibility to take the ministry—the work of the church—to the community, instead of waiting for people to show up at the church's door.

Some immigrants emphasized the church's social engagement.[7] When asked if the church should be involved in denouncing social injustices, for instance, they generally responded affirmatively, for they thought this was one of the main missions of the church. Ramón, in Washington, explained: "It is only natural that the church should denounce injustices. Christ taught us to do so. If we don't, then we're not following Jesus' teachings, and if that happens, we're no longer a church." In fact, according to Julio, also in Washington, active involvement in helping the marginalized should be the church's priority. "As Saint Paul says, 'it is necessary to feed the hungry before you teach them the scriptures.' It is necessary to start with the basics. You can't expect the hungry to respond to your message if they haven't eaten, right?"

As the words of Ramón and Julio suggest, these immigrants' views of their church's involvement with social issues are closely linked to religious teachings. When informants said that the church has a mandate to help those in need, they cited biblical parables to support their views. Carlos, in Washington, explained how a Catholic should live as follows: "The true work of a [Catholic] person is to live a life with and for others, not only in the [rituals of the] church. Remember? When the apostles went up the mountain and told Jesus, 'Oh look how pretty it is up here, we can build a couple of huts and stay here.' And Jesus told them no, 'You need to come down, you need to be down here, in the world, doing your work.' To me that means that we need to imitate Jesus in everything, and we need to do it in our daily lives, not only in the [rituals of the] church." And Claudia, in Phoenix, when asked why she thought the church should be involved in helping immigrants, responded: "There's a simple reason for that. Our faith tells us that we have to help our *prójimo* (fellow human beings), our brothers and sisters, and we are all brothers and sisters, and since the church is our leader in our faith, it should take the lead, the responsibility to set the example for the rest of us."

I do not mean to paint an excessively positive image of religious institutions in the eyes of these immigrants, for there were a few who did not feel particularly attracted to religious institutional activities and were a bit cynical in their views of church activities. When asked if he thought churches should be involved in helping immigrants, Manuel, in Phoenix, responded: "Of course they should. With all the money they take from people, that's the least they can do." Manuel's mother had a similar view, which she held in common with a small minority of informants present in all three locations. She explained: "I don't think the church should be involved in anything. Priests should only do what they're supposed to. To God what is God's and to man what is man's. They should only dedicate themselves to their churches and that's it. Well, if they have the means to help, then I think they could do a little bit more, to provide financial help, which we all need, especially at the beginning. But no, I am not inclined to trust the church. So I wouldn't want any priests involved in anything that doesn't concern religion. I don't trust them with anything, much less with things like immigration [smiles and shakes her head]."

A Collective Approach

Importantly, calls to action on the part of the Catholic leadership are expressed institutionally as collective. Like some of their leaders,

---

[7]This is particularly the case among those who did political work or were active in progressive brands of Catholicism in El Salvador. They believed that the Catholic Church they have encountered in the United States resembles the more conservative Catholic Church in El Salvador. In fact, one informant argued that those Salvadoran Catholics who were used to progressive— or even radical—forms of Catholicism have joined other, mostly mainline Protestant, churches where they have found more support fot their views.

members of the congregations believed that the most effective way to reach their goals was through different forms of collective action (though they did not term their efforts as such). A priest in Washington invoked his religion's "communitarian ethic" (Greeley 1989:486), to explain this view. "I see our work as being truly, fundamentally community-oriented; we have to encourage and to create community. We only do that when we recognize the origins of our congregation, where they come from, and at the same time unite them in Christ, which is our mission." In fact, the Catholic leaders, in reaching out to the immigrants, made carefully balanced efforts to allow the parishioners to express their faith in culturally relevant ways (see Menjívar 1999). At the same time, they kept the unity of the flock under the umbrella of "Hispanics" or "Latinos," a sensible approach in an ethnically heterogeneous congregation. Among efforts to unite the Latino congregation (because the parishes were usually composed of a plurality of ethnicities and nationalities), a priest in Washington held weekly meetings to read the Bible from a "Latino" or "Hispanic" perspective. During these sessions, as they read passages and interpreted them in light of their current (immigrant) situation vis-à-vis their environment, they were challenged to think of ways to confront many issues, mostly looking at how such issues affect them as a group and, in turn, how they can respond to them from within this unifying perspective.

The parishioners more actively involved in the church (who were not the majority in all three cities) often mentioned a personal relationship with God or with Christ and understood their mission as part of a collective effort. They referred to their work and themselves as part of a community, a view reflected in the language they used to describe their experiences. When using biblical passages to describe their mission, they would often identify with the Apostles' work, which they saw as having been carried out collectively. Jorge, in Washington, explained that his church had been effective in reaching

youngsters through a program to combat drugs because they had organized it as a group effort. For Ramón, also in Washington: "We are the church of the poor, of the needy, so the church does not have the economic resources to carry out its mission fully. We need to be congregated as a community to be able to solve our problems. If we live in community and try to solve our problems as a community, we'll do much better."

An important exception to this pattern among active Catholics are the charismatic groups (present in the three sites), who adhere to less socially oriented teachings. Instead of the social teachings and community-action approaches that prevailed among other Catholics, charismatics viewed their mission as contained within the confines of the church, and were more prone to emphasize prayer and church rituals as viable measures to combat problems in the neighborhood. They were also likely to mention individual responses and recommend them in dealing with how to live their faith. However, even the less collectively oriented charismatics agreed that the best way to live their lives was by trying to make a difference in the world. Elizabeth, in Washington, observed: "To be able to reach the Kingdom of God one has to make a difference in this life, to be able to do something so that when I present myself to God I can say that I did something."

The Evangelical Churches

The approach and organization of the Evangelical churches in this study, in many respects, seemed to be the opposite of the Catholic churches. Rather than focusing on the efforts of the collectivity to attempt to change the immigrants' situation, the Evangelicals promoted individual spiritual discovery that led to Christian growth. Instead of the Catholics' socially oriented teachings, the Evangelical churches emphasized ritual and prayer. In contrast to the Catholic churches, the absolute leadership in the Evangelical churches rested on the pastor. In the Catholic congregations, the priests acted as guides, aided by committees of laypersons. In the Evangelical churches, even though pastors had assistants (not committees as in the Catholic churches) to help them carry out some of the work, they assumed many other responsibilities, which made them indispensable in the members' lives. I do not mean to underplay the importance of the participatory nature of the Evangelical churches—an organizationally less hierarchical church than the Catholic—where members refer to one another as "brothers and sisters" and treat one another as family. However, the pastor's authority and his centrality in the lives of the members are unmatched. Under the circumstances in which many Salvadoran immigrants live (e.g., their uncertain legal status, their long hours of backbreaking jobs, their stress from multiple demands for help, and their nostalgia for loved ones in El Salvador) a person who knows them and can listen and demonstrate concern and who understands their worries—in their language—becomes invaluable. So the Evangelical pastors often served as counselors, spiritual guides and confidants. They dealt with concerns on a case-by-case basis and took an active stance to guide their members. Oftentimes the pastors acted as father figures and advised and scolded their followers. The services were often infused with admonishments to the members to keep from "bad company" that could entice them to sin, particularly drinking and infidelity among the men, and coquettish behavior and "unladylike" manners among women. The pastors seemed to be "on call" at all hours of the day to tend to their flocks' concerns, always stressing the benefits for those who accept Christ as their savior.

Thus a pastor in Washington was there to comfort a woman who called him in the middle of the night because of a dispute with her husband. He was also there to console a church member whose relative had been detained by the Immigration and Naturalization Service; the pastor even took a collection in church to pay for this person's bail. He had helped some church members with immigration applications and had referred a family who lacked medical insurance to a community clinic. Thus, following the personal influence strategy that pervades Evangelicalism (see Smith 1998), this pastor stressed that he was there to help his congregation, but that he had no "programs" set up to assist them; he took each case one at a time because he was familiar with each person's special circumstances and individual problems.[8] Personal knowledge of the members was largely possible because these Evangelical churches were much smaller than the Catholic ones. The fact that he personally knew most of the church's members, he believed, qualified him to provide personal and, therefore, more effective solutions. As a church member put it: "It is a wonderful thing but very tough on our pastor because he has to deal with everything, from the personality of the people to everything that happens to them. He takes care of everything; he visits hospitals, he has to give advice and, if he's called in the middle of the night, even if he's tired, he has to go where he's needed. But when a person has God's calling, the person has to be ready to respond."

"Accept Christ as Your Savior"

Similar to the Catholic, the Evangelical churches' teachings helped their members to make sense of the world around them. In the Evangelicals' case, however, this was tied to the idea that the individual, through deeds that glorify God, could find his or her own spiritual salvation. For instance, when Cleotilde, in Phoenix, was asked about her decision to migrate, she recounted:

---

[8]This pastor was so familiar with each person in the congregation that he knew who was working and who was not and, if they were employed, what their approximate income was. So when it came time to tithe, the pastor knew how much each person should give.

God revealed everything to me in a dream many years before I left. I knew everything, even what happened at the American Embassy in San Salvador before I even went there. God had a purpose for me to come here because He wanted me to serve Him. He has enriched my life. Through my experiences here I have served Him. I am very happy because there is so much need here, there are a lot of Hispanics to whom I can take the good news, and I can do that because of the language. I can talk about the Lord's Word to them because we speak the same [Spanish] language. So we have a lot of work to do here.

Because most Evangelicals—in the three locales where I conducted this study—were converts (usually from Catholicism), events related to their conversion were some of the most important in their lives (as opposed to those of the Catholics who cited marriages, births, deaths, and the separation from loved ones as a result of migration). Evangelicals often referred to having accepted Christ (meaning their conversion) as the most consequential moment in their lives. They were likely to recount the conditions under which this happened, usually after a tragedy or in attempts to mend their ways. Along these lines, they also mentioned that their faith could help those, who, like themselves, "had fallen to the temptation and vices of the [nonconvert] world."

An important difference from the Catholic expressions of faith and organization of religious activities is that when a person decides to accept Christ, he or she is encouraged (sometimes required) to attend religious services at least once, but preferably several times, per week. The services that I attended in the Evangelical churches were on average three times as long as a regular Catholic mass. They were also usually family affairs which everyone, even the smallest children, attended. Participants were required to bring their Bibles to the services, where they would read passages and chant along with the pastor. Thus, religious activities and expressions of faith in Evangelical churches were conducive to greater individual involvement in the institutional structure of the church than was the case among Catholics. Marcela, in San Francisco, who had attended Catholic and Evangelical churches, explained this difference as follows: "Look, I see it like this. If you're a Catholic, you can say that you're a Catholic even if you never go to church. Then one day you're in need or something happens, and you start going [to church] again. But then you get a job or move to a different place and you don't go to church for a long time, but you're still the same Catholic. If you're an Evangelical, no, you can't say today I'll go to the service and tomorrow say I'm tired or I have to work, so I can't go. You go all the time, or else you're not part of the church. There are no in-betweens here like [there are] among Catholics." And Maria Elena in Phoenix, who also attended a Catholic and an Evangelical church, echoed Marcela in the following words: "I am Catholic, and since I'm used to going to church only on Sundays I tried to do the same at the Evangelical church. But [the Evangelical church] is different. You need to be there more, not only on Sundays. I like to go because they have helped me a lot. Spiritually, you know, a lot. It's helpful to go all the time." One wonders whether the success of the Evangelical churches in helping people straighten their ways (e.g., keeping the men from alcohol and infidelity, and both the men and the women from going to parties, which, the pastors argued, simply open opportunities to sin) rests at least partially on this high demand for the time of its members—requiring that they spend many hours a week in church, particularly on weekend evenings.

Individual Solutions?

These congregations generally were not inclined to speak of collective solutions for their problems. This point is similar to what scholars have noted among other Evangelicals (cf. Smith 1998). In fact, many would not even discuss a solution to a problem—personal or not—as coming from individuals or the congregation because only the Lord had the power to act on such matters. For instance, members often mentioned that the best way to deal with the problems that afflicted their neighborhoods, and even the country, was to pray and to convince people to accept Christ. In the words of a pastor (and one of the founders of a church) in Washington: "We are united in prayer, all of us pray for everyone, for our [political] leaders, those who govern, so that one day they can be saved and if they want a special, personal prayer, we'll say it. But even if they don't request them, we'll pray anyway, because we pray for our environment, for our race, every week." Some of these members thought that one of today's major problems was spiritual decadence, which leads to drug use and other social problems. Thus, a logical solution was to save people through conversion; if more people accepted Christ, there would be fewer social problems. Bernarda, a church member, echoed the pastor's words adding: "What we need to do is to accept that we cannot live without God. We need to accept Him because without Him we cannot do anything."

Interestingly, as the previous cases indicate, in spite of the Evangelicals' concentration on the individual and on personal conversion as a means to combat all problems, it seems that a large portion of their activities are geared to the community. In fact, a pastor in Washington pointed out that their work is indeed community-oriented. In his words: "If the government would let us go out and spread the Gospel around more publicly, it would need fewer ambulances, fewer policemen, and fewer hospitals, because Christ can save many more people than the authorities can." In doing their work, however, the Evangelicals do not invoke social teachings—but rather concentrate on the individual and conversion—emphasizing prayer and church ritual, which underscores the uniqueness of their personal involvement. In contrast to Catholic views (and in line with what has been observed among Evangelicals in general [see Smith 1998]), neither the pastor nor the congregation believed that they should participate in the collective solutions to address social problems that so often surfaced in conversations with the Catholics; achieving the

higher goal of personal conversion would take care of the rest. When asked if his church should be involved in denouncing injustices, a pastor in Phoenix responded: "The church should not get involved in any of that directly; the [nonconvert] world can do as it pleases. What we need to do is to work hard so that more people accept Christ as their savior. This is the only thing that can change everything."

The Congregation

When asked if their church should seek solutions to social problems, Evangelicals in all three locations overwhelmingly answered negatively, as they did not readily see how such actions could be of more benefit than a conversion, which guarantees not only salvation but also better people in general. Lucia, in Phoenix, explained:

> I think that we as Christians should not denounce anything, it is better that we seek God and let Him take care of things. We are peregrines here on earth, we're only here temporarily, and the days that we're allowed to spend here, we should spend them seeking our objective, which is to find Christ. Instead of talking about all those problems and getting involved in those things, we need to put all those things, all problems before God because the Word tells us "there is nothing impossible for God." But if we start dealing with these problems ourselves, we'll never get anything done because only God's magnanimity can solve it all.

Elsy, from Washington, was not even interested in discussing social problems, much less how to confront them, because she deemed them "political" and reasoned that dealing with such problems was beyond the capacity of humans. She explained that she could not address those questions because she was not competent in, nor particularly attracted to, discussing those areas. When asked if the church should be engaged in community organizing to deal with social problems, she replied:

> You see, the church is only in charge of that which deals with the diffusion of the Word, the Lord's

Word. The church does not get involved in other problems because only God is our judge. We first must recognize that He is just, our only justice, and justice for us will come when He deems it's time to. But no, I don't think we should get involved in trying to change things that only God can. No, our church shouldn't participate in a protest or that kind of thing, you know, like sometimes people do with immigration issues. Yes, our church can do something for us Salvadorans, for immigrants. What it can do is preach the Gospel to all, to gain more souls for our Lord and pray for our leaders. But not to go out in the streets shouting political things, no, that's not for us.

Thus, evangelicals did not interpret their teachings in ways that justified collective solutions or actions, nor did they believe that their mission was to be engaged in any action that could be interpreted as political. For instance, when issues with political content—particularly linked to experiences in El Salvador and still very much alive in the minds of many of the members—would come up, the Evangelical pastors attempted to remove the political content in the immigrants' concerns. One afternoon during a service in Washington, a woman recounted a terrifying nightmare from which she had woken up crying and very shaken. She described how in her dreams she saw military trucks passing by her town at night and forcibly taking people from their homes, people who were later found tortured and dead. Even though this woman's nightmare might have been based on real events in her hometown in eastern El Salvador—where she personally knew people who had been abducted and where the overwhelming majority of the congregation originated—and could have been a symptom of post-traumatic stress disorder (not uncommon among Salvadoran immigrants), the pastor (a Salvadoran from the same small town) chose a very different interpretation. The church was undergoing internal turmoil, and two months later it split into two. Thus the pastor took this woman's nightmare as a sign to alert the congregation to a danger emanating from members who were not true believers. In his view, these members should stop sinning and "accept Christ in their hearts fully," or else they could bring disaster to their church.

When asked if their church has helped them to effect changes in the conditions in which they live, the Evangelicals in all three cities overwhelmingly responded affirmatively. For instance, Virginia in San Francisco intimated that she has been able to carry on in spite of the infinite difficulties she has encountered in the United States because her "brothers and sisters in Christ" have been there to help her even more than her own family. Elizabeth, in Washington, is convinced that her faith has helped her to cope with many problems in her life in the United States. She explains: "My faith has helped me get through in my life. God, through the Holy Spirit, has given me everything I have in my life now. The enemy tried to get in my way, so that I wouldn't have a home to live in, but God, in His infinite mercy, has been with me." And Maria and her husband Esteban in Phoenix maintained that their church had saved their lives. They invited me to a service so I could witness the miracles that their church works on people, but also to encourage me to contemplate my own conversion, which the other Evangelicals I came to know also asked me to consider.

Discussion and Concluding Remarks

There are a few points that can be made in assessing the importance of religious institutions in the lives of the Salvadoran immigrants in this study. My observations in San Francisco, Washington, D.C. and Phoenix show that religious institutions are focal points in the lives of many Salvadoran immigrants, regardless of the specific receiving points where they live. Even though the immigrants in this study have arrived in a city with several generations of Salvadoran immigrants—like San Francisco—in a city where they are the majority of the Latino population—like Washington, D.C.—and in a new destination point where they are a minority and often "pass" for Mexicans—like Phoenix—Catholic and Evangelical churches play a key role in their lives. An important reason for this finding is that the broader politico-economic framework is constant in all locations and its influence permeates every aspect of the immigrants' lives. The legal context affects these immigrants' opportunities in the labor market, where they usually find low-paying jobs, and thus, not surprisingly, their socioeconomic standing is very similar in all three cities. In the absence of government aid for the Salvadorans' resettlement as refugees (which the U.S. government normally provides to people escaping political violence), churches have stepped in to fill this void.[9] Churches also have worked to change immigration policy and, in doing so, to change the broader context of reception for this group. Thus, religious institutions play a key role, particularly when immigration policies are hostile to a group (as in the case of the Salvadorans in this study). It is therefore not surprising that regardless of the specificities of the destination point, religious institutions remain crucial for these immigrants. Indeed, the vital place of the church in Salvadoran immigrants' lives has been found to differ from other Latino groups as well. In a comparative study of Guatemalans, Salvadorans and Cubans in Phoenix, Salvadorans (and Guatemalans) had received more types of assistance from the church and thus deemed the place of the church as vital in their lives, whereas Cubans saw the church mainly as a source of spiritual comfort (Menjívar 2001). Therefore, regardless of particular community dynamics in specific locations, the church (and its activities) is key in these immigrants' lives; it is an effective antidote to forces that may undermine these immigrants' emotional, spiritual, material strength and resilience.

Importantly, these religious institutions provide immigrants with resources that the immigrants *themselves* deem necessary for the goals they seek to achieve—from legal counsel to financial assistance for a month's rent, from organizational strategies to deal with problems in their neighborhoods to a kind word in a desperate moment. Thus, from the point of view of the immigrants, religion, as was the case historically, may continue to provide avenues for groups to improve their lot (Warner 1993:1068). Moreover, within the social milieu of the churches, Salvadoran immigrants are able to forge networks that provide them with some of the most important forms of support (Menjívar 2000). Therefore, for these immigrants, as Andrew Greeley (1997:592–3) has observed more generally, religion can be a powerful resource of desirable social capital.[10]

Although there were no discernible differences by destination point in how Salvadorans perceive the church in their lives, important differences between the two churches emerged as more significant in this study and these were present in all three locales. The Catholic Church, in efforts to reach out to a large and ethnically heterogeneous flock, encourages collective actions to transform the conditions in which immigrants live and fosters models for community action. Such an approach combines community- and socially oriented teachings with attempts on the part of the leadership to become more relevant to an increasingly ethnically diverse membership. In this way the Catholic Church encourages different ethnic and cultural expressions of the faith without compromising the unity that it is attempting to forge, and it helps immigrants in their efforts to change the conditions they face (Menjívar 1999). Whereas the Evangelical churches also promote the active

---

[9]The absence of an infrastructure to protect Salvadoran immigrants is directly linked to U.S. foreign policy in El Salvador during the war, as it would not accept as refugees (and offer protection) those fleeing a government that it was supporting (Menjívar 2000).

[10]A word of caution is in order here. Simply having friends or acquaintances at church should not be misinterpreted with their actually generating social capital, as this depends on other factors, particularly the resources to which the immigrants have access (Menjívar 2000).

participation of the membership (through frequent services where everyone prays and chants together), such participation is geared to bring the comfort of individual salvation (with hopes for material improvement) to those who accept Christ as their savior. The engagement of the membership in this church is largely a result of smaller and more ethnically homogeneous congregations, in which the pastor often develops personal relationships with the members and provides them with individualized support; the congregation becomes a family for each member. Thus, both Catholics and Evangelicals produce community-level changes, the former through communitarian teachings to reach the parishioners who come to join established churches, the latter through ritual and prayer in churches that they or other recent immigrants have founded. In both cases religious teachings and the organizational structures of the churches shape the provision of support for the immigrants.

The two churches examined help to shape the immigrants' views of their own position in the host society, but do so in dissimilar ways. The communitarian approach of the Catholic Church can advance pan-ethnic models (in multicultural parishes) and encourage members to look for collective solutions to their problems—which may lead to coalition building and a sense of ethnic identity with the potential to impact the immigrants' long-term integration. The Evangelicals forge strong ties among coreligionists and with leaders, which often make the church the single most important institution in their lives. This church can promote strong bonds among ethnically homogenous groups under the umbrella of a Christian identity. Thus, both churches provide avenues for their members to develop group identities—be it ethnic or religious.

The ethnic composition of the churches is important. Immigrants, like the Salvadorans in this study, develop important ties within the spaces that the churches provide because for them the church is an important social arena, not just a purely religious one. An ethnically heterogeneous church, Catholic or Evangelical, provides spaces

for the immigrants to interact with coethnics, with other immigrants, and with natives—interactions that impact the immigrants' identities as well as integration. The number of contacts alone might not be a good indicator of immigrants' interactions with coethnics, other groups or natives; rather the *quality* of such contacts may be more pertinent. If the immigrants' contacts with natives or groups outside religious spaces are limited to employers, bureaucrats (in hospitals, schools, the immigration service), landlords or service providers (a bus driver or a clerk), regardless of their frequency, these will never be of the same quality (and social importance) as those the immigrants establish within the spaces of friendlier institutions, like the church.

Might these churches impact the long-term integration of these immigrants? The Catholic Church has institutionalized programs to help immigrants learn English, regularize their legal status, and even lobby for less stringent immigration laws. This helps them to acquire the resources needed for socioeconomic mobility. The Evangelical churches assist immigrants, but on a smaller scale. Their aim is to change individuals through conversion and this approach tends to relegate more pragmatic objectives (such as securing legal residence and economic advancement) to a second place, though Evangelical churches sometimes help individual immigrants to attain these more worldly benefits on a case-by-case basis. The institutional aspects of the churches, such as the expression of different doctrines, the organization of their manifestation, and the composition of the churches themselves might impact the long-term prospects of the immigrants. Scholars may argue that an all-encompassing situation, such as several of the churches in this study, may stand in the way of immigrants' assimilation in the host society, since immigrants can find abundant solace, friendship and spiritual comfort within them. Others, such as W. I. Thomas (Janowitz 1966), have pointed out that institutions (such as churches), far from isolating newcomers from American life, provide organizational vehicles that allow them to participate in it. But whether churches—their doctrines and institutional organization—pave the way for the immigrants to realize their objectives is intimately related to the resources of the receiving families and communities and how the body of law reconstitutes each immigrant group. Different religious spaces may promote immigrants' incorporation in different ways, but this is hardly a unilinear process where all groups begin and end in the same place—even if they belong to the same church. Immigrants "assimilate" only to the milieu that their resources—what they bring with them and what they encounter—allow them to and not all do so at the same rate. Thus, whereas different churches may guide immigrants along different paths, the end result remains conditioned by the structure of opportunities available to the particular immigrant group in the context and time they arrive.

REFERENCES

Barnouw, A. J. 1937. Dutch Americans. In *Our racial and national minorities: Their history, contributions, and present problems,* edited by F. J. Brown and J. Slabey Roucek, 137–50. New York: Prentice Hall.

Bau, I. 1985. *The ground is holy: Church sanctuary and Central American refugees.* Mahwah, NJ: Paulist Press.

Berger, P. 1967. *The sacred canopy: Elements of a sociological theory of religion.* Garden City, NY: Doubleday and Company.

Berger, P., and T, Luckmann. 1966. *The social construction of reality: A treatise in the sociology of knowledge.* Garden City, NY: Doubleday and Company.

Dolan, J. 1975. *The immigrant church: New York's Irish and German Catholics.* Baltimore: The Johns Hopkins University Press.

Ebaugh, H. R., and J. S. Chafetz. 2000. *Religion and the new immigrants: Continuities and adaptations in immigrant congregations.* Walnut Creek, CA: Altamira Press.

Gerth, H. H., and C. W. Mills. 1946. *From Max Weber: Essays in sociology.* New York: Oxford University Press.

Gleason, P. 1968. *The conservative reformers: German-American Catholics and the social order.* Notre Dame: Notre Dame University Press.

———— 1992. Immigration, religion, and intergroup relations: Historical perspectives on the American experience. In *Immigrants in two democracies: French and American experience,* edited by D. L. Horowitz and G. Noiriel, 167–87. New York: New York University Press.

Greeley, A. 1989. Protestant and Catholic: Is the analogical imagination extinct? *American Sociological Review* 54:485–502.

———. 1997. Coleman revisited. *American Behavioral Scientist,* 40 (5):587–94.

Herberg, W. 1960. *Protestant, Catholic, Jew: An essay in American religious sociology.* 2nd ed. Garden City, NY: Anchor.

Janowitz, M. 1966. *W. I. Thomas on social organization and social personality: Selected papers.* Edited and with an introduction by M. Janowitz. Chicago: University of Chicago Press.

Kim, K. J. 1991. The role of the Korean Protestant immigrant church in the acculturation of Korean immigrants in Southern California. Ed.D. diss., University of Southern California.

Kim, Y. 1994. The correlation between religiosity and assimilation of first-generation Korean immigrants in the Chicago metropolitan region. Ph.D. diss., Loyola University of Chicago, 1994. Abstract in *Dissertation Abstracts International* 55–05A:1388.

Levitt, P. 2001. *The transnational villagers.* Berkeley: University of California Press.

Litt, E. 1970. *Ethnic politics in America: Beyond pluralism.* Glenview, IL: Scott Fresman.

Menjívar, C. 1999. Religious institutions and transnationalism: A case study of Catholic and Evangelical Salvadoran immigrants. *International Journal of Politics, Culture, and Society* 12 (4):589–612.

———. 2000. Fragmented ties: *Salvadoran immigrant networks in America.* Berkeley: University of California Press.

———. 2001. Latino immigrants and their perceptions of religious institutions; Cubans, Salvadorans and Guatemalans in Phoenix, Arizona. *Migraciones Internacionales* 1 (1):65–88.

Mol, J. J. 1961. *Churches and immigrants (A sociological study of the mutual effect of religion and emigrant adjustment).* The Hague, The Netherlands: REMP Bulletin, Supplement 5, Vol. 9.

Mullins, M. 1987. The life cycle of ethnic churches in sociological perspective. *Japanese Journal of Religious Studies* 14:321–34.

Nelli, H. S. 1970. *Italians in Chicago, 1880–1930: A study of ethnic mobility.* New York: Oxford University Press.

Portes, A., and R. G. Rumbaut. 1996. *Immigrant America: A portrait.* Berkeley: University of California Press.

Portes, A., and M. Zhou. 1993. The new second generation: Segmented assimilation and its variants. *Annals of the American Academy of Political and Social Science* 530:74–96.

Rollwagen, J. 1975. Introduction: The city as a constant, a symposium. *Urban Anthropology* 4:1–4.

Smith, C. 1998. *American evangelism: Embattled and thriving.* Chicago: University of Chicago Press.

Smith, T. L. 1978. Religion and ethnicity in America. *American Historical Review* 83:1155–85.

Tomasi, S. M. 1970. The ethnic church and the integration of Italian Americans in the United States. In *The Italian experience in the United States,* edited by S. M. Tomasi and M. H. Engel, 163–93. New York: Center for Migration Studies.

Warner, R, S. 1993. Work in progress toward a new paradigm for the sociological study of religion in the United States. *American Journal of Sociology* 98:1044–93.

_____. 1998. Immigration and religious communities in the United States. In *Gatherings in diaspora; Religious communities and the new immigration,* edited by R. S. Warner and J. G. Wittner, 3–34. Philadelphia: Temple University Press.

Warner, R. S., and J. G. Wittner, eds. 1998. *Gatherings in diaspora: Religious communities and the new immigration.* Philadelphia: Temple University Press.

Wiltfang, G., and D. McAdam. 1991. The costs and risks of social activism: A study of sanctuary movement activism. *Social Farces* 69:987–1010.

A Focus Group Study of the Motivation to Invest

"Ethical/Green" and "Ordinary" Investors Compared (2001)

Alan Lewis

1. INTRODUCTION

Why do people invest? At one level the answer is obvious: to increase their stock of wealth. If one adheres to the notion of a rational self-interested economic actor (*homo economicus)* in its narrow form the answer can be fledged out a little by adding in the factor of risk. No one knows for certain whether a particular investment will show a profit or a loss. An 'expert,' such as an Independent Financial Advisor (IFA) will have historical and other data to guide investors about risk and return. The conundrum is that risk and return, to some extent, pull in opposite directions: relatively 'safe' investments provide unspectacular returns, while riskier ones can produce sizeable gains (and losses). Many people are risk averse (with notable exceptions, e.g., as demonstrated

by the 'framing' effects of Kahneman & Tversky, 1979) but want to earn some money as well, settling for a mixed portfolio combining 'safe' investments with 'riskier' ones.

Keynes (1936) speculated a little more about underlying motivations, coming up with eight, namely Precaution, Foresight, Calculation, Improvement, Independence, Enterprise, Pride, and Avarice. Empirical investigation of investment (and saving) motivation is rare (exceptions are Furnham, 1985, Warneryd, 1999) and usually relies on the interpretations people place on their own behavior and consequently are prone to what social psychologists refer to as 'attributor bias' (Ross, 1977). Some survey research using questionnaires (Lewis & Mackenzie, 1997) reveals that the top three motives are Precaution (the need to save for the purposes of security and stability);

SOURCE: "A Focus Group Study of the Motivation to Invest: 'Ethical/Green' and 'Ordinary' Investors Compared" by Lewis, A., in *Journal of Socio-Economics, 30* (2001), 331–341. Reprinted with permission.

Foresight (in particular making provisions for old age); Calculation (capital growth, rather than providing income for the present). As anticipated, respondents are loath to endorse 'Avarice' as a motive even when toned down in the questionnaire to read 'Desire to accumulate.'

While some economists are happy to agree that a 'richer' model of economic motivation is required beyond a narrowly based *homo economicus,* for the sociologist Etzioni (1988) in particular, economists have not gone far enough as they ignore, what for him, is the most important consideration of all: morality. Etzioni (1988) has persuasively argued that dispassionate economic decisions are the exception rather than the rule and that the market is more commonly a moral one governed by social rules and expectations of fairness and trust.

How might morality be relevant to investment decisions? Ethical/green investing provides an excellent example. These investors (usually in consultation with Independent Financial Advisors (IFA's) take into account the 'normal' financial considerations of risk and return additionally requiring that certain companies are avoided in the construction of the portfolio; particularly companies which manufacture arms, use animal testing, or pollute the environment. The first U.K. ethical unit trust (EUT) was launched in 1984 and there are now more than forty of them ('social' investment has a longer history in the U.S.A. and represents a larger section of the investment market). There can be little doubt that the demand (and supply) of these products is growing. It is very difficult to explain this with recourse to self-interest, narrowly defined, alone.

Are ethical/green investors cranks or are their motivations similar to 'ordinary' investors and therefore informative more generally?

2. WHAT IS KNOWN ABOUT ETHICAL/GREEN INVESTING?

The author has been involved on a recent Economic and Social Science Research Council funded project on ethical investing in the U.K.: this section reflects this work and builds on research conducted

in the U.S.A. (e.g., Domini & Kinder, 1984; Lowry, 1991) as well as the U.K. (Anand & Cowton, 1993). A comprehensive review of the relevant literature can be found in Mackenzie, 1997.

A questionnaire survey of 1146 ethical investors in the U.K. (Lewis & Mackenzie, 2000a) revealed that the profile of ethical investors is much the same as for 'standard' investors: the majority being over 45 with professional qualifications. What makes them unusual is that many more of them than you would expect by chance, vote for the Liberal Democrats and the Labour Party, work (or have worked) in 'caring' professions such as health and education, and are active members of major charities, religious and environmental groups. This hardly makes them cranks: ethical/green investing is an important part of their lifestyle.

When given a choice between avoiding companies which are failing ethically and retaining investments in these companies while seeking (through the activities of ethical fund managers) to improve the ethical performance of the miscreants, 41% select avoidance, 27% more active engagement (a further 32% remain uncommitted: Lewis & Mackenzie, 2000b). When asked whether they would be prepared to take a 20% loss on their return for ethical investments, over 80% of respondents said they would (and over 40% believe they currently take a loss in any case: Lewis & Mackenzie, 2000a). So while a clear majority of ethical/green investors are prepared to take a loss in order 'to put their money where their morals are' it must be underlined that 80% of respondents have 'ethically mixed' portfolios holding 'clean' and 'not so clean' investments at the same time (Lewis & Mackenzie, 2000a). Leading to the speculation, from qualitative telephone interviews, that these investors are driven (perhaps like the rest of us) by mixed motives and are maximizing neither their wealth nor their moral commitment (Mackenzie & Lewis, 1999; Lewis, Mackenzie, Webley & Winnett, 1998). We have some ideas, from these same telephone interviews, how people explain the 'social dilemmas' brought about by mixed motives. There is evidence that the 'unethical' portions of the portfolio are sometimes explained as historical accidents; inheritances which recipients have yet to disinfect. Being able to bequeath as much as possible to ones offspring was put forward as a moral obligation of equal value (or even greater value) than being completely scrupulous, in ones ethical investment practices. These explanations are valuable but are based on a restricted sample of people who invest in Shared Interest, an ethical investment vehicle with consistently low returns, who are frequently religiously committed or have been recruited by the Ethical Investment Research Information Service (EIRIS) (Mackenzie & Lewis, 1999). What is required is an examination of more 'mainstream' ethical investors compared to 'standard' ones, in a social context.

3. Aims, Objectives and Methodological Rationale

The aims and objectives of the study are to assess how both 'ethical/green' and 'standard' investors explain their motives to invest and any moral dilemmas, confusions or inconsistencies they face: in what sense (if at all) does investing have a moral dimension? This paper is part of a larger project funded by the Economic and Social Research Council in the U.K. Other strands of the project have produced quantitative results from questionnaire studies (Lewis & Mackenzie, 2000a,b) and computer simulations (Webley, Lewis & Mackenzie, 2000). Qualitative methods have been employed for example, participant observation, in the examination of the authenticity and workings of ethical unit trusts (Mackenzie, 1997). Of more direct relevance to us here are the qualitative data produced from the telephone interviews with ethical investors (Mackenzie & Lewis, 1999). All these approaches have their respective strengths and weaknesses and the value of focus groups as a method has been discussed elsewhere (Lunt, 1996; Krueger, 1994). It was felt that focus groups were a highly appropriate and innovative method for exploring motivation and moral

dilemmas as they provided an opportunity for investors to air their views, in their own words, in a social context with fellow investors (rather than in the comparatively isolated one of a telephone interview). Participants were not invited to reach any consensus, in fact facilitators encouraged speakers to comment on the contributions of others and discuss them as a group. It was hoped in this way that explanations would emerge which were not solely in the possession of individuals, and allowed participants to even question the motivations they attributed to themselves.

4. Method

4.1. Participants

There were fourteen focus groups altogether, seven comprising 'standard' investors ($n = 45$) and seven ethical/green investors ($n = 49$). The average focus group size was seven. Participants were recruited with the help of IFA's in Bristol and Exeter and through local newspaper advertisements. The groups were conducted on the university sites at Exeter and Bath. Participants were paid a small fee to cover travel and expenses.

As would be expected from previous survey work, the majority were over fifty years of age. There were fairly even numbers of males and females. Again as anticipated the occupation profiles of the 'green/ethical' and 'standard' investors differed somewhat: the former comprised a fair number of teachers, nurses, and other health professionals, social workers and people who volunteered the information that they were Christians; there were representatives from the 'caring' professions in the 'standard' group as well but there was much more diversity; participants included industrialists, company directors, small business owners, a meteorologist and a retired soldier.

4.2. Design and Procedure

Participants were told before arrival (either by their IFA or in the newspaper advertisement) that the research was about investment decisions, conducted by university researchers, interested in the replies of nonexperts. On arrival at the focus group location, participants were given a cup of tea or coffee, introduced to one another and the researchers, and the purposes of the research repeated. Confidentiality was assured. The facilitator (Craig Mackenzie, the research officer on the project) explained what a focus group was, that people were invited to air their views, whatever they were, and to comment on the views of others; the purpose of the group was *not* to reach consensus. It was also explained that the role of the facilitator was not to pass judgment, but to make sure that everyone had their say and that the 'conversation' was a directed one that 'stayed on track.' The facilitator and investors sat in a circle around a central table. The focus groups were all tape recorded. The author sat separately taking notes and was not, in a direct sense, a participant. This was also explained to investors.

At the start each contributor filled out a form (one page) saying a little about themselves and why they invest. These were used to give everyone the confidence to contribute, allowing them to use the form as an *aide memoire* if they chose. These were collected at the end to supplement (and as a check) for the author's notes. The groups lasted 45 min on average and all the tape recordings were transcribed producing over 150 pages of typed script (excluding the author's notes and forms). The author was then engaged in a number of 'readings' of the transcript with the help of his notes taken at the time. In addition, the transcripts were all coded using the NUDIST software program. Each 'bit' of information was placed into Textual Units which comprised complete, uninterrupted talk. Each T.U. was classified. A further 'reading' was also provided by John Phillips, an independent researcher (who also did the NUDIST coding). The synthesis provided is therefore a sum of all of these. The data and the coding has been stored in the ESRC qualitative data archive and is open to other researchers to access. Given the time and other resources put into this analysis it is the view of the author that while other researchers might put a different gloss on their interpretations of the data, something radically at variance with the results and commentary presented here would be difficult to justify.

5. RESULTS AND COMMENTARY

5.1. Reasons for Investing

In this section informative textual units (T.U.'s) are reproduced complete and verbatim, where the T.U.'s have been edited, usually because they were too long, this is indicated. The asterisks mask personal details of participants.

Those who agreed straightforwardly, that they invested to make money were in a small minority. It was primarily the nonethical investors who agreed to it in any form. Contexts were used to moderate the idea of raw acquisitiveness and greed. They included the need for reliable pensions and for emergency funding: the change to necessary self-reliance was cited more than once. The most common reasons for investing comprised a combination of 'precaution' and 'foresight' using the terms of Keynes, 1936. All had, however, a flavor of appropriate preservation of self in weakening circumstances. They included those where the desire was to avoid being "a burden to others."

> "I'm old enough now that I'm not too worried about making more money for myself but I have three children and a lot of our financial arrangements has been to try to avoid as much inheritance tax as possible, so I'm thinking of leaving it to them as well, plus there is this point about going to the home, I would hope that if one of us had to go to a home we'd be able to invest enough in say an annuity which would more or less cover it plus pensions that we have. Because this, I think, is a big worry with elderly people nowadays, the cost of going into a nursing home especially." (Nonethical)

There were fewer economic explanations among ethical investors whose reasons for investing, as one might expect were largely ethical. Where economic explanations were present, after 'precaution' and 'foresight' came the motive to bequeath and the need for independence.

> "Well the only thing is, I'm sure I'm not normal in this is that I'm not really concerned about how much I get back because I'm elderly and because I have a house and I have a pension, I'm all right, and I have some money saved. I'm hoping to die before it's spent so that my nieces will inherit it because I'm quite happy living a very modest life now. I don't want to go into an old people's home and have them whip it all away, I'm praying I won't do that. Because it must be lovely to get a nice little nest egg from some elderly aunt. I never got one and I think it would be so nice if someone said 'oh whoopee Auntie **** died, she's left us all this to enjoy.' That isn't the usual point I know." (Ethical)

Ethical investors were reluctant to agree to any characterization, direct or implied, that could impute "economically rational" interests to themselves. Providing for children; providing for health; providing for independence; providing for old age and any weakening in their ability to look after themselves, was seen as sufficiently not-self based as to mitigate any notion of self-interest. In spite of their more free acceptance of rational economic motives, nonethical investors in turn used these same conceptual strategies to mitigate any undesired characterization. In addition "force majeure"—Government 'cut-backs' on welfare provisions—has encouraged investors (especially but not exclusively ethical investors) to reluctantly make provision for themselves which they would have preferred to remain the responsibility of the state in the U.K.

5.2. Ethical Concerns of Investors

Unsurprisingly ethical/green investors readily mentioned ethical concerns when explaining their reasons and motives for investing. For the nonethical group, motives such as wanting to bequeath to offspring came up but not the specific ethical motives common among ethical investors. After the initial discussion with the nonethical group the facilitator mentioned ethical investments

and the form that they took, asking participants to say what they thought of the idea. This generated a good deal of discussion, indeed more so than in the ethical groups where there was more consensus. Textual Unit counts revealed that ethical investors most commonly talked about munitions and armaments, environmental issues and business conduct; nonethical investors about exploitation generally (although closely followed by business conduct and armaments).

Ethical investors did not—and hardly needed to elaborate their reasons for investing ethically in the context of these focus groups. It was clear, however, that the conclusion in parallel work (Lewis & Mackenzie, 2000a) that they saw that decision as consistent with other life (or lifestyle) choices was confirmed.

> "Because it's against what the rest of my life stands for and I want my—I don't want it to be divided into two parts that the money does one thing and I do something else. I mean it's part of me and therefore it should follow the same sort of principles that I want to in the rest of my life. So supporting the campaign against the arms trade and investing in an arms company is total—I mean I should pull out of one or the other." (Ethical)

6. ETHICAL PROBLEMS OF ETHICAL INVESTMENT, MIXED MOTIVES AND PORTFOLIOS

6.1. What Problems Do Ethical Investors Find With Investment?

6.1.1. Worries about investment in general (all ethical)

> "Don't you think we all of us have to believe that decisions we make do have some kind of positive effect otherwise we wouldn't vote or we wouldn't ethically invest. What I put down, one of the things I think I am probably doing when I invest in an ethical fund is producing a certain 'feel good factor' which perhaps offsets any guilt. So maybe those of us who are driven to a certain extent by guilt also need to do something to compensate for that—from an economic point of view this is our way of doing it."

It is clear, then, that for some ethical investors there was an initial reluctance to invest at all, and for some this remains an unresolved issue. In the case of the last quotation, the speaker contrasts a "legitimate" ethical positivity, including a reference to the nonrational act of voting, with a generated good feeling which may be illegitimate, and a mere compensation. This illustrates perfectly the self-denials implicit and explicit in the paradoxes of ethical investment.

6.1.2. Inevitable compromise and mixed portfolios (almost all ethical)

Quantitative evidence reveals that many ethical investors have 'standard' (or 'unethical') investments as well (Lewis & Mackenzie, 2000a). Is this a dilemma for these investors? And if so how can it be resolved?

"Well having said what I said I must say that I feel guilty about my banking account. I've got two bank accounts, one with the Co-op Bank and one with Barclays and I have Barclays because it is convenient if I need to go to the machine to get cash."

Facilitator: "And does it cause you an extreme amount of guilt or a little amount or what?"

"I wouldn't say an extreme amount of guilt but it often crosses my mind ought I to do something about this and so far I haven't." (Ethical)

"Vaguely yes. My name's ***** and I really invested ethically because I wanted to avoid particular things in particular the arms trade. It seems stupid to me to go out protesting against things and then to put my money into something that was supporting it. I'm not sure I've solved the whole problem because I can't say that all my money is invested in ethical funds, but I hope I'm avoiding the worst excesses. I want to." (Ethical)

"And I think it could be imprudent for a group of people or individuals to put all their money in this one ethical basket because that can go out of fashion and if you want money because you were ill or you wanted it for other reasons you may not be able to get it because you've put all your eggs in the ethical basket. So I think it would be very imprudent." (Ethical)

6.2. Can Ethical Investing Make a Difference?

In the telephone interviews reported in a previous study (Mackenzie & Lewis, 1999) respondents admitted that what they were doing by investing ethically was 'salving their consciences.' Beyond this respondents were not very articulate about the broader issues and implications of ethical investing, explaining their actions in terms of individual attributes for example, 'because I am a Christian.' Telephone interviews can be stilted. Did the focus group give a greater opportunity to explore the likely social consequences and causes of this kind of investment? The examples below suggest the answer is 'Yes.'

"I will go back to what we said before: I mean, I'm with you entirely, I'm totally opposed to the present economic system and I find it difficult to operate within it. The little bits of money that I have invested are not invested in order to make a profit. I invest them to encourage causes in which I believe and I'm not interested in any return but I am interested in giving some encouragement to causes and things in which I believe. Frankly it's as simple as that." (Ethical)

Many thought that progress towards acceptance and social influence would be slow (60 T.U.'s). Nonetheless, it was worth the effort.

"And if more people make the statement that they're going to ethically invest then that may in turn have an influence on other people and change the pattern of investment to make the unethical firms start to look at their practices and change. I mean it's a very dripping–water dripping on a stone effect, I don't think investing ethically has a major effect but it may have a timely effect if enough of us decide to do it." (Ethical)

There was a clear view that awareness was growing: (116 T.U.'s)

"It's come a long way since it started when the ethical funds were laughed at by the mainstream and now at least they are considered to be part of the mainstream and they are starting to have an effect as far as I can see." (Ethical)

"It is true but you've got to do something haven't you? You can't just turn a blind eye even though you've only got a little voice. If enough little voices say enough then perhaps something will change. And certainly government policy ought to change." (Ethical)

"Well I think if enough people are investing ethically I mean surely businesses are going to say,' well there's a lot of people who do care about these things we'd better start cleaning up our act.' I think it needs to be–it's obviously a carrot and a stick and there also needs to be regulations as well but I think that it does help. Yes." (Ethical)

"I see it as part of the wider thing as well like buying organic produce which I do sometimes but not always and fair trade, you know if I can, and then I'll buy fair trade stuff—I mean I must admit it depends how much money I've got at the time and various other things, but I see it as part of the wider thing." (Ethical)

"It's why have we chosen that fund? Because it's ethical and because it is in tune with what we want. We're not doing it as a game. It's not—well certainly not for me it's not toy money that I can throw around, it's something that I hope is meaningful and one day I hope it will have an effect." (Ethical)

Participants were generally clear that although it might be a long haul, there were similar examples that gave grounds for optimism, and that there is evidence of a growing awareness and influence. They wanted to feel, and felt, as if they were part of a new self-sustaining movement.

7. Some Conclusions and Speculations

Very few people, it seems are particularly keen to see themselves as the embodiment of rational economic man (in the narrow sense, as a wealth maximizer). Even 'standard' (nonethical) investors are faintly embarrassed by the notion that they invest primarily, for income and capital growth. 'Precaution,' 'foresight,' avoiding being a 'burden to others' in old age and the motive to bequeath are frequently mentioned by ethical and nonethical investors alike. There is a feeling that individuals are now required to make provisions for themselves which they would prefer to remain the responsibility of the state: something particularly, but not exclusively, remarked upon by ethical investors.

Ethical/Green investors naturally have a different agenda and there is a considerable consensus among them about the importance of avoiding munitions, exploitative and polluting businesses and those that test their products on animals. There is a feeling here too that the perceived lack of government initiative in tackling problems of pollution and exploitation of various kinds has been the spur to action.

Standard investors, on the whole, are not against the notion of ethical investing when introduced to the idea and some are quick to say that while their investments may not be particularly ethical, neither are they that obviously unethical either. The prime differences between the two groups is that the ethical investors have put their sympathies into action, thereby maintaining a coherent 'lifestyle' given their career choices and other connections. But it is not a simple matter of putting ones money where ones morals are, as generally ethical investors see the performance of their investment as acceptable; nonethical investors not only have less moral commitment they also perceive ethical investments as poorer performers and are unconvinced, on occasions, of their real ethical status. What is abundantly clear is it is not only ethical investors, but 'standard' ones as well who see making investments as more than just a financial decision.

Many ethical investors have mixed portfolios of ethical and not so ethical investments at the same time. This is variously accounted for by inertia, a 'lack of interest in money,' and the information costs involved in 'getting it right.' While a few investors say they are prepared to lose money in order to invest consistently with their moral commitments, others say it is imprudent to put all ones money in a single ethical egg basket (which fits closely with the evidence form questionnaire studies: Lewis and

Mackenzie, 2000a). Not all ethical investors are the same and clearly this 'dilemma' is more troublesome to some than others. There were those who were fairly comfortable with their positions while others felt 'guilty' and 'selfish' about investing at all. A way of avoiding these feelings was to think of investments as providing for oneself because of government 'failure,' to bequeath to others, and for the benefit of some 'future self.' There were instances where participants got themselves in knots: it was wrong to enjoy investments selfishly yet one still could get a 'warm glow' by investing ethically.

Explanations were not solely individualistic; there was evidence that ethical investors saw themselves as part of a social movement. There was a common belief that the market could not be changed overnight but that slowly but surely, like water dripping on stones the moral commitment of ethical investors would make a difference.

In a sense this study has been an examination of 'practical ethics' where people do the best they can given motives and responsibilities which do not always pull in the same directions. The Mackenzie and Lewis (1999) paper concluded that ethical investors where neither maximizing their morals nor their wealth and similar conclusions (based on a larger and less restricted selection of participants) are reached here. There is one important exception: in the earlier paper there was a tone of disappointment among the authors for the way participants were behaving and it is hoped that a more positive note is struck here. Participants frequently felt confused with current ideological debate, where the relatively old certainties of socialism in the U.K. have broken down; they did not know where they stood on the new pragmatic 'third way.' Consequently what they were doing was well-meaning but was not driven by any consensual ideological position. In this way they presented themselves as driven by mixed motives with which many readers will now be familiar. What participants have told us should not be up for criticism, rather what they have said is a mirror to wider social issues and contradictions.

REFERENCES

Anand, P., Cowton, C., 1993. The ethical investor: Exploring dimensions of investment behaviour. *Journal of Economic Psychology 14* (2), 377–385

Domini, A., Kinder, K., 1984. *Ethical investing.* Addison-Wesley, Reading, MA.

Etzioni, A., 1988. *The moral dimension.* Free Press, New York.

Furnham, A., 1985. Why do people save? Attitudes to, and habits of saving money in Britain. *Journal of Applied Social Psychology 15,* 493–502.

Kahneman, P., Tversky, A., 1979. Prospect theory, an analysis of decision making under risk. *Econometrica 47,* 263–292.

Keynes, J.M., 1936. *The general theory of employment, interest and money.* Macmillan, London.

Krueger, R., 1994. *Focus groups: A practical guide for applied research.* Sage, London.

Lewis, A., Mackenzie, C., 2000a. Money, morals, ethical investing and economic psychology. *Human Relations 53* (2), 179–191.

Lewis, A., Mackenzie, C., 2000b. Support for investor activism among UK ethical Investors. *Journal of Business Ethics 24,* 215–222.

Lewis, A., Mackenzie, C., 1997. Morals, motives and money: the case of UK Ethical Investing. Unpublished manuscript available from authors.

Lewis, A, Webley, P., 1994. Social and ethical investing: Beliefs, preferences and the willingness to sacrifice financial return. In: Lewis, A., Warneryd, K.-E. (Eds.), *Ethics and Economic Affairs.* Routledge, London.

Lewis, A., Mackenzie, C., Webley, P., Winnett, A., 1998. Morals and markets: Some theoretical and policy implications of ethical investment. In: Taylor-Gooby, P. (Ed.) *Choice and public policy.* Macmillan, London.

Lowry, R., 1991. *Good money: A guide to profitable social investing in the '90's.* Norton, New York.

Lunt, P., 1996. Rethinking the focus group in media and communications research. *Journal of Communication 46,* (2), 79–98.

Mackenzie, C., 1997. Ethical investment and the challenge of corporate reform. Unpublished Ph.D. thesis: University of Bath, U.K.

Mackenzie, C., Lewis, A., 1999. Morals and markets: The case of ethical investing. *Business Ethics Quarterly 9* (3), 439–452.

Ross, L., 1977. The intuitive psychologist and his shortcomings. In: Berkowitz, L. (Ed.), *Advance in experimental social psychology (Vol. 10).* Academic Press, New York.

Warneryd, K.-E., 1999. *The psychology of saving.* Edward Elgar, Cheltenham, U.K.

Webley, P., Lewis, A., Mackenzie, C., 2000. Commitment among ethical investors: An experimental approach. *Journal of Economic Psychology 22* (1), 27–42.

The Pub and the People [Excerpt] (1942)

Mass Observation

In Worktown more people spend more time in public houses than they do in any other buildings except private houses and work-places. Why?

Of the social institutions that mould men's lives between home and work in an industrial town, such as Worktown, the pub has more buildings, holds more people, takes more of their time and money, than church, cinema, dance-hall, and political organizations put together.

The pub, reduced to its lowest terms, is a house where during certain hours everyone is free to buy and drink a glass of beer. It is the only kind of public building used by large numbers of ordinary people where their thoughts and actions are *not* being in some way arranged for them; in the other kinds of public buildings they are the audiences, watchers of political, religious, dramatic, cinematic, instructional or athletic spectacles. But within the four walls of the pub, once a man has bought or been bought his glass of beer, he has entered an environment in which he is participator rather than spectator.

In six religious sects (five of them new), the ordinary man or woman has also a higher degree of participation, even extending to speaking in tongues. They are the only other institutions in Worktown which supply a similar participation, except the "clubs"—and the word "club" has become synonymous locally with drink; and especially with obtaining drink after hours.

The relation of the pub to the place as a whole may be indicated by a general account from a person who has been working with the study unit; his impressions are thus:

There are 300 pubs in Worktown: 200 police: nearly 200 churches and chapels: 30 cinemas: about 24 prostitutes: 180,000 other people.

The major industry of this industrial town is cotton, but iron, leather, machinery, coal, and tripe are also important industries. Chimneys are the outstanding landscape feature. Most of them smoke, and all day long soot dirties all the faces. It is the most prosperous of all the cotton towns, for it does fine spinning, and so has been least affected by foreign competition. In 1938, 15,000 workers were unemployed, which is approximately one in every nine of the working population. Work is predominantly done in the mills, whose employees include a high percentage of women (with high maternal and infant mortality rates). There are extremely few "upper class" people: there is a constant tendency for people who are economically or intellectually successful to leave the town and the district. The M.P.s are Conservative. There is very little local art, and if you go into the municipal Art Gallery, the attendant comes and has a good look to see that you are all right. The local evening paper is the intellectual dominant, reaching some 96 per cent of homes: it is "impartial," with a strong liberal-conservative slant, old established, first-rate journalism and production. The Unilever combine sales departments regard this as one of their black spots. Local patriotism is strong; though the town (incorporated as a borough in

---

SOURCE: From *The Pub and the People* by Mass Observation. Reproduced with permission of Curtis Brown Group Ltd, London on behalf of The Trustees of the Mass Observation Archive.

1838, now getting a strong city urge) is one of an endless chain across the north, it in no sense identifies itself with other adjacent towns. It has a culture essentially its own, and available for uniform study—the solid background and smoky foreground of the industrial revolution and the vast, intricate technical civilization that has grown up around the basic industries. Worktown has a saying which has been heard from two consecutive mayors in public: "What Worktown says to-day, the North says to-morrow, and London the day after." Neither the tram service labyrinth that greets the new arrival outside the huge, hollow station, nor the architecture along the main streets (wider than in other towns), nor the women's hats, lend much colour to this thesis.

Very few workers have holidays with pay. Sunday is strict, and no trams or buses run in the morning. There are some 55,000 houses, and the same number of Co-op. members. The houses stand mainly in long, continuous rows, with narrow backs, across which washing flaps, soot-gathering, on Mondays.

The streets are mostly cobbled—and so is the bed of the town's river, the only paved river in England. Innumerable clogs clatter before daylight on their way to cotton's 48 hour week, cotton spinners with wages from 18 to 80 or so shillings, weavers averaging 32. A third of the workers are in Unions. There is no local branch of the Catering Section of the Transport and General Workers, the Union that takes in barmen. The Isolation Hospital and the Technical School are years out of date, must soon be replaced to save local disgrace. Water supply good. Rates just up Is. *2d.* partly because of the new huge extension to the Town Hall, white, ornate, Bradshaw, Gass and Hope (architects) crescent, with lions and arcades. This is in town centre, bordering a huge waste space, fringed on another side by the new and very striking cinema, and a decomposing interstitial industrial belt, with slums immediately adjacent—they also run off from the main shopping streets. The Casual Ward is in the town centre too. The Public Assistance Committee's

Mental block is well outside, though, and inadequate; people have to be recertified every few weeks in accordance with law because there's nowhere to shift them to. Most people are sane, pleasant and straightforward, without southern sophistication, local-minded but curious, reasonably credulous, reasonably optimistic, fairly mean and suspicious—these generalizations don't really mean much about any town, and equally cover all.

The dialect is at first unintelligible to the stranger. Full of fine shades of meaning, reversed grammar, and regular good humour. On the whole people care about their own homes, and their few personal dreams (security, a holiday week at orientalised Blackpool, a fortune in the Pools) and nothing else matters very much except the progress made by the town's famous football club, whose stadium draws each Saturday more people than go into pubs or churches, in a once-a-week mass manifestation of enthusiasm, fury, and joy.

Things are made in this dirty town. That justifies it. Why they are made no ordinary citizen knows. In this mess of goodwill, misunder-standing, effort, insecurity, thought for the day, *Victoria the Great* as biggest film draw of the year, the pub stands on any corner. The frequent tide of adult folk sends long temporary pseudopodia into the doors of each, to drink and talk, then retract in darkness to smaller but not dissimilar houses where they sleep. Why do they go there? Because people have done before? Because other people are there? Because there are things there that are nowhere else ? Because people go everywhere there is to go? Because the pub is as much a part of this civilization as the font or forge or diesel engine? Because they like to change the rate of living, to alter the tempo of muscle and eye, trained now in such exact and even exacting routines—but people with no such exactness, cannibals and so on, also take rate changers, stimulants, drugs? They go there to drink.

But there is more to it than that.

It is no more true to say that people go to public houses to drink than it is to say they go to private houses to eat and sleep. These are the things that people do in pubs:

SIT and/or STAND
DRINK

TALK	about	betting sport
THINK		work people
SMOKE		drinking weather
SPIT		politics dirt

Many PLAY GAMES
   cards
   dominoes
   darts
   quoits
Many BET
   receive and
   pay out losings and winnings.
   PEOPLE SING AND LISTEN TO SINGING: PLAY THE PIANO AND LISTEN TO IT BEING PLAYED.
    THESE THINGS ARE OFTEN CONNECTED WITH PUBS ...
... weddings and funerals.
   quarrels and fights.
   bowls, fishing and picnics.
   trade unions.
   secret societies. Oddfellows. Buffs.
   religious processions.
   sex.
   getting jobs.
   crime and prostitution.
   dog shows.
   pigeon flying.
PEOPLE SELL AND BUY
   bootlaces, hot pies, black puddings, embrocation.
Also

   LOTTERIES AND SWEEPSTAKES
   happen. PREJUDICES gather.

All these things don't happen on the same evenings, or in the same pubs. But an ordinary evening in an ordinary pub will contain a lot of them.

Here is a characteristic record of such an evening:

This pub is at the corner of a block of brickfronted houses, whose front doors open directly on to the pavement. The road is cobbled; the bare, flat façades of the houses are all tinted to the same tone by the continual rain of soot from the chimneys of the mill opposite and the chimneys of all the other mills that stand in all the other streets like this.

The pub isn't much different from the other houses in the block, except for the sign with its name and that of the brewing firm that owns it, but its lower windows are larger than those of the others, and enclosed with stucco fake columns that go down to the ground; and the door, on the corner, is set at an angle; it is old-looking, worn, brown; in the top half is a frosted-glass window with VAULT engraved on it in handwriting flourishes; at the edges of the main pane are smaller ones of red and blue glass.

The door opens with a brass latch, disclosing a worn and scrubbed wooden floor, straight bar counter brown-painted with thick yellow imitation graining on the front panelling; at its base is a scattered fringe of sawdust, spit-littered, and strewn with match-ends and crumbled cigarette packets. Facing the bar a brown-painted wooden bench runs the length of the room.

Four yellowish white china handles, shiny brass on top, stand up from the bar counter. This is important, it is the beer engine, nerve-centre of the pub. Behind the bar, on shelves, reflecting themselves against mirrors at the back of their shelves, are rows of glasses and bottles, also stacked matches and Woodbine packets. Beer advertising cards and a notice against betting are fixed to the smoke-darkened yellowish wallpaper; and on the wall, beside the door, is a square of black glass, framed in walnut, that has painted on it, in gilt, a clock face with roman numerals, and the letters NO TICK. (The clock can't tick, it has no works; but if you are a regular the landlord will give you credit.)

Five men, in caps, stand or sit, three at the bar, two on the bench. They all have pint mugs of mild.

From the back parlour can be heard the sound of a man singing a sentimental song. In here they are discussing crime, man-slaughter, and murder. A small, thin man (whose name subsequently turns out to be X) appears to be a little drunk, and is talking very loudly, almost shouting. Another chap, called Y, also has a lot to say.

X (to Y): " If a man says you're a jailbird he's no right to say it—if he is a man."

Another man: "He can have you oop for defamation."

Y: " I've seen cases in the paper where a man's been found guilty and it's a bloody shame."

X (very slowly): "I'll tell you a bloody case, I'm telling you . . ."

Y: "Awright."

X: "There were two navvies————"

Another man, who has been quiet up to now, suddenly says, in indignant sounding tones "No, they weren't navvies," to which X simply replies "Ah'm sober enough" and goes on, apparently irrelevant— "There isn't a law made but what there's a loop'ole in it. Marshall Hall said that afore 'e was made a Sir—some big trial it were, for murder, an' it lasted a week, he'd strangled 'er wi' a necklace, it were that Yarmouth murder. He 'a won t´case, too, but for that courtin'couple, they were passing and they 'eard 'er screamin' and they thought they were only, you know, 'avin' a bit. Instead o' that 'e were stranglin' 'er. D'you know why there's a loophole in these 'ere laws. Well, them there M.P.s—'ave you ever noticed there's always some lawyer puts up. Now the reason for that————" He looks up and sees, through the serving hatch at the back of the bar, a man going into the parlour, and shouts out "Eh, Dick, lend us two an' six. We're skint." Dick shouts back something inaudible and goes on into the parlour.

X stands silent for a moment, beerswallowing. One of the men on the bench says to him "Are you workin'?"

X: "I'll never work no more. I've an independent fortune every week."

Questioner turns to the barmaid, who has now come in from the parlour, and says "Molly, you don't know Mr. X, do you?" (Meaning that she knows him pretty well.) She laughs and replies:

"No, I don't know him."

X: "None of that, Mr. X. I call 'er Molly, not Mrs. . . ." He trails off, not knowing her surname.

The chaps begin to talk about swimming. X, irrepressible, knowing everything, chips in "I'll tell you 'oo were a good lad—Bob Robbins."

The singer in the parlour, who has been steadily working through three verses, now finishes with a prolonged and loud note, and there is the sound of some clapping.

The talkers have now divided into two groups, one around X, the other around an old man who is arguing about the age of the swimming baths. He keeps on saying "I remember it being built," to which another chap replies, disagreeing, "My father works there."

X: "That lad could fly through t' water like a bloody fish."

Y: "Bill Howard, that's 'is name."

X: "Goes into water like a bloody fish."

Old man (loud): "I remember it being built."

X: "I'll tell you what 'e could do—you know when you're walking along the towing path, you an' me walking along the towing path, 'e'd keep up wi' you, you an'me, walking decent tha knows, 'e'll keep up wi' you."

X stops, drinks, and the old man can be heard stubbornly reiterating: "I remember it being built."

X: "I'll tell you the hardest feat that was ever known—for a man to fall off the top of the bath and not go to the bottom and not go to the top, as long as 'e can 'old 'is breath—I've seen (name inaudible) do that, 'e could do a 'undred yards in eleven seconds—wi'out any training. What could 'e do wi' training? I'm telling you, he could stay in t' water, not go to the top and not go to the bottom—an' I'll tell you 'ow 'e did it."

Y (interrupting): " 'ave another."

X: "Aye."

While he is getting his drink a chap stands up, and says "I swim that road," demonstrating convulsive sidestroke movements with his arms.

The old man looks up from his argument and remarks "I go left 'and first." And returns to the swimming bath discussion.

X, now with another beer, carries on: "He'd drop into the water and neether go to the bottom or go to the top . . ."

In the parlour they are singing the chorus of a jazz song, which the barmaid hums loudly.

It is now half past eight, and more people are coming in. Two old men arrive; both have gaps in their front teeth; wearing clogs, dark scarves knotted round pink wrinkled necks, white hair raggedly protrudes from behind their old caps; their coats, trousers, and waistcoats are all different yet appearing alike to be made of a shapeless greasy grey-blue cloth. They sit together, talking in undertones. Their beermugs are placed on the edge of the bar counter, and they have to reach forward, half standing up, to get at them. They both smoke pipes, from which drift the ropey smell of cheap twist. At regular intervals they shoot tidy gobs of spittle across into the sawdust. They reach for their mugs together, and drink the same amount at each swig. The mugs stand untouched for several minutes, with a last inch of beer in them; then one of the men stands up, drains his mug, and bangs it on the counter:

> The barmaid has gone out, and the landlord takes her place. (He is large, redfaced, clear blue eyes, about 45, wears a clean dark-grey suit, no coat, clean white shirt, sleeve rolled up, no collar or tie.) He draws off two halfpint glasses from one of the middle taps; the old man pays him, and the two empty the glasses into their mugs. During this transaction no one has said anything. Both men, standing, take a long, simultaneous swig, and sit down. One remarks, suddenly loud "Well, of all the bloody good things at Ascot t'other week anyone following Aga Khan t'other week would 'ave 'ad a bloody picnic."
>
> X bawls across at him "What dost tha know about bloody horses. I'll bet thee a bloody shilling and gie thee two thousand pound start an' I'll 'ave bloody Lawson agen 'im. Why, 'e's seven bloody winners at meeting, you bloody crawpit." The old man says nothing.
>
> A group of four men has gathered round the table, and is playing dominoes. Each has a pint mug at his elbow. At the end of the round they turn the dominoes face downwards and stir them noisily. They play with a lot of loud talking and joking.
>
> One says "'oo went down then?"
>
> "Jimmy."

> "Oh, Jimmy went down."
>
> "I did."
>
> "My down—one an' one."
>
> "If we're down we're down, that's all. What's the use of worrying."
>
> "Come on, man, don't go to bloody sleep. Th'art like a bloody hen suppin' tea; when th'art winnin' it's awreet, but when th'art losin' it's all bloody wrong."
>
> They talk about the holidays, which begin next week.
>
> "I'm not savin' oop twelve bloody months for t' sake a gooing away fer a week. Wife's always asking what I do wi' me overtime, and I towd 'er—why, I bloody well spend it, what dost think—and she says—Tha owt t' 'ave more bloody sense."

So on, until, at about 10.20, they leave; standing for from one to three minutes outside, and calling "Good night" as they walk, at about two miles an hour, to their private houses, which are seldom more than three minutes' walk away.

We shall presently come to all the different things that are done in the pub, from brawls to Royal and Ancient Order of Buffalo initiations; from the fading folk-lore of Pigeon Racing to the growing rage for darts. It is only necessary to point out here, that betting and gambling are largely centred in the pub, with a whole social group around the bookmakers' runner; but that the other things are found to some extent in other institutions. There are few things which are peculiar to the pub in Worktown, other than draught beer and spittoons. It is essentially a social group around widespread and commonplace social activities. These attain new angles, new point, and a close integration with other aspects of industrial life by being pressed into the service of satisfying, or dissatisfying, these numerous small communities bound together by the bond of beer habits.

There are, on the other hand, certain things which are not found in pubs in Worktown, though they occur in pubs elsewhere. The following might be expected:

Billiards.

Whist Drives.

Dances.

Skittles.

Shove ha'penny.

Literature.

Billiards, dancing and whist drives never occur in Worktown pubs. They are a regular feature of church and political life, and often a major source of church and party revenue. There are also separate dance and billiard halls, well patronized: interest in billiards tends to decline, in dancing to increase. The patrons of both are often regular pub-goers, and frequently leave the halls to have a drink. Skittles and shove ha'penny are apparently unknown in the town, and the pub has apparently given up its one-time function of a reading place; few even have an evening paper for their patrons. Bearing these qualifications in mind, it should incidentally be possible from the particular study of Worktown pub life to appreciate something of the function of the pub in all English industrial communities.

"Afterword" From *Sidewalk* by Mitch Duneier (2000)

Hakim Hasan

The streets that are the focus of these pages are places of metropolitan refuge, where the identities of the men and women who work and live are hidden in public space. In the pedestrian's eye these men and women are reduced to a horrific *National Geographic* photograph come to life. It is as if they were born on these streets and have no past, or other life experiences.

My decision to leave the corporate world and sell books on Sixth Avenue was incomprehensible to my family and friends. One of my black former co-workers saw me selling books one evening, walked over to me and asked with comic disbelief, "So this is what you are doing now?" I did not want to answer this embarrassing question, so I replied, "No. I'm just watching the stuff for a friend of mine. He went to the bathroom."

In effect, I went into exile on the street. I began the process of exile long before I arrived on Sixth Avenue. In an attempt to avoid the everyday formalities of corporate life, in 1988 I began working as a legal proofreader on the night shift in the word-processing department of the law firm Robinson, Silverman. Nothing made the futility of my efforts more evident to me than an incident that occurred one evening when I had no work to do because of an upcoming holiday. I sat at a secretary's work station and read a copy of *Business Week*. A white attorney walked over to me. He leaned over my shoulder, saying not a word, and began to read. The crumbs from the popcorn he was eating fell on my head. I thought to myself, "Man, I should stand up and slap this guy senseless." In the moments that it took for me to weigh this option, I imagined paramedics working on his limp body and a phalanx of television reporters and police officers interviewing my co-workers in the corridor. I did not say a word to him. My silence was simply another in a series of concessions I made to those who provided me with my daily bread.

I was abruptly fired during an employee-review meeting in 1991 by the director of administrative services, a middle-aged white woman. Why? I had been accused of being incompetent, she said, by an attorney she refused to identify. I still remember the cadence of her words: "I'm so sorry, but we're going to have to let you go," as if it were a refrain to a song; and I recall the way I sat in a chair opposite her desk, statue-still, paralyzed by their unforeseen and immediate implications. I recall the way she stared at my face and the way my silence prompted her to say, "You seem to be taking this so calmly."

The director of administrative services was not my supervisor. How did she conclude that I was incompetent? What were her criteria? I worked on the night shift and saw her rarely—only when she was working late. The night-shift proofreaders and word processors had very little contact with her or the members of the legal staff, as it was my supervisor's responsibility to deal with them.

Prior to this meeting, my supervisor and I traded the normal office banter. She never gave me any verbal or written notification, during the time she was my supervisor, that my work was not satisfactory, nor was she present at the meeting.

Incompetent? What about those three years, working under deadlines and enormous pressure, proofreading legal documents inside a room the size of a prison cell with three other proofreaders? The director of administrative services believed the expression on my face was one of calm. It was an expression of shock. That night I left this insular world in order to salvage whatever was left of myself and forge a new identity.

Mitchell Duneier recalls that he was thoroughly surprised when, during our first conversation at my book-vending table, I told him that I had a Rolodex. His surprise was a matter of social context. But what if I had not mentioned the word Rolodex to Mitch? Because the word Rolodex is associated with people who work in offices, and because I was perceived as a "street person," my use of it stood out. It caused

a shift in Mitch's perceptions of me. I am now inclined to suggest that this book would not have been written if it had not been for this conversation, which challenged his assumptions about me and my social status.

In the first chapter Mitch recalls his difficulty in convincing me to become a subject—at that time the sole subject—of the book. Indeed, I found myself hearing the decree of my mother, whenever she had to leave my siblings and me at home alone: *Do not open the door for anyone while I'm gone.*

If I defied the maternal decree and opened *this* door, on what basis would I weigh Mitch's intentions? How could I prevent him from appropriating me as mere data, from not giving me a voice in how the material in his book would be selected and depicted? How does a subject take part in an ethnographic study in which he has very little faith and survive as something more than a subject and less than an author?

Because I believe my disastrous experience in the corporate world was the effect of racism (a claim many whites these days liken to that of the proverbial boy who cried "Wolf!"), I asked myself, "Can I expect Mitch, as a white sociologist, to understand why that experience led me to work as a book vendor on Sixth Avenue in the first place?" The idea of race as a lived experience could not be avoided; at the same time, if I made the mistake of denying Mitch *his* humanity on the basis of race, without giving him a fair chance, there would have been no way for me to know whether he could write about my life accurately.

I did not know how Mitch would construct an account of my life on these blocks. Would he conduct his research as a descendant of a sociological tradition which historically has found it all but impossible to write and theorize about blacks, especially poor blacks, as complex human beings? I worried this way, oddly enough, even after reading Mitch's book *Slim's Table,* despite its insights into the lives of working-class black men, because my life, not the lives of the men depicted in that book, was at stake.

Over several weeks, I talked with Mitch informally at my book-vending table, and whenever possible at a restaurant where we could speak candidly without being interrupted. These exploratory conversations revolved around the basic facts of my life and, more to the point, the circumstances that prompted me to become a street bookseller, and they were emotionally charged. Mitch did not react to what I had to say with the cool, clinical detachment I had imagined to be the sociologist's stock-in-trade. He listened attentively. I came to respect his sensitivity, and soon I trusted him to write about my life.

After reading the original manuscript three years ago, I concluded that the events and conversations that took place at my book-vending table could not convey, by themselves, the complexity of the social structure that existed on these blocks. I sent Mitch a long, handwritten letter outlining my concerns. I expected him to think I had overstepped my bounds as "subject." True, I knew Mitch's research agenda had been shaped by my reference to Jane Jacobs's intriguing idea of the "public character." But, since I was a subject, how far did my right to theorize go?

Not long afterward we spoke on the telephone—I from a public telephone as I watched my table, he from his office. Mitch told me that he appreciated my sociological insights and that he was grateful for the letter. He wondered aloud if it might be productive for us to co-teach a seminar where we would discuss the issues raised by the book with students and each other. Shortly thereafter, Mitch received permission to invite me as a paid lecturer to co-teach a ten-week undergraduate seminar with him. This course marked the beginning of a process whereby the other men and women on Sixth Avenue would no longer be mere data.

I literally found myself selling books on Sixth Avenue one day and on the next seated opposite Mitch at a huge conference table at the University of California at Santa Barbara. This was new terrain, since I had no formal experience whatsoever teaching in a university environment. Up until that point, I had jokingly told Mitch that the sidewalk had been my classroom, so to speak, and that I was contemplating charging tuition.

The nineteen students whom Mitch and I had selected on an "instructor approval" basis to enroll in this seminar represented diverse ethnic backgrounds and demonstrated a keen interest in the way the seminar was structured, as well as a willingness to tackle an arduous series of reading assignments. Race, of course, was an unavoidable component of our meetings. This was due to the choice of reading materials and to the issues that emanated from the street.

We encouraged class participation based upon the assigned reading materials so that individual seminars would not be reduced to "rap sessions." The reading material we assigned was twofold: some books provided structural and conceptual understanding of issues of street life (*The Death and Life of Great American Cities, Streetwise, Urban Fortunes,* and *The Homeless),* others were "black books" that working and middle-class blacks purchased at my book-vending table (*Pimp, Dopefiend, Volunteer Slavery, Africa: Mother of Civilization, Makes Me Wanna Holler, Breaking Bread, Race Matters,* and *Confronting Authority,* to name a few).

Co-teaching this seminar with Mitch was not easy. Not only was there a tremendous amount of preparation involved, but it gave me a firsthand understanding of the magnitude of his responsibilities as a college professor. Teaching undergraduates, where a professor must contend with the occasionally base intellectual instincts of some students, is a difficult enterprise. Standards and critical thinking are of the utmost importance.

I was given an office in which to work and conduct meetings with students during my office hours. Before each of the first four seminars, I would sit in my office stricken with such anxiety that I would find myself taking two Tylenols to help ease the onslaught of a headache, even though I had spent years at my book-vending table conversing with ordinary and famous people day after day.

And yet I adapted easily to this new social context. The seminar proceeded wonderfully, with Alice and Marvin visiting us in the middle of the academic quarter for two weeks. What became evident from the questions and responses of students was the shortcomings of the book. Why were the lives of the magazine vendors not included in the first draft? What about the panhandlers? What about homelessness? Why didn't these people simply find jobs? What did the whites have to say to these people? What were their interactions like with neighborhood residents? How did I get my books? Could a white professor really be trusted to write about black men without succumbing to stereotypes? These were difficult questions, and Mitch and I talked about them at length in between sessions. As a result of the seminar and our conversations, Mitch began writing this book all over again, returning to Sixth Avenue to document the lives of the other men.

My telephone communiqués back to New York proved to be meaningless as Alice recounted the general assessment of my trip to me. The men on Sixth Avenue could hardly believe that I was actually co-teaching a class with Mitch. They thought I was in Santa Barbara vacationing and enjoying the high life.

The social hierarchy of the book vendors and magazine vendors was characterized by long-standing antagonisms (as described in the chapter on the space wars), and I had a good but far from perfect relationship with the magazine vendors. In order for Mitch to gain access, he needed a sponsor among them—both to help him gain their trust and to ensure his safety. This is why Marvin was crucial. As a sponsor, he had greater credibility than I would have had, because he and Mitch had had no prior relationship.

Marvin and I briefed Mitch on what to expect and avoid as he initially moved about these blocks conducting fieldwork. Many of these men believed that Mitch was "rich" (that is the word I often heard) and they were prepared to take advantage of him. On these blocks, life is measured on a day-to-day basis, often in terms of the money one can obtain from people of goodwill. In those early days of fieldwork, the question of whether or not Mitch was really writing a book about the meaning of their lives was secondary. Their question was: How much money can I get out of him?

Some of them had earned as much as one hundred dollars apiece selling magazines the day before, but had spent that money on crack or alcohol before dawn. They invariably asked Mitch for money to buy breakfast, which had a variety of shaded meanings: a two-dollar ham, egg, and cheese sandwich from Gray's Papaya, a bottle of St. Ides malt liquor, or a hit or two of crack.

As far as money goes, none of these men were aware that Mitch had covered all of the costs associated with the research for this book out of his salary. He did not have a research grant, and would not wait to get one before conducting his research. Marvin was shocked when I told him this, but I knew that it would not have mattered if I told it to the other men.

Mitch eventually learned how to say no to requests for money from seemingly desperate people. He established goodwill through his seriousness of purpose and sincerity as a sociologist. I watched him gain access to the magazine vendors as I periodically peeked around the corner from my table and sometimes looked from the second-floor window of Userfriendly (a pay-by-the-hour computer center, now closed). I could see him working for Marvin and slowly but assuredly easing his way into the life that existed at that table. There was an "invisible" social world there unknown to most pedestrians and, as I would later learn, even to me. Through intensive fieldwork, Mitch managed to document this subtle and complex social structure. It is fair to say, in retrospect, that his reception among these men was actually far easier than I anticipated it would be.

Alfred Robinson, who was among the "first generation" of men to make their lives on Sixth Avenue, told me that Mitch would have become a "victim" on these streets had there not been a consensus among the men and women that what he was trying to do was important. In the end, any sociologist who simply believes that time spent in the field qualifies him as "one of the boys" is not only sadly mistaken but in grave trouble. The street is the street. Make no mistake about it. Mitch understood this from the outset. He never pretended to be anything other than he was: a human being and sociologist attempting to understand the meaning of our lives.

Not one of these men or women (including myself) had any coordinates for this kind of undertaking, but in order for Ovie Carter to photograph these men and women, they had to put their faith in him too. People who work and live on the street, as a general rule, do not like, let alone permit, photographs to be taken of them. Some do not like the idea of their lives being reduced to a tourist attraction, while others see photographs as an aspect of police surveillance. Many think that unless they "get paid" the photographer is "getting over" on them.

Ovie is a black staff photographer for the *Chicago Tribune*. He is a soft-spoken man who has spent over twenty-five years photographing the inner city, with a particular focus on problems like drug abuse. This would be the third major project on which he and Mitch would collaborate. I can say with assurance that Ovie's status as a black man was not the sole criterion for his admission into the lives of these men and women. Jamaane, for example, initially expressed his reluctance to be photographed. I recall Ovie talking to Jamaane about his reluctance in front of Store 24 (now Go Sushi) on Greenwich Avenue, the very block I work on. It was an intense yet cordial conversation. Within fifteen minutes, Jamaane changed his mind. Jamaane, who is a man of great integrity, had come to respect Ovie and his intentions as they related to this project. The wealth of Ovie's Chicago experience photographing men and women very much like those on Sixth Avenue had never really occurred to me in my own assessment of how he would manage to be accepted on these blocks. Compared to Mitch's, his rapport with the men and women was almost instantaneous.

When Mitch had written another draft of this book and photographs had been carefully selected, he came back to New York, rented a room at the Washington Square Hotel, and brought each and every man and woman involved with this project there. He read chapters of the book to them and solicited their opinions. This was not easy, but it proved (particularly when everyone involved had heard their own words) that the book was a work in progress that portrayed their lives accurately. Mitch had made his own judgments after listening to everyone first.

There was no way for me to know that my desire to survive as something more than a subject and less than an author *would* influence the way this book was conceived and written. Let me elaborate: my determination to participate in this project forced me to discover that a dialogue with Mitch, in his capacity *as a social scientist,* was possible. This was no small achievement. This was a departure from the "scholar knows best" paradigm. The romanticized idea of "the subject's voice" that I often hear about from graduate students studying at New York University and the New School for Social Research who come to my table is one thing. The radical willingness of the social scientist to listen is quite another.

Mitch's research compelled me to realize that I knew less about the lives of the men and women on these streets than I thought, although I had spent years working right next to them. For instance, I was quite surprised to learn that a sub-group of these men had actually known one another for over fifteen years and had "migrated" to Sixth Avenue after having lived in and around Pennsylvania Station. Because of social distinctions that exist between the magazine and book vendors, I was not privy to this fascinating information. Had Mitch failed to talk to each and every man who inhabited these blocks, there would have been no way to determine, let alone document, their shared history and their migration from Penn Station to Sixth Avenue.

The story of their migration raised profound questions for me, since it demonstrated their tremendous adaptability and ability to create a milieu in public space in which they could survive. Perhaps, in the final analysis, migration of any kind is a story of survival and adaptability. But this seems never to occur to people who encounter these persons, including policy makers, who think street vendors can be eliminated with laws that cut vending space or ordinances that make the world less comfortable for them.

When I read the first draft of the chapter "A Scene from Jane Street," I found it unimaginable that Billy Romp and his family are allowed to live in a camper on Jane Street (an unusually narrow street, no less) and that residents think so much of the Romps that they give them keys to their apartments. I explained to Mitch, I have never been offered keys to any resident's apartment, and even if I were, I doubt that I would have accepted. The limitations that I place upon trust would not allow me to do so. Maybe this is not important. What is important is the keys, which symbolize that the Romps are accepted by the residents.

The juxtaposition of Ishmael being told by the police officers that he could not sell his magazines on Christmas Day and Billy Romp selling his Christmas trees made me angry. Let me say something about the comparison between Billy Romp and me as public characters: while it is admirable that he is widely accepted on Jane Street, and undeniable that his presence creates a sense of "eyes upon the street," the role I came to play on Sixth Avenue is markedly different from his. Without the signs of race, class, and family stability (I have no children) that might have allowed me to gain immediate acceptance on Sixth Avenue, I had to earn my place there through my wit, presence, and perseverance. There is no indication that I, or any of the other men and women, have ever been accepted altogether on Sixth Avenue.

Despite the fact that it was a labor of love, working on the Avenue for over seven years took a toll on me. Two days after Alice handed me a letter on the sidewalk notifying me that our relationship was over and that she was romantically involved with another vendor on *our* block, I decided to leave Sixth Avenue. While this news was a precipitating factor, I had endured poverty and the lack of health insurance long enough, and the prospect of entering middle age with no financial security was frightening. I had to leave.

My departure from Sixth Avenue was no easier than my arrival. One does not spend seven years working on the sidewalk and make a swift foray back into the formal economy. I thought that I could. My attempt now to move into publishing, public school education, or urban policy research is marred still by bitterness and my contempt for corporate whites who thwarted my ability to simply earn a living, which is what brought me to Sixth Avenue in the first place. This conflict between my aspirations and my bitterness is the essence of my story. It has not been resolved. It may never be.

I am still trying to understand how Mitch and the people whose lives he documented developed relationships on several New York City streets where race and class conflicts derail most efforts to transcend such barriers. Does this mean that people sometimes find ways—the will, actually—to work through their phobias and prejudices on these streets? Is it a matter of being willing to listen to one another with respect? Does it hinge on the sheer willpower of a subject, in this case myself, who was determined not to be reduced to a theoretical formulation or mere "data"? Given the vast inequalities, racial misunderstandings, and violence found on the street at every turn, I believe there was some measure of good luck involved here—the kind of luck that scholars and "subjects" of different races, classes, and genders will need when they encounter one another "in the field."

Section VI

QUANTITATIVE DATA ANALYSIS

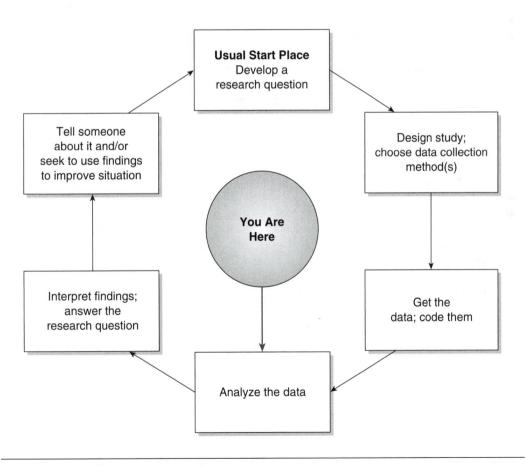

FIGURE 6.1 A Different View of the Map

By this point, we should have made it clear that researchers plan their data analysis before collecting the actual data (or at least they should have and are sorry if they haven't). Data themselves are just piles of raw materials that may or may not contain something useful. They must be coded into some usable format and examined to turn them into information. So the questions that we must ask ourselves at the start are:

What data do we need to answer the research question, and, once we have those data, how will we answer our question?

The selections in this section and the following one address the second question—how do we use data to answer our questions? In each case you will see the authors worked purposefully from the initial data collection plan to the last word of their conclusions in which "what we know" meets "how we know." That is, given a question about how action X relates to result Y, the authors first defined X and Y, then determined what data they needed to represent X and Y, and then planned a data collection method that would get them those data. The strength of each analysis relies on having appropriate, reliable, and valid data organized in a usable form. (Where those data come from was the subject of an earlier section.)

By convention, we tend to distinguish between *quantitative* and *qualitative* techniques. Quantitative analysis refers to all of the ways that we work with numerical data, which usually involve statistics. One advantage of quantitative analysis is the precision of measurements between two or more variables. We will look at that here. Qualitative analysis refers to our techniques for dealing with all of the rest of our data and interpreting intersubjective meanings. Qualitative analysis is the subject of the next section.

Quantitative data refers to things measured as numbers. Heights, weights, rates, percentages, and counts fall naturally into this category. The size of a population, the percentage of voters in a county favoring something, or the average amount by which gas prices rise just before a major holiday are good quantitative data. Other, more abstract ideas can be put on a numeric scales—quantified—as well. If you have ever indicated whether you thought a film was "(1) great (2) good (3) neutral (4) poor, or (5) terrible," then you have seen how this works. The point of quantifying data is to collect a lot of it, and use statistical analysis to find the trends and patterns within the numbers.

Statistical analysis used to be the most frightening part of studying sociology, given that statistics rely on some fancy algebra, and sociology students were sometimes not as comfortable with the formulae and procedures as they might have liked. Happily, computer programs such as SPSS and SAS, to name a couple of popular ones, do the calculations for us now, so we only need to know why we should tell the computer to perform a particular statistical analysis, how to tell the computer what to do, and then how to understand and explain what the computer tells us in response. This arrangement allows sociologists to focus more on the ideas of the research and less on the mathematical computations. One good set of data (called the "data set"), a few clicks of the mouse, and you have a color-coded multiple regression analysis with estimates of interaction effects and relational significance. All that remains is for you to tell people what that means. (Of course, first we have to make sure that we know what to tell the computer, and know what it means, so that we can tell others about it.)

In 1954, Darrell Huff wrote a lively book called *How to Lie With Statistics.* As you can gather from the title, Huff demonstrated statistics' uses and misuses.[1] For example, take the image of money bags in the old cartoons. One can say that the large bag is twice as big as the

---

[1]Today, much of the work of Professor Joel Best from the Department of Sociology at the University of Delaware has followed in Huff's tradition.

other, and seemingly holds twice the money. But think back to your geometry: As the height of the bag increases by two, the cubic volume increases by far more than that. Thus, while the description might say that the cartoon illustrates twice the money, a casual observer is likely to come away with the impression that it really is many times that amount. One could use an illustration like that to give a false impression.

FIGURE 6.2   Bags of Money

Similarly, we can be slippery with percentages if the audience is not thoughtful. For example, if I take away 25% of your salary, but then give you a 25% increase, you will not end up in the same place. How can that be? Easy. If you are making $40,000 and I take 25% away, you now have $30,000 left. If I then give you a 25% increase, you get that additional 25% based on your new salary of $30,000, which equals $7,500. You now have $37,500. That's clearly less than $40,000.

Or, consider graphs. If I change the scale of the Y axis, even if the numbers remain identical, I can make a relationship look strong or weak. The two graphs below show the exact same numbers, but because of the differences in the Y axis scale, the top graph looks like a dramatic drop whereas the lower one looks like a slow decline. (See Figure 6.3.)

The message of *How to Lie With Statistics* is not that you can lie with statistics, but that you can fool people who don't look very carefully at the statistics. Those who carefully examine the graphs or percentages or illustrations will not be fooled. In fact, they will call attention to the actual numbers, and discredit authors who are sloppy, ignorant, or intentionally deceptive.

As researchers, or even as students reading research, we must be alert to the iconic status of statistics. This is especially true today, when every other first grader seems to have his or her own laptop that can generate elegant graphs and fancy-looking calculations. Related to which, we often confuse *precision* with *truth*. Computers are precise, meaning that they can give you exact answers to highly complex problems, calculated out to 10 decimal places. But if you input poorly estimated data, or numbers based on dubious assumptions, or even fake data for two variables, and ask a statistics program to calculate exactly how well the variables correlate to one another, you will get a very precise answer. It just won't be true.[2] This is called **false precision.**

So, before we look at some of the useful things that we can do with statistics, it is worth remembering that what matters is the quality of the information, the clarity of the question, the appropriateness of the statistical method, and the transparency of the research process—not the complexity of the analysis.

Statistical techniques are extremely powerful at reducing very large mountains of data to their underlying patterns. This helps us to see the patterns in the data, patterns that reveal social trends and relationships.

---

[2]You may have seen Spock, on *Star Trek,* calculate the precise odds of overcoming an enemy force without actually knowing the size, weaponry, or preparedness of that force. He was lying.

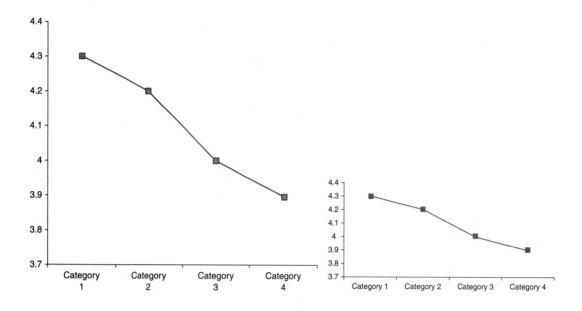

FIGURE 6.3

THE LANGUAGE OF STATISTICS

It is possible that some of you have not yet studied statistics. It is even possible that some of you have taken a course on the subject, but don't remember it in detail. In order to smooth your way through the selections and discussion in this section, we will present a very brief review of some of the key terms and concepts of statistical analysis.

Univariate Description. When looking at even *one* variable in social statistics, we tend to look for two factors: (1) a summary measure to describe the entire distribution of the variable, be

it median height, average reading scores, median income, modal hair color, or whatever;[3] and (2) the estimate for how the distribution of scores/ numbers/values is spread around the **mean, median,** or **mode**. You could also say it's a measure of how well the trend represents the whole.

For example, consider a class of 12th-grade students. The average age would be about 17, and the dispersion around that age—the ages above and below—would be very tight. Or, consider the average age of the high school teachers. Some are as young as 22 and some are in their 70s. The average might be 41, but the dispersion around the mean would be very great. In fact, we use medians rather than means when the scores may be very

---

[3]Mean is the arithmetic mean, which is usually called the "average." Median is the halfway point in the distribution—one half of the scores are above the median and one half are below the median. Mode is the most common score or value: For example, if you knew everyone's hair color, you might find that brunette was the modal color.

disparate. For instance, we might use medians when describing a small town's average age of first marriage so as not to be mislead by a few 82-year-olds who get married for the first time.

We call these average values measures of **central tendency;** they allow us to replace thousands of data points with a "typical" value. For many numbers, like reading scores and number of miles driven per year, the measure of central tendency is usually the mean, which is an arithmetic average. The median and the mode are the two other measures often used for ordinal and categorical data.

The measures of dispersion around the measure of central tendency—the mean, median, or mode—reflect the entire distribution and the shape of the distribution, as in the example above with the high school students and their teachers. The statistics that relate the central tendency to the whole distribution of values are called **measures of dispersion.** The measure most commonly provided is the **standard deviation**.

Bivariate Description. Once we have taken the measure of something (by reducing it to the univariate statistics that describe it), we generally like to know how it relates to other things. If one group of donors to a politician is younger than another, does that predict that they will give less? Or does it mean that their decisions about who and what to support depend on different criteria or interests? How do the two variables—age and giving—relate to one another? What is the *pattern of association* between our measures?

Measures of association tell us the *strength* and *direction* of association between two variables. Looking at data about the U.S. population in general, for example, we find that as age increases, income increases. So the direction of the relationship is positive. If that relationship were consistent across the life course, then we would say it was a "positive, linear relationship." Figure 6.4a shows this. In reality, however, income tends to drop off significantly around and beyond retirement age,

usually 60–65. This makes the relationship positive, *curvilinear*—rising at first, then falling off. Figure 6.4b is positive curvilinear.

A negative relationship, not surprisingly, goes the other way. As one thing (X) increases, the other (Y) decreases. An illustration of this is smoking and health. The more smoking there is in the population, the worse our overall health. See Figures 6.4c and 6.4d.

All of the relationships pictured here are relatively strong. That is, if we know how X is changing, we can make fairly confident predictions about Y. A weak relationship is one in which there may be some pattern of association, but the two variables also change independently of one another. A weak positive relationship might state that as X increases a lot, Y will, on average, increase a little.

Statistics that describe how the values of variables distribute across a lot of cases are called **descriptive statistics**. Most social research is more concerned with the relationships among the things we measure. If we know something about the ages of a group's members, can we predict something about their incomes? If we know their ages, gender distribution, and income, can we infer anything about how they will cast their votes? Does a change in the value of X *cause* a change in the values of Y? Statistics that address questions like these are called **inferential statistics**.

Inferential statistics tell us how certain we can be about generalizing from our sample's findings to the larger population. Inferential statistics are presented in terms of probability, as in when we say "there is a 5% probability this finding could have been generated by chance, or sampling error." Sometimes you see probabilities attached to a range of numbers around the estimated statistic. Thus you'll see something like, "There is a 95% probability that the true mean (average) is plus or minus 3 points from our estimate (statistic)."

When you study statistics (if you haven't already) you'll learn a lot more about inferential statistics and probability theory. For now, this is probably enough.

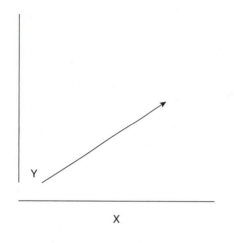

FIGURE 6.4a   Positive, linear relationship

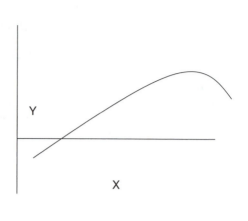

FIGURE 6.4b   Positive, curvilinear relationship

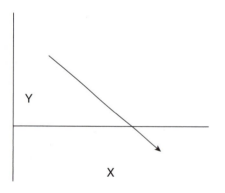

FIGURE 6.4c   Negative, linear relationship

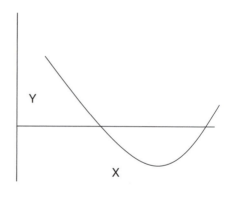

FIGURE 6.4d   Negative, curvilinear relationship

STATISTICAL ANALYSIS

In the selection by Higgs, Weiller, and Martin, "Gender Bias in the 1996 Olympic Games: A Comparative Analysis," the authors examine the televised coverage of the 1996 Summer Olympic Games to determine gender bias—not in the games, but in the way the TV producers and reporters presented the men and women in the games. Higgs et al. look at the amount of time devoted to men's versus women's sport activities, the "quality" of the coverage, the background stories told about the athletes, and the types of adjectives used to describe the participants. The authors also compare the amount of time devoted to men's versus women's Olympic activities in 1992 compared to 1996. The article therefore provides numeric examples of both quantitative data (e.g., numbers of minutes and seconds of air time) and qualitative data (e.g., percentage of words about women's personal histories vs. their athletic abilities).

The first comparison is on the amount of time spent in 1992 versus 1996 on men's sports versus women's sports. As can be seen in Higgs et al.'s Table 1, in 1996, the percentages devoted to women's sports were far more than four years earlier, in 1992. In fact, in 1996 the time spent on each type of sport was rather balanced. Also, there was more balance in some of the key terms used to describe athletes. In 1992, male players were more likely to be described as "strong" or "aggressive" whereas women players were more likely to get terms like having "plenty of game and grit" or showing "perfect execution." Also, by 1996 most women athletes were far less likely to be called "girls" as compared to "women" or "young women" than they were in 1992, except for the gymnasts who were consistently diminished in this way.

Gymnastics and Gender Typing. Despite the greater balance noted above, there were many examples of gender bias in the presentation of the 1996 Olympics. Male gymnasts were usually referred to by their last names, whereas women athletes were consistently called by their first names—a clear demeaning of status. First names were used for women 177 times, but for men only 16 times. Similarly, the male gymnasts were never called "boys," but always "men" or "young men." The women, in contrast and as noted above, were often called "girls."

Narratives/Short Stories. The TV producers introduced small three-minute documentaries about the athletes. These were designed to increase interest in the participants by telling stories, usually including struggle and the triumph over adversity. Higgs et al. compared the men's and women's narratives. In general, the women's segments included more about their relationships (e.g., marriages, close bonds to trainers, parents) than were included in the men's segments, which tended more to center on "drive," "training," and "competitiveness."

SECONDARY ANALYSIS

When you design your own research, collect your own data, and analyze those data, you are conducting a **primary analysis**, a first analysis of data that you have in hand. Most likely, your analysis aims at answering your research questions, and you structure your data collection around this goal. But often there is much more to learn from your data. There are combinations of variables that aren't part of your question, or reams of text that do not directly address your issues. Other researchers may wish to borrow your data after you are done with them to address their own questions, questions that are different from the ones you have already addressed. This is a **secondary analysis** of data collected at an earlier time.

More often, data used in secondary analyses are collected by large, comprehensive research projects and then made publicly available for further analysis. Much of this data collection is sponsored by government agencies, including the Census Bureau, the National Institutes of Health, the National Institute on Drug Abuse, the Bureau of Justice Statistics, and many more. In addition, a number of ongoing research projects take wide "snapshots" of the nation every few years, providing researchers with a broad range of behavioral, attitude, or economic data collected in a consistent fashion over an extended period of time (**longitudinal** data). Examples include the General Social Survey (GSS), the Monitoring the Future Study (MTF), and the National Longitudinal Study of Adolescent Health (Add Health). Finally, comparable data are collected in most other nations throughout the world and are useful for cross-national comparisons. Examples of publicly available datasets include the United Nations' World Economic and Social Survey and the World Bank's World Development Indicators.

Snapshot studies such as these are not focused on specific research questions. Rather, they measure a host of related issues and demographics with which researchers can address new questions. In our next selection, Denton and Villarrubia use a single new census question to investigate theoretical questions of race, class, and identity in Puerto Rico. Residents of the island have several distinct "identity constructs" available to them, and several different narratives about how collective identity and difference are understood. Sociologists, for our part, have a good number of different theories with which to explain these narratives. But how do the residents identify themselves, given a fair number of choices and a neutral setting for answering? From this simple question, Denton and Villarrubia are able to examine the nature *and meaning* of racial segregation in contemporary Puerto Rican society.

The U.S. census provides particularly useful data for this question since it provides data on ethnic identity, socioeconomic status, and neighborhood of residence. Thus, the authors are able to compare the degree of racial segregation with the degree of class segregation. As well, they can test whether there are differences in the integration of those who choose to define themselves as "white," those choosing "black," and those choosing "*mestizaje*," a category indicating multiple ethnicities.

Writing for a primarily American readership, the authors must present their *conceptual definition* of ethnicity carefully. That is, they note the casual American discourse on race and ethnicity is different from the ways in which these terms are used on the Island of Puerto Rico, and that academic definitions, for purposes of research, aim to be more precise and limited than either of those cases. Neither race nor ethnicity have clear-cut and obvious meanings, and as the census bureau found, even asking the question may be threatening or controversial.

This brings us back to the issues of validity and reliability that we looked at in an earlier section. We want to study ethnic identity by asking people to identify their ethnicity. But just asking is not as simple as it sounds. The term *ethnicity* means one thing to the people writing the question, another to the people answering it, and something a little different to social theorists. This, then, is the great strength and the great weakness of secondary analysis: Because you have access to something as comprehensive as the census, you get a large amount of highly *reliable* data measured in a clear and consistent fashion in different places and different times. But, because the questions are very general and because they were not designed for your purposes, it is often tricky to ensure that your interpretation of the data is *valid*. Clearly, had Denton and Villarrubia designed their own large-scale survey of ethnic identity in Puerto Rico, they would have asked different questions. So secondary analysis opens some doors to the intrepid and creative researcher, but closes others.

It takes a certain amount of work to translate information about the world into numeric format. This is **coding**. And, as we have just seen, it takes more work to translate numeric data back into information. Call this *decoding*. So what do we accomplish with all of this? In simple terms, coding translates each individual piece of information into a number, while decoding finds the patterns among all of the data together. Analysis involves first finding those patterns, and second, interpreting them.

BOX 6.1 EMILE DURKHEIM (1858–1917)

Durkheim was a French sociologist who contributed to our understanding of social order, social processes, religion, criminology, and education. Some of his major methodological contributions were developed in his book *Suicide* (1897), in which he used a quantitative analysis of suicide rates among Catholics, Protestants, and Jews in France to derive a theory of anomie, or normative conflict, within social groups. In his *Rules of the Sociological Method* (1895), Durkheim proposed a formal approach to sociological inquiry. His Rules influenced the development of functionalism and social control perspectives in the social sciences. Like Weber, Durkheim is famous for developing and operationalizing a number of enduring sociological concepts, such as anomie, "social facts," and the forms of social integration (or social solidarity).

CONCLUSION

The reading by Higgs, Weiller, and Martin offers a range of simple statistics—comparisons of percentages, ratios, and simple counts (e.g., number of seconds of TV time). However simple, they illustrate the power of these calculations to take a lot of information and reduce it to patterns we can understand and compare. Fancier statistics do exactly the same thing, but the calculations are more involved, the assumptions are more numerous (e.g., the assumption that the relationship you are studying is linear), the characteristics of the statistics are more complicated, and the restrictions on interpretation may be more stringent. Ultimately, however, statistics are the best ways we have for dealing with large quantities of information and for findings patterns that would otherwise remain obscured or even invisible. Used intelligently, statistics are both microscopes and telescopes, enabling us to see both what is there and, critically, what is *not* there. Even if you never intend to compute statistics yourself, you must be able to understand what they say and how they are used. Absent that ability, you are forever at the mercy of others' interpretations and conclusions—an unenviable and unnecessary limitation. Whether you embrace statistics only with trepidation, like the odd aunt your parents obliged you to greet, or warmly, they are essential tools of research, of science, of logical debate, and of much public discourse.

DISCUSSION QUESTIONS

1. Why do we say statistics enable us to "reduce" a large amount of information? Give examples of what this "reduction" means in relation to:
   - The height of the people in your class;
   - The relationship in the United States between the general population's amount of education and the level of earnings.

2. Why is it important that we understand at least the basics of statistics? Give two examples from current discussions or debates about public policy that are informed by statistical information.

3. Describe the difference between inferential and descriptive statistics. When might you use each kind?

4. Statistics may be extraordinarily helpful, but they are not magic. In Puerto Rico, the conceptualization of race appears to differ from that in the mainland United States. How would the presentation of statistics about perceived racial differences distort more than clarify if the researchers did not modify their measures and definitions?

WEB RESOURCES

The following links can provide you with more detailed information on the topics discussed in this section. You may also go to www.sagepub.com/lunestudy where you will find additional resources and hot-links to these sources.

The General Social Survey: http://www.norc.org/GSS+Website
Monitoring the Future Study (MTF): http://www.monitoringthefuture.org
National Longitudinal Study of Adolescent Health (Add Health): http://www.cpc.unc.edu/projects/addhealth
World Economic and Social Survey: http://www.un.org/esa/policy/wess/
World Development Indicators: http://web.worldbank.org/WBSITE/EXTERNAL/DATASTATISTICS/0,,contentMDK:21725423~pagePK:64133150~piPK:64133175~theSitePK:239419,00.htmlCensus Bureau: http://www.census.gov
National Institutes of Health (NIH): http://www.nih.gov
National Institute on Drug Abuse (NIDA): http://www.nida.nih.gov
Bureau of Justice Statistics (BJS): http://www.ojp.usdoj.gov/bjs/

Gender Bias in the 1996 Olympic Games

A Comparative Analysis (2003)

Catriona T. Higgs, Karen H. Weiller, and Scott B. Martin

Market forces are largely responsible for the underrepresentation of women's sports by television or, for that matter, in all aspects of the communications media (Hilliard, 1984). Where women are covered, the media has largely focused attention on those sports that are traditionally viewed as conveying a feminine image (e.g., gymnastics and figure skating) and enhancing existing societal norms (Shifflett & Revelle, 1994).

Researchers suggest that sports media influences how people view participation in sports. By emphasizing certain facets of female participation in sports while ignoring others, the sports media effectively shapes the public agenda and influences the public's judgment about the world of sport, and the athletes who are a part of that competition (Coakley, 1998). NBC experienced an enormous ratings success (Coakley, 1998) and were afforded extraordinary ratings, the best since 1976. Part of the ratings success can be attributed to the United States' hosting of these games, yet as noted by Remnich (1996) and Coakley (1998), NBC provided viewers with a reality that was designed to "bring a tear to the eye and billions to the coffers" (Remnich, 1996, p. 26). Furthermore, Remnich (1996) suggested NBC framed events, specifically withholding information, therefore deliberately shaping their broadcasts to appeal to a female audience.

Previous studies of the media coverage of women have demonstrated a significant difference in the way that male and female athletes are covered by televised media (Duncan, Messner, Williams, & Jensen, 1990; Higgs & Weiller, 1994; Kahn & Goldenberg, 1991; Theberge, 1991). Duncan et al. (1990) have suggested that the Olympic Games is an event that attempts to target female spectators through the coverage of feminine sports in an attempt to attract female viewership. Daddario (1997) noted the focus by the media on "women's spectator sports" in the first week of NBC's 1992 Olympic coverage. In fact, NBC's highest rating for the 2-week period of coverage was for the night of a gymnastics telecast (Daddario, 1997). Daddario (1997) further emphasized NBC's programming strategy of pretaping events and packaging them for a specific type of storytelling approach. This approach served to personalize the lives of the athletes, both male and female, to build an emotional identification with the athletes. Daddario described this as a "feminine narrative form" (p. 107), similar in nature to that used in television soap operas to draw audiences into the focus of the character and plot. The concept of narrative has been used persuasively by televised media to lure viewers into maintaining interest in a desire for further viewing (Harris & Hills, 1993). The intent of this type of programming in the 1996 Olympic Games was to "emphasize the human drama of the Summer Games . . . to reach their target

SOURCE: From "Gender Bias in the 1996 Olympic Games: A Comparative Analysis" by Higgs, C. T., Weiller, K. H., & Martin, S. B., in *Journal of Sport and Social Issues* 2003; *27*.1; 52–64. Used with permission of Sage Publications.

audience, in which the 25 to 54 year old female figured prominently" (Daddario, 1997, p. 112).

A previous study by Higgs and Weiller (1994) demonstrated that although women were given greater coverage in individual sports during the 1992 Olympic Games, that coverage was divided into shorter and more heavily edited segments. In addition, commentaries centered on gender marking, biased and ambivalent reporting, and focused on personalities as opposed to athletic abilities when covering women's sports.

The phenomenal success of the American women athletes in the 1996 Olympic Games clearly demonstrated to the American public the quality, depth, and progress of women's sports in America since the advent of Title IX (Kane & Parks, 1992). The question that remains is, With such a heightened focus on women's sports, and on women athletes, was the television coverage of the 1996 Games less stereotyped and gender hierarchical than the coverage in 1992?

PURPOSE

The purpose of this study was to examine televised coverage of the 1996 Summer Olympic Games in Atlanta to determine the amount of coverage time, quality of coverage devoted to men's and women's same sport activities, and to compare this coverage with that of the 1992 Summer Olympic Games.

METHOD

NBC televised more than 150 hours of Olympic coverage. All coverage was taped and a content analysis was conducted on only those segments that featured same-sport activities for men and women. A total of 60 hours was then randomly selected as an appropriate sample from the total coverage. A content analysis was then performed on those segments that featured same sport activities for men and women. Randomness was

assured by selecting time segments at various times in the day/evening coverage. Quantitative analysis focused on the amount of running time devoted to male and female sports, length of segments, number of slow-motion replays used, and the use of onscreen statistics. Qualitative analysis focused on one particular characteristic, the narrative, by examining adjectives used by the commentators to describe male and female athletes, and the themes stressed by commentators in the course of weaving narratives about the events.

RESULTS

Of the total 60 hours of taped material, 30 hours and 28 minutes was devoted to same-sport activities. Same-sport events analyzed were the team and individual sports of basketball, volleyball, gymnastics, swimming and diving, track and field, and minor sports of cycling, tennis, kayaking, rowing, and soccer. Compared with our previous study (Higgs & Weiller, 1994) results demonstrated that women were afforded more televised media coverage in the 1996 Olympics than men in same-sport activities. A comparison between the quantitative time totals of same-sport competition from the 1992 and 1996 Olympic Games revealed that women's sport coverage increased in 6 out of the 11 sports analyzed, whereas male sport coverage declined in 4 out of the 11 sports analyzed. This is a notable result in comparison with previous studies, which have demonstrated that women are usually covered less and for shorter time periods than men (Higgs & Weiller 1994).

In the present study, total and segment broadcast times devoted to men's and women's basketball, gymnastics, track and field, volleyball, swimming, diving, cycling, tennis, kayaking, rowing, and soccer were examined. Results indicated that time coverage totals for men's track and field was the most televised competition, whereas men's volleyball was the least (see Table 1).

TABLE 1 Quantitative Time Totals of Same Sport Competition From the 1992 and 1996 Summer Olympic Games

	1992			1996		
Sport	Male %	Female %	Total Time	Male %	Female %	Total Time
Basketball	74	26	18.23	48	52	2.23
Volleyball	75	25	3:05	6	94	2:48
Gymnastics	16	84	5.48	26	74	9:55
Swimming	48	52	3:35	43	57	6:00
Diving	44	56	2:11	26	74	3:27
Track & Field	63	37	9:10	74	26	4:48
Cycling	40	60	:52	0	100	:22
Tennis	33	67	:18	93	7	:36
Kayaking	81	19	:27	86	14	1:48
Rowing	33	67	:12	0	0	:00
Soccer	*	*	*	77	23	:21

NOTE: In 1992, women's soccer was not a medal sport. Men's soccer was a medal sport but was not analyzed by Higgs & Weiller, 1994.

Most notably, coverage for women increased in team sports of basketball (26%) and volleyball (69%), whereas these same sports saw a decrease in time allotted for men. Other sports analyzed in both 1992 and 1996 remained fairly comparable. Time coverage totals for women indicate that gymnastics was the most televised competition, and tennis was the least televised competition.

BASKETBALL

Gender Differences

Denial of power, which was a central theme in the coverage of women's basketball in the 1992 Olympic Games, was far less blatant in the 1996 televised coverage. Slow-motion replays, gender marking, and commentators' use of adjective differentials were found to be fairly balanced. Although slow-motion replays were shown more often in the men's games (four per game) than in the women's games (three per game), the disparity was not as great as in the 1992 Olympics where the intense focus on the "dream team" precipitated far more coverage and interest in the men's competition. Although gender marking was evident throughout the coverage, with phrases such as "U.S. Women's team," the use of the word girl was minimal (3 X total).

Strength/Weakness Descriptors

Commentators' use of adjectives to describe the strengths and weaknesses of men and women were fairly similar. In the 1992 coverage, the words *aggressive* and *powerful* to describe the male athletes were used numerous times (185) versus only 68 times in the women's competition. In the coverage of the 1996 Olympic basketball competition, a total of 52 strength descriptors were used to describe the male players versus 47 for the women. The ambivalence that was used in the 1992 coverage to describe the women's competition was not as evident. Women players were more often described in positive terms as having plenty of game and grit, being tough, and showing perfect execution in scoring a point.

Narrative

The emotional narrative that had accompanied the "run for gold" by the 1992 dream team was replaced in the 1996 coverage with a focus by the commentators on the success of the women's team prior to the Olympic competition. The U.S. women's basketball team had come into the competition unbeaten for a period of 2 years and the male commentators mentioned this fact numerous times (14) in their commentary. Similar statements used to describe the dream team of 1992 were evidenced in the narrative of the 1996 women's competition. In 1992, the "dream team rolled over Croatia," in 1996 the women "rolled past Cuba." It is interesting that comparisons were made in the men's games to some of the U.S. women players; a situation that was largely reversed in the 1992 coverage. "Mini" narratives were used to enhance the drama of the competition, allowing viewers to identify with the athletes on a more personal level. Interviews with Karl Malone and Reggie Miller highlighted the extraordinary aspects of the athletes' lives, their successes in the National Basketball Association (NBA) and their hopes and dreams of an Olympic medal. Through such narrative devices, Daddario (1997) comments "mediated sports invite the predominantly male audience to identify with athletes" (p. 166). Although no personal interviews were conducted with the women players during the time frame

analyzed, commentators discussed aspects of the women's lives; including colleges attended, degrees earned, playing level (professional/semi-professional), and successes at the collegiate level (i.e., National championships). The lack of emphasis on the feminine form and their personal lives was a sharp deviation from coverage of the 1992 Olympic Games, where there was a great deal of focus on gender stereotypic behaviors and characteristics. The marginalization of women's sports, as evidenced in so many previous studies of media coverage was not as evident in NBC's coverage of the 1996 Women's Olympic Basketball competition.

VOLLEYBALL

As with basketball, depictions of power were fairly evenly dispersed between the men's and women's competition. Again, this is in sharp contrast to the coverage of the 1992 Olympic volleyball competitions.

Gender Differentials

More slow-motion replays were used in the women's games than in the men's games (24/11). In addition, men's first names were used more often than women's first names (8/1). Hierarchy of naming (Duncan et al., 1990) was not evidenced in this portion of the analysis. Commentators used only men's surnames 40.6% of the time compared with 46.3% of the time for women. In general, first and last names were used equally to describe the athletes (55.2% men; 53.3% women).

Strength/Weakness Descriptors

Strength descriptors in both events outweighed weakness descriptors (men 34/4; women 25/5), a result that mirrors that of the coverage in 1992.

Narratives

Narratives in the men's and women's games in the 1992 Olympics revealed a strong distinction in presentation of male dominance and strength (Higgs & Weiller, 1994), whereas narratives of the 1996 competition were far less distinctive. Comments such as "two of the best middle blockers in the game" and "they have raised the level of this game substantially" are examples of the nature of the narrative. The focus on the men's games was equally interesting. The men's squad was described as "emotional" and "frustrated," "struggling for recognition and respect." Audiences were not left wondering as they were in 1992 about the viability of the women's team events as legitimate competition. Rather, women's events were presented in such away that no systematic discrimination between the men's and women's coverage was discernible. This finding is in distinct contrast to previous studies (Duncan et al., 1990; Higgs & Weiller, 1994), which have suggested that coverage of women's team sports have traditionally been trivialized.

GYMNASTICS

The major theme that seems to emerge from an analysis of the men's and women's gymnastics coverage of the 1996 Olympic Games is that the traditional trivialization of women's athletic performance was still strongly represented in the coverage of this event.

Gender Differentials

First-name descriptors were used frequently in the women's events. Female athletes were referred to by their first name 177 times versus only 16 times for the male athletes. Although, the coverage of the men's gymnastic events was still less in total time than that for the women, these figures still suggest a disparity in this particular area.

Strength/Weakness Descriptors

Verbal attributions of strength and weakness descriptors contrasted. In discussing the female gymnasts, 42 descriptors suggested strength, compared with 100 suggesting weaknesses—a ratio of almost 3 to 1. In the men's competition, there were fewer strength descriptors than in the women's competition (26); however, the narrative that accompanied the use of these descriptors left the audience with little doubt about the power of the male gymnast. He was described as *very aggressive, amazing,* "going all out from the start to the finish." She was described as the "little girl dancing for gold at the Olympic Games" who was "a little messy on the landing." It is interesting that a total of 67 slow-motion replays were used in the women's competition compared with only 2 in the men's. These segments served to magnify the drama of the event and to build anticipation for the next performance.

Narratives

As with the 1992 competition, the narrative that accompanied the 1996 Olympic coverage of the gymnastics competition was characterized by conflict and controversy. In attempting to heighten the audience's interest, commentators presented human interest stories on the main U.S. contenders and their European rivals. The injury of Kerry Strugg on the vault was replayed numerous times for the audience, while commentators built up her heroic status as the person who had bravely won the all-around medal for the U.S. team. In reality, at that point, the U.S. women's team had already won the gold medal and there was no need for Strugg to have even vaulted.

As the commentators lauded and praised the injured heroine, the camera panned to the crestfallen Russian team as the commentators discussed "the little girls in tears" who "cried these same tears four years ago in Barcelona." The commentators ended the evening with a montage of images from the team competition and with the words "tonight she (Kerry Strugg) was there for Bella (Karoli), for her team, for her country, and for herself"; "there are tears, but I think they are because of joy as well as pain."

The term *girl* was used numerous times to describe the female gymnasts. This held true for all female gymnasts, regardless of age. Male gymnasts were largely described as *men* or *young men*. Although some of the male gymnasts were older than the female gymnasts, equity in this area would help eliminate disparity. There was a focus on the artistic and graceful nature of the gymnastic event as female gymnasts were described as *artistic, beautiful, elegant,* and *passionate.* The drama of the comparison was enhanced by the focus on the competition between the Americans and Russians for the team competition. The commentators began the segment by stating "Russia, no longer the specter of evil, but still the threat of beauty and perfection." Thus, the coverage of the women's competition was enhanced by a soap opera or storytelling theme and was "replete with interpersonal conflict as well as personal catastrophe" (Daddario, 1997).

The men's competition was largely ignored by NBC. However, in the brief coverage analyzed, the difficulty of the equipment was mentioned (largely ignored in the women's competition), as was the aggressiveness of the participants. In the team compulsory competition, one of the gymnasts was said to have "put on a clinic." The drama of the men's event was enhanced by the focus on a Russian gymnast whose wife was nearly killed the previous summer. Every performance by this gymnast was judged by the commentators as an effort to "win gold for her" (his wife) who is "waiting at home." Thus the framing of the men's competition was done in the context of consequential sensationalism.

SWIMMING AND DIVING

As with coverage of the 1992 Olympic Games, the swimming and diving coverage was fairly equitable in terms of total time and individual time segments.

Gender Differentials

Slow-motion replays in the swimming competition (26 for men versus 19 for women)

and in the diving competitions (35 for men and 21 for women) were similar. Both ambivalent and sexist comments were used consistently to describe the women swimmers. These included "she's a glamour girl as well as an Olympic champion," "the queen of American swimming" (used to describe Janet Evans), and "look at those long blue fingernails." Both male and female divers were described by words such as *beautiful, flawless,* and *graceful.* Male commentators appeared to be far more critical of the female American divers than the male divers when mistakes were made. Comments such as "not the strongest twisting dive" and "a disastrous third round dive" were used to describe the women divers versus "a forceful dive that took a lot of guts to perform" and "very safe, but a little slow" (men) were examples of the different ways that the male commentators described a poor dive.

In the 1992 games, the word *girl* was used repeatedly to describe the female swimmers. In the 1996 games, this tendency did not continue as the word *girl* was only used 15 times to describe female swimmers.

Narrative

As opposed to the blatant sexist comments used to describe the women's events in the 1992 Olympic Games, the narrative used in the 1996 games was quite different. Women swimmers were described as "having a mission" and "very powerful," who "dominated the event." It is conceivable that the success of the women's team in the 1992 games engendered more respect for the 1996 athletes and therefore led to the observed differences between Barcelona and Atlanta. Much was made of Janet Evans' age in comparison with the younger swimmers. The success of this swimmer was also noted by the commentators and her age was discussed at length.

In diving, as with the 1992 competition, the athletes appeared to be covered in a more androgynous manner. Similar adjectives were used to describe both competitions, even the appearances of the athletes were discussed equitably. For example, "she and Tom Dolan have no fat" and "his body is immature like the young Chinese girls." Commentators praised the "guts," "skill, and courage" of Mary Ellen Clarke who was in her 30s. Commentators also described the "power of another dream" that had fueled Mary Ellen Clarke's need to compete in the diving competition.

TRACK AND FIELD

Time Differentials

Disparity in amount of coverage of the women track and field athletes was still evident in the 1996 Olympic Games. Of the total 4 hours and 48 minutes of track and field coverage analyzed, men were featured for more than twice the amount of time women were featured.

Gender Differentials

The lack of overtly sexist comments in the track and field competition was a positive change from the blatant sexist manner in which these events were reported in the 1992 games (Higgs & Weiller, 1994). Gender marking however continued with comments such as "she was the fastest woman in the world" where he "was the world's greatest all around athlete." Male athletes were still lauded for their accomplishment with comments such as "the Joe DiMaggio of long jumpers," "a legend already," and "history being made"; however, women were also recognized for their considerable successes at the games. She was "running very well and very consistently" and "they looked like rockets racing those hurdles" are examples of these types of comments. Overall, there appeared to be greater similarity in the manner in which these athletes were covered.

Narrative

Depictions of women's personal lives by the commentators were not as overt as in the 1992 competition. Contrasts in presentation of individual biographies of athletes were noted. For example, commentators reported Jackie Joyner Kersee was focusing on her marriage and relationship with her husband, who also happened to be her coach. In a contrasting sketch on Michael Johnson, the focus was purely on his athletic talent. The piece depicted him as a "feared" fighter and the Olympic Games was where "the battle lines would be drawn." After Johnson won his first event, he was highlighted again as a man "whose mission was halfway accomplished," and who was focusing on "making Olympic history" and "thinking "only about gold." For Joyner Kersee, the focus was on her doubts, fears, and family. Such differences in the portrayal of these elite athletes serve to highlight the inequities that still exist in the coverage of men and women in Olympic competition and further served to highlight a "storytelling approach" (Daddario, 1997), particularly for the female athletes.

TENNIS, CYCLING (MOUNTAIN BIKING), SOCCER, BASEBALL, AND SOFTBALL

Relatively little time was devoted to these five sports. The only notable exception was the women's softball competition. Perhaps greater coverage of women's softball was due to the dominance of the American women in this event and the fact that this was the first time this sport had been offered at the Olympic level. The focus of attention during the softball competition was on Dot Richardson as the "oldest player on the team." A biographical sketch showed her as a doctor working with children "and loving it." In the United States versus Puerto Rico game, the commentators called the women's softball team "the other dream team." Comparisons were made to male baseball players like "she's kind of the Cal Ripken of her sport." The baseball competition was very poorly covered, however updates emphasized the "power" of the athletes and how the "1996 games was a record setting Olympics for home runs." In the women's road race, one of the French cyclists was called "arrogant" because of her "fiery competitiveness and focus of attention." This was compared with an equally dominant male athlete in the mountain biking competition whose competitive fervor was praised and viewed as "so impressive." The male commentators focused on the personal lives of the female cyclists calling one "Mommy medalist" and describing how a woman managed to work out a training schedule "while still being a mom." In describing one of the female cyclist's family arrangements, a male commentator jokingly referred to her family as "hearing about Mom's trip to Atlanta" and how "it's time for the others to help with the dishes." The drama of the cycling competition was enhanced by the focus on the comparison of women cyclists. In attempting to weave an interesting tale, the commentators talked about how much one cyclist was hated by her peers and that "they would ride the next 64 miles filled with this emotion." Highlights of the women's soccer competition were accompanied by very positive comments such as "the U.S. women are very good" and "she is the best U.S. player and probably the best in the world." Similarly, in the canoeing and rowing competitions, women racers were described as "well disciplined" and "very efficient."

CONCLUSIONS

Commentators have the power to maximize or minimize both men's and women's athletic participation, athletic abilities, and athletic achievements in televised sport events. The importance and relevance of how the mass media chooses to feature athletes aides in shaping popular beliefs, attitudes, and values (Lee, 1992).

In the past, it has been characteristic of televised sports media to highlight men's and women's sporting events in different ways (Duncan et al., 1990; Harris & Hills, 1993; Higgs & Weiller, 1994). Emphasizing these differences reinforces messages that amplify male hegemony not only in sport but in other

realms of life (Lambo & Tucker, 1990). In comparison with the 1992 Olympic Games (Higgs & Weiller, 1994), findings of the present study suggest the following:

1. Coverage for women increased in two team sports (basketball and volleyball) and in 6 of 11 sports analyzed.

2. Traditional coverage of gymnastics was still evident with disparities in strength/weakness descriptors and an emphasis on human drama, particularly from the female gymnasts.

3. Qualitatively, basketball and volleyball were more evenly presented in the 1996 Olympic Games, with gender marking being the single disparity evident.

4. Swimming and diving continued to be fairly evenly presented; however, both ambivalent and sexist commentary was still employed to describe female swimmers.

5. There was a lack of overtly sexist commentary in track and field as compared with the 1992 Olympic Games; however, some gender differentials in presentation of the narrative was still evident.

6. Overall, narrative analysis revealed a solid focus on the athleticism of the female athlete; however, for both male and female athletes, an intense focus on personal information (background, college attended, playing experience) was noted.

DISCUSSION

As the pinnacle of amateur performance, the Olympic Games are viewed and respected by millions. The findings of the present study suggest there have been notable changes both quantitatively and qualitatively in the way female athletes were presented in the 1996 Olympic Games, although similarities in the manner of presentation noted in the 1992 Olympic Games (Higgs & Weiller, 1994) were still evident. Perhaps part of NBC's extraordinary ratings were derived from the focus on the female athlete, both from an athletic and personal perspective. Emphasizing the human drama of the event, utilizing a programming strategy that served to build an emotional identification with the athletes, (Daddario, 1997) and highlighting a specific target audience, may, in part, account for the more positive nature of media presentation of the female athletes. Certainly, findings from this study do suggest there was a definite effort on the part of televised media to present female athletes in a stronger manner.

There is little doubt that the improvements seen in the quality of coverage of the women's events in the 1996 Olympic Games mirrors the advancements made by women in sport since 1992. The increase in opportunities for women to participate at all levels in sport has led to a new understanding of the role of women in international competition. The success of the women's teams in the 1996 Olympic Games undoubtedly enhanced the reputation and image of women at this level of competition. In addition, as Coakley (1998) suggests, NBC experienced a great rating success when they targeted coverage toward women during these 1996 Games. The improvement in media coverage is encouraging, however, the positive changes that are suggested by this study must be viewed with caution. A limitation of the present study was the limited number of hours analyzed. Although results in the present study may be representative of the total coverage, generalizations to the entire broadcast of the 1996 Olympic Games cannot be made.

Time segments increased in many of the sports analyzed between the 1992 and 1996 Games. However the qualitative analysis of the 1996 Games continues to reveal many disparities, particularly in the coverage of women's sports that traditionally appeal to the media audience (e.g., gymnastics), and perhaps a female audience. It is perhaps this fact that should be most carefully scrutinized. The media is effectively telling us that it is now "OK" to compete in sports, but the image of women in some types of competition remains stereotypically fixed. Despite the "cultural messages" that suggest that sport is an appropriate avenue for women to now compete in, there remains an underlying message that while competing, women should still conform to society's image of what is deemed appropriate. Until the media can totally view women as "athletes" and not "bodies," it is likely that this situation will continue. Old attitudes persist and although the attitudes toward women's sports are changing, the expectations of the behavior and appearance of women athletes remains largely the same.

REFERENCES

Coakley, J .J. (1998). *Sport in society: Issues and controversies.* Boston: McGraw-Hill.

Daddario, G. (1997). Gendered sports programming: 1992 Summer Olympic coverage and the feminine narrative form. *Sociology of Sport Journal, 14,* 103–120.

Duncan, M.C., Messner, M. A., Williams, W., & Jensen, K. (1990). *Gender stereotyping in televised sports.* Los Angeles: Amateur Athletic Foundation.

Harris, J., & Hills, L. A. (1993).Telling the story: Narrative in newspaper accounts of a men's collegiate basketball tournament. *Research Quarterly for Exercise and Sport, 64,* 108–121.

Higgs, C. T., & Weiller, K. H. (1994). Gender bias and the 1992 Summer Olympic Games: An analysis of television coverage. *Journal of Sport and Social Issues, 18,* 234–246.

Hillard, D. C. (1984). Media images of male and female professional athletes: An interpretive analysis of magazine articles. *Sociology of Sport Journal, 1,* 251–262.

Kahn, K. F., & Goldenberg, E. N. (1991). The media: Obstacle or ally of feminists. *ANNALS, AAPSS, 515,* 104–113.

Kane, M. J., & Parks, J. B. (1992).The social construction of gender difference and hierarchy in sport journalism—few new twists on very old themes. *Women in Sport and Physical Activity Journal, 1,* 49–83.

Lambo, R., & Tucker, K.W. (1990). Cultures, television and opposition: Rethinking cultural studies. *Critical Studies in Mass Communication, 1,* 97–116.

Lee, J. (1992). Media portrayals of male and female Olympic athletes: An analysis of newspaper accounts of the 1984 and the 1988 summer games. *International Review for Sociology of Sport, 27,* 197–222.

Remnich, D. (1996, July). Inside-out Olympics. *Newton Massachusetts News Tribune,* pp. 26–28.

Shifflet, B., & Revelle, R. (1994). *Gender equity in sports media coverage: A review of the NCAA news.* Thousand Oaks, CA: Sage.

Theberge, N. (1991).A content analysis of print media coverage of gender, women and physical activity. *Journal of Applied Sport Psychology, 3,* 36–48.

Residential Segregation on the Island

The Role of Race and Class in Puerto Rican Neighborhoods (2007)

Nancy A. Denton[1] and Jacqueline Villarrubia

INTRODUCTION

There is little doubt that the topic of race on the island of Puerto Rico is complex. One observer says "apart from small groups of the upper or middle class, any ordinary gathering of Puerto Ricans represents a striking example of the complete acceptance of social intermingling of people of different color and racial characteristics" (Fitzpatrick, 1987:104–105). Discussions of the significance of race in Puerto Rico are often tied to the island's history and the mixing of aspects of Spanish, African, and Taíno culture into a nationalist ideology of *mestizaje* or blending (Torres, 1998). Although the importance of *indigenismo* is sometimes contested because few Taíno survived contact with the Spanish, and the African influence is frequently overlooked, most observers still focus on the *mestizaje* (Godreau, 2002; Safa, 1998; Torres, 1998). Many people argue that class is far more important than race. However, the widespread acknowledgment of the importance of the process of whitening, known as *blanqueamiento* (Torres, 1998), clearly suggests the importance of race, as do informal accounts of the lack of blacks in high positions (Rodriguez-Cotto, 2004), the low socioeconomic status of blacks (Rivera-Batiz, 2004), and poverty in traditionally black areas of the island (Godreau, 2002; Gordon, 1949). Puerto Ricans

also use numerous words to describe variations in skin color: *moreno, trigueño, café con leche, jabao,* or *prieto* among others (Duany, 2002:238; Fitzpatrick, 1987:105; Rodriguez, 2000:108–109), indicating their awareness of race.

To date there have been few empirical investigations of race on the island, no doubt in part due to a lack of data about race among the entire population. Fortunately, for the first time in 50 years, the 2000 Census of Population and Housing in Puerto Rico contained a question about race as well as Hispanic origin, providing a unique opportunity for the direct study of race on the island. In addition, it was the first census to allow people to choose more than one race and thus allow for the direct expression of *mestizaje*. In this paper, we use these new data to examine how race and class operate to structure neighborhood segregation in the metropolitan areas on the island. Neighborhood segregation is an ideal place to examine the influence of race versus class, as real estate transactions usually take place between relative strangers, thus giving a good opportunity for discrimination based upon skin color. In Puerto Rico, as almost everywhere, neighborhoods are stratified on the basis of socioeconomic status and the new race data allows us to see if the racial characteristics of the population are linked to the socioeconomic status of their neighborhood. In other words, are black

[1]Department of Sociology, University at Albany, SUNY, 1400 Washington Ave., Albany, New York 12222; e-mail: n.denton @albany.edu.

Puerto Ricans segregated from white Puerto Ricans on the island? What about Puerto Ricans who chose Indian, other, or more than one race on the Census? Is racial segregation higher or lower than segregation by socioeconomic status; in other words, does class really trump race on the island? Are the neighborhoods of black Puerto Ricans of poorer quality than those occupied by white Puerto Ricans?

THEORETICAL BACKGROUND AND LITERATURE REVIEW

The questions above flow in part from what we know about how race operates to structure neighborhoods in the United States. The study of the links between socioeconomic status, race, and neighborhood is referred to as the process of spatial assimilation (Alba and Logan, 1991; Logan and Alba, 1993; Massey and Denton, 1985; 1993). Although assimilation usually refers to the incorporation of new groups into U.S. society, spatial assimilation describes a process of socioeconomic mobility that anyone can experience. As they improve their human capital, people get ahead by moving to better neighborhoods, which improves their local environment and services, as well as the schools to which they have access, and often the rate of appreciation of their house if they own it. To the extent that people's race limits their access to certain neighborhoods, their ability to derive these spatial returns on their human capital is blocked. In the United States, researchers have questioned the applicability of the spatial assimilation process to all groups, pointing to the exceptionally high segregation of blacks and argued that there is really a system of "place stratification" whereby certain groups live in certain neighborhoods (Logan and Alba, 1993). Although we have found only one published study of socioeconomic segregation in Puerto Rico (Schwirian and Rico-Velasco, 1971), the existence of "good" and "bad" neighborhoods is frequently acknowledged by residents. Thus, there is no reason to suspect that the

process of spatial assimilation operates differently on the island of Puerto Rico than in the United States. The analyses of this paper will provide important baseline data for the study of the process of residential segregation in the metropolitan areas in Puerto Rico.

Studies of residential segregation by the Mumford Center (2002) reveal that among Puerto Ricans living on the U.S. mainland, Puerto Rican segregation from non-Hispanic whites averages 56.5 and from non-Hispanic blacks 50.2. Puerto Ricans are more segregated from non-Hispanic whites than Cubans and Mexicans, though less segregated than Dominicans. Puerto Rican segregation from non-Hispanic blacks is higher than that of Mexicans, but lower than that of Cubans and Dominicans. More specifically, in 2000 the segregation of Puerto Ricans in New York from non-Hispanic whites is 68.6 and from non-Hispanic blacks is 54.2; whereas the corresponding segregation scores for Dominicans are 80.8 and 64.3, respectively. Nationally, Hispanics who identify as white are segregated from those who identify as black at a level of 34, while white Hispanic segregation from those of some other race (as opposed to white) is 17.3. Earlier research also showed higher segregation levels for Hispanics who identified as "other" or black than their white counterparts (Denton and Massey, 1989; Massey and Bitterman, 1985). In addition, black Hispanics live in neighborhoods with higher poverty and fewer homeowners (Mumford Center, 2003). So race and residence are clearly linked on the mainland, the question is whether there is a linkage between race, residential location, and economic status on the island.

On one hand, one could argue that no relationship would be observed between race and socioeconomic status on the island because the racial system in Puerto Rico, and for that matter, Latin America, is quite different from that of the United States (Rodriguez, 2000). Numerous authors have pointed out that in the Caribbean race is seen as a continuum, not as a dichotomy, as the "one drop" rule in the United States presupposes (Rodriguez, 2000; Fitzpatrick, 1987). Fitzpatrick argues that in part racial discrimination was tempered by the fact that Spain had a long history of contact with dark-skinned people, upper-class men in the Spanish colonies recognized illegitimate children born to them by colored women (Fitzpatrick 1987:106–107). Previous research has shown that there are differences between the mainland and the island in how people racially identify themselves, but these researchers have not linked these differences to residential outcomes (Landale and Oropesa, 2002; Rodriguez, 1989). Yet another reason that we may expect to find no relationship between race and socioeconomic status in Puerto Rico is that there is no dominant non-Hispanic white group on the island with which to residentially assimilate. Indeed, segregation between Hispanics of different races in U.S. cities where the Puerto Rican population is large is much lower than the segregation of white, other, or black Hispanics from non-Hispanic whites (Denton and Massey, 1989; Mumford Center, 2003). As the island is overwhelmingly Puerto Rican (96.3%), then segregation there may be more similar to that observed among Puerto Ricans in the United States (Census 2000, SF1, Table QT-P9, from American Factfinder).

On the other hand, despite many denials of the importance of race to getting ahead on the island, there is evidence of black isolation in low SES communities with poor housing conditions (Duany, 2002; Godreau, 2002; Torres, 1998), which suggests that linkages between race, neighborhood location, and socioeconomic status would be observed on the island. Recent research has also shown support for a link between occupational status and race (Rivera-Batiz, 2004). Emphasis on the process of whitening (*blanqueamiento*) also suggests the linkage between race and socioeconomic status, as does the fact that people have different races in different contexts (Fitzpatrick, 1987:108). Given that the history of Puerto Rico has emphasized whitening and downplayed African heritage, it seems reasonable to hypothesize

lighter skinned Puerto Ricans live in areas of higher status and better other amenities such as schools, services, and safety. A final reason to hypothesize a relationship between race and socioeconomic status on the island is the fact that Puerto Ricans, despite having their own conception of race, are well acquainted with the United States racial system or one-drop rule as well due to considerable migration between the two places (Duany, 2002; Flores, 2000:11; Rodriguez and Codero-Guzman, 1992).

Race is clearly a politicized issue in Puerto Rico, and one that people prefer not to discuss. As Rosario and Carrion noted over half a century ago "the discussion of the problem of the black has been kept in a humid and unhygienic obscurity" (1951). The national identity of *mestizaje* promotes integration, yet people of European descent and those with "white" features (hair texture and nose) are privileged (Torres, 1998). Despite claims that they are taught in school that Puerto Ricans are a blend of Spanish, Indian, and African (Hovland and Buckley-Ess, 2003), it seems the blending is emphasized mainly when convenient, and remarks that the African traces will be gone in a few more decades are common (Torres, 1998). For Puerto Ricans, race is viewed as a continuum between white and black rather than as a dichotomous variable (Rodriguez, 1989:52–53). In Puerto Rico, cultural identification as Puerto Rican takes precedence over racial identification to the point that someone black may become white by achieving higher socioeconomic status or by becoming one's friend (Rodriguez, 1989:53). This is not to say that Puerto Ricans are unaware of racial differences, but rather that they perceive them more fluidly than most U.S. non-Hispanic whites do.

It is important to note that the reason the question on race was added to the Puerto Rican Census in 2000, after having been absent for half a century, was not because there was any official interest in the race of the population of the island residents. Rather, the government of Puerto Rico asked the U.S. Census Bureau to use the same questionnaire on the island as on the mainland in order to have Census 2000 data for the island available sooner and more easily accessible. By using the same questionnaire, the Census Bureau was able to process the Puerto Rican data along with all the other U.S. data, thus saving time and effort for the Bureau. As a result, Puerto Rico is listed as one of the states on the Census website and in American Factfinder, the Puerto Rican data are much more widely available than was the case in prior censuses, and exactly comparable data are available for Puerto Ricans on the island and the mainland.

As part of their evaluation and testing program after Census 2000, the Bureau ran focus groups to find out why people did not return their census form or did not fill it in completely (Hovland and Buckley-Ess, 2003). In these groups, participants mentioned that the race question was "divisive and insensitive to the 'mixed' realities of Puerto Rico" (p. 13) and "that the existing race categories did not match their Puerto Rican identity" (p. 15). Further discussion revealed confusion as to how race was being defined (color, features, etc.) and the possibility that different members of the same family could have different races. Even though one of the three components of Puerto Rican national identity comes from the Taíno Indians, there is evidence of confusion about whether the Native American category on the census could be used to indicate Taíno (Torres, 2000). Past research had found that Hispanics may feel pressure to respond that they are white, even though they do not feel that it describes them or that others in their country consider them white (Hovland and Buckley-Ess, 2003). Focus group respondents for Census 2000 pointed out that "White was the best answer among inappropriate alternatives, Black was only for those who were pure Black, and that there is still a stigma to being identified as Black in Puerto Rico" (Hovland and Buckley-Ess, 2003:18). No doubt all of these factors affected some respondents. Compared with mainland residents, Puerto Rican

islanders have little experience in reporting their race on official forms. However, rates of imputation for race were only about 5% for the island and each metropolitan areas, so despite the issues just discussed, people did answer the question on race on the Census.

DATA AND METHODS

Data for this study comes from Summary File 3 of the 2000 Census of Population and Housing (U.S. Census Bureau, 2003a,b). Census tracts, small, non-overlapping geographical units averaging about 4,000 persons are used as a proxy for neighborhoods (U.S. Census Bureau, 2003a,b). As the concept of neighborhood has more validity in more densely populated areas, we confine our study to the metropolitan portion of Puerto Rico, where 84% of the island population lives. Six metropolitan areas are included: Arecibo, Caguas, and San Juan-Bayamón PMSAs, (which together make up the San Juan-Caguas-Arecibo CMSA), and the Aguadil-la, Mayagüez, and Ponce MSAs.

To examine the relationship between neighborhood location and race (or socioeconomic status) in these six metropolitan areas, we use the dissimilarity index (Massey and Denton, 1988). Dissimilarity measures how evenly a population is distributed across the neighborhoods in an area. It can be interpreted as the percent of either group that would have to change neighborhoods in order for each neighborhood to have the same overall composition as the metro area as a whole. It ranges between 0 and 100, and values less than 30 are considered low segregation, between 30 and 60 are moderate, and over than 60 are high. The index compares two groups, a disadvantage in a place as racially complex as Puerto Rico. Unfortunately, there are no alternatives that do not make unreasonable assumptions about the relative sizes of the groups. As we are interested in the relationship between race and socioeconomic status, the dissimilarity index will be computed by income, occupation, and educational attainment as well as race. We also conduct correlation and principal components factor analyses among the indicators of socioeconomic status and race to determine their relationship at a bivariate and multivariate level.

Once we have examined the segregation patterns in the metropolitan areas overall, we then analyze how race and socioeconomic status play out at the neighborhood level since as noted above, there is acknowledgment of the generally poorer conditions in areas where darker-skinned Puerto Ricans live. As San Juan-Bayamón is the largest and most diverse of the metropolitan areas, we focus on it to allow for more detailed neighborhood analysis. First, we classify the neighborhoods into groups based on racial composition or socioeconomic status and then compute averages of particular tract characteristics, weighted by the population living in that tract. This is an adaptation of the weighting strategy used in the P-star indices and can be interpreted as the experience of the average person living in a tract of the type defined by the grouping characteristic. For example, if tracts are divided into low, medium, and high groups based on median household income, and we examine racial composition, then we can discuss the average percent black in low-income neighborhoods compared with high-income neighborhoods. Next we examine neighborhoods representing the areas where blacks live and where Dominicans (the largest non-Puerto Rican group on the island) live and compute the characteristics of those neighborhoods, comparing them to a similar subset of neighborhoods that are overwhelmingly white.

METROPOLITAN PUERTO RICO

As relatively little has been written in English about the metropolitan areas located on the island of Puerto Rico, Table I presents some basic demographic characteristics of them. As mentioned above, 84% of the total population of 3,808,610 persons live in these metro areas. In terms of location, San Juan-Bayamón is on the eastern side of the island, Ponce on the southern side, Mayagüez and Aguadilla are on the west coast, Arecibo is on the northern coast, and Caguas is in the mountainous area on the eastern side of the island. In terms of size, San Juan-Bayamón, at nearly two million people, is clearly the largest metropolitan area, almost five and one-half times the size of Ponce, the second largest metropolitan area. San Juan is the center of government for the island and the second oldest city in the New World, behind Santo Domingo in the Dominican Republic. Ponce, on the other hand is known for its political and economic influence in the southern region of the island, as well as for being the birthplace of three of the island's former governors.

The other four metro areas range in size from 308,365 in Caguas to 146,424 in Aguadilla. The majority of the 78 municipios of the island are within these six metro areas, with the exception of the municipios in the interior and southeastern part of the island. All but Caguas are coastal, reflecting the mountainous interior of the island, which is sparsely populated. In terms of economy, Aguadilla, Arecibo, and Mayagüez still depend on the manufacturing sector as a significant source of revenue, while Caguas, Ponce, and San Juan-Bayamón have shifted to a service sector economy. Of all the six metro areas, San Juan has the highest degree of economic development and is also the center of the island's financial district. Both San Juan-Bayamón and Mayagüez saw their populations increase about 17% in the previous decade, much smaller than the 55% increase in the population of Ponce. The other areas experienced no change in population size, or in the case of Aguadilla, a 12% population loss.

In terms of their demographic characteristics, San Juan-Bayamón stands out from the other areas with the highest educational attainments, median household income, housing value, and lowest poverty rate. Over one in five of its

TABLE I Demographic Profiles of Metropolitan Areas in Puerto Rico, 2000

Metropolitan Area	No. of Tracts	Total Population	% Change 1990–2000	Education HS or BA or More		Median Income ($)	% of Families in Poverty	Median Year Housing Built	Median Value of Housing ($)
Aguadilla MSA	28	146,424	−12.4	53.3	14.1	11,385	53.9	1980	60,900
Arecibo PMSA[a]	33	174,300	−1.2	55.4	15.2	12,616	48.8	1978	64,800
Caguas PMSA[a]	65	308,365	1.1	60.1	18.3	15,275	42.5	1977	81,000
Mayagüez MSA	57	253,347	18.2	56.0	17.0	12,707	44.8	1977	68,400
Ponce MSA	82	361,094	55.0	58.9	17.3	12,505	50.9	1976	63,400
San Juan-Bayamón PMSA[a]	426	1,967,627	16.5	63.7	20.9	16,728	39.6	1974	86,700

SOURCE: U.S. Census Bureau, Census 2000, Tables DP-1, DP-2-PR, DP-3, and authors' calculations from SF1 and SF3 data.
[a]Part of the San Juan-Caguas-Arecibo CMSA.

residents have a bachelor's degree or higher, and the median housing value is $86,700. Caguas, a part of the San Juan-Caguas-Arecibo CMSA, is next, with just over 18% of its residents with a bachelor's degree or more, and a median housing value of $81,000. Arecibo, Mayagüez, and Ponce all have relatively similar socioeconomic indicators, a bit below those of Caguas. Aguadilla has the lowest education, income, and housing value and highest poverty. Interestingly, it has the newest housing, which is usually associated with population growth, though as noted above, this area lost population. It is important to note that the poverty rates shown here are based on the United States standard, whereas the cost of living is substantially lower in Puerto Rico. As a result, 45% of families on the island are officially poor (Census 2000, SF3, Table DP-3, from American Factfinder).

PUERTO RICANS CHOICE OF RACE ON CENSUS 2000

Despite the national emphasis on the blending of Spanish, African, and Taíno ancestry on the island of Puerto Rico, 80.5% of the population reported themselves as "white only," and if multiple races are included 84%, 11%, and 8% reported themselves white, black, or "other," respectively (Census 2000, SF1, Tables QT-P4 and QT-P6, from American Factfinder). Although the culture argues for *mestizaje* and the census question allowed the expression of all three races, the vast majority of the population chose a single race. The prominence of circular migration notwithstanding this overwhelming identification as white is in stark contrast to the racial identification of Puerto Ricans on the mainland, where only 49% identified as white, 42.8% as "other," and 8.2% as black (Mumford Center, 2003).

In Table II we present data on the racial identification of the population in each metropolitan area to see how they differ from the data for the entire island. Not surprisingly, the population of Puerto Rico is overwhelmingly Hispanic, less than 2% of San Juan's population is non-Hispanic and in the other metropolitan areas it is 1%. The Hispanic population overwhelmingly chose "white alone" as their race, ranging from almost 90% in Arecibo to 83% in Caguas and Ponce. Only 75% of the San Juan-Bayamón population chose "white alone."

After "white only," the most common choice in all metropolitan areas save San Juan was "other race," followed by "black only." The choice of "other race" could reflect the designation of "mixed" or "multiracial," or it may be that islanders consider "Puerto Rican" their race. Over 7% of those in Caguas and San Juan-Bayamón chose "other" as their racial designation. San Juan is distinct in that more people there, 10.3%, chose "black alone" as their race. Indian was chosen by fewer than half of 1% in all the metropolitan areas listed.

In short, Census 2000 provided the opportunity for the Puerto Rican people to choose more than one race and one would have expected that in a nation that emphasizes *mestizaje* many people would choose more than one race. However, the results in Table II clearly reveal that this did not happen. If anything, they suggest the importance of *blanqueamiento* in the overwhelming choice of only one race, "white," though only longitudinal data could reveal if individuals actually change their racial identification over time. Only in Ponce did over 5% choose more than one race, and fewer than 5% did so in San Juan-Bayamón and Mayagüez. Less than 3% did so in the other three metropolitan areas. The limited use of the option of checking more than one race (which would then have been tabulated as "two or more races" in this table) indicates that the ideology of being

a nation made up of Spanish, Indian, and African parts does not seem to extend to racial self-identification. This is also true with the fact that so many chose only black, as opposed to black and something else. If the blending were uppermost in people's minds, one would have expected all the single race groups to be seldom chosen, as was the case for only the Indian category. Given that the national ideology is based on the combination of Spanish, Indian, and African, it is interesting that only 4,557 people on the island chose these three races, with another 3,458 choosing white, black, and other, out of a population of 3.8 million (Census 2000, SF2, Table PCT-1, from American Factfinder).

A word of caution is in order, however, for though the numbers in the table support the interpretation just given, there is evidence that there was confusion about whether or not people with Taíno Indian background could use the "Indian" designation (Torres, 2000). The focus groups conducted by the Census Bureau reported people saying that they did not realize they could choose more than one race (Hovland and Buckley-Ess, 2003), though given how clearly this option was stated on the Spanish questionnaire, it seems unlikely that so many people could have not seen this as an option. More likely, as discussed above, even the option to choose multiple categories did not seem appropriate to capture the reality of how Puerto Ricans think of race. In addition, as they had not been asked to report their race in half a century, the whole question of race seems to have generated confusion on the part of some, particularly as members of the same family can be of different races (Fitzpatrick, 1987; Hovland and Buckley-Ess, 2003).

However, the fact remains that nearly two out of every 10 people reported a race other than white, so we turn now to an analysis of patterns of residential segregation in the metropolitan areas on the island of Puerto Rico.

TABLE II Puerto Rican Population by Hispanic Ethnicity and Race, Metropolitan Areas, 2000

Metropolitan Area	Total Population	% Non-Hispanic	Hispanics							
			% White	% Black	% Indian	% Asian	% NHOPI	% Other Race	% Two or More Races
Aguadila	146,424	1.3	85.9	3.9	0.1	0	0	5.9	2.8
Arecibo	174,300	1.0	88.9	3.4	0.2	0.1	0	3.7	2.6
Caguas	308,365	0.9	82.9	5.8	0.2	0.1	0	7.3	2.8
Mayagüez	253,347	1.0	84.9	4.2	0.2	0.1	0.01	4.8	4.7
Ponce	361,094	1.0	82.6	5.2	0.2	0.1	0.01	5.8	5.1
San Juan	1,967,627	1.7	75.2	10.3	0.3	0.2	0.01	7.5	4.7

SOURCE: Authors' calculations from SF1 and SF3 data, Census 2000, U.S. Census Bureau.

SEGREGATION BY RACE

Data on residential segregation by race in each of these metropolitan areas, using the well-known index of dissimilarity, are presented in Table III. As Puerto Rican identity is grounded in Spanish (or white), Indian (Taíno), and black (African) roots, the segregation of Hispanic whites from Hispanic blacks and Hispanic Indians are shown in the first two columns. It is clear that Hispanic whites are not very segregated from Hispanic blacks, with the index of dissimilarity ranging from a high of 33.3 in San Juan to a low of 17.1 in Caguas. The numbers suggest much more segregation of Hispanic whites from Hispanic Indians, above 50 in all the metropolitan areas and above 70 in Aguadilla.

The segregation of Hispanic whites from those Hispanics who chose "other" (which could be a term for mixed race) or "two or more races" (a direct measure of people who view their race as mixed) is shown in columns three and four of Table III. Again, there appears to be a low level of segregation between these groups, as only one

of the indices is above 30. Hispanic white segregation from Hispanic others is lower than Hispanic white segregation from Hispanic blacks in Arecibo, Mayagüez, and San Juan-Bayamón and about the same in Aguadilla and Ponce. Hispanic whites' segregation from those of two or more races is lower in the same four metro areas, but their segregation from both groups is higher in Caguas and Ponce. However, as all these numbers are in the "low" range (below 30), these differences probably do not have much substantive meaning. The segregation of Hispanic whites from those who reported two or more races is lower than that from Indians, and in general very low everywhere but in Ponce and San Juan-Bayamón.

Although less than 2% of the population of Puerto Rico is non-Hispanic, it is of interest to see the segregation between the Hispanic and non-Hispanic populations as this population is presumably the most culturally different. Segregation of Hispanic whites from non-Hispanics is moderate, ranging from a low of 26.3 in Arecibo and 26.5 in Caguas to

TABLE III   Segregation by Race and Hispanic Ethnicity, Metropolitan Areas, 2000

Dissimilarity								
Of Hispanic Whites From:						*Of Hispanic Blacks From:*		
Metro Area	Hispanic Blacks	Hispanic Indians	Hispanic Others	Hispanics Two or More	Non-Hispanics	Hispanics Others	Hispanic Two or More	Hispanic Indians
Aguadilla	24.3	71.4	23.4	17.2	33.3	18.8	28.6	74.4
Arecibo	21.7	54.8	15.1	15.3	26.3	21.5	25.4	57.9
Caguas	17.1	57.8	18.2	20.5	26.5	19.4	25.1	55.7
Mayagüez	19.8	53.5	15	19.7	30.9	20.6	21.5	54.6
Ponce	21.4	58.9	22	28.2	28.9	24	26	58.5
San Juan	33.3	51	28.6	32.4	37.2	26.8	36.7	49.6

SOURCE: Authors' calculations from SF1 and SF3 data, Census 2000, U.S. Census Bureau.

a high of 37.2 in San Juan, and in most cases it is higher than the segregation of Hispanic whites from either Indians and those of two or more races, both of which are also very small populations.

The segregation of Hispanic blacks from Hispanic others and Hispanics of two or more races are likewise all in the low range (Columns 6 and 7) of Table III, reaching above 30 only for segregation between black Hispanics and those of two or more races in San Juan-Bayamón at 36.7. Black Hispanics' segregation from Indians is again much higher (column 7), as it was from whites, ranging from 74.4 in Aguadilla to 49.6 in San Juan-Bayamón.

Overall, these indices reveal what can only be described as moderate to low segregation by race in the metropolitan areas of Puerto Rico. To scholars accustomed to looking at the segregation of blacks from whites, or even Puerto Ricans from whites, in mainland metropolitan areas like New York, they no doubt appear very small. At the same time, one must remember that these are the usual range

for segregation by most socioeconomic statuses except race in the United States (see White, 1987 for a presentation of segregation indices by different socioeconomic statuses in the United States; Pamuk, 1985 for segregation indices by occupational status in Great Britain). Segregation at these low levels is in line with the cultural identity claims of being a mixed nation. We turn now to an analysis of segregation by socioeconomic status, in order to examine the claim that class matters more than race.

SEGREGATION BY SOCIOECONOMIC STATUS

As noted above, Puerto Ricans maintain that class is more important than race. As class can be measured in numerous ways, and we are limited by the tabulations available at the census tract level, Table IV presents segregation by household income, educational attainment, and occupational status, three common measures of socioeconomic status. Segregation by income[2] (shown in the first panel) is generally low, particularly in the smaller metropolitan areas. In Ponce and San Juan-Bayamón, there is more evidence of class segregation as the lowest income group, those making less than $10,000, are segregated from the highest, those making $50,000 or more, with indices of 35.3 and 44.7, respectively. Similarly, the next income group ($10,000–14,999) is segregated from the highest with indices of 40.4 in San Juan-Bayamón and just over 30 in Caguas and Ponce. Segregation of households with incomes from $15,000 to $24,999 from those with incomes $50,000 or more is 36.6 in San Juan-Bayamón, but in all other cases, the segregation is generally around 20, near the bottom of the low range. Although segregation by income is generally higher than segregation by race, it is still not sizable, especially when compared with segregation in the United States.

The next panel of Table IV presents segregation indices by educational attainment. These only exceed 30 in two instances, the segregation of those who have not completed high school from college graduates in Ponce and San Juan-Bayamón. These two groups are segregated at about 24 in Caguas and Mayagüez. High school dropouts are segregated at about 23 from those with some college in Ponce and San Juan, and high school graduates are segregated from college graduates at about 20 in Caguas, Mayagüez, and Ponce, and 26.6 in San Juan-Bayamón. Comparing the segregation of Hispanic whites and blacks from Table III to the segregation of high school dropouts from college graduates, reveals that racial segregation is higher than educational segregation in Aguadilla and Arecibo, but educational segregation is higher in the other four metro areas.

The bottom panel in Table IV presents data on occupational segregation. As only 1.1% of the employed population is engaged in farming, only non-farm occupations are presented. The segregation of occupation groups is moderate, in line with what we found for segregation by education. Looking at the end points, the segregation of management and professionals from production workers ranges from a high of 34.8 in San Juan-Bayamón to a low of 17 in Aguadilla and Arecibo. In general, occupational segregation in highest in San Juan-Bayamón, regardless of the occupational groups being compared, and if it is not the highest there, it is close to the higher segregation found in Ponce. It should be remembered that the occupational classifications used here are very broad, and there are many different types of occupations in each, which no doubt affects the segregation. Still, as was true for the segregation by other characteristics, segregation by occupation is moderate on the island of Puerto Rico.

On balance, it appears that segregation by socioeconomic status is somewhat higher than segregation by race, particularly in San Juan-Bayamón and Ponce, in line with the claim that social class is more important than race in Puerto Rico. If we compare the segregation between Hispanic blacks and Hispanic whites to the segregation between the bottom and top of the three socioeconomic status measures, income segregation is higher than racial segregation in all six of the metropolitan areas, and educational segregation and occupational segregation are higher than racial segregation everywhere but in Aguadilla and Arecibo. Segregation by income is 19 points higher than segregation by race in Caguas, 14 in Ponce, and 11 points higher in San Juan-Bayamón. All the other differences are more modest. Were we able to further subdivide the lowest income category (< $10,000) into which one-third of the households fall, no doubt segregation between the richest and the poorest would be higher.

Given the generally low levels of segregation seen in Tables III and IV, we explored the relationship between race and socioeconomic

---

[2]It should be noted that the income categories used on Census 2000 resulted in 31.4% of Puerto Rican households being in the lowest category, less than $10,000 and 44.6% of families below the official poverty line.

TABLE IV Segregation by Socioeconomic Status, Metropolitan Areas, 2000

Panel (a) Dissimilarity Indices by Income

Metro Area	Less than $10,000 from				$10,000–14,999			$15,000–24,999		$25,000–49,999
	$10,000–14,999	$15,000–24,999	$25,000–49,999	$50,000 or More	$15,000–24,999	$25,000–49,999	$50,000 or More	$25,000–49,999	$50,000 or More	$50,000 or More
Aguadilla	10.1	11.3	15.2	30.1	10.5	11.8	27.6	14.0	27.3	20.8
Arecibo	10.5	10.7	16.7	22.1	8.7	14.1	22.7	10.5	19.0	16.2
Caguas	10.5	13.7	21.3	35.8	8.7	15.8	31.5	12.4	29.3	22.2
Mayagüez	12.5	14.1	20.4	28.6	9.4	15.8	26.6	11.2	23.9	20.0
Ponce	13.0	15.9	28.1	35.3	11.4	21.2	30.3	15.6	25.7	21.4
San Juan	14.0	17.0	27.3	44.7	11.7	20.9	40.4	15.5	36.6	26.3

Panel (b) Dissimilarity Indices by Occupation

Metro Area	Management From:				Services From:			Sales From:	Construction From:
	Services	Sales	Construction	Production	Sales	Construction	Production	Construction	Production
Aguadilla	17.9	9.7	22.2	17.2	13.8	13.5	12.3	15.7	12.2
Arecibo	13.8	9.6	20.7	17.1	12.4	14.0	12.2	17.4	11.7
Caguas	22.7	14.5	23.2	23.8	14.9	14.7	15.1	20.2	14.4
Mayagüez	19.4	14.0	26.3	24.6	13.5	16.3	15.2	20.5	14.0
Ponce	24.9	13.4	28.1	22.3	21.3	15.9	13.9	24.3	15.7
San Juan	29.0	17.3	34.2	34.8	19.4	18.2	20.9	26.5	16.9

(Continued)

TABLE IV (Continued)

Metro Area	Less than High School From:			High School From:		Some College From:
	High School	Some College	Four Years of College or More	Some College	Four Years of College or More	Four Years of College or More
Panel (c) Dissimilarity Indices by Education						
Aguadilla	10.0	13.6	18.7	8.7	13.5	8.5
Arecibo	11.8	14.3	17.4	12.9	15.4	8.6
Caguas	12.8	18.8	24.2	14.2	19.4	10.4
Mayagüez	10.7	16.6	24.6	11.5	19.8	12.3
Ponce	14.0	22.2	30.1	12.7	19.6	11.6
San Juan	13.9	24.4	34.3	15.1	26.6	17.0

SOURCE: Authors' calculations from SF3 data, Census 2000, U.S. Census Bureau.

status using bivariate correlations presented in Table V. For all metropolitan areas together, there is a statistically significant relationship between the three racial indicators, percent Hispanic white, percent Hispanic black, and percent Hispanic non-white and the four indicators of socioeconomic status, percent professional workers, percent with a BA or more, percent with income greater than $50,000, and median housing value. The correlations with percent white are all positive, while those with percent black and percent non-white are negative as would be expected if there were discrimination based on race. Substantively, though, the size of the coefficients is small, ranging from 0.08 to 0.28. When we ran the matrix separately for each metropolitan area (data not shown), though all the correlations were of the expected sign, none were statistically significant in Aguadilla and Arecibo. In Caguas, only the correlations with race and housing value were significant, while only those with household income were significant in Mayagüez. In short, the phenomenon of a relationship between race and socioeconomic

status is found only in San Juan and Ponce. As these two areas account for the vast majority of the neighborhoods, they dominate the correlations in Table V. In these metropolitan areas, the correlations also tend to be higher in value, ranging from 0.22 to 0.32 in Ponce and 0.25 to 0.38 in San Juan. These were also the metropolitan areas, which most often had the highest racial segregation. It thus appears that race may occasionally be important, but that its importance does not operate as strongly through the traditional measures of socioeconomic status in Puerto Rico as it does in the United States.[3]

It seems clear that overall, the relationship between race and residence in Puerto Rico is not strong. This conclusion is reinforced by looking at the substantial variation across neighborhoods in terms of racial composition. In all six metro areas combined, the percent Hispanic white ranges from 10.6 to 96.5, the percent Hispanic black from 0.19 to 86.7, and the percent Hispanic non-white from 3.3 to 89.4. Furthermore, in contrast to the United States where the distribution of neighborhoods by black racial

TABLE V Correlation Between Race and Socioeconomic Status for Neighborhoods in Puerto Rico, 2000

	% Professional Workers	*Median Housing Value*	*Income $50,000 or More*	*% BA or More*
% Hispanic white	0.21856	0.08564	0.11679	0.19392
% Hispanic black	−0.24865	−0.11831	−0.16172	−0.23263
% Hispanic non-white	−0.28383	−0.14299	−0.18599	−0.26737

All are significant at $p < .0001$.

SOURCE: Authors' calculations from SF1 and SF3 data, Census 2000, U.S. Census Bureau.

---

[3]To see the relationship among the variables in Table V in a multivariate context, a principal components factor analysis was run for each metropolitan area separately to see if the racial percentages loaded on the socioeconomic status measures. Percent black did not load with any of the SES indicators, and emerged as a third weak factor everywhere but in Aguadilla and Caguas, where it loaded only with percent homeowners.

composition tends to be U-shaped, with most neighborhoods with either a very low or a very high black proportion, and few in the middle, the distribution of neighborhoods in Puerto Rico is not skewed, but rather the number of neighborhoods and a particular racial composition is linear. As segregation was highest there, we turn now to an examination of the characteristics of the neighborhoods in San Juan-Bayamón.

RACE AND CLASS IN NEIGHBORHOODS IN SAN JUAN-BAYAMÓN

As San Juan-Bayamón is by far the largest and most diverse of the metropolitan areas, we focus on it to explore a bit further the issue of race and class in Puerto Rican neighborhoods. Although the pattern of low segregation at the metropolitan area level is clear from the analyses presented so far, there could still be small groups of neighborhoods that are heavily black and of low socioeconomic status. San Juan-Bayamón also offers the advantage of a comparison group, namely the presence of immigrants from the Dominican Republic, many of who are black or of other mixed races as well. Although Puerto Rico has a relatively small foreign born population (2.9%), they are overwhelmingly located in San Juan-Bayamón (84%), and predominately from the Dominican Republic (56%), so that three of every five foreign born in San Juan-Bayamón are Dominicans.

To explore the relationship between race and socioeconomic status in San Juan-Bayamón neighborhoods, we first compute "profiles" of the average characteristics of neighborhoods to see if non-white Puerto Ricans reside in worse quality neighborhoods. The top panel in Table VI groups the neighborhoods by percent Hispanic black and examines median education, percent professional, percent poor, median household income, median housing value, and percent of home that are owned. It is

clear that as the percent black in the neighborhood rises, median education, professional workers, and all the other indicators of socioeconomic status decline. The percentage with a BA degree or more falls from 26 to 11, and median housing value from $114,668 to $68,367. Similar declines are seen for professional workers and household income. Although the percent poor is 38 in neighborhoods that are less than 5% black, it rises to 54% in those that are more than 20% black. Clearly, neighborhoods with higher proportions of black residents are worse places to live, though the differences between the lowest and the highest percents black are not as large as one would see in a similar grouping of U.S. neighborhoods because segregation is not as high.

As the literature argues that social class supercedes race, in Table VII we group the neighborhoods by socioeconomic status, measured as percent with a bachelor's degree or more.[4] The average neighborhood percent with a BA or more was divided into the five categories shown. Looking at the percent Hispanic whites and Hispanic blacks, there is a large difference between neighborhoods where less than 5% of the population has a BA degree or higher, but the differences at other educational levels are less clearly distinguished by either race. This again suggests that overall race is not strongly linked to socioeconomic status. Other measures of socioeconomic status, however, increase as the percent with a BA degree increases, reflecting the fact that different measures of SES are highly correlated.

WHAT ABOUT LARGELY BLACK AND LARGELY WHITE AREAS?

Numerous observers, from Gordon (1950) to current residents, note that there are poor areas in Puerto Rican cities where the population is also black. Dominicans also tend to live predominantly

---

[4]Grouping by household income and occupation showed similar patterns.

TABLE VI   Average Neighborhood Socioeconomic Status by Percent Hispanic Black San Juan-Bayamón Metropolitan Area, 2000

Percent Hispanic Black	*< 5*	*5%–10%*	*10%–15%*	*15%–20%*	*> 20%*
Median Education	13.28	12.72	12.66	12.28	12.07
% BA or More	26.34	20.39	19.24	13.50	10.92
% Professional	33.09	27.88	25.71	20.32	18.72
% Poor	38.00	42.27	42.80	47.68	53.99
Median Household Income	$22,519	$18,525	$17,365	$14,902	$13,172
% Home Ownership	76.78	74.80	68.39	65.80	66.87
Median Housing Value	$114,668	$91,118	$88,374	$75,889	$68,367
Number of Tracts	104	146	92	44	40

SOURCE: Authors' calculations from SF1 and SF3 data, Census 2000, U.S. Census Bureau.

TABLE VII   Average Neighborhood Racial Composition by Socioeconomic Status, San Juan-Bayamón Metropolitan Area, 2000

	Percent with a BA or More:				
	< 5	*5%–10%*	*10%–15%*	*15%–20%*	*> 20%*
Median Education	11.13	11.84	12.19	12.59	13.78
Percent Professional	10.46	16.44	21.31	25.66	38.43
Percent Families in Poverty	69.76	57.63	51.29	40.55	29.06
Median Household Income	$8,318	$11,707	$13,344	$17,280	$26,527
Percent Home Ownership	49.93	76.71	74.34	72.68	72.04
Median Housing Value	$44,253	$61,441	$70,493	$86,549	$130,358
Percent Hispanic Black	22.05	12.85	9.45	11.03	8.12
Percent Hispanic Non-White	41.23	26.2	21.81	23.86	20.14
Number of Tracts	24	63	103	76	160

SOURCE: Authors' calculations from SF1 and SF3 data, Census 2000, U.S. Census Bureau.

in one area. Despite the ideological attempts to explain them away via *mestizaje,* they do appear to reflect a linkage between race and socioeconomic status. To examine this argument directly, we selected neighborhoods that were more than 50% black, those more than 30% Dominican, and those more than 90% white in San Juan and computed average tract characteristics. These three groups of neighborhoods represent the "extremes" of segregation to the extent that it exists in San Juan (Table VIII).

The first thing that we noticed was that there were only eight tracts with more than 50% black, and these comprise the area known as Loíza, a largely black area settled by Nigerian slaves, and there were nine heavily Dominican tracts. There were 39 tracts that are more than 90% Hispanic white, though none that are more than 95% Hispanic white. The comparison among the three areas is stark: Loíza and the Dominican neighborhoods are substantially worse on every single socioeconomic indicator, and worse than the

TABLE VIII Neighborhood Characteristics of Largely Black and Largely White Neighborhoods in San Juan-Bayamón

Neighborhood Characteristic	More Than 50% Hispanic Black	More Than 30% Dominican	More Than 90% Hispanic White
Median Education	12.05	11.92	12.45
Percent BA or More	6.58	13.01	17.46
Percent Professional	15.92	18.37	26.52
Median Income	$9,193	$13,329	$16,381
Percent Earning $50,000 or More	3.72	5.84	10.19
Percent Families in Poverty	66.96	47.28	50.71
Median Year Housing Built	1981	1957	1979
Median Housing Value	$58,874	$75,222	$85,760
Percent Homeowners	82.47	33.72	80.37
Percent Hispanic White	20.4	51.55	91.66
Percent Hispanic Black	66.36	21.74	3.07
Percent Dominican	0.96	34.00	0.44
Number of Tracts	8	9	39

SOURCE: Authors' calculations from SF1 and SF3 data, Census 2000, U.S. Census Bureau.

results shown in Table VI. Compared with the white neighborhoods, the black neighborhoods average about one-third as many college graduates, almost 50% fewer professional workers, and median incomes of just over $9,000 compared with $16,381. The only variables for which Loíza has higher scores than the heavily white neighborhoods are homeownership and median year housing was built, and in both cases the difference is not large. On some indicators, such as percent with a BA or more and median household income, the heavily Dominican neighborhoods are intermediate between the heavily black and the heavily white neighborhoods. But they are more similar to the white neighborhoods in terms of their percent in poverty. The most striking contrast is their low homeownership, 34% compared with over 80% for the other two groups of neighborhoods. No doubt this reflects in part that they have arrived relatively recently.

The role of homeownership in the analyses done for this paper is interesting. Quite the opposite of the situation in the United States, it does not appear to be related to race nor does it appear to have a strong relationship to socioeconomic status. While homes do tend to be relatively cheap in Puerto Rico, incomes are also very low, as about one-third or more of the population in each of these metro areas has a household income of less than $10,000 per year.

Summary and Conclusions

In this paper, we used the racial data available for the first time in 50 years to examine the links among race, socioeconomic status, and residential location in Puerto Rico. It is clear that Puerto Ricans overwhelmingly chose white as their race, and that they chose only one race, not a combination of races that would seem more in keeping with the ideology of *mestizaje*. It will take much more research than this simple analysis of the aggregate results from Census 2000 to figure out why this was so. One explanation, as suggested by the focus group member cited above, as well as numerous academics, is that the races listed on the Census form do not fit with the Puerto Rican continuum of race, so white was chosen as the best among a bad lot of alternatives. Another is that the process of *blanqueamiento*, noticed early in the twentieth century, is continuing apace, not because it reflects anything about phenotype or social status, both of which are important to the determination of race in Puerto Rico, but because Puerto Ricans have learned that white is associated with privilege and power in the world in which they live. The migration of Puerto Ricans between the island and the mainland would certainly help to foster this idea.

The primary aim of this paper was to investigate whether the linkage between race and socioeconomic status, so prevalent among groups in the United States including Puerto Ricans, resulted in residential segregation. The results presented here show that segregation by race is generally lower than segregation between the lowest and highest income categories in all metro areas, but that the results for education and occupational status differ by metropolitan area. In Aguadilla and Arecibo, segregation by race is higher than segregation by education or occupation, whereas in Caguas, Mayagüez, Ponce, and San Juan-Bayamón, segregation by education or occupation is higher than that by race. Overall, however, segregation by race, as well as segregation by the other socioeconomic indicators can only be described as quite modest. The fact that so many people on the island chose white as their race, and that within the same family people can differ by race, may help to explain these modest levels of segregation. But using aggregated data does not allow us to look at family racial composition.

To address the fact that observers often mention the poverty of black and Dominican areas, we investigated average neighborhood characteristics. We find that as the percent black increases, the socioeconomic status of the neighborhood declines. In looking at the extremes, Loíza, home to a community of black Puerto Ricans, and some heavily Dominican areas, these neighborhoods are decidedly worse. So across all neighborhoods, there is a modest relationship between race and socioeconomic status, but neighborhood sorting by socioeconomic status is a bit stronger. And there do exist, in San Juan at least, specific areas that match the poverty and race association observers report, but measuring neighborhoods as census tracts, there are not many of them.

What we have not learned is what this means. On the optimistic side about the future of race relations, it is tempting to argue that these results clearly demonstrate the success of racial integration in Puerto Rico, as many have argued. However, the process of *blanqueamiento,* best thought of as the fact that someone's race may be redefined based on his or her socioeconomic accomplishments, could also produce these results. If the highly successful (high educational attainment, high income, and high occupational status) people are more likely to report their race as white, then it would be very difficult to find a relationship between race and socioeconomic status. "Individuals with similar family backgrounds, economic status, political affiliation, and phenotypical variation in the family are considered equals. Income, occupation, education, social relationships, and material wealth are all taken into account in identifying the economic and social standing of individuals and their families. This view of a local-level stratified system blurs distinctions and perpetuates the view that socioeconomic status overrides concerns regarding an individual's racial and family heritage. But indicators of socioeconomic status are themselves racialized" (Torres, 1998:197).

The poor blacks in poor areas may have been the victims of discrimination and suffer from a lack of return on their human capital, but to the extent that they are able to change their race once their fortunes improve, it complicates the issue of linking race with socioeconomic status. Paradoxically, the absence of relatively fewer high-status blacks compared with whites, makes it difficult to determine if race is the cause of the low status of some blacks in certain areas of the island. Certainly, however, the lack of any other explanation leaves the racial one still available.

Race is linked with culture in Puerto Rico. "The view here is that upward mobility cannot be achieved if a black identity is maintained because there are negative cultural ascriptions associated with blackness. *Gente negra,* black people, are perceived to be culturally unrefined and lack ambition" (Torres, 1998:197). It has long been noted that Puerto Ricans do not like to talk about race. Torres (1998:198) argues, "By collapsing racial and class distinctions under the broad concept of *una buena familia* or *una buena persona,* Puerto Ricans can neatly avoid the extent to which issues of race, gender, and class permeate every day life."

Clearly, the next step is to analyze individual-level data (from the 2000 PUMS file) to examine how individual characteristics translate into socioeconomic status to give insight into our findings about neighborhood outcomes. One key question which we cannot answer with summary data is how race is distributed within families, for if each family has members of different races, then segregation would by definition be low because families live together in households. It would also be of interest to compare Puerto Ricans on the island and on the mainland in terms of neighborhood location by socioeconomic status and race. Still, it is very clear that the analyses thus far demonstrate the complexity of race in Puerto Rico, and highlight how different the racial landscape is should they migrate to the United States. Researchers accustomed to the U.S. pattern of association between neighborhoods and socioeconomic status and race will have to be open to new questions if they want to help explain how race operates in the social structure of Puerto Rico.

REFERENCES

Alba, Richard D., and John R. Logan

1991 "Variations on Two Themes: Racial and Ethnic Patterns in Attainment of Suburban Residence," *Demography* 28: 431–453.

Denton, Nancy A., and Douglas S. Massey

1989 "Racial Identity among Caribbean Hispanics: The Effect of Double Minority Status on Residential Segregation," *American Sociological Review* 54: 790–808.

Duany, Jorge

2002a "Mobile Livelihoods: The Sociocultural Practices of Circular Migration between Puerto Rico and the United States," *International Migration Review* 36(2): 355–388.

Duany, Jorge

2002b *Puerto Rican Nation on the Move: Identities on the Island and in the United States.* Chapel Hill, NC: University of North Carolina Press.

Flores, Juan

2000 *From Bomba to Hip-Hop: Puerto Rican Culture and Latino Identity.* New York: Columbia University Press.

Godreau, Isar P.

2002 "Changing Space, Making Race: Distance, Nostalgia, and the Folklorization of Blackness in Puerto Rico," *Identities. Global Studies in Culture and Power* 9: 281–304.

Gordon, Maxine W.

1949 "Race Patterns and Prejudice in Puerto Rico," *American Sociological Review* 14(2): 294–301.

Gordon, Maxine W.

1950 "Cultural Aspects of Puerto Rico's Race Problem," *American Sociological Review* 15(3): 382–392.

Hovland, Idabelle, and Julie Buckley-Ess

2003 "Puerto Rico," *Census 2000 Testing, Experimentation, and Evaluation Program. Topic Report Series, No. 14. U.S. Bureau of the Census* (http://www.census.gov/pred/www).

Landale, Nancy S., and R. S. Oropesa

2002 "White, Black, or Puerto Rican? Racial Self-Identification among Mainland and Island Puerto Ricans," *Social Forces* 81(1): 231–254.

Logan, John R., and Richard D. Alba

1993 "Educational Returns to Human Capital: Minority Access to Suburban Community Resources," *Demography* 30: 243–268.

Massey, Douglas S., and Brooks Bitterman

1985 "Explaining the Paradox of Puerto Rican Segregation," *Social Forces* 64(2): 306–331.

Massey, Douglas S., and Nancy A. Denton

1985 "Spatial Assimilation as a Socioeconomic Outcome," *American Sociological Review* 50: 94–105.

Massey, Douglas S., and Nancy A. Denton

1988 "The Dimensions of Residential Segregation," *Social Forces* 67: 281–315.

Massey, Douglas S., and Nancy A. Denton

1993 *American Apartheid: Segregation and the Making of the Underclass.* Cambridge, MA: Harvard University Press.

Mumford Center

2002 "Hispanic Populations and Their Residential Patterns in the Metropolis." Issued May 8, 2002. Accessed April 17, 2005 (http://mumford.albany.edu/census/HispanicPop/HspReportNew/page1.html).

Mumford Center

2003 "How Race Counts for Hispanic Americans." Issued July 14, 2003. Accessed April 17, 2005. (http:// mumford.albany.edu/census).

Pamuk, Elsie R.

1985 "Social Class Inequality in Mortality from 1921 to 1972 in England and Wales," *Population Studies* 39: 17–31.

Rivera-Batiz, Francisco

2004 *Color in the Tropics: Race and Economic Outcomes on the Island of Puerto Rico.* New York: Russell Sage Foundation Research Report.

Rodriguez, Clara E.

1989 *Puerto Ricans: Born in the U.S.A.* Boston: Unwin Hyman.

Rodriguez, Clara E

2000 *Changing Race: Latinos, the Census and the History of Ethnicity in the United States.* New York: New York University Press.

Rodriguez, Clara E., and Hector Cordero-Guzman

1992 "Placing Race in Context," *Ethnic and Racial Studies* 15(4): 523–542.

Rodriguez-Cotto, Sandra

2004 "En Evidencia el Racismo Hacia la Mujer Negr" *El Nuevo Dia* April 20, p. 26.

Safa, Helen

1998 "Race and National Identity in the Americas," *Latin American Perspectives* 25: (3) 3–20.

Schwirian, Kent P., and Jesus Rico-Velasco

1971 "The Residential Distribution of Status Groups in Puerto Rico's Metropolitan Areas," *Demography* 8(1): 81–90.

Torres, Arlene

1998 "La Gran Familia Puertorriquena "Ej Prieta de Belda" (The Great Puerto Rican Family IS Really Really Black)," in Torres, Arlene, and Norman E. Whitten Jr (eds.), *Blackness in Latin America and the Caribbean: Social Dynamics and Cultural Transformations: Volume II: Eastern South America and the Caribbean.* pp. 285–306. Bloomington, IN: Indiana University Press.

Torres, Chief Pedro Guanikeyu

2000 "A Report on the United States Census Bureau Meeting." Accessed February 13, 2004 (http://www.taino-tribe.org/us-census.html).

U.S. Census Bureau

2003a "Census 2000 Summary File 1 Technical Documentation." SF1/12 RV (September 2003). Accessed September 30, 2003 (http://www.census.gov/ prod/cen2000/doc/sf1.pdf).

U.S. Census Bureau

2003b "Census 2000 Summary File 3 Technical Documentation." SF3/11 RV (September 2003). Accessed September 30, 2003 (http://www.census.gov/prod/cen2000/doc/sf3.pdf).

White, Michael

1987 "Neighborhoods and Urban Society," in Michael White (ed.), *American Neighborhoods and Residential Differentiation:* pp. 1–23. New York: Russell Sage.

Section VII

QUALITATIVE DATA ANALYSIS

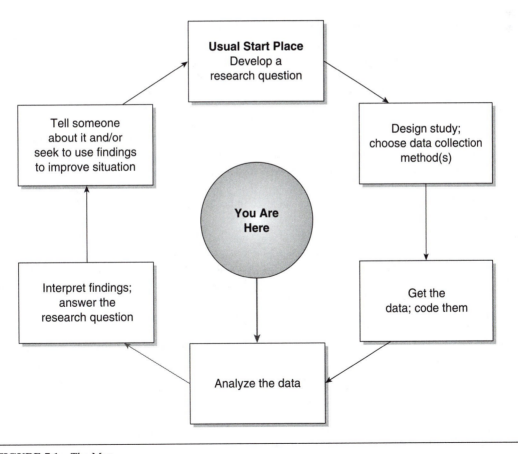

FIGURE 7.1 The Map

In the previous section, we talked about quantitative data. In this section, we look at qualitative data analysis. Qualitative data are information about the social world that is usually not coded as numbers. Using a Likert scale, we might be able to make a numeric distinction between "agree" (4 points) and "strongly agree" (5 points). But if we want to distinguish between "I guess I would be willing to go along with that" and "I felt that I had been preparing for this opportunity my whole life," then it's probably a distortion to reduce that information to numbers. Qualitative data analysis often focuses on the *meaning* of information or of relationships among variables.

The logic of qualitative analysis is similar to that just discussed for quantitative data: How do you take a mass of stuff (numbers, words, images) and find the meaningful patterns? In qualitative analysis, we are trying to find patterns in events and interactions, words and images, or in *social artifacts,* such as street signs, maps, graffiti, TV programs, newspaper articles, comic strips, greeting cards, and garbage. Unlike quantitative analysis, which reduces huge amounts of data to their underlying numeric patterns, qualitative analysis looks very closely at the details of cases, finding a world of information in the events of everyday life. And whereas quantitative snippets of information from around the social world form indicators of things that are often shared across contexts, qualitative data tend to be highly valid but more specific to the social context in which they were produced. Qualitative analysis examines how the particular context shapes social action and experience.

We analyze social action and context by **coding the information so that we can understand and explain it.** That is, we try to pull all of the separate observations and information together into something we can see and try to get our minds around. Reality is usually messy and volatile; analysis requires coalescing the separate findings into something more coherent and sensible. Coding and decoding lie at the heart of all qualitative research. Our coding schemes translate social artifacts—words, images, and the like—into data indicating social phenomena. For example,

we could look at the transcript of a business meeting and code all of the different ways that people make references to either the group or to themselves as individuals. Some of the phrases we might identify would look like "we can do this," or "we are the ones who . . ." or "what is our policy on . . ." or "I think I can handle the Jones account," or "I dropped the ball" or even, "I think these data show . . ." We can then analyze the patterns of these indicators to reveal more widely held expectations, values, preferences, and priorities. We can identify conditions under which people are more likely to accept or deflect personal responsibility or to invoke shared interests. (For instance, some research shows business*men* are more likely to say, "*We* dropped the ball," whereas business*women* are more likely to say, "*I* dropped the ball.") These, of course, are *qualities* of the social world. Coding consists of defining the social context of our analysis, specifying the *types* of data that occur in that context, and designing a system for recognizing each data type as it occurs. Below, we provide a summary of an assortment of studies and their coding schemes.

In each case, the creative work is in the coding and in developing the coding schema. A coding scheme separates the vast array of words, images, and/or events into a foreground (things that indicate our concepts) and a background (when, where, how, and why the events, etc., occurred). The background in Goffman's study of print ads, for example, includes such things as the setting (family, work, outdoors) and the products. The foreground is the images of the people and their physical relationship to each other. Goffman's coding scheme translates a still image (man and woman in a house) into measures of centrality and authority (man in center of image, woman peripheral; man standing, woman sitting).

CODING INTERVIEW AND OBSERVATIONAL DATA

Much of our qualitative data come to us in the form of words, usually recorded as text in a file

TABLE 7.1 Qualitative Coding Schemas

Research Question	Social Context	Types of Data	Coded Instances
Who has more or less informal authority in a small group? (W. F. Whyte 1943. *Street Corner Society: The Social Structure of an Italian Slum*)	Groups of working-class Italian American men interacting almost daily as a group in a "slum" neighborhood.	Patterns of exchange, such as casual conversation, making plans, or dealing with money.	Who gets to interrupt whom, and how often? Who initiates ideas that the group pursues? Who initiates plans that they don't pursue?
How do men and women present themselves in personal ads? What are they looking for? (Willis and Carlson 1993. "Single Ads: Gender, Social Class and Time")	Norms of "desirability" are gendered. Are men and women presenting themselves according to stereotypical norms, or seeking others who meet those norms?	Language used in ads that conform to, challenge, or ignore stereotypical attributes.	Desirable characteristics (money, attractiveness), desired characteristics (attractiveness, money), ages, ages sought, personality.
How do advertisers present men and women in interaction? (E. Goffman 1979. *Gender Advertisements*)	Commercial print advertisements—in which men are shown as independent & superior vs. women who are shown as smaller and adoring.	Pictures portray men displaying power, dominance, or superiority. Visual layouts, relative position of figures, size, posture.	Whose images are larger in the photos? Who takes "leadership" positions? Men look at the camera; women look at the men. Men stand, women sit.

or in notebooks or on tape. Such data include interviews, court transcripts, public speeches, dialogue from films or plays, jokes, advertising text, or published books. Of course, almost any written or recorded materials may be examined as text, from street graffiti to blogs to the naming of towns. These data are usually information that has been compiled for some other reason, whether entertainment or marketing or memoir, which we then code and analyze. The text is the surface meaning, the unexamined *what* of the data. By systematically analyzing the materials in ways that allow us to visualize patterns and processes—looking at word choices and phrases, defining the flow of ideas and images—we seek to reveal the *subtext*, the *why*

and *how* of the data. Content analysis assumes that written and visual communications express the ideas that guide social action. The set of techniques that we apply to this kind of information is called **content analysis**. It's the act of translating text from information, in the general sense, to coded data that can be summarized, compared, and interpreted.

Coding Interview Data

Here's a scenario. You want to know how people feel about their jobs and how their dreams and aspirations have changed over time with their work experience. So you interview 60 people of different ages at different career stages.

One of them tells you a long story about her struggle from almost unpaid copyediting at a small newspaper in the 1950s to her eventual success as a writer at a respected city newspaper in the 1980s, only to see the paper fold in the 1990s. Another subject talks about his basic lack of interest in his office job, but that he finds his emotional needs met through the time he spends with friends and family. A third has a decent temporary job teaching, but would rather get a graduate degree in psychology and start a new career. Altogether you have a lot of words, but do you have *data you can understand in a meaningful way?* Where is the part that can be analyzed, and how do you do that?

Interviews provide subjects' *accounts* of events, experiences, and memories as well as interpretations and justifications of those accounts. Interview data are not simply facts; nor are they lies (usually). They are patterned and mostly meaningful stories about various topics. The interviewees provide the stories. The researcher's job is to extract and explain the underlying meanings, from some given theoretical perspective.

In the first reading in this section, one of us looked at the difficulties faced by emerging organizations working in areas that are viewed with suspicion and hostility by the state and city agencies on which they depend. The article presents a historical argument that syringe exchange programs faced unique difficulties and even organized opposition as they sought legitimacy and routine encounters with public health agencies. Although the health benefits of syringe exchange had been established, and the law had changed in order to allow their operation, the political context in which they worked was almost universally hostile. Thus, program planners and managers at the exchange programs had to develop political strategies to protect and preserve their groups.

The author conducted a series of interviews with organizers at syringe exchange programs in New York City in the late 1990s. The topic of the interviews was the organizational identity of the programs. This included questions about which

agencies they work with, how they maintain their networks, how they define their programs, and what challenges they face. The interview data (foreground) were coded for any and all references to the political environment in which they worked, evidence of either hostility or compromise from that environment, and strategies adopted by the organizers to cope with these conditions. Notice that while the analysis centered on the question of "survival strategies" for organizations that face opposition, the interviews were much broader. Within those interviews, patterns of responses, shared experiences, and particular types of language use emerged. By coding and comparing all of the indicated responses, the researcher is able to define and analyze the underlying conceptual patterns.

As usual, the introduction and literature review establish the background of the study and the context for the analysis. Issues discussed there include the costs and benefits of working with political institutions, and the nature of relationships between social movements and the state. While the primary—foreground—data analysis concerns organizational survival strategies, these strategies are evaluated qualitatively in relation to the background context. Thus, the various strategies—repudiating a movement identity, cultivating invisibility, helping communities, providing a gateway to healthcare, and deflecting attention—all represent an interpretation of the informants' comments coded to indicate the costs and benefits of working with, or against, state institutions. The background, as defined by the researcher, identifies the themes that need to be explored. The data are then coded into categories that address these themes. The primary task of the analysis, then, is to find the patterns among these categories, thereby discovering the relationships among the themes.

Although the data come from the interview subjects, the researcher should not assume that the subjects could answer the research questions we pose in our terms. While we might be interested in whether external pressures have caused an organization to alter its priorities, individuals within the organization may not have the information available to address that question, or even think of the events in those terms. We are able to answer such questions by systematically and consistently defining and measuring the variety of narratives that indicate either external pressures or the lack of external pressures, and to relate that to narratives that reflect organizational missions and priorities. We saw the same process at work with quantitative data collection and analysis: If we want to measure the effect of A on B, we don't ask "what is the effect of A on B?" We measure A, measure B, and compare the patterns of results. It is the researcher's job, not the subject's, to put the pieces together. In fact the subject may understand less about the relationship to be examined than most people.

Just as we can examine words to discern and define patterns of meaning through our coding processes, we can also interpret and code observational data. Data gathered through observation—with or without participation—reflects behaviors and actions without explanations. Observational data let us see patterns in *what* happens. We cannot observe *why* things occur, but by relating the patterns of observed action to the conditions under which they occur, we can draw conclusions about the social processes behind our behaviors.

Consider the observational data presented in *The Pub and the People* (see Section V, Reading 3). The background to that study is broad, and yet detailed, with an emphasis on working-class culture and neighborhood life. Within that, we might wonder about gender relations. English pubs in the 1930s were often segregated by gender, officially or otherwise. With this research question in mind, the researchers could *observe* the interactions among men and women within the informally organized space of the pub. Code categories might include anything that indicated that some men or women were deliberately avoiding mixing by gender, or deliberately seeking to mix. What happens when a woman walks through the men's area (or the other way around)? How are the social boundaries maintained or broken? Are there insults, jokes, or other ways of simply calling attention to the "transgression?" Are certain men or certain women given more leeway to move across the spaces? If so, who are these people? Many indicators of male–female relations (in public) can be observed, coded, and analyzed without requiring interviews or other self-report data.

BOX 7.1 ERVING GOFFMAN (1922–1982)

Erving Goffman was a modern leader of the study of microsociology: personal behavior, small-group interactions, and the symbolic acts through which we "frame" those interactions. Goffman's primary methodological contributions were to ethnographic research, particularly through the participant observation method. He also pioneered a dramaturgical approach to the study of face-to-face communication. In his research, Goffman was a tireless advocate for the analysis of context as a key component of the research process. He viewed public behavior as a kind of performance, and he called our attention the underlying meanings in these performances that we tended to take for granted. Finally, Goffman's work was influential in the development of such conceptual ideas as "institutionalization," "labeling," and most important, "framing" or the strategic depiction of reality. These three conceptual developments dramatically revised the symbolic interactionist perspective and have revolutionized every field of sociology. Goffman was a steward of the "second Chicago School," continuing the Chicago tradition of small, cultural studies. He served as the 73rd president of the American Sociological Association.

TEXT ANALYSIS

We collect interview data to analyze them for social research. A great deal of the text that we examine, however, was written for some other purpose. For example, when we look at the representation of gender roles in advertisements, we are taking materials that were created for one purpose (selling stuff) and using them for another purpose (examining conventions about gender). Television shows may represent popular ideas about torture, or they may seek to influence those ideas. Humor often reveals social taboos by making use of them for comic effect. Occasionally, attempts at humor concerning social taboos provoke powerful backlashes that reveal how deeply held those taboos are.

Song lyrics are often deliberately constructed to convey messages or represent identities. This has certainly been the case for hip-hop, a genre in which the autobiography of the singer is a frequent theme. While social critics have decried the various messages that they perceive in some of the more sensational hip-hop songs (anti-women, pro-crime, etc.), these controversies tend to focus on individual songs. In contrast, "industry watchers blamed the profit motivation of major record labels" (Lena 2006:486) for the most "puerile" song content. We still need to ask what patterns of meanings or ideas occur regularly within the musical form and why.

In our next reading, Jennifer Lena examines the contrasting patterns of hip-hop themes in works produced by the "major" corporate labels versus the ones produced by independent labels. Her rather straightforward argument is that the context in which the music is produced (major corporate or independent settings) significantly affects, or limits, the content of the work. Specifically, she finds that much of the outlaw culture that is so often discussed is favored in works produced by major labels, while the independently produced songs are far more likely to address the corporate influence on what initially had been a personally and socially motivated form of musical expression. The *content* for this analysis are the song lyrics. The major themes that are examined are the messages, claims, and scenarios presented in these lyrics. And the context for this analysis is the business model under which the work was recorded and distributed.

Notice that Lena's content analysis contains both quantitative and qualitative results. The quantitative part is used to establish the styles and patterns of music that are most popular, primarily in terms of sales. These subgenres represent the music that most consumers favor. The qualitative analysis then asks what these songs are about.

What isn't coded? The researcher doesn't ask who is right or wrong, true or false. She doesn't judge whether certain songs "send the right message or not." She does not address the value question of what rappers "ought" to do, or what it means to consumers. Her question concerns the outside forces that encourage or discourage the rise and fall of particular styles of musical expression.

VISUAL ANALYSIS

"Content" does not always mean text. Films, photographs, advertisements, and even architecture communicate through visual means. We need to code images in order to analyze the content of that communication.

Looking at both visual content and text in comic strips, a medium that doesn't rely heavily on words, Ralph LaRossa and colleagues are able to track changing patterns in the popular understanding of fatherhood in the United States over a period of 60 years. The authors do not claim that representations of fathers in comics exactly match what readers were thinking during those times, or that they match what fathers were doing. The question is whether and how the "culture" of fatherhood—defined as "the norms, values, beliefs, and expressive symbols pertaining to fatherhood"—changed over time. No one comic strip can capture all of that, and we could not expect hundreds of comics to agree. The authors, therefore, look at the distribution of images and jokes over time to measure changing patterns in their coded categories, as reflections of changing patterns in gender perceptions.

Gender-based roles of men and women appear to change more rapidly than "traditional" role designations. Men participate in "traditionally female" activities, including parenthood, while women participate in "traditionally masculine" activities such as working to support their families. Yet, these nontraditional activities are sometimes celebrated and encouraged, at other times met with hostility and scorn. Jokes about parental incompetence, for example, were far more likely to make fun of fathers than mothers throughout the 20th century in the United States. But, as this study shows, the nature and pattern of these jokes change in systematic ways. What is revealed by these shifts?

The authors answer this question carefully, noting that the "messages" revealed by their coding and analysis are not "the meaning" of the strips, but rather part of the spectrum of meanings that a reader could find within them. The fact that certain interpretations occur often does not mean that they represent "the truth" or that they are shared by all cartoonists and readers. It does, however, mean that those interpretations are readily available to readers at those times, that the interpretations are not significantly or widely questioned, and that the joke must depend on "mutually understood and shared definitions of a comedic situation that are held by many, if not most, of the inhabitants of that culture." That is, for a joke to work, people have to "get it."

The authors describe a number of methodological choices that they made to avoid potential problems with their analysis. First, they choose their sample of comics from a limited number of popular sources over a particular time period. This allowed them to analyze literally every comic strip in that sample that was on their topic rather than having to decide which cartoons to

include or not from more newspapers. Further, they deliberately chose to look only at comics published on certain days, for reasons they explain in the article. And, since the study question involved changes over time, they hid the dates of publication from the researchers who were coding the data. That is, the coders' decisions about which comic was more or less traditional, more or less supportive or incompetent, were made without knowledge of when the comic came out. If you knew that a certain comic was from the 1950s or the 1970s, you might have certain expectations about it. Your expectations would influence how you interpreted the comic, which would alter the pattern of data. Hiding the publication dates guards against this problem. This is called **blind analysis**.

The researchers' analysis includes both coded categories anticipated by the authors and ones discovered by them during analysis. They also incorporate information about the time periods in the analysis. Thus, they look for evidence that the women's movement had a direct effect on gender role images, or that changes in the official status of Father's Day would alter the pattern of Father's Day cartoons. The authors also took steps to ensure a high **interrater reliability** for their coding decisions. That is, having agreed upon the categories into which the comics would be coded, they had multiple coders independently assign each comic. Wherever different coders made different assignments, the four authors discussed the comic together. Thus, while the process of interpreting the meaning or nature of a comic is a subjective process, a valid and reliable coding scheme can be applied to it with fairly consistent results. In concrete terms, it is unlikely that all four authors would be able to agree that a certain set of comics showed incompetence or nurturing qualities unless the depictions were reasonably consistent with the ways in which people in that culture tend to understand competence or nurturing.

Finally, the visual analysis presented here is able to compare decades and find patterns wherein some themes appear, disappear for a while, and then appear again later. This allows researchers and readers to find similarities among times that were otherwise quite different. It also provides data with which to question simpler narratives about gender roles over time, particularly the conventional idea that each decade relies less on popular prejudices. Instead, as we see here, popular ideas remain in easy circulation for long periods of time, even after their social desirability or accuracy has been called into question.

CONCLUSION

Learning to be a part of our social world includes learning the codes through which so much of our communication takes place. From handshakes to smirks, physical posture to saber rattling, we infuse our words and actions with endless layers of coded meaning. As sociologists, our job is to decode these meanings. We bring the hidden layers of meaning to the surface. We do so through deep "readings" of the multiple meanings of words and acts in conjunction with more mechanical acts of labeling and counting.

Qualitative analysis is neither psychoanalysis nor police work. Layers of meaning are hidden only in the sense that we don't explicitly state one exact factual sense for each utterance. For the most part, we would be unable to do so. But this doesn't mean that we are trying to hide our intentions. On the contrary; we use subtle and sophisticated symbol systems in order to communicate more, not less. But this subtlety and individual variety make it hard to see the broader social patterns of meanings, expectations, values, and the like, that members of a shared culture can recognize and use as easily as we use words. Qualitative analysis both defines and discovers the patterns of shared ideas.

As with anything else in sociology, the recurring patterns are more important than the individual cases. Qualitative analysis does not tell us exactly what a single person had in mind when she said or wrote something. But it does tell us a great deal about what most listeners or readers are likely to take away from the words or images in question. If each cultural group has its own sets of codes, qualitative analysis is our decoder ring.

DISCUSSION QUESTIONS

1. You are asked to analyze a movie, looking especially at who interrupts whom when they are speaking. You expect that the people in power (e.g., bosses, leaders, rich people) are more likely to interrupt others than to be interrupted. What other categories might you code for in your analysis? Consider how roles and social positions are portrayed on the screen. Consider also that movies are art, not reality. How might that influence your interpretations?

2. The old line goes: "Women speak to communicate emotion with other women; men speak to establish hierarchy." Ignoring the fact that such sweeping generalizations about gender are rarely true, how would you go about studying this hypothesis? What methods, categories (codes) of speech or action would you use? Why?

WEB RESOURCES

The following links can provide you with more detailed information on the topics discussed in this section. You may also go to www.sagepub.com/lunestudy where you will find additional resources and hot-links to these sources.

UCLA Center for the Study of Urban Poverty: http://www.sscnet.ucla.edu/issr/csup/index.php
University of Pittsburgh Qualitative Data Analysis: http://www.qdap.pitt.edu
Choosing Qualitative Data Analysis Software: http://www.socresonline.org.uk/3/3/4.html
The Qualitative Report: http://www.nova.edu/ssss/QR/web.html

Weathering the Storm

Nonprofit Organization Survival Strategies in a Hostile Climate (2002)

Howard Lune

The provision of health and social services to unpopular population groups has a long history, much of it defined by moral debates and questions of deservedness. The desirability of various constituencies has an effect on the willingness of governments and communities to take responsibility for their needs, or even to acknowledge an association with them. Prior to the development of the modern welfare state, responsibility for "the needy," was often left to churches, local communities, and families (Dobkin-Hall, 1992). Under present U.S. policy, the federal government has taken responsibility for a variety of social protections and economic safety nets. But, typically, policy makers have distinguished between the "deserving poor" and "the general poor" (Lin, 2000), or between those who are in need "through no fault of their own" and those who can be said to have brought their problems on themselves (Waxman, 1977). It always has been easier to invest public money in the well-being of sympathetic groups rather than those who are too closely identified with social problems or social ills. Not surprisingly, within the United States, there also has been a significant racial component to the moral distinctions (Quadagno, 1994).

This study analyzes strategies for organizational survival among community-based nonprofit organizations (NPOs) operating in an institutional environment hostile to their constituency and antithetical to their missions. I approach this question through an organizational ethnography of syringe exchange programs (SEPs) in New York City. In particular, I ask how SEPs have negotiated a relationship with government agencies that allows them to operate despite conditions of hostility and disenfranchisement. I examine the presentation of forms chosen by the groups in question, their political tactics, their interorganizational relations, and the manner of claims made or not made by representatives of SEPs in the political arena. This work also evaluates the relationship between their institutional dependencies and their strategies, and it examines the limitations inherent in these decisions.

Throughout the past 20 years, HIV prevention has been one of the largest growth areas of need throughout the United States and much of the rest of the world. In contrast, the greatest increases in federal spending during this period have related to the "war on drugs." Under the rhetoric of "zero tolerance," which is central to

SOURCE: From "Weathering the Storm: Nonprofit Organization Survival Strategies in a Hostile Climate" by Lune, H., in *Nonprofit and Voluntary Sector Quarterly, 31*(4): 463–483. Used with permission of Sage Publications.

our anti-drug strategies (Office of National Drug Control Policy, 2000), the majority of HIV prevention efforts for drug users, as well as virtually all forms of harm reduction, have been labeled as "attempts to legalize drugs" (Office of National Drug Control Policy, 1999, p. 52). In this environment, SEPs, which have expanded and had moderate success throughout much of Europe, have been described by government officials as a misguided policy that "sends the wrong message to our children by condoning illegal drug use" (Whitman, 1998). Although increased syringe availability has been endorsed by numerous health agencies, including the surgeon general, the Centers for Disease Control and Prevention, the American Medical Association, the National Institutes of Health, the American Bar Association, and the American Public Health Association, it has received almost no support from any elected official and is routinely derided by prominent legislators.

The prevalence of HIV/AIDS among injecting drug users raises a number of difficult social, political, and public health questions. Within the public health sector, these questions occur at the intersection of many much older problems including disease prevention, poverty, racism, drug use, moral contests, long-term financial burdens, adaptation to crisis, and the inconsistent needs of public health versus law enforcement in policies concerning drug users. Underlying this conflict is the problem of state support for private initiatives whose clients and participants are neither represented nor desired in discussions of public policy. Proposals for controversial interventions such as syringe exchange—in which injecting drug users are given sterile syringes in exchange for used ones in order to reduce the transmission of blood-borne disease—have generated tension between public health advocates and supporters of the war on drugs. Most significant, efforts to implement syringe exchange have forced us to confront our commitment to the welfare of a subpopulation defined principally by their association with a criminal activity.

In recent decades, the prioritization of social welfare spending has become a matter of great political contention. Private organizations that advocate on behalf of disadvantaged and disenfranchised groups define population needs, demonstrate the effectiveness of various interventions, and help to support the growth of mutual aid and empowerment organizations. Many ethnic or cultural minority groups have achieved a place in policy debates only through long-term organized activism targeted against the state (Meyer & Tarrow, 1998). These efforts have successfully redirected some government money, as well as increased the participation of community advocates in policy-planning processes. Among social movements, however, the successful integration of activists into policy processes has been shown to create structural dilemmas for the collective actors involved, as they find themselves compelled to "professionalize" their organizations in order to work with state agencies (Kleidman, 1994). In other cases, elite support may be directed away from the organizations that originally defined the programs and issues toward new groups that distinctly do not share the political perspectives of the initiator movements (Tierney, 1982). More ironically, an increase in popular support and funding opportunities creates pressures on activist organizations to channel their activities into issues with mainstream appeal (Jenkins, 1998). That is, once organized outsiders successfully gain access to political institutions, they often choose to behave more like insiders, shifting their goals from their initial oppositional stances toward claims and forms that are less threatening (Lebon, 1996; Morrill & McKee, 1993). Yet, outsider groups often find it difficult to operate as insiders (Arnold, 1995; Reinelt, 1995).

Institutional theories (old and new) offer a conceptual framework for understanding the complex interactions between institutional centers of power and "outsider" or marginal claimants. At the simplest level, political and social elites have every reason to feel threatened by, and to suppress or co-opt, outsider mobilizations (Selznick, 1949). Because any collective action for the empowerment of marginal groups inherently seeks to redistribute power and influence, those with the most power have the most to lose. Yet, although the direct suppression of challengers may undermine the legitimacy of elite authority, authorities can maintain legitimacy by incorporating selective portions of the outsiders' goals and methods (Jenkins & Eckert, 1986). In certain cases, elites have been shown to increase their support for the least threatening challenges in response to the presence of a far more threatening claim, a process known as the "radical flank effect" (Haines, 1984). In other cases, the successful professionalization of a radical organization can create spaces for newer, more radical groups to grow (Lune & Oberstein, 2001). In such cases, the overall field of work associated with the challengers benefits by the presence of a group that does not compromise.

There are many reasons why challenger mobilizations might prefer to remain outside of institutional political processes. As the radical flank effect suggests, the vanguard of a collective mobilization can serve the interests of the collective community by honing its edge and by refusing to be the part of the field that collaborates. Alternatively, a radical vanguard also could broker its "activist identity" as a form of cultural capital that elites will pay to share. Described as "radical chic," this process refers to the dynamic by which elites will choose to support challenger movements in order to improve their own image, as long as the radicals are perceived to be socially constructive and the tangible threats to elite privilege are minimal (Silver, 1998). Like channeling, however, both the radical flank effect and the radical chic effect presume that (a) social change requires elite support and (b) that real change will only occur within the comfort zone of the elite supporters.

The interorganizational dynamics cannot be the same for communities, and claims, that lie inherently outside of this comfort zone. This raises new questions about the process of institutionalization. What are the costs to an organization or set of organizations that seek compromise with the state when those efforts are rebuffed? How much goal displacement can a community-based mobilization endure in pursuit of institutional acceptance? How can groups that are politically beyond the pale survive when the institutional elites on whom they depend continue to view their very existence as illegitimate?

METHOD

Research for this study is based on interviews, site visits, and both participant and nonparticipant observations at seven of the quasi-legal SEPs in New York City, and with activists from three illegal exchange operations. A total of 15 interviews were conducted, half of which were on-site at the exchanges. Informants included program directors, outreach coordinators, and street-level service providers. Interviews followed a "focused, unstructured" format (Merton, Fiske, & Kendall, 1989), in which informants are encouraged to use their own terms, definitions, and priorities to address a common set of topics. Informants were asked to address their personal and organizational histories, the nature of any opposition that they faced, who their allies were or are, and the nature of their relationships with program participants, neighborhoods, community boards, elected officials, police, the Department of Health, and the general public. Although some of the informants spoke only of their present groups, most had worked with a number of different exchange programs over the years and spoke of their experiences with each. All informants were offered confidentiality. Most chose to speak on the record for much of the time, with certain statements kept off the record or simply not for attribution. Therefore, almost all identifying information has been removed from quotes and descriptions, although all of the participating organizations are named.

Interviews and site visits were conducted at ADAPT, New York Harm Reduction Educators/Bronx-Harlem NEP, CitiWide Harm Reduction Program, Foundation for Research on Sexually Transmitted Disease (FROST'D), Lower East Side Needle Exchange Program, and St. Anne's Corner of Harm Reduction (SACHR). Several additional interviews were conducted with former volunteers of the ACT UP/NY Needle Exchange Program, the National AIDS Brigade, and Moving Equipment. Each of these three organizations had been active in the creation of the underground exchange network in New York City, although none of them operates legal exchanges in New York.

The terms "needle exchange program," or NEP, and "syringe exchange program," or SEP, are used analogously by different sources and are treated as interchangeable in this document.

WHY EXCHANGE SYRINGES

U.S. law targets criminal acts, not criminal types. The former may be legislated against; the latter not. Although the use of controlled substances is a crime, being a person who uses or has used drugs is not. Laws against addiction have been enacted on a few occasions in several states, yet, due precisely to the legal distinction between behavior and identity, such laws have not endured. With the 1962 case of *Robinson v. State of California*,[1] the Supreme Court established that laws against addiction as an identity status violated the Eighth Amendment (Pascal, 1988, p. 120). As with homosexuality under antisodomy laws, the courts have affirmed that one can be prosecuted only for engaging in illegal acts, not

for being the sort of person who would do that or who has done so in the past. Comparable attempts to criminalize homelessness throughout the country have been challenged or overturned for similar reasons (Ades, 1989; Simon, 1982).

In each of these examples, however, the law may still be used to restrict the visibility of the target populations, be they homeless, gay, drug using, or otherwise marginalized. As long as particular behaviors associated with the groups invite legal sanctions, their individual and collective acts are limited. Since the 1970s, anti-drug legislation has targeted virtually every drug-related activity with a specific law. Apart from the laws against the possession, sale, purchase, transportation, and consumption of controlled substances, most states and many cities have additional laws and ordinances restricting the possession of drug paraphernalia such as bongs, pipes, roach clips, syringes, cookers, and other implements that are designed to assist in drug use. In the United States, 49 states and Washington, DC, have enacted drug paraphernalia laws, and many states have additional prescription laws concerning "dual use" items, notably syringes, which can have both legal and illegal purposes. Extending this logic slightly, drug users found carrying used syringes have been charged with drug possession based on the traces of drug measurable in the syringe (Abdul-Quader, Des Jarlais, Chatterjee, Hirky, & Friedman, 1999, p. 285). Such laws may be read as attempts to recriminalize addiction as an identity status. Under paraphernalia laws, it is not necessary to catch drug users in the act of purchasing, carrying, or using illegal drugs. If they are carrying drug paraphernalia, such as syringes, then they are subject to arrest. For drug users with previous convictions, this infraction also is sufficient to revoke an existing parole or probation and could lead to lengthy periods of incarceration.

---

[1]370 U.S. 660, 82 S. Ct. 1417 (1962).

The fear of arrest for syringe possession does not appear to have measurably reduced drug consumption, but it has discouraged injecting drug users from carrying clean needles (Bluthenthal, Kral, Erringer, & Edlin, 1999). Instead, they must either purchase syringes with the drug, which can be done in some shooting galleries but rarely in the streets, or they must reuse others' needles. The motivation to reuse a syringe is rational, and its practical, rather than cultural, significance has been verified by current research on HIV/AIDS prevention. As Koester (1994) summarized, "Syringes are shared because they are scarce, and they are scarce because they are illegal to possess without medical justification" (p. 287). Because syringes are designed to capture, protect, and redistribute blood and blood-borne agents, syringe reuse has been a remarkably efficient means of HIV transmission. HIV may remain viable in a syringe for 4 weeks or more (Abdala, Stephens, Griffeth, & Heimer, 1999).

In response to this situation, drug users and harm reduction advocates have established SEPs, or NEPs, in cities throughout the country since the late 1980s. Injecting drug users can bring their used syringes to the exchange sites and swap them for sterile ones. The used equipment may be tested prior to safe disposal, by which means researchers track HIV prevalence among drug injectors. At most U.S. sites, users also may receive HIV tests if they wish, or receive a referral for medical care or drug treatment, if available. But the primary benefit of SEPs is as an HIV/AIDS prevention measure.

> As needles are removed from circulation (exchanged), the means of circulation time of the needles declines, which is associated with a decline in probability of infection. The provision of sterile needles in exchange for used ones reduces sharing, the number of times contaminated syringes are shared, limiting the number of viral transmission events. (Needle, Coyle, Normand, Lambert, & Cesari, 1998, p. 7)

THE POLITICAL ENVIRONMENT

Throughout the period of SEP formation, particularly the first 10 years, the programs faced considerable political resistance. Congress enacted and repeatedly reinforced bans on federal funding for SEPs or any prevention education that "condones or promotes" syringe exchange. Between 1988 and 1995, Congress voted on nine separate occasions to block funding of SEPs (Donovan, 1996, p. 2). Revisions to the Anti-Drug Abuse Act of 1988, introduced in 1998, specified that SEPs could not be funded until the Secretary of Health and Human Services determined that they effectively reduced the spread of HIV without encouraging further drug use. When the secretary did just that (Shalala, 1998), the law was amended to state that funding would be prohibited regardless of the secretary's evaluation. Legislative and federal policy debates equated harm reduction in general, and syringe exchange in particular, with drug legalization, and dismissed harm reduction policy proposals as "a half-hearted approach that would accept defeat" in the drug war (Office of National Drug Control Policy, 1999, p. 53). Advocates for syringe exchange were routinely branded "soft on drugs."

Government action on HIV/AIDS prevention among drug users has not been entirely one sided, however, and state legislatures have shown more flexibility than the federal level. Furthermore, as the existing programs age, they

---

[2]Expanded Syringe Access Demonstration Project, 10 NYCRR 80.137. The change was initiated by the state Department of Health with active support from the governor, and relatively passive support, but only small opposition, from the state assembly. With the Republican governor taking a visible, and somewhat surprising, stance in support of greater syringe access, organized opposition was limited.

are increasingly able to refute the worst fears of their critics. Some past opponents, including former New York City Mayor David Dinkins, have even come around to endorsing the programs. Following changes in state law enacted in 2001, pharmacies in New York State now have the option to sell syringes without prescriptions.[2] It is too soon to tell what the impact of this development will be, but over-the-counter sales of syringes are unlikely to replace SEPs for most addicts. As a precedent, however, it represents a tangible case in which government has chosen to overturn an anti-drug policy in favor of an HIV-prevention measure. This change may be considered a measure of the success of SEPs, as syringes themselves appear to be less stigmatized. Comparable challenges to other "zero tolerance" policies also have arisen in the latter half of the 1990s. California and Arizona have approved the use of marijuana for medical purposes, for example, choosing a harm reduction approach in favor of the strict criminal justice policy. And a public discourse on the reform of drug laws has gained ground in many states, including New York (Purdy, 2000).

Syringe exchange itself, however, has not become sufficiently institutionalized into the public health domain to grow or expand. Nine quasi-legal SEPs presently operate in New York City, engaging in three different SEP modalities. Each of these modalities is geographically limited. Storefront exchange sites have fixed locations and offices where participants can come for syringe exchange or a variety of other harm reduction services, counseling, education, or social activities. Street corner (or street-side) exchanges operate smaller, mobile units out of vans or trailers. At a scheduled time and location, mobile exchange vehicles park on out-of-the-way streets, and workers set up tables, tents, bins, and so forth to construct temporary service

offices. Mobile street-based outreach exchanges seek out injecting drug users (IDUs) and others in need of services and try to initiate contact with new potential participants. Street outreach programs target "hard-to-reach" populations, including prostitutes, juvenile IDUs, and homeless people with HIV.

New York SEPs operate under a state waiver from syringe prescription laws. The waiver was enacted in 1992 as part of a declaration by the commissioner of the State Department of Public Health finding New York City to be in a state of emergency with respect to HIV/AIDS. Syringe exchange is not legal under the waiver system, but a limited number of supervised programs, and their participants, are protected from prosecution. The first waivers were granted to formerly underground programs, or to the new agencies formed by underground providers to replace the illegal operations.[3]

The prelegal work constituted a form of civil disobedience. Volunteers referred to these activities as "the underground needle exchange movement." Activists distributed syringes as a form of political protest to call attention to the neglect of HIV/AIDS prevention among this population and, eventually, to force a legal challenge to the state's paraphernalia laws (Elovich & Sorge, 1991). Since 1992, most of the formerly underground programs have reorganized and redefined their exchange operations. Organizations that were once managed by recovering addicts are now run by professional managers with no prior experience in drug issues. Instead, they have implemented formal policies to seek input from the target client population. The conditions for above ground work require a degree of professionalism and accountability in accordance with the interests of those outside of the affected communities rather than those within. Such organizational changes

---

[3]Not every underground exchange program that applied for a waiver received one. The differences among the various underground programs and how this affected the selection process is but one of the complex issues surrounding the transition of syringe exchange from illegal to quasi-legal status that has yet to be written about. A proper treatment of the interorganizational relations among the prelegal programs is, unfortunately, beyond the scope of this work.

have been accompanied by operational changes that are more difficult to classify.

SURVIVAL STRATEGIES

In addition to formal changes in organizational structure, the groups operating SEPs have made further accommodations to the change in their legal status. They have altered their goals and tactics, and fundamentally changed the ways in which they present themselves to the outside world. As the priorities of the field have shifted from challenging the law to ensuring survival, the exchange programs have adopted different forms of organization. Although there was a great deal of variability in the informants' views on where syringe exchange was heading, or how best to get there, the interviews demonstrated general agreement as to where the programs had come from and how they presently operate.

The following strategies for organizational survival emerged through interviews and observations at SEPs in New York City. Each of the strategies was evidenced to some degree at each of the study sites. All of the organizational changes described here demonstrate one characteristic in common: They all represent a move from "challenger" practices that sought to undermine state policy and practices toward conciliatory practices that implicitly or explicitly legitimate the interests of political elites, even at the cost of delegitimating their own constituency. These developments represent more than the familiar practices of professionalization. They indicate active pressures to deny or suppress the political component of syringe exchange in pursuit of institutional détente, and not of institutional acceptance.

REPUDIATE MOVEMENT IDENTITY

Now that the underground exchange movement has become an authorized part of the health care delivery system, its relationship to state agencies has fundamentally shifted. The programs do not make demands or issue threats anymore. Several informants have stated in various ways that although SEPs used to be "a kind of movement," now they rarely attempt to form collective strategies or even to develop consensus positions on policies or practices. Organizers and advocates seldom, if ever, sit down together except in meetings called by the city, to which they are all invited but for which they are not setting the agenda. Under the present arrangement, they discuss catchment areas and budgets, but not policy. You "can't talk openly about needle exchange," according to one long-time participant. And they cannot, or do not, act collectively. As the New York Academy of Medicine found, "While many SEPs have developed effective interventions to reach particular subpopulations of IDUs, no mechanism exists for SEPs to share expertise with one another, or to integrate their expertise and services with the many HIV programs unable to develop effective programs for active IDUs" (Finkelstein & Vogel, 1999, p. 6).

More significant, according to informants' descriptions, the SEPs have become isolated and inner directed, worrying more about their own continuity than about their former missions. Sources at programs that have faced difficulties expressed a particular disappointment that they could not look to one another for support. When the media launch attack stories at one site, for example, most of the other programs try not to get involved, and the targeted program itself will not respond aggressively. Even when deliberate abuses (of fact or reportage) are revealed, the programs are loath to make an issue of it. This change has not been described as competition among organizations so much as a shared pragmatism. "Under [Mayor] Guiliani . . . we wouldn't want to make front page news or the whole thing will be shut down."

Instead, the SEPs have turned toward a quieter style of advocacy aimed at reducing the atmosphere of hostility and distrust, and trying to forge lasting, undemanding relations with other agencies in the health and human services. As one program director explained, "My board has always been a board that has insisted upon a very low profile for the organization. We don't make a lot of waves and as result I don't know that we have the kind of adversarial relationship with the political system that other programs may have . . .

You've got to distinguish between political advocacy and the advocacy that is more program related. And I think we do a lot of the latter and we do almost none of the former. I am on the [name withheld] committee of the citywide PPG, and I'm head of the [name withheld] workgroup, and so we push our agenda in that way. And I think that agenda is . . . 'you've got to let these people in, you've got to work with them, and we have the ability to teach you how to do that.' We do advocacy in that way, and I think that's much more powerful than the other way of yelling and screaming and doing whatever you need to do."

Cultivate Invisibility

The principal survival-oriented strategy of the SEPs has been to minimize their visibility. They avoid political entanglements by trying not to be seen and by encouraging communities to forget that they exist. This strategy also allows political elites and state agencies to ignore them. On the streets where the programs operate, organizers had begun to develop this approach long before the waiver. Discussing the early days of the ACT UP/NY and SACHR programs in the Bronx, a former volunteer, now a professional organizer, recalled that "both exchanges had a 'Brigadoon' aspect. . . . A discreetly organized social service entity that appeared weekly in a public landscape."

FROST'D provides harm reduction services to streetwalkers from a mobile site, based in a van. Although they travel to where their target population can be found, they do not do outreach. For although the local communities have grown accustomed to the streetwalkers, organizers fear that syringe exchange might be a problem. Asked about community relations, the program director replied, "I don't think people know we're there."

CitiWide Harm Reduction is unique in that they visit people in their homes, in single-room occupancy hotels. Part of their motivation for this approach is to reach another segment of the target population. Specifically, they are seeking out the most underground subgroup of drug users. But they also are responding to the conditions that keep their participants hidden. CitiWide perceives their mission to be a response to police strategies that makes it dangerous for these clients to visit a street-based program. "Police tend to target people based on how they look." The poor, homeless drug users invite examination and interrogation. Their lives constitute probable cause. They are therefore at greater risk to be caught with paraphernalia and to receive harsh treatment from the criminal justice system. The goal of the CitiWide approach is to allow their participants to remain behind closed doors. CitiWide has designed its operational procedures with the explicit goal of providing services without being seen to provide services.

Program invisibility extends beyond the strategies of individual organizations and encompasses most of the policy processes that enable their operation.

> Every year there's a certain amount of state funding for AIDS which doesn't get spent. Those are called the reappropriation dollars, and that's what syringe exchange programs get their money out of. Because that's not part of the budget that gets signed off on. Therefore, it doesn't have to be debated. . . . So that gives you an idea. None of the elected officials are really willing to touch it. And even the ones who are willing to touch it are really only comfortable doing it in indirect ways.

A variant of this strategy, and a reversal of their earlier goal, has been to keep their issues off of the political agenda. In the early days of the Bronx-Harlem program, there was "no need for elite allies." The message to the Dinkins administration was to "just leave us alone." Program organizers sought help merely to "get Dinkins to not oppose it." When they needed additional funding for ancillary health services at the exchange sites, they "sought personal connections through informal networks."

City officials have been willing to assist the development and expansion of syringe exchange in New York, but not in public. One agency director described his system of working with the mayor's office and the Department of Health.

> They help me package the idea and ultimately, help me get some of the money. . . . There is this discretionary money out there, people who are willing to meet with you in some restaurant in Morningside Heights to talk about where do we need to go.

Several of the above-ground programs replaced sites that had been opened by activists prior to the waiver system. The transition from political activism to health intervention meant a shift in strategy from public activism to private acts. SACHR, for example, replaced an ACTUP/NY demonstration site in the Bronx. ACT UP worked "in a public thoroughfare, hence, appropriation of space. . . .SACHR . . . entered into a community space" that was "already organized." SACHR therefore had to make promises and offer protections to their participants and others who allowed them to work there. In contrast, one of their ACT UP contacts, who was still operating as an activist, did press interviews and sought to bring camera crews into the sites. The authorized program had to oppose the activists in order to maintain the acceptance

of the local community. They had to channel the work away from a public political model toward a private health services one.

HELP COMMUNITIES MANAGE THEIR DRUG PROBLEM

The population affected by syringe exchange is perhaps the most stigmatized one in the country right now. Not only are drugs repeatedly called the number one problem that the nation faces, but drugs and drug users have been blamed for literally all social ills.[4] They are reviled in popular culture and in politics. Public figures have literally asked why we do not support more policies to kill them rather than protecting their lives.[5] SEP organizers rarely try to mobilize support for HIV prevention among the injecting drug users themselves. Instead, they emphasize the potential benefits that the program provides to others in the community.

The first targets of this new strategy of representation were the police. Despite the state waiver, programs can be shut down easily if the police in the community choose to do so. At one Brooklyn site, the precinct commander "took it upon himself to close the site" on any pretext. Because the waiver is limited to syringe distribution, but the programs also provide clean bottle caps (cookers), this location was temporarily shut down for distributing other paraphernalia. In the early years, one program found that the exchange "exposed users to law enforcement. [The police] would sit on the corner and see who came. They knew that after we left they could get them with paraphernalia." In some cases, the police "used to rip up the

---

[4]As of this writing, the war on terrorism has superceded the war on drugs in popular discourse and law enforcement priorities, but the present text reflects "normal" conditions. See, for example, the 1989 National Drug Control Strategy, which blames poverty, violence, unemployment, and "the fact that vast patches of the American urban landscape are rapidly deteriorating" on the advent of crack cocaine, as though these issues had not existed before 1985 (The White House, 1989, p. 3).

[5]Television's Judge Judy famously stated that we should "Give 'em all dirty needles and let 'em die!" (DrugSense, 1999). Former Los Angeles Police Chief Daryl Gates opined that we should take users and shoot them (Kirp & Bayer, 1993, p. 80).

cards" that identified users as legitimate exchange participants. But organizers found that the waiver system also provided an opportunity to educate the police.

Program organizers encourage the police to view them as local resources, not threats. Most of the SEPs conduct formal outreach to local police precincts in which they emphasize their ability to serve police interests without undermining enforcement of drug laws. Paramount among these is the legitimate fear of being stuck by an infected needle while patting down a suspected drug user. Outreach workers emphasize that, if the police are known to respect the needle exchange protections, they can simply ask the users to dump their needles before frisking them. Many of the programs also provide the beat cops with sharps disposal boxes into which the users may empty their syringes without any direct contact by the police at all. In a similar vein, but with less discussion, the programs also provide many of the local police with condoms, which also are distributed by the SEPs.

In their dealings with both police and residents, program organizers often find themselves implicitly endorsing negative imagery about drug users in order to project a positive image for the exchange. They phrase their accomplishments in terms of protecting the community from their clients. A concern frequently expressed by community boards, for example, is that the needle exchange will somehow cause an increase in stray needles, particularly in playgrounds. Notwithstanding the fact that used needles have commodity value only at the needle exchange, residents often fear that the program will introduce additional needles into their communities. In response, some programs have asked community boards to identify the high-risk spaces and existing areas of concern. They can then make a show of sending volunteers out into parks and playground areas collecting and counting syringes. If the areas are found to have improperly disposed sharps, the programs identify those locations to their

participants, many of whom will stop off there on the way to the exchange site in hopes of picking up additional needles. In this way, the exchange site can define itself as a program to protect children from needle sticks, with the implication that closing the site would place children at greater risk.

SEPs have had immense difficulty expanding their operations, and very few new sites have been approved since 1992. This means that they have to seek invitations or support from community elites in order to package a successful application. In Bedford-Stuyvesant, for example, informants indicated that the SEP was able to open only because a local doctor who had influence with the community board personally made the case for the health need. Whereas the illegal exchanges used to take over public space, as a political act and a legal challenge, the legal programs negotiate through intermediaries for access to private spaces.

Programs also require acceptance by the injecting drug users in the target communities. Most programs try to identify intermediaries there as well, to smooth the way. One organization explicitly applied the community outreach strategy to a local drug lord. "I educated him on HIV/AIDS to the point that he was asking what he should do about it, which was supporting needle exchange." A Brooklyn expansion site was opened by an informant who used to cop drugs there during his time as a user. He knew the street users, and he could talk with locals to make sure people wanted the exchange program to come in. "The first thing the people there noticed was 'Oh, a Hispanic.' " This gave the program street credibility there that the earlier activist site had lacked.

Present the SEP as a Gateway to Health Care

The provision of accepted forms of health care, at public expense, to indigent drug users has faced considerable controversy and resistance. HIV/ AIDS prevention has received little or no popular support anywhere, and it has been opposed in many forms by Congress and local legislatures. The prospect of reducing the spread of HIV/AIDS is not enough to counter these trends. Programs have therefore encouraged the state and other observers to view SEPs as the conduit by which IDUs would be linked to a wide variety of services, treatment, and care. In many cases, these expectations have become requirements for funding and quasi-legal status (Kochems et al., 1996).

In discussing their work, and in program brochures, SEPs emphasize their other accomplishments, such as linking street people to health and social service organizations. Even so, informants acknowledge that their referrals network only flows in one direction. Health care agencies and high threshold drug treatment programs do not openly send clients to syringe exchanges. One activist endorsed the goal of linking SEPs to the rest of the health care system, but did not feel that these efforts had borne fruit. "Needle exchange programs are regularly funneling people into drug treatment. Drug treatment programs are not funneling anybody back. When you get kicked off the program they don't tell you go to the syringe exchange." Program volunteers also have expressed concerns that some of the health agencies to which they send participants do not want to deal with a drug-using population.

Within New York City, however, there are many agencies whose goals are to find and help the people in need who are the hardest to reach. In many forums, exchange organizations emphasize their unique frontline position and their ability to bring disenfranchised groups into contact with health care. This presents the SEP as a resource to the rest of the public health care system.

> Twenty-five percent of what we do is needle exchange. Seventy-five percent is everything else. [We're] more of a conduit because we have a

fundamental belief that lots of the folks we deal with have a deficit in terms of ability to navigate the [public health] system.

DEFLECT ATTENTION FROM GOVERNMENT OFFICIALS

Public health officials and politicians who have advocated on behalf of drug users have been branded soft on drugs or soft on crime. In some cases, law enforcement officials have suggested that the advocates be locked up with the addicts. Those elected officials who take a different view rely on exchange organizations to introduce the necessary data to legislative debates at the appropriate time, so that the officials themselves do not have to do it. Program organizers recognize that as a key component of their viability.

> So M. calls us up and says, "Send someone over here to talk to me, and have them bring all the literature and all the evidence." And so I go over there. . . . Here's the public health information and the Academy of Medicine and the this and the that, all the federal stuff. . . . What she said is, "Look, I don't want to get into a controversy about your program," and I said, "I don't want you to be drawn into it, because if our reputation, our ability to survive becomes hinged to the rise or fall of an elected official, that means that when M. is out of office, our program gets shut down." . . . So we saw completely eye to eye.

One informant described his organization's interactions with government health agencies when they were working on their application for the state waiver. "There were people in the CDC [Centers for Disease Control and Prevention] who wouldn't open their mouths. They pushed it clandestinely. They ghost wrote it. They told us how to do it."

Another source explained that they must understand and to some extent take advantage of the tensions that public officials face in negotiating their own survival.

You have to distinguish between public behavior and private behavior. In many ways, whether they like it or not, the political establishment supports programs like this . . . because they recognize the problem but they can't say so publicly. We get a lot of support from the city. We don't get direct support for syringe exchange. We get support for supportive services.

Just because people work for a particular administration does not mean they necessarily share. . . . And there are a lot of people in policy-making positions in this administration who really believe that the [SEPs] are right and good and valuable, they can't say so in many words but they can help you out, they can provide you with funding, with moral support and technical assistance and lots of other things.

SEPs have little direct contact with elected officials, and they eschew direct challenges. Most of the underground workers had little or no experience with formal political processes. As one informant noted, "If you're a minority . . . and you're trying to convince White, male legislators, you're not on your home turf." Even after the change in legal status for the exchange programs, neither workers nor politicians sought direct contact. Negotiations, exchanges of information, and program planning usually take place through intermediaries, such as staff members. This gives the SEPs an insider advocate while maintaining an environment of plausible deniability for elected officials.

Discussion

SEPs depend on the ongoing support of state agents, including the police, the mayor's office, the city council, and local district representatives. Although the programs have been endorsed by city, state, and federal health officials, almost no elected official has been willing to visibly support them while in office. Long-time participants, those who have made the transition from activism to services, see this as a defining condition for the operation of all SEPS.

There is no support from elected officials, or minimal. I can think of some city council members, and some state assembly people, and some state senate people, who've actually been outspoken in their support of the idea of syringe exchange. . . . So I won't say that it's completely hostile. But those guys are definitely operating in a hostile environment.

A crucial aspect of this scenario is that elected officials could face sanctions for appearing soft on drugs if they proposed to assist active drug users, even in a health emergency. The political liability appears to relate to the extent of the disenfranchisement of drug users in the United States. Questions about the logic of syringe exchange as a public health intervention rarely came up during the interviews. Identity politics was ubiquitous.

SEPs have responded to the present political climate by adopting forms of behavior and self-representation that affirms public disdain for drug users, even as they organize on behalf of this population. SEPs thus endorse the conditions that limit their own work, rather than attempt to bring their constituency into the political arena. They serve their present clients, but they do so in a manner that makes it more difficult to reach new populations or new neighborhoods. In particular, SEPs visibly protect the interests of the state officials who invisibly protect theirs.

All of the programs in New York City have adapted their forms and actions to accommodate the hostile environmental conditions, although not all interpret these changes in the same manner. One program director, for example, focused on the long-term viability of syringe exchange as a form of work.

We need people who are going to try to mainstream it. We need to mainstream it, because if we don't mainstream it we're going to marginalize the people we serve. And those marginalized people are powerless, and the more marginalized you are, the more powerless you are.

In this perspective, the population of active drug users whom the SEPs serve will eventually gain acceptance in the public health care system through the efforts of the exchange programs to foster institutional linkages. There is evidence that this may be occurring, but slowly.

In contrast, a field-worker from a different agency suggested that SEPs could not make a significant difference as long as the users themselves were excluded from the health policy process.

> I think that needle exchanges are partly to blame for this. In the process of saying "there's politics," they cop to the game that somehow it's the injectors' lives we're saving, as though injectors' lives were really ours to give or take, and now we're going to choose to save them even though the injectors themselves have so clearly "put themselves on the course of death."

From this point of view, the professionalization of SEPs can only minimally benefit drug users or affect drug policy. Greater change will require a new discourse on drugs and drug use.

SEPs are tolerated, for the moment, but they can be shut down any time the state withdraws its unusual protection.[6] SEPs are effectively excluded from much of public health services and the drug treatment field. Publicly supported health service agencies, including hospitals and drug treatment programs, could potentially be accused of violating the terms of their funding if they were to refer clients to an SEP. The hostile legal environment for SEPs further discourages support from other sources, including foundations, potential collaborative agencies, and banks and insurance companies (Burris, Finucane, Gallagher, & Grace, 1996). As a result, SEPs cannot exist without public support from the institutional forces most clearly antithetical to them.

Despite the institutional incompatibility, it has been possible for syringe exchanges to collaborate with state agencies. SEPs and government agencies share an interest in depoliticizing needle exchange. Many elected officials and most public health officials recognize the role of syringe exchange in limiting HIV transmission, just as program organizers recognize the political liability inherent in supporting them. The experience in New York City suggests that political opposition to SEPs has derived more from the unpopularity of their constituency than from disagreement with their basic social role. The problem has been one of political accountability. Within both city and state government, SEPs have found closeted supporters. As SEP advocates and organizers have moved away from visible challenges in the political domain, government agencies have responded by providing other points of access.

For any existing organization, this arrangement has obvious merit. But the pragmatic, short-term benefits carry a considerable political cost. With a legislative sword of Damocles hanging permanently over their heads, exchange programs do what they can to ensure their survival, which necessarily has entailed a depoliticization of their work. The integration of the former underground movement into the margins of the public health care system has placed significant barriers between the advocates and their communities. What was once the syringe exchange movement in New York City has distanced itself from the population in whose name they act. Having won the right to exist, they have retreated from pursuing virtually any other (political) goal. Thus, SEPs have had to participate in their own marginality and invisibility as a condition for what amounts to a reduction of hostilities with state agencies.

---

[6]Since the time of this research, New York State repealed its syringe prescription laws, clearing the way for over-the-counter sales at pharmacies. Paraphernalia laws remain in effect, but the motivation for threatening SEPs has been greatly diminished.

CONCLUSION

The founders of syringe exchange in this country were social activists engaged in high-risk activism. Not surprisingly, the quasi-legal programs are run on very different principles and practices. What is surprising is how much the groups have changed and how little they may have received in return. Among other goals, movements for social and political change seek to alter the manner in which their issues are perceived and discussed. They engage in public acts, such as rallies or media events, in order to challenge the status quo and possibly to delegitimate the processes by which routine policies have become routine. In many prominent cases, a period of outsider activism is followed by a period of compromise or collaboration in which challengers and state actors make concessions to each other and, thereby, acknowledge the legitimacy of each other's interests. This has long been perceived to create problems for challenger groups that do not wish to legitimate state practices. But it may be as great a problem for challenger groups whose legitimacy, or existence, remains unacknowledged by the state.

To some degree, the gradual acceptance of SEPs in the arena of HIV/AIDS prevention has eased the burden on the less radical elements of the field, improving prospects for an ongoing discourse on prevention. But, as a form of compromise, it has not served the SEPs themselves or their primary constituency as well. The professionalization of syringe exchange has not created the exchange of support that many earlier mobilizations have negotiated. In contrast to the civil rights movement, activism for gay rights, and environmental activism, SEPs have yet to even be co-opted.

This process of political retreat is not uncommon, but neither is it inevitable. It does not follow a natural course of development from community-based organization to political player, along the lines of Michels's (1935/1968) "Iron Law of Oligarchy." For SEPs, the course

was charted in the early 1990s when New York State declined to reexamine its paraphernalia laws and, in effect, obliged private funding agencies to keep a lid on the groups' activities. By repudiating any responsibility for the public health goals of syringe exchange, placing the burden of protecting the continuity of the waiver system on the volunteers and activists, the state compelled the movement, as a movement, to extinguish itself.

The professionalization of syringe exchange led the SEPs to define themselves in mainstream terms while they were still perceived by others as radical, thereby limiting their options on both fronts. The programs could not have remained radical or refused to work with the waiver system. Such a course likely would have brought an end to the entire form of work. But there might have been other options. Could the groups have held out longer, or somehow negotiated a better deal? That is, could they have bargained their radical chic? Would they have done more if they had received more external support? Even within HIV/AIDS work, many groups were loath to involve themselves in needle exchange politics. Perhaps the field of community-based services for drug-using populations would have been better served by making a greater show of support for the SEPs early on. Finally, might the groups have maintained more of a radical flank while professionalizing? One could speculate that the aboveground SEPs could have done more to preserve and propagate, rather than replace, the underground SEPs. The continued operation of SEPs has contributed to the wider acceptance of other innovations in HIV/AIDS prevention and drug policy. Perhaps the SEPs would have more voice in urban politics if there were someone farther out on the edge than themselves.

This study has examined the ways in which nonprofit community-based organizations have attempted to persevere in their underlying mission in a political and organizational climate that is defined by its public insistence that they be stopped. The question is not whether SEPs can operate or even if they achieve their goals. The SEP experience reflects the highly constrained options for self-organization and mutual aid available to stigmatized and unpopular population groups. Although we might admire the innovations of the organizational leaders who have managed to operate under adverse circumstances, we cannot fail to notice that New York City formally provides SEPs without actually making a significant dent in the need for clean syringes or the prospects for controlling the HIV/AIDS epidemic. The groups exist, but they are, in some respects, more of a hidden population than the drug-injecting population that they set out to serve.

REFERENCES

Abdala, N., Stephens, P. C., Griffeth, B. P., & Heimer, R. (1999). Survival of HIV in syringes. *Journal of AIDS and Human Retroviruses, 20*(1), 73-80.

Abdul-Quader, A., Des Jarlais, D., Chatterjee, A., Hirky, E., & Friedman, S. (1999). Interventions for injecting drug users. In L., Gibney, R. J., DiClemente, & S. H. Vermund, (Eds.), *Preventing HIV in developing countries: Biomedical and behavioral approaches.* New York: Plenum.

Ades, P. (1989). The unconstitutionality of "antihomeless" laws: Ordinances prohibiting sleeping in outdoor public areas as a violation of the right to travel. *California Law Review, 77,* 595-627.

Arnold, G. (1995). Dilemmas of feminist coalitions: Collective identity and strategic effectiveness in the battered women's movement. In M. M. Ferree & P. Y. Martin (Eds.), *Feminist organizations. Harvest of the new women's movement.* Philadelphia: Temple University Press.

Bluthenthal, R., Kral, A. H., Erringer, E. A., & Edlin, B. R. (1999). Drug paraphernalia laws and injection-related infectious disease risk among drug injectors. *Journal of Drug Issues, 29*(1), 1-16.

Burris, S., Finucane, D., Gallagher, H., & Grace, J. (1996). The legal strategies used in operating syringe exchange programs in the United States. *American Journal of Public Health, 86*(8), 1161-1166.

Dobkin-Hall, P. (1992). *Inventing the nonprofit sector and other essays on philanthropy, volunteerism and nonprofit organization.* Baltimore: Johns Hopkins University Press.

Donovan, M. C. (1996, August 29-September 1). *The needle exchange: AIDS, drugs and political competition.* Paper presented at the meeting of the American Political Science Association.

Elovich, R., & Sorge, R. (1991). Toward a community-based needle exchange for New York City. *AIDS & Public Policy Journal, 6*(4), 165-172.

Finkelstein R., &Vogel, A. (1999). *Towards a comprehensive plan for syringe exchange in New York City.* New York: New York Academy of Medicine.

Haines, H. H. (1984). Black radicalization and the funding of civil rights: 1957-1970. *Social Problems, 32,* 31-43.

Jenkins, J. C. (1998). Channeling social protest: Foundation patronage of contemporary social movements. In W. Powell & E. Clemens (Eds.), *Private action and the public good.* New Haven, CT: Yale University Press.

Jenkins, J. C., & Eckert, C. M. (1986). Channeling Black insurgency: Elite patronage and professional social movement organizations in the development of the Black movement. *American Sociological Review, 51,* 812-829.

Judge Judy sees death for addicts as justice. (1999, December 8). *DrugSense FOCUS Alert, 139.*

Kirp, D. L., & Bayer, R. (1993). The politics. In J. Stryker & M. D. Smith (Eds.), *Dimensions of AIDS prevention: Needle exchange.* Menlo Park, CA: Henry J. Kaiser Family Foundation.

Kleidman, R. (1994). Volunteer activism and professionalism in social movement organizations. *Social Problems, 41,* 257-276.

Kochems, L. M., Paone, D., Des Jarlais, D. C., Ness, I., Clark, J., & Friedman, S. R. (1996). The transition for underground to legal syringe exchange: The New York City experience. *AIDS Education and Prevention, 8*(6), 471-489.

Koester, S. K. (1994). Copping, running, and paraphernalia laws: Contextual variables and needle risk behavior among injecting drug users in Denver. *Human Organization, 53*(3), 287-295.

Lebon, N. (1996). Professionalization of women's health groups in São Paulo: The troublesome road towards organizational diversity. *Organization, 3*(4), 588-609.

Lin, P.Y.C.E. (2000). Citizenship, military families, and the creation of a new definition of "deserving poor" in Britain, 1793-1815. *Social Politics, 7*(1), 5-46.

Lune, H., & Oberstein, H. (2001). Embedded systems: The case of HIV/AIDS nonprofit organizations in New York City. *Voluntas, 12*(1), 17-33.

Merton, R. K., Fiske, M., & Kendall, P. (1989). *The focused interview. A manual of problems and procedures.* New York: Free Press.

Meyer, D. S., & Tarrow, S. (1998). A movement society: Contentious politics for a new century. In D. Meyer & S. Tarrow (Eds.), *The social movement society: Contentious politics for a new century.* New York: Rowman & Littlefield.

Michels, R. (1968). *Political parties: A sociological study of the oligarchical tendencies of modern democracy* (E. Paul & C. Paul, Trans.). New York: Free Press. (Original work published 1935)

Morrill, C., & McKee, C. (1993). Institutional isomorphism and informal social control: Evidence from a community mediation center. *Social Problems, 40*(4), 445–463.

Needle, R., Coyle, S., Normand, J., Lambert, E., & Cesari, H. (1998). HIV prevention with drug-using populations—Current status and future prospects: Introduction and overview. *Public Health Reports, 113*(Suppl. 1), 4–18.

Office of National Drug Control Policy. (1999). *The national drug control strategy: 1999*. Washington, DC: Author.

Office of National Drug Control Policy. (2000). *The national drug control strategy: 2000*. Washington, DC: Author.

Pascal, C. (1988). Intravenous drug abuse and AIDS transmission: Federal and state laws regulating needle availability. In R. J. Battles & R. W. Pickens (Eds.), *Needle sharing among intravenous drug abusers: National and international perspectives* (Monograph Series 80). Washington, DC: National Institute on Drug Abuse.

Purdy, M. (2000, May 21). For judges, drug laws can mean having to say you're sorry. *The New York Times*, p. A35.

Quadagno, J. S. (1994). *The color of welfare: How racism undermined the war on poverty*. New York: Oxford University Press.

Reinelt, C. (1995). Moving onto the terrain of the state: The battered women's movement and the politics of engagement. In M. M. Ferree & P. Y. Martin (Eds.), *Feminist organizations. Harvest of the new women's movement*. Philadelphia: Temple University Press.

Selznick, P. (1949). *TVA and the grassroots*. Berkeley: University of California Press.

Shalala, D. (1998, April 20). *Research shows needle exchange programs reduce HIV infections without increasing drug use* [Press Release]. Washington, DC: Department of Health and Human Services.

Silver, I. (1998). Buying an activist identity: Reproducing class through social movement philanthropy. *Sociological Perspectives, 41*(2), 303–321.

Simon, H. (1982). Towns without pity: A constitutional and historical analysis of official efforts to drive homeless persons from American cities. *Tulane Law Review, 66*(4), 631-676.

Tierney, K. J. (1982). The battered women's movement and the creation of the wife beating problem. *Social Problems, 29*(3), 207–220.

Waxman, C. I. (1977). *The stigma of poverty*. New York: Pergamon.

The White House. (1989). *National drug control strategy*. Washington, DC: Government Printing Office.

Whitman, C. T. (1998, April 21). *Governor lauds U.S. drug czar's opposition to needle exchange programs* [Press Release]. State of New Jersey: Office of the Governor.

Reading

Social Context and Musical Content of Rap Music

1979–1995 (2006)

Jennifer C. Lena

Over the past three decades, scholars produced important evidence on the role of industry, organizational structure and markets in the creation of cultural goods. However, the consequences of these structures for creative people and the content of the cultural objects they produce are not yet well understood, as noted by Cerulo (1984) and Peterson and Anand (2004). This gap in the literature is striking given the emphasis of lead production of culture scholars on the impact of the context of production on artistic work (Becker 1982, White and White 1965). Yet, there is much evidence for the effect of market concentration and the organization of firms on the production of rap music.

The structure of the contemporary recorded music industry is oligopolistic, controlled by multi-national firms with diversified holdings across multiple media and consumer product markets (Burnett 1995; Burnett and Weber 1989; Dowd 2000, 2004; Frith 1987, 1988). These firms restructured their bureaucratic infrastructure in the past several decades, establishing semi-autonomous divisions that oversee subsidiary labels. Subsidiary labels are typically run by freelance producers, who are *"delegated* the responsibility of producing marketable creations, with little or no interference from the front office beyond the setting of budgetary limits" (Hirsch 1972:644). Recently, Dowd (2004) found one effect of this "de-centralized" production was to attenuate the negative effect of oligopolistic markets on musical diversity.[1] De-centralized production allows subsidiary labels to imitate independent labels' ability to seek out new talent and musical styles; at the extreme, they are able to co-opt the type of musical products independent labels offer (Dannen 1990, Negus 1999).

Scholars do not agree, however, on the source of diversity in music markets. Anderson and Hesbacher (1980) found independent labels often introduce new genres to the marketplace, but these genres have little variability. Independent labels introducing new genres typically record new artists (Dowd 2003, Kennedy 1994, Lopes 1992, Peterson 1997); however, Dowd (2000) found that hits of new performers are not as musically varied and dissimilar as those of established performers. Disagreements over the source of diversity are partly attributable to the lack of a standard

measure: the literature relies both on a variety of proxy measures and direct measures of musical content. Proxy measures of musical diversity include the appearance of new artists (Lopes 1992, Peterson and Berger 1975, Rothenbuhler and Dimmick 1982), the appearance of new firms and artists (Dowd 2004, Lopes 1992, Peterson and Berger 1975), and the number of female (Alexander 1996, Anderson and Hesbacher 1980) and African-American (Dowd and Blyler 2002) performers. Direct measures of musical content include lyrical diversity (Peterson and Berger 1972, 1975), melodic and chordal structure (Dowd 1992), musical dissimilarity (Dowd 2000), and musical material (Alexander 1996).

This research seeks to contribute new measures of diversity, an analysis of lyrical and sub-genre musical content. It offers the first analysis of R&B music charts and population data on charted rap music as well as evidence of the effect of decentralized production by oligopolistic firms on the content of music. There are consequences of social context on art production.

RAP MUSIC

Rap music was the best case for this study for several reasons. First, the link between record label management practices and rap music content has been a focus of highly publicized criticisms of the genre. Sen. Joe Lieberman (D-Conn.) captured national attention with a letter writing and radio campaign aimed at pressuring record companies to cease production of "obscene" rap music (Holland 1996:8). Lieberman was joined by fellow Sen. Sam Dunn (D-Ga.) and C. Delores Tucker (National Political Congress of Black Women). This followed two years of anti-rap record store demonstrations and

---

[1]Using a range of historical and ecological factors hypothesized to effect musical diversity, Dowd (2004) found growing levels of decentralized production reduced the negative effect of concentration on carriers of diversity, and at the most expansive levels of decentralization, concentration no longer had any impact on these carriers (2004:1444). In fact, Dowd found distinct effects on two forms of "producer" diversity: the number of new performers was more sensitive to contextual factors than the number of new firms.

Congressional Hearings on the issue. There is evidence that record labels encouraged rap artists to produce prurient content. For example, during this period, Carmen Ashhust-Watson described the development strategy of rap label Def Jam: "Right now gangsta rappers are the big thing. If [a hypothetical rap group] look like the kind of group that has the capacity to do that, then [our label] might suggest they do some gangsta-style songs" (quoted in Rose 1994b:124). The link between (objectionable) rap content and record labels is thus of interest to policy makers and the public. Second, rap music charted earliest on the *Billboard Magazine* weekly R&B charts, a data source scholars have ignored. Drawing upon these charts provides the most complete temporal snapshot of charting rap songs and includes more sales heterogeneity than other studies of music markets, with the notable exception of Dowd (2004).[2]

DATA AND METHODOLOGY

The primary data are all rap singles that appeared in the weekly *Top 100 R&B Billboard Magazine* charts from Jan. 1, 1979 through Dec. 31, 1995.[3] The compilers of the *Billboard* charts have based their rankings on a weekly sampling of wholesale record sales, jukebox plays and airplay on radio stations since Aug. 4, 1958. Although the formula coordinating these three sources of data has changed over time (Hesbacher 1974), experts agree that the *Billboard* charts are the fairest and least subjective of the published music charts (Anderson et al. 1980, Denisoff 1986, Dowd 2004, Lopes 1992, Peterson and Berger 1975).

Four criteria were used to determine if R&B singles were included in the population of rap songs: chart designation, rap interludes, shelving designation and expert opinion. First, a song was included if it was designated "rap" in the official compilation of these weekly charts (Whitburn 1996). R&B songs with rap interludes were designated thusly: "featured performer MC X (rap)," indicating a rap within the song, and this was sufficient for inclusion in the population. If the text indicated neither the rap genre nor the presence of any interlude, the shelving designation on the back cover of the album/CD was considered; if either "rap" or "hip-hop" were listed among the first two genres, all the songs that charted from that album were included in our population.[4] Finally, several rap music experts, including major retailers of rap music and radio professionals, were asked to determine the genre of ambiguous songs. In total, 1,221 songs met at least one of these criteria for inclusion.

The record label of each rap single was recoded to identify it with the appropriate parent corporation. Following Peterson and Berger (1975), Lopes (1992), and Dowd (2004), these corporations were determined by issues of the *Annual Billboard International Buyers Guide* and on information from the Securities and Exchange Commission (in particular, 10-K Forms and annual reports to stockholders). Corporations typically under-report limited partnerships with recording companies, but errors were reduced by supplementing these sources with *Standard and Poor's Daily News* reports and trade press articles.

Rap music content was classified into mutually exclusive, exhaustive and independent categories that reflect producers' and consumers' axes of differentiation. Sociologists of culture

---

[2]Lopes (1992) remains the only author to have investigated rap music diversity in light of market and industry structure; however, he relied on year-end charts of the top 100 singles and albums.

[3]The charts used in this study were variously entitled "Hot Soul Singles" (1979–1982), "Hot Black Singles" (1982–1990), and "Hot R&B Singles" (1990–1995).

[4]"Hip-hop" is a more expansive term than "rap," including particular styles of language, music, dress, dance, and occupation of physical space; however, "rap" is the preferred term here because the focus is on the music.

have provided evidence of the differentiation of artistic tastes that constitute consumers as fan communities (Bourdieu 1984, 1993, 1995; DiMaggio 1991; Frith 1996; Mark 1998; White 1993; White and White 1965). Audiences sense— literally *hear* (or see, etc.)—genres and sub-genres in music and by audibly mapping the system and choosing their preferences they contribute to these communities. The link between sub-genres of rap music and audience groups is established in the work of Schusterman (1991), Gilroy (1993a, b), Rose (1994a), Brennan (1994), and Walser (1995). Krims (2000:3) argues, "the degree to which a rap (or more generally, hip-hop) fan will defend the authenticity, originality, and sophistication of her/his favorite rap style/genre/artist/album/song is virtually unparalleled."

Little musicological analysis has been done to obtain the dimensions of comparison used by rap audiences with the exception of Krims (2000), and it is from this work that sub-genre classifications were taken. Krims (2000) performed a content analysis of articles and advertisements in popular magazines, interviews with artists, conversations with fans and the music itself to generate the musical and lyrical components that distinguish rap sub-genres. His categories reflect the "remarkable consistency in how the field of. . . rap music is divided and that characteristics are attributed to each [sub-genre]" (Krims 2000:47). These distinctions reflect criteria used by producers and consumers to organize the field of production into sets of contrasts between songs, artists and albums. From these distinctions, a taxonomy based on four criteria was developed. When applied to a song, this sorted it into a sub-genre group with a unique admixture of attributes:

1. *Flow* is "the verbal wordplay of rap"—the rhythmic pattern and meter used by the rapper in delivering spokenword texts. There are three kinds of flow: a *sung flow* is marked by rhythmic repetition, on-beat accents and regular pauses, and gives the effect of a sing-along. A *percussion saturated flow* employs a sharply attached or crisp delivery and offbeat attacks to push the boundaries of meter, spilling the text past the cæsura of the metric line. A *speech saturated flow* resembles spoken language, but with a great number of rhyming syllables. Rappers often begin a new four-measure unit with the end of the previous measure or rhyme complex, and commonly omit a metric pulse.

2. *Musical Style* distinguishes the function performed by the "background" music. If instrumentation is background or rhythm for the primary voice or voices then that rap has a *rhythmic musical style*. When pre-recorded music ("samples") is foregrounded in the composition (even if the sound or tempo is distorted), this is a *memory musical style*. When instrumentation or samples function as the "speaking voice," this is an *interlocutor musical style*. This technique is most recognizable when *scratching*, the practice of using a body part or object to slide a record back-and-forth under a needle to create a percussive distortion of the music.

3. *Rhythmic Style* is characterized by the regularity of rhythm. One crucial role for rhythm in rap songs is to make possible the audibility of layering, or the multiplication of musical tracks within a recording through the assemblage of disparate musical sources, creating polyrhythmic (and polytimbral) textures (Krims 2000, Rose 1994a).[5] Rap songs are distinguished based on whether they have a *unitary rhythm style* (one dominant beat), or use *multiple* rhythms. For example, a song with a *multiple rhythm style* will permit the listener to distinguish a piano from a guitar from a drum.

4. *Semantic Content* distinguishes songs based on lyrical content. There are more than 10 tropes found in rap music between 1979 and 1995,

---

[5]There is a close relationship between timbre and rhythm in rap music: timbre is the quality of sound that allows a listener to distinguish sounds that have the same pitch and loudness (Krims 2000). It is determined by the harmonic content of a sound and its dynamic qualities (like vibrato or attack).

including sex, love, violence, gender roles, politics, race, partying, money, comedy/parody and boasting. These categories are not mutually exclusive and exhaustive.

The complete audio recording or majority segments of each of the singles in the population and lyrical content were secured from several archives.[6] It is possible that inaccessible sonic segments of some singles may have caused a partial coding to result, and thus an erroneous allocation of those singles to sub-genre groups. It is possible that inaccuracies in the text of lyrics could have caused errors in the lyrical coding. In addition, the coding of lyrics was complicated by the use of slang, metaphor and irony. However, errors of this kind are likely to be random, and will affect only the magnitude of effect, not its presence or absence.

Each single was allocated to a sub-genre group using a "best fit" method, according each single one and only one category for three of the four coding criteria (except *semantic content*). In order to establish the reliability of the coding procedure, 25 percent of the data was recoded a second time after an interval of nearly three years. The simplest estimate of stability is the percent of codes on which the two waves agree; published articles typically have a minimum of 90 percent coding reliability, although scores in the high 80th percentile are not uncommon (Wimmer and Dominick 1997). The reliability score of this coding was 88 percent, indicating adequate reliability. After songs were sorted into sub-genres, sub-genre names were assigned that matched the content and style of the songs and are commonly used to refer to those songs by fans. Thirteen sub-genre groups were identified: booty rap, crossover rap, don rap, dirty south rap, east coast gangsta rap, g funk, jazz rap, new jack swing, parody rap, pimp rap, race rap, rock rap and west coast gangsta rap (see Table 1).

RESULTS

Sub-Genre Development

There were several notable characteristics of sub-genre development. Almost half of the charting singles were crossover raps, including the first rap single to chart, "Rapper's Delight" (Sugarhill Records 1979) (see Table 2). This is unsurprising given that crossover rap's musicological attributes (fast-paced with intelligible lyrics and thin instrumentation) resemble popular music of the period. In contrast, *dirty south* rap, a genre notable for its lyrical focus on sex, partying and a twangy "southern" enunciation, had the fewest charting songs; this is unsurprising given its late development and the right-censoring of the data (Miller 2004). The other 11 charting rap sub-genres achieved parity in terms of chart success, relative to these two sub-genres.

The second notable characteristic of rap sub-genre development between 1979 and 1995 is the evolution of stylistic characteristics out of older sub-genres and into new ones. For example, in 1982 *parody* rappers expanded the musical and rhythmic styles of crossover rappers to include *interlocutor* and *multiple rhythmic styles*, but narrowed the lyrical focus to include only parodies of other rap songs, or song-length "toasts."[7] This stylistic transition was smooth compared to the break between the first *pimp* rap in 1983 and its peer genres: *new jack swing, west* and *east coast gangsta*, and *booty* rap. While *pimp* raps resemble *crossover* raps in the use of a *sung* flow, *unitary* rhythmic style and *rhythmic* background music, the lyrical focus on sex, money, boasting and violence demarcated it from the rest of 1983's charted raps. The single remained sonically and lyrically distinct until 1988 when six *pimp* rap songs charted and were joined by singles in other, new rap sub-genres

---

[6]http://www.ohhla.com. http://www.lyrics.com.

[7]Toasts, or long, profane vernacular narrative pieces performed orally, and their connection to rap lyrics is discussed by Kelley (1997) and Rose (1994a).

TABLE 1   Content and Count of Rap Sub-Genres, 1979–1995

Sub-Genres	Flow	Background	Rhythmic Style	Semantic Content	#
Crossover	Sung	Rhythm	Unitary	Partying	549
Parody	Sung	Rhythm, interlocutor	Unitary, multiple	Sex, humor, parody	86
Rock	Sung	Rhythm, memory, interlocutor	Unitary	Romance, sex, partying, humor, parody	37
Booty	Sung	Rhythm, memory	Unitary	Sex, humor, partying, boasting	52
Pimp	Sung	Rhythm	Unitary	Sex, money, boasting, violence	90
Don	Speech effusive	Rhythm, memory	Unitary, multiple	Sex, violence, money	27
Jazz	Speech effusive, sung	Memory	Unitary	Romance, parody, race, gender roles, politics	57
New Jack Swing	Sung	Rhythm	Unitary	Romance, boasting, partying, money	43
Race	Sung, percussion effusive, speech effusive	Rhythm, memory, interlocutor	Unitary, multiple	Race, gender roles, politics	66
G Funk	Sung	Rhythm, interlocutor	Multiple	Sex, parody, boasting, money	52
Dirty South	Sung, speech effusive	Rhythm, memory	Unitary	Sex, boasting, partying, violence	19
E. Coast Gangsta	Speech effusive	Memory, interlocutor	Multiple	Violence, boasting, race	83
W. Coast Gangsta	Sung, percussion effusive	Memory, rhythm	Unitary	Politics, race, violence, boasting	79
TOTAL:					1221

TABLE 2   Count of Rap Sub-Genres by Year, 1979–1995

	Year																	
Subgenre	79	80	81	82	83	84	85	86	87	88	89	90	91	92	93	94	95	Total
Crossover	1	4	8	13	12	29	45	28	22	33	37	42	57	60	46	55	57	549
Rock			2		1	5	5	8	4	4	1	3	2		2			37
Parody				1	1	3	5	8	5	9	9	9	8	8	5	4	11	86
Jazz											4	1	4	11	12	18	7	57
Race			1	3	1	5		2	3	4	6	3	9	10	11	4	4	66
Pimp					1			1	1	6	16	9	11	9	11	3	3	71
New Jack								2		5	7	4	7	8	5	5		43
W. Coast								2	1	4	6	4	3	9	17	19	14	79
E. Coast									1	6	7	9	8	8	11	10	23	83
Booty										4	4	3	7	5	16	9	4	52
G Funk											1	1	4	4	8	12	22	52
Don													1		2	10	14	27
D. South													1	1	4	7	6	19
Total	1	4	11	17	16	42	55	51	37	75	98	88	122	133	150	156	165	1221

that contained similarly graphic depictions of sex and violence.

CORPORATIONS AND PUERILE CONTENT

Did major record labels produce the majority of puerile rap? The perceived abundance of this lyrical content prompted anti-rap crusaders like Robert H. Bork to describe the genre as a "knuckle-dragging sub-pidgin of grunts and snarls, capable of fully expressing only the more pointless forms of violence and the most brutal forms of sex" (1996:125). Industry watchers blamed the profit motivation of major record labels; they concluded that as long as there were customers willing and able to buy, "record labels will continue to put ethics and morality aside to release [violent or sexist rap]" (McAdams and Russell 1991: R-22). The shock value of this music contributed to its success on the charts (Perkins 1996): *Billboard Magazine* editors argued that corporations invested in puerile rap "because [it] was sleazier as a lure, easier as an enterprise, and more speedily remunerative at the end of the day" (Anonymous 1996:4).

For the purposes of evaluating this contention, songs were recoded in eight sub-genres (*pimp, new jack swing, west* and *east coast gangsta* rap, *booty, g funk, don* and *dirty south*) as "hardcore" rap because their lyrics contained graphic descriptions of sex or violence. The strength of similarity between these sub-genres rests in their distinctiveness in the field of rap music production —in comparison to other charting rap sub-genres. Scholars have noted that across sub-genre styles, hardcore rap lyrics feature a "hustler" as a protagonist (Krims 2000, Rose 1994a). The hustler dominates or victimizes others using force and seduction; hustlers are either "baaadmen" who dominate through force and intimidation or pimps (macks or players). The pimp and the baaadman are anti-heroes—representations of men who can control others physically or lyrically. As anti-heroes, pimps and baaadmen personify accomplishment against the odds; they live in a world of reverse power where the oppressed are powerful (Gates 1988, Kelley 1996, Roberts 1989, Smitherman 1997, Toop 1991).[8] The protagonists of hardcore rap have one foot in the world of extreme bourgeois consumption and success and the other in the ghetto.

Among singles charting in the late 1980s, there is a striking profusion of sub-genres utilizing very different styles of *flow*, background music and rhythm, but all featuring hustler protagonists. Sub-genres differed in how they deployed the hustler narrative. *Booty* rappers like Miami group 2 Live Crew epitomized sexual anti-conformity (in songs like "Dick Almighty," "Me So Horny," and "The Fuck Shop" (as Nasty as They Wanna Be, Little Joe Records 1989), while *pimp* rappers foregrounded money and placed sex as a correlate (Sean "P. Diddy" Combs' work is an example,

particularly "It's All About the Benjamin's" (No Way Out, Bad Boy/Arista Records 1997). In contrast, *gangsta* rappers emphasized the violent antisocial behavior of the baaadmen. For example, on the inner sleeve of their album *Straight Outta Compton* (Priority Records 1988), gangsta rap group N.W.A. (Niggaz Wit Attitude) thanked:

> All the gangsters, dope dealers, criminals, thieves, vandals, villains, thugs, hoodlums, killers, hustlers, baseheads, hypes, winos, bums, arsonists, police, maniacs and bad ass kids for listening to our shit...

Finally, *don* rappers (like Master P and Junior M.A.F.I.A.) combined *gangsta* rap's violence with the emphasis on wealth, individuality and the sexual dominance of the pimp persona.

Table 3 reveals that starting in 1988 the largest record corporations charted substantially more "hardcore" rap songs than independent labels. In the eight years between 1988 and 1995, majors charted up to five and a half times as many hardcore rap singles as all their independent competitors combined. Major record labels produced the majority of puerile rap, consistent with the hypothesized trend.

Authenticity and Identity

While coding the data on lyrics, strong similarities across sub-genres during the period before 1988 were readily apparent. Charting artists in *crossover, parody* and *rock* rap shared a lyrical emphasis on partying, romance, humor and parody, and upon closer inspection appeared to use similar slang and regional argot as well as references to specific personalities, places, events and concerns. Songs that described romantic entanglements identified specific community members, as in UTFO's "Roxanne, Roxanne" (*U.T.F.O.*, Select

---

[8]Kelley (1996:130) suggests that rappers parallel white-collar crime with street crime, thus "'reversing' dominant discourses legitimating entrepreneurship, hostile takeovers and a global corporate culture more concerned with profits than committed to a national community... gangsta rappers hold up the illicit economy as a mirror image of American capitalism."

TABLE 3 "Hardcore" Rap Singles by Label Type, 1979–1995

	79	80	81	82	83	84	85	86	87	88	89	90	91	92	93	94	95	Total
Independents	0	1	0	3	1	2	0	6	6	10	10	5	10	8	27	23	14	126
Majors	0	0	0	0	1	3	0	1	0	20	38	28	40	45	59	57	74	366
Total	0	1	0	3	2	5	0	7	6	30	48	33	50	53	86	80	88	492

Records 1985). Lyrical competition, or battling, was organized largely around neighborhood boundaries as in the contest between Queensbridge and The Bronx captured in MC Shan's "The Bridge" (*Down by Law*, Cold Chillin' Records 1987) and Boogie Down Productions' answer "The Bridge Is Over" (*Criminal Minded*, B-Boy Records 1987). Cautionary tales like Dr. Jeckyll and Mr. Hyde's "Fast Life" (Profile Records 1981) or Grandmaster Flash's "The Message" (*The Message*, Sugarhill Records 1982) were located in particular surroundings and evoked the physical and social deprivation faced by many rappers and their families. These rap lyrics linked "representin' the ghetto" with "keepin' it real." Sincerity and a ghetto identity were deeply associated in early rap lyrics, a facet of "authenticity work" (Peterson 2005). The early focus of rap lyrics on local people, places and things could reasonably be a function of familiarity alone. These artists used for inspiration the source material in their environments.

Rappers were particularly likely to respond to the impact of the increasing commercialization of rap on their local environment. Rappers often forswore the corrupt values of commercial enterprise and instead promoted an ethos akin to Bourdieu's conception of "art for art's sake" (1989). Rapper JDL (Cold Crush Brothers) captures the sentiment of many old school rap musicians:

See, we came from the origin of hip-hop, when it wasn't a money thing. It wasn't a political structure that the record company builds around hip-hop. It wasn't about getting paid and all that. It was about something you loved. (Fernando 1994:14)

In the distinction of "money" and "love," JDL contrasts rappers who work in a "political structure" that is run by the "record company," to "original" legitimate rappers. Early rappers repeatedly echoed the positive value of marginal commercial status. Remarkably, even Rick Rubin, producer of several of the earliest gold and platinum rap albums, lamented the commercialization of rap:

At the time that I started it was still kind of a pure thing… [people] were doing it out of love for it. And I think that changed to people thinking they could get something from it. And when that happened the art kind of went away, and it became commerce, and people trying to put records together to sell. And that's what really ruined it for me. (Rubin quoted in Fernando 1994:169)

Beyond its ubiquity, what is striking about this anti-commercial ethos is the productive context in which it emerged. The rap industry had entered a period of consolidation, and rap artists were aware of the oligopolization efforts of corporations as early as 1983 when Sugar Hill Records, the earliest and most successful rap label, established a contract making it a subsidiary of CBS Records (Lena 2003). Early rap artists noted a rise in the number of major label contracts and chart spots allocated to rap groups (Fricke and Ahearn 2002). A number of high visibility contract disputes during this period still fuel morality tales that warn new rap artists of the pitfalls of doing business with the "majors" (e.g., Fricke and Ahearn 2002:212–15, 271, 324).

Rappers developed particular tropes of artistic legitimacy to cope with the threat of corporate incursion into the market reflected by the "hustler" character. The large-scale shift toward hardcore rap lyrics after 1988 may have been promoted by ex-independent rap artists who sought to reconcile their earlier espousal of anti-commerciality with their new status as "corporate" artists. They felt pressure to craft an identity suitable (and saleable) in the mainstream recording industry while "keepin' it real," remaining congruent with an older value system. The hustler is still an outsider, but one with a comfortable relationship to commercial culture and material success. Despite the surface-level tension that exaggerated violence in hardcore rap provokes between reality and art, it still manages to represent "a religion and ideology of authenticity" (Perkins 1996:20). To wit, hardcore identity is deeply rooted in "being real" (especially found in slogans of "real niggaz," "niggaz for life" and "bein' and stayin' real"; see Perkins 1996: 19–20). The shift toward hardcore rap may reflect a re-alignment of rap identity, one that reconciles "old school" authenticity with "new school" profits.[9]

CONCLUSION

These results suggest an unanalyzed dimension of research on market concentration and musical diversity: artists react to this environment and this affects musical content. In the early period of rap production, lyrics emphasized features of the local environment, and producers emphasized anti-corporate values as an extension of their vision of authentic artistic production. In contrast, the major-label dominated market for rap music featured lyrics that effectively blended "street" credibility and commercial success in the hustler protagonist. These results suggest artists' perceptions of the R&B market effect artistic content.

This research has three goals: (1) to contribute new lyrical and sub-genre measures of musical diversity, (2) to offer a novel analysis of

R&B charts and rap music, and (3) to offer evidence of the contemporary music market's effect on rap content. Production and artistic content are clearly linked. While the diversity of rap sub-genres over 16 years of production is undeniable, an analysis of rap lyrics suggests strong similarities across sub-genre styles. Taken singly, either level of analysis would contribute only a partial understanding of the relationship between market concentration and musical content. Using past proxy measures (e.g., the appearance of new songs, artists and firms), and some direct measures of musical content (e.g., background music, flow and rhythm) would lead one to conclude that diversity is thriving in post-1988 rap music. However, this analysis moves beyond such a partial understanding by illustrating critical and strong similarities across styles and artists.

Future research necessitates case studies of artistic production. Only by turning to the reflections of artists and experts was the nature of the link between social context and musical content in rap made clear. These results illustrate the critical need for studies that join specific social contexts to the production of art works. Following Cerulo (1984:886), I exhort sociologists to engage in this research because "if a composer is a product of a particular environment, and hence, subject to its influences, it is reasonable to expect that a specific social context will provide insight into the processes of musical construction."

REFERENCES

Alexander, Peter. 1996. "Entropy and Popular Culture: Product Diversity in the Popular Music Recording Industry." *American Sociological Review* 61(1):171-74.

Anderson, Bruce W., and Peter Hesbacher. 1974. "Popular American Music: Changes in the Consumption of Sound Recordings: 1940-1955." Unpublished manuscript. University of Pennsylvania Press.

Anderson, Bruce W., Peter Hesbacher, K. Peter Etzkorn, and R. George Denisoff. 1980. "Hit Record Trends, 1940-1977." *Journal of Communication* 30:31.

---

[9]Kelley (1996) offers an alternative interpretation, arguing that these are masculinist narratives that use metaphorical and playful descriptions of violence, and also that they are "street ethnographies," functioning as an alternative vision of American life. This sentiment is echoed in other work, notably that of Tricia Rose (1994a).

Anonymous. 1996. "Thug Life: Where Do the Children Play?" *Billboard* September 28:4.

Becker, Howard S. 1982. *Art Worlds*. University of California Press.

Bork, Robert H. 1996. *Slouching towards Gomorrah: Modern Liberalism and American Decline*. Regan Books, Harper Collins.

Bourdieu, Pierre. 1984. *Distinction: A Social Critique of the Judgment of Taste*. Richard Nice, translator. Routledge and Kegan Paul.

_____ . 1989. "Flaubert's Point of View." Pp. 221-29. *Literature and Social Practice*. Priscilla Parkhurst Ferguson, translator. Philippe Desan, Priscilla Parkhurst Ferguson and Wendy Griswold, editors. University of Chicago Press.

_____ . 1993. *The Field of Cultural Production*. Columbia University Press.

_____ . 1995. *The Rules of Art: Genesis and Structure of the Literary Field*. Susan Emanuel, translator. Stanford University Press.

Brennan, Timothy. 1994. "Off the Gangsta Rip: A Rap Appreciation, or Forgetting about Los Angeles." *Critical Inquiry* 20(4):663-93.

Burnett, Robert, and Robert Phillip Weber. 1989. "Concentration and Diversity in the Popular Music Industry 1948–1986." Paper presented at the annual meeting of the American Sociological Association in San Francisco, CA. August.

Burnett, Robert. 1995. *The Global Jukebox: The International Music Industry*. Routledge.

Cerulo, Karen A. 1984. "Social Disruption and Its Effects on Music: An Empirical Analysis." *Social Forces*. 62(4):885-904.

Dannen, Frederic. 1990. *Hit Men: Powerbrokers and Fast Money Inside the Music Business*. Random House.

Denisoff, R. Serge. 1986. *Tarnished Gold: The Record Industry Revisited*. Transaction.

DiMaggio, Paul. 1991. "Cultural Entrepreneurship in Nineteenth-Century Boston: The Creation of an Organizational Base for High Culture in America." Pp. 374-97. *Rethinking Popular Culture: Contemporary Perspectives in Cultural Studies*. Chandra Mukerji and Mchael Schudson, editors. University of California Press.

Dowd, Timothy, and Maureen Blyler. 2002. "Charting Race." *Poetics* 30:87-110.

Dowd, Timothy. 1992. "The Musical Structure and Social Context of Number One Songs, 1955 to 1988: An Exploratory Analysis." Pp. 130-57. *Vocabularies of Public Life: Empirical Essays in Symbolic Structure*. Robert Wuthnow, editor. Routledge.

_____ . 2000. "Musical Diversity and the U.S. Mainstream Recording Market, 1955 to 1990." *Rassegna di Italiana di Sociologia* 41:223-63.

_____ . 2003. "Structural Power and the Construction of Markets: The Case of Rhythm and Blues." *Comparative Social Research* 21:147-201.

_____ . 2004. "Concentrations and Diversity Revisited: Production Logics and the U.S. Mainstream Recording Market, 1940-1990." *Social Forces*. 82:1411-55.

Fernando, S.H. Jr. 1994. *The New Beats: Exploring the Music, Culture, and Attitudes of Hip-Hop*. Anchor/Doubleday.

Fricke, Jim, and Charlie Ahearn. 2002. *Yes Yes Y'all: Oral History of Hip-Hop's First Decade*. Da Capo/Perseus.

Frith, Simon. 1987. "Towards an Aesthetic of Popular Music." Pp. 133-49. *Music and Society: the Politics of Composition, Performance and Reception*. Richard Leppert and Susan McClary, editors. Cambridge University Press.

_____ . 1988. "Video Pop: Picking Up the Pieces." *Facing the Music: Essays on Pop, Rock and Culture*. Pp. 88-130. Simon Frith, editor. Pantheon.

_____ . 1996. *Performing Rites: On the Value of Popular Music*. Oxford University Press.

Gates, Henry Louis. 1988. *The Signifying Monkey: A Theory of Afro-American Literary Criticism*. Oxford University Press.

Gilroy, Paul. 1993. *The Black Atlantic: Modernity and Double Consciousness*. Verso.

Hesbacher, Peter. 1974. "Sound Exposure in Radio: The Misleading Nature of the Playlist." *Popular Music and Society* 3:189.

Hirsch, Paul M. 1972. "Processing Fads and Fashions: An Organization-Set Analysis of Cultural Industry Systems." *American Journal of Sociology* 77(4): 639-59.

Holland, Bill. 1996. "Anti-RAP Campaign to Be Directed at 5 Major Record Labels." *Billboard* 108(23):11.

Kelley, Robin D.G. 1996. "Kickin' Reality, Kickin' Ballistics: "Gangsta Rap" and Postindustrial Los Angeles." Pp. 117-58. *Droppin' Science: Critical Essays on Rap Music and Hip Hop Culture*. William Eric Perkins, editor. Temple University Press.

_____ . 1997. *Yo' Mama's Dysfunkional!: Fighting the Culture Wars in Urban America*. Beacon.

Kennedy, Rick. 1994. *Jelly Roll, Bix, and Hoagy*. Indiana University Press.

Krims, Adam. 2000. *Rap Music and the Poetics of Identity*. Cambridge University Press.

Lena, Jennifer C. 2003. *From 'Flash' to 'Cash': Producing Rap Authenticity, 1979-1995*. Doctoral dissertation, Department of Sociology, Columbia University.

Light, Alan. 1992. "Ice-T." *Rolling Stone*. P. 32. Aug. 20.

Lopes, Paul D. 1992. "Innovation and Diversity in the Popular Music Industry, 1969 to 1990." *American Sociological Review* 57:56.

Mark, Noah. 1998. "Birds of a Feather Sing Together." *Social Forces* 77:2.

McAdams, Janine, and Deborah Russell. 1991. "Rap Breaking through to Adult Market." P. 4. *Hollywood Reporter*. Sept. 19.

Miller, Matt. 2004. "Rap's Dirty South: From Subculture to Pop Culture." *Journal of Popular Music Studies* 16:175-212.

Negus, Keith. 1999. *Music Genres and Corporate Cultures*. Routledge.

Perkins, William Eric. 1996. "The Rap Attack: An Introduction." Pp. 1-45. *Droppin' Science: Critical Essays on Rap Music and Hip Hop Culture*. William Eric Perkins, editor. Temple University Press.

Peterson, Richard A., and David Berger. 1972. "Entrepreneurship in Organizations: Evidence from the Popular Music Industry." *Administrative Science Quarterly* 10:1.

_____. 1975. "Cycles in Symbolic Production: The Case of Popular Music." *American Sociological Review* 40:158.

Peterson, Richard A., and N. Anand. 2004. "The Production of Culture Perspective." *Annual Review of Sociology* 30:311-34.

Peterson, Richard A. 1997. *Creating Country Music*. University of Chicago Press.

_____. 2005. "In Search of Authenticity." *Journal of Management Studies*. 42:5.

Roberts, John W. 1989. *From Trickster to Badman: The Black Folk Hero in Slavery and Freedom*. University of Pennsylvania Press.

Rose, Tricia. 1994a. *Black Noise: Rap Music and Black Culture in Contemporary America*. Wesleyan University Press.

_____. 1994b. "Contracting Rap: An Interview with Carmen Ashhurst-Watson." Pp. 122-44. *Microphone Fiends*. A. Ross and T. Rose, editors. Routledge.

Rothenbuhler, Eric W., and John W. Dimmick. 1982. "Popular Music: Concentration and Diversity in the Industry, 1974-1980." *Journal of Communication* 32:143.

Shusterman, Richard. 1991. "The Fine Art of Rap." *New Literary History* 22:613.

Smitherman, Geneva. 1997. "'The Chain Remain the Same': Communicative Practices in the Hip Hop Nation." *Journal of Black Studies* 28:1.

Stinchcombe, Arthur L. 1959. "Bureaucratic and Craft Administration of Production: A Comparative Study." *Administrative Science Quarterly* 4:168-87.

Toop, David. 1991. *Rap Attack 2: African Rap to Global Hip-Hop*. Pluto.

Walser, Robert. 1995. "Rhythm, Rhyme and Rhetoric in the Music of Public Enemy." *Ethnomusicology* 39:193.

Whitburn, Joel. 1996. *Top R&B Singles 1942–1995*. Record Research.

White, Harrison C., and Cynthia A. White. 1965. *Canvasses and Careers: Institutional Change in the French Painting World*. Wiley.

White, Harrison C. 1993. *Careers and Creativity: Social Forces in the Arts*. Westview Press.

Wimmer, R.D., and J.R. Dominick. 1997. *Mass Media Research: An Introduction. Fifth edition*. Wadsworth.

Reading

The Changing Culture of Fatherhood in Comic-Strip Families

A Six-Decade Analysis (2000)

Ralph LaRossa, Charles Jaret, Malati Gadgil, and G. Robert Wynn

How do popular portrayals of fathers in the 1970s, 1980s, and 1990s compare with popular portrayals of fathers in the 1940s, 1950s, and 1960s? Have the portrayals improved? Have they gotten worse? Is there any variation at all?

SOURCE: From "The Changing Culture of Fatherhood in Comic-Strip Families: A Six-Decade Analysis" by LaRossa, R., Jaret, C., Gadgil, M., & Wynn, G. R., in *Journal of Marriage and the Family, 62*:375–387. Copyright © 2000. Reprinted with permission.

The issue here is not whether the conduct of fatherhood has shifted, but whether the culture of fatherhood has changed (LaRossa, 1988). When it comes to conduct, studies have shown that with the increase in the number of dual-earner families, more fathers are spending large blocks of "quality time" with their children, although men still lag behind women in this regard (Pleck, 1997). On the other hand, because of the long-term escalation in divorce, many nonresident fathers have only minimal contact with their daughters and sons. The behavioral picture of the contemporary male parent thus can be said to have both a good side and a bad side (Furstenberg, 1988).

What about the culture of fatherhood (i.e., the norms, values, beliefs, and expressive symbols pertaining to fatherhood)? How much change can be discerned here? Scholars may be better equipped today to answer this question than they were 15 years ago, but a careful examination of the four studies that have directly tested "the changing-culture-of-fatherhood hypothesis" (Day & Mackey, 1986; LaRossa, Gordon, Wilson, Bairan, & Jaret, 1991; Atkinson & Blackwelder, 1993; Coltrane & Allan, 1994) indicates that much still remains unknown.

In the first effort to systematically tackle the question, Day and Mackey (1986) compared single-panel family cartoons published in the *Saturday Evening Post* between 1922 and 1968 with similar kinds of cartoons published between 1971 and 1978 to see whether "the role image of the American father" in popular culture had been transformed. They found that up to the late 1960s, fathers were significantly more likely than were mothers to be characterized as incompetent (e.g., as "awkward," "unhandy," or "gawky"), but in the 1970s, the incidence of incompetence for men and women was statistically similar. Because of the convergence in how cartoons portrayed fathers and mothers during the second period in contrast to the disparity of their portrayals in the first, Day and Mackey concluded that the 1970s marked a paradigmatic shift in the culture of fatherhood. As they saw it, the percentage of mothers in the labor force, the decline in birth rates, and the

fervent advocacy of gender equality in the 1970s (brought on by the feminist movement) had prompted the traditionally minded *Saturday Evening Post* cartoonists to reduce their satirical attacks on fathers. A new, improved version of fatherhood had come on the scene.

Social scientists have long recognized that humor can reveal patterns of stratification (e.g., see Mulkay, 1988; Wilson, 1979), hence the premise that the incompetence level of cartoon characters could be used as a barometer of social trends does have validity. Nonetheless, were Day and Mackey (1986) correct about the 1970s? Had the image of the American father basically been consistent until then?

In a follow-up study, LaRossa et al. (1991) examined the same kinds of *Saturday Evening Post* cartoons that Day and Mackey (1986) had, but focused more closely on the years 1924, 1928, 1932, 1936, 1940, and 1944, when historical conditions were analogous to those in the 1970s (i.e., the labor force participation rate of mothers had increased, birth rates had alternated, and the first wave of the 20th century women's movement was reverberating). LaRossa et al. discovered that whereas fathers were significantly more likely than were mothers to be depicted as incompetent in the 1920s, the disparity with respect to incompetence had disappeared in the 1930s and especially the early 1940s. If gender parity in cartoon humor is a sign of "role image" change, as Day and Mackey suggested, then it would seem that the 1970s were not the first time fathers were taken seriously. The paradigmatic shift that Day and Mackey had assumed was peculiar to the 1970s also may have occurred in the 1930s and 1940s. Synthesizing the findings from the two studies, LaRossa et al. inferred that a fluctuating pattern was a more accurate model of how the culture of fatherhood had changed over the course of the 20th century.

Next, in another study that relied on print media but not on cartoons, Atkinson and Blackwelder (1993) examined popular magazine articles published in the middle years of every decade from the early 1900s to the 1980s to see what had happened to "fathering role definitions" in the interim. Calculating the ratio of articles accentuating "nurturant fathering" to articles accentuating "providing fathering," they found that in the 1920s and 1930s, the emphasis on "providing fathering" was predominant, but that from the 1940s through the 1980s "nurturant fathering" was the more common theme. They also noted that for the latter part of the 20th century, the ratios moved up and down, reporting scores of 2.5, 1.3, 1.4, 3.3, and 2.8 for the 1940s, 1950s, 1960s, 1970s, and 1980s, respectively (i.e., fathers were 2.5 times more likely in the 1940s to be defined as "nurturing," and so on). These figures suggest that traditional gender roles were more likely to be endorsed in the 1950s and 1960s and that the concept of the "New Father" (i.e., the more involved father) was strongest in the 1970s. The pattern would appear to support both Day and Mackey's (1986) claim that the 1970s were a high water mark for nurturant fathering and LaRossa and colleagues' (1991) contention that the culture of fatherhood had fluctuated. Left unanswered, however, was why there would be a lower ratio in the 1980s than there was in the 1970s. Interesting, too, was the similarity between the 1950s and 1960s. Did the feminist movement of the 1960s have no immediate effect on definitions of fatherhood?

In the most recent study, based on electronic rather than print media, Coltrane and Allan (1994) compared representations of fatherhood and motherhood in television advertising in the 1980s with representations in the 1950s. Characters appearing in "classic" and award-winning commercials were judged on a variety of criteria, including whether they were parents or paid workers and whether they were nurturant and supportive when performing the parental role. On the first measure, Coltrane and Allan found that in the 1950s, men were six times more likely to be shown as workers than as parents, whereas women were twice as likely to be shown as parents than as workers. In the 1980s, the portrayal of men had changed only slightly, whereas the portrayal of women had become more similar to that of the men; three decades later, men were almost four times as likely, and women were twice as likely, to be shown as workers than as parents. The convergence in the portrayal of men and women as workers indicated that some change had occurred, but Coltrane and Allan pointed out that gender differences continued to be visible in that "men were still more likely to be pictured in occupational roles than were women" (p. 51).

Coltrane and Allan's (1994) study revealed little change on the issue of whether men and women were depicted as nurturant and supportive. In the 1950s, 75% of the fathers and 89% of the mothers displayed nurturant and supportive behaviors; in the 1980s, 71% of the fathers and 78% of the mothers displayed nurturant and supportive behaviors. In other words, most of the advertisements tended to present fathers and mothers as "warm and fuzzy," but there was no greater tendency to do so in the 1980s, which is unexpected if one were looking for evidence of an increase in the concept of the "New Father." Coltrane and Allan concluded that previous research had probably overestimated the extent of change: "Our findings must be considered tentative because of sampling limitations [e.g., only four men and nine women were pictured as parents in the 1950s], but we challenge the common perception that the popular culture of fathering was transformed in fundamental ways during the 1980s" (p. 61).

Taking the studies together, what can be said about the culture of fatherhood in late-20th-century America? First, it appears the researchers agree that change has occurred but disagree on the magnitude of change. Whereas Day and Mackey (1986) described a "paradigmatic" shift in the "role image of the American father," and Atkinson and Blackwelder (1993) referred to the amount of change in "the popular conceptualization of parenthood" as "remarkable" and "important," Coltrane and Allan (1994) were of the opinion that the change in "fatherhood imagery" was minimal at best and largely overstated. Second, there is an absence of consensus among the researchers on the timing and duration of change. Day and

Mackey and Atkinson and Blackwelder offered evidence that the 1970s were critical years in the cultural history of fatherhood, but if Coltrane and Allan were correct, the moment must have been short lived. The downturn that Atkinson and Blackwelder reported for the 1980s also would suggest a dampening effect. Third, there is a lack of clarity on the shape of change. Is there a fluctuating pattern, as LaRossa et al. (1991) and Atkinson and Blackwelder believe? If so, how do we make sense of Coltrane and Allan's findings, which imply that the 1950s and 1980s were similar?

OBJECTIVE

The goal of this article is try to answer the above questions and, in so doing, reduce some of the confusion that now exists. Drawing on a six-decade content analysis of 490 comic strips published on Father's Day and Mother's Day, we endeavor to determine whether and how the culture of fatherhood has changed since World War II

Why comic strips? More than 100 million people read comic strips every day (Wood, 1987, p. 186), and, as with television sitcoms, they occupy a central place in American society. A study of comic strips thus has the potential to tap into a nation's collective consciousness. Also, because comics have been around for more than a century (Inge, 1979, 1990), they lend themselves to the investigation of long-term cultural trends (Harrison, 1981; Kasen, 1979, 1980). Given how often they revolve around domestic situations, they have proven an especially valuable index of family ideologies and gender stereotypes (e.g., see Brabant, 1976; Brabant & Mooney, 1986, 1997).

Interestingly enough, despite the role that political cartoons have played in exposing the foibles of the powerful, comic strips often perpetuate rather than challenge gender stereotypes (Chavez, 1985; Mooney & Brabant, 1987, 1990). Choosing comic strips for our database thus made it more likely that we would not find any historical differences. With comic

strips as our criterion, the changing-culture-of-fatherhood hypothesis faced a stiffer challenge.

As for deciding to examine comic strips published on Father's Day and Mother's Day, this carried with it several advantages. First, we felt that chronological comparisons would be more meaningful if we focused on comics published on the same day from one year to the next. Second, Father's Day and Mother's Day are public rites or ceremonies that cryptically symbolize the social value of fatherhood and motherhood in America. Third, content analyzing comic strips on Father's Day and Mother's Day allowed each holiday to serve as a point of reference for the other.

One may ask the question, what connection do comic strips have to public attitudes and behaviors? One answer is they have no connection at all. That is, some may say that comic strips are too oblique and too divorced from everyday life to have any relationship to what is "really going on." But then why are they funny? Humor essentially entails a paradoxical juxtaposition of two realities, conventional and unconventional (Macionis, 1989). Thus, it could be argued that a father making a mess of the kitchen while preparing a Mother's Day breakfast was a recurring theme in the comics we studied because of both its familiarity and its absurdity (the gift, sincerely offered, backfires). The fact that, in contrast, there was not a single comic that had a mother mismanaging a Father's Day breakfast—and that if there were, it probably would seem odd (unless it were ingeniously crafted)—says something about how fathers and mothers are portrayed in American culture and about how they think and act. The many published studies that have shown empirically how comic strips reflect gender, race, and class divisions, among other realities, also make a strong case for taking them seriously in social science.

To say that there is a connection between comic strips and everyday life is not to say that the connection is simple. Internalizing culture, of which comic strips are a part, is not akin to downloading software on a computer. Rather, the socialization process is more selective and more interactive. Culture basically operates as a framing device—channeling, not determining, attitudes and behaviors (W. Griswold, 1994; Zerubavel, 1991, 1997). Culture, therefore, is "more a 'tool kit' or repertoire" from which people choose assorted "pieces" to construct "strategies of action" (Swidler, 1986, p. 277). One could say that comic strips are part of a society's cultural supermarket. A strip's presence "on the shelves" makes its stories and vocabularies (e.g., "Good grief!" from *Peanuts*) available for selection and incorporation into the amalgam of norms, values, beliefs, and expressive symbols that influence people's perceptions and behaviors.

METHOD

Comics and Characters

We carefully reviewed the humorous comics (i.e., the funnies as opposed to the dramatic serials) published in the *Atlanta Journal and Constitution* on Father's Day and Mother's Day from 1940 to 1999 and marked for coding those comics that (a) explicitly mentioned or implicitly alluded to Father's Day or Mother's Day or (b) had fatherhood, motherhood, or parenthood as a theme. We limited the study to humorous comics because when we first scanned the comic-strip pages, it appeared to us that humorous comics were more likely to present the kinds of stories that would reveal attitudes toward fatherhood and motherhood. When we completed the review, 216 Father's Day and 274 Mother's Day comics were found to fall into one category or the other. These 490 comics were then individually photocopied, making them black and white, and randomly numbered so as to disguise their publication dates.

In our analysis, we focused on the designated Father's Day or Mother's Day parents; if the comic did not explicitly mention or implicitly allude to one of the holidays, we focused on the parents who were the most central (if identifiable). The focus also could be a grandparent or stepparent or, in a few cases, a father or mother figure. Fathers and mothers could be humans, animals (e.g., ants), or even machines (e.g., robots). Among the 490 comics, there were 357 fathers and 389 mothers who were singled out for "observation."

Because the comics analyzed in this study included every comic in the *Atlanta Journal and Constitution* published on Father's Day and Mother's Day that mentioned or alluded to the holiday or that focused on fatherhood, motherhood, or parenthood, we had the entire population of relevant comics, rather than only a sample of them. Our comparisons of the Father's Day and Mother's Day comics thus do not require significance tests because the percentages derived are not subject to sampling error.

Although we relied on a single newspaper, the fact that Sunday comics are syndicated meant that many of the comics appeared in hundreds, if not thousands, of newspapers nationwide. The recognizability and range of the comics also are indicative of a set that is more representative than idiosyncratic. Some of the comics selected were: *B.C., Blondie, Bloom County, Cathy, Dennis the Menace, The Family Circus, For Better or Worse, Garfield, Gasoline Alley, Hagar the Horrible, Hi and Lois, Little Orphan Annie, Peanuts, Pogo, The Wizard of Id,* and *Ziggy,* (among others). The oldest syndicated comic in the grouping was *Gasoline Alley,* first published in 1919. The second oldest was *Blondie,* first published in 1930 (Goulart, 1995, pp. 96, 125; Kinnaird, 1963, pp. 92–93).

Men penned the majority of comics under investigation, reflecting the patriarchal culture of the newspaper industry. Women drew some of the newer comics, however (e.g., *Cathy, For Better or Worse,* and *Stone Soup*), suggesting movement toward gender equality, albeit slight. Also, until recently, all the comic-strip characters appear to be White. Only in the 1990s, with the addition of comics such as *Curtis, Jumpstart,* and *The Boondocks,* have we seen more frequent representations of people of color. In total, 5.1% of the 490 comics in our sample feature an African American parental figure. Finally, we had hoped to determine whether socioeconomic status might be a factor but soon discovered that almost all the comic-strip families were middle class (based on the quality of the furnishings inside the home, among other indicators). The typical Sunday comic strip thus resembles the typical popular magazine article or television show in at least one respect: Each tends to offer a homogenized portrait of social life.

Coding

What messages, relevant to the culture of fatherhood, can be found in a comic strip? First of all, it is important to recognize that there are no messages "in" a comic. Rather, there are various meanings that the reader may give to the pictures and words on the page. To the cartoonist, a particular comic may symbolize one thing. To the publisher, it may symbolize something else. Among the audience, multiple readings may exist. As with any text (whether it be a painting, a poem, or a historical or legal document), a comic can be subject to a variety of interpretations (Mukerji & Schudson, 1991).

We take the issue of multiple messages in texts seriously. Nonetheless, we also believe that, with care, it is possible for someone immersed in a culture to reliably and validly ascertain (i.e., code) the mutually understood and shared definitions of a comedic situation that are held by many, if not most, of the inhabitants of that culture. Indeed, we would contend that the ability to accomplish this feat is what makes a successful cartoonist.

With an awareness of the challenges involved, coding was a multistep process. First, MG and GRW would independently code the comics. Then, the four of us would meet to discuss the comics and reconcile any discrepancies that had emerged in the first round. These group sessions provided a forum where we would toss back and forth how best to approach some of the more subtle comics.

Although RL and CJ were aware of the goals of the project from the beginning, MG and GRW were deliberately not told what the study was about while they were coding, and they were asked not to read any of the previously published literature on the subject. Because of the nuances in comic-strip humor and the complexity of the codes employed, coding took longer than was originally planned. Contemplating how to "speed things up," we considered bringing in another coder to serve as a tiebreaker. After a while, however, we came to realize that our team approach and in-depth familiarity with the comics greatly enhanced the reliability and validity of the coding process. Our different disciplinary ties and diversity in gender, age, and national and regional background also contributed positively to the content analysis. (Note: The set of comics published in 1999 were a late addition to our sample and were coded by RL and CJ. The rules that had become institutionalized in the group sessions were applied to the 1999 set.)

Measures

Attention Given to Father's Day and Mother's Day. How much attention was given to Father's Day and Mother's Day from 1940 to 1999? To address this question, we counted for each year the number of comic strips that explicitly mentioned or implicitly alluded to Father's Day or Mother's Day. More often than not, if Father's Day were mentioned or alluded to at all, it was in a comic published on Father's Day; and more often than not, if Mother's Day were mentioned or alluded to at all, it was in a comic published on Mother's Day. But there were instances where an acknowledgment of Father's Day would appear on Mother's Day, or an acknowledgment of Mother's Day would appear on Father's Day. (Sometimes a single comic would give attention to both, for example.) We also included these crossovers in our counts.

Incompetence. To measure the level of incompetence exhibited by the fathers and mothers in the strips, we built upon the coding scheme that LaRossa et al. (1991) used. In that study, coders were asked: "Is the father in this family (whether he is pictured in the cartoon or not) being depicted as incompetent?" Each cartoon was given one of the following codes: 0 *Not applicable* (Father is not in the cartoon, and no reference is made to him or about him); 1 *Not incompetent* (Father is in cartoon or is referenced in the cartoon, but he is not depicted as incompetent); or 2 *Incompetent* (Father is in cartoon or is referenced in the cartoon, and he is depicted as incompetent). The question was then repeated so that it applied to the mother. To be "incompetent," the father or mother would have to behave in a way that could be classified as ignorant, inadequate, incapable, ineffectual, inefficient, inept, stupid, unable, unfit, or weak (first-order synonyms for incompetence in the Wordperfect thesaurus).

In this study, coders reviewed 27 activities that fathers and mothers could enact and made the following judgment: "Is the Father's Day (FD) Father/Grandfather or the male spouse of the Mother's Day (MD) Mother/Grandmother in this comic (whether he is pictured in the comic or not) enacting any of the following activities; if so, is he depicted as incompetent in the activity?" Each cartoon was given one of the following codes: 0 *Not applicable* (FD/MD father is not in comic and no reference is made to him or about him); 1 *Activity not enacted* (FD/MD father is in comic or referenced in comic, but is not involved in the activity); 2 *Incompetent* (FD/MD father is in comic or is referenced in comic, and he is depicted as incompetent on this particular issue); or 3 *Activity enacted competently or enacted in such a way that competence or incompetence is not an issue* (FD/ MD father is in comic or referenced in comic, is involved in the activity, and is competent in his performance, or the question of competence or incompetence is not relevant on this particular activity). The question was then repeated so that it would apply to the mother. The synonyms for "incompetence" used in the LaRossa et al. (1991) study also were used in this study. The list of activities included not only child-care activities (e.g., verbally or physically expresses affection toward children), but also marital activities (e.g., engages in

negative emotional interaction with spouse), household activities (e.g., does traditionally feminine household chores), employment-related activities (e.g., performs paid work), gender-socializing activities (e.g., shows a child what it means to "be a man"), and activities related to Father's Day or Mother's Day (e.g., gives or is about to give Father's Day or Mother's Day gift).

Mocked. Recognizing that it is possible for a parent to be made to look foolish even though he or she is not acting foolishly, we decided to ask more globally, and without focusing on any specific activities: "Does this comic make a deliberate point to mock anyone in particular or in general?" Children and others were sometimes mocked in the comics, but for this analysis, we will report only the numbers for fathers and mothers.

Nurturant and Supportive Parenting Behaviors I. Coltrane and Allan (1994) operationalized nurturant and supportive parenting behaviors as verbally or physically expressing affection toward a child, serving or caring for a child, verbally encouraging a child, or comforting a child or inquiring about the child's feelings and thoughts. To compare what Coltrane and Allan found when they looked at television ads with what we might find when we looked at comic strips, we included their four examples of nurturant and supportive behaviors in our list of 27 activities.

Nurturant and Supportive Parenting Behaviors II. While pretesting our coding instrument, we discovered that comic-strip fathers and mothers also could be nurturant and supportive by praising a child for a completed task or activity or for a job well done, listening to a child's problem, or purposefully teaching a child. We thus added these three nurturant and supportive behaviors to Coltrane and Allan's (1994) four nurturant and supportive behaviors to construct a seven-item composite measure, Nurturant and Supportive Parenting Behaviors II. For this measure, as well as the previous measure, verbally encouraging a child meant explicitly "during a task or activity," so as to distinguish it from praising a child "for a completed task or activity."

RESULTS

Attention Given to Father's Day and Mother's Day

Table 1 reports the number of comics by half decade that explicitly mentioned or implicitly alluded to Father's Day or Mother's Day. (We opted for half-decade cutting points because of significant intradecade variations uncovered in our analysis.) Several trends are revealed, the most important of which are: (a) the shift from the 1940–1944 period when there were no comics that acknowledged Father's Day or Mother's Day to the 1945 and after period when there were many that did, (b) the general rise over time in the number of comics that acknowledged the holidays, (c) the greater attention given to Mother's Day compared with Father's Day overall (for every 10 acknowledgments of Mother's Day, there were about 8 acknowledgments of Father's Day), and (d) the much greater attention given to Mother's Day compared with Father's Day from 1995 to 1999 (the difference in the late 1990s accounts for almost half of the difference in the totals).

Incompetence

Table 2 reports how the fathers and mothers in the entire sample were portrayed (i.e., among the 357 fathers and 389 mothers pictured or referenced in the 490 comics that explicitly mentioned or implicitly alluded to Father's Day or Mother's Day, or had fatherhood, motherhood, or parenthood as a theme).

The first-row totals indicate that over all the years, 10.9% of the fathers and 5.7% of the mothers in the comics were depicted as incompetent. These percentages are fairly small and mean that the parents in the Father's Day and Mother's Day comics were much more often than not depicted as capable, efficient, and so forth, or they were shown performing activities in which competence or incompetence was not an issue. Given the higher scores for father and mother incompetence in studies of single-panel *Saturday Evening Post* cartoons (Day & Mackey, 1986; LaRossa et al., 1991), we surmise that the cartoonists were less inclined to portray parents as incompetent on holidays intended to honor them.

The reluctance to disparage parents on Father's Day and Mother's Day makes the difference between fathers and mothers in the comics all the more relevant. Over time, the tendency to depict mothers as incompetent generally remained at a

TABLE 1 Number of Comics That Explicitly Mentioned or Implicitly Alluded to Father's Day, or Mother's Day, 1940–1999

	40–44	45–49	50–54	55–59	60–64	65-69	70–74	75–79	80–84	85–89	90–94	95–99	Totals
Father's Day	0	6	5	8	14	9	14	17	20	28	37	35	193
Mother's Day	0	8	7	8	15	16	19	19	22	35	40	56	245
Difference	0	–2	–2	0	–1	–7	–5	–2	–2	–7	–3	–21	–52

TABLE 2 Percentage of Fathers and Mothers Depicted as Incompetent, Mocked, or Shown to Be Nurturant and Supportive Parents in Comics Explicitly Mentioning or Implicitly Alluding to Father's Day or Mother's Day, or Having Fatherhood, Motherhood, or Parenthood as a Theme, 1940–1999

	40–44	*45–49*	*50–54*	*55–59*	*60–64*	*65-69*	*70–74*	*75–79*	*80–84*	*85–89*	*90–94*	*95–99*	*Totals*
Incompetent													
Fathers	—	21.4	33.3	0.0	14.3	21.1	8.3	8.0	3.6	14.9	5.4	12.3	10.9
Mothers	—	28.6	0.0	7.1	5.0	4.5	6.7	0.0	3.0	4.0	9.2	3.2	5.7
Difference	—	–7.2	33.0	–7.1	9.3	16.6	1.6	8.0	0.6	10.9	–3.8	9.1	5.2
Mocked													
Fathers	—	14.3	11.1	13.3	33.3	31.6	12.5	12.0	25.0	19.1	18.9	19.8	18.8
Mothers	—	21.4	0.0	7.1	5.0	4.5	0.0	0.0	3.0	4.0	10.5	8.4	6.0
Difference	—	–7.1	11.1	6.2	28.3	27.1	12.5	12.0	22.0	15.1	8.4	11.4	12.8
Nurturant and Supportive Parenting Behaviors I													
Fathers	—	35.7	33.3	6.7	19.0	15.8	12.5	12.0	14.3	17.0	23.0	38.3	23.0
Mothers	—	28.6	20.0	42.9	20.0	18.2	16.7	44.0	12.1	36.0	39.5	36.8	31.6
Difference	—	7.1	13.3	–36.2	–1.0	–2.4	–4.2	–32.0	2.2	–19.0	–16.5	1.5	–8.6
Nurturant and Supportive Parenting Behaviors II													
Fathers	—	42.9	55.6	20.0	28.6	31.6	20.8	16.0	28.6	36.2	36.5	53.1	36.4
Mothers	—	42.9	50.0	64.3	30.0	22.7	23.3	48.0	21.2	48.0	48.7	51.6	42.9
Difference	—	0.0	5.6	–44.3	–1.4	8.9	-2.5	–32.0	7.4	–11.8	–12.2	1.5	–6.5
ns													
Fathers Pic/Ref	—	14	9	15	21	19	24	25	28	47	74	81	357
Mothers Pic/Ref	—	14	10	14	20	22	30	25	33	50	76	95	389
Difference	—	0	–1	1	1	–3	–6	0	–5	–3	–2	–14	–32

stable low, whereas the tendency to depict fathers as incompetent fluctuated. Note the large gender difference in the early 1950s and late 1960s and the near convergence in the early 1970s and early 1980s, all due largely to changes in how the fathers were portrayed. The fact that mothers were depicted as more incompetent than were fathers in the late 1940s, late 1950s, and early 1990s is also interesting.

Fathers and mothers also diverged in the kinds of activities that, when performed, had higher rates of incompetence. For fathers, these activities included showing a child what it means to "be a man," doing feminine household chores, nonphysically disciplining a child, and playing sports. For mothers, these activities included physically or nonphysically disciplining a child, giving a Father's Day gift, and comforting a child.

Mocked

The second-row totals in Table 2 indicate that 18.8% of the fathers and 6.0% of the mothers were mocked. These totals corroborate the cartoonists' tendency not to make fun of parents on Father's Day and Mother's Day, but they also demonstrate, from another vantage point, that if any parent were to be targeted on the holidays, it was likely the father and that the propensity to disparage men fluctuated. Note the large gender difference in the 1960s and 1980s, compared to the 1950s, 1970s, and 1990s. Note, too, that mothers were mocked more than fathers were in the late 1940s.

Nurturant and Supportive Parenting Behaviors I

The third row in Table 2 reports the results for our first measure of nurturant and supportive parenting behaviors. Overall, 23.0% of the fathers and 31.6% of the mothers were shown verbally or physically expressing affection toward a child, serving or caring for a child, verbally encouraging a child, or comforting a child or inquiring about the child's feelings and thoughts. The half-decade percentages for the fathers exhibited a U-shaped pattern, whereas the percentages for the mothers spiked in the late 1950s and late 1970s.

Nurturant and Supportive Parenting Behaviors II

The fourth row in Table 2 reports the results for our second measure of nurturant and supportive parenting behaviors. When we added to the activities listed above the additional activities of praising a child for a completed task, activity, or a job well done; listening to a child's problem; and purposefully teaching a child, the percentages increased across the board: 36.4% of the fathers and 42.9% of the mothers were shown to be nurturant and supportive. The longitudinal pattern of the first measure was repeated,

however. The percentages for the fathers looked more-or-less U-shaped, and the percentages for the mothers spiked in the late 1950s and late 1970s. Significant is the fact that this parenting measure showed fathers increasing in nurturance and support beginning in the 1980s and continuing through the 1990s.

DISCUSSION

Has the culture of fatherhood changed over the past six decades? Viewed through the prism of Father's Day and Mother's Day comic strips, it would appear that it has, but not in a linear or simple way.

Changes in Attention Given to Father's Day and Mother's Day

When we looked at the amount of attention given to Father's Day and Mother's Day, we found that Father's Day was generally acknowledged less frequently. In this respect, the comics parallel other indicators of "popularity": regardless of how the holidays are compared (by number of phone calls made, cards sent, meals eaten out, or cartoonists' recognition) Father's Day comes up short (see Ward, 1993).

When we looked at the amount of attention given to Father's Day and Mother's Day over time, we found the amount of attention generally going up. This increase, we learned, was not because the number of comics published in a given year had risen but because family-oriented comics had come to dominate the comic-strip page. Publishers may have decided that readers prefer these kinds of comics to the more serious strips (e.g., *Brenda Starr* or *Mary Worth)* or adventure strips *(Tarzan* or *Steve Canyon).*

We did wonder whether the amount of attention given to Father's Day would increase in the 1970s, given that 1972 marks the year President Richard Nixon signed Father's Day into law. (Previously, Father's Day was on the calendar, and presidential proclamations acknowledging the holiday were a matter of routine, but it was not until 1972 that Father's Day was made "legal." Mother's Day was certified a federal holiday in 1914.) The data do show that the amount of attention given to Father's Day started to climb in the 1970s, but we would be hard pressed to say that the upward movement had anything to do with the government's actions. We do know that none of the comics parodied the signing.

The large difference in the amount of attention given to Father's Day, compared with Mother's Day, in the late 1990s is puzzling, given the higher level of nurturant and supportive parenting behaviors exhibited by fathers in this period. The reason for the gap is that the number of comics that explicitly mentioned or implicitly alluded to Father's Day leveled off (from 37 to 35), whereas the number of comics that explicitly mentioned or implicitly alluded to Mother's Day continued to rise (from 40 to 56). Something else happened as well, something that is not apparent from the tables. Even though the number of comics acknowledging both Father's Day and Mother's Day was fairly high in the 1990s, the comic strips referring to these parental holidays actually constituted a smaller share of the family-oriented comics overall. That is, the proportion of comics that did not acknowledge Father's Day or Mother's Day but did have fatherhood, motherhood, or parenthood as a theme mushroomed, from only a minute fraction in the years before to nearly 25% overall in the 1990s. Also, the proportions differed for Father's Day and Mother's Day and for the first and second half of the decade. For Father's Day, the proportions were 22% in the early 1990s and 34% in the late 1990s. For Mother's Day, the proportions were 25% in the early 1990s and 19% in the late 1990s. In other words, cartoonists were more likely in the 1990s than they were in decades before to craft stories about parenthood without mentioning or alluding to either holiday, and they were more likely in the late 1990s than they were just a few years before to craft stories about fatherhood without mentioning or alluding to Father's Day.

One possible explanation is that cartoonists in the 1990s were more adept at communicating their viewpoints without framing the comic as a holiday message. Another possibility is that the fragility of family ties in the 1990s made the acknowledgment of both Father's Day and Mother's Day problematic. Because it could be awkward for children and others who are separated or estranged from their fathers or mothers to be reminded of Father's Day and Mother's Day, some cartoonists may have tried to display sensitivity by not bringing attention to the holidays. Still a third possibility, not exclusive of the others, is that cartoonists in the late 1990s had difficulty reconciling the concept of the "New Father" with its opposite, the nonresident "Absentee Dad," a manifestation of both the good and bad sides of male parenthood in the late 20th century (Furstenberg, 1988). Some attitudinal shift, whatever the cause, does seem to be at work because the changes in the scores cannot be attributed to changes in the composition of comic-strip families. There was, for example, no increase in single-mother characters.

Changes in the Portrayal of Fathers and Mothers

Regardless of whether the comics are about Father's Day, Mother's Day, or family life in general, one thing is clear. In recent years, there have been many more comic-strip characters who are parents and thus many more opportunities for readers to view fictitious fathers and mothers engaged in child-care activities. This expansion is important. If, hypothetically speaking, the number of fathers in a set of comics were to increase significantly from one decade to the next, while the percentage of nurturant and supportive fathering behaviors were to remain the same, there would still be more nurturant, supportive fathers in the comics for readers to observe. This, in turn, could affect the social reality of fatherhood because observing more male comic-strip characters acting fatherly could lead people to assume that the same kind of activity was occurring among their neighbors and friends. (These assumptions need not be correct. What people believe fathers do and what fathers actually do is the difference between the culture and conduct of fatherhood; LaRossa, 1988.)

Similarly, Coltrane and Allan (1994) made the point that "[t]he salience of a few men cuddling babies ... [can] create the impression that things have changed dramatically," even if "quantitative findings indicate that viewers continue to be bombarded with even more images of men as heroes, lovers, and loners" (p. 55). Coltrane and Allan reported that although the percentage of fathers in television ads who were nurturant and supportive did not increase between the 1950s and 1980s, the percentage of parents who were fathers did: in the 1950s, men accounted for 31% of all parents pictured in ads, but in the 1980s, they accounted for 71% of all parents pictured in ads. The 1980s profile could have inflated viewers' estimates of the prevalence of the "New Father," despite the fact that the more standard comparison (percentage of nurturant, supportive fathers then and now) suggested no change.

When we looked at how often fathers and mothers in the comics were portrayed as incompetent, we found that incompetence was not a usual theme, indicating a reluctance on the part of cartoonists to lampoon parents on Father's Day and Mother's Day. The few cases there were, however, were not randomly distributed across the decades. Consider the small difference between the portrayal of fathers and mothers in the 1970s. Day and Mackey (1986) found that fathers were no more likely than were mothers to be depicted as incompetent in the 1970s. We found this, too, but we also found additional support for the proposition that the portrayal of fathers has wavered over time. If we place chronologically the results from LaRossa and colleagues' (1991) study of the early 20th century alongside the results of this study of the late 20th century, we can see that the relative gender parity in the 1930s and early 1940s

(compared with the 1920s) reported in the first study, coupled with the relative gender parity in the 1970s (compared with the 1960s) reported in the current study, makes for a fluctuating pattern in the culture of fatherhood.

A picture of fluctuation also emerged when we looked at how frequently comic strips mocked fathers and mothers. With the single-item mocking question, which is more sensitive than is the incompetence measure to satirical nuance, the shift upward from the 1940s–1950s to the 1960s and the shift downward from the 1960s to the 1970s are unmistakable. With this variable, it also appears that the fluctuating pattern continued after the 1970s. Fathers were more likely to be mocked in the 1980s and 1990s than they were in the 1970s. Both Day and Mackey (1986) and Atkinson and Blackwelder (1993) offered evidence to suggest that the 1970s were a time when fatherhood was more likely to be culturally validated. If the extent to which fathers are mocked is a guide, our results reinforce their rendition of this decade.

With regard to nurturance and support, Coltrane and Allan (1994) found continuity when they examined the nurturant, supportive behaviors of fathers and mothers in television advertising in the 1950s and 1980s. Using their operational definition of nurturant, supportive behavior, we also found some degree of continuity when we aggregated the two decades and compared them. We do not infer from this, however, that no transformation in fatherhood imagery has occurred. For one thing, the continuity between the 1950s and 1980s on this particular measure belies the discontinuity between other decades on the same measure. Second, the half-decade analysis indicates that the fathers' up-down pattern for the early and late 1950s was not the same as the fathers' relatively stable pattern for the early and late 1980s. Third, a modified version of the Coltrane and Allan measure, what we called Nurturant and Supportive Parenting Behaviors II because of the addition of three child rearing activities, yielded results that showed sharper differences between the 1950s and 1980s, especially when we employed a half-decade analysis.

Critical, too, was the dramatic increase in paternal nurturance and support beginning in the 1980s and continuing through the 1990s. Although the gender disparities did not vanish—for the most part, mothers were depicted as more nurturant and supportive than were fathers—the concept of the "New Father" did seem to gain ground, even though it did so, ironically, at the same time that the attention given to Father's Day was becoming more ambiguous.

Equally interesting was the high level of maternal nurturance and support in the late 1980s and early and late 1990s. The cartoonists may have tried to acknowledge the concept of the "New Father," but they did not do so at the expense of motherhood. Indeed, if anything, they seemed to pay homage to both fatherhood and motherhood at the end of the millennium. Keep in mind, however, that the families in the comics were mainly White, middle class, and nuclear in structure. Single fathers and mothers, among others, were largely absent and not praised.

Knowing that we would also be making comparisons with the 1950s, as well as with the late 1940s, and because we were familiar with how scholars and popular writers have characterized the post-World War II era (sometimes called the Cold War or Baby Boom era), we fully expected that the comics published in these years would offer unequivocal displays of paternal buffoonery and maternal domesticity. However, our results turned out to be more complex. First, we found differences between the late 1940s and early and late 1950s. In the immediate postwar period, fathers were less likely than were mothers to be depicted as incompetent (by one character) and less likely to be mocked (by one character), but they were also more likely, or as likely, to be nurturant and supportive (depending on whether Nurturing and Supportive Parenting Behaviors I or II is used). We suspect men's relatively positive portrayals in

the late 1940s, were a continuation of the development of the concept of the "New Father" that accelerated in the 1920s and 1930s and that was at full throttle in the early 1940s, helped by a war accentuating men's role as the defenders of the nation (LaRossa, 1997). Women's less positive portrayals were another matter. In the 1940s, childrearing experts were disparaging mothers for being overprotective and for stifling independence. Philip Wylie, in *Generation of Vipers* (1942), coined the term "momism" to denote "the [smother] mother problem" (p. 196). Edward A. Strecker, in *Their Mothers' Sons* (1946), charged that women had turned millions of men into "sissies" unfit for combat. Cartoonists may have been swayed by the negative propaganda.

Then, there were the contrasts between the 1950s and 1960s. Although fathers during the 1950s were more likely to be mocked than were mothers of the day, the disparity between fathers and mothers in the 1950s was actually smaller than it was in the 1960s. The changes in the level of nurturant and supportive behaviors, considered in conjunction with the changes in the extent to which fathers were mocked, highlights the significance of this decade in the cultural history of fatherhood. As it turns out, the 1960s were a time when fathers were as likely as mothers to be depicted as nurturant and supportive, but they were also more likely to be mocked. When we look at the change in percentages, we see that the convergence in nurturant and supportive parenting behaviors was not because the fathers in the comics increased their "warm and fuzzy" quotient between the 1950s and 1960s, but because the mothers decreased theirs. Nonetheless, it was the fathers, not the mothers, whom the cartoonists ostensibly targeted in the 1960s.

In this regard, the parallels between the 1920s and the 1960s are striking. In the 1920s, there was much talk not only about the "New Father," who was supposed to become more involved with his children, but also about the "New

Woman," who was perceived as having less to do with hers; simultaneously, there were more jokes manifestly at men's expense (LaRossa et al., 1991). However, things are not always what they seem. In a society in which motherhood is the more sacred and fatherhood is the more profane and in which attitudes toward fathers and mothers are so intertwined, satire manifestly aimed at one quarry can be implicitly aimed at another. Hence, the real targets of the almost exclusively male cartoonists in the 1920s—and the 1960s—may not have been men or fathers per se, but the "battle of sexes," that, to some pundits, epitomized the two decades.

In general, our study supports the conclusions of Atkinson and Blackwelder (1993) and LaRossa et al. (1991) more than it supports the conclusions of Coltrane and Allan (1994) and Day and Mackey (1986): Fluctuation is the mode. Apart from the different data sets employed, the conflict in views may come down to the fact that Coltrane and Allan and Day and Mackey used a binary historical approach, examining only two points in time (the 1950s vs. the 1980s in the first case, 1922–1968 vs. 1971–1978 in the second), whereas Atkinson and Blackwelder, LaRossa et al., and the current study used a multiple-points-in-time approach. Two waves of data may be said to provide some information about social change and, strictly speaking, "constitute a longitudinal study," but such designs have serious methodological limitations (Rogosa, 1995). Multiwave studies are more sensitive to the complexities of cultural history.

Why the fluctuation? There are so many contradictory economic and political factors that have contributed to the ebb and flow of fatherhood in the late 20th century, it would be difficult to imagine events moving in a straight line (see Coltrane, 1996; R. Griswold, 1993). The changes that we uncovered, however, were not entirely the result of materialist conditions. Ours is a study of comic strips, of authored texts. Comics and other cultural objects are created by people and do not appear out of the blue (W. Griswold, 1994). Thus, another question to ask

is, was there anything about comic strips as a genre or about the comic-strip artists that might explain the fluctuation? One thing we discovered is that two comic strips dating back to the 1950s— *Dennis the Menace* and *The Family Circle*— wavered hardly at all from one decade to the next. The consistency of these strips prompted us to reflect on the fact that comic strips are similar to soap operas in which stories are dictated by the characters' personalities and the fictitious families' routines. Even minor modifications can alter the flow of a successful comic and mean audience disapproval and cancellation.

If, indeed, some principle of inertia and caution prevents long-running strips from altering their narratives in response to structural trends, then the historical changes that we report would have to be a partial function of different comics with different authors entering and leaving the comic-strip section of the newspaper. The changes in the 1990s, for one, may have mirrored the changing gender and age composition of the cartoonists themselves. As more women and more artists from different age cohorts broke into the comic-strip trade, the tableaus of fatherhood and motherhood in the comics were literally and figuratively redrawn and "updated."

The lesson to derive from this is that studies of the culture of fatherhood must focus more on how the various norms, values, beliefs, and expressive symbols pertaining to fatherhood are manufactured. It is not just a question of "what" is produced about fatherhood, but also a question of "who" produces it (LaRossa, 1997). What would we have learned had we interviewed the cartoonists about their work? What were the cartoonists contemplating when, pen in hand, they sat at their drawing tables preparing the comics that would be published on Father's Day and Mother's Day? Studies of the culture of fatherhood also must focus more on how the various norms, values, beliefs, and expressive symbols pertaining to fatherhood are read and interpreted. Virtually every day, the populace is bombarded with "information" about fathers, some of it comedic.

How much is known about what goes on in people's minds when they see this material? (Two excellent examples of cultural studies, although not of fatherhood, that look at these issues are Radway, 1984, and Simonds, 1992.)

Ultimately, researchers must not lose sight of the relationship between the "objectivation" of fatherhood and the "externalization-internalization" of fatherhood (Berger & Luckmann, 1966). Whereas the former refers to a cultural product, the latter refers to a process through which that product is constructed and incorporated into people's consciousness on an ongoing basis. Fully comprehending the first will require detailed studies of the second.

REFERENCES

Atkinson, M. P., & Blackwelder, S. P. (1993). Fathering in the 20th century. *Journal of Marriage and the Family, 55,* 975–986.

Berger, P., & Luckmann, T. (1966). *The social construction of reality: A treatise in the sociology of knowledge.* New York: Anchor/Doubleday.

Brabant, S. (1976). Sex role stereotyping in the Sunday comics. *Sex Roles, 2,* 331–337.

Brabant, S., & Mooney, L. A. (1986). Sex role stereotyping in the Sunday comics: Ten years later. *Sex Roles, 14,* 141–148.

Brabant, S., & Mooney, L. A. (1997). Sex role stereotyping in the Sunday comics: A twenty year update. *Sex Roles, 37,* 269–281.

Chavez, D. (1985). Perpetuation of gender inequality: A content analysis of comic strips. *Sex Roles, 13,* 93–102.

Coltrane, S. (1996). *Family man: Fatherhood, house-work, and gender equity.* New York: Oxford University Press.

Coltrane, S., & Allan, K. (1994). "New" fathers and old stereotypes: Representations of masculinity in 1980s television advertising, *masculinities, 2,* 43–66.

Day, R. D., & Mackey, W. C. (1986). The role image of the American father: An examination of a media myth. *Journal of Comparative Family Studies, 3,* 371–388.

Furstenberg, F. F., Jr. (1988). Good dads—bad dads: Two faces of fatherhood. In A. J. Cherlin (Ed.), *The changing American family and public policy* (pp. 193–218). Washington, DC: Urban Institute Press.

Goulart, R. (1995). *The funnies: 100 years of American comic strips.* Holbrook, MA: Adams Publishing.

Griswold, R. L. (1993). *Fatherhood in America: A history.* New York: Basic Books.

Griswold, W (1994). *Cultures and societies in a changing world.* Thousand Oaks, CA: Sage.

Harrison, R. P. (1981). *The cartoon: Communication to the quick.* Beverly Hills, CA: Sage.

Inge, M. T. (1979). Introduction. *Journal of Popular Culture, 12,* 631–639.

Inge, M. T. (1990). *Comics as culture.* Jackson, MS: University Press of Mississippi.

Kasen, J. H. (1979). Exploring collective symbols: America as a middle-class society. *Pacific Sociological Review, 22,* 348–381.

Kasen, J. H. (1980). Whither the self-made man? Comic culture and the crisis of legitimation in the United States. *Social Problems, 28,* 131–148.

Kinnaird, C. (1963). Cavalcade of funnies. In D. M. White & R. H. Abel (Eds.), *The funnies: An American idiom* (pp. 88–96). New York: Free Press. (A revision of an article that appeared in *The Funnies, Annual No. 1,* 1959, King Features Syndicate, Inc.)

LaRossa, R. (1988). Fatherhood and social change. *Family Relations, 37,* 451–457.

LaRossa, R. (1997). *The modernization of fatherhood: A social and political history.* Chicago: University of Chicago Press.

LaRossa, R. Gordon, B. A., Wilson R. J., Bairan, A., & Jaret, C. (1991). The fluctuating image of the 20th century American father. *Journal of Marriage and the Family, 53,* 987–997.

Macionis, J. J. (1989). What makes something funny? In J. J. Macionis & N. V. Benokraitis (Eds.), *Seeing ourselves: Classic, contemporary, and cross-cultural readings in sociology* (pp. 109–113). Englewood Cliffs, NJ: Prentice-Hall.

Mooney, L., & Brabant, S. (1987). Two martinis and a rested woman: "Liberation" in the Sunday comics. *Sex Roles, 17,* 409–420.

Mooney, L., & Brabant, S. (1990). The portrayal of boys and girls in six nationally-syndicated comic strips. *Sociology and Social Research, 74,* 118–126.

Mukerji, C, & Schudson, M. (Eds.). (1991). *Rethinking popular culture: Contemporary perspectives in cultural studies.* Berkeley, CA: University of California Press.

Mulkay, M. (1988). *On humor: Its nature and its place in modern society.* Oxford, England: Basil Blackwell.

Pleck, J. H. (1997). Parental involvement: Levels, sources, and consequences. In M. E. Lamb (Ed.), *The role of the father in child development* (pp. 66–103). New York: John Wiley.

Radway, J. (1984). *Reading the romance: Women, patriarchy, and popular literature.* Chapel Hill, NC: University of North Carolina Press.

Rogosa, D. (1995). Myths and methods: "Myths about longitudinal research" plus supplemental questions. In J. M. Gottman (Ed.), *The analysis of change.* Mahwah, NJ: Erlbaum.

Simonds, W (1992). *Women and self-help culture: Reading between the lines.* New Brunswick, NJ: Rutgers University Press.

Strecker, E. (1946). *Their mothers' sons: The psychiatrist examines an American problem.* Philadelphia: Lippincott.

Swidler, A. (1986). Culture in action: Symbols and strategies. *American Sociological Review, 51,* 273–286.

Ward, B. (1993, May 9). The changing face of Mother's Day. *Atlanta Journal and Constitution,* p. C3.

Wilson, C. (1979). *Jokes: Form, content, use and function.* London: Academic Press.

Wood, A. (1987). *Great cartoonists and their art.* Gretna, LA: Pelican.

Wylie, P. (1942). *Generation of vipers.* New York: Holt, Rinehart, & Winston.

Zerubavel, E. (1991). *The fine line: Making distinctions in everyday life.* New York: Free Press.

Zerubavel, E. (1997). *Social mindscapes: An invitation to cognitive sociology.* Cambridge, MA: Harvard University Press.

Section VIII

MIXED METHODS AND ADVANCED TOPICS

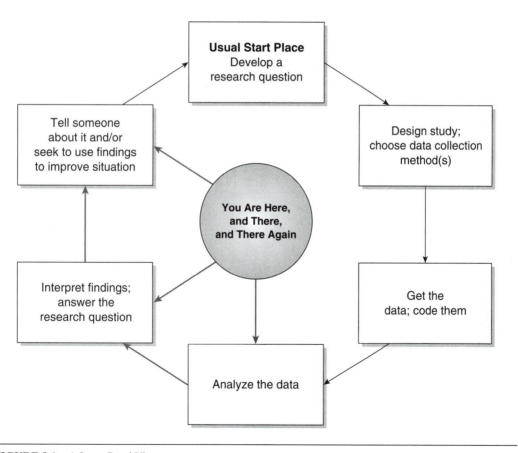

FIGURE 8.1 A Long Road View

The division between quantitative and qualitative methods is often a matter of personal conviction and theoretical preference. Most researchers are trained in both, and, as we have emphasized, tend to choose the data collection and analysis methodologies that are best suited to the research question at hand. Often this requires creative combinations of both quantitative and qualitative approaches.

In this last section, we will introduce three additional kinds of studies that deserve their own discussions and presentations. They do not fit clearly under any of our previous headings. Many researchers use the term "mixed methods" to refer to purposeful blending of qualitative and quantitative approaches to highlight the strengths and overcome the limitations inherent in each. We use **mixed methods** a bit more loosely here, addressing instead several more advanced approaches to research that tend to rely on multiple forms of data: case studies and comparative–historical research. In this section we also review evaluation research, which often, but by no means always, employs mixed research methods.

EVALUATION RESEARCH

Evaluation studies apply research methods and data analysis techniques to assess the viability and efficacy of programs, policies, and intervention strategies. Evaluation research is an *applied* research strategy, undertaken with the intention that the findings should have a direct impact on the policies and programs that are studied. Evaluation studies inform decision makers, help reduce costs, facilitate consideration of multiple strategic options, and realign implementation strategies with an agency's or institution's goals. Ultimately, data from evaluation studies should help policymakers avoid costly mistakes like those that were revealed in the aftermath of the *Challenger* disaster and Hurricane Katrina.

The popularity of evaluation research grew during the 20th century in conjunction with the expansion of social policies and federal programs following the Depression. Federal programs required a high degree of accountability to justify their growth. This required that formal evaluations had to be built into the program planning. In addition, technological innovations facilitated the collection, analysis, and dissemination of major evaluation findings and recommendations, adding to the popularity of this research technique. Demands for scientific and technological expertise after the 1950s, coupled with the inception of President Johnson's Great Society programs in the 1960s consolidated the reputation of applied research and expert knowledge within the public policy domain. Ironically, during the 1980s, evaluation studies were also instrumental in the various efforts to shrink the size of government, streamline policies, and retool entitlement and federal programs (Pumar 2009).

Social scientists' ability to observe and analyze a wide assortment of data makes these scholars ideal candidates to conduct evaluations. This is evident in our next selection, Diane Vaughan's discussion of her work on behalf of the commission investigating the *Challenger* disaster. Through ethnographic research, Professor Vaughan found that the underlying causes behind this horrific accident were what she refers to as "the dark side of organizations," creeping misunderstandings about risk amid the myriad decisions made by many departments and individuals—rather than the malfunctions attributed by engineers or the political deliberations of public officials. She also found that few of the individuals or agencies involved in studying the disaster were equipped to view NASA's actions at a sufficient level of abstraction to recognize the nature of the failures. The article we present here is not her evaluation study itself, but a conceptual "revisitation" she recently undertook in search of sociological lessons learned.

At the start of this study, Vaughan was confronted with preexisting explanations based in the structure of NASA, the culture of administration, the economics of government programs, and the assumption of individual misconduct. In order to provide a more comprehensive understanding of the events leading to the decision to launch the *Challenger* space shuttle on January 28, 1986, she drew upon the *Report of the Presidential Commission on the Space Shuttle Challenger Accident* (content analysis); the interview transcripts that went into that report, including videotapes of subsequent Congressional testimony by the same sources (interview analysis); a historical analysis of NASA's program to develop and utilize solid fuel rocket boosters (mostly content analysis); and her own organizational ethnography of the decision-making culture at the agency, including interviews with many of the key personnel. In sum, Vaughan perceived a serious limitation in the approach taken by the President's Commission. Using a combination of the best already available data and a new round of data collection, she reevaluated the evaluation report.

Social scientists are often perceived as outsiders to the policy and program development realms. In this instance, this perception could offer advantages for evaluators because, in conjunction with the status associated with their expert knowledge, it minimized any conflict of interests and bypassed the **stakeholders'** blinding subjectivity. As original Commission member Richard Feynman noted in his memoir of the study, insiders to a political process rely on outsiders to deliver bad news.

The phases of the evaluation processes parallel those of any other research, but with added emphasis on the involvement of the participants and/or sponsors to whom we are reporting. Evaluators must develop valid evaluation criteria and a baseline from which to begin to measure the effects of the project or policy being assessed. The research question itself will depend on the nature of the evaluation design.

Evaluation research consists of four different design approaches. These are: (1) **monitoring**, (2) **needs assessment**, (3) **impact assessment**, and (4) feasibility studies or **cost–benefits analysis**

(Rossi, Freeman, and Lipsey 1999). Monitoring assesses the degree to which intervention strategies fulfill the mission statement. With this strategy, evaluators develop monitoring criteria to measure the implementation of goals and then develop a mechanism to track how well the project approaches these goals. Monitoring takes place either periodically or when important milestones are scheduled. Keeping a project on schedule and on task minimizes the risk that some of the mission goals will be left unfulfilled. Needs assessment is another of the evaluation designs. With needs assessment the aim is to appraise a situation to ensure that the recommended actions address the identified problems. Needs assessment studies sometimes reveal that the problem local stakeholders were focused on is not the one that requires the most resources or attention. Thus the evaluator is often confronted with having to propose tasks and solutions that others have not envisioned.

Perhaps the most of popular of the evaluation designs is impact assessment: measuring what the program or policy has done. One reason for the attractiveness of impact studies is that this is the most visible of the evaluation designs. Whether intended or not, social science research routinely informs public debates on policy, law, and programs for social change. It is probably fair to state that the development of applied social research has more to do with impact assessment than with any other evaluation strategy.

The last evaluation approach we consider is the feasibility study or the cost–benefits analysis. This evaluation strategy attempts to estimate cost effectiveness and whether or not an initiative, regardless of its social implications, can be accomplished. This type of evaluation relies on quantitative tools, such as econometrics, and is often employed by decision makers to weigh multiple options or to endorse the feasibility of moving forward with one recommendation. Cost–benefits estimations provide the rationale supporting the decision to continue, amend, or terminate a policy or program.

BOX 8.1 WILLIAM FOOTE WHYTE (1914–2000)

Bill Whyte's major work was in the development of participant observation methods and of what is today called urban ethnography. His book *Street Corner Society* (1943) is still regarded as a touchstone in the field of urban sociology, community studies, and ethnic studies. More important, Whyte revolutionized the Chicago approach to sociology by demonstrating that, contrary to the assumptions of some in the early Chicago School, ethnic enclaves are also governed by social norms that sustain the social fabric in those communities. These findings continue to fuel multiple urban ethnographies today. His triangulation of (1) participant observation, (2) in-depth interview strategies, and (3) skillful handling of gatekeepers in the field are still regarded as pathbreaking developments for ethnographers. Whyte also conducted some of the most interesting research in workplace ethnography. Like Durkheim, Weber, and Merton, William Foote Whyte was committed to applying the methods of sociology to improve societal conditions.

CASE STUDY

Depicted as one of the most economical of the mixed method strategies, the case study focuses on a single case as the **unit of analysis**. Case studies are popular across the social sciences, but ethnographers are especially linked with them. Ethnographic case studies typically entail one or more researchers spending considerable amounts of time at a single research site, often armed with questionnaires, observation plans, and **interview schedules**. With the recent resurgence of urban and community studies, case studies, popularized by the Chicago School in the 1920s, have regained currency in the social sciences.

One of the many advantages of the case-study approach is that it offers the opportunity to triangulate multiple methods and theories, providing rich contextual explanations. There are, however, two major risks associated with case studies. First, there is a tendency among some researchers to tilt the balance of their work in favor of description, thereby sacrificing explanations and limiting generations and comparability from one case to the other. Second, researchers must be mindful to select representative cases. The same unique features that make some cases so compelling to researchers often make it that much more difficult to generalize their implications to any other settings.

Another challenge of case studies is that you cannot anticipate the number of cases necessary to support widely applicable assertions. Case-study methodologists have countered this apparent limitation by applying mixed methods, by making use of statistical techniques to discern social trends, and by using a technique called within-case comparisons. This technique compares multiple situations within a single case. A good illustration of this strategy is Peter Gouveritch's (1986) analysis of the American state responses to financial crises in the late 19th century, the 1930s, and the 1970s. Although Gouveritch examined a single case, that of political responses within a single domain and a single nation, he was able to use the variation in circumstances over time to measure its impact on the policy outcomes.

The case-study approach works best when it is employed to analyze cases that are deviant or defined by situational knowledge. The first regards circumstances that do not conform to familiar patterns of behaviors or goals. Deviant cases are unique situations, such as the contentious social whirlwind of 1968 or the *Challenger* disaster. We can use counterfactual logic to discern the forces behind these unique cases and in doing so better understand the normal state of affairs. That is, we study the question of what makes this case so different.

Situational knowledge refers to cases that are not entirely unique, but that are highly dependent on the circumstances of their environments. As Gallant and Cross (1993:241) expressed it, "The case study provides an in-depth understanding of what takes place in a closed world." Multiple case studies of comparable cases across different situations are also used to construct theories of the overall "type" that each case represents. We also use theoretical explanations derived from one case to make sense of a number of similar historical occurrences despite the visible changes in the environments.

Such logic is at work in our next reading, Pershing's study of hazing at the U.S. Naval Academy. Elite military academies are necessarily a unique set of organizations whose cultures are closed off from much of the outside world. While findings from a study of the Naval Academy can suggest questions for research at other institutions such as colleges and athletic teams, the many studies of hazing throughout the nation's colleges may not apply to the special case of a top program for military preprofessional training. This case is different because it depends so much on its particular setting.

In this study, Pershing uses a combination of quantitative surveys and qualitative interviews to explore the place and meaning of hazing at the Academy. Since hazing is both commonplace and forbidden, it seems that it must have great meaning to the midshipmen and the institution. A survey can hint at the frequency of its occurrence, though, as the author notes, there are powerful norms against even admitting that it exists. But to understand the meaning of hazing in that institution, the author also needs deep qualitative data collected from recent graduates who are still close to the Academy, and defined by their participation in it, yet not still living there.

Pershing's 40 interviews lasted about an hour each, and some were more than two hours. Clearly the author did than simply collect hazing stories. She studied the circumstances and meanings of the events. Interviews covered the nature of rules, regulations, and expectations at the Academy, as well as incidents where the rules were violated, and impressions and experiences related to reporting these violations. In other words, "the purpose of these interviews was to acquire detailed information about the social context and culture in which hazing is sustained." The interviews also drew upon the survey data to solicit respondents' attitudes toward forms of hazing that are common but that they had not experienced themselves. In this way, respondents had the opportunity to discuss their own attitudes and beliefs in the context of the institutional norms. Further, by incorporating gender differences in both the sample and the subject matter, the author was able to assess the role of informal discipline in terms of the midshipmen's ideas about the place of women at the Academy. Not surprisingly, this detailed case study found more than just behavioral trend. Respondents were able to explore and reveal inconsistent and ambivalent feelings about rituals and practices that they had willingly adopted.

MACRO COMPARATIVE HISTORICAL ANALYSIS

The macro-historical or comparative historical strategy investigates systemic spatial transformations over time. The unit of analysis for such studies is generally at the level of states or regions. In some cases, even larger units may be employed, such as the study of interactions between the most industrialized nations and less industrialized nations. Despite the elegance of this methodology and its intriguing conclusions, its general appeal has been constrained by several factors. First, students of the macro-historical approach must be well versed in history to be able to grasp how the trajectories of long processes unfold over time. This is no easy task, as the work of Wallerstein and his former collaborators at the Braudel Center for the Study of Economies, Historical Systems, and Civilization at Binghamton University testifies. Second, since the data collected in these studies are historical, and most likely not primary, there are several concerns about their validity and reliability. Third, and perhaps more important, the historical nature of this strategy limits its application to trajectories with a long past, discounting more current events that lack such historical precedence. Hence, one could not apply the macro-historical approach to study the development of neoconservatism or the results of the recent elections in the United States, for example.

One such illustration of this strategy in the social sciences is the work of Immanuel Wallerstein, as seen in our next reading. Inspired by Fernand Braudel and the French *Annales* School, Wallerstein has dedicated most of his career to the analysis of the rise and transformation of capitalism since the 16th century, and the effects of those systemic changes on the relations among nation-states and the global structural organization. Wallerstein, and others who have adopted this approach, call it a "world systems" model. As is evident in his discussion of the capitalist world economy after 1945, this research examines broad economic patterns that characterize the overall nature of the system and that determine differences in the quality of life around the globe. Since this approach is concerned with macro-historical transformations, skeptics point to all of the historical details that are overlooked and the political considerations that often unfold independently from the economic forces Wallerstein and others emphasize. World system theorists and others defend this methodological approach by emphasizing the weight of history on current events and the significance of structural effects on social action.

CONCLUSION

Mixed methods offer researchers opportunities to combine some of the methodological and analytical approaches discussed in this book. The readings included in this chapter only hint at the versatility of these combined approaches. Mixed methods encompass many different fields of study. Evaluation techniques, for instance, are popular among policy studies researchers. The world systems approach, on the other hand, is usually more academic. Triangulation is used in many fields, and is sought to improve our understanding of a problem and increase our confidence in our findings by combining differing perspectives and techniques. Mixed methods, thus, give us an opportunity to be creative and expansive in our approach to understanding, to data collection, and to analysis. Even if different methods should suggest alternative findings, that result, too, is usually valuable and remarkably suggestive of further insights. In sum, we suggest that combining methods—mixed methods—is almost always useful and increasingly appreciated by researchers and others.

DISCUSSION QUESTIONS

1. In what respects is evaluation research just like any other social research? What makes it different?

2. Much has been said about the case of "American exceptionalism" or the unique historical development of the United States. What sorts of data would you want to look at about the histories of other nations in order to evaluate this idea? What other countries would you want to include in your study? Why?

WEB RESOURCES

The following links can provide you with more detailed information on the topics discussed in this section. You may also go to www.sagepub.com/lunestudy where you will find additional resources and hot-links to these sources.

The Fernand Braudel Center: http://fbc.binghamton.edu
Journal of World System Research: http://jwsr.ucr.edu/index.php
American Evaluation Association: http://www.eval.org
Comparative Methods: http://poli.haifa.ac.il/~levi/method.html
Society for Comparative Research: http://www.yale.edu/scr

Theorizing Disaster

Analogy, Historical Ethnography, and the Challenger Accident (2004)

Diane Vaughan

When NASA's Space Shuttle Challenger disintegrated in a ball of fire 73 seconds after launch on 28 January 1986, the world learned that NASA was not the pristine citadel of scientific power it had seemed. The Presidential Commission appointed to investigate the disaster quickly uncovered the cause of the technical failure: the O-rings that seal the Solid Rocket Booster joints failed to seal, allowing hot gases at ignition to erode the O-rings, penetrate the wall of the booster, and destroy Challenger and its crew. But the Commission also discovered a NASA organization failure of surprising proportion. In a midnight-hour teleconference on the eve of the Challenger launch, NASA managers had proceeded with launch despite the objections of contractor engineers who were concerned about the effect of predicted cold temperatures on the rubber-like O-rings. Further, the investigation indicated that NASA managers had suppressed information about the teleconference controversy, violating rules about passing information to their superiors. Worse, NASA had been incurring O-ring damage on shuttle missions for years. Citing 'flawed decision making' as a contributing cause of the accident, the Commission's Report (Presidential Commission on the Space Shuttle Challenger

Accident, 1986) revealed a space agency gone wrong, forced by budget cuts to operate like a cost-efficient business. Apparently, NASA managers, experiencing extraordinary schedule pressures, knowingly took a chance, moving forward with a launch they were warned was risky, willfully violating internal rules in the process, in order to launch on time. The constellation of factors identified in the Report—production pressures, rule violations, cover-up—indicated amorally calculating managers were behind the accident. The press fueled the controversy, converting the official explanation into historically accepted conventional wisdom.

These revelations attracted my attention. Always fascinated by the dark side of organizations, in 1986 I began to investigate the political, economic, and organizational causes of the disaster. This research culminated in a book, The Challenger Launch Decision: Risky Technology, Culture, and Deviance at NASA (Vaughan, 1996). Contradicting the Report in both fact and interpretation, I concluded the accident resulted from mistake, not misconduct. In 'Revisits,' Burawoy (2003) writes about the ethnographic revisit, in which the researcher returns to the field site for another look. It could be the next day or ten years hence—or possibly

SOURCE: From "Theorizing Disaster: Analogy, Historical Ethnography, and the Challenger Accident," by Vaughan, D., in *Ethnography*, 5: 315–347. Copyright © 2004. Reprinted with permission.

another researcher visits the same site, seeking to depose the first. Exploring the variety of revisits, Burawoy identifies the archeological revisit: the ethnographic practice of digging into the past, deliberately reconstructing history in order to identify and then track the processes connecting past and present. Distanced from action by time and space, the ethnographer working in this mode relies, to a greater or lesser extent, on documentary records. My NASA research was an archeological revisit—an historical ethnography —but this article engages me in a different kind of a dig. I return not to my research site, but to my research experience to think reflexively about my interpretive practices as I theorized disaster in a revisionist account published in 1996.[1]

Theorizing is the process of explaining our data; theory is the result. In this article, I focus on theorizing, retracing how I developed the concepts and theory that accounted for this event, showing the utility of analogical comparison, mistakes, and documentary and historical evidence in my theorizing. Too often we read only the finished product of research, the theory fully formed and perfectly polished, while the cognitive manoeuvres behind that theoretical explanation remain invisible.[2] Perhaps it is because we are not trained to think about how we theorize as we arrive at certain interpretations and theoretical conclusions.[3] Perhaps it is just difficult to articulate an intuitive cognitive process that is tacit knowledge. Perhaps it is because the path to developing theory is through making mistakes and that publicly admitting our mistakes is not easy.[4] Ironically, the documentary record that made my research possible also led to my mistakes. Significantly, my mistakes were about social factors that were central to my explanation. So it is useful for the methods of ethnographers engaged with history to think reflexively about the construction of the documentary sources I used, how I read culture, structure, and history in that archival record, and the mistakes, contradictions, and differences that drove my frequently shifting explanation.

These analytic reflections have relevance for all ethnographers, however. They reveal analogical comparison to be a useful method for elaborating theory.[5] To the extent that all ethnography can be conceptualized as ethnography-as-revisit, analogical comparison and theorizing is foundational to the enterprise. Second, although certain problems I faced are distinctive because of the peculiarities of the organization and event I was studying, the social factors that were important to my analysis are found in all social settings. Following the trail of my mistakes shows how the same social factors that explain our research questions can be obstacles to our analysis. Yet we benefit from recognizing the sources of misunderstanding: mistakes are the turning points in the research process that open up cultural meaning making and symbolic understandings, driving the development of theory.

---

[1]In this article, I reproduce selected aspects of my 1996 findings in condensed form to track down how I came to them. In order to focus on the theorizing process, I use citations only when the point is specific enough to warrant doing so, rather than citing the original evidence or the relevant literature from the 1996 book to support every point.

[2]There are, of course, exceptions. See, for example, Whyte (1955) and Burawoy (1979), who, long before it was acceptable to write in first person, integrated into the text explanations of how their concrete experiences in the setting led to specific theoretical insights.

[3]Becker (1998), Mitaugh (2000), and Katz (2001) are three recent works that explore the cognitive process of theorizing. However, my point is that graduate training in theory is institutionalized; training in theorizing is not.

[4]Specifically I mean mistakes and confusions in theorizing. Ethnographers, probably more than researchers using other methods, do discuss mistakes and dilemmas while in the field and after. Perhaps the most well-known example is Whyte's description of his illegal voting (1955).

[5]See also Snow et al. (2003).

ANALOGICAL THEORIZING, MISTAKES, AND HISTORICAL ETHNOGRAPHY

In a late-night epiphany in 1981 as I reworked my dissertation on organizational misconduct for publication, I discovered that my own process of theorizing was analogical. I was revising three not-very-good, disconnected literature chapters when I saw that my case study data resonated with Merton's Anomie Theory (1968), which he developed to explain rates of individual deviance. With growing excitement I dived into Merton's writing, weighing every aspect of his scheme against the details of my case and the published research on corporate crime, ultimately reorganizing and converting my three lacklustre, stand-alone chapters into three inter-related parts of a causal theory (Vaughan, 1983: 54–104). Not only did the major components of Merton's theory fit the data on organizations, but the comparison showed differences that allowed me to critique and reconceptualize his theory, which, as it turned out, better explained the deviance of organizations than that of individuals. I realized that what I had done was switch units of analysis, taking a societal level theory designed to explain individual deviance and applying it to organizations. It worked! But why?

As a graduate student, I was strongly influenced by Simmel's argument that the role of the sociologist is to extract essential social forms from content, as he so brilliantly did in his writing, in particular with 'dyads and triads' (Wolff, 1950). Returning to Simmel, I noted that his position legitimized developing theory by comparing analogous events, activities, or incidents in different social settings! Theorizing by analogical comparison also made sense to me because forms of social organization have characteristics in common, like conflict, hierarchy, division of labor, culture, power and structured inequalities, socialization, etc., making them comparable in structure and process. I concluded that it was sociologically logical to, for example, develop a theory of organizational dissent, defined as one

person speaking out against authority, from such seemingly disparate cases as the corporate whistle-blower, the prison snitch, sexual harassment, and domestic violence (Vaughan, n.d.). Searching for precedent, I found a neglected passage in Glaser and Strauss (1967) that suggested comparing similar activities in different social settings as a way of formulating general theory. With few exceptions, however, grounded theory had evolved in practice to explain a single case, or multiple incidents within a case, the comparison being limited to the back-and-forth interplay between data and the case explanation rather than developing general theory. I had theorized from the ground up, as their model suggested, but it did not fully explain what I had done. Grounded theory tied scholarship to the local, with no directions about pursuing the structural or political/economic contexts of action. Also, Glaser and Strauss suggested that having a theory in mind invalidated the procedure. Finally, their inductive method gave no insights about the cognitive principles involved in theorizing itself.

Fascinated to discover how other people theorized, I turned to the classics, finding that analogical theorizing across cases was frequent but unacknowledged by those who used it (e.g., Blau, 1964; Coser, 1974; Goffman, 1952, 1961, 1969; Hirschman, 1970; Hughes, 1984). Stinchcombe (1978) discussed the search for analogy and difference as a method for social history, but for units of analysis belonging to the same class of objects (e.g., all nation-states). My own experience convinced me that not only was analogical case comparison useful for theorizing across different cases, but also that analogy drove our more spontaneous tacit theorizing: linking a known theory or concept to patterns in our data, deploying examples, even the simple act of citation. I was taught in graduate school to theorize by comparing all hospitals, or all nation states, or all families. I was taught that in case analysis, you start 'theory free.' I was taught that you can not generalize from a case study. I was no longer convinced. I believed that if analogical comparison, which I and other scholars were intuitively using to theorize, could be made explicit and systematic, the cognitive processes underlying it could be identified and taught.

So my experiment in analogical theorizing began. By the time of the 1986 Challenger accident, it had progressed to a book-in-progress that compared corporate crime, police misconduct, and domestic violence as a step toward developing a general theory of organizational deviance and misconduct. From experience with the three cases, I had arrived at the following working principles (for elaboration, see Vaughan, 1992). A case is chosen because an event or activity appears to have characteristics in common with other cases, but also because the social setting varies in size, complexity, and function. The individual case must be explained first, however, for it may not turn out to be an example of what we thought. Thick description produces the detail that guarantees discovering differences, thus guarding against forcing the case to fit a theory or a previous case. The cross-case comparison is done after the case analysis, but the way is paved at the outset by loosely sorting data for the new case into categories known to be associated with the comparison cases, thus drawing attention to analogies and differences as the analysis progresses.

Moreover, each case is analyzed using a combination of diverse qualitative methods known to illuminate differences as well as similarities: a) analytic induction (Robinson, 1951; Znaniecki, 1934), b) Blumer's (1969) sensitizing concept, and c) Glaser and Strauss's (1967) grounded theory, the latter amended to acknowledge that we always have some theories, models, or concepts in mind; by making them explicit we are enabled to either reject, reconceptualize, and/or work toward more generalizable explanations. Once the case analysis is complete, then we do the cross-case comparison, searching for structure and process equivalences.

But differences also matter. I had learned that selecting cases to vary the social setting (corporation, police department, family) produces different kinds of data—historical, political, economic, organizational, social psychological. Thus, the end result has a distinctive sociological scope: a general theory that situates individual interpretation, meaning, and action in relation to larger complex and layered forces that shape it (see Vaughan, 1998, 2002).

Coincidentally, when the Challenger accident occurred I was looking for a case of misconduct by a complex organization that was not a corporate profit-seeker to add to my project. The data analysis was guided by my 1983 theory, which can be summarized thus: the forces of competition and scarcity create pressures on organizations to violate laws and rules (Vaughan, 1983, Chapter 4); organization structure and processes create opportunities to violate (Chapter 5); the regulatory structure systematically fails to deter (Chapter 6), thus the three in combination encourage individuals to engage in illegality and deviance in order to attain organization goals. To draw attention to analogies and differences, I used these three causal principles as sensitizing concepts to organize the data. But the data dragged me in new directions, changing the project in its theoretical explanation, size, and method.[6] Although the case seemed at the outset to be an exemplar of organizational misconduct, I was wrong. It was mistake, not misconduct. In the process of getting from one theoretical explanation to the other, the analysis outgrew my first idea for a chapter in a book of four case comparisons, outgrew my second idea for a slender volume that would be done in a year, and finally ended as a 500-page book that I had to rush to complete by the accident's ten-year anniversary.

---

[6]Analytic induction (AI) typically is used as a tool by social psychologists analyzing social processes who treat individuals as cases (Robinson, 1951). If the case does not fit the hypothesis, either a) the hypothesis is reformulated or b) the phenomenon to be explained is re-defined, excluding the deviant case, sometimes seeking replacement cases that fit the hypothesis. Excluding deviant cases is not an option, in my view, because retention drives theory elaboration in new directions, preventing automatic verification (see also Burawoy, 1998).

Analytic induction, which forces researcher attention to evidence that does not fit the hypothesis, is nothing more nor less than learning by mistake. Repeatedly, I came across information that contradicted both my factual and theoretical assumptions, keeping me digging deeper and deeper, so the analysis was changing all the time. I was forced by confusion and contradiction from Volume 1 of the Commission's Report to Volumes 4 and 5, containing transcripts of the public hearings, and to NASA documents describing procedural requirements. A critical turning point came in the 13th month of the project. To determine whether this case was an example of misconduct or not, I had decided on the following strategy: Rule violations were essential to misconduct, as I was defining it. The rule violations identified in Volume 1 occurred not only on the eve of the launch, but on two occasions in 1985, and there were others before. I chose the three most controversial for in-depth analysis. I discovered that what I thought were rule violations were actions completely in accordance with NASA rules! This was not my last mistake, but it was perhaps the most significant because the Commission's identification of rule violations was the basis for my choice of the launch decision as an example of organizational misconduct. My hypothesis went into the trash can, and I started over.

My discovery of the Report's mistaken assertion of rule violations transformed my research. I now suspected that NASA actions that outsiders—the Commission, the press, the public, me—identified as rule violations and therefore deviant after the accident were defined as non-deviant and in fact fully conforming by NASA personnel taking those actions at the time. Immediately, the research became infinitely more complex and interesting. I had a possible alternative hypothesis—controversial decisions were not calculated deviance and wrongdoing, but normative to NASA insiders—and my first inkling about what eventually became one of the

principle concepts in explaining the case: the normalization of deviance. The Commission identified 'rule violations' related to the Solid Rocket Boosters from the beginning of the Space Shuttle Program. Were these alleged rule violations true violations? Or would investigating them reveal the gap between outsider and insider definitions of these actions, too? I realized that understanding NASA culture and the meaning of events to insiders as they made decisions would be crucial. I shifted my focus from the 1986 launch and my singular examination of rule violations and began reconstructing a chronology of all decision making about the Solid Rocket Boosters (SRBs), 1977–85.

Thus, the research became an historical ethnography: an attempt to elicit structure and culture from the documents created prior to an event in order to understand how people in another time and place made sense of things. My work was in harmony with the work of many social historians and anthropologists who examine how cultures shape ways of thinking by analyzing documents. However, my research was distinctly ethnographic in the centrality of culture and the theoretically informed sociological/ethnographic writing and interpretation of it. My purpose was to connect the past to the present in a causal explanation. I wanted to explain individual meaning making, cultural understandings, and actions on the eve of the Challenger launch in relation to a) previous SRB decisions and b) historic institutional, ideological, economic, political, and organizational forces. In contrast to some archeological revisits that focus on social change across generations,[7] my research setting was distinctly modern: a complex organization in which the technology for producing records and the process of record keeping were valued, thus creating the artifacts for its own analysis. But the research still would not have materialized were it not for the fact that the accident was a politically controversial, historical event. A Presidential

---

[7] See, for example, Haney (2002), Hondagneu-Sotelo (1994), and Kligman (1998).

Commission was convened with the power to mandate the retrieval of all documents related to the SRBs, require technicians, engineers, managers, administrators, astronauts, and contractors to testify in public hearings, and later deposit evidence at the National Archives, Washington, DC. The available data were certainly not all the evidence; however, far more were publicly available than for previous research on alleged or confirmed cases of organizational misconduct, where the usual problem is getting access to written records. More important was the unique content of the archival record, which allowed me to track the cultural construction of risk at NASA for nearly a decade, making historical ethnography possible.

My data sources were over 122,000 pages of NASA documents catalogued and available at the National Archives; Volumes 1, 2, 4, and 5 of the Report, with Volumes 4 and 5 alone containing 2500 pages of testimony transcripts from the Commission's public hearings (Presidential Commission, 1986) and the three-volume Report of the subsequent investigation by the Committee on Science and Technology, US House of Representatives, which included two volumes of hearing transcripts (US Congress. House. Committee on Science and Astronautics, 1986a, 1986b). In addition, I relied upon transcripts of 160 interviews conducted by government investigators who supported Commission activities, totaling approximately 9000 pages stored at the National Archives. These were important because separate interviews were conducted for each person on the two topics that interested me: the Challenger teleconference and the history of SRB decision making. Nearly 60 percent of those interviewed by these investigators never testified before the Presidential Commission. Video recordings of all public hearings, available at National Archives' Motion Picture and Video Library, aided my interpretation of hearing transcripts. Using the Freedom of Information Act, I obtained copies of engineering risk assessments used in NASA's pre-launch decision making for all shuttle launches. Also, I conducted interviews in person and by telephone. Primary sources were key NASA and contractor personnel involved in SRB decisions, a Presidential Commission member, and three staff investigators. After initial interviews, all remained sources whom I consulted throughout the project as needed. I also interviewed NASA safety regulators, journalists, secretaries, space historians, and technical specialists, many of them more than once. The result was numerous conversations with the same people throughout the project that makes any tally of 'number of interviews' impossible.

THEORIZING: TURTLES ALL THE WAY DOWN

Clifford Geertz tells this Indian story to draw an analogy with ethnography:

> An Englishman who, having been told that the world rested on a platform which rested on the back of an elephant which rested in turn on the back of a turtle, asked (perhaps he was an ethnographer; it is the way they behave), what did the turtle rest on? Another turtle. And that turtle? 'Ah, Sahib, after that it is turtles all the way down.' (Geertz, 1973: 28–9)

Geertz tells the story to point out that cultural analysis is necessarily incomplete, and the more deeply it goes, the less complete it is. When historical ethnography combines with a layered structural analysis that frames individual action and meaning making in a complex organization and its historic, political, economic, and institutional context, the result is sure to be, as the Indian said, 'turtles all the way down.' What matters is going beyond the obvious and dealing with the contradictions produced by going below the platform and the elephant. Here I show how going deeper into the archival record uncovered mistakes of fact and interpretation in Volume 1 of the Report, revealing NASA culture and the meaning of actions to insiders. I show the utility of mistakes in theorizing by tracing how my own mistakes revealed the Commission's mistakes and led me away from misconduct to mistake as an explanation. In keeping with the working principles of analogical theorizing, after explaining the case I discuss the theoretical results of comparing the NASA case with other cases in the conclusion.

I began the research analyzing newspaper accounts of the Presidential Commission's public hearings, but when the 250-page Volume 1 was published in June 1986, I treated it as primary data, a mistake on my part. It was far superior to press accounts, but when the other four volumes and data at the National Archives became available in September, I recognized it for what it was: a summary and the Commission's construction/interpretation of original documents, testimony, and interview data. The discursive framing and data in Volume 1 misled me on many issues. From the outset, culture was a central research question: was NASA's a risk-taking culture, where production pressures pushed schedule ahead of safety, as the Report implied? Culture was the question, but culture was also an obstacle to my analysis. Understanding events at NASA depended upon my ability to grasp NASA's technology, organization structure, bureaucratic and engineering discourse, and norms, rules, and procedures.

Immediately I had problems translating the technology and technical discourse (Figure 1). I knew nothing about engineering or shuttle technology. Volume 1 was full of illustrations and explanations for the lay reader of how the technology worked, so I began with the utmost confidence that I would be able to master the necessary technical information. I underestimated the challenge. Much of it was seat-of-the-pants learning: I studied memos and engineering documents, including the engineering charts showing SRB risk assessments for all launches. The interview transcripts at the Archives and public testimony were helpful because in them engineers and managers carefully and patiently tried to explain to confused government investigators and Commission members how the technology worked and why they decided as they did. Also, a NASA engineer, Leon Ray, and a contractor engineer, Roger Boisjoly (both with long experience working on the O-rings and key players in the post-accident controversies), helped me over the hard spots in telephone conversations over the years.

Uncovering cultural meanings also required translating NASA's bureaucratic discourse, a mind-numbing morass of acronyms and formalisms, designed for social control of both technological risk and people. By the documents reproduced in Volume 1 and the Commission's interpretation, the Report portrayed a culture of intentional risk-taking. But was it? Commission member Richard J. Feynman expressed astonishment at finding the words 'acceptable risk' and 'acceptable erosion' in pre-launch engineering charts for the SRBs. Feynman stated that NASA officials were playing 'Russian roulette': going forward with each launch despite O-ring erosion because they got away with it the last time (Presidential Commission, 1986, Appendix F: 1–5). However, I noticed that the Commission had examined engineering charts for the SRBs only; I found the words 'acceptable risk' and 'acceptable anomalies' appearing in charts for other shuttle components throughout the program! At the National Archives, I stumbled across a document that explained this bizarre pattern. Written before the first shuttle launch, it was titled 'The Acceptable Risk Process' (Hammack and Raines, 1981). In it, NASA acknowledged that the shuttle technology, because of its experimental character, was inherently risky. Even after they had done everything possible to assure safety of all technical components before a launch, some residual risks would remain. Prior to a launch, the document continued, engineers had to determine whether or not those residual risks were acceptable—thus the language of 'acceptable risk' appeared in all engineering risk assessment documents. Part of the bureaucratic routine and discourse, 'The Acceptable Risk

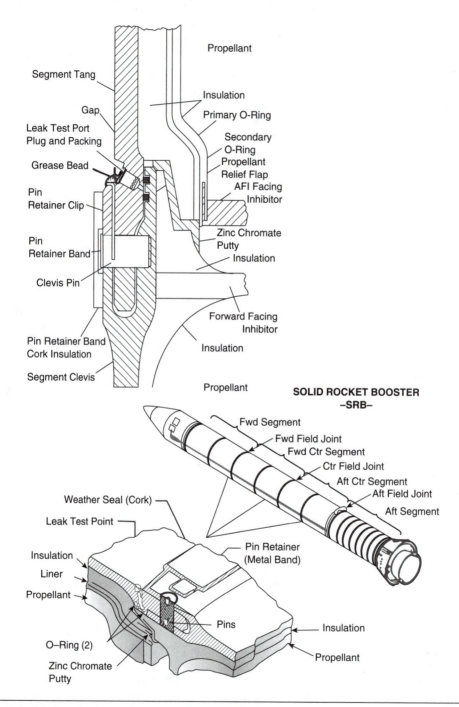

FIGURE 1 My Introduction to the Solid Rocket Booster Joint, Presidential Commission on the Space Shuttle Challenger Accident, Report, 1986, Volume 1: 57.

Process' and the words 'acceptable risk' on all documents indicated that engineering safety procedures had been followed, not violated, as Feynmann thought. For insiders, flying with known flaws was routine and taken-for-granted activity that conformed to NASA rules, not wrongdoing.

NASA's institutionalized rules and procedures were part of the culture and thus critical to my interpretation of it. At the National Archives, a video of the Commission's public hearings brought life and meaning to the hearing transcripts. One example will suffice. In 1985, after extensive O-ring damage during a mission, NASA managers imposed a 'Launch Constraint' on the SRBs. A Launch Constraint is an official status at NASA assigned in response to a flight safety issue that is serious enough to justify a decision not to launch. But NASA's Solid Rocket Booster Project Manager waived the launch constraint prior to each of the shuttle flights remaining in the year before Challenger, without fixing the O-ring problem. The video showed Commission members angered by what they concluded was a violation of the Launch Constraint rule. Repeatedly, Commission members used the word 'waive' as a verb— 'Why would you waive a Launch Constraint?'— their use of it indicating that they were equating 'waive' with 'ignore,' or, more colloquially, 'blow it off.' However, digging deeper, I again found NASA rules and procedures that contradicted the Commission's interpretation. I learned that 'waiver' is a noun at NASA. A Launch Constraint is a procedure to assure that some items get an extra review prior to a launch, not to halt flight, as the Commission believed. A waiver is a formalized procedure that, upon completion of the extra review and based on extensive engineering risk assessment, allows an exception to some rule. Waivers are documents, signed and recorded, indicating rules have been followed, not a surreptitious inattention to rules as the Commission concluded.

These discoveries strengthened my conviction that actions that appeared deviant to outsiders after the accident were normal and acceptable in NASA culture. One contradiction between Volume 1 and the archival record sent me in a direction that solidified the normalization of deviance as a concept. In the Report's discursive frame, managers were portrayed as the bad guys, production-oriented and ignoring dangers in order to meet the schedule. Engineers were the good guys, safety-oriented and insisting all along that the design was flawed and needed to be fixed. Reinforcing that dichotomy, Volume 1 reproduced memos and excerpts of memos from worried engineers warning managers about the booster problems long before the Challenger launch. As early as 1977, Volume 1 reported, NASA technician Leon Ray wrote a memo stating that the booster design was 'unacceptable.' And in a 1985 memo, contractor engineer Roger Boisjoly warned of impending 'catastrophe' if the design problems were not fixed. The Commission concluded that NASA managers were so dedicated to meeting the schedule that in the history of decision making, as on the eve of the launch, they had ignored the concerns of their engineers.

Another misrepresentation of the archival record on the Commission's part! When I found Ray's memo, it did not say that the booster design was unacceptable. Instead, Ray wrote that 'no change' in the design was 'unacceptable.' Then he listed a number of design options that would make it acceptable (Figure 2). Moreover, it turned out that Ray later became part of a team that implemented those same design options. Like Ray's memo, Boisjoly's warning of 'catastrophe' held a different meaning in NASA's culture. The word 'catastrophe' was a formalism, stripped of emotional meaning by its function in a bureaucratic tracking system for ranking failure effects by seriousness. 'Catastrophe' was an official category of risk and loss, one of several in a gradient of failure effects that were assigned for each of the shuttle's 60,000 component parts and recorded. Over 700 shuttle parts were assigned the same category as the SRBs. Boisjoly was simply stating the known failure consequences of an item in that category.

To NASA managers and engineers, the memo was not the strong warning it appeared to be to the Commission. The words risk and catastrophe were neutralized by repeated bureaucratic use that had routine, taken-for-granted understandings. Testimony and interview transcripts showed that when managers and engineers wanted to convey concerns about risk to each other, they resorted to euphemism: if we do x, we will have 'a long day,' or 'a bad day.'

Contradicting the Commission's portrayal of a continuing struggle between managers and engineers, prior to the teleconference Ray and Boisjoly both agreed that the SRBs were an

ORGANIZATION:	MARSHALL SPACE FLIGHT CENTER	NAME: LEON RAY
EP25	SRM CLEVIS JOINT LEAKAGE STUDY	DATE: OCTOBER 21, 1977

DESIGN OPTIONS	
OPTIONS	REMARKS
1. NO CHANGE	○ UNACCEPTABLE -TANG CAN MOVE OUTBOARD AND CAUSE EXCESSIVE JOINT CLEARANCE RESULTING IN SEAL LEAKAGE. ○ ECCENTRIC TANG/CLEVIS INTERFACE CAN CAUSE O-RING EXTRUSION WHEN CASE IS PRESSURIZED.
2. SHIMS BETWEEN TANG AND CLEVIS (OUTSIDE)	○ <u>ACCEPTABLE SHORT-TERM FIX IF PROPER SHIM SIZE IS USED.</u> ○ PROBABILITY OF ERROR IN CALCULATING PROPER SHIM SIZE. ○ REQUIRES INCREASED ASSEMBLY TIME FOR SHIM INSTALLATION AND JOINT CENTERING.
3. OVERSIZED O-RINGS	○ UNACCEPTABLE SOLUTION – HIGH PROBABILITY OF O-RING DAMAGE OR CLEVIS DISTORTION DURING ASSEMBLY. ○ DEPARTS FROM RECOMMENDED DESIGN PRACTICES.
4. REDESIGN TANG AND REDUCE TOLERANCE ON CLEVIS	○ BEST OPTION FOR LONG-TERM FIX - ELIMINATES USE OF SHIMS WHEN ALL REDESIGNED HARDWARE IS USED. ○ PREVENTS THE TYPE OF ERROR WHICH COULD RESULT IN CALCULATING JOINT CLEARANCE FOR SHIM INSTALLATION.
5. COMBINATION OF REDESIGN (AS IN OPTION 4) AND USE OF SHINS	○ ACCEPTABLE APPROACH. SHIMS WILL BE REQUIRED IN SOME CASES WHEN REDESIGNED HARDWARE AND PRESENT HARDWARE IS JOINTED. ○ SHIMS WILL BE DISCONTINUED WHEN PRESENT HARDWARE IS PHASED OUT.

FIGURE 2   NASA technician Leon Ray's 1977 Memo. Report, 'SRM Clevis Joint Leakage Study,' NASA, 21 October 1977, PC 102337, National Archives, Washington, DC.

acceptable risk. Further confirmation was forthcoming. Reconstructing the decision history, I discovered a five-step decision sequence in which technical deviations—anomalies found in the booster joint O-rings after a mission—first were identified as signals of potential danger, then, after engineering analysis, were redefined as an 'acceptable risk.' This decision sequence repeated, launch after launch. Here, full blown, was the evidence showing how O-ring erosion repeatedly was normalized! The first decision to accept risk established a quantitative engineering standard that, when followed by a successful mission, became a precedent for future decisions to fly with recurring anomalies. No one was playing 'Russian roulette'; engineering analysis of damage and success of subsequent missions convinced them that it was safe to fly. The repeating patterns were an indicator of culture—in this instance, the production of a cultural belief in risk acceptability. Thus, the 'production of culture' became my primary causal concept at the micro-level, explaining how they gradually accepted more and more erosion, making what I called 'an incremental descent into poor judgment.' The question now was *why*.

The surprise was that managers and engineers arrived at these decisions together and agreed. The engineering charts and risk assessments that were the basis for this pattern were created by the same engineers who opposed the Challenger launch. Because of the well-documented economic strain and schedule pressures at the agency, the Commission's finding of disagreement between managers and engineers in the years before Challenger made sense to me. After all, managers and engineers had different social locations in the organization and were thus subject to and responsible for different organization goals, managers for cost and schedule, engineers for safety. Were engineers bullied into agreement? Were they, too, susceptible to deadline and schedule pressures, in contradiction to the appearance of being defenders of the true and the good, as Volume 1 indicated? In an interview, a NASA manager told me, 'We are all engineers by training, so by training we think alike and our thought processes are alike.' I had been thinking much too locally about the effects of position in a structure. Although differently located in the NASA organization hierarchy, managers and engineers were similarly located in the engineering profession.

From the research on the engineering profession and how those characteristics were made visible in my data, an explanation of the similar viewpoints took shape. Engineers typically work in technical production systems that are organized by the principles of capitalism and bureaucratic hierarchy. Perucci (1970) explains that engineers are trained in the application of technology in production by technical schools and university programs underwritten by corporations and government projects that effectively monopolize technical intelligence. 'Servants of power,' they develop a cultural belief system that caters to dominant industrial and government interests. The engineering worldview includes a preoccupation with 1) costs and efficiency, 2) conformity to rules and acceptance of hierarchical authority, and 3) production goals.

Specialization limits professional mobility, so identity and loyalty are tied to the employer. Engineers adopt the belief systems of the organizations that employ them, a transition for which their training prepares them.[8] Engineers expect a workplace dominated by production pressure, cost cutting, and limited resources. Conflict between cost and safety is an ongoing struggle (Zussman, 1985). Decision making is a

---

[8]Bensman and Lilienfeld (1991), in *Craft and Consciousness: Occupational Technique and the Development of World Images*, examine professional training, noting the systematic production of particular worldviews associated with various crafts. 9 Emerson (1983) describes the importance of 'holistic effects' in decision making, noting how a single decision is shaped by its position in a decision stream.

story of compromise: 'satisficing,' not maximizing, is the norm (Simon, 1957). NASA was not a corporate profit-seeker, but as part of a capitalistic system was subject to competitive pressures for space supremacy internationally and nationally that required NASA compete for a chunk of the federal budget. Further, at the inception of the Space Shuttle Program, historic political and budgetary decisions by powerful actors in the White House and Congress slashed NASA budgets and made efficiency the measure of success. To assure continued funding, NASA leaders accelerated the launch schedule and minded costs, thus altering the agency's pure science culture to operate more like a bureaucratic production system—the kind that engineers normally inhabit.

The fit between my data and the ideology of professional engineering showed the connection between the political/economic forces in NASA's institutional environment, the organization, and decisions about the boosters. Analogical theorizing is not restricted to tacking back and forth between cases of similar events in social settings that vary in size, complexity, and function. We import theories and concepts of other scholars as a project progresses either because they are analogical with our data or show a contradiction, in either instance illuminating our analysis. The new institutionalism describes how non-local environments, such as industries and professions, penetrate organizations, creating a frame of reference, or worldview, that individuals bring to decision making and action (Powell and DiMaggio, 1991). The theory has been criticized for its absence of agency, and so its authors proposed Bourdieu's habitus as a possible connective piece to explain action at the local level (Powell and Dillaggio, 1991: 15–27; Bourdieu, 1977; Jepperson, 1991). Once a student asked me, 'How do I know habitus when I see it?' We see it operating in what people say and do. First, the history of decision making itself was evidence: it was one of compromise between safety, cost, and schedule, in which launches continued while the scarce resources of

a budget-constrained agency went to 'more serious' problems and the implementation of a permanent fix for the O-rings was repeatedly delayed. The consensus of managers and engineers about 'acceptable risk' showed the conjunction of the cultural beliefs of professional engineering, the organization culture, and practical action. Second, evidence supporting this theoretical connection was in the verbatim testimony and interviews, which showed NASA managers and engineers expressing the worldview of professional engineering, impressed upon them during their training and reinforced in the workplace. The following examples illustrate, respectively, conformity to bureaucratic ruling relations, satisficing, rules and protocols, cost and efficiency, and production goals:

> And if I look back on it now what I should have done is I should have done everything within my power to get it stopped . . . but, you know, really I'm not of that grade structure or anything. (Engineer, interview transcript, National Archives, 9 March 1986: 28–9)

> Engineering-wise, it was not the best design, we thought, but still no one was standing up saying, 'Hey, we got a totally unsafe vehicle.' With cost and schedule, you've got to have obviously a strong reason to go in and redesign something, because like everything else, it costs dollars and schedule. You have to be able to show you've got a technical issue that is unsafe to fly. And that really just was not on the table that I recall by any of the parties, either at Marshall or Thiokol [the contractor]. (Chief Engineer, Solid Rocket Booster Project, personal interview, Marshall Space Flight Center, Huntsville, Alabama, 8 June 1992)

> The problem was the increasing launch rate. We were just getting buried under all this stuff. We had trouble keeping the paperwork straight, and were accelerating things and working overtime to get things done that were required to be done in order to fly the next flight. . . . The system was about to come down under its own weight just because of the necessity of having to do all these procedural things in an ever accelerating fashion. (Manager, Solid Rocket Booster Project, Marshall Space Flight Center, telephone interview, 5 August 1992)

I was spending far more time each day dealing with parachute problems. This was a serious problem because it had economic consequences. If the parachutes didn't hold, the SRBs were not recoverable and this was expensive. They sank to the bottom of the sea. On the joints, we were just eroding O-rings. That didn't have serious economic consequences. (Manager, Solid Rocket Booster Project, Marshall Space Flight Center, personal interview, Huntsville, Alabama, 8 June 1992)

No one has to tell you that schedule is important when you see people working evenings and weekends round the clock. (Engineer, interview transcript, National Archives, 14 March 1986: 37)

Similarly located in the engineering profession, managers and engineers shared categories of understanding that were reproduced in NASA's organization culture, affecting the definition of the situation for managers and engineers, driving launches forward. I called these macro-political/economic forces the 'culture of production.' Within the culture of production, cost/schedule/safety compromises were normal and non-deviant for managers and engineers alike. More and more, the explanation of NASA's history of booster decision making was shaping up to be one of conformity, not deviance or misconduct.

Now I had two concepts. The production of culture explained how managers and engineers gradually expanded the bounds of acceptable risk, continuing to fly with known flaws; the culture of production explained why. But a piece of the puzzle was still missing. The O-ring problems had gone on for years. Why had no one recognized what was happening and intervened, halting NASA's transition into disaster? Neither NASA's several safety organizations nor the four-tiered Flight Readiness Review, a formal, adversarial, open-to-all process designed to vet all engineering risk assessments prior to launch, called a halt to flying with O-ring damage.

Although the Commission indicated that NASA middle managers had suppressed information, I concluded that structural secrecy, not individual secrecy, was the problem. Everyone knew about the recurring O-ring damage: the question was, how did they define risk? Aspects of structure affected not only the flow of information, a chronic problem in all organizations, but also how that information was interpreted. The result undermined social control attempts to ferret out flaws and risks, in effect keeping the seriousness of the O-ring problem secret.

Patterns of information obscured problem seriousness. In retrospect, outsiders saw O-ring damage as a strong signal of danger that was ignored, but for insiders each incident was part of an ongoing stream of decisions that affected its interpretation.[9] As the problem unfolded, engineers and managers saw signals that were mixed (a launch had damage, engineers implemented a fix, then several launches with no damage signaled that all was well); weak (e.g., damage resulted from a contingency unlikely to recur); and when damage became frequent, signals became taken-for-granted and routine, the repetition diminishing their importance. Organization structure created missing signals, preventing intervention. Safety oversight was undermined by information dependence. In Flight Readiness Review, thick packages of engineering charts assessing risk and daylong arguments at the lowest tier gradually were reduced to two pages and ten minutes by the time they arrived at the top review. By then, the risk assessment was condensed, contradictory data and ambiguity gone. Instead of reversing the pattern of flying with O-ring erosion, Flight Readiness Review ratified it. The structure of safety regulation also resulted in missing signals. External safety regulators had the advantage of independence, but were handicapped by inspection at infrequent

---

[9]All Flight Readiness Review documents were signed by participants at each level of the four-tiered process. Letters, memos, technical reports also identified people and their participation. The amount of paper and bureaucracy involved in all this internal tracking also conveyed an important message about the culture.

intervals. Unless NASA engineers defined something as a serious problem, it was not brought to regulators' attention. As a result of structural secrecy, the cultural belief that it was safe to fly prevailed throughout the agency in the years prior to the Challenger launch.

THE CONVENTIONAL WISDOM AND A REVISIONIST ACCOUNT

I had the third concept explaining the normalization of deviance: the production of culture, the culture of production, and structural secrecy. No one factor alone was sufficient, but in combination the three comprised a theory explaining NASA's history of flying with known flaws. The behavior—the normalization of technical deviation on the SRBs—led to a new concept, the normalization of deviance, that explained what had happened as a socially organized phenomenon. This was progress. However, I worried about the surprising number of discrepancies between Volume 1 of the Commission's Report and the archival record. As I learned culture, I was revising history. My book was going to contradict everything in print—including the Report of a Presidential Commission. Careful documentation was essential. I also needed to explain the discrepancies between my account and these others to substantiate my developing argument to myself, first, but also eventually I had to convince readers: what accounted for the Commission's construction of documentary reality? Despite press concerns about cover-up when President Reagan named former Attorney General William Rogers as head, the other Commission members came from diverse backgrounds. Watching videos of the public hearings at the Archives convinced me that the Commission was trying hard to get to the bottom of things. The hearings began in a spirit of peaceful collaboration with NASA, but became harshly adversarial in tone and line of questioning after the Commission learned of the fateful teleconference, about which NASA

had not informed them. Throughout the remainder of the hearings, several Commission members displayed emotion ranging from incredulity, disgust, and shock, to outrage, which could not have been feigned.

Turning to investigate the organization of the official investigation, I found that the Commission had made mistakes that, analogous to NASA, originated in structural secrecy and production pressure. Time constraints and the resulting division of labor created information dependence. The President mandated that the Commission complete its investigation in three months. They elected to conduct public hearings in which they interviewed witnesses, but to expedite the investigation they also recruited experienced government investigators to help them. These investigators conducted 160 interviews that averaged 40–60 pages each when transcribed. The archival database of supporting documents was huge, because the Commission asked NASA for every document related to the SRBs from the beginning of the Space Shuttle Program. From the interview transcripts and collection of documents, these investigators briefed the Commission on what topics were important to pursue and recommended witnesses to be called. In the briefing process, information was condensed, lost, and removed from its context.

A second source of mistakes was hindsight, which biased the sample of evidence the Commission considered and therefore their findings. Knowing of some harmful outcome, the tendency is to focus in retrospect on all the bad decisions that led to it (Starbuck and Milliken, 1988). The government investigators thus suggested calling witnesses who could explain the flawed decisions about the SRBs. Hindsight distorted their selection process: of the 15 working engineers who participated in the eve of launch teleconference, only the seven who opposed the launch were called to testify; those engineers in favor of launching were not. This obscured the complexity of making decisions about the shuttle's experimental technology at the same time it reinforced the evil managers/ good engineers picture of the debate that night. Hindsight bias also explains two incidents mentioned earlier: pulling only flight readiness engineering charts for the boosters, not charts for other shuttle parts that would have showed that 'acceptable risk' was on all NASA engineering risk assessments; and taking Leon Ray's memo out of its context in the historical trajectory of decisions, obscuring Ray's later participation on a team that corrected the design problems his early memo identified. All data were available to the Commission by computer. However, time limits restricted their ability to do a thorough reading of the archival record. Instead, Commission members typed in key words or names, a strategy that also severed information and actions from its social, cultural, and historic setting.

The Commission's construction of documentary reality had directly affected mine. The organization of the investigation and hindsight had prevented the Commission from grasping NASA culture. I had duplicated the Commission's errors in my starting hypothesis. Working alone, I could never have amassed the amount of data the Commission did, but tenure gave me a resource they did not have: the gift of time to reconstruct the history of decision making chronologically, putting actions, meanings, and events back into social, historical, and cultural context, revising history, leading me to different conclusions. However, it was now 1992. I had not even begun to analyze the launch decision that initially drew me to this research. I had not predicted my difficulty in learning culture, the many contradictions challenging my main contentions, the constantly shifting terrain of my explanation, or the length of time the analysis was taking. I worked with an uncertainty unknown to me. I was an ethnographer, not an historian, yet I spent years with archival data, constructing a history, but not a normal history, a socio-cultural technical history. The research became a causal analysis, not of a single decision resulting in a cataclysmic event, as I had originally imagined,

but of a gradual transition into disaster that extended nearly a decade (1977–86). I had analyzed the longitudinal process of a gradual transition out of intimate relationships by identifying turning points (Vaughan, 1986), but little else in my background prepared me for this. The combination of technology, complex organization, and historical ethnography had me inventing method as I went along.

In addition to the Report volumes of hearing testimony, I had a five-drawer file filled with photocopies of official interview transcripts, engineering charts of risk assessments for Flight Readiness Reviews, and other documents from the National Archives. How to deal with such an unwieldy documentary mass? Studying transitions out of relationships, I had coded interviews, marking key constructs and turning points in the margins, identifying patterns with a system using 4 X 6 index cards. I could remember who said what, remember the context, and the index cards enabled me to track the patterns. I began coding the Challenger interview transcripts, but after a month I realized that if I followed my old method the coding alone would take a year or more. Worse, so much information was there that I couldn't devise a short-cut tracking system that functioned as the index cards had (this was before computerized analytic tools for qualitative research). More important, my previous strategy was ill-suited for this project. Aggregating statements from all interviews by topic (a practice I had often used to identify patterns) would extract parts of each interview from its whole. But memory, which previously had preserved context if not in entirety at least sufficiently to guide me to the appropriate interview transcript, would not suffice with 9000 pages of transcripts. Each person was giving a chronological account of 1) the history of decision making, and 2) the eve of the launch. Keeping the decision stream of actions and interpretations whole was essential to see how people defined risk and why they decided as they did, incident to incident.

So I proceeded chronologically, analyzing launch decisions and other controversial decisions—the turning points—one by one. I examined documents to identify the people who participated in a decision or event and others who knew about it.[10] I compared their testimony and interview transcripts with documents showing what they did at the time, writing from all relevant transcripts and documents for each decision, integrating them to show all actions and perspectives. Because I wanted to know how interpretations varied depending on a person's position in the structure and their specialization, this strategy was complicated by NASA's matrix system, which increased the number of people and points of view.[11] Putting together all these pieces was interesting because the reconstruction of each turning point was shattering the construction of facts in Volume 1 at the same time it was revealing the production and reproduction of the cultural definition of 'acceptable risk' inside NASA. The process was like solving many small puzzles, each one a piece of a larger one. However, the larger one was distant. Analyzing the decision history was essential to making my case, but tedious and time consuming, requiring analysis of many pages of engineering charts of risk assessments for each launch—not exactly a 'good read.' Not only was the process uncertain, it seemed endless. I wondered when I would finish.

Analysis, writing, and theorizing are not separate processes, as we are taught. Some discovery—another technical mistake, a misunderstood procedure, an unforeseen contingency, action, or actor—would require correcting an interpretation in a previous chapter. Jettisoning outline after outline, I began writing the decision history but found myself constantly rewriting. What I intended as one chapter showing how managers and engineers normalized technical anomalies in the years prior to Challenger had, by 1992, grown into three chapters. Because observation of actions and culture prior to the accident were impossible, interviews were critically important. My interviewing was driven by the historical chronology, so ebbed and flowed throughout the project. The interviewees, subject matter, and timing were dictated by the gradually unfolding picture and the questions that arose.[12] I deferred interviews with the five key NASA managers until 1992. The Commission's interpretation of these managers' actions was the core of the conventional wisdom. When I began the research in 1986, however, I believed that interviews would not produce anything different than what was already on the public record. Only if I asked them different questions, based on a thorough understanding of the organization, its technology, and the archival evidence, would it benefit me to talk to them. By 1992, when the decision chronology was in

---

[10]A matrix organization is one designed on principles of flexibility across formal organizational boundaries. Specialists from other parts of NASA were 'matrixed in' to join those permanently assigned to work on a shuttle part when problems or controversies arose that required additional expertise. This strategy is often used by organizations to manage large complex technical projects (see Davis et al., 1978).

[11]For example, in 1988, I did telephone interviews with 18 people responsible for safety regulation who had official oversight responsibilities at NASA headquarters, at several space centers, on external safety panels, and Congressional committees because I needed to know the scope of safety regulation at the time. Whenever I had questions about the Presidential Commission's investigation, I contacted a Presidential Commission member, who had agreed to be an anonymous informant, or one of the Commission's investigative staff; when I was reconstructing decisions that required evaluating testimony about wind and temperature conditions at the Florida launch site, I contacted the National Climatic Data Center in Maryland and the National Weather Service in Titusville, Florida to secure temperature records for Cape Canaveral. As mentioned earlier, I consulted Roger Boisjoly and Leon Ray regularly on technical issues, but I also consulted them about procedural, cultural, organizational, and social, economic, and political influences on decision making.

[12]I thank Rachel Sherman for this observation.

decent shape, I felt I could ask informed questions that went beyond what the Commission had asked. The initial interviews, in person and four to eight hours in length, captured both their NASA and Commission experiences in-depth, clarified technical and organizational procedures, tested my interpretation of culture and theoretical explanation, and raised new issues. I did telephone interviews with these managers as needed for the rest of the project.

Even the book's architecture was an experiment. As my analysis began to look more like conformity than deviance, more like mistake than misconduct, I realized my construction of documentary reality would have to contend with the one created by the Commission's Volume 1. How to present my revisionist account? Through trial and error, I settled on a writing strategy that was analogical to my own theorizing process. The first chapter would be persuasive support for the Commission's amorally calculating manager, rational-choice explanation. The chapter would begin with a 5–10-page reconstruction of the eve of the launch teleconference that matched the Commission's historically accepted explanation, followed by the extensive post-accident evidence in the press and Volume 1 establishing NASA's political and economic constraints and the pressures to get the Challenger launch off on time. Chapter 2 would be a first-person account in which I dissuaded the reader of the straw argument in Chapter 1. I would walk the reader from my first hypothesis through all my mistakes and the evidence I found that contradicted the conventional wisdom, then lay out the argument of the book. The next chapters would map the interrelated parts of the causal theory. Chapters 3, 4, and 5 on the history of decision making—'The Production of Culture'—would show how NASA defined and redefined risk, normalizing technical deviations. Chapter 6, 'The Culture of Production,' would show the macro-level forces explaining why this normalization continued unabated despite the accumulation of incidents. Then Chapter 7, 'Structural Secrecy,' would explain why no one

had intervened to alter the definition of the situation.

The last chapter would be 'The Eve of the Launch Revisited.' The book's structure set the launch decision itself in historical context as one decision in a chain of decisions defining O-ring erosion as an acceptable risk. In bold font, I would reproduce verbatim the historically accepted conventional wisdom presented in Chapter 1, but divide it into short segments at critical turning points in decision making. Following each bold font segment, in regular font I would reconstruct that same chunk of time in thick description, using the testimony and interview transcripts of all participants, thereby restoring actions to their full context and complexity. The two constructions of documentary reality, the Commission's and mine, side by side, would be read by many readers who, I assumed, would have begun the book believing as the Commission's Volume 1 and press coverage led me to believe initially: production pressures and managerial wrongdoing. By this last chapter, however, readers would have been led to a different position than they held at the beginning of the book. Writing is teaching. As they read, they would have learned NASA technology, structure, and culture—rules, procedures, allegiance to hierarchy and authority relations, cost/efficiency/safety conflicts, and ideology of professional engineering. They would be acculturated. They would, as much as possible for an outsider, know the native view, or at least my interpretation of it. They would understand this reconstruction. When the moment of the Challenger launch arrived in my chronology, readers would know why the launch decision was made, requiring no further interpretation from me. The End.

But even when I thought I was at the end, I was not. I worked on the last chapter, reconstructing this event in a chronological play-by-play of the launch decision from interview transcripts of all 34 participants. I was excited and fascinated by the complexity of my reconstruction and the contrast with the bold font of the Commission's version. In contrast to the arduous writing of technical detail in the three decision-making chapters, I loved re-creating this pivotal social scene: where to make the breaks in the stereotyped version; how to write a chronology that showed people on a teleconference in three separate geographic locations where actions were happening simultaneously; incorporating the people omitted from the Volume 1 account who by their presence or absence that night played an important role. I realized that this was the first time I had ever assembled all the data about the eve of the launch teleconference! The act of writing produced still more theorizing. In the second epiphany of my career, when the event was reconstructed I saw how the same factors that explained the normalization of deviance in the history of decision making explained the decision making on the eve of the launch! The production of culture, the culture of production, and structural secrecy worked together, as before, normalizing yet another anomaly—unprecedented cold temperature—and systematically producing a decision to proceed with the launch. I expected that the chapter would show the decision to be a mistake, but I had not imagined the form of the mistake nor that the social causes of previous decisions would be so perfectly reproduced in that fatal decision. It was conformity, not deviance, that caused the disaster. I added Chapter 9, 'Conformity and Tragedy,' explaining the fateful teleconference described in Chapter 8 by showing how the patterns of the past were reproduced in that single event. Although the discussion that night was heated and adversarial, the outcome was a cooperative endeavor: all participants conformed to the dictates of the culture of production, thus expanding the bounds of acceptable risk one final time.

Theorizing and Theory: History, Analogy, and Revisits

This revisit has been a doubling back in time to reconsider my process of theorizing disaster and the utility of analogical comparison, mistakes, and

documentary evidence in that process. I turn now to what these analytic reflections mean for theorizing, theory, and ethnography. Ethnographers who engage with history have a unique translation problem, in that they theorize culture, structure, and history from documents created by others. When ethnography reaches into history, the completeness or incompleteness of the documentary record affects theorizing. Scarcity and abundance present different challenges. My research was surely unique, both in the volume of original documents available and the fact that they were conveniently located in one place. Although many organizations were involved in this event—three NASA space centers, two contractors, regulatory agencies, the Commission—for documents I only had to travel to the National Archives, where the Commission stashed them, or use the Freedom of Information Act. My problem was abundance, not scarcity. In both circumstances, however, ethnographers must consider what went unrecorded, what documents are missing, and what the effect of this historic sifting and sorting is upon the record available to us. The construction of the surviving documentary record also must always be questioned. Many of the mistakes I made in this research were a consequence of the Commission's framing discourse and data that comprised Volume 1 of the Report. Time constraints, the division of labor, and hindsight biased the Commission's sample of evidence; ethnographers reconstructing history must be wary of how these same factors bias their own selection process.

The mistakes I made in this research were not only due to the construction of Volume 1, but also because of my difficulty as an outsider interpreting NASA culture from the documentary record. My mistakes could be explained because NASA was unique—a completely foreign culture to me, and unlike ethnographers who do their research in distant countries, I could not prepare by learning the language or something about the culture in advance because the accident was unexpected. On the other hand, in a practical sense the difficulties I had were hardly exceptional. They originated in factors common to all socially organized settings. Analyzing my mistakes, I realized that the aspects of NASA culture that caused me to stumble were the same factors that explained NASA decisions. The value of mistakes is in recognizing the social source of them. The experience of making mistakes is the experience of being behind; the result, however, is that they drive the explanation ahead.

Some mistakes in theorizing are recognizable prior to publication, when we make what Burawoy (2003) calls the 'valedictory revisit:' with some trepidation, we give the completed draft to the cultural insiders as a means of correcting our interpretation. This strategy can be counted on to produce new data in the form of criticism, validation, and visceral emotional reaction. I mailed the manuscript to my NASA and contractor interviewees, following up on the phone. Uniformly, they were surprised, some even shocked, by Chapter 8, 'The Eve of the Launch Revisited'. In three geographic locations for the teleconference, participants' understandings of what happened that night were blocked by structural secrecy that was never remedied. Neither NASA nor the corporate contractor ever got all teleconference participants together after the accident to collectively discuss and analyze the sequence of events during the crisis. Until they read my reconstruction, they only knew what was happening at their location and what others said on the teleconference line. Reading my draft renewed their experience of grief, loss, responsibility, and the wish that they had acted differently. I was surprised that their criticisms were primarily minor and factual. No one contested my interpretation or conclusions, instead saying that I had helped them understand what happened, what they did, and why they did it. The single objection came from Roger Boisjoly, who said, 'You make us sound like puppets.' As the contractor engineer who most vigorously objected to the Challenger launch, he was angry. He felt stripped of his capacity to act by my culturally, politically, and historically deterministic explanation.

Some mistakes in theorizing may only be realized years later, on reflexive revisits such as this one. A reviewer for this journal asked if all mistakes were corrected, did no mistakes go unnoticed, were there no flaws in the book? At the time of publication, I felt the book's length, detailed technical information, and theoretical complexity, though necessary, were failings. Would anyone really read a 500-page academic book? Because the book was published on the 10th anniversary of the 1986 disaster, however, it received an extraordinary amount of press attention. The wide readership and positive reception were completely unexpected. NASA engineers, former and current, wrote validating my interpretation, but I heard nothing from NASA officials, a likely result, a space historian told me, of the agency's perennial barrage of criticism, resulting bunker mentality, and unwillingness to take advice from outsiders. Perhaps, but length and complexity also may have been an impediment. More than this, however, the reviewer's question caused me to revisit, not theorizing, but the theory itself. Could it have been different?

I was initially struck by the absence of women in the archival database. None occupied positions shown in the diagrams of NASA and contractor organizations. None testified before the Commission or participated in engineering decisions at any level. Only four women were connected to the accident: Challenger astronaut Judith Resnick and Teacher-in-Space Christa McAuliffe, former astronaut and Commission member Sally Ride, and Emily Trapnell of the Commission's investigative staff. Among the factors mentioned in post-accident press speculation about the causes was a 'can-do' attitude at NASA that drove the agency to take risks, but I did not incorporate gender into my explanation. If NASA's culture were a macho, risk-taking culture, then launch delays would have been infrequent. However, delays were so frequent that NASA often was chastised by the press. Indeed, Challenger was delayed three times, and Columbia, launched before it, was delayed seven times. The very SRB engineers who opposed Challenger's launch had previously initiated a two-month launch delay. I concluded that gender was not a factor driving launch decisions, thinking also that if women had been participating in engineering decisions, they would have been subject to the same cultural beliefs of professional engineering as men. Because of the absence of women's viewpoints in the data, gender was not visible to me. In a perfect example of how the aspects of social settings that explain our research also can be obstacles to understanding it, the testimony and my interviews with men in a male-dominated culture did not enlighten me on this issue. Having 'resolved' the macho culture issue by the frequency of launch delays and the engineering evidence behind those delays, I went no further. Had I sought NASA women employees outside the archival database for interviews (i.e., non-technical staff), I would have been able to further clarify the question.

The final important reason to revisit the theory of the book is to examine the results of analogical theorizing as a method. After explaining the case, the next step is the cross-case comparison. How is this case analogous to and different from the guiding theory, which was an outgrowth of other cases? Have any generic structures and processes been identified? What are the theoretical implications? (For full assessment, see Vaughan, 1996: 395–415.) Recall that the three interrelated parts of the theory of organizational misconduct guiding this analysis worked as follows: historical political/economic forces create structural pressures on organizations to violate; organization structure and processes create opportunities to violate; the regulatory environment systematically fails, thus the three in combination encourage individuals to engage in illegality and deviance in order to attain organization goals. This case was not an example of misconduct as I originally thought: rules were not violated. Still, harm was done. Moreover, NASA's actions were deviant in the eyes of outsiders, and, after the accident, also in the eyes of those who made decisions. Affirming the deviance behind NASA's mistake is the remarkable extent to which the case conformed to the theory. Consider how the explanatory concepts support the generalizability of the theory across cases. The culture of production is analogous to the forces of the political/economic

environment: the ideologies of professional engineering and historic shifts in policy decisions of Congress and the White House at the start of the Shuttle Program combined to reproduce in NASA the capitalistic conditions of competition and scarcity associated with corporate crime. The production of a cultural belief in acceptable risk was a key organizational process that allowed NASA to continue launching with flaws. Reinforced by the culture of production, this cultural belief drove launch decisions despite increasing concern about safety as O-ring damage increased. Structural secrecy described how both organization structure and the structure of safety regulation were systematic sources of regulatory failure. They precluded agents charged with monitoring risk assessments from deterring NASA from disaster by suppressing the seriousness of the O-ring problems. Exposing macro-, meso-, and micro-connections, these three factors in combination perpetuated the decisions that resulted in the accident.

How was this case different from other cases? The logic of comparing cases of similar events in a variety of social settings is that each case produces different data, thus bringing into focus social dimensions not previously noted. The NASA case produced differences that elaborated the original theory at all levels of analysis. First, history emerged as a causal factor. Zald has pointed out that organizations exist in history, embedded in institutional environments, and they exist as history, products of accumulated experience over time (1990). History was cause at both the institutional and organizational level, and also a third: the history of precedent-setting decisions about O-ring erosion. This finding shows the importance of longitudinal studies of organization processes, suggesting that historical/ documentary evidence might productively be incorporated into traditional ethnographic work in organizations or communities, possibly producing revisionist accounts that transcend other conventional wisdoms.[13] Second, culture comes alive as a mechanism joining political/ economic forces, organizations, and individuals, motivating action. My analysis shows how taken-for-granted assumptions, dispositions, and classification schemes figure into goal-oriented behavior in a prerational, preconscious manner that precedes and prefigures individual choice. It affirms a theory of practical action that links institutional forces, social location, and habitus to individual thought and action (Vaughan, 1996: 222–37, 402–5, 2002). Third, the case produced extensive micro-level data that showed how unexpected technical deviation was first accepted then normalized at NASA.

This latter discovery shows that analogical theorizing can uncover generic social processes, previously unidentified, that generalize across cases. Although no rules were violated, the normalization of deviance in organizations helps to explain misconduct in and by organizations when it does occur. The persistent question about organizational misconduct is how educated, employed, apparently upstanding citizens can become amorally calculating managers, engaging in illegality to achieve organization goals. The socially organized processes by which deviance was normalized at NASA show how people can be blinded to and insulated from the harmful consequences of their actions because those actions are culturally consistent and conforming within that setting. We see additional evidence of the role of conformity in deviant outcomes in Arendt's *Eichmann in Jerusalem* (1964) and Kelman and Hamilton's *Crimes of Obedience* (1989). These two works identify the historic and organizational forces at work in the normalization of deviance, but do not trace the incremental process behind it. Recall that NASA's long prelude to disaster was typified by anomalies occurring at intervals across time, no single incident appearing significant, the time between them reducing the salience of each. My research on uncoupling showed an analogous pattern, revealing that when relationships end, warning signs are mixed, weak, and routine, obscuring problem seriousness so that the partner being left behind fails to notice and act until too late (Vaughan, 2002). The concept also suggests how social work institutions come to normalize evidence of foster families abusing children; for nation states, it may explain cultural shifts in political ideology or, at the societal level, the transition from Victorian repression of sexuality to media expression that is uncensored and routine. These examples suggest the normalization of deviance as a generalizable concept showing that the gradual routinization and acceptance of anomalies, driven by invisible socially organized forces, is part of all change.

On the other hand, the theory that explained the normalization of deviance at NASA was a theory of systematic reproduction and sameness, not change. What was striking was the repetition of decisions despite changing personnel and increasing O-ring damage. The Challenger disaster was an accident, the result of a mistake that was socially organized and systematically produced. Contradicting the rational choice theory of the amorally calculating manager argument, the accident had systemic causes that transcended individuals and time. In the last chapter of the book, I argued that strategies for change must address the social causes of a problem. Because the causes of Challenger were in NASA's organizational system—the layered structures and processes of the agency's historic political and budgetary environment, the organization itself, and individual sense making—simply firing personnel or moving them to other positions at the agency would not prevent future accidents because new people in the same positions would be subject to identical forces. The flawed system would produce another accident. I concluded the book with these words:

> After the Challenger disaster, both official investigations decried the competitive pressures and economic scarcity that had politicized the space agency, asserting that goals and resources must be brought into alignment. Steps were taken to assure that this happened. But at this writing, that supportive political environment has changed. NASA is again experiencing the economic strain that prevailed at the time of the disaster. Few of the people in top NASA administrative positions

exposed to the lessons of the Challenger tragedy are still there. The new leaders stress safety, but they are fighting for dollars and making budget cuts. History repeats, as economy and production are again priorities. (Vaughan, 1996: 422)

I predicted another accident, but I did not predict the consequences of such an event for me. On 1 February 2003, NASA's Space Shuttle Columbia disintegrated upon reentry to earth's atmosphere. As a consequence, my Challenger research revisited me, making me an expert to consult about this second NASA accident. Theory, analogy, and history again played themselves out, as the causes of Challenger repeated to produce Columbia. Reconsidering the causal theory that explained the loss of Challenger and the ethnographic practices that led to a theory that generalized from the first accident to the second prepares the way for an ethnographic account in this journal of this revisit, begun immediately at Columbia's loss, showing the connection between ethnography, theory, public discourse, and policy.

REFERENCES

Arendt, Hannah (1964) *Eichmann in Jerusalem: A Report on the Banality of Evil.* New York: Viking.

Becker, Howard S. (1998) *Tricks of the Trade.* Chicago, IL: University of Chicago Press.

Bensman, Joseph and Robert Lilienfeld (1991) *Craft and Consciousness: Occupational Technique and the Development of World Images.* New York: Aldine de Gruyer.

Blau, Peter M. (1964) *Exchange and Power in Social Life.* New York: John Wiley.

Blumer, Herbert (1960) *Symbolic Interaction.* Cambridge: Cambridge University Press.

Bourdieu, Pierre (1977) *Outline of a Theory of Practice.* Trans. Richard Nice. Cambridge: Cambridge University Press.

Burawoy, Michael (1979) *Manufacturing Consent.* Chicago, IL: University of Chicago Press.

Burawoy, Michael (1998) 'The Extended Case Method', *Sociological Theory 16*(1): 4–33.

Burawoy, Michael (2003) 'Revisits: An Outline of a Theory of Reflexive Ethnography', *American Sociological Review 68*(5): 645–79.

Cerulo, Karen (ed.) (2002) *Culture in Mind: Toward a Sociology of Culture and Cognition.* New York: Routledge.

Coser, Lewis (1974) *Greedy Institutions.* New York: Free Press.

Davis, Stanley M., Paul R. Lawrence and Michael Beer (1978) *Matrix.* Reading, MA: Addison Wesley.

Emerson, Robert M. (1983) 'Holistic Effects in Social Control Decision Making', *Law and Society Review 17*: 425–55.

Geertz, Clifford (1973) *The Interpretation of Cultures.* New York: Basic Books.

Glaser, Barney G. and Anselm L. Strauss (1967) *The Discovery of Grounded Theory.* New York: Aldine.

Goffman, Erving (1952) 'On Cooling the Mark Out: Some Aspects of Adaptation to Failure', *Psychiatry 15*: 451–63.

Goffman, Erving (1961) *Asylums: Essays on the Social Situation of Mental Patients and Other Inmates.* New York: Anchor.

Goffman, Erving (1969) *Strategic Interaction.* Philadelphia: University of Pennsylvania Press.

Hammack, J.B. and M.L. Raines (1981) Space Shuttle Safety Assessment Report. Johnson Space Center, Safety Division, 5 March. *National Archives*, Washington, DC.

Haney, Lynne (2002) *Inventing the Needy: Gender and the Politics of Welfare in Hungary.* Berkeley and Los Angeles: University of California Press.

Hondagneu-Sotelo, Pierrette (1994) *Gender Transitions: Mexican Experiences of Immigration.* Berkeley and Los Angeles: University of California Press.

Hirschman, Albert O. (1970) *Exit, Voice, and Loyalty: Responses to Decline in Firms, Organizations, and States.* Cambridge, MA: Harvard University Press.

Hughes, Everett C. (1984) *The Sociological Eye.* New Brunswick, NJ: Transaction Books.

Jepperson, Ronald L. (1991) 'Institutions, Institutional Effects, and Institutionalism', in Walter W. Powell and Paul J. DiMaggio (eds.) *The New Institutionalism in Organizational Analysis*, pp. 143–59. Chicago, IL: University of Chicago Press.

Katz, Jack (2001) 'From How to Why: On Luminous Description and Causal Inference in Ethnography, Part 1', *Ethnography 2*(4): 443–73.

Katz, Jack (2002) 'From How to Why: On Luminous Description and Causal Inference in Ethnography, Part 2', *Ethnography 3*(1): 63–90.

Kelman, Herbert C. and V. Lee Hamilton (1989) *Crimes of Obedience.* New Haven, CT: Yale University Press.

Kligman, Gail (1998) *The Politics of Duplicity.* Berkeley and Los Angeles: University of California Press.

Meiksins, Peter and James M. Watson (1989) 'Professional Autonomy and Organization Constraint: The Case of Engineers', *Sociological Quarterly 30*: 56–85.

Merton, Robert K. (1968) Social Theory and Social Structure. New York: Free Press.

Mitaugh, Dennis E. (2000) *Learning to Theorize.* Thousand Oaks, CA: Sage.

Ortner, Sherry B. (2003) *New Jersey Dreamin': Capital, Culture, and the Class of '58*. Durham, NC: Duke University Press.

Perucci, Robert (1970) 'Engineering: Professional Servant of Power', *American Behavioral Scientist 41*: 492–506.

Powell, Walter W. and Paul J. DiMaggio (eds.) (1991) *The New Institutionalism in Organizational Analysis*. Chicago, IL: University of Chicago Press.

Presidential Commission on the Space Shuttle Challenger Accident (1986) Report to the President by the Presidential Commission on the Space Shuttle Challenger Accident. 5 vols. Washington, DC: Government Printing Office.

Ragin, Charles C. and Howard S. Becker (eds.) (1992) *What Is a Case? Exploring the Foundations of Social Inquiry*. Cambridge: Cambridge University Press.

Robinson, W.S. (1951) 'The Logical Structure of Analytic Induction', American *Sociological Review 16*: 812–18.

Simon, Herbert (1957) *Models of Man*. New York: Wiley.

Snow, David A., Calvin Morrill and Leon Anderson (2003) 'Elaborating Analytic Ethnography: Linking Fieldwork and Theory', *Ethnography 4*(2): 181–200.

Starbuck, William and Frances Milliken (1988) 'Executives' Perceptual Filters: What They Notice and How They Make Sense', in Donald C. Hambrick (ed.) *The Executive Effect*, pp. 35–65. Greenwich, CT: JAI.

Stinchcombe, Arthur L. (1978) *Theoretical Methods in Social History*. New York: Academic Press.

US Congress. House. Committee on Science and Astronautics (1986a) *Investigation of the Challenger Accident: Hearings*, 2 vols. Washington, DC: Government Printing Office.

US Congress. House. Committee on Science and Astronautics (1986b) *Investigation of the Challenger Accident: Report*. Washington, DC: Government Printing Office.

Vaughan, Diane (1983) *Controlling Unlawful Organizational Behavior*. Chicago, IL: University of Chicago Press.

Vaughan, Diane (1986) *Uncoupling: Turning Points in Intimate Relationships*. New York: Oxford University Press.

Vaughan, Diane (1992) 'Theory Elaboration: The Heuristics of Case Analysis', in Charles C. Ragin and Howard S. Becker (eds.) *What Is a Case? Exploring the Foundations of Social Inquiry*, pp. 173–202. Cambridge: Cambridge University Press.

Vaughan, Diane (1996) *The Challenger Launch Decision: Risky Technology, Culture, and Deviance at NASA*. Chicago, IL: University of Chicago Press.

Vaughan, Diane (1998) 'The Dark Side of Organizations: Mistake, Misconduct, and Disaster', *Annual Review of Sociology 25*: 271–305.

Vaughan, Diane (2002) 'Signals and Interpretive Work: The Role of Culture in a Theory of Practical Action', in Karen Cerulo (ed.) *Culture in Mind: Toward a Sociology of Culture and Cognition*, pp. 28–54. New York: Routledge.

Vaughan, Diane (n.d.) Theorizing: Analogy, Cases, and Comparative Social Organization. In preparation.

Whyte, William Foote (1955) *Street Corner Society*. 2nd ed. Chicago, IL: University of Chicago Press.

Wolff, Kurt (trans. and ed.) (1950) *The Sociology of Georg Simmel*. New York: Free Press.

Zald, Mayer N. (1990) 'History, Sociology, and Theories of Organization', in John E. Jackson (ed.) *Institutions in American Society: Essays in Market, Political, and Social Organizations*, pp. 81–108. Ann Arbor: University of Michigan Press.

Znaniecki, Florian (1934) *The Method of Sociology*. New York: Farrar and Rinehart.

Zussman, Robert (1985) *Mechanics of the Middle Class: Work and Politics among American Engineers*. Berkeley and Los Angeles: University of California Press.

Reading

Men and Women's Experiences With Hazing in a Male-Dominated Elite Military Institution (2006)

Jana L. Pershing

Highly publicized cases of hazing in the military have predominated in the American media over the past century, dating back to 1899 when Douglas MacArthur, one of the U.S. military's most decorated generals, disobeyed orders to disclose the names of cadets guilty of hazing him during a West Point hazing scandal (Leon 2000). More than a century later, publicized cases involving the mistreatment of students attending West Point as well as other U.S. Department of Defense (DOD) service academies continue to raise questions about the pervasiveness of hazing and the extent to which it is formally addressed (U.S. General Accounting Office 1994).

While research on military culture reveals that various forms of hazing are viewed as a critical component of the resocialization process from civilian to military life (Firestone and Harris 1999; Lenney 1949; U.S. General Accounting Office 1992), no research to date has examined the relationship between gender and hazing for students attending DOD service academies, including the Military Academy (West Point), the Naval Academy, and the Air Force Academy. Each of these educational/ military institutions serves the primary purpose of training future officers for a specific branch of the military (e.g., army, navy), providing nine percent of the military's newly commissioned officers (U.S. General Accounting Office 1992). Not only are the service academies lauded as the standard for military professionalism, they are also considered one of the most direct routes for achieving upward social mobility within the military structure.

In contrast to other military institutions and civilian organizations, DOD service academies also serve as unique settings in which to examine the pervasiveness of hazing because of the structure of daily living. For instance, little is known about hazing in elite military institutions where men and women live together, work together, attend university classes together, and are being trained to serve alongside one another as military officers. Not only are students relatively isolated from the civilian community for four years, they may only leave campus grounds during approved periods of liberty. And though military service academies are clearly not representative of other organizations, the benefit of studying total institutions (Goffman 1961) is that they closely approximate social experiments and thus allow one to study behavior within a relatively closed environment. In comparison, one of the challenges in studying social problems in other organizational settings is that it is difficult to isolate case studies from the social structure, community, and culture in which they exist (Vaughan 1983).

A fundamental component of military training at DOD service academies is the indoctrination system for fourth classmen (freshmen), which includes traditions and rituals passed down through several generations. Because these systems are primarily student-run by upperclassmen (juniors and seniors), and since the distinction between hazing and legitimate military training has sometimes been ambiguous in the past, the fourth class indoctrination systems are subject to potential abuse. While the prevalence of hazing at the service academies has been documented in historical accounts and personal biographies, no research has compared men and women's experiences with hazing since women's entry in 1976. And although their numbers have increased steadily compared to the first graduating classes of 1980, women today remain a minority population.[1]

In response to the lack of research on gender and hazing in these military training institutions, this article presents the findings of a case study of hazing at the U.S. Naval Academy, which is the Department of Defense's service academy for training Naval and Marine Corps officers. There are three primary lines of inquiry: (1) to examine

---

[1]Although women are underrepresented at all Department of Defense service academies, their proportions vary. At the Naval Academy, 16 percent of the 2006 graduating class are women, whereas women comprise only 6 percent of the 2006 graduating class at the Military Academy (West Point). While recent admissions data are not available for the Air Force Academy, 15 percent of 1999 graduates were women.

the extent to which men and women experience hazing during their freshmen year, (2) to examine men and women's attitudes about the appropriateness of hazing, and (3) to analyze men and women's perceptions about the potential consequences of reporting hazing and the extent to which grievances are actually filed.

BRIEF REVIEW OF PRIOR RESEARCH ON GENDER INTEGRATION AND HAZING IN THE MILITARY

Social scientists first approached the entry of women into the DOD service academies in 1976 from the perspective of previous research on racial integration in the military during World War II, which had found that racial prejudice decreased among whites in integrated platoons because they had close associations with African Americans (Moskos 1971; Stouffer 1949). In examining gender, researchers hypothesized that men in sex-integrated companies would be less prejudiced toward women than men in all-male companies. However, the results of research conducted on the first gender-integrated class were mixed (Durning 1978). Men in integrated squads or platoons developed the most egalitarian gender attitudes, whereas men in mixed companies but not mixed platoons or squads were the most traditional. And men in all-male companies fell between these two groups.

Research today continues to find that contact does not necessarily decrease prejudice toward the minority group if men and women do not initially agree on the changing roles of women (DeFleur 1985; Kimmel 2000; Stiehm 1996; Yoder, Adams, and Price 1983). In other words, studies have demonstrated that, in general, men attending the academies have very traditional

attitudes about women's roles, particularly their ability to serve as effective military leaders. In contrast, women entering the academies hold nontraditional gender-role attitudes. Furthermore, differences in the types of leadership positions available to women (i.e., combat positions) not only fail to create an environment where men and women are seen as equals but may actually exacerbate conflicts (DeFleur 1985; Segal and Hansen 1992). Likewise, women's relatively recent entry into formerly all-male, private, officer-training institutions like the Citadel and the Virginia Military Institute has raised questions about whether women's presence disrupts male cohesion by interfering with the "adversative method" whereby students are subjected to psychological rigors and hardships in an effort to resocialize them from civilian to military life (Kimmel 2000). Consequently, proponents of returning to an all-male U.S. military argue that gender equality and women's integration pose a threat to military effectiveness (Segal and Hansen 1992).

Aside from studies examining the impact of women's presence on men's gender-role attitudes, comparing men and women's experiences with nonsexual hazing has not been a specific topic of inquiry in DOD service academy studies.[2] Instead, the most recent accounts of hazing date back to the 1800s and early 1920s, prior to women's entry. These testimonials and accounts demonstrate that the line between legitimate military training and hazing has historically been blurred at both the Naval Academy and other service academies and that, in some instances, hazing was so severe that it resulted in serious injuries and sometimes death (Benjamin 1900; Lenney 1949; Leon 2000; Puleston 1942). Since the vast majority of these cases were directed at fourth classmen

---

[2]It should be noted that while hazing may be conceptualized as a form of harassment, the present study is restricted to examining nonsexual hazing. Not only do Naval Academy regulations distinguish hazing from sexual harassment, prior research has demonstrated that the vast majority of Academy students who experience sexual harassment are women (Pershing 2003b; U.S. General Accounting Office 1994).

(freshmen), hazing that targeted freshmen was eventually outlawed by Congress in 1874.[3] Notwithstanding, hazing continued for more than a century until the Naval Academy instituted further changes in 1990 following several highly publicized scandals involving severe hazing (U.S. General Accounting Office 1992).

Similarly, while no recent empirical studies have examined the extent to which the active-duty military population directly experiences hazing, some research on military culture reveals that nonsexual harassment is viewed as a critical component of resocializing new initiates (Firestone and Harris 1999; Lenney 1949; U.S. General Accounting Office 1992). In addition to employing conventional training methods, a number of nonconventional methods, including hazing, are sometimes used to promote group cohesion, cooperation, and interdependence (Firestone and Harris 1999). In other words, the process of military resocialization involves creating an environment of shared struggle and suffering which in turn leads to increased comradery and loyalty between peers. Moreover, research on military men serving in all-male combat units reveals that group bonding is often intensified because men feel that their lives and personal well-being depend upon one another given the potential dangers of their jobs (Wilson 1999). And while group bonding may serve positive functions during wartime and periods of combat through instilling values of self-sacrifice and reliability, it can become dysfunctional during peacetime when inappropriate behaviors are promoted and wrongdoers are protected by an informal "code of silence" that prohibits reporting peer misconduct (Janowitz 1974; Pershing 2002; Wilson 1999). Therefore, group loyalty and bonding create a culture where reporting wrongdoing is unlikely given potentially negative consequences, including social ostracism and other retributive actions (Pershing 2002, 2003a; Wilson 1999). And unlike members of civilian organizations, military personnel cannot readily leave the group if they disagree with military training methods or directly experience mistreatment.

In contrast to the lack of empirical research on hazing in the U.S. military, several case studies in a variety of male-dominated civilian organizations have documented that hazing is pervasive and unlikely to be formally addressed. For example, research on initiation rites into secondary schools, colleges, and fraternities find that hazing rituals reinforce peer loyalty, emphasize hegemonic masculinity, and promote sexism (Anderson and Noesjirwan 1980; Brown 1976; De Los Reyes and Rich 2003; Jones 1999; Leemon 1972). And although the majority of research on civilian campuses focuses on men's experiences with hazing, some studies have documented the use of hazing rituals in rites of initiation into sororities, reporting similarities in the use of alcohol as well as support for behaviors that reaffirm a sexist ideology (Anderson and Noesjirwan 1980; Drout and Corsoro 2003; Nuwer 1999). However, no study has directly examined the relationship between gender and hazing victimization on college campuses. And while DOD service academies share similarities with college fraternities insofar as being male-dominated as well as supporting a "code of silence" in hiding misconduct (Leemon 1972; Nuwer 1990), military academies differ because they are total institutions and have been coed since 1976. More importantly, instead of being seen as simply rites of initiation, hazing rituals have historically been viewed as a critical component of officer training programs for first-year students (Benjamin 1900; Lenney 1949; Leon 2000; Puleston 1942).

In sum, while some research has examined men's attitudes about and experiences with nonsexual hazing in active-duty military populations and the formerly all-male officer training institutions, no study to date has compared men and women's experiences with hazing at DOD service academies. Instead, research on

---

[3]Act of June 23, 1874, c. 453, 18 stat. 203.

women's integration into the service academies has emphasized the impact of women's entry on men's gender-role attitudes and their acceptance of women in general. Lastly, since hazing has historically been viewed as a traditional male-bonding ritual in military institutions, the question arises as to what extent students' experiences with hazing vary by gender.

THE U.S. NAVAL ACADEMY: WOMEN'S ENTRY, PLEBE YEAR, AND HAZING POLICIES

Although the Naval Academy opened its doors in 1845, women were not admitted until 1976 following turbulent congressional hearings that resulted in President Ford's signing of public law mandating that women be allowed to attend all U.S. Department of Defense service academies.[4] This first cohort of women included eighty-one members, of which fifty-five went on to graduate in 1980 (Disher 1998). While the proportion of women attending the Naval Academy has slowly increased as a result of changes in combat-exclusion rules, women are still underrepresented. At the time the present study was conducted, the proportion of women admitted was sometimes as high as 13 percent. However, with high attrition rates, the proportion of women was typically around 10 percent. More recently, women represented approximately 15 percent of the Academy population during the 2002–2003 academic year, whereas men comprised 85 percent of the student population.

The Academy population is relatively small, comprised of fewer than 4500 students. Daily life inside this total institution is organized around class/company divisions, consisting of thirty-six midshipmen. For mixed-gender divisions, six women are typically assigned to a group. Within each division, there is a "chain of command" whereby upperclassmen (juniors and seniors) are

responsible for socializing, training, and assigning military performance grades to underclassmen (freshmen). Not only does the structure of the student chain of command provide upperclassmen with the opportunity to practice leadership skills, it serves as a period of resocialization for freshmen. This period of transition from civilian life to military service begins during a seven-week intensive military training period the summer preceding freshman year and continues through the end of the first academic year. A freshman's military performance during this time is reflected in his or her military performance grades—grades which affect class rankings, which in turn affect his or her military job opportunities upon graduation.

Freshman year is considered so fundamental to the development and training of military officers that it has been termed *plebe year*. In addition to referring to a fourth classman (freshman), the term *plebe* is also defined in the Naval Academy's student handbook as "that insignificant thing that gets all the sympathy and chow [food] from home" (U.S. Naval Academy 1989, 287). Since the Academy is interested in retaining only those midshipmen who are committed to enduring four years of intensive academic, military, and physical training, plebe year is designed to be difficult both physically and psychologically (Pahl 1987). In fact, one of the Navy's most highly decorated admirals, Admiral Elmo R. Zumwalt, was once quoted as saying, "On my first day as a plebe I called my father and told him, 'I'm leaving here.' On the way back from the phone booth I changed my mind and I never looked back" (*United States Naval Academy, 1845* 1987, 30). And although the majority of midshipmen do not leave despite thoughts about doing so, the rigors of Academy life are reflected in the relatively high attrition rates of students during their first two years. Approximately 23 percent of men and 33 percent of women leave the Academy (U.S. General Accounting Office 1993). Beyond their second

---

[4]Public Law 94-106 (10 U.S.C. 6954) was signed on 7 October 1975.

year, however, midshipmen may not simply drop out of the Academy. Only under rare circumstances are resignation requests approved by the Academy's superintendent. In these instances, midshipmen would be required to either pay back the full cost of their education or serve as enlisted personnel for the same length of time that they attended the Academy. Unless they are expelled or approved to resign, midshipmen's legal commitment mandates that they graduate and serve in either the Navy or Marine Corps for a designated number of years.

Today hazing is prohibited at the Naval Academy by Public Law 10 U.S.C. 6964, which defines hazing as "any authorized assumption of authority by a midshipman whereby another midshipman suffers or is exposed to any cruelty, indignity, humiliation, hardship, or oppression, or the deprivation or abridgement of any right." In addition to delineating what types of behaviors constitute hazing, upperclassmen in charge of plebe indoctrination are required to participate in workshops and training courses that emphasize positive leadership behaviors.

Victims of hazing have two potential courses of action to formally report grievances. First, they may report the incident to the student chain of command, which is how other conflicts and problems between midshipmen are addressed.[5] Given that the student chain of command is a fundamental component of the Academy's officer training program, designed to reflect the hierarchy that midshipmen will work within as military officers, this course of action is encouraged before pursuing other options. If, however, this avenue does not resolve the problem, victims may then report the incident to the officer chain of command. When grievances are filed, Academy regulations recognize two broad categories of hazing-related offenses. The more serious category is defined as "repeated hazing" with the corresponding punishment being permanent expulsion from the Academy. In the second category, hazing is described as "abuse of the Fourth Class Indoctrination System through unauthorized use of physical contact, ordering performance of personal services, or humiliation of fourth classmen" (U.S. General Accounting Office 1992). Perpetrators found guilty of this type of hazing typically receive demerits on their military records.

DATA AND METHODOLOGY

The case study reported here is based on a descriptive analysis of two data sets: data from a U.S. General Accounting Office Survey of Naval Academy midshipmen and semistructured interview data collected from Naval and Marine Corps officers who graduated from the Academy. Data from both sources were collected from midshipmen attending the Academy within the same general time frame.

U.S. General Accounting Office Survey of Academy Midshipmen

In November and December of 1990, the U.S. General Accounting Office (GAO) administered a survey to a stratified random sample of midshipmen from the classes of 1991 to 1994. The sample consisted of 82 percent men, 18 percent women, 64 percent whites, and 36 percent who were members of racial minority groups. In comparison, the brigade (student population) included 91 percent men, 9 percent women, 81 percent whites, and 19 percent who were members of racial minority groups. The percentages for men and women include both whites and members of racial minority groups. Similarly, the percentages for members of racial minority groups include both men and women. The survey response rate was approximately

---

[5]Although faculty, staff, and commissioned officers are involved in the enforcement of Academy rules and regulations, the Code of Conduct is largely self-regulatory, which means that midshipmen are expected to monitor both their own behavior as well as the behavior of their peers.

85 percent, resulting in a sample of 527 midshipmen including 434 men and 93 women.[6]

Since the GAO survey was part of a broader review of all DOD service academies, it covered a variety of topics related to the treatment of students. Items relevant to the present study include nine questions about midshipmen's experiences with hazing during their plebe (freshman) year. Regardless of whether they experienced hazing, respondents were also asked whether each form of hazing should be allowed to occur at the Naval Academy. Also included in the survey are questions about midshipmen's opinions regarding the purpose of plebe (freshman) year and their perceptions about negative consequences of reporting hazing. The survey data may be generalized to all Academy midshipmen and also may serve as a validity check for comparable data collected from interviews with graduates.

Interviews With Naval and Marine Corps Officers

In 1994, I interviewed forty Naval and Marine Corps officers who had graduated from the Naval Academy in either 1992 or 1993. For the remainder of the article, these officers will be referred to as *graduates*. Access to Academy graduates was first gained through snowball sampling techniques that began with both personal contacts and individuals whom I did not personally know. Although snowball sampling techniques do not produce random population samples, the interview sample is varied with regard to background characteristics like gender, race/ethnicity, academic major, grade point average upon graduation, military rank while

attending the Academy,[7] and current billet or job in the Navy or Marine Corps.

Because this study compares men and women's experiences at the Academy, I oversampled on women. Although women comprised only 10 percent of the Naval Academy population, fourteen women were interviewed, or 35 percent of the sample. Of these women, four were members of racial minority groups, and ten were white. Approximately 20 percent of Naval Academy midshipmen were members of racial minority groups, yet they comprised 25 percent of the interview sample. Six minority men were interviewed. The remaining 20 graduates were white men, representing 50 percent of the sample.

Open-ended, semistructured interviews were conducted and all graduates were asked a core set of questions about their personal experiences at the Naval Academy. Because the interviews were part of a broader study of the U.S. Naval Academy, they covered a variety of topics related to student misconduct, including the perceived treatment of students during plebe year. Interview questions that were designed to acquire information about the following are relevant to the present study: (1) background characteristics of graduates; (2) structure of daily life at the Academy; (3) Academy rules and regulations, including guidelines for handling cases of misconduct; (4) personal experiences involving various forms of misconduct, including hazing; and (5) personal experiences related to gender. Depending on their responses, graduates were asked additional questions that probed for clarity. Interviews ranged from 30 to 150 minutes in length, with an average of 60 minutes. The purpose of these interviews was to acquire detailed information about the social

---

[6]The 1990 GAO study remains the most recent survey of Naval Academy midshipmen's experiences with hazing. Interaction effects of gender and race on hazing victimization cannot be analyzed since only fourteen women surveyed were members of racial minority groups.

[7]The sample contains a disproportionate number of graduates who were high-ranking midshipmen. This is important in terms of addressing a common critique leveled at snowball samples. It is sometimes argued that relying on informal and personal contacts may produce a sample of peripheral rather than central members of a social group. Given the variation in the sample, especially with regard to military rank, there is no reason to assume that the graduates interviewed were peripheral members of the Academy.

context and culture in which hazing is sustained. These data are also used to compare men and women's experiences at the Academy. It should be noted that while the survey and interview data provide a descriptive account of midshipmen's experiences with hazing during their freshmen year, they do not allow for a comprehensive analysis of all factors related to hazing.

FINDINGS

Pervasiveness of Hazing

Despite the integration of hazing prevention training programs into the Naval Academy's curriculum, the GAO survey data reveal that the majority of midshipmen reported experiencing minor forms of hazing at least a couple times per month or more during their freshman year (see Table 1). For example, 77.4 percent of men and 76.1 percent of women responded that they had upperclassmen scream in their face on a recurring basis. Hazing activities related to upperclassmen exacerbating the time constraints faced by freshmen were also regular occurrences, with 72.7 percent of men and 72.8 percent of women indicating that they had to frequently memorize and recite trivia to upperclassmen. In contrast, physically abusive hazing appeared to be the least common with only 2.8 percent of men self-reporting being tied up, taped, or restrained, and 0.7 percent of men indicating that their heads had been dunked in toilets. Although gender differences are not significant, women in the general population sample did not self-report experiencing these forms of hazing on a recurring basis.

Moreover, the results of chi-square tests suggest that men and women are equally likely to experience each of the nine forms of hazing summarized in Table 1. This finding is particularly noteworthy because it raises the question of whether women have been accepted through their inclusion in traditional Academy hazing rituals (DeGroot and Peniston-Bird 2000). On the other hand, it is also possible that the lack of gender differences in hazing victimization are unique to freshman year, which would suggest that one's status as a plebe overrides one's gendered status in a male-dominated institution.

Perhaps the greatest limitation of this study is that the GAO survey does not measure midshipmen's experiences with hazing beyond plebe year. Therefore, the data cannot ascertain whether men and women remain equally likely to experience hazing during their sophomore, junior, and senior years. Furthermore, since the survey only includes questions about hazing victimization rather than perpetration, students' motivations for hazing particular freshmen based on gender or other personal characteristics cannot be examined. Despite these limitations, prior research that finds that women have not yet been fully integrated into the service academies (DeFleur 1985; Pershing 2001; Stevens and Gardner 1987) lends support to the latter explanation—that is, the absence of gender differences in hazing victimization are most likely unique to freshman year. This interpretation is further substantiated by the interviews because the majority of graduates indicated that gender was a less salient factor of differentiation during plebe year. For example, one female stated,

> Plebe year everyone is more gender-neutral. People are more in a mode to help each other, but after plebe year the guys tend to go to their little groups and, unless they're extremely comfortable with women as equals, they tend to congregate with just guys.[8]

Furthermore, during interviews with graduates, plebes were simply referred to as "plebes." References to gender were not typically made. In contrast, when sophomores, juniors, and seniors were discussed, graduates often referred to either

---

[8]Interview quotations are not assigned numbers or pseudonyms, primarily because several graduates expressed concern that readers would be able to match information and uncover their identities.

TABLE 1 Types of Hazing Experienced by Naval Academy Men and Women, as Occurring a Couple Times per Month or More (in percentages)

Types of Hazing	Men (n = 434)	Women (n = 93)	Total (N = 527)
Had an upperclassman scream in face?	77.4	76.1	77.2
Had to memorize and recite trivia to upperclassmen?	72.7	72.8	72.7
Had to "brace" for an extended period of time?	56.0	47.3	54.4
Had to endure verbal harassment, insult, or ridicule?	47.8	41.9	46.8
Had to participate in a prank?	24.8	17.2	23.5
Had to do multiple sets of push-ups in short succession?	20.9	25.0	21.6
Missed a meal reciting plebe rates or performing some other activity for upperclassmen?	12.1	17.2	13.0
Was tied up, taped, or restrained?	2.8	0.0	2.3
Had head dunked in toilet?	0.7	0.0	0.6

SOURCE: U.S. General Accounting Office (1990). The response categories for each survey item were *never, one or two times a year, a couple times a semester, a couple times a month, a couple times a week*, and *daily or almost daily*. In this table, the last three categories have been combined to include *a couple times a month or more often*, which represents hazing-type treatment on a recurring basis.

NOTE: Chi-square tests were performed on each survey item and yielded no statistically significant differences in men and women's experiences with hazing-type treatment (both before and after combining response categories).

"male midshipmen" or "female midshipmen." In other words, plebes, who are at the bottom of the midshipman chain of command, appear to occupy a unique status since they have not yet proven that they belong at the Academy. One graduate described the relationship between plebes and other midshipmen:

It's hard to explain the relationship between plebes and everyone else, even third classmen [sophomores]. It's very formal. Plebes have to refer to everyone above them as "sir" and "ma'am." You

don't really think of them as even being human—they're just plebes. They shouldn't even eyeball you [look you in the eye] because they're inferior. In addition to dressing differently, they had to walk differently.

Another graduate explained, "third classmen [sophomores] are expected to guide plebes, while everyone else's job [juniors and seniors] is to shit on them." Therefore, anyone who deviated from plebe rules and regulations was quickly singled out and humiliated. For example, one graduate explained that "plebes have to walk in the dorm with their knees high and are not allowed to look around. Every time they turn a corner, they have to say, 'Go Navy. Beat Army.' " Since this graduate failed to look straight ahead while rounding a corner in the dormitory on one occasion as a plebe, an upperclassman ordered him to look around each time he turned a corner and say, "Gee, this place is nice. I wonder how much it cost?" Another graduate had difficulty remembering the names of senior midshipmen the first time he was told them, so he was ordered to wear all their name tags for several weeks. Interviews revealed that these types of degradation and humiliation rituals are weekly occurrences and are ultimately designed to send the message that plebes are not yet legitimate members of the Naval Academy.

Midshipmen's Attitudes About Hazing

Although men and women are equally likely to experience hazing during their freshman year, men and women's attitudes about hazing are not necessarily similar. Table 2 summarizes the proportion of men and women who responded in the GAO survey that specific hazing activities should not be allowed at the Academy. Responses vary depending on the severity of the offense. The majority of midshipmen indicate that physical forms of hazing such as being tied up, taped, restrained, or having one's head dunked in a toilet should not be allowed. However, women are significantly more likely than men to indicate that physically abusive hazing should not be allowed. For example, 83.6 percent of women compared to 65.9 percent of men indicate that having one's head dunked in a toilet should not be allowed. Women are also more likely to disapprove of severe forms of verbal hazing, with 65.6 percent of women compared to 41.0 percent of men responding that verbal insults and ridicules should not be allowed. In contrast, there are no significant differences in men and women's attitudes about

the appropriateness of four types of hazing, including reciting plebe rates and doing multiple sets of push-ups in short succession. Only 33.7 percent of women and 29.5 percent of men self-report that memorizing and reciting trivia to upperclassmen should not be allowed.

Gender similarities in attitudes about the appropriateness of minor forms of hazing may be related, in part, to men and women's shared opinions about using plebe year to ascertain whether a midshipman possesses the attributes to succeed as a military officer. For example, the GAO survey revealed that men and women are equally likely to agree (75.9 percent and 71.0 percent, respectively) that "fourth class year should be used to identify and eliminate midshipmen who are not committed to the Academy or cannot function effectively under pressure" (see Table 3). The interviews reflected this sentiment insofar as several male and female graduates expressed concern with detecting and removing midshipmen who "did not belong." These individuals were viewed as "subperformers" in need of being "weeded out" of the system for both their own good as well as for the good of the brigade (student population). Graduates also explained that since "the chain is only as strong as the weakest link," the rigors of plebe year were seen as one way to identify and remove subperformers in an effort to make the chain stronger.

In contrast, gender differences in attitudes about whether five of the nine hazing activities should be allowed may be related, in part, to differences in men and women's attitudes about the primary purpose of fourth class year. Although 45.9 percent of men and 49.5 percent of women view this system as "primarily a leadership development tool," 15.7 percent of men and 5.4 percent of women view plebe year as a "rite of passage" (see Table 3). And while more men than women view plebe year as a rite of passage, a significant proportion of midshipmen view plebe year as evenly balanced between serving as a rite of passage and as a leadership development tool (38.5 percent of men and 45.2

TABLE 2 Naval Academy Men and Women Indicating That Specific Hazing Activities Should Not Be Allowed (in percentages)

Types of Hazing	Men (n = 434)	Women (n= 93)	p
Had an upperclassman scream in face?	9.4%	21.7%	>.01
Had to memorize and recite trivia to upperclassmen?	29.5	33.7	ns*
Had to "brace" for an extended period of time?	21.2	31.2	>.001
Endured verbal harassment, insult, or ridicule?	41.0	65.6	>.001
Had to participate in a prank?	29.0	33.7	ns
Had to do multiple sets of push-ups in short succession?	11.9	16.5	ns
Missed a meal reciting plebe rates or performing some other activity for upperclassmen?	73.1	76.1	ns
Was tied up, taped, or restrained?	62.4	84.8	>.001
Had head dunked in toilet?	65.9	83.7	>.01

SOURCE: U.S. General Accounting Office, 1990 (*N* = 527). The response categories for each survey item were *definitely be allowed*, *probably be allowed*, *can't decide*, *probably not be allowed*, and *definitely not be allowed*. In this table, the last two categories have been combined to include *probably or definitely not be allowed*.

NOTE: Chi-square tests (*p*) were performed on each survey item to test for statistically significant differences between men and women's attitudes about whether hazing-type activities should be allowed to occur at the Naval Academy. Results were the same for each item both before and after combining response categories;* = not statistically significant at *p* .05.

percent of women). If midshipmen are more likely to view plebe year as a rite of passage, or as an endurance test of an individual's desire to become a Naval officer, they may be more likely to support hazing activities including physically abusive hazing. Furthermore, viewing plebe year as a rite of passage could affect attitudes about the appropriateness of hazing such that the distinction between acceptable fourth class indoctrination and improper treatment may be unclear.

Differences in men and women's attitudes about the appropriateness of some forms of hazing may also be indirectly related to the effects of one's gendered status as either a relatively new or long-standing population at the

Academy. In other words, since women have only attended the Academy since 1976 and comprise only 10 percent of the student population, they may be less likely to support behaviors that have historically been associated with traditional male-bonding rituals (Kimmel 2000). In contrast, as members of the majority population, men may be more likely to uphold what they believe to be traditional military values and norms passed down from previous generations, dating back to a time period when the Naval Academy was an exclusively male institution. For example, one male graduate said that he "would have liked to have attended a military school that was all male." When I asked why, he explained,

When there were no women, some of the antics that went on were much less controlled and much more challenging. The physical stress and challenging nature of the training would have been more extreme, including everything from outright hazing and humiliation. I don't know how to describe it without throwing private parts into the description of things that went on in the older days. Everyone knows how things used to be at the Academy before women came.

Similarly, another male graduate indicated that although the Naval Academy is still a prestigious institution, the caliber of students declined when women were admitted:

Our top guys, the top third of our class, are as good as they've ever been. It's that the bottom is falling out because of all the political changes since they let women in. I wish I could have gone to an all-male Academy like my father. It was better then in terms of what you could do to plebes. Thirty years ago you

TABLE 3   Men and Women's Opinions About the Purpose of Fourth Class (Freshman) Year (in percentages)

	Men (n = 434)	Women (n = 93)	p
"Fourth class year should be used to identify and eliminate midshipmen who are not committed to the Academy or cannot function effectively under pressure."			
Strongly agree	37.8%	26.9%	ns*
Agree	38.1	44.1	
Undecided	8.6	10.8	
Disagree	11.8	12.9	
Strongly disagree	3.7	5.4	
"Should the fourth class system be primarily a rite of passage, a leadership development tool, or a combination of the two?"			
Primarily a rite of passage	15.7	5.4	>.05
Evenly balanced between rite of passage and leadership development tool	38.5	45.2	
Primarily a leadership development tool	45.9	49.5	

SOURCE: U.S. General Accounting Office Survey, 1990 (N = 527). The response categories for the second survey item were a rite of passage only, a combination with more emphasis on rite of passage, evenly balanced between rite of passage and development, a combination with more emphasis on development, and a leadership development tool only. In this table, the first two categories were combined to include primarily a rite of passage, and the last two categories were combined to include primarily a leadership development tool.

NOTE: Chi-square tests (p) were performed to test for statistically significant differences between men and women's opinions about the purpose of fourth class year. Results were the same for the second item both before and after combining response categories; * = not statistically significant at p .48205.

could stress them [plebes] a lot more without having to worry about hazing and harassment. Today, it's a lot more touchy-feely and sensitive.

Moreover, for male graduates who argued that the Naval Academy should be an all-male officer training institution, antifemale sentiments were more pronounced for men assigned to mixed-gender class/company divisions. A minority male commented on this issue since he was in a mixed-gender division:

> Women at the Academy is a touchy situation. It made a difference for us. A lot of it had to do with the basic social interaction between men and women. Let's face it—there are differences between men and women. Everyone can see that. When you're in a closed environment like that, and when they're only 10 percent of the population, it makes a big difference in terms of the company. It was easier for guys in all-male companies because they didn't have to worry about gender.

It should be noted that the majority of male graduates said that they were "O.K." with women's presence at the Academy as long as they could "hold their own." One male graduate explained that there were three types of men at the Academy: "There were guys who didn't want girls there and only talked to them because they had to. Then there were the guys who didn't have a problem with them being there, and there was a third group of guys who were dating them." However, even for men who accepted women's presence, they often described Academy women as being qualitatively different from other women they knew. One male graduate said, "I thought women were well accepted [at the Academy]. They're not like the girls I know. They go there and they do everything we do. I

got nothing against women, believe me. I have a bunch of sisters."

Although the majority of male graduates claimed that they accepted women's presence, interviews also revealed that women were informally isolated despite being formal members of the Academy. Social isolation manifested itself primarily in looking at the development of friendships, which were intragender but not intraracial. As previously discussed, male graduates emphasized that friendships began to form on the first day they arrived for plebe summer training and that male comradery developed as a result of shared daily experiences. When I asked men to describe who their best friends were while attending the Academy, the majority indicated that they were midshipmen in their same class/company division and also of the same gender. When I asked men who were members of racial minority groups about the racial status of their closet friends, they reported that they had both minority and white male friends and emphasized that race was not a factor at the Academy.[9]

However, women stated that, beyond plebe year, they learned that their gender set them apart from "bonding," or forming close friendships, with men. Not only did female graduates indicate that they were either on the periphery of, or completely excluded from, male friendship networks, but, when asked about their positive experiences at the Academy, very few mentioned friendship and loyalty—this, in contrast, was the most commonly cited benefit of having attended the Academy for both minority and white men. When I specifically asked women about who their closest friends were, the following was a typical response: "Most people probably had close friends starting on Day 1, but I really didn't."

---

[9]During the interviews, minority men indicated that their racial status was not an issue at the Academy. Likewise, minority women indicated that their gender rather than racial status was an issue in terms of how other midshipmen treated them. GAO survey data do not reveal significant racial differences in either students' experiences with hazing or their attitudes about it, which is consistent with prior research documenting that the integration of minority men has been relatively successful compared to the integration of women (Moskos 1971; Stouffer 1949). However, other research demonstrates that racial integration is far from complete (see Bodnar 1999).

Since friendship is an intragender phenomenon, one of the challenges that women face is having close contact with only a relatively small group of women. In other words, women are placed in companies with one to five other women and, therefore, have a smaller pool of people with whom to choose to be close friends and roommates. If they happen to be placed in a group of women with whom they are not necessarily compatible, then their options are limited in terms of finding other women with whom to room and be friends. Because friendship does not cross gender boundaries and because women are less likely to form friendships with one another, female graduates indicated that they felt excluded from midshipmen networks and, subsequently, like "outsiders." In turn, since women report feeling like outsiders, they may be more likely to view hazing as another form of exclusion or alienation. In contrast, men may be more likely to interpret hazing as a form of peer bonding or inclusion by virtue of their male friendship networks or status as "insiders."

Midshipmen's Perceptions About Reporting Hazing

Although midshipmen have ample opportunities to report hazing given the high proportion of freshmen who experience it on a recurring basis, grievances are infrequently filed, according to a report issued by the U.S. Navy Inspector General and U.S. General Accounting Office (1992). A review of Naval Academy records from 1986 to 1990 revealed that only a few students had been charged with "repeated hazing," an offense for which a student can be permanently expelled (U.S. General Accounting Office 1992). The review also found that even when midshipmen were officially reported for engaging in hazing-like behaviors, charges were reduced to lesser offenses, which means that no student was convicted of "repeated hazing" during this time period. And while the GAO survey did not include a question about formally reporting hazing, no

graduates filed grievances despite frequently experiencing hazing during plebe year.

The disparity between the proportion of plebes who self-report experiencing hazing and the number of officially reported cases may be explained by several factors including the belief that plebe year should be a rite of passage or an endurance test of one's desire to become a military officer, viewing some forms of hazing as acceptable, and ambiguity about what constitutes hazing as opposed to appropriate military training. The confusion over the difference between "hazing" and "training" was raised during several interviews and is exemplified in the following graduate's account of plebe year, where he uses the terms interchangeably:

> You don't have any time to yourself during plebe year because you're hazed all year. Well, I don't know if I'd call it hazing. It's also training. You have responsibilities you have to do for the upperclassmen like learning things about the military and strategy.

Another consideration is that the Naval Academy operates using a system of self-regulation whereby peers are expected to monitor one another's behavior. However, an underlying dilemma in institutions that rely on self-regulation is that peers must be willing to violate informal norms regarding peer loyalty to uphold formal norms, or to report misconduct (Akerstrom 1991; Heck 1992; Pershing 2002). At the Naval Academy, even though midshipmen are provided channels to file grievances, graduates uniformly discussed the informal "code of silence," which discourages midshipmen from "snitching" on peers who engage in any form of misconduct, including hazing. Those who violate this code of silence by reporting wrongdoing risk not only social ostracism but possibly retaliation from peers. Furthermore, because midshipmen live and work within a strict hierarchy that is dictated by class rank, plebes are even less likely to report upperclassmen for misconduct because they are at

TABLE 4 Men and Women's Perceptions of Negative Consequences of Reporting Hazing (in percentages)

	Men (n = 434)	Women (n = 93)	P
"Midshipman would be shunned by other midshipmen."			
Extremely likely	7.7%	20.7%	>.01
Likely	38.9	37.0	
Not sure	27.2	23.9	
Unlikely	21.5	17.4	
Extremely unlikely	4.7	1.1	
"Midshipman would be subjected to more of the same actions."			
Extremely likely	3.5	7.5	>.01
Likely	14.0	28.0	
Not sure	21.3	22.6	
Unlikely	38.8	29.0	
Extremely unlikely	22.4	12.9	
"Nothing would be done."			
Extremely likely	3.1	5.4	>.05
Likely	13.9	25.8	
Not sure	18.8	16.1	
Unlikely	39.3	33.3	
Extremely unlikely	24.9	19.4	

SOURCE: U.S. General Accounting Office Survey, 1990 (*N* = 527).

NOTE: Chi-square tests (*p*) were performed to test for statistically significant differences between men and women's perceptions of negative consequences of reporting hazing.

the bottom of the student chain of command. One graduate explained,

> If you're a plebe, you would never turn in a first classman. If you reported something, all the other firsties [seniors] in the company would be pissed off that their friend had been snitched on. All the firsties would have made the plebe's life even harder. It was already hard enough. They would have yelled and screamed at him everyday. They never would have let him forget what he did.

Because of the centrality of friendship and peer loyalty at the Naval Academy and since reporting misconduct becomes "common knowledge" in the brigade, the majority of midshipmen are not willing to "snitch," particularly plebes who are struggling to prove that they belong at the Academy. As one graduate emphasized, "no one likes a snitch because they can't be trusted." And since female freshmen occupy a "double-outsider" status by virtue of their plebe status and their gender, women are significantly more likely to perceive negative consequences of filing grievances relative to their male counterparts. For example, GAO survey data reveal that 46.6 percent of men and 57.7 percent of women indicate that it is likely that a "midshipman would be shunned by other midshipmen" for reporting hazing (see Table 4). Likewise, 17.5 percent of men and 35.5 percent of women perceive that a "midshipman would be subjected to more of the same actions." And, 17.0 percent of men compared to 31.2 percent of women indicate that it is likely that "nothing would be done." Consequently, for a substantial proportion of midshipmen, the perception is that the potential unintended consequences of reporting hazing are likely to exacerbate the situation rather than remedy it.

SUMMARY

In response to the lack of research on how gender is related to nonsexual harassment, specifically in male-dominated institutions where women are a relatively new population, this case study has examined men and women's experiences with hazing at the U.S. Naval Academy. Several trends emerge from an analysis of survey data collected from midshipmen and semistructured interviews with Naval and Marine Corps officers who graduated from the Academy.

First, despite attempts to eradicate hazing, the majority of midshipmen self-reported experiencing minor forms of hazing at least a couple times a month or more during their freshman year. The most frequently experienced forms of hazing involved upperclassmen screaming in their faces and being required to recite trivia to upperclassmen. In contrast, physically abusive hazing was the least common form, which suggests some improvement relative to historical accounts of severe hazing that resulted in serious injuries and sometimes death (Lenny 1949; Leon 2000). Notwithstanding, it is clear that the distinction between hazing and legitimate military training at the Academy remains ambiguous and that the largely student-run system is still sometimes abused. Interviews with graduates also reflect findings from prior research on military culture, which documents that hazing has traditionally been viewed as a critical component of socializing new initiates. Graduates described the benefits of the stresses and rigors of the fourth class indoctrination system as promoting peer bonding as well as removing midshipmen who do not belong in an officer training institution (Firestone and Harris 1999; Lenney 1949; U.S. General Accounting Office 1992). Moreover, survey data reveal that male and female midshipmen are equally likely to agree that plebe year should be used to detect and eliminate those who cannot function under pressure.

What is most notable about the current research is the lack of gender differences in freshmen's experiences with each of the nine forms of hazing included in the GAO survey, which of course raises the question of whether women have been accepted through their inclusion in traditional hazing rituals. Alternatively, the lack of gender differences could be unique to freshman year, which would suggest that one's status as a plebe overrides one's gendered status. However, as discussed previously, one of the limitations of this study is that the GAO survey does not measure midshipmen's experiences with hazing beyond plebe year. In other words, data cannot ascertain whether men and women remain equally likely to experience hazing during their sophomore, junior, and senior years. Nor can students' motivations for hazing particular freshmen based on gender or other personal characteristics be examined since the survey only includes questions about victimization rather than perpetration.

In spite of these limitations, interviews with graduates suggest that gender is a less salient factor of differentiation during freshman year since plebes are at the bottom of the student chain of command and occupy a status as "outsiders" who have not yet proven that they belong at the Academy. Interviews with female graduates also reveal that the peer bonding experienced as plebes is short-lived and does not extend beyond their first year at the Academy. In addition to women's exclusion from male friendship networks, some male graduates directly expressed antifemale sentiments and argued that the Naval Academy should be an all-male officer training institution. These findings are consistent with prior research on women's integration that finds that women have not yet been fully integrated into the service academies (DeFleur 1985; Pershing 2001; Stevens and Gardner 1987), lending support to the explanation that the absence of gender differences in hazing victimization is most likely unique to freshman year.

Third, although midshipmen's attitudes about the appropriateness of minor forms of hazing do not vary by gender, women are significantly more likely than men to indicate that both physically abusive hazing and severe forms of verbal hazing should not be allowed. These differences may be explained, in part, by gender differences in attitudes about the primary purpose of fourth class year. Women are more likely to view the fourth class system as primarily a leadership development tool, while men are more likely to regard plebe year as an initiation rite or as an endurance test of an individual's desire to become a Naval or Marine Corps officer. Since men are more likely than women to view plebe year as a rite of passage, they may be more likely to support behaviors that have historically been associated with traditional male-bonding rituals as well as interpret those behaviors as a form of inclusion (Kimmel 2000; Wilson 1999). In contrast, as a socially isolated population, women may interpret severe forms of hazing as another form of exclusion and, therefore, be more likely to agree that these types of activities should not be allowed at the Academy.

A final key finding of the present study is that despite freshmen experiencing hazing on a recurring basis, formal grievances are infrequently filed. This disparity may be related to several factors, including attitudes about the purposes of the fourth class indoctrination system, opinions about the appropriateness of specific hazing behaviors, confusion over the difference between hazing and legitimate military training, and perceptions about negative consequences of filing grievances. Regarding the latter issue, an important consideration is that the Naval Academy operates using a system of self-regulation whereby peers are expected to monitor one another's behavior (Pershing 2002). Given the emphasis on peer loyalty, an informal "code of silence" discourages midshipmen from "snitching" on peers who engage in any form of misconduct, including hazing. As a consequence, the majority of midshipmen are not willing to report wrongdoing, particularly plebes who are at the bottom of the midshipman hierarchy and are struggling to prove that they belong at the Academy. And, consistent with the observation that female freshmen occupy a "double-outsider" status by virtue of their plebe status and their gender, women are significantly more likely than men to perceive negative consequences of reporting hazing, including not only social ostracism but possibly retaliation from peers.

Filing grievances with the student chain of command is also problematic because the perpetrators of hazing are usually upperclassmen. And even though incidents may be reported to the officer chain of command if the student chain of command fails to resolve the problem, midshipmen do not typically pursue this avenue because it is likely to draw unwanted attention. Furthermore, unlike members of civilian organizations, Academy students cannot readily remove themselves from the situation. An alternative solution would be to eliminate the student chain of command as a first course of action in reporting hazing, which is a strategy that has been employed at the Naval Academy for victims of sexual harassment. However, prior research demonstrates that midshipmen are not likely to pursue this avenue given that it bypasses standard military procedure and also draws unwanted attention (Pershing 2003b). In sum, while formal policies are clearly necessary, they alone cannot reduce the pervasiveness of hazing since midshipmen are unlikely to pursue formal avenues because of concern that doing so will exacerbate the situation rather than remedy it. Further research would be useful toward identifying specific cultural and structural causes in an effort to provide information that could be used in developing comprehensive policies to reduce hazing.

The present study has compared men and women's experiences with hazing in a male-dominated military institution, highlighting that hazing is not a uniquely male experience. Not only are male and female initiates equally likely to experience hazing victimization, they also share opinions about the appropriateness of minor forms of hazing and the importance of using the rigors of plebe year to weed out misfits, which are cultural attitudes that promote and sustain hazing. In closing, the findings of this case study call for an expansion of hazing research to include gender comparisons in integrated military and civilian organizations while taking into account the impact of men and women's shared experiences as initiates or new members of formal institutions. In addition to explaining *how* gender is related to hazing victimization and corresponding attitudes, future research could clarify *why* there are either similarities or differences.

REFERENCES

Act of June 23, 1874, c. 453, 18 stat. 203.

Akerstrom, M. 1991. *Betrayal and betrayers: The sociology of treachery*. New Brunswick, NJ: Transaction.

Anderson, A.M., and J. A. Noesjirwan. 1980. Agricultural college initiations and the affirmation of rural ideology. *Mankind* 12:341-47.

Benjamin, P. 1900. *The United States Naval Academy, being the yarn of the American midshipman (naval cadet)*. New York: G.P. Putnam.

Bodnar, J. W. 1999. How long does it take to change a culture? Integration at the U.S. Naval Academy. *Armed Forces & Society* 25:289-306.

Brown, D. L. 1976. Organizational change from the bottom up. *Education & Urban Society* 8:159-71.

DeFleur, L. B. 1985. Organizational and ideological barriers to sex integration in military groups. *Work and Occupations* 12:206-28.

DeGroot, G., and C. Peniston-Bird, eds. 2000. *A soldier and a woman: Sexual integration in the military*. New York: Longman.

De Los Reyes, G., and P. Rich. 2003. Housing students: Fraternities and residential colleges. *Annals of the American Academy of Political & Social Science* 585:118-23.

Disher, S.H. 1998. *First class: Women join the ranks at the Naval Academy*. Annapolis, MD: Naval Institute Press.

Drout, C. E., and C. L. Corsoro. 2003. Attitudes toward fraternity hazing among fraternity members, sorority members, and non-Greek students. *Social Behavior and Personality* 31:535-43.

Durning, K. P. 1978. Women at the Naval Academy. *Armed Forces & Society* 21:25-43.

Firestone, J. M., and R. J. Harris. 1999. Changes in patterns of sexual harassment in the U.S. military: A comparison of the 1988 and 1995 DOD surveys. *Armed Forces & Society* 25:613-32.

Goffman, E. 1961. *Asylums: Essays on the social situation of mental patients and other inmates*. Garden City, NY: Anchor.

Heck, W.P. 1992. Police who snitch: Deviant actors in a secret society. *Deviant Behavior* 13:253-70.

Janowitz, M. 1974. *Sociology and the military establishment*. Beverly Hills, CA: Sage.

Jones, R. L. 1999. The hegemonic struggle and domination in black Greek-letter fraternities. *Challenge: A Journal of Research on African American Men* 10:1-33.

Kimmel, M. 2000. Saving the males: The sociological implications of the Virginia Military Institute and the Citadel. *Gender & Society* 14:494-516.

Leemon, T. A. 1972. *The rites of passage in a student culture: A study of the dynamics of transition*. New York: Teachers College Press.

Lenney, J. J. 1949. *Caste system in the American Army: A study of the Corps of Engineers and their West Point system*. New York: Greenberg Publisher.

Leon, P. W. 2000. *Bullies and cowards: The West Point hazing scandal, 1898-1901*. Westport, CT: Greenwood Press.

Moskos, C. 1971. Minority groups in military organizations. In *Handbook of military institutions*, ed. R. Little. Beverly Hills, CA: Sage.

Nuwer, H. 1990. *Broken pledges: The deadly rite of hazing*. Atlanta, GA: Longstreet Press.

———. *Wrongs of passage: Fraternities, sororities, hazing, and binge drinking*. Bloomington: Indiana University Press.

Pahl, D. 1987. *Annapolis: The United States Naval Academy*. New York: Exeter Books.

Pershing, J. L. 2001. Gender disparities in enforcing the honor concept at the U.S. Naval Academy. *Armed Forces & Society* 27:419-42.

———. 2002. Whom to betray? Self-regulation of occupational misconduct at the United States Naval Academy. *Deviant Behavior* 23:149-75.

———. 2003a. To snitch or not to snitch? Applying the concept of neutralization techniques to the enforcement of occupational misconduct. *Sociological Perspectives* 46:149-78.

———. 2003b. Why women don't report sexual harassment: A case study of an elite military institution. *Gender Issues* 21: 3-30.

Public Law 10 U.S.C. 6964.

Public Law 94-106 (10 U.S.C. 6954).

Puleston, W. D. 1942. *Annapolis: Gangway to the quarterdeck*. New York: D. Appleton-Century Co.

Segal, M. W., and A. F. Hansen. 1992. Value rationales in policy debates on women in the military: A content analysis of congressional testimony. *Social Sciences Quarterly* 73:296-309.

Stevens, G., and S. Gardner. 1987. But can she command a ship? Acceptance of women by peers at the Coast Guard Academy. *Sex Roles* 16:181-88.

Stiehm, J. H., ed. 1996. *It's our military too! Women and the U.S. military*. Philadelphia: Temple University Press.

Stouffer, S. A. 1949. *The American soldier: Adjustment during army life*. Princeton, NJ: Princeton University Press.

United States Naval Academy, 1845. 1987. Louisville, KY: Harmony House Publishers.

U.S. General Accounting Office. 1992. *DOD service academies: More changes needed to eliminate hazing*. Document #GAO/NSIAD-93-36. Washington, D.C.: U.S. General Accounting Office.

———. 1993. *Naval Academy: Gender and racial disparities*. Document #GAO/NSIAD-93-54. Washington, D.C.: U.S. General Accounting Office.

———. 1994. *DOD service academies: More actions needed to eliminate sexual harassment*. Document #GAO/NSIAD-94-6. Washington, D.C.: U.S. General Accounting Office.

U.S. Naval Academy. 1989. *Reef points 1989-1990: The annual handbook of the brigade of midshipmen*. Annapolis, MD: U.S. Naval Academy.

Vaughan, D. 1983. *Controlling unlawful organizational behavior: Social structure and corporate misconduct*. Chicago: University of Chicago Press.

Wilson, D. 1999. Rites of passage and group bonding in the Canadian airborne. *Armed Forces & Society* 25:429-57.

Yoder, J. D., J. Adams, and H.T. Prince. 1983. The price of a token. *Journal of Political and Military Sociology* 11:325-37.

Reading

The World-System After the Cold War (1993)

Immanuel Wallerstein

1. INTRODUCTION

The certainties of the post-1945 era are now over, in particular two. (1) The United States dominated the capitalist world-economy, being the most efficient producer and the most prosperous country. This is no longer true. (2) The USA and the USSR were engaged in an all-encompassing 'Cold War,' which shaped all interstate relations. The Cold War is no more. Indeed, the USSR is no more. To understand what this portends, we have three relevant pasts: the past of the US hegemonic era, 1945–90; the past of liberalism as the dominant ideology of the capitalist world-system, 1789–1989; the past of capitalism as an historical system, which started in 1450 and will perhaps be no more by 2050.

2. THE THREE RELEVANT PASTS

The story of the US hegemonic era is the easiest to tell. At the end of World War II, the USA found itself in an exceptional position. Its basic economic forces had been growing steadily stronger

SOURCE: From "The World-System after the Cold War" by Immanuel Wallerstein in *Journal of Peace Research*, 1993; 30.1: 1–6. Reprinted with permission of Sage Publications, LTD.

in terms of technology, competitiveness, and quantitative share of world production for 100 years. World War II resulted in enormous physical destruction throughout the Eurasian land mass, and thus among all the potential economic rivals of the USA, both those who had been allies and those who had been foes during the war.

The USA was thus able to establish a new world order, a pax americana, after the long disorder of 1914–45. The pax americana had four pillars. The first was the reconstruction of the major industrial powers, not only its long-time allies in western Europe, but its recent foes, Germany and Japan. The motives were multiple. The world-economy needed the reentry of these countries both as major producers and as major customers for US production. The USA needed a network of associates to maintain the world order. And, ideologically, the USA needed to propagate the idea of a 'free world' that was prosperous as a symbol of hope and therefore of moderation for the world's lower strata.

The second pillar was an arrangement with the only other serious military power in the world, the USSR. The Soviet Union was ostensibly an ideological rival and potentially an expanding power. In fact, it was quite easy to come to an arrangement in which the Soviet Union had its reserved zone (the 'socialist bloc'). There were four conditions to the deal: there would be absolute peace in Europe; the two blocs would be territorially fixed; the two great powers would maintain internal order in their blocs; the socialist bloc would expect no help in reconstruction from the USA. There were, to be sure, many noisy quarrels, but since none of them ended in breaking the arrangement, we may assume that their purpose was largely for show.

The third pillar was US internal unity built around the acceptance of US 'responsibility' in the world-system, anti-Communism at home and abroad, and the end of racial segregation. The fourth pillar was the slow political decolonization of the Third World and modest efforts for its so-called economic development. The emphasis was on the adjectives 'slow' and 'modest.'

If we turn to the second past, that of 1789–1989, we start with the geocultural shock of the French Revolution and its Napoleonic aftermath. The French Revolution changed France less than we believe, but it changed the world-system fundamentally. The French Revolution changed mentalities by imposing the belief that political change was 'normal' and legitimated by 'popular sovereignty.' The attempt to deal with this new reality took the form of the creation of the three ideologies: conservatism, liberalism, and socialism. The ostensible difference was in their attitude towards such normal change: the conservatives dubious and wishing to slow it down maximally, the liberals wishing to manage it rationally, and the socialists wishing to speed it up maximally. In theory, all three ideologies looked with disfavor on the state. But, in practice, all three ideologies found that they had to strengthen the state vis-à-vis society in order to achieve their objectives. In the end, all three ideologies united around the liberal program of orderly 'reform' enacted and administered by 'experts.' The conservatives became liberal conservatives and the socialists became liberal socialists.

In the 19th century, in Europe, liberalism promoted two great reforms: the extension of the suffrage and the creation of the social welfare state. By 1914 both reforms were in place or in process, and widely accepted as legitimate throughout western Europe and North America. The object of the reforms was the integration of the working classes in a way that would tame their anger but not threaten the continuing functioning of the capitalist world-economy. This program was superbly successful, for two reasons. The governments could mobilize their working classes around a double nationalism: an intra-European nationalism and the nationalist superiority of the 'Europeans' to the 'backward' peoples of the world. And, second, the costs of the social welfare state could be borne without too much disruption because of the expanded exploitation of the periphery.

World War I marked the beginning of a long intra-'European' struggle between Germany and the USA as the successor hegemonic power to Great Britain. It would end with US victory and world hegemony in 1945. World War I also marked, however, the moment when the peoples of the periphery began to try to reassert themselves against the European domination of the world-system. The North-South struggle we know today took shape then. The ideological response of the North to this new political reality was Wilsonianism, or the liberal program applied on a world scale. Wilsonianism offered the world equivalent of suffrage, the self-determination of nations. And 25 years later Roosevelt added the world equivalent of the social welfare state, the program of the economic development of the Third World, assisted by Western 'aid.' Leninism, which posed itself as the radical opponent of Wilsonianism, was in fact its avatar. Anti-imperialism was self-determination clothed in more radical verbiage. The construction of socialism was economic development of the Third World clothed in more radical verbiage.' One of the reasons 'Yalta' was possible was that there was less difference in the programs of Wilson and Lenin than official rhetoric maintained.

In the heyday of US hegemony after 1945, this world liberalism also seemed superbly successful. The decolonization of Asia and Africa was rapid and, for the most part, relatively painless. The 'national liberation movements' were full of hope for the future. The United Nations proclaimed the 1970s the 'Development Decade.' But something essential was lacking in the attempt to repeat in the 20th century at the world level what had been the 19th-century success of liberalism within Europe. There was no Third World for the Third World. One could neither mobilize the 'patriotism' of the Third World against a 'Third World' nor count on the income from exploiting a periphery to pay for their social welfare state. The taming of the working classes, so successful within Europe, was a chimera at the world level.

If we now turn to the third past, that between 1450 and today, we see a third 'success story,' that of capitalism as an historical system. The raison d'être of capitalism is the endless accumulation of capital. The historical system that has been built, slowly and steadily, has been remarkable in its accomplishments. It has sustained a constant expansion of technology permitting an incredible growth in world production and world population. The capitalist world-economy was able to expand from its initial European base to incorporate the entire world and eliminate all other historical systems from the globe. It has developed a political framework of 'sovereign' nation-states within an ever more codified interstate system which has developed the right proportion of state power vis-à-vis the market so as to permit the maximal accumulation of capital. It has developed a complex system of the remuneration of labor, combining wage and non-wage forms, thereby keeping world labor costs down but offering incentives for efficiency. It has institutionalized both sexism and racism, enabling the construction of a hierarchical labor force which is self-sustaining politically.

Capitalism has been a dynamic system. It has been based not on a stable equilibrium but on a pattern of cyclical swings wherein the 'animal spirits' of the entrepreneurial classes, in pursuing their own interests, regularly and inevitably create mini-crises of overproduction which lead to downturns or stagnations in the world-economy. This is in fact very functional for the system, weeding out the weak producers and creating constraints on the ability of the working classes to pursue their incessant claims for greater reward.

There are, however, some basic contradictions in this historical system, as in all historical systems. The dynamic of the system requires constant spatial expansion; this has reached its limits. The dynamic of the system requires constant externalization of costs by individual producers; this may be coming close to reaching its limits. The dynamic of the system requires the constant, if slow, proletarianization of the working classes of the world; but proletarianization is a negative process from the point of view of the capitalists, in that it increases labor costs and creates political risks. Liberalism as an ideology was a very effective means of containing unrest and 'democratization,' but over time it inevitably has put enormous strains on state budgets and created a public debt pyramid which threatens the stable functioning of the system.

3. THE TRANSITIONAL PRESENT

The late 1960s was a turningpoint in many ways. It marked the beginning of the downturn ending the incredible post-1945 Kondratieff A-phase expansion. The basic economic reason was obvious. The remarkable economic recovery of western Europe and Japan plus the economic development of the Third World led to such a great increase in the production capacities of the previously most profitable industries (steel, automobiles, electronics, etc.) as to create a profit crunch. We have been living in this Kondratieff B-phase ever since. What has happened is what always happens in B-phases: acute competition among the core powers in a situation of contraction, each trying to maximize its profit margins and minimize its unemployment at the expense of the others; a shift of capital from seeking profits in production to seeking profits in financial manipulations; a squeeze on governmental balance of payments, resulting in debt crises (of the Third World, the ex-socialist bloc, and the United States). There has been a relocation of production at the world level. There has been an intensive search for new product innovations which can be the basis of future quasimonopolies. As in all B-phases, the effects of the downturn have not been felt evenly; some do better than others. In this downturn, the relative success story has been that of Japan and the East Asian 'dragons,' which are linked.

At the same time, in 1968, there began a world revolution which, it is now clear, was a revolution against liberalism as the dominant ideology of the world-system. At the time, the social unrest, which occurred throughout the world—France and Germany, the USA and Japan, Czechoslovakia, and China, India and Mexico—seemed to have two common themes everywhere: opposition to US hegemony in the world-system and Soviet collusion; denunciation of the so-called Old Left (Communist and social-democratic parties, national liberation movements) for their complicity with the dominant forces. This revolt of 1968 in fact culminated with the overthrow in 1989–91 of the Communist governments in eastern Europe and the USSR. It is today clearer than it was in 1968 that the two themes—opposition to US hegemony and opposition to the Old Left—are in fact but a single theme, the opposition to reformist liberalism as a justification of the workings of the world-system.

The two principal changes in the geopolitics of the world-system in the 1970s and 1980s have been the decline of the relative power of the USA and the great disillusionment with developmentalism in the Third World. The first is a normal cyclical occurrence. The economic strengths of the European Community and Japan have been steadily rising since the mid-1960s, and the USA has not been able to keep pace. This has of course political and cultural implications. The world policy of the USA has for the past 20 years been centered around ways to slow down this loss of hegemony by exerting pressure on its allies. The second is not a cyclical occurrence at all. It marks the breakdown of the Wilsonian liberal enticement to the working classes of the periphery. The collapse of 'statism' in both the Third World and the ex-socialist bloc is the collapse of liberal reformism, and hence the undermining of a crucial pillar in the stability of the capitalist world-economy.

The collapse of the Communist bloc is thus a double setback for the world-system. For the USA, it is a geopolitical catastrophe, as it eliminates the only ideological weapon the USA had to restrain the EC and Japan from pursuing their self-defined objectives. For the capitalist world-economy as an historical system, it marks the onset of an acute crisis, since it lifts the

Leninist justification of the status quo without replacing it with any viable substitute.

4. THE UNCERTAIN FUTURE

We have now entered into the post-American era, but also the post-liberal era. This promises to be a time of great world disorder, greater probably than the world disorder between 1914 and 1945, and far more significant in terms of maintaining the world-system as a viable structure. What may we expect?

On the one hand, we may expect the capitalist world-economy to continue to operate in the short run in the way it has been operating for 500 years, but operating in this way will only exacerbate the crisis. Once this current Kondratieff B-phase is finally over (which will only be after one last downward swing), we shall as previously enter into a new A-phase, in which Japan, the USA, and the EC will struggle to obtain quasi-monopolistic control over the new leading industries. Japan stands a good chance of coming out on top, and it is probable that it will make a world economic alliance with the USA as junior partner to ensure this. In this new era of prosperity, the new main areas of economic expansion will be China for the Japan-US grouping and Russia for the EC. The rest of the periphery will be largely excluded from any benefits, and the polarization of world wealth will grow markedly more acute, as will the polarization of population growth.

A further problem is that the collapse of Wilsonian liberalism has led worldwide to a collapse in the faith in the 'state' as the central locus of social change and progress. It has also meant the collapse of long-term optimism, which has long been a key stabilizing political factor in the operation of the system. Polarized wealth without hope leads to generalized fear and the search for structures of security. These are being sought in identity politics, whose meaning is ambiguous but whose force is quite apparent.

There are three obvious sources of major instability in the world-system over the next 50 years. One is the growth of what I shall call the Khomeini option. This is the assertion by states in the periphery of total otherness and rejection of the rules of the interstate system as well as the geocultural norms governing the world-system. This particular option has been largely contained for the moment in Iran, but it is quite likely that other states will resort to it (and not only Islamic states), and it will be much more difficult to contain it if several states try it simultaneously.

The second source of instability is what I shall call the Saddam Hussein option. This is the attempt to challenge militarily the dominance of the North in the world-system. While Saddam Hussein's attempt was stopped cold, it took an extraordinary mobilization by the USA to do it. It is not at all clear that, as the decades go by, this can be repeated, especially if there are several such attempts simultaneously. US military strength will decline because the USA cannot sustain it either financially or politically. The states of the North are looking for a long-term substitute, but there is no clear one in sight. And acute economic and political competition among the core powers during the next upturn of the world-economy may not render such military collaboration too likely.

The third source of instability will be an unstoppable mass movement of people from South to North, including to Japan. The growing polarization of wealth and population makes this an option which no amount of border guards can successfully police. The result will be internal political instability in the North, coming doubly from right-wing anti-immigrant forces and from the immigrants themselves demanding political (and hence economic) rights; and all this in a context where all groups will have lost faith in the state as a means of solving social inequities.

This is a picture of world turmoil, but it is not necessarily a pessimistic one. Obviously, such world disorder cannot go on indefinitely. New solutions will have to be found. This will undoubtedly mean creating a new historical system to replace the one that has been so efficacious for 500 years, but which is now crumbling because of its very success. We come therefore to the historical choices before us: what kind of new historical system to build, and how? There is no way to predict the outcome. We shall find ourselves in what scientists today are calling a bifurcation far from equilibrium, whose resolution is intrinsically unpredictable, but in which every intervention has great impact. We are thus in a situation of 'free will.' The world of 2050 will be the world we create. We have a considerable say about that creation. The politics of the next 50 years will be the politics of this restructuring of our world-system.

REFERENCES

My views in this article are stated more elaborately in several places:

Arrighi, Giovanni, Terrence K. Hopkins & Immanuel Wallerstein, 1989. *Antisystemic Movements.* London: Verso.

Wallerstein, Immanuel, 1991. *Geopolitics and Geoculture. Essays on the Changing World-System.* Cambridge: Cambridge University Press.

Wallerstein, Immanuel, 1992. "The Concept of National Development, 1917–1989; Elegy and Requiem," pp. 79-88 in Gary Marks and Larry Diamond, eds. *Reexamining Democracy; Essays in Honor of Seymour Martin Lipset.* Newbury Park, CA: Sage.

Wallerstein, Immanuel, 1992. "The Collapse of Liberalism," pp. 96–110 in Ralph Miliband and Leo Panitch, eds. *Socialist Register 1992: New World Order?* London: Merlin.

Section IX

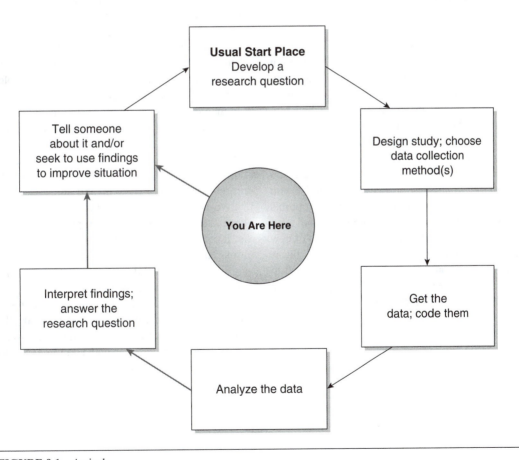

FIGURE 9.1 Arrival

Now that you have completed the journey from your original question to an answer (even if you don't like it), it's time to let people know what you have found. True, you may have completed only a course paper, and you might not have confidence that your work needs to see the light of day. But if you have completed the whole cycle with integrity and care, then you are in possession of findings that no one else has seen. You should share them. Why not take your work on the road? Submit it to a conference. Send it to a journal. More to the point, there isn't much benefit to doing research if no one sees the results.

How do you know if there is any benefit to your work? Recall what we said in Section I about motivation. If you have chosen a subject matter that has some meaning, and a research question that we don't already know the answer to, then there is a need to know the answer. In fact, there might be a whole world of people out there who are doing whatever they do based on some assumption that you have just called into question. But even if your research only confirms a widely held suspicion, it is still one new puzzle piece for the big board.

Having completed the research journey, you might be wondering what's next. Well, if you notice that the last arrow on our map points forward to the first square, then you will also realize that each set of answers raises a lot of new questions. Having explored your topic as far as you have, you are now much better equipped to raise all kinds of questions that might not have occurred to you before. For every variable that you have measured in your study, there is a host of others that you chose not to address at that time. Each reader who has looked at your work has probably raised a few more questions or possibilities. Even as you wrote your conclusion, you might have been thinking of all the questions that are left unanswered. If you've shown that Y really does depend on X, then how exactly does that work? And why didn't we know that already? And what about X and another combination of variables?

The fact is that any given sociologist never gets the last word in. In fact, no social scientist or any scientist ever gets the last word in. There are simply too many unknowns, too many new and interesting ideas to explore, too many great questions to ask, and too much change in the world for anyone to think that anything is settled for good and all. That's the whole point of science and research. We are building theory by examining reality as carefully as we can. Then we consider our findings in relation to the theories that guide us. Research methods help us examine that reality in ways that are verifiable, reproducible, and transparent. The methods are not magical, but they are the best humankind has developed. In the words of Andrew Abbott (2004:3), "Science is a conversation between rigor and imagination. What one proposes, the other evaluates. Every evaluation leads to new proposals, and so it goes, on and on."

We hope that these readings and our words have shown you how human a process research is. It's just people being very careful when they look at what is happening. Our work is significantly helped by the extraordinarily thoughtful insights and methods of those who have come before us. But, ultimately it's a researcher—perhaps you—armed with the theory and tools of the trade, trying to answer a question to help us better understand our world, our society, and ourselves.

GLOSSARY

Aggregate: Combining groups or scores from different samples to form a larger data set. You might, for example, have samples of boys and of girls at a school, which you then aggregate to reflect the entire school. Or, you might combine different scores in various subjects to reflect combined measures.

Anonymity: Protecting your research subjects by not collecting their names or other identifying information. See also **confidentiality**.

Bias (sample bias): An aspect of the sampling process that prevents random selection; for example, if you wanted to interview a sample of everyone in your county, but relied on phones, you would bias the sample in favor of those with phones. If you interviewed only people who spoke English, you would bias the sample in ways that did not reflect the entire population.

Blending In: Blending in refers to the strategy in fieldwork research to enter the field by appearing to assimilate with the population or group you are studying. The goal of blending in is to minimize the differences between the researcher and the study population so that you seem less of an outsider.

Blind Analysis: Blind analysis occurs when information about the source or nature of data is withheld from the researchers who are analyzing it. This approach avoids conscious or unconscious biases that could otherwise influence the analysis.

Case Study: A broad and extensive analysis of a single instance of something intended to represent crucial aspects of phenomena of that type. One can conduct a case study of a place with certain characteristics (e.g., a refugee camp) to understand all such places better or of an event (e.g., a wildcat strike) in order to understand such events.

Central Tendency: This is a statistical measurement that reports the single value that represents the most typical value in a distribution of values. It can be the mean (the arithmetic average), the median (half of the scores are below this point and half are above), or the mode (the most common value). The central tendency represents the "trend" of the distribution. See **descriptive statistics.**

Closed-Ended: In questionnaire design, closed-ended, or fixed-format questions allow respondents to select responses from only a fixed set of options. Contrast with **open-ended**.

Confidentiality: Protecting your research subjects by not revealing their names or other identifying information. The researcher knows the identity of the subjects, but suppresses this information when writing about the research. See also **anonymity**.

Coding: The process whereby data are recorded in some standardized form, usually conforming to a numerical format, for comparison and analysis. Coding assigns responses, observations, interactions, or other information to categories that are relevant to the research question.

Comparative–Historical Research: Research using multiple methods and data sources in order to compare states, cultures, or regions across time and place.

Composite Variable: A variable that is composed of several factors, or **dimensions**. For example, "socioeconomic status" (SES) is usually made up of a person's occupation, education, and income.

Conceptualization: The process whereby the researcher refines the ideas and definitions to be used in the research. Conceptualization translates abstract and imprecise concepts into specific items or variables that can be measured.

Content Analysis: The process of coding text, images, or other materials to reveal the patterns through which key concepts appear, or to discern and identify the significant themes in that content.

Control: To isolate a variable or set of variables or hold their values constant throughout the course of research. Factors that could have an effect on the relationship being studied are controlled so that the measures that remain reflect only the variables of interest. To control for the effects of age, for example, one can study the effects of variable X on variable Y within similar age groups.

Control Group: The control group is a group of subjects who participate in an experiment without being subjected to the experimental stimulus. Having a control group allows us to observe the effects of the experimental setting and other, exogenous factors by distinguishing changes that occur with and without the stimulus. The classic example of a control group is the placebo group in a drug trial who take a dummy pill while the experimental group takes the actual medicine. See **experimental group.**

Cost–Benefits Analysis: The cost–benefits analysis is an evaluation strategy that measures the effectiveness of policies or programs in relation to their financial and other costs. The question is not whether the program has a positive effect, but whether the effect is sufficient given the cost of the program. Often, measuring effects becomes an exercise in values clarification.

Data Collection: Data collection is the phase of the research process where the researcher systematically gathers all the data on which the study will be based. The data collection plan typically relies on a clearly specified research method and includes detailed specification of the research sample, **instruments,** and the schema for coding and recording the data.

Data Collection Instruments: Data collection instruments are tools the researcher employs to collect data during the data collection phase. They might be survey forms, (questionnaires), observation forms, coding forms, a Web-based questionnaire, or any tool that helps systematically collect information for research.

Deductive Reasoning: Deductive logic is the process whereby we formulate explanations from general principles or assertions. We deduce hypotheses based on theories. Deductive logic is one of the two approaches that help us formulate hypotheses in social research. See **inductive reasoning**.

Dependent Variable: In any given cause and effect relationship, the dependent variable (Y) is the latter. If we measured amount of homework in relation to grades, then "grades" would be the dependent variable. The distribution of values of this variable depends on the values of the **independent variable** (amount of homework).

Descriptive Statistics: Descriptive statistics describe the characteristics of a particular population or dataset. Univariate descriptive statistics present the information on one variable. Other statistics allow examination of the strength and direction of relationships among variables. See **inferential statistics** and **central tendency**.

Development Economics: Theories concerning the path to industrialization; the causes of poverty and economic inequality among nations, societies, and the world economy; and obstacles to economic growth at the national level. Development economics also examine the consequences of economic changes and the ideologies associated with economic policies.

Dimension (also, one-dimensional variable): A dimension is a specific aspect of a concept identified during the process of conceptualization. The concept of "good student" might include several dimensions, such as motivation, homework effort, and paying attention in class. Each dimension must be measured independently.

Dysfunction: In a functionalist analysis, dysfunction refers to the adverse or unexpected activities that impair or undermine the desired outcomes within a social system. The market economy, for example, functions to distribute goods throughout a society, but also creates dysfunctional outcomes such as poverty, inequality, and the inefficient distribution of resources.

Ethnography: A study of the culture of a group or community, typically conducted through extensive fieldwork. The goal is to capture the nuances and meanings of the lives of people.

Evaluation Research: A study of some program, designed intervention, or policy change to determine whether it is having the intended effect. The research is guided by the design and stated goals of the program, intervention, or policy.

Experimental Group: The experimental group is the group of subjects that receives the stimulus in an experiment to assess the effects of that stimulus. The effects in this group are assessed in relation to the **control group**.

Experimental Research: Experiments are a research strategy that involves the application of a stimulus, in a controlled environment, to measure the effects of the stimulus. A classic experimental design exposes an **experimental group** of subjects to a change in the value of some **independent variable** in order to measure the resultant change in the value of one or more **dependent variables**. Sometimes the experimental group is called the "test" group.

False Precision: Refers to a level of accuracy (precision) that is not reflected in the data. It is possible to make a rough guess appear precise by simply adding decimal places to the estimates.

Fieldwork: Fieldwork is the research strategy and practice where researchers are actively involved in collecting data. This may involve the researchers' personal interviews or participant observations, or it may encompass supervision of a staff of observers, surveyors, interviewers, and so on.

Focus Group: This methodology involves prompting discussion through open-ended questions in a small group setting. Data are collected on the participants' responses to the researcher's questions and their interactions with each other. At its best, it solicits information from participants because they are encouraged by other participants to think about and express their views.

Functionalism: Functionalism is a perspective in the social sciences that views society as a social system composed of interrelated parts, norms, and organizational functions in which the parts serve the whole system. The functionalist perspective includes the assumption of "self-correction"—that societies tend to move organically toward stable and sustaining social arrangements whether we perceive the underlying system of order or not. This perspective evolved from Emile Durkheim's sociology and went on to dominate American social sciences for most of the 20th century.

Gaining Entry: Gaining entry refers to the series of steps and strategies researchers usually take to begin, or gain entry to, the fieldwork they have chosen to collect data for their study. See **blending in**.

Gatekeeper: The gatekeeper is a person, identified by the researchers, who facilitates gaining entry to, and collecting data in, the field. Gatekeepers are usually deeply familiar with the population and setting where fieldwork takes place and therefore are indispensable to the researcher.

Generalizable: Research findings are generalizable when the lessons we draw from them can be applied to multiple settings and situations; for example, to the larger population or to other populations.

Hypothesis: A testable proposition about the relationship between two or more variables. Hypotheses must be structured such that they can be shown to be unsupported by the data. Note that we do not say hypotheses are proven or disproven. Rather we say supported or not supported. Real scientists are humbled by the process of scientific inquiry. Hypotheses about variables typically derive from theories about concepts. Note the etymology of the word: little thesis.

Impact Assessment: Impact assessment is one of the most popular evaluation techniques in the social sciences. It usually involves measuring the social and/or economic effects of a specific policy or program to determine whether, and how well, the program or policy worked.

Independent Variable: In any cause and effect relationship, the independent variable (X) is the former. It is sometimes viewed as the presumed cause of the issue being studied where the effect is the change in the values of the **dependent variable**. The values of this variable change independently of the relationship that is studied.

Indexes: Indexes are multiple and combined measurements that summarize and order more

than one observation. They are composite scores reflecting more than one measure or variable.

Indicator: An empirical observation that reflects a variable or concept. In some cases, there may be more than one indicator for a variable. For instance, indicators of a quarterback's effectiveness might be his passing rating, his win/loss ratio, and his sack rate.

Inductive Reasoning: Inductive logic is the process whereby the researcher develops conclusions based on many individual observations or collected data. We induce theories from the patterns of individual observations. See **deductive reasoning**.

Inferential Statistics: Inferential statistics consist of the computations that permit us to draw conclusions and generalizations from data we select following one of the random sampling techniques. We make inferences about the population based upon findings in the sample.

Informed Consent: The process whereby the researcher tells the research subjects what participation in the research will involve and seeks their agreement prior to beginning the data collection.

Institutional Review Board (IRB): IRBs are committees established within institutions and organizations that seek to protect research subjects in studies conducted by members of those institutions. They focus on research ethics. Today, any organization wishing to receive federal funding must set up an IRB to review the ethical implications of human subject (or other vertebrate animal) research conducted by the institution.

Instruments: In social research, instruments are tools, such as questionnaires, that facilitate data collection and analysis. The data collection instruments indicate how to code the information that is collected, thereby translating it into a coded format.

Interrater Reliability: The level of agreement among multiple "raters," researchers applying an agreed upon procedure to the evaluation of a **subjective** measure or coding scheme.

Interval: A statistical measure that describes the values of variables that are hierarchical and of equal distance from each other. A ruler or a weight scale is an interval measure.

Interview: A "conversation with a purpose." An exchange of questions and answers with the subject or subjects being studied related to the research topic.

Interview Schedules: The list of question topics and possible probes (follow-up questions) asked by the interviewer of the interviewee. Interview schedules indicate an oral interview (as compared to a **questionnaire)** that may be self-administered via paper and pencil or a computer. An interview schedule may specify the exact wording of the questions, or it may be used as a guideline for topics to ask about.

Key Informants: These are indispensible individuals we identify during our fieldwork to provide us with information about the population and social setting we study.

Latent Function: The unintended consequences or side effects of a social system or process. The latent function is often accepted as the necessary cost of doing things the way we want, though such outcomes can often go unnoticed. See **manifest function**.

Longitudinal: Longitudinal studies or trend analyses examine how a particular attribute unfolds over time. We might look at individuals' political views as they evolve over many years.

Manifest Function: The intended or obvious function of a social system or process. The manifest function of some way of doing things represents the motivation for doing things that way. See **latent function.**

Mean: Commonly known as the average, the mean is one of the measures of central tendency. It describes the arithmetic average (all scores added together divided by the number of observations). See **central tendency**.

Measures of Dispersion: A way of counting the scores or observations that fall above and below the mean and that also reflects the range of those scores or observations. Measures of dispersion tell us how well the **measure of central tendency** represents the entire distribution.

Median: The midpoint in a distribution. The measure of central tendency that splits the set of values in half. The median can be measured only for data that have an inherent order to them.

Mixed Methods: Strategic combinations of quantitative and qualitative data collection and analysis techniques designed to exploit the strengths of each for maximum validity and reliability.

Mode: The most commonly occurring observation or value in a univariate distribution. A measure of central tendency. See **central tendency**.

Monitoring: An element of the evaluation process whereby the researcher systematically tracks and records the results or actions of the program, policy, or organization being monitored. It is often a necessary element of evaluation.

Naturalist Paradigm: The idea that social research must be verified in the "real" world where social actors are fully embedded in the relevant environments. The naturalist paradigm seeks to account for all of the complexity of the context and the moment, in contrast to the **positivist paradigm**.

Needs Assessment: In evaluation research, a needs assessment is an exploratory study undertaken prior to designing a program or intervention. Its goal is to establish the range of needs of the target population, and to prioritize goals for future programs.

Nonparticipant Observation: An unobtrusive research strategy for data collection in a public setting. The researcher attempts to **blend in** with the setting in order to observe a variety of activities, both predetermined and unexpected. See **participant observation** and **fieldwork.**

Norms: Socially constructed rules of behavior within a society that shape the values, attitudes, and behaviors of members of the society. They vary from subtle and informal (e.g., face the door in an elevator) to codified and strenuously enforced (e.g., thou shalt not kill).

Objective: Not influenced by one's interests, preferences or assumptions. Objective measures do not require additional judgment calls from researchers. See **subjective**.

Observations: Data gathered by a field researcher either participating in a social situation or **unobtrusively** standing back just to watch. Observation data may include people's actions and encounters, conversations, movements, or reactions, but it does not include any **self-report** indicators of their intentions, feelings, or motivations.

Open-Ended: In questionnaire design, open-ended questions allow respondents to write in (or speak) their responses in their own words. Contrast with **closed-ended**.

Operationalization: Precisely defining the research concepts and variables so that they can be measured. The operationalization of a concept yields a single variable for that concept.

Ordinal: A property of a variable that reflects hierarchy but not equidistant values; for example, good, better, best. Note that "best" is not some specific metric better than "good."

Oversampling: Sometimes, when conducting a large survey, you sample a disproportionately larger percentage of some subgroup so that you are not restricted by small sample sizes of that subgroup. For example, if you had a school with only 200 females and 800 males, and you were going to take a 10% sample, then you would have 80 males and only 20 females. Concerned that you could not generalize from the small N of females, you might oversample them. Of course, when you recombine the two samples, you must adjust the findings so you don't overemphasize the women's responses.

Paradigm: An overarching system of meaning or set of ordering assumptions. We do our research and derive our theories about the world within the framework of meanings established by the dominant paradigms of our society. Paradigms are sometimes referred to as perspectives.

Paradigm Shift: A widespread reconsideration of a broad array of assumptions about some part of the world. A paradigm shift represents a significant change in society's perspective on a subject, undermining a great deal of what was previously assumed to be true. The classic example of paradigm shift is moving from seeing the universe as revolving around the Earth to seeing it as revolving around the sun (heliocentric).

Participant Observation: Joining the group you are studying, or at least appearing to join the group you are studying.

Positivist Paradigm: A belief that the world is knowable and measurable by factual observation or other empirical techniques. This perspective emphasizes the importance of objective measures and downplays the relevance of any measure that is inherently subject to interpretation.

Primary Analysis: The first intended analysis of the collected information. It is in contrast to **secondary analysis** where researchers not associated with the original data collection effort examine the database (for the same or for very different purposes).

Purposive: As in purposive sampling: Sampling cases in a nonrandom fashion to ensure that the researcher includes those cases that reflect specific attributes; for example, interviewing only baseball pitchers who played in World Series games.

Qualitative Research: Techniques for data collection, coding, and analysis that work with the data in a form that is close to the original, preserving much of the context and meaning from the data source.

Quantitative Research: Techniques for data collection, coding, and analysis that rely on recording the data in a numeric format that is amenable to statistical analysis.

Random Sample: A sampling method that ensures every sampling element (e.g., person or thing) has an equal chance of being selected. The classic example is putting all of the names in a hat and pulling out some of them. In real life, achieving a random sample is a serious and often difficult effort.

Reification: To reify is to make real, or to assume something is real when it is only a concept. As W. I. Thomas noted, if a situation is believed to be real, it will be real in its consequences. Many **social constructs** are treated as though they were immutable and based in physiology, for example, "momentum" as applied to a movement is still a concept and not a physical reality.

Reliability: The likelihood that an observed measure or relationship will be consistent across different times and places.

Representative: A term embodying the hope that our sample reflects the characteristics and attributes of the population we wish to study.

Research Design: The strategy researchers create to collect the data, ensure accuracy, and produce appropriate conclusions.

Research Question: The question or questions that guide(s) a research project and design. An entire research cycle from design through data collection through analysis derives from a central question that the data analysis is intended to address. Not all research questions can be definitively answered.

Respondent: A research subject in a study involving **self-report** data collection. The subject responds to the researcher's questions, either in person or via some other communication media (paper, e-mail, etc.).

Sampling Frame: The list of all elements from which you derive the sample. If you want to sample all the faculty in your college, you may find that you have to use the faculty phone directory. Faculty without listed phones will not be in the sampling frame even though they are in the population you wanted to interview.

Scale: A set of measures that each indicates the same concept, but in slightly different ways. They may be **aggregated** (added, or averaged, or otherwise combined) to form a single scale variable that best represents the overall concept. This is different from a **composite** variable in which each indicator measures a unique dimension of the concept.

Scientific Revolutions: A scientific revolution occurs as a result of a **paradigm shift** within some branch of science. Einstein's postulate that light travels as both a wave and a particle, for example, revolutionized much of astronomy and physics.

Secondary Analysis: A quantitative data collection method in which the researcher performs a new statistical analysis of data from an existing data set, or some combination of existing data sets.

Self-Reports: Data about research subjects that are collected by asking or allowing the subjects to report the data themselves. **Interviews** and **surveys** rely on self-reports.

Semistructured Interview: An interview where the researcher has a list of issues and perhaps some questions, but there is room for additional questions, follow-ups, and digression. See **structured interview** and **unstructured interview.**

Social Constructs: We "construct" social categories by imbuing them with meaning. A social construct is some part of the social world to which we assign particular uses, meanings, or value, which we then treat as the inherent use meaning or value of those categories.

Spurious: An observed relationship is spurious if the reasons for the association among variables are due to some outside factor such that the associated variables are actually independent of one another.

Stakeholders: The people or organizations that have consequential (real life) involvement with the policy, program, or issues you are studying. Those affected by changes or continuation of policies or programs.

Standard Deviation: The measure of dispersion around the mean. A very specific way of measuring the observations or scores that fall around the arithmetic mean of all of the observations or scores. Standard deviations have properties that allow us to compare the dispersions around the means from one sample to another.

Structured Interview: Generally realized in an "interview schedule," it is the carefully crafted list of questions and perhaps probes the interviewer is required to follow. It is the one-on-one version of a questionnaire. See **semistructured interview** and **unstructured interview.**

Subject: As in research subject, human subject: The individuals who are studied or who provide data for a study. Subjects may be voluntary participants in the study, as in surveys, interviews, experiments, or the subjects may be part of the public in an observation study.

Subjective: Open to interpretation, requiring judgment, or dependent on one's perspective or situational knowledge. Subjective measures rely on the researcher's ability to validly gauge the intent or underlying meaning of data when multiple interpretations are possible.

Survey: A quantitative data collection method that relies on a questionnaire containing set questions with mostly fixed format response categories.

Theory: An explanatory framework that explains or predicts how different phenomena relate to one another.

Unit of Analysis: What we are measuring and analyzing. The usual units of analysis in the social sciences are individuals, groups, organizations, and social artifacts. Each unit of analysis has different properties. For example, you can't share clothing with yourself but you can with your siblings. There the unit of analysis is "groups" (in this case, a family). Crossing units of analysis often leads to logical and empirical errors; for example, assuming properties of a group are found in all of the individuals in that group.

Unobtrusive: As in unobtrusive measures: Ways of collecting data that do not influence the respondents. For example, when you ask questions via a survey, you affect the way people think and talk about the topic. But if you observe them from a hidden place, you are not likely to influence their behaviors. You can ask people if they liked the food (obtrusive) or you can see how much they leave on their plates (unobtrusive).

Unstructured Interview: An **interview** with no script, where the researcher allows the subject to lead the conversation, steering it back to the intended topic only when necessary. See **semistructured interview** and **structured interview.**

Validity: The claim that one's measures meaningfully reflects one's research concepts. There are many subcategories of validity: Does the variable reflect the full range of concepts and ideas, does it comport with other measures, does it predict?

References

Abbott, Andrew. 2004. *Methods of Discovery. Heuristics for the Social Sciences.* New York: Norton.

The ASA Code of Ethics 1999. Downloaded from http://www.asanet.org/galleries/default-file/Code%20of%20Ethics.pdf

Blau, Peter. 1977. "A Macrosociological Theory of Social Structure." *American Journal of Sociology* 83.1:26–54.

Dalton, Harlon L. 1989. "AIDS in Blackface." *Daedalus* 118.3:205–27.

Denton, Nancy, and Jacqueline Villarrubia. 2007. "Residential Segregation on the Island: The Role of Race and Class in Puerto Rican Neighborhoods." *Sociological Forum* 22.1:52–77.

Duster, Troy. 2006. "Comparative Perspectives and Competing Explanations: Taking on the Newly Configured Reductionist Challenge to Sociology." *American Sociological Review* 71:1–15.

Epstein, Cynthia Fuchs. 2007. "Great Divides: The Cultural, Cognitive, and Social Bases of the Global Subordination of Women." *American Sociological Review* 73:1–22.

Feynman, Richard P. 2001. *What Do You Care What Other People Think? Further Adventures of a Curious Character.* New York: Norton.

Foschi, Martha, and Shari Buchan. 1990. "Ethnicity, Gender, and Perceptions of Task Competence." *Canadian Journal of Sociology* 15.1:1–18.

Gallant, Mary J., and Jay E. Cross. 1993. "Wayward Puritans in the Ivory Tower: Collective Aspects of Gender Discrimination in Academia." *Sociological Quarterly* 34.2:237–56.

Gans, Herbert. 1975. "The Positive Functions of Poverty." *American Journal of Sociology* 78.2:275–89.

Goffman, Erving. 1979. *Gender Advertisements.* New York: Harper & Row.

Gouveritch, Peter. 1986. *Politics in Hard Times: Comparative Responses to International Crisis.* Ithaca, NY: Cornell University Press.

Grzywacz, Joseph G., and Dawn S. Carlson. 2007. "Conceptualizing Work–Family Balance: Implications for Practice and Research." *Advances in Developing Human Resources* 9.4:455–71.

Hasam, Hakim. 2000. "Afterword" from *Sidewalk* by Mitch Duneier. New York: Farrar, Straus and Giroux.

Higgs, Catriona T., Karen H. Weiller, and Scott B. Martin. 2003. "Gender Bias in the 1996 Olympic Games: A Comparative Analysis." *Journal of Sport and Social Issues* 27.1:52–64.

Inglehart, Ronald. 2006. "Mapping Global Values." *Comparative Sociology* 5.2–3:115–36.

Kidd, Sue Monk. 2008. *The Secret Life of Bees.* New York: Penguin.

Lena, Jennifer C. 2006. "Social Context and Musical Content of Rap Music, 1979–1995." *Social Forces* 85.1:479–95.

LaRossa, Ralph, Charles Jaret, Malati Gadgil, and G. Robert Wynn. 2000. "The Changing Culture of Fatherhood in Comic-Strip Families: A Six Decade Analysis." *Journal of Marriage and the Family* 62.2:375–87.

Lewis, Alan. 2001. "A Focus Group Study of the Motivation to Invest: 'Ethical/Green' and 'Ordinary' Investors Compared." *Journal of Socio-Economics* 30:331–41.

Lune, Howard. 2002, "Weathering the Storm: Nonprofit Organization Survival Strategies in a Hostile Climate." *Nonprofit and Voluntary Sector Quarterly* 31.4:463–83.

Mass-Observation. 1970. *The Pub and the People.* London: Curtis Brown.

Menjívar, Cecilia. 2003. "Religion and Immigration in Comparative Perspective: Catholic and Evangelical Salvadorans in San Francisco, Washington, D.C., and Phoenix." *Sociology of Religion* 64.1:21–45.

Musick, Mark A. 2000. "Theodicy and Life Satisfaction Among Black and White Americans." *Sociology of Religion* 61.3:267–87.

Pershing, Jana L. 2006. "Men's and Women's Experiences With Hazing in a Male-Dominated Elite Military Institution." *Men and Masculinities* 8.4:470–92.

Platt, Jennifer. 1998. *A History of Sociological Research Methods in America 1920–1960.* Cambridge, UK: Cambridge University Press.

Pumar, Enrique S. 2009. "The War on Poverty." *Encyclopedia of World History.* Santa Barbara, CA: ABC-CLIO.

Rossi, Peter, Howard E. Freeman, and Mark W. Lipsey. 1999. *Evaluation: A Systematic Approach.* 6th edition. Thousand Oaks, CA: Sage.

Solovey, Mark. 2001. "Project Camelot and the 1960s Epistemological Revolution: Rethinking the Politics-Patronage-Social Science Nexus." *Social Studies of Science* 31.2:171–206.

Swift, Jonathan. [1729] 1973. "A Modest Proposal." Pp. 502–09 in *The Writings of Jonathan Swift,* edited by Robert Greenberg and William B. Piper. New York: Norton.

Turner, Stephen. 2007. "A Life in the First Half Century of Sociology: Charles Ellwood and the Division of Sociology." Add pages in *Sociology in America: A History,* edited by Craig Calhoun. Chicago: University of Chicago Press.

Vaughan, Diane. 2004. "Theorizing Disaster: Analogy, Historical Ethnography, and the *Challenger* Accident." *Ethnography* 5.3:315–347.

Waltermaurer, Eve. 2005. "Measuring Intimate Partner Violence." *Journal of Interpersonal Violence* 20. 4:501–06.

Weschler, Henry, Adrea Davenport, George Dowdall, Barbara Moeykens, and Sonia Castillo. 1994. "Health and Behavioral Consequences of Binge Drinking in College." *Journal of the American Medical Association* 272.21:1672–77.

Whyte, William Foote. 1943. *Street Corner Society: The Social Structure of an Italian Slum.* Chicago: University of Chicago Press.

Willis, Frank N., and Roger A. Carlson. 1993. "Single Ads: Gender, Social Class and Time." *Sex Roles* 29.5/6:387–404.

Wratten, Ellen. 1995. "Conceptualizing Urban Poverty." *Environment and Urbanization* 7.1:11–38.

Name Index

Subject Index

About the Editors

Howard Lune is an Associate Professor of Sociology and the Director of the Graduate Social Research Program at Hunter College, CUNY. His areas of study include organizations, collective action, collective identity, and community-based mobilizations. He is the author of *Urban Action Networks: HIV/AIDS and Community Organizing in New York City*, as well as numerous papers on related topics.

Enrique S. Pumar is an Associate Professor of Sociology and Fellow at The Life Cycle Institute at The Catholic University of America. His areas of research are race and ethnic relations, migration, and economic sociology. He has published numerous papers on social class and assimilation among migrant communities, national development and democracy, and other related topics. In 2008–2009 he was elected President of the District of Columbia Sociological Society.

Ross Koppel is on the faculty of the Sociology Department at the University of Pennsylvania, where he has taught research methods, statistics, medical sociology, and sociology of work for the past 17 years. For the past seven years, he has been the principal investigator of Penn's study on hospital workplace culture and medication errors, at the Center for Clinical Epidemiology and Biostatistics (School of Medicine). Much of his recent work focuses on the impact of technology on the workplace and on medication errors. He is the recipient of the William Foote Whyte Award, the Robert E. Park Award, and the Distinguished Career Award in applied sociology.

Supporting researchers for more than 40 years

Research methods have always been at the core of SAGE's publishing program. Founder Sara Miller McCune published SAGE's first methods book, *Public Policy Evaluation*, in 1970. Soon after, she launched the *Quantitative Applications in the Social Sciences* series—affectionately known as the "little green books."

Always at the forefront of developing and supporting new approaches in methods, SAGE published early groundbreaking texts and journals in the fields of qualitative methods and evaluation.

Today, more than 40 years and two million little green books later, SAGE continues to push the boundaries with a growing list of more than 1,200 research methods books, journals, and reference works across the social, behavioral, and health sciences. Its imprints—Pine Forge Press, home of innovative textbooks in sociology, and Corwin, publisher of PreK–12 resources for teachers and administrators—broaden SAGE's range of offerings in methods. SAGE further extended its impact in 2008 when it acquired CQ Press and its best-selling and highly respected political science research methods list.

From qualitative, quantitative, and mixed methods to evaluation, SAGE is the essential resource for academics and practitioners looking for the latest methods by leading scholars.

For more information, visit **www.sagepub.com**.